Studies in Economic Transition

Series Editors
Jens Hölscher
The Business School
Bournemouth University
Bournemouth, Dorset, UK

Horst Tomann
Department of Economic Policy and Economic History
Freie Universitaet (FU) Berlin
Berlin, Germany

This series brings together theoretical and empirical studies on the transformation of economic systems and their economic development. The transition from planned to market economies is one of the main areas of applied theory because in this field the most dramatic examples of change and economic dynamics can be found. It is aimed to contribute to the understanding of specific major economic changes as well as to advance the theory of economic development. The implications of economic policy will be a major point of focus.

More information about this series at
http://www.palgrave.com/gp/series/14147

Sylvia Sztern

Russia on the Move

Railroads and the Exodus from Compulsory Collectivism, 1861–1914

palgrave
macmillan

Sylvia Sztern
Department of Economics
Hebrew University of Jerusalem
Jerusalem, Israel

ISSN 2662-6675 ISSN 2662-6683 (electronic)
Studies in Economic Transition
ISBN 978-3-030-89284-5 ISBN 978-3-030-89285-2 (eBook)
https://doi.org/10.1007/978-3-030-89285-2

This Palgrave Macmillan imprint is published by the registered company Springer Nature Switzerland AG.
The registered company address is: Gewerbestrasse 11, 6330 Cham, Switzerland

Foreword

Introduction

Who was the Sick Man of Europe when the continent was slipping into that terrible World War I? The term was coined by Tsar Nicholas in the middle of the nineteenth century. Yet it seems now that it should also have applied to Tsarist Russia herself, an empire that, like its Turkish sister, was also about to be transformed by World War I, starting a roller coaster ride whose imprints are still visible, a century later, on today's Russia. What started off as Tsarist autocratic rule turned into the Leninist-Stalinist repression and ended up in Putin's rule, where the law of the ruler rather than the rule of law still prevails.

These events form the stage on which Dr. Sylvia Sztern's PhD dissertation, the basis of this volume, charts the passage of the Russian village into the modern world. Sztern shows that, contrary to what is still widely believed, this transition was gathering steam long before World War I, possibly since the middle of the nineteenth century. Furthermore, the Tsarist autocratic government itself catalyzed this process; in essence, its own demise, by the construction of railway lines, intended to strengthen the country externally and improve conditions of life while preventing the revolutionary ferment. Yet the railroads unleashed the rise of civil society. Even though a different, wider gauge was selected to protect Russia from invasion and also isolate it from the winds of change blowing from the west, Industrialization and, in particular, the rails, imported science, and the spirits of enlightenment and freedom that flowed along the rails and helped undermine the *ancient regime*. The very grant of economic rights to the peasant amplified the demand for political rights, propelling Tsarist Russia toward constitutional monarchy. In other words, the Tsarist government helped to undermine autocracy, a central tenet of Tsarism,[1] and dig its own grave.

This is the background to Sztern's story, whose hero is the Mir (the Russian village community. Its basic unit was the village commune, the *obshchina*, whose vital role was to provide the peasantry with insurance. Given the extreme uncertainty of Russian climate, characterized by a short growing season and unpredictable yield, local variations in precipitation between adjacent fields—where one might shrivel while its neighbor was flooded by rain—it was essential that those whose climatic draw in a given year was lucky share with the unlucky ones—who may be the winners in coming years. Yet the commune had a dynamic side to it. Over time family sizes varied and their resources diverged. The periodic land redistribution, the so-called reallotments, was at the heart of the flow over time of the nineteenth-century Black Earth commune. Families that grew in size and those who were temporarily unlucky and suffered from ill-health had to be supported and be allocated increased resources. This was achieved by periodic reallotments as well as by transfers (see "pomoch'" below).

Yet reallotments had their costs. If today's holding may not be yours tomorrow, why invest in it? Your neighbors may reap the fruits of what you ploughed, planted, and tended. The benefits of investment in land were too tenuous, and the maintenance and improvement of land were neglected. Sztern's thesis challenges this understanding. The income transfers from the growing towns to the village following the peasants' use of the railroads to work in urban centers allowed rural households to invest in their land and stabilize their yields, reduced the risk of starvation, and resulted in rising productivity and improving peasant living standards. Sztern shows how the pros and cons of these alternatives were affected by the winds from the west. The easier means of communication—the telegraph, and cheaper and faster, predictable and reliable means of transportation—the rails, took over much of the insurance upon themselves and reduced the perceived advantage of the commune. The threat of death from starvation receded where there were railroad lines; the only advantage of the commune was to reduce real income swings. The commune's hold on its members weakened. Its main resource, the land, effectively began to be privatized.

[1] Figes (1996).

This leads us into interesting debates. Sztern shows how the village commune, the *obshchina*, was being nibbled up from within by the *muzhik*, the Russian peasant, who was following his own interests. In this, she counters Gerschenkron, who is widely accepted as the final arbiter of Russian history and who claimed that the commune had atrophied and would not change unless shaken from above; Sztern shows that younger peasants were responding to market signals and freeing themselves from the shackles maintained by the elders and seeking alternative occupations that may better their conditions in towns where new industries were being launched. In this, she counters the idea that change had to be imposed from above and that Stalin's cruel war against the peasantry was necessary in order to lead Russia into the twentieth century. Sztern shows that not only was Stalin not necessary but that his restructuring broke down the peasant's entrepreneurial spirit and froze up Russian agriculture for many decades. This is a subject that is being discussed in depth in the Chap. 9 of this book.

These are the main messages of this volume, yet they build upon a wide-ranging description and analysis of the Russian village under the Tsars.

Chapter 2 prepares the ground by detailing the historical background, from Peter the Great to Nicholas II, the last Tsar. Peter founded the absolutist state; Catherine II tried to depersonalize Tsardom, to constitutionalize the highly hierarchic empire. Attempts at reform came after the debacle of the Crimean War of the 1850s, which showed that the weakness of the muzhik as the foot soldier of the autocratic Tsar's army was an important cause of the defeat. Alexander II tried to free the muzhik to improve him as a soldier, yet the statues of 1861–1863 enforced the peasant commune, that is, the rule of the elders and the tying of the peasant to his village and his elders' estate or farm. Gerschenkron believes that the Russian village that ensued had thereby atrophied into "immutable backwardness." Sztern shows that the Russian peasant did not differ from peasants, nay, from people everywhere, and followed their economic incentives. And these were affected by the changes in the west, imported, *inter alia*, by industrialization.

Industrialization, launched by the rulers, was necessary for several reasons. Firstly, it was to help prepare Russia for impending confrontations, but also to relieve the pressure of population growth on the land. Yet it was industrialization that started the erosion of autocracy. Industry required workers, namely peasants. These peasants, having been freed from their isolation in the commune by commuting by rail to the new urban centers, were exposed to the libertarian ideologies that accompanied Western technicians and engineers servicing the imported machinery and technologies. They catalyzed the acquisition of skills, and transformed the muzhik into a political agent. This resulted in effective demands for equality before the law and for universal suffrage. Industrialization thus joined the invading rails and the telegraph to corrode the rusty foundations of Tsarist autocracy.

A significant aspect of the story is Sztern's critique of Gerschenkron. The very fact that young *muzhiks* did not await an official *ukaz* but followed market signals and left their commune shows that, when freed by the rails from the threat of starvation, the yoke of the commune could be relaxed and Russian peasants became able to follow their economic interests and to move to where better life was beckoning. They acted rationally, no longer being the prisoners of their old environment. The environment was evolving and with it the actors' habits and strategies.

How did the Tsarist government respond to the evolving village? As mentioned above, shortly after the Crimean war, the Tsar and his ministers realized that an important element of Russian weakness lay in the backwardness of the Russian soldier, that is, the muzhik. To improve him, he was to be emancipated from the bondage and granted some rights. Reforms were started in 1861. In the first step peasants were granted rights in their land and received options to purchase the land they were working, yet at a price that imposed a hardly bearable burden on them. Most of the land, though, stayed communal; as long as the village was cut off from its urban environment, the commune served as an insurance in times of droughts, frost, floods, and other natural calamities that are very frequent in Russia. These calamities are also highly uneven: they may hit one field but not its neighbor; thus, mutual insurance in a village may alleviate its dangers. As long as starvation as a result of drought and other natural calamities was a threat, the commune had vital value. Yet once the rails were constructed, they took upon themselves this task and the commune as an insurer became dispensable. The result was a process of privatization that was legalized in 1906 with the Stolypin laws that offered a menu of several forms of landholding. By 1913, the only year for which Sztern has obtained the relevant data, privatization was taken up where the rails replaced the commune as a provider of insurance. Sztern takes this up in greater depth in Chap. 9.

Why was privatization so important? Each household in the commune was continuously evolving in size and fortunes. Different hazards that affected households' composition and resources would lead to the evolution of inequalities that would undermine the sense of community. Too extreme a spread of income would have made the commune unmaintainable, unsustainable. Thus, in the pre-railroad era, the landlord, the state, and the peasantry were all interested in maintaining periodic, leveling reallotments, that is, a redistribution of the means of production. In their absence, a modicum of equality was impossible to maintain over time. Thus, reallotment was at the heart of the Black Earth nineteenth-century commune. Yet the commune was increasingly perceived by the entrepreneurial peasant households as an oppressive social institution. The custom as understood by Gerschenkron stipulated that the elders who stood at the top of the hierarchical social structure enforced uniformity that did not permit any individual initiative and suffocated incentives. Once an individual household had become the master of its land, freed from the periodic redistribution, he (because women as heads of households were very rare) could be sure that the fruits of his investments would be harvested by himself and not by other members of the commune. The social change brought about by the weakening of the commune is therefore also an essential cog in the machinery that made change possible.

Privatization provided incentives for land improving investment that allowed households to determine what and how to produce, permitting them to participate in production for the urban market and enabling specialization—impossible before the arrival of the rails. And the rails, enabling timely shipments of grain from distant locations, provided insurance against starvation, yet naturally not the financial loss of a poor harvest (which the commune had provided).

This is the picture at large that emerges from the first three chapters of this book. Some color and greater detail are provided by the remaining ones.

Chapter 4 details the institutional–cultural evolution that industrialization and railroads construction led to. The highly personal and arbitrary nature of Tsarist rule was not conducive, to understate the case, to large-scale investment in heavy industry. Legal reform was a prerequisite. Yet this ran counter to the last Tsars' own conception of their rights. This was also the ground on which tensions grew between Tsardom and the developing legal institutions. Finally, following the 1890 industrialization spurt and the debacle in the Russo Japanese War of 1904, as well as the upheaval of 1905, rights were granted to classes, or *estates*, that had never had any; workers were able to complain against maltreatment and peasants received the rights to appeal against incursions into their property. This had wide-ranging effects on social relations and led to the weakening of the oppressive autocracy. Sztern also shows that productivity of both industry and agriculture was improving and that internal migration protected peasants against the reduction in their standard of life. This is further discussed in the following chapter.

The debate between Gerschenkron and Gregory is detailed in Chap. 5. Gerschenkron, true to his belief in the necessity of governmental intervention prior to any change, insists that the peasantry was dormant and immobile in the stagnant commune; Gregory's data show that the agricultural productivity was growing, albeit at a slower rate than industrial production, that is, structural change was taking place amid the Tsarist industrialization drive. From this Sztern derives that labor mobility barriers were low enough to be bridged and there was transition from extensive to intensive growth. With the end of land reallotment, in spite of the growth in population, real income on the land has been growing.

Chapter 6 goes more deeply into the nature of serfdom and the commune and into how it was affected by the arrival of the railroads. Communes' members in the Black Earth regions were all serfs. Serfdom was introduced at the very end of the sixteenth century and has been a major distinguishing feature of Russia and of Tsardom until the liberation of serfs after the Crimean war. Serfs were tied to the land, that is, land was transferred by either sale or grant with the serfs tied to it. As the property of the owner, they could be subjected to corporal punishment at his whim and escaping serfs were apprehended and severely dealt with.

The above detailed harsh climatic conditions of Russia led the serfs who peopled the commune to insure themselves, as said above, by a significant degree of cooperation, whose characteristics are described in this chapter. The whimsical tale of crust sharing, in which bread is shared with those whose crops failed (p. 176), and pomoch' extended to households temporarily calamity stricken (p. 146) is a case in point. The commune thus served as life insurer—that is, income provided at certain pre-defined events—calamities that were impossible to obviate or avoid but whose ill effects were ameliorated. Taxes were imposed on the village as a whole and were allotted to the households for payment, thus adding a coercive element of cohesion to the commune. For the owners, this meant that their chattels, the serfs, were easy to control and tax, once the serfs were sure to be kept at home. The mutual assistance in the commune survived the emancipation of the serfs in 1861, proving that it did not depend solely on imposition from above. Yet the arrival of the rails that reduced the risks of the environment and enabled the freed serfs to seek their fortunes outside their village began the breakup of the commune.

The twin institutions of church and the army were always the mainstay of the Russian Empire. The entry of whiffs of enlightenment with the railroads helped start the rot that was to undermine them. Muzhiks who left their commune were exposed to information from which they had been isolated in the commune. They met and associated with fellow peasants in their *landsmannschaften* and with others who had arrived from other communes and they were "infected" by literacy, useful both to keep in touch with their families and required in their new environment. The new environment introduced them to a changing world where novel options, such as apostasy or adherence to alternative "subversive" religious sects, were an option. From their new abode, some traces of the new freedom of thought must have reached their place of origin, the now less isolated village commune. These are the nuggets I take from Chap. 7.

Chapter 8 introduces us to the tension between the advancing institution building and the existing rigid hierarchical structures. In consequence of Peter's modernization and importation into Russia naval technology (with the construction of the Baltic Fleet). The intelligentsia among the nobility had looked to the west, whence they adopted their habit, their dress, and their nick names, even their language of conversation, French, as we learn from Tolstoy and Russian dramatists; this did not extensively impinge on the village other than through butlers and maids. In fact, it seemed to strengthen the muzhiks' adherence to old norms and customs, and feel even more alienated from their "betters" whom they regarded as alien, almost non-Christian heretics. Some elements of institutionalization tended to strengthen the old structures. Taxes—mentioned in the previous chapter—were imposed on the village commune as a whole, to save bureaucratic costs, yet thereby they strengthened the hold of the elders on the young generation. The continued use of corporal punishments inhibited the search for new methods and innovation in production.

The rails, whose *raison d'être* was military, became by the law of unintended consequence the subversive element that, in time, would threaten the hierarchical edifice. This is the theme of Chap. 9 that opens the empirical part of this volume. This chapter, in which the writer of this Introduction has taken part, summarizes much that was said in the previous chapters; its main contribution is the econometric study that indicates that the rails were instrumental in the breakdown of the commune by leading to an accelerating drive of privatization of its land, that is, of members opting out. This process must probably have started in the nineteenth century, in the Penza, the studied province 1874, 39 years before the advent year of the data (Penza zemstvo self -government statistics 1913) that were the basis of our econometric tests, but was institutionalized thereby legalized by the Stolypin reform of 1906, just eight years before World War I. The author argues that it is obvious that the seven years that had elapsed between the codification of the reform and its second stage were too brief to effect the radical change in landholding. Yet we can observe that within that short span of time changes were taking place, changes induced by that harbinger of modernity, the railroad.

This volume bears a message: Russian agriculture was not dormant in those last days of peace before the revolution. Privatization was gathering steam, leading to a rise in agricultural output. Had there been no war and revolution, history might have been very different. Could the Romanovs have stayed in the saddle, could regal autocracy have survived, when a modern agriculture would have joined a modern industrial structure and an educated middle class, necessary to run these sectors, would have taken root? Perhaps not—today's Putinesque rule shows that even though these steps forward have taken place, Russia has not yet acquired the rule of law that is the basis of real democracy.

Yet one point can be taken from this story: there was no need for Stalin's cruelty to waken the Russian village. It was modernity flying in from the west that was already gnawing at the rotting structure of rural life and stoking the engines of progress. Stalin has done the opposite: his road to collectivization has broken the muscles and the spirit of the Russian peasant, who is still trying to find his way to becoming an enterprising farmer. To paraphrase Regan, Stalin was not the solution; Stalin deepened the problem of agriculture in Russia.

Department of Economics, Hebrew University, Jerusalem, Israel

Michael Keren

References

Figes, O. G. (1996). *A People's Tragedy*. Kindle Edition.

Preface

In line with Revisionist schools of thought, led by the Neoclassical analyses of Gregory, Mironov, Borodkin, and Leonard, this monograph tackles the widely accepted concept of Late Imperial Russia as seen through the prism of European industrialization in Alexander Gerschenkron's iconic panoramic analysis. Gerschenkron tells the story of a backward land, tethered to its serfdom past by the shackles of the coercively imposed commune, that steered the post-Revolution Eurasian empire, understood through the lenses of materialism, into Stalin's clutches while envisaging a historic continuity from its Imperial past of bondage ordained by Peter I.

My contribution challenges this conception by describing what happened wherever railroads were built: growing and discontinuously emergent cognitive and cultural alternative value of human, economic, and political capital acquisition, along with a revolution in de facto and de jure rights manifested by modernization in the pre-Revolution Euro-asian Empire. According to my empirical hypothesis, and co-authored by my academic adviser Professor Kerens challenge, access to railroads was significant at more than 30 percent explanatory power in the response of the Povolzhe peasantry (which cultivated lands near the Volga River system) to the opportunities embedded in the 1906 Stolypin land reform. Dwindling distance from railroad stations explains the shift to individualistic forms of landholding. My initial metaphysical Kantian scientific assumption, which questions the notion of constant and stable peasant and non-peasant predispositions, is at least tentatively legitimized and corroborated. Thus, it should inspire additional novel research.

Western schools of thought emphasize Russian collectivism; my thesis, in contrast, seeks to understand its origins and its metamorphosis. By first impression, I am following the footsteps of neoclassical "safety first" theoreticians such as Scott, Eggertsson, and McCloskey, supplementing the Northian NIE school, by which population changes (land-to-labor ratios, as Kolchin explains) determine institutionalized dependencies and structures. The novelty of my theoretical model lies in its integration of theories as a method, while secondary sources in NIE clusters boost the inductive input to higher matrixes of abstract complementary synergy from which new insights are deduced. I consider the Critical Realist school, which sees structures as preceding individual interaction, but I suggest that the extent of the priority of this downward causation is determined by compliance with authority as a function of the evolutionary level of the studied population. The infusion of spatial-mobility technology to Imperial Russia allowed multi-institutional flux, incentivized literacy, and promoted the acquisition of matter-of-fact knowledge, changing the register of individual opportunity choice and increasingly allowing rational deliberation, voluntary cooperation, and individualism to take place. At this stage, the explanatory value of American Evolutionary Institutionalism declines, leaving more and more room for New Institutional Economics with its Neoclassical notion of core equilibrium. The compulsory authoritarian collectivist structures of serfdom and their post-emancipation legacies came under challenge as harbingers of an insurance-providing experience. Compliance with authority no longer constituted an Evolutionarily Stable Strategy of Survival. The autocracy, following Hayekian political rationality, tried to obviate the challenge to the historical hierarchies of coercion, thereby occasioning the January 9, 1905, massacre. Applying the Regulationist school, I propose that this tragedy triggered the "general collapse" of the previously stable status of the anointed Tsar as an intermediary between the human and the divine. The Greek Orthodox mainstream pillar of stability of the Empire had been from within shaken by the rise of secularized ideologies as well as pious sectarian subversion. I emphasize the Baccunian rather than the Marxian root of the Old Believers, mingled with their heritage of ascetic monks and ostensibly Socialist Revolutionary peasant subversion. The railroads facilitated mass gatherings, wider meeting spaces, and spiritual and intellectual exchange and regrouping, allowing market integration, specialization, and temporarily rising transaction costs to occur. All these factors, in view of the debacle of the 1904 Russo-Japanese War, forced the Tsarist government to make the concession of transforming Tsarist patrimony lands into a peasant entitlement—a dispensation that it codified in Stolypin's reform. Individual property rights in land, albeit still within the peasant estate, challenged Tsardom's monolithic hegemony, allowing democratization. The seeds of the peasant exodus from the mutually insuring commune to individual family farms, and the translation of communal cooperation in the *obshchina* and *artel* craft forms into urban trade unions that could withstand organized lockouts the railroads, incentivized peasant literacy, information handling capacity, and tacit knowledge of the kind that labor organizations harbor. These, in turn, collectively challenged the autocracy and induced it to ratify the constitution and allow the first Duma to convene. Following Freeze, Pipes, and Boyer and Orlean, I theoretically and empirically argue, in terms of measurable history, that the railroads initiated modernization in Late Imperial Russia such as to legitimately claim that Stalin's "big-bang," socially costly attempts to modernize the country should be delineated and defined as costs of dictatorship.

Bournemouth, UK — Jens Hölscher
Berlin, Germany — Horst Tomann

Acknowledgments

This monograph was written from its inception as a statement of profound homage and dedication to the scholars at the Department of Economics at the Hebrew University of Jerusalem. I begin my tribute by acknowledging the continual and topical academic advice of Professors Michael Keren (Economics) who inter alia has been working on the Economics of Transition and Gur Ofer (Economics and Russian Studies), both of whom I uniquely to each of those grand scholars honor in particular among my mentors. In the preliminary stages of this work, I benefited from the advice and invaluable inspiration of Professor Michael Confino of the Cummings Centre at Tel Aviv University. My public doctoral dissertation event at Lund University, Sweden, was chaired by the faculty opponent, Professor Judith Pallot of the Department of Geography at Oxford University—to whom I owe gratitude as well.

In the context of the revisionist challenging Alexander Gerschenkrons authority on Late Imperial Russian in European Mirror industrialization typology, I especially thank Professors Leonid Josephovich Borodkin, Lomonosov State University in Moscow Carol Scott Leonard Oxford University and Professor Michail Abramovich Davydov Humanitarian University in Moscow.

I was privileged to have Professors Keren and Ofer as my academic advisors, and Professor Confino, who had personally worked with Gerschenkron, and supported and legitimized me to challenge Gerschenkron's general continuity model.

In their Talmudic wisdom, my academic advisers Michael and Gur saw their pedagogy and intellectual generosity as an idealistic mission, and imparted to their student much more than a tradition of formal and tacit knowledge. They were supportive of my thinking on every line of the pages that follow, tirelessly commenting and always offering encouragement to keep up the good work while affirming the scientific value of my contribution.

By co-authoring Chap. 9 and naming me the lead author, Professor Keren privileged me with useful knowledge for future research. His scientific guidance and Veblenian parental bent gave me precious tools with which to embark upon pioneering individual investigations of the quantitative causality of spatial mobility and human-capital formation in Chaps. 10 and 11.

The Hebrew University's moral support enabled me to handle the overwhelming sorrow of solitude that, had it accompanied my writing in Lund, might have occasioned an irreparable tragedy. Professor Ofer ushered an editor of telepathic capabilities: Mr. Naftali Greenwood, whose good will, proficiency, and useful questions turned the almost unreadable sesquipedalian sentences of my original manuscript into an elegant and easily followed book. I, of course, am solely responsible for any shortcomings that may remain.

For the theorem combinations that challenge the established schools of thought, I am indebted, beyond my own idle curiosity and the quest for novelty that steered me to the Regulationist School, to Professor Geoffrey Martin Hodgson, chair of the Institutional, CRIE, and GROE workshops at the University of Hertfordshire, for his useful comments and inspiration in the search for source material that enriched the theoretical foundation of the dissertation that underlies this monograph. For their encouraging comments upon the presentation of my Master's thesis with its supplement, I warmly thank Professors Jane Hartley and Roger Bartlett.

In 2008, the Svenska Institutet (Swedish Institute), in conjunction with the Axon Johnsson Foundation, gave me a small research grant that allowed me to spend a semester of study at Lomonosov Moscow State University. There I was most generously advised by my host, Professor Leonid Josephovich Borodkin, and by Professor Mikhail Abramovich Davydov of the Moscow State Humanitarian University, who, upon receiving the previous, yet untested version of my model, steered me to what Professor Keren and I would consider our main primary source: Zemstvo (Rural Self-Government) Statistics for Penza Province in 1913. I was even able to collect sources at the Historical and Lenin Libraries in Moscow and enjoy the archival advice and services of the latter.

Professors Leonid Josephovich Borodkin and Carol Scott Leonard provided invaluable comments and advice as well as evaluations of my post-doctoral work at the Hebrew University of Jerusalem.

During my Post Doctorate at the Department of History, the Hebrew University of Jerusalem which I owe to Professor Yitzkhak Brudny 2018–2019, the Department of Russian Studies at the Hebrew University awarded me the honored Matwei Gunsbourg Foundation for Fellowship in Russian and Slavic Studies, which allowed me to participate in the PEDD Political Economy of Dictatorship and Democracy conference at the University of Münster and the GranaSlavic2019 conference at the University of Granada, resulting in precious publications.

My mother Cecylia Dereczynska, a specialist in neurology, and my deceased violinist father, Dr. Mojzesz Sztern through their generous upkeep, afforded me a standard of living during my doctoral and post-doctoral research that was on par with my colleagues worldwide who earn a wage or receive lavish stipends. Thanks to their sacrifice, I was able to gather source materials at the libraries of the Hebrew University of Jerusalem, the Cummings Centre at Tel Aviv University, and the British Library in London, as well as replenish my own inventory of sources, precious library. By their virtue, I could also present my progress at EHES, EACES, ASEEES, CRIE, and GROE, FRESH meetings, and Sound Economic History conferences and workshops. I can never repay my Jewish parents for their gift of love as well as their closest relations, always being there for me in Israel.

These chapters constitute a documentary tribute to my teachers and mentors at Ironi Alef High School in Tel Aviv and the Rubin Academy of Music/Buchmann-Mehta School of Music at Tel Aviv University, with special emphasis on Dr. Fishler and Professors Alexander Volkov, Miriam Boscovich and Jonathan Zak and the families (Goldberg and Rozenberg), classmates (Eitan and Ronit and Nissim), friends (Ilan, Frieda and Meir, Ida and Adi), and lovers (Omri and Sinai) who, during my years of indescribable happiness (1972–1987), enriched my senses with immense and invaluable intellectual and emotional inspiration, energy, and ennoblement. I lovingly thank my Mom, my Dad, and Leon Sztern.

Finally, I thank Moni for his concern, his moral support, and The Hope. I conclude in homage to his father, my apothropus Gad Goldberg, who at my ardent request afforded me my Israeli identity in memoriam.

Haifa, August 27, 2021 Dr. Sylvia Sztern

Contents

List of Figures

List of Tables

CHAPTER 1

Russia on the Move: Railroads and the Exodus from Compulsory Collectivism, 1861–1914

The advent of the railroad in Tsarist Russia in 1842 would precondition the institutions of the Russian autocracy in its final decades. In this monograph, I propose that the post-emancipation interaction between this insensitive-to-climate transport technology and the Tsarist-era rural commune made the latter redundant. I further argue that the railroads revolutionized the opportunity cost of time in travel while reducing the risk to life and property. The qualitative and quantitative discontinuity that railroadization created posed an irreversible challenge to peasant conventions that had been evolutionarily stable until then. The subversive force that embodied the challenge was pious-rural or nihilistic, rather than something structured on Marxian ideology.

Aims and Contents of This Monograph

As a grandchild of two men of honor who were slain by totalitarian, enslaving social perversions—the Stalinist and the Nazi, respectively—I have since childhood been intensely fascinated by the magnificent human urge to freedom and dignity, the quest for novelty and creative endeavor, and the omnipresent exodus from yesterday's institutional shackles toward unprecedented spatial, temporal, and cognitive personal mastery over the collectivist environment and the oppression it imposes through dependency and domination. Here the pious subversives Isaac Levitan and

S. Sztern, *Russia on the Move*, Studies in Economic Transition,
https://doi.org/10.1007/978-3-030-89285-2_1

Fyodor Dostoyevsky share a commonality with Mikhail Bakunin: profound abhorrence and rejection of the hierarchy of oppression of men by men. Paradoxically, Russia has been the playground of multiple expressions of the ultimate escape from and rejection of bondage.

My dissertation combines New Institutional Economics (NIE) and American Evolutionary Institutionalism (AEI) to study the transition of the Tsarist Russian village commune, the *obshchina*, from evolutionarily determined obedience of patriarchal elder authority to individuals' rational participation in a cooperative mechanism of their choosing. The uncertain harvests in Russia's climatically precarious agrarian environment, coupled with a high land-to-labor ratio, explain the state of bondage that existed under compulsory coercive peasant collectivism (Milov, 2001; Kolchin, 1987; Hoch, 1986). This structure allowed *samosud*, barbarian village mob rule, to sanction individuals for defecting from custom and redistributing surpluses (Frank, 1999), if any, from the younger to the eldest generation in order to attain a premium and use it to control uncertainty. Peasants, in turn, practiced mutual insurance against famines and other calamities in collectivist redistribution networks. The guiding philosophy encouraged rather low productivity and a stable probability of survival by all under the structured control of landlords who, without exception, leaned on the peasant eldest generation (Eggertsson, 1990; Scott, 1976; McCloskey, 2009).

The Tsarist autocracy introduced railroad technology in 1837–1843. Its thinking in so doing was dual-purpose: military strategy and mitigation of peasant households' risk of dying in frequent famines and other calamities while raising peasant standards of living through access to urban markets and income. The iron horse would indeed power spurts of industrialization following the emancipation of the serfs (1861–1890–1907–1914), taking over the risk-insurance function of the pre-modern collective. In due course, I argue,[1] the coercively collectivist village evolved into a voluntary rationalist cooperative network. I conceptualize Pyotr Stolypin's agrarian reform (1906–1917) as the *ex post* codification of an *ex ante* emergent peasant rationalist individualism in landholding that was the cumulative result of the interaction of *mirs* (by origin, self-governing communities composed of peasant households) with railroads. The world of the peasantry widened under growing

[1] Contrary to the expectations of Alexander Gerschenkron—a point I will emphasize repeatedly.

individualized control—spatial, spiritual, intellectual, and cultural—in tandem with cognitively dwindling distances to factories and courts of law. The increasingly literate cohort of *otkhodniks* (peasants who turned to urban wage labor) gained even more than monetary income as they faced less and less risk of death due to violence, famine, and miscellaneous calamities.

I propose that Stolypin's reform be understood as the result of market formation, integration, and specialization, coupled with a temporal increase in transaction costs, that compelled the Tsarist state to acknowledge individual household-head property rights in land, triggering a mass exodus of the peasantry from compulsory collectivism. When economic civil rights are awarded, political bargaining power changes hands (Martens, 2004, p. 194; Pipes, 1999). In the aftermath of the Stolypin reform, the Tsarist autocracy unintentionally metamorphosed into a constitutional monarchy.

In the empirical section of this book, I and my cherished co-author and academic advisor, Professor Michael Keren, prove econometrically that the closer peasants were to railroads, the more frequently they adopted, through rational choice, individually farmed landholding. If so, the modernization of Russia was engineered by the Tsarist steam locomotive and not by Stalin's Five-Year Plan and collectivization. The latter tragedy was not necessary for developmental parity between Russia and the West.

Theoretical Framework: The Composite NIE/AEI Model

American Evolutionary Institutionalism (AEI), introduced by Veblen (1931) and interpreted by Hodgson (2004), and New Institutional Economics (NIE), represented by North (1973, 1981, 1990, 2005), North et al. (2009), are widely treated as separate and distinct. In contrast, I find them to have complementary properties. The AEI paradigm advises that institutions, subject to natural selection and adaptation to the physical conditions of life, precondition socially shaped "habits of thought" (Veblen, 1931, p. 188; Lawson, 1997, pp. 27–35; Hodgson, 2004 with Hodgson & Knudsen, 2004, March 4). According to NIE, it is hedonistic, individual utility-maximizing interaction that brings the institutional structure into being. Although both theories emphasize interaction between agency and structure (Hodgson, personal communication, 2007), NIE, with its relatively strong emphasis on agency, is in fact complementary to AEI, with its orientation to a reconstitutive downward-causation structure. As a general proposition, technological novelty challenges the homogeneity of inherited structures. In the case of the Tsarist railroads, two factors have these revolutionizing progressive properties. The first is their ability to reduce the risk of death and mitigate uncertainty. In the second, repeated and spatially dispersed interaction among rural and urban economies caused the perceived cognitive distance to the agglomerates of knowledge (Fujita et al., 2001) and jurisprudence (Burbank, 2004) to narrow while incentivizing the acquisition of human capital (Brooks, 2003). The perceived easing of access to justice facilitated the enforcement of rights, occasioning a transition from personalized to impersonalized institutions that allowed anonymous trade to take place and the grasp of the market to widen (Martens, 2004; Smith, 1998). The emerging multiplicity of institutions, occasioned by spatial mobility, incentivized the acquisition of matter-of-fact as opposed to ceremonial knowledge (Veblen, in Hodgson, 2004). The acquisition of literacy, general education, and skills not only facilitated entrepreneurial risk-taking but also set cultural cognitive evolution in motion (Brooks, 2003; Eklof, 1986; Kahan, 1989; Sztern, 2018). Subservience to authority and its reservoirs of experience-based knowledge (Engelgardt, in Frierson, 1993) became redundant as matter-of-fact options and egalitarian rationalism in decision-making rose to predominance (Shevzov, 2004, p. 39; Sheshinski, 2010, p. 3; Gintis, 2009, pp. 1, 2). The railroads allowed national markets to form and prices to converge, reducing transaction costs and uncertainty, enhancing specialization, and jolting the structure of individualist exclusion from property rights, thus enhancing increases in investment and productivity (Metzer, 1972). I define the ensuing transformation from personalized coercion hierarchies to impersonalized institutions as flowing from evolving rational choice among alternative informal institutional structures, subsequently codified into laws and statutes, as North (1990) proposes.

Endogenous and Exogenous Explanatory Factors

In this context, I distinguish between endogenous and exogenous factors on the basis of their time frame. The endogenous physical factor that preconditioned village-commune collectivism was the high land-to-labor ratio that structured in the serfdom milieu (Kolchin, 1987, p. 2). This factor, combined with climatic conditions, raised the opportunity cost of labor employed in conflict (Eggertsson, 1990, p. 291; Kahan, 1985, p. 13, and 1989, Appendix Table 3A, pp. 139–41) and, thereby, increased the value, high to begin with, of internal harmony (Ma, 2006, p. 11). This was manifested in mutual assurance of asset redistribution, a condition that endogenously fostered material egalitarianism (Atkinson, 1983, p. 54; Vanberg, 1994, p. 55, Eggertsson, 1990, p. 291). Railroad construction facilitated the endogenous "translation" of the material egalitarianism of the village commune into an abstract demand for equality before the law (Boyer & Orlean, 1993, p. 22). My understanding of the 1905 Revolution is congruent with the non-materialist conception advanced by Gregory (1994, p. 48) and Mironov (1999, p. 475)—the latter, again, in contradistinction to Gerschenkron's proposal. The subversive demand, I suggest, centered on abolishing the estate system and the patriarchal commune and bringing on equal civil rights (Ascher, 1988, pp. 87–89) rather than protesting against the impoverishment occasioned by an alleged agrarian crisis. An exogenous factor that catalyzed structural revolution clusters, I posit, was railroad construction, which played the pivotal role of an "external invasion" (Boyer & Orlean, 1993, p. 22) of libertarian ideology that accompanied the importation of Western technology, and the consequent "general collapse" (Boyer & Orlean, 1993) of theretofore stable Evolutionary Strategies of Survival (ESS). In the course of the industrialization spurt that the state-led railroad construction animated, this "collapse" was occasioned by a non-Malthusian, Boserupian synergy of population increase, cognitive discontinuity abetted by the peasantry's spatial mastery (Shivelbusch, 1986), human-capital accumulation that increasingly challenged the autocracy, and the secularization of the conception of the Tsar as the nation's fatherly defender, caused by the Bloody Sunday affair on January 9, 1905. The upturn in pious subversion, conditioned by the new spatial mobility, instigated a process of democratization within ecclesiastic structures (Shevzov, 2004) that, for this reason, ceased to provide the Tsarist autocracy with its intellectual–spiritual plinth of stability. As peasants' territorial mobility ushered them into urban and rural economies as well as divergent climatic and topographic land-to-labor ratio zones, households' risk of death diminished. The consequent transition from extensive to intensive growth patterns amid rising individualism and rationalism powered increases in marginal value product of labor (Hesse, 1993) and total factor productivity (Leonard, 2011). Supplementing Gerschenkron and Gregory, I merge the quantitative-turned-qualitative role of the railroads into a single exogenous modernizing factor.

In this chapter, I propose that the 1890 industrialization spurt triggered a transition from personalized–collectivist–hierarchical to impersonalized–individualist–egalitarian institutions (Raeff, 1984, pp. 90, 91). The population increase during the eighteenth century initiated this process (Kahan, 1985) and set a chain reaction in motion. This induced railroad construction for strategic and economic reasons, causing the land-to-labor ratio to fall even more due to population increase and weakening households' mutual dependency within the communal village as interaction with the urban economy raised the rising marginal value product of labor. Resources came under increasingly intensive use. Proximity to urban markets made investment returns more predictable (see also Leonard, 1990), raising land values and creating lending collateral as the Peasant Bank (est. 1882) allowed additional innovative investment to take place (North, 1973, pp. 28–30; Gregory, 1982, pp. 6.1, 141, 1994, p. 53; Hesse, 1993, p. 51). In a virtuous cycle, income variances stabilized in cumulative terms—lowering transaction costs, mitigating uncertainty, and intensifying demand for exclusively delineated property rights in land (Sahlin, in Bates, 1989, p. 42) in tandem with rising investment incentives (Poznanski, 1992). The upturn in productivity mitigated insurance interdependency, triggering a transition from a patriarchal hierarchy of coercion to voluntary egalitarian cooperation. The transformed village commune that emerged, through a nexus of voluntary rationalist cooperation, became a vehicle of subversion.

These aspects of my argument are congruent with and complementary to—as I suggest by adding peasant spatial mobility as an explanatory variable—Nafziger (2006) on Neoclassical utility maximization, the ethos that structured the flexible late-nineteenth-century village commune, and the response of this commune to population changes. The Tsarist gendarmes' violent reactionary response on January 9, 1905, to the public quest for egalitarian rights drove the Evolutionary Stable Strategy to general collapse. The norm of obeying the anointed Tsar was shaken irreversibly.

The Gerschenkronian–Szternian–Gregorian Conception

This subchapter fills the conceptual gap between the Gerschenkronian theory on the modernizing substitution of the state for the market and Gregory's (1982, 1994) revisionist emphasis on peasant rationalism. The autocracy's demand for goods and services, Gerschenkron claims, compensated for the deficiency in peasant purchasing power caused by instability of ownership. Land redistribution was managed on the basis of eldest authority, namely, by a hierarchy. Gregory (1994, p. 52) maintains that rational redistribution of movable capital, as in monetary "side payments," allowed the land-repartition custom to be sidestepped and enabling hereditary household landholding to prevail de facto over authoritarian collectivism. According to Gregory, Tsarist Russia insinuated itself into European business cycles, indicating full institutional integration rather than coercive backwardness. I argue, contrarily, that peasant household individualism cannot be assumed as given. During the initial post-emancipation period, considering the long-term legacies of serfdom, the Gerschenkronian conception should be credited. From 1842 onward (the dawn of railroad construction), anticipating its emancipation two decades later, however, the peasantry's transition to rationalism was increasingly driven by falling subsistence risk (Scott, 1976, p. 4).[2] Credit for this belongs to the railroads, reaching peaks in the industrialization spurt of 1890: By creating multiple material and immaterial choice opportunities, the "iron horse" set in motion a transition from risk-averse obedience to authority to mutual insurance in terms of rationalist voluntary cooperation (Sheshinski, 2010; Gintis, 2009; Poznanski, 1985). This, in turn, caused the domestic market for industrial goods to develop beyond Gerschenkron's expectations, rendering "state substitution" superfluous (Metzer, 1972, pp. 6–8; Bideleux, 1990, p. 204).[3] Emphasizing the costs of dictatorship (Gerschenkron, 1968, pp. 315, Points 1–5), I argue—contrary to Gerschenkron's proposal—that in the long run the Tsarist autocracy hindered, rather than promoted, the transition to modern economic growth (Fig. 1.1).

I now turn to historiography and propose the applicability of the continuous transformation theory. Descriptions informed by the Critical (of atomism) Realist school center on social structure and emphasize the identity-constituting authority of rulers and superiors in relation to subjects (Lawson, 1997, p. 247). Thus, the Critical Realist school delivers relatively high explanatory value where pre-modern societies are concerned. Gerschenkron proposes a rationalism restricted by custom, namely,

[2] I assume that allowing for risk diversification the railroads reduced "the subjective probability of maximum loss" (Hodgson, 2004; Veblen, 1931; McCloskey, 2009).

[3] On agriculture productivity growth as a proxy for the growing market for industrial produce, see Gregory (1982, p. 169, 1994, p. 31). Russia's agriculture/industry labor–productivity ratio compared rather well with that of European countries (Gerschenkron, 1962, Table, 355).

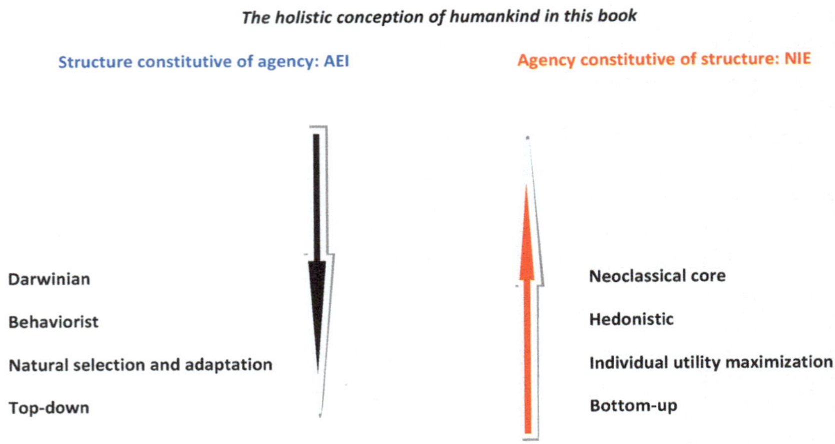

Fig. 1.1 Veblen (1931), Hodgson (2004)—Gerschenkron vs. Gregory–Sztern as a doctrinal historical bridge between the established schools. (Sources: Veblen (1931), Hodgson (2004), North (1973), Gregory (1982, 1994), Hamilton (1999))

a bounded rationality.[4] Applying my integrated AEI/NIE theory to his work, I find that reconstitutive downward causation (AEI) outweighs NIE. My contribution applies the findings of Sheshinski (2010) and Gintis (2009). I explain the reason: The explanatory weight of rationalist accounts rises in tandem with technological progress that rests on the widening availability of choice (see also Nelson & Winter, 1982). Gregory represents the Rationalist extreme, in which an atomistic independent peasant household practices a hedonistic utility-maximizing calculus. These schools cannot be seen as mutually challenging and exclusive. Applying the NIE/AEI framework, I emphasize that the railroads, supplemented by the telegraph (Chandler, 1977, p. 89), affected the peasants' cognitive and physical perceptions of distance (Crafts, EHES, 2007; Martens, 2004, p. 55). Reduced costs of travel measured in time units lowered the opportunity cost of labor employed in learning as the relative value of tilling the land declined. They lowered the costs of litigating disputes in court,[5] raising peasants' self-dignity perception and, in turn, their

[4] Williamson (1991) clarify this concept of human beings as "intendedly rational," though only limitedly so.

[5] Gaudin (2007, Table 3-3, p. 103, and Table 3-4, p. 104) gives evidence of escalating litigation rates in 1861–1913. See also, Engelgardt in Frierson (1993, p. 36).

factor productivity. Through natural selection and adaptation, household routines and individuals' habits of thought transformed toward higher tolerance and demand for individual rights (Worobec, 1995, p. 103). The instinctive predisposition to workmanship was increasingly selected by attracting more social approval than patriarchal protection (Hodgson, 2004, p. 186; Hoch, 1986, p. 129), which was deflated by its exploitive property. Freedom of exit transformed the commune into a vehicle of subversion (Barkai, 1987, p. 1).

Structure of the Monograph

Chapter 2. From Hierarchy to Egalitarianism: From Gerschenkron to Gregory—Deduction and Induction from NIE/AEI Complementarity and the Regulationist Model

This chapter answers the question of why the explanatory weight of Rationalist arguments rises in tandem with technological progress that involves the growing availability of choice. While Gerschenkron's account emphasizes the restriction of rational deliberation due to obedience of authority as dictated by custom, Gregory's work represents the Rationalist extreme, in which a peasant household atomistically practices a hedonist utility-maximizing calculus. The two schools cannot be seen as mutually challenging and excluding. I propose here that the spurt in industrialization in 1890 triggered a transition from personalized–collectivist–hierarchical to impersonalized–individualist–egalitarian institutions (Raeff, 1984, pp. 90, 91; Boserup, 1965). Such a perspective challenges the Marxist conceptualization of the post-emancipation Russian institutions.

Chapter 3. Through the Lenses of Theory: New Institutional Economics and American Evolutionary Institutionalism—The Railroads, National Market Formation, and Democracy in Late Tsarist Russia

Here I apply the integrated framework of NIE (New Institutional Economics), which views agency as the source of structure, and AEI (American Evolutionary Institutionalism), in which structure brought about by natural selection and adaptation preconditions individual agency. In this manner, I emphasize that the railroads, supplemented by the telegraph, affected cognitive and physical perceptions of distance, allowing income risk to diversify and facilitating the use of the legal system for dispute resolution (Chandler, 1977; Shivelbusch, 1986; Burbank, 2004). Combine the Neoclassical, NIE, and Evolutionary Cognitive Economics (Martens, 2004) approaches, I explain that the railroads triggered a hazard- and uncertainty-reducing market integration, leading to specialization and a temporary increase in net transaction costs. Seeking to lower these costs, the Tsarist government delegated property rights in land to individual heads of household under the aforementioned Stolypin reform. This transfer of economic rights amplified the demand for political rights, propelling Tsarist Russia toward constitutional monarchy.

Chapter 4. Industrialization and Tensions Between Tsardom and Nascent Civil Society

The discourse in this chapter addresses the social costs of the Gerschenkronian substitution pattern of Tsarist industrialization. This is done in terms of the Tsarist state's enforcement of coercive authoritarian hierarchies in view of the "endogenous" egalitarianism and the "external invasion" of the demand for participation that they occasioned. The patriarchal authority embedded in the popular conceptualization of the anointed Tsar and emulated by the village elder structures transmogrified into rationalist cooperation in which the premium for membership, in terms of the alternative returns on the options forgone, could not exceed the risk-insuring benefits of cooperation. The railroads played a crucial role in this as the *artel* ethos evolved endogenously into the forerunner of organized labor. I conclude by arguing that the autonomous Tsarist "commitment devices" (Greif, 2006) were of rural and kinship, rather than of Marxist-class, origin.

Chapter 5. The Peasant and His Ties to the Land in the Tsarist Industrialization

In this chapter, I argue that population increase in the Russian hinterland necessitated more intensive use of resources and presented the Tsarist government with novel internal and external challenges to its territorial control. This stimulated railroad construction for strategic reasons, unintentionally reducing the land/labor ratio and the interdependency of households in villages along the railways from the middle to the last decade of the nineteenth century. Central in the discussion are quantitative indicators of industrialization and the effects of this process on the peasantry's ties to the land and, conversely, its labor mobility. The revisionist studies of Gregory (1982, 1994) and Bideleux (1990) challenge Gerschenkron's claim that the obstacles to industrialization originated in rural collectivism. I posit that the interaction between the railroads and the communal custom and its corollary, the growing accessibility to urban industrial employment, caused barriers to peasant rural–urban and center–periphery migration to erode through the rise of peasant rationalism. The latter facilitated the transfer of labor from agriculture to industry, the accumulation of industrial skills, and the diversification of income sources, while lowering dependency on mutual insurance against calamities and its consequence, collectivism within the communal villages.

Chapter 6. The Railroad and the Metamorphosis of the Mir: Westernizer and Slavophile Conceptions Revisited

This chapter encapsulates the challenge to Gerschenkron's proposal. Conceptualized in the combined NIE/AEI paradigm, the railroad changed the character of the peasant commune during the post-emancipation period. The commune transformed itself from a compulsorily collectivist institution, structured on patriarchal authority, that embodied the legacy of serfdom with its heavy reliance on corporal punishment, to a hedonistic, rationalistic, and voluntary unit based on mutual insurance and cooperation following the industrialization spurt of 1890. The village commune formally dissolved during the Stolypin reform in accordance with what preceded it: an informal, voluntary peasant choice of the mixture of collectivism and individualism that would optimize productivity growth. The NIE/AEI model suggests complementarity between the Slavophile and Westernizers' conception of the commune.

This chapter concludes with a summary of the long-term decrease in risk occasioned by Imperial Russia's imports of Western technology for strategic purposes. Unlike the maritime technology that was absorbed during the reign of Peter I, which in greater part equipped the nobility with navigation skills, the dual-purpose railroads abetted increases in peasant literacy, geographic and social mobility, standards of living, and, ultimately, individualization of landholding rights, paving the way to productivity-raising agrarian entrepreneurship.

Chapter 7. Secularization and Pious Subversion: To the Constitution by Rail

Contrary to Fogel's (1964) proposal concerning the American railroads, Bajkov (1954) acknowledges the crucial role of railroads in the modernization of Russia, specifying their role in facilitating Tsarist industrialization by linking populations with centers of natural resources. Supplementing Baykov's focus on tangible aspects of modernization, I argue that the new technology also introduced an element of genuine choice that set a cultural revolution in motion: a transition among the peasantry from obeying authority to applying rationalism. Challenges by rival spiritual cultures were thrusting the Greek Orthodox legitimacy base of the autocracy[6] into a state of flux. Massive canonization gatherings, defections to the revolutionary Old Belief—*Starovery*—and retreats to other piously subversive sects, as well as secularization, challenged the basis of the empire's spiritual stability as well (Freeze, 1996, p. 311; Burds, 1998, p. 217). The resulting institutional rivalry caused the intra-ecclesiastical structure to metamorphose from hierarchical–authoritarian to an egalitarian and participatory parish (Shevzov, 2004, p. 39). The Russo-Japanese War, instigated to distract discontent, ended in 1904 in a debacle that destabilized the army. To re-legitimize the empire, Nicholas II launched a land-title reform in 1906 that aimed to improve the peasantry's living standards (Freeze, 1996, p. 309). Bearing in mind the incongruence of individual property rights and autocratic rule, I argue that the railroads established a direct line to the Constitution.

Chapter 8. Tsarist Modernization, the Peter-to-Nicholas-Continuity, and Progress through Reform

This chapter emphasizes the tension between Gerschenkron's (1968) notion of abstract continuity in history and Confino's (Personal communication, Discussion, 1997) historical-uniqueness approach. To allocate physical and human capital to military use—always a precipitant of backwardness—the primacy of the common welfare over individual welfare, typical of a war economy, has to be institutionalized (Anisimov, 1993; Sztern, 1994). This condition historically legitimizes individual subservience and degradation, hampering innovation (Mokyr, 1990, p. 177).[7]

[6] Freeze (1996, p. 309) relates to the political-stability function of the Church, the army, and the Tsar's personality cult.

[7] On this basis, I propose that the enforcement of individual property rights provides assurance against degradation.

This explains why, in a historical vicious cycle, Tsarist Russia became a backward importer of technology. Following the historical-uniqueness approach, however, I distinguish between Peter I's earlier version of modernization and that under Nicholas II. The "dual purpose" nature of railroad technology, as opposed to the eighteenth-century Baltic fleet, allowed and incentivized broad population strata to acquire human capital, bringing on a cultural revolution. The railroads stimulated the growth of domestic commodity markets, resulting in a short-run increase in net transaction costs originating in specialization. The ensuing Stolypin land reform, instituted at the Hayekian political rationality lag that, according to the Coesian paradigm, accumulated the costs of transactions, was incongruent with the Tsarist system of non-participatory rule (Pipes, 1999, p. 98).

Chapter 9. Was Stalin Necessary? The Railroads and the Crumbling of the Obshchina in Tsarist Russia

This chapter, co-authored by Michael Keren, uses a primary database: second-stage statistics for the Penza region and its rural self-government (*zemstvo*) in the Stolypin reform (1913), including the distance from each group of communal villages (*selo)* to the nearest railroad station, and fifteen land categories. Each category embodies a different and chronologically decreasing degree of collectivism versus individualism in the landholding mode that emerged from the emancipation of the serfs (1861) to and beyond the implementation of Stolypin's reform (1913).

The transformative impact of the railroad technology, expressed in the distance from each *selo* to the nearest railroad station, is an exogenous explanatory variable that influences the choice of landholding type—land category—and the congruent increasing over time degree of individualism versus collectivism that each of the fifteen post-Stolypin categories embodies. The degree of coercion versus voluntary cooperation that results in collectivism versus individualism in landholding, manifested in the mode of land cultivation chosen, is the dependent variable in the impact of Stolypin's reform as documented by the rural *zemstvo* (self-governing authority of Penza province—namely, the 1913 data applied). The landholding category is defined as the percent of the specific land category in the total land area in the *selo*. The results of the inquiry are as expected: the closer the peasants are to the nearest railroad station, the more individualistic is the land category that they choose. This also indicates that the peasantry's transition to rationalism took place in tandem with its use of the railroads. Thus, it was the advent of the Tsarist railroads that thrust the Russian economy into modernization mode; Stalinism was not necessary to instigate the process.

Chapter 10. Individualism and Collectivism: Measuring the Transition to Modernity in Tsarist Russian Peasant Society, Penza Province, 1913

This discourse defines human dignity as the determinant of human performance, making it a vital production factor. The aspect of individual human-dignity perception that unleashes creative productive performance is a socioeconomic choice driven by individuals' access to information and their ability to communicate and voluntarily organize. In a peasant society, spatial mastery and the acquisition of literacy and education are the means to the perception of human dignity, manifesting a structural change that heralds the transition to modernity. Empirically I support my argument with regressions of literate wage labor in relation to the population of Russian peasants as they shifted their modalities of landholding from collectivistic to individualistic ones after the emancipation (the dependent variable). The transition to individualism is a conceptual proxy for creative risk-taking that indicates a measure of reduced degradation. My data material originates in the 1913 statistics of the *zemstvo* (rural self-government) of Russia's Penza Povolzhe (province).

Unlike Robert Schumann, who sensed that human creative performance thrives mushroom-like "in humidity and darkness," I argue here that productive performance—delineated as a declining input-to-output ratio amid rising quality of production, resulting in rising standards of living and quality of life—is dependent on personal dignity. Applying the insight of Kazimierz Poznanski (1985, 1992), I argue that Imperial Russia's dependence on technology imports (Sztern, 2017) was occasioned by individual degradation, restrictions on freedom of thought and movement, growing risk of poverty, and analphabetism. I disclose two sets of conditions: those under which collectivism insulates against individual degradation and those that render collectivism the source thereof (Fig. 1.2).

This chapter calls attention to the conundrum of spatial mobility, literacy, and demand for education, catalyzed by the railroads, as the levers that gave peasant households and their members the ability to shake off the yoke of pre-modern insurance imposed under a hierarchy of coercion.

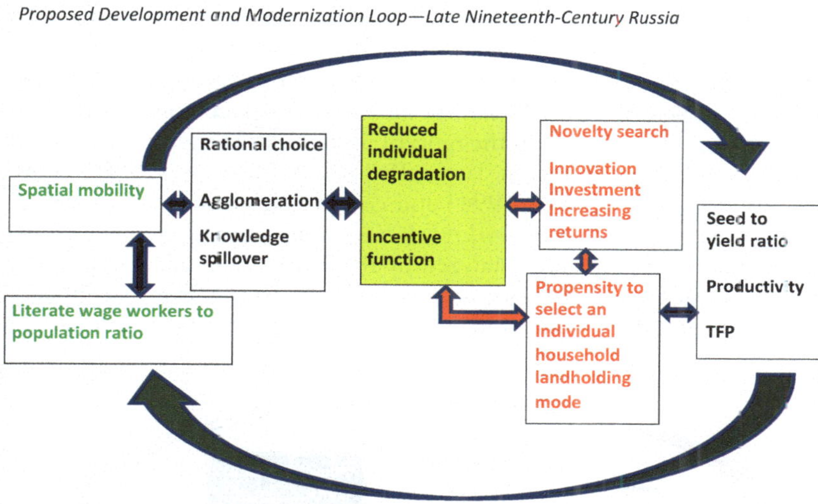

Fig. 1.2 Proposed development and modernization loop—late-nineteenth-century Russia. (Sources: Kahan (1989), Penza self-government (*zemstvo*) statistics (1913), Sheshinski (2010), Gintis (2009), Fujita et al. (2001), Hesse (1993), Mokyr (1990), Poznanski (1985, 1992), Brooks (2003), Leonard (2011), Gregory (1994))

Chapter 11. Measurable Power: Railroads, Literacy, and the Crafts Artel—Hierarchy in Disarray in Late Imperial Russia

Here I propose a way to measure the heretofore unexplained techno-cultural "translation" of the traditional rural non-agricultural production organization—the mutually insuring skilled workers' cooperative, the *artel*—into the historically continuous core of industrial trade unions, the institutional harbingers of modernization in pre-1905-Revolution Russia. The ratio of spatially mobile literate wage laborers to population, and to working men, is an explanatory variable for the transition to individualism and rationalism. Peasants' choice of individualistic landholding, in turn, is positively correlated to the share of children learning to read in the population—which I introduce as a proxy for the human-capital aspects of the modernization of development. By generating non-agricultural peasant income while incentivizing contractual literacy and lowering the costs of collective action, the *artel* paved the way toward the Constitution. To anchor these proposals in data, I use *zemstvo* (rural self-government) statistics for the Penza region, pertaining to the population of literate wage laborers (*gramotnye otkhodnikii*), the distance of village communes from railroad stations, and data on the ratio of households that engaged in craft production to households at large. Following Mironov (1999, 2000, 2012) and Gregory (1982, 1994) and countering Gerschenkron (1962, 1968), I argue that *the cultural revolutions that occurred* (Kahan, 1989) were non-violent and were catalyzed by the Tsarist railroads—setting the peasant population in motion, incentivizing its exodus from analphabetism, enhancing its skill accumulation, and predating 1905 (Fig. 1.3).

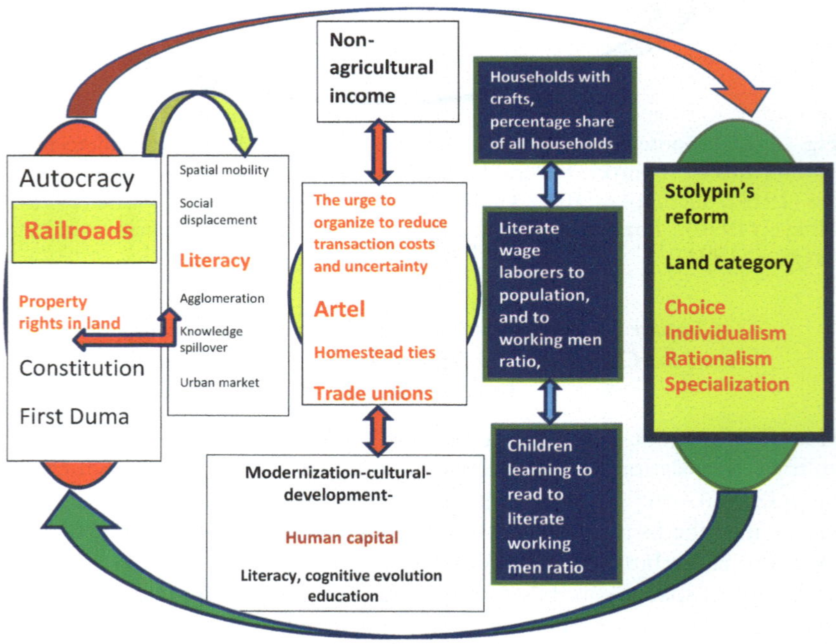

Fig. 1.3 The autocracy–railroads–modernization loop. (Sources: Ascher (1988), Gerschenkron (1962), Sztern (2017, 2018), Anderson (1980), Mironov (2012), Johnson (1979), Eklof (1986), Markievich and Castaneda (2017), Martens (2004))

References

Anderson, B. A. (1980). *Internal Migration During Modernization In Late Nineteenth-Century Russia*. Princeton UP.

Anisimov, V. E. (1993). *The reforms of Peter the great: Progress through coercion in Russia*. Sharpe.

Ascher, A. (1988). *The revolution of 1905. Part I: Russia in disarray. Part II: Authority restored*. Stanford University Press.

Atkinson, D. (1983). *The end of the Russian land commune 1905–1930*. Stanford University Press.

Bajkov, A. (1954). The economic development of Russia. *Economic History Review, 7*(2), 137–149.

Barkai, H. (1987). *Kibbutz efficiency and incentive conundrum*. The Maurice Falk Institute for Economic Research, The Hebrew University of Jerusalem.

Bates, R. (1989). *Beyond the miracle of the market: The political economy of agrarian development in Kenya*. Cambridge University Press.

Bideleux, R. (1990). Agricultural advance under the Russian village commune system. In R. Bartlett (Ed.), *Land commune and peasant community in Russia: Communal forms in imperial and early soviet society*. Macmillan in Association with the School of Slavonic and East European Studies.

Boserup, E. (1965). *The conditions of agricultural growth: The economics of agrarian change under population pressure*. Allen Unwin.

Boyer, R., & Orlean, A. (1993). How do Conventions Evolve? In Witt U. Ed. (1993) *Evolution in Markets and Institutions*. Physica-Vlg.

Brooks, J. (2003). *When Russia learned to read: Literacy and popular literature 1861–1917*. Northwestern UP.

Burbank, J. (2004). *Russian peasants go to court: Legal culture in the countryside, 1905–1917*. Indiana University Press.

Burds, J. (1998). *Peasant dreams and market politics: Labor migration and the Russian village 1861–1905*. Universitey of Pittsburgh Press.

Chandler, A. (1977). *The visible hand: The managerial revolution in American business*. Belknap Press of Harvard University Press.

Crafts, N. (2007). *Lecture*. EHES conference.

Eggertsson, T. (1990). *Economic behavior and institutions*. Cambridge University Press.

Eklof, B. (1986). *Russian peasant schools: Officialdom, village culture, and popular pedagogy, 1864–1914*. University of California Press.

Engelgardt, P. N. (1993). *Letters from the country, 1872–1887* (C. Frierson, Trans. & Ed.). Oxford University Press.

Fogel, R. (1964). *Railroads and American economic growth*. John Hopkins University Press.

Frank, S. (1999). *Crime, cultural conflict and justice in rural Russia 1856–1914.* University of California Press.

Freeze, L. (1996). Subversive piety: Religion and the political crisis in late Imperial Russia. *Journal of Modern History, 68*(2), 308–350.

Fujita, M., Krugman, P., & Venables, A. I. (2001). *The spatial economy; cities, regions and international trade.* The MIT Press.

Gaudin, C. (2007). *Ruling peasants: Village and state in late imperial Russia.* Northern Illinois University Press.

Gerschenkron, A. (1962). *Economic backwardness in historical perspective.* The Belknap Press of Harvard University Press.

Gerschenkron, A. (1968). *Continuity in history and other essays.* The Belknap Press of Harvard University Press.

Gintis, H. (2009). *The bounds of reason: Game theory and the unification of the behavioral sciences.* Princeton University Press.

Gregory, P. R. (1982). *Russian national income 1885–1913.* Cambridge University Press.

Gregory, P. R. (1994). *Before command. An economic history of Russia from emancipation to the first five-year plan.* Princeton University Press.

Greif, A. (2006). *Institutions and the path to modern economy: Lessons from medieval trade.* Cambridge University Press.

Hamilton, D. (1999). *Evolutionary economics: A study of change in economic thought.* Transaction Publishers.

Hesse, G. (1993). Land use systems and property rights. Evolutionary versus institutional economics. In U. Witt (Ed.), *Evolution in markets and institutions.* Physica-Vlg.

Hoch, S. (1986). *Serfdom and social control in Russia. Petrovskoe, a village in Tambov.* University of Chicago Press.

Hodgson, G. M. (2004). *The evolution of institutional economics, agency, structure and Darwinism in American institutionalism.* Routledge.

Hodgson, G. M., & Knudsen, T. (2004). *The replication of habits.* Paper Presented at the 6th International Workshop on Institutional Economics, The University of Hertfordshire.

Johnson, R. (1979). *Peasant and Proletarian - The Working Class of Moscow in The Late Nineteenth Century.* Leicester UP.

Kahan, A. (1985). *The plow, the hammer and the knout: An economic history of eighteenth-century Russia.* University of Chicago Press.

Kahan, A. (1989) *Russian economic history: The nineteenth century* (R. Weiss, Ed.). University of Chicago Press.

Kolchin, P. (1987). *Unfree labour, American slavery and Russian serfdom.* The Belknap Press of Harvard University Press.

Lawson, T. (1997). *Economics and reality.* Routledge.

Leonard, C. S. (1990). Landlords and the mir: Transaction costs and economic development in pre emancipation Russia (Iaroslav gubernia). In R. Bartlett (Ed.), *Land commune and peasant community in Russia: Communal forms in Imperial and early soviet society*. Macmillan in Association with The School of Slavonic and East European Studies.

Leonard, C. S. (2011). *Agrarian reform in Russia: The road from serfdom*. Cambridge UP.

Ma, D. (2006). *Law and commerce in traditional China. An institutional perspective on the "Great Divergence"*. Seminar Paper, Department of Economic History, Lund University.

Markievich, A., & Castaneda, D. (2017). *The Stolypin reform and agricultural productivity in late Imperial Russia*. Working Paper No 239 CEFIR/ NES Working Paper Series.

Martens, B. (2004). *The cognitive mechanics of economic development and institutional change*. Routledge.

McCloskey, D. (2009, February 23). *Talk on bourgeois ethics. Economic history seminar*. Lund University.

Metzer, J. (1972). *Some economic aspects of railroad development in Tsarist Russia*. Unpublished doctoral dissertation. University of Chicago.

Milov, L. (2001). *Velikorusskiipakhariosobennostirossijskogoistoricheskogoprotsessa*. Biblioteka Gumer-istoria. http://www.gumer.info/bibliotek_Buks/History/milov/01.php

Mironov, B. N. (1999). *SocialnayaistoriaRossiiperiodaImperii (XVIII-nachalo XX v) genezislichnostidemokraticheskojsemiigrazhdanskogoobshchestvaipravovogogosudarstva: v dwuchtomach*. DimitrijBulanin.

Mironov, B. N. (2000). *A social history of imperial Russia, 1700–1917* (Vol. I). Westview Press.

Mironov, B. N. (2012). *Nabljudalsia li v PozdnieImperskojRosiiMalthusianskijkrizis :DochodyipovinostiRossijskogokrestianstva, v 1801–1914 gg*.

Mokyr, J. (1990). *Lever of riches. Technological creativity and economic progress*. Oxford University Press.

Nafziger, S. (2006). *Communal institutions, resource allocation, and Russian economic development*. Unpublished doctoral dissertation, summary. Yale University.

Nelson, R., & Winter, S. (1982). *An evolutionary theory of economic change*. The Belknap Press of Harvard UP.

North, D. C. (1973). *Västerlandets Uppgång*. SNS.

North, D. C. (1981). *Structure and change in economic history*. WW Norton and Company.

North, D. C. (1990). *Institutions, institutional change and economic performance*. Cambridge University Press.

North, D. C. (2005). *Understanding the process of economic change*. Princeton University Press.

North, D. C., Wallis, J. J., & Weingast, B. R. (2009). *Violence and social orders: A conceptual framework for interpreting recorded human history*. Cambridge University Press.

Pipes, R. (1999). *Property and freedom*. Harvill Press.

Poznanski, K. (1985). *The environment for technological change in centrally planned economies*. World Bank Staff Working Papers.

Poznanski, K. (1992). A property rights perspective on the evolution of communist-type economies. In K. Poznanski (Ed.), *Constructing capitalism. The re-emergence of civil society and liberal economy in the post-communist world*. Westview Press.

Raeff, M. (1984). *Understanding Imperial Russia*. Columbia University Press.

Scott, J. (1976). *The moral economy of the peasant. Rebellion and subsistence in Southeast Asia*. Yale University Press.

Sheshinski, E. (2010). *Limits in individual choice*. The Hebrew University of Jerusalem.

Shevzov, V. (2004). *Russian orthodoxy on the eve of revolution*. Oxford University Press.

Shivelbusch, W. (1986). *The railway journey: The industrialization of time and space in the 19th century*. University of California Press.

Smith, A. (1998). *An inquiry into the nature and the causes of the wealth of nations*. Regnery Publishing.

Sztern, S. (1994). *Det socioekonomiska systemets institutionella desintegration och omvandling Sovjetunionen/Ryssland*. Unpublished candidate paper. Lund University, Department of Economic History.

Sztern, S. (2017). *Russia on the move; the railroads and the exodus from compulsory collectivism 1861–1914*. Lund university Press.

Sztern, S. (2018). *Steam engine on the rail and landholding system in-nineteenth century Russia*. Lomonosov State University Economic History Seminar. (in Russian).

Vanberg, V. (1994). *Rules and choice in economics*. Routledge.

Veblen, T. (1931). *The theory of the leisure class*. Viking.

Williamson, O. E. (1991). The Logic of Economic Organization. In Williamson, O. E., & Winter, S.G. Ed. *The Nature of the Firm-Origins, Evolution and Development*. Oxford UP.

Worobec, C. D. (1995). *Peasant Russia family and community in the post-emancipation period*. Northern Illinois University Press.

CHAPTER 2

From Hierarchy to Egalitarianism: From Gerschenkron to Gregory—Deduction and Induction from NIE/AEI Complementarity and the Regulationist Model

An Institutional Transition from Personalized to Impersonalized Rights

Russia's historical transition, described in this monograph, and the recent one—dating from 1985 or so—have one feature in common: a shift from personalized to impersonalized institutions. Thus, my historical investigation of the Tsarist modernization centers on the dissolution of personalized hierarchies of coercion.

The transitional reform embodied in this commonality comprises a set of corrective measures triggered by change in informal institutions (conventions), to which the general defining elements of the institutional superstructure adjusted at a lag. It is assumed in the following discussion that during the Tsarist period, as well as in the institutional disintegration and transformation of the Soviet Union, "bottom-up" informal institutional adjustments that strove to mitigate uncertainty—to lower transaction costs—preceded the actual "top-down" reform. Thus, society's demand for decentralization was the novelty and the formal institutional restructuring of property rights was a lagged—path-dependent—incorporation of this novelty into the formal institutional infrastructure. The

S. Sztern, *Russia on the Move*, Studies in Economic Transition,
https://doi.org/10.1007/978-3-030-89285-2_2

Back to the relatively modern *concluding stage,* 1890–1914

Planned economy to market economy, *from 1985 to the present writing (2021)*

Commonality: from personalization to impersonalization of rights

Fig. 2.1 The two Russian transitions

Personalized **Impersonalized**

Time range / quality of rights

Fig. 2.2 Impersonalization of the law. (Sources: Bakunin, 1970; Raeff, 1984; Barzel, 1989)

popular demand for institutional change in the late Tsarist period represented society's adjustment to the increase in population density and the state-led industrialization, namely, a technology-driven change in the production possibility frontier (Eggertsson, 1990, p. 319).

The argument that follows rejects the Marxian paradigm, which considers class conflict the way to conceptualize the effects of industrialization on institutions, and vice versa, in Tsarist Russia. Instead of discussing the consequences of the development of an ostensible disequilibrium between the relative weights of competing class interests, I believe it more appropriate to address the contradiction between the *subjectivization* of the society-specific concept of rights over time generally and of property rights specifically, and its *objectivization*.

Picture a continuous time axis along which the transition of a society, manifested through systemic metamorphoses observable at two discrete points, is defined by degrees of subjectivization/personalization versus objectivization/impersonalization of the process that distributes and enforces rights. The qualitative variable defined by this principle assumes the following polar dichotomy (Fig. 2.2):

The quality of rights, in principle, is commensurate with their distribution and the probability of their enforcement. Personalization of a right means that the ruler bestows a right on a particular person and no one else. Thus, it assumes the form of a personal privilege, the terms and durability of which are constrainable by changes in the nature of a particular ruler–subject relationship. In this case, the probability of enforcement is zero. The opposite is a right distributed under a specific and relatively permanent set of rules to any person who meets foreknown criteria. The right would be fully transferable and predictable; the probability of its enforcement would equal 1.

In historical time, these qualitative proportions have evolved from personalized, hence subjective, privilege in pre-modern society to objective rights in modern society. The probability of enforcement makes the following transition:

$0 \leq \Pr(e) \leq 1$.[1]

Transaction costs rise when property rights are insufficiently delineated in terms of reliability (Barzel, 1989, pp. 3–12). Plain intuition indicates

[1] Let us summarize this in symbolic form:

Probability of enforcement = $0 \leq \Pr(e) \leq 1$
Transferability = $0 \leq \Pr(f) \leq 1$
Predictability = $0 \leq \Pr(c) \leq 1$
System-specific transaction costs = TR(S)

The system-specific transaction costs are a function of the expected value of the variables defined above:

$$TR(S) = f\left[E\left(\Pr(e), \Pr(f), \Pr(c)\right)\right]$$

It also stands to reason that the system-specific transaction costs, TR(S), are positively related to the proportion of personalization/subjectivization, $0 \leq \Pr(P) \leq 1$, and are negatively related to the proportion of objectivization, $0 \leq \Pr(O) \leq 1$, of rights:

$$\Pr(O) = 1 - \Pr(P)$$

$$\Pr(P) = 1 - \Pr(O)$$

In symbolic form:

$$TR(S) = f\left[\Pr(P)\right] \text{alt.} TR(S) = f\left[1 - \Pr(O)\right]$$

that personalized subjectively legitimized property rights are insufficiently delineated. Generalizing this theory of property rights to other kinds of rights—civil rights, for instance—one ends up assuming that rising system-specific transaction costs in a society are a symptom of vaguely delineated rights. In our case, this means that when restrictions as well as rewards depend on the nature of personal relations, by no means excluding those between ruler and subjects, no set of such rights can endow life and property with long-term security.

Generally speaking, the objectivization of the distribution of rights and obligations requires the establishment of instances that can play an autonomous legislative role vis-à-vis the sovereign without incurring personal risk. A legal code consistent with a set of fundamental principles, judicial uniformity, sundry administrative praxis, and equality before the law may be thought of as necessary, although not sufficient *per se*, for the objectivization of rights.

Locus and Type of Rule in Tsarist Russia

A feature that clearly distinguishes the Tsarist Russian institutional tradition from its West European counterparts is the lack of decision-making power centers that are both legally constituted and autonomous relative to the Tsar. Muscovy's late-medieval policies were defined by attempts to attain national unification by legitimizing the unconstrained authority of the autarchy. Tsardom was built atop foundations of the patrimonial principle, which allowed all state lands to become the personal *votchina* (patrimony) of the ruler (Pipes, 1995, p. 70). State governance was restricted to the performance of *posylki*—"errands" assigned to the crown, from which the nation could benefit via personal service to the Tsar (Raeff, 1966, p. 90). This absolved government officials of personal responsibility for the quality of judicial and other administrative services performed on the sovereign's behalf.

The absence of a coherent legal code of conduct randomized the discharge of governmental functions, placing it at the mercy of competing personal rent/favor-seeking interests. It also raised communication barriers in relations with the crown and hindered coordination among different arms of the autarchy in the systematized managing of its subjects' conduct (Raeff, 1966; Wagner, 1994; Wortman, 1989, pp. 12–31).

Due to delayed and distorted information flows, the personalized distribution of obligations as well as of rights (or, more appropriately termed, "privileges") was unpredictable, resulting in insecurity of life and property even at the highest levels of the social hierarchy. Expressed in modern Neo-Institutionalist terms, one may state that the personalized rule of the absolute autarchy, contrary to expectations at the time of its enforcement, was characterized by high transaction costs occasioned by traditionally vaguely defined rights (Barzel, 1989, pp. 3–12). The notion of the person of the Tsar as the sole mediator between the human and the divine and an executor of the latter's wish—by definition, satisfying the highest moral requirements—was considered instrumental for a formally strengthened Greek Orthodox national identity, the unification of all conquered ethnicities under the European Russian rule of God's go-between with man, and the uniformity of governance that would enhance personal security. Paradoxically, however, this very notion resulted in a volatile institutional setting and unpredictable outcomes even for Tsarism's most intimate servants.

Peter I and His Notion of the Rule of Law: Militarized Absolutism

It is true that Russia had experienced a relative separation of Tsar and state before the period discussed here. The first, engineered by Peter the Great (r. 1682–1725), oriented the guidelines of government administration toward rationalization and universalization of the legal framework (Wortman, 1976, p. 9; Raeff, 1966, pp. 92, 93, 98). Institutional adjustments in the eighteenth and nineteenth centuries, such as greater autonomy for the Senate, were brought on by the exigencies of war, leading to the adoption of the military hierarchy as an organizing model for state administration (Wortman, 1976, pp. 12, 13, 71). Since the concept of an impersonalized state, distinguished from the Tsar's personalized rule, clashed with custom, a regression toward the latter followed the cessation of Peter's coercive reign (Wortman, 1976, pp. 12, 13, 71; Raeff, 1966, pp. 92, 93, 98). The prevalence of traditionally established ways of conduct over formally introduced innovations verifies North's postulates about the historical durability of informal institutions and their impact on adaptability to systemic changes in general (North, 2005, p. 117). The need to transition from conformity to custom to an innovation-adjusted set of available skills limits the de facto effectiveness and durability of reforms. The more quickly the transition occurs, the greater the risk of regression (North, 1990, 1993).

Thus, the personalized distribution and modification of civil and property rights re-emerged as a manifest and distinctive feature of the Russian institutional superstructure and persisted for decades to come. Furthermore, the inquisitorial procedure—a relic of the Petrine era that remained identifiable until the judicial reform of 1864—severely restricted the autonomy, that is, the purview, of judges. The subordination of civil law to a military concept of law that centralized the power of implementation in the hands of the Tsar was itself a seventeenth-century institutional innovation that eventually attained the status of tradition (Wortman, 1976, p. 14).[2]

Catherine II: Ambivalent Steps Toward the Impersonalization of Law

Catherine II (r. 1762–1796), cognizant of the political need to ratify the nobility's de facto strengthened position, absolved landed subjects of compulsory state service in 1762. These subjects' allodial property rights were codified in the 1785 Charter to the Nobility, which ostensibly assured her erstwhile servants—the *khlopy*, a historical category of landed subjects prior to 1785—the nobility's allodial property rights. Initiated in the Petrine era (1714), the Charter bestowed freedom from state service, enhancing the security of the nobles' lives and property (Bartlett, 1999). The informal restrictions inherent in the intermediary executive echelons, however, prevented these acts from allowing a consolidated estate, one that could influence the crown's decisions and legislation, to emerge. Still, concern for property and civil rights during the eighteenth century—inspired by Western philosophers—was not restricted to reforming the conditions of the nobility. The contemporary debates also turned their attention to aspects of an incentive structure composed of a codified set of rights that would address the institutional environment problems of state peasants who lived on land owned by the Tsarist State (Moon, 1999, p. 22). Thus, a Lockean "instrumental" version of the property rights concept was adopted to free the nobles, who, according to the Charter, were formally assured *polnaya sobstvennost* (full ownership) and propositions to grant the right of possession and use—*vladenie i polzovanie* (transferable only through hereditary tradition and distinct from ownership

[2] The institutions that guided the courts, inspired by Swedish, Danish, and German military codes, were introduced in the Military Process section of the Military Statute of 1716.

rights)—were expressed in regard to the state peasantry. Finally, through codification in the *Svod Zakonov* (the Tsarist law book), state peasants were formally given property rights—*krestianskaya sobsvennost*—that shared the characteristics of nobles' rights, although not fully applied (Crisp, 1989, pp. 34, 36).

Generally speaking, the contents of Catherine's formal reform may be seen as progressive. Its inclusiveness suggests that one should treat the question of legitimacy and attempts to implement the rule of impersonalized law as the key variables in addressing the metamorphoses of the Russian system, instead of promoting a conflict perspective that focuses on the various "class-specific" proportions of rights granted. The personal talents, concepts, and aspirations of the Tsar, and his ability to effectively dominate the informal institutions—the essence of autarchy—were crucial in any institutional change in Imperial Russia.

While the Petrine legislation bore evidence of the Tsars' signature *imennye ukazy* (Hughes, 1998, p. 93), the enlightened Catherine II subordinated the institution of the Tsar to the rule of law by strengthening the role of the Senate and autonomous local government by giving sway to systematized and impersonal law, albeit not superseding the dignity of anointed Tsars' rulings. Hosking explains that as a matter of administrative novelty European Russia was to be divided in *gubernii* (provinces populated by 200,000–300,000 souls) and, within each gubernia, *uezdy* (districts populated by 20,000–30,000 souls). Each gubernia would be structured by a governor responsible to the Senate and entitled to appeal directly to the Tsar. The institution of the governor embodied controlled autonomization of the tax collection, police, and trade monopolies functions (Hosking, 1997, pp. 101, 102). Catherine's attempt to create exclusively judicial institutions, such as local courts of the *uezd*—administrative district—established in 1775 (Wortman, 1976, p. 13), may be interpreted as an effort to decentralize, namely, to autonomize the judiciary in the manner necessary for the impersonalization of law. These attempts, however, were counterbalanced by the supremacy of the procurator general, an official inaugurated in Petrine times whose task it was to head the judicial hierarchy and closely supervise the activity of the Senate in accordance with Tsarist directives (Wortman, 1976, p. 13). Thus, in principle, the Tsar remained the unchallenged source of all law (Raeff, 1966, pp. 98, 103–107).

Did the 1864 Judicial Reform Institute the Rule of Law?

One would assume that the formal codification of rules in 1833, the 1864 judicial reform, and the subsequent professionalization of the judicial services would have combined to further the de facto objectivization of the principles that informed the distribution of obligations and rights. All this notwithstanding, however, the imperial institutions evolved unpredictably. Their patterns of conduct were dictated by the ad hoc preferences of the sovereign, which he communicated to his subjects in the form of decrees unrestricted by any aspiration to consistency within the general legal framework.

Patriarchal Authority as the Source of Law, Personalized Institutions, and Erosion of Estate Cohesion

As late as the nineteenth century, the state and the Orthodox Church considered the family the cornerstone of the social and political order (Wagner, 1994, p. 3; Hughes, 1998, p. 94) and, at the micro level, invoked the guiding principle of the sovereign's unquestionable authority and patriarchalism as its metaphor (Wagner, 1994, pp. 5, 6).

Confusion between birthrights (presumably personalized in their origin) and privileges (which rewarded specific members of the nobility for meritorious service) mired the huge seigniorial clans in perpetual internal conflicts (Raeff, 1966, pp. 98, 99), not to mention institutionalized hurdles against the development of solidarities that would delineate broader strata such as a gentry. Consequently, the crown's most vigorously promoted objective was to prevent, systematically, the formation of any alternative power centers such as powerful estates defined by a homogeneous set of goals, including a center composed of nobility. Russian society, including the gentry as well as the commune-bound peasantry (Crisp, 1989), was conflict-ridden, atomized, and, where property rights were concerned, chaotic at its highest levels. To explain the weakness of the concept of property rights in Russia, one must note both the codification of rights and its absence. Several examples bear this out: An act passed in February 1803 proposed to award full individual title in specified parcels of land to serf householders by the *pomeshchik*, their former owner, who individually decided to free them. Legislation in 1848 allowed serfs to acquire and possess immobile assets in their own names, not merely in that of their master. Prototype reforms ahead of the 1861 Emancipation Act, however, did not delineate the full individual right to property. It established hereditary use rights only and institutionalized the customary law, which was based on collective ownership (Crisp, 1989, p. 37). Given the erratic nature of the statutory praxis, the question of who held rights (title) to a given parcel of land could be answered, de facto, on a personalized basis only. In the case of serfs, until the general emancipation the answer depended simply on the strength of the *pomeshchik's* memory. Thus, in the Russian context, the codification of laws by no means guaranteed their objectivization.

Laws in the Service of Political Goals

Laws of whatever kind, written as well as customary, had no superior dignity over political ends and were reconciled with such ends ad hoc. Differences in ownership status between one seignior's emancipated serfs and another's, which presumably existed, prevented the formation of a peasant estate and abetted perpetual internal conflicts instead of class solidarity. The delegation of political power for the purpose of legitimizing, through the franchise, autonomous legislative and executive instances and allowing for the establishment of a bureaucracy that would take governmental actions according to a consistent, rational, and predictable set of rules—a legal code of higher dignity than the autarchy's short-term ends—was paradoxically thought to have destabilizing characteristics. As independent public courts were introduced during the 1864 judicial reform, the autocrat termed the emerging institutional innovation "the usurpation of autocratic prerogatives, threatening the very basis of the Tsar's power." In other words, the Tsar as the source of a personalized institutional system never came to terms with the impersonalization of law. This created an inherent contradiction in the reform process, impeding progress and, in the eyes of the autarchy, legitimating repression (Wortman, 1976, pp. 2, 5; Ascher, 1988).

It would be no exaggeration to assume that Russia's defeat in the 1853–1856 Crimean War called the Tsarist Government's attention to the dire need to modernize and to delegate legislative and political power. Thus, the communication problems between the Tsar and his subjects could be addressed and the imperial administrative efforts could be coordinated. The debates that heralded the emancipation of the serfs in 1861 erupted presumably in response to the importance—acknowledged by the ruling elites, the intelligentsia, and the government—of the subjects' loyalty and participation, not least in battle. Another factor that should not be neglected is the effect of an endogenous change in attitudes toward the concept of legality that had been occurring gradually since the middle of the eighteenth century (Wortman, 1976).

Skill Accumulation As the Source of Corporate Demand for Legality

Any top-down reform presumably creates a lagged increase in adaptability, namely, an enriched spectrum of skills at the executive levels. This process, although hampered, strengthens the demand "from below" for institutional innovations.[3] An example of such requested changes in our context might be society's commitment to equality before the law, which one may understand as a "translation" (Boyer & Orlean, 1993, p. 22) of a form of egalitarianism specific to Russian culture. Theoretically, the institutional innovations could have been induced indirectly by confronting the crown with a credible threat of a disorganized, knowledge-determined challenge to its supremacy. The voice of the enlightened among the nobility and the intelligentsia, which rejected the notion of serfdom as such (Gerschenkron, 1968, p. 155), as well as the urgency of the political threat inherent in the serfs' poverty and backwardness, did assume weight in Tsarist considerations.

Viewed from a historical perspective, the Emancipation Act of 1861 and the gradually strengthened position of the gentry, including the establishment of rural self-government—the *zemstvo* assemblies—implied recognition of the autarchy's interdependence of the existence of cohesive social strata loyal to the crown. The mere acknowledgment of this state of affairs restricted the scope of despotic rule. The institutionalized protection of the interests of landowning strata, contrary to a particular noble's interests, may be seen as the onset of de facto recognition of the importance of objectivizing rights in land. This process, as well as the attention given to the peasantry's need for socioeconomic subsistence, amounted to a forced concession by the totalitarian ruler to his subjects, in the shape of a modernizing land reform, for his long-term aim of self-preservation. The origins of Stolypin's land reform are put into theoretical conceptualization in Chap. 3. Although peasants endured hardships at the time of its

[3] A deeper discussion of this issue in our context is found in Chap. 8.

implementation, the rapid industrialization program personified by S.I.U. Witte, the enlightened Minister of Finance (1892–1903), was widely expected by the Tsarist Government, the ruling elites, and the Westernized intelligentsia to raise the masses' standard of living in the long run and, in turn, guarantee the supremacy of autocratic rule.

Emancipation and Redemption in the 1861–1863 Statutes: Enforcement of the Peasant Commune as an Unintended Paradoxical Challenge to Totalitarian Atomization

Admittedly, the imperial government never intended to attenuate the country's social atomization unless forced to do so. On the contrary,[4] the consolidation that occurred within the agricultural and industrial production units was a byproduct of the modernization that industrialization brought in train. Cultural modernization driven by the industrialization process, in turn, inspired reactionary elements among the entrepreneurial class and the landowning nobles to intensify their demand that the autarchy formally redefine the principles of its rule (Atkinson, 1983, p. 19).

The cause of this social imbalance was manifested in the redemption acts, which favored the gentry, implicitly acknowledged the political need to secure the nobles' loyalty, and appeared to amplify the importance of the peasant commune. These features, *in the Russian context*, may be considered unintentionally progressive and representative of a liminal stage, suggesting the transformative possibility of creating consolidated and, in relation to autarchy, reasonably autonomous power centers that would influence policy. There was in fact a causal connection between the consolidation of the post-emancipation commune and autonomous demand for political negotiation power.[5] The developing entrepreneurial sector

[4] Atkinson (1983, pp. 12, 13), elaborates. The Tsar's highly personalized rule imposed a top-down restriction on the bureaucracy's modus operandi. Instead of following a predictable impersonalized law, the imperial bureaucracy is said to have "served at the sovereign's pleasure," that is, it was controlled by the Tsar's will from the very top to the very bottom. *Freedom of association was not recognized*; the operative idea was to exacerbate social atomization and render the creation of an organized opposition to the autocracy impossible. The institution that supplied imperial rule with its legitimacy, the Orthodox Church, was itself restricted by the Tsar in its practical endeavors, as "The administrators of the Orthodox Church were servants of the state appointed, personally, by the Tsar." Atkinson emphasizes the "weakness of public institutions" relative to the crown. If so, the pro-atomization forces were represented by the "extended hand" of the tradition-oriented order.

[5] It is discussed in Chaps. 3 and 5.

and the professionalization of judicial services oriented to Roman law implied the *possibility* of development toward a pluralistic society (Raeff, 1966; Gerschenkron, 1968, p. 124; Ascher, 1988, p. 18) that could absorb and institutionalize an objectivized code of socioeconomic conduct. The intelligentsia's rejection of ownership of men by men may be regarded as a first step toward the de facto implementation of the principle of equality before the law. Growing awareness of the need to establish an independent judiciary may be seen as the beginning of a transition toward the impersonalization of law. Concurrently, a gradual change in favor of privatization on a household basis and the individualization of property rights occurred in the interpretation and implementation of the emancipation and redemption statutes of the 1860s (Crisp, 1989, p. 41).

Now that the peasants enjoyed freedom (relative to serfdom conditions that had limited them to being a supply of cheap labor for the landed gentry), they increasingly demanded modernization. Thus, despite institutional anachronisms inherent in rural customs, the abolition of serfdom and the judicial reform of 1864 paved the way to the 1890 industrialization program peak, which in turn fostered an innovation-oriented set of skills that placed the autarchy under additional and decisive pressure for change (Gerschenkron, 1968, p. 132).

Industrialization as the Foremost Challenge to Personalized Institutions Until 1906

Nevertheless, the problem of objective rights—the de jure and de facto implementation of the rule of law as a supreme principle—remained largely unresolved until 1906. During the decades preceding the industrialization effort, the relation between ownership structure and economic performance received emphasized attention amid open debate (Ermolov, 1906; Pravilova, 2014). Viewed from this perspective, nineteenth-century Russian society cannot be criticized for lack of intellectual consciousness of socioeconomic issues. The hindrances to development lay in the inability of the professionals and intellectuals to effectively influence policy outcomes in accordance with the conclusions they had reached without questioning the rationality of preserving the autarchy. This, in turn, suspended the autarchy on the horns of an ancient dilemma that totalitarian states face: Disregarding the perceived need for change, absolutist Tsardom could not reform itself from within without jeopardizing its fundamental legitimacy and self-destructing in the process.[6]

Since Petrine times, the scope of institutional innovation in Russia was restricted to a range of Tsarist prerogatives bounded by leaving the autarchy in place as an omnipotent, personalized institution or serving merely as the sole guardian of justice. Within this ambit, the authority of the crown could concentrate on legislating and executing justice or could lay down institutional guidelines through reform and guarantee the executive functions of the judicial system. As the matter played out, the crown traditionally eyed the general independence of courts and the professionalization of service with suspicion. The bolder a Tsar's decision to introduce impersonalized law in Russia was, the more severe the personalized restrictions that were imposed on its implementation.[7]

Thus, the country's legal culture yielded a Russia-specific dualism. Progressive reforms were accompanied by an intensified effort to control the Tsarist judicial system, officialdom and all, thereby impeding the skill-acquisition process that was needed for the successful implementation of the new statutes. Corruption and lack of professional knowledge at the intermediary levels were exploited by the "head" to legitimize additional control and repression. Russians lived constantly under the illusion that the Tsar was their just protector whereas the judges, the advocates, and the clerks who applied the law were their tormentors and despoilers. Willfully erected barriers to the development of intellectual integrity in the judicial system prevented the secularization that was needed to demystify the institutional role of the Tsar and limit the scope of despotism, impairing the predictability that would enhance socioeconomic progress (Wortman, 1976, p. 12). The ruler, according to the conservative mindset that held sway—supported by the Orthodox Church for reason of its own interests—had to be perceived as the source of moral order. Judicial autonomy and the objectivization of rights, if successful, would strip the cherished Father (*Batjushka*), the Tsar, of the stability that illiteracy and custom assured him. The implementation of an impersonalized legal code would deprive the sovereign, as a source of law, of its raison d'être.

[6] Gerschenkron (1968, p. 113). See also my essay, *Det socioekonomiska systemets desintegration och omvandling Sovjetunionen/Ryssland* (Sztern, 1994.

[7] Wortman (1976, pp. 10, 11) calls attention to Catherine the Great's *nakaz*—instruction—to the 1767 legislative commission, demanding an absolutely literal interpretation of law and total subservience of judges, severely restricting executors' personal responsibility and the autonomy of the judicial system.

The role of the 1890 industrialization effort in strengthening innovative thinking and, in turn, the challenge that it posed to the autocracy, should not be ignored in this context—especially if one bears in mind Gerschenkron's depiction of the process as having been spearheaded by imports of technology. Viewed in this manner, one may assume that this process led, by necessity, to intensified interaction and intellectual interdependence between Russia and the West. Given the ongoing transition to constitutional government in Western and Central Europe, the Russian hereditary monarchy, based on the 1832 Fundamental Laws that affirmed the Tsar's rule as one of divine right (Ascher, 1988, p. 12), may have been perceived by more and more constituencies as an anachronism by the turn of the twentieth century.

The abolition of serfdom in Russia was followed by a legal opportunity for peasants to transform their use rights in land into ownership rights through a redemption procedure.[8] Intuitively, one might expect these two measures to have created the necessary incentives for investment and productivity increases in agriculture, thereby freeing labor for industrial production in urban centers. As Gerschenkron emphasizes, however, matters in Imperial Russia were not quite so simple (left-hand side of Fig. 2.3). An ancient custom in rural life erected a major impediment to labor mobility and, in turn, imposed a development barrier of formal nature (Gerschenkron, 1968, pp. 122, 187). The custom originated partly in the survival strategies of the non-urban population (Alexandrovich, in Bartlett,

[8] Generally speaking, the annual redemption payment reflected the maximum rate of interest permissible for the period—6 percent—and the regressive allotment quitrent, which was set according to "the law of diminishing returns to land." Consequently, the quitrent was higher for the first *desyatina* (2.7 acres) of land than for the next one. Nevertheless, the additional burden relative to the pre-reform quitrent obligations concerned the 20–25 percent of redemption debt that was not taken over by the state. The peasants' post-reform economic hardships originated largely in their dependency on the goodwill of the gentry as well as that of the state, the latter charged *de jure* with protecting the interests of the former. The redemption process was carried out collectively by the *mir*, a village of former serfs belonging to the same seignior, which might contain several village communes (Atkinson, 1983, p. 23). According to the 1861 Imperial Manifesto, the nobility retained property rights in land even after the abolition of serfdom under a formally maintained fiction. The Emancipation prescribed the granting of permanent use rights in land that would be collectively allotted to peasants. The same land could be transferred to a *selskoe obshchestvo*, a "rural society," in exchange for payment, 80 percent of which was to be made by the state and repaid by the peasants over a forty-nine-year period. Gerschenkron (1962, pp. 120, 171–182) concludes that the redemption procedure did involve the transformation of use rights into ownership rights.

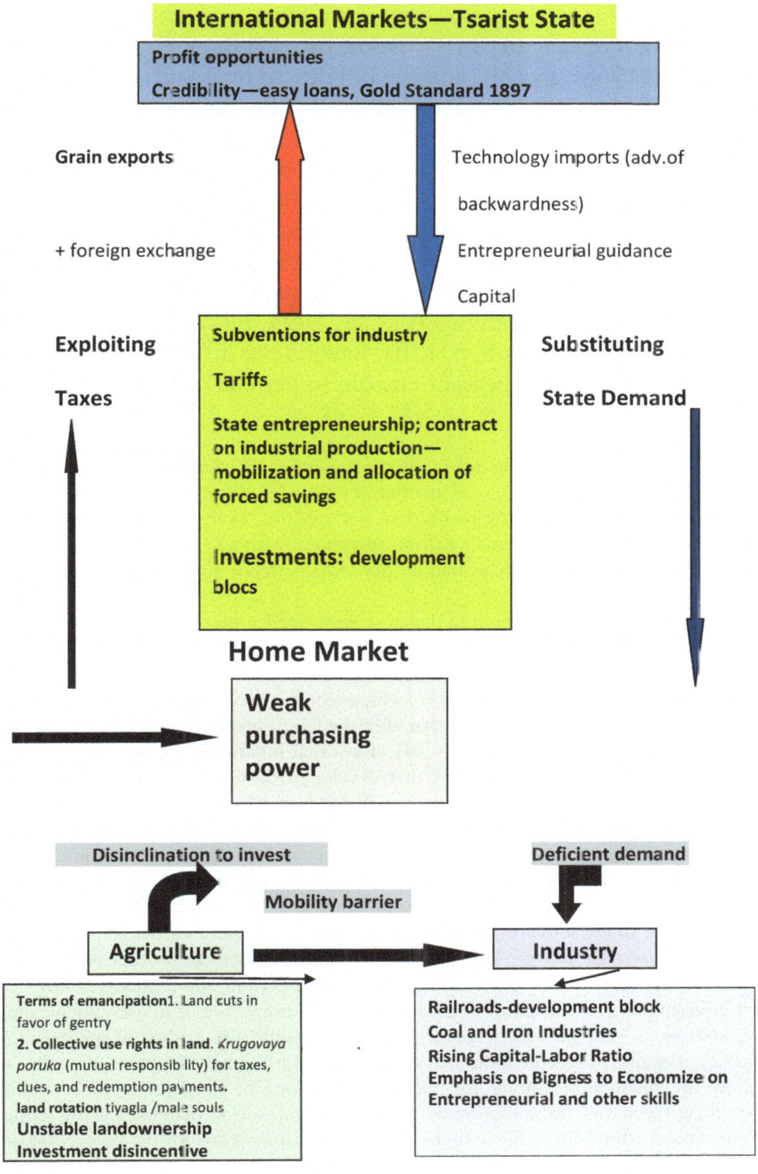

Fig. 2.3 The Gerschenkronian perspective modeled: summary of Gerschenkron's substitution theory of the state. (Source: Gerschenkron, 1962, 1968)

1990, pp. 36, 37), partly in taxation procedures, and partly in the aspirations of the autarchy (the Tsar) (Atkinson, 1990, p. 9; Gerschenkron, 1965 [reprint 1968], p. 189) and the nobility to maintain social and political control of land collectively held and cultivated by the *obshchina* (communal village).[9] Thus, a tense coexistence ensued between institutionalized collectivism[10] and attempts to individualize land ownership. It was inherent in communal landholding[11] as well as in the dichotomy of conformity versus contradiction in preserving the *obshchina* amid the pursuit of the industrialization goals of the late nineteenth century—well before the "second emancipation" in 1906. An additional player in this tension was the patriarchal family hierarchy (Wagner, 1994, pp. 3–5; Frierson, 1990, p. 303; Gerschenkron, 1968, p. 120). Beyond the differences between the positive imperial law and peasant custom in general (Crisp, 1989, p. 40),

[9] Bartlett (1999, pp. 1, 2). The terms *mir*, *obshchina*, and *obshchestvo* all denote a commune. The distinction among them is attributed to the nineteenth-century Russian intelligentsia. "Obshchestvo," according to Bartlett, denotes the "body of peasants to whom the land was to be given under any emancipation agreement with an estate owner." This is relevant mostly after the 1861 Emancipation Act, which defined the abolition of serfdom in Russia.

[10] Crisp (1989, p. 49). In addition to the aforementioned sources concerning the "ancient custom of collectivism" in the rural ownership structure, collective responsibility or "mutual guarantee" is said to have had its roots in the treaty between the Kievan Prince Oleg and the Byzantine Greeks. Thus, the established risk-dispersion practice was ancient indeed. Its continuity was broken by a statute in 1903 that abolished joint responsibility for taxes and dues.

[11] Alexandrovich, in Bartlett (1999, p. 39), notes that inheritable household land ownership was granted through common law that developed during the "disintegration of the tribal commune." The custom applied even to "*odnodvortsy* living under state feudalism" in pre-Emancipation Russia. An egalitarian "system of redistributive ownership" was adopted to prevent internal conflicts, thereby increasing the probability of survival. The inheritable right to household land may in itself be seen, relative to the commune, as partial privatization of ownership. However, the family-based right to land is but an *intermediary* stage to its individualization. In the short run, household ownership imposes a barrier to the individualization of property right (Crisp, 1989 pp. 43, 44). The Emancipation Edict of 1861 makes provisions for (1) *obshchinnoye pol'zovanie*—common or community tenure, (2) *mir*—peasant self-government, comprised of elected officials and assemblies of householders, and (3) *sel'skoye obshchestvo*—village society (*volosc*), which, in a vague way, embraced the units under (1) and (2). Alexandrovich concludes that the inherently arbitrary attempt to generalize does not allow the distinction among the different functions of those units to be clarified. Furthermore, the status of the *obshchestvo* as a legal person was ill-defined, leaving scope for intervention and arbitrariness. Since there was "no provision in law for the protection of the rights of individual against the collective," the application of the Statute with regard to the individual was random.

the principles of patriarchalism[12] and patrimonial inheritance,[13] as well as the tradition of property through the generations, restricted the legal status of family members in relation to the male head of household. These norms affected all subjects of the empire until the 1917 Revolution.

The Labor-Mobility Barrier to Industrialization

Consequently, considering the Gerschenkronian conception of the post-emancipation village commune, the right to land within the commune was doubly controlled: through family law, following the aforementioned principles, and via the decision-making power that the communal assembly wielded de jure (as in requiring approval of 2/3 of members before a division of land could take place [Frierson, 1990, p. 303]) as well as by peasant custom. Thus, the institutional foundations of family conduct acted in concert with the economic disincentive that household elders faced when adult family members asked them for permission to leave the commune (Gerschenkron, 1962, p. 120).[14] Even when such consent was given, the quitrents that the *obshchina* assembly demanded (Gerschenkron,

[12] Wagner (1994, pp. 61–81). The Orthodox Church as well as imperial law, the legitimacy and authority of the latter additionally strengthened by the religiously determined legitimacy of the former, defined the code of conduct within the family nexus, in which nearly total compliance of females and offspring with husbands' rule was required and legally enforceable. Thus, to obtain an internal passport or work outside of the household, a married woman needed permission from her husband and a single woman needed the same from her father (Gerschenkron, 1962, p. 120). Even a male member of the family could not leave the commune without permission from the head of the household (Frierson, 1990, p. 303). Finally, the consent of the eldest male, the head of the family, was necessary to divide a family holding into separate households.

[13] Wagner (1994, pp. 228–230) remarks: "The property became identified with the kin-group (*rod*)," meaning that as a rule it should be passed on to the male heirs of the family, who in the case of sale could exercise preferential right of redemption. In the case of an heiress, the right of inheritance concerned 1/14 of immovable property and 1/8 of movable, with the remaining 13/14 of the immovable property equally divided among the male descendants. A widow had no right of inheritance. The patrimonial principle seems to have restricted testamentary power, as "the legal status of the latter remained uncertain."

[14] The periodic formally induced repartitions of land were conducted on the basis of man-power/household. If an adult male left the *obshchina* permanently, his household might be entitled to less land than otherwise in a future repartition. Therefore, in keeping with the principle of patriarchal authority, the departure of males from village communes was restricted by the need to obtain the consent of heads of households, who had a disincentive to grant it (Gerschenkron, 1965, reprint 1968, pp. 165, 166).

1965 [reprint 1968], pp. 180–181, 194–196)—as the law allowed it to—created an institutionalized impediment to the allocation of labor to non-agricultural production,[15] obstructing urbanization and industrialization in the last quarter of the nineteenth century (Gerschenkron, 1968, p. 211). In a nutshell, despite the abolition of serfdom by Legislative Act in 1861, restrictions on the individualization of ownership[16] within the family and the commune hierarchy curtailed the inclusion of the peasantry in the late nineteenth-century modernization of Russia.

Since the sanctions created by imperial civil law constrained the division of household land, one might argue that the relative stability of ownership that had been achieved would have satisfied the necessary preconditions for investment in agricultural production, providing prerequisites for productivity increases and subsequent wealth accumulation within the

[15] The peasants were mutually responsible for collectively assigned land and its corresponding tax liability. Formally, even a temporary departure entailed the consent of the *obshchina* assembly for the issue of an internal passport. Thus, the collective tax responsibility could constitute a mobility barrier due to the discrepancy between the market value of allotted land and its redemption value (Atkinson, 1983, pp. 26, 27; Gerschenkron, 1968, p. 180).

[16] Atkinson (1983, p. 23). The Redemption Acts of 1861, 1863, and 1866, concerning the gentry, the appanage, and the state peasantry respectively "(1) recognized communal land tenure, (2) The newly unbound peasant was in effect now bound to the commune" (p. 27). An example is presented as an illustration: A peasant who wished to redeem his allotment land from the commune was obliged, apart from having to obtain the head of household's consent, to pay a price set not relative to the productive capacity of the land but according to its taxable value, which was set above the allotment market price. The commune assembly could block such redemption even though half of the assessment had been paid. The redemption payments exceeded land rental costs. Notably, despite the institutionalized acceptance of the commune as the basic form of peasant holding, the possibility of a transition to private ownership in the future was recognized by *the granting of hereditary rights on a family/household basis.* If such rights had not been implemented earlier by custom, they could be legalized by a two-thirds majority vote of the commune assembly. According to Atkinson (1983, p. 24), the elders' consent in this matter may be seen as an *intermediary step toward the individualization of ownership.*

Gerschenkron (1968, p. 177) notes that under the provisions of the 1863 Redemption Act, the transformation of use rights into ownership rights would, as a rule, be conducted on a family basis. Thus, he concludes that the statute "irreversibly" legalized "the establishment of *family farms* in Imperial Russia" (pp. 186, 187). Article 36 of the General Statute of the 1863 Redemption Act, quoted by Gerschenkron and reproduced in Chap. 2 of this monograph, gives the impression that joint/communal ownership was voluntary on the member's part. According to Article 165 of the Redemption Statute, subsequently quoted by Gerschenkron, however, one needed the consent of the commune to secede from the commune. If so, it remains true that the requirement of permission *per se* constituted an exit barrier.

commune. This, by extension, would have attenuated the effect of economic disincentives to the migration of labor to urban industries. The initial effect of household ownership would then have been offset in the long run by the increase in mobility of labor. Unfortunately for such a line of reasoning, the *obshchina* was a very convenient instrument for the imperial government to use in securing its tax revenues (Crisp, 1989, p. 39; Gerschenkron, 1965 [reprint 1968], pp. 189, 190), especially in the post-serfdom era. By nullifying landlords' responsibility for peasant taxes, the 1861 Emancipation Act left the state and the peasantry without the mediator that until the reform had helped to enforce the serfs' fiscal obligations.[17]

Gerschenkron and the Immutable Backwardness of the Peasantry: A Critique

Gerschenkron's analysis depicts an utterly backward peasant economy that was trapped by active de jure and de facto popular support for the *obshchina*, a setting oriented to recognition and political stability. This economy was hampered by poverty and misery due to population growth, onerous redemption payments, and heavy taxation. If so, the subsequent economic hindrances and institutional disincentives for innovation and investment magnified the effect of the growing numbers of eaters, an effect that should have been offset by greater productivity and higher levels of agricultural production. Such an economy could not possibly sustain the domestic market and satisfy the theoretical prerequisite for industrialization.

[17] Until the emancipation, "The landlords served as agents of the state, collecting taxes and levying recruits" (Leonard, 1990, pp. 122, 123). Leonard's assumptions about the effects of the costs of "exercising authority over the labor force" conform to the Northian explanatory framework. Supported by both approaches, one may assume that the transaction costs inherent in the need to closely survey and supervise the communes through paid officials subjected the landed nobility to a growing burden and gave it a motive to accept the peasants' emancipation (Atkinson, 1983, pp. 22, 25, 27). The *volosc* assembly, headed by a *starshina* (eldest) and its court, seems to have taken over some intermediary functions, as its domain expanded in the wake of the emancipation. This form of joint representation for several rural societies (almost the equivalent of communes) is seen by Atkinson as a compromise between "tendencies of local autonomy and autocratic centralization." A similar function on behalf of the nobility was assigned to the zemstvo, the rural self-government. Notably, however, one-third of the seats in the zemstvo were reserved for representatives of the peasants (Gerschenkron, 1965 [reprint 1968], p. 189).

Nevertheless, a great spurt began in 1890 under such conditions of backwardness as almost to coincide with the crop failures and famine of 1891–1892 (Atkinson, 1983, p. 33). It happened due to institutional improvements favoring free trade, railroad construction, and an upsurge of complementary industries that created Dahménian "development blocs" (Gerschenkron, 1968, p. 125) that were supported and utilized by a dramatic change of governmental attitudes in favor of industrialization. Restricted peasant consumption freed growing shares of national output for investment. Domestic demand was replaced by demand for exports, improving the balance of payments and making foreign credit and loan servicing possible (Gerschenkron, 1968, p. 125).

Gerschenkron identifies a substitution pattern that characterizes industrialization under conditions of backwardness (Fig. 2.1). In the Russian case, restrictions on peasant consumption through taxation, redemption payments, and the diversion of agricultural output to export created a budget buffer that could be used to import technology. Thus, the initial deficiency of the domestic market generally, and of the large rural sector particularly, was counterbalanced by the "surplus" accrued by the boldness of the political decision to give the growth rates of industrial output a sharp upward push.

The Gerschenkronian conception emphasizes the short-term ability of railroad construction and railroad-related industries to satisfy the government's demand for larger industrial output. As the railroads in Russia were constructed, the government directed its attention at the strategic-military advantages of this technology. The primary role of the railroads, thus conceived, was to effectuate the territorial claims of the autocracy and, in turn, to prop up the autocracy's legitimacy base (Freeze, 1996, p. 309). The dual-purpose (military/civilian) effects of railroad construction, however, had the consequence, unforeseen by the government, of causing a cultural and economic revolution that liberated most of the Tsarist Russian population from the vicious cycle of compulsory collectivism and poverty. I emphasize this repeatedly and devote most of Chap. 9 to demonstrating it via econometric tools.

Understanding the effect of the dual use of railroad construction, Gerschenkron (1962, p. 126) selected the substitution of expanded government industrial investment, and demand—that is, savings forced through fiscal pressure—for the general lack of domestic demand.

My thesis, complementing Gerschenkron's analysis in a manner touched upon neither by this scholar nor by his followers, is this: The railroads abetted the emergence of membership ties that were autonomous relative to estates such as peasantry and *zemliachestvo* (landsmanship) (Johnson, 1979, p. 69), along with spontaneous anonymous trade (Martens, 2004, pp. 161, 163)—by which I mean trade coordinated by the price mechanism under a trans-regional price convergence that mitigated transaction uncertainty and cost while enhancing the formation of national markets (Metzer, 1972, p. 12). Paradoxically, government demand and credit did not, in and of themselves, substitute for deficient domestic demand and capital formation within the scope of private enterprise, respectively. Railroad construction triggered a transition from the pre-modern economy of the self-sustaining patriarchal household, which had been oriented to subsistence while being structured by the common use value of production as defined by the patriarchal head of household, to the personalized intra- and inter-household barter of goods and services under the mutual-insurance systems of the village (Eggertsson, 1990, p. 303). Under the impact of railroads and of the growing incidence of peasant wage labor, the ultimate outcome of this transition was the impersonalized, individualized, specialized mixed agrarian–urban–industrial market exchange of goods and services in anonymous trade. Moreover, the railroads enhanced the transition from extensive to intensive growing. Traditional self-sustaining household farming, endowed by "common knowledge" (Martens, 2004, pp. 11, 106), caused the input/output ratio to rise continually at this time, necessitating the appropriation, most often through conquest of an additional quantity of factor inputs for the same amount of output—which may partly explain the redistribution of villages' land allotments in accordance with labor teams per household. Specialization of production under a newly absorbed technology, with prices of goods and services as the coordinating mechanism, inevitably lowers the input/output ratio, meaning that it *raises factor productivity*. In the late Tsarist case, this transition from a risk-averse, low-productivity modus operandi—extensive farming[18] restricted by a common pool of knowledge—to the anonymous exchange of specialized production (Martens, 2004, pp. 106, 162) amid rising factor productivity should be attributed to railroad construction. Challenging Gerschenkron's proposal, I suggest that the effects of the state-led industrialization, an exploitive process in the fiscal pressure that it imposed on the peasantry, were offset by the rising accessibility of

[18] Consider Ricardo's corn model on diminishing marginal factor productivity under static conditions (Poznanski, 1985, p. 41; Backhouse, 1985, p. 27).

the railroad technology, which assumedly had a crucial impact on factor productivity by affecting the prevailing growing method. This assumption is congruent with findings of the revisionist school, represented by Gregory, on the rising and not declining living standards of the post-emancipation peasantry.

Abstracting from these transitions, Gerschenkron maintains that the Tsarist government made subsidized investments in the iron, steel, and machinery industries. He argues that lack of skilled entrepreneurs and labor, the latter due to the institutional barriers that prevented an exodus from the rural sector to the urban, was offset by the centralization of industry at high capital/labor ratios. Capital and the quality of entrepreneurial talent made up for the shortage of skilled labor. The main advantage of backwardness was the absence of vested interests and other retarding factors that ordinarily accompany general transitions from obsolete to new technology (Gerschenkron, 1968, p. 120). Russia, as an industrial latecomer relative to England, Germany, and the United States, benefited from the lag by importing the most advanced technological equipment extant. Accordingly, its industrial growth raced ahead at an 8 percent average annual pace in the 1890–1900 decade (Gerschenkron, 1962, pp. 127–129). This investment-driven growth, unique to Russia during this period, was financed largely by additional pressures on the peasant economy, says Gerschenkron (1962, p. 130).[19] Ultimately, however, the fiscal burden imposed by the Tsarist autocracy to finance railroad construction was offset by the improvement in peasant living standards that railroad construction itself afforded for those served by the rails.

Indirect evidence supports the effect of rails on income. Studies indicate an increase in standard of living related to railroad use during the post-emancipation era. Frierson (1990) finds that the closer a population was to railroad lines, the more frequent were nuclear families as opposed to an extended family structure. The extended family served as a living form of insurance for its numerous dependents and was historically typical of European Russia. It is possible to infer from Worobec (1995, pp. 98, 101) that such a family structure was a peasant response to uncertainty. In this context, Frierson's causality implying finding—that proximity to the railroads occasioned rising incomes that resulted in more widespread formation of nuclear families, eroding the extended-family structure—clearly

[19] According to Atkinson (1983, p. 34), Finance Minister I.A. Vyshnegradskii (1887–1892) "insist[ed] that grain be exported even at the cost of going hungry."

indicates that the closer the families were to the railroads the lower was the uncertainty due to stable income streams and, in turn, the higher were the living standards.

Relatedly, an econometric analysis in Chap. 9 of this monograph demonstrates a connection between village-commune proximity to a railroad station and literacy levels, themselves prerequisites of higher income and living standards, and Chap. 9 illuminates statistically the shift to more individualized forms of peasant landholding.

Here I note that the railroads made peasant households relatively less dependent on each other for insurance against famines and other calamities, a condition that abetted the transition to individualism in landholding—the main source of livelihood. The assumed economic emancipation occasioned by the function of the railroads interacted with cognitive, intellectual, and spiritual changes that also facilitated transition to individualism and rationalism. This, in turn, lowered transaction costs, allowing returns on invested capital to rise in a virtuous circle that boosted standards of living. The focus on the railroads sustains the challenge to Gerschenkron's postulates on peasant impoverishment in the industrialization era, as well as the hypotheses of other scholars who, in the Gerschenkronian tradition, emphasize the agrarian crisis.

Witte's System and Gerschenkron's Entrepreneurial-State Theory

Gerschenkron's Theory of Relative Backwardness

This theory (Gerschenkron, 1962, p. 355) is oriented toward an explanation of the dynamism of economic development. Couched in Coase's and North's transaction costs and uncertainty mirror, it incorporates relative changes in factor scarcity over time and the corresponding place-specific restrictions on economic performance, namely, the institutional and, therefore, economic effects of cultural patterns—disclosing a diachronic dimension. Gerschenkron's theory, based on induction from a long-term comparative analysis of continuity and discontinuity—identifiable spurts of industrialization in European, including Russian, economic development—may be understood as complementary in providing a basis for a theory that slides along a "moving equilibrium" (Coase, 1937, p. 55). Such a theory would explain why entrepreneurial units get larger or smaller

(p. 55), or, alternatively expressed, why "islands of conscious power rise expand and disintegrate" (pp. 35, 53–55).

The higher the degree of relative backwardness, says Gerschenkron,

> *the greater is the part played by* special institutional factors *designed to increase the supply of capital to nascent industries and, in addition, to provide them with* less decentralized and better informed entrepreneurial guidance; *the more backward a country, the more pronounced was* the coerciveness and comprehensiveness of those factors. (Gerschenkron, 1962, p. 354, emphasis added)

By "special institutional factors," Gerschenkron means formal institutions in the Northian sense, those designed by the state. The more severe the relative backwardness of a country is, the more restricted is its domestic market for industrial goods provided by increased productivity and surpluses in agriculture. Summarizing Gerschenkron's argument, I would add that the more acute the backwardness, the more intrusively state activity would substitute for market transactions. As for defining the degree of backwardness with regard to sources of capital supply, Gerschenkron sketches the following (Fig. 2.4):

According to Gerschenkron's theory of relative backwardness, the degree to which an economy is coordinated by a state bureaucracy should correlate positively with the degree of backwardness. By implication, the state's threat to "take over" should escalate/de-escalate in tandem with

Stage of transition to modern economic growth	Advanced area	Area of moderate backwardness, e.g., Germany	Area of extreme backwardness, e.g., pre-Revolution Russia
I	**Factory**	**Banks**	**State**
II		Factory	Banks
III			Factory

Fig. 2.4 Gerschenkron's substitution theory in a European context. (Source: Gerschenkron, 1962, p. 355)

the degree of backwardness. Such a takeover may occur in various ways: nationalization; intervention via subsidies and dictates in industries, transportation activities, and commercial service units that are temporarily uncompetitive but politically perceived as key; concentration of industry in large production units; and/or geographical concentration of industry in centers of bureaucratic control (Owen, 1995, p. 33).

Gerschenkron in a Coasian Mirror

A purely theoretical question follows: How would Gerschenkron's substitution theory relate to Coase's 1937 theory of the firm?

To attain an in-depth understanding of Gerschenkron, I begin by positing our venerated scholar's "entrepreneurial state substituting for the market" theory against the transaction costs and uncertainty theory of the firm, which explains the rise, expansion, and fall of an entrepreneurial unit from a time- and culture-neutral perspective, depicting discrete equilibrium points for static or synchronic analysis. Viewed through this lens, the scope of the state in the role of entrepreneur–coordinator in Coase's sense, substituting for the coordinative function of the market, should be related positively to the degree of backwardness. Since economic backwardness also indicates institutional backwardness and the latter implies greater uncertainty due to greater arbitrariness, information scarcity, higher risk, and more uncontrollable and therefore more costly external effects (higher transaction costs), the entrepreneurial coordinating state should initially expand its purview to internalize those costs. Then, if the state is a rational agent, it will downscale its entrepreneurial functions as institutional and economic development increases. The essence of this combination of Gerschenkronian and Coasian theory implies that the state's initial attempts to internalize transaction costs within its purview until socioeconomic equilibrium (in the combined Coasian and Gerschenkronian sense) is attained do promote development. Afterward, however, continued attempts to internalize transaction costs until *political* equilibrium is attained, meaning the stage at which the costs of additional surveillance equal or surpass the benefits of additional centralization to the ruler—when the effects of excess internalization become politically manifest through an observable threat to internal stability—burden society with the costs of state entrepreneurship. Russia's corrective measures in 1906, as stated, lagged behind those that society demanded. Therefore, one might expect a "rational state" to have introduced a reform meant to lower transaction costs, thereby strengthening the incentive function of property rights *before* industrialization. It might, for example, have reformed land rights and liberalized the state's concessionary policy toward corporations in 1860–1880 (Owen, 1995, p. 21). On the formal level, the crown did introduce these reforms, but it was too late (Fig. 2.5).

Economic equilibrium is derived from the combined Coase–Gerschenkron theory (Coase, 1937, p. 42; Gerschenkron, 1962, p. 126); political equilibrium is defined by Hayek (1944, pp. 80, 81).

The hypothesis put forward here is that Russia's conventions and informal habits changed precisely in the direction of these corrective measures. Individual motives and informal (custom-determined) institutions are

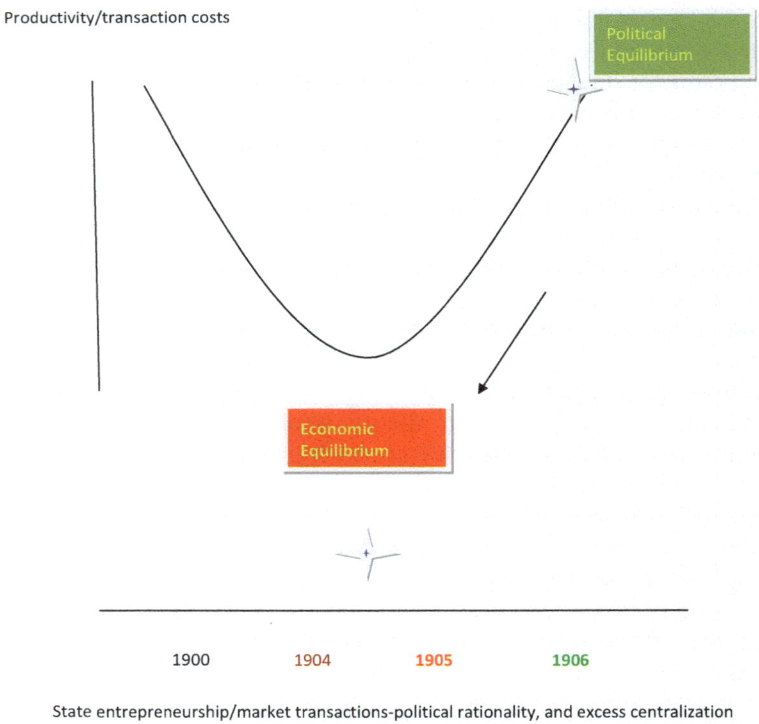

Fig. 2.5 Costs to society: political rationality supersedes economic rationality

thought to adapt faster than formal institutions to population increase and subsequent industrialization, invoking social sanctions in the direction to promote the novelty—the individualization and, therefore, the objectivization of rights. The institutional change in Russia was led from below by the autonomization process. State activity, guided by internal political stability goals, promoted progress through lagged top-down reforms but impeded it by controlling the process of adjusting to the changed scarcity relations and repressing the adjustment to the formal state-led transition to modern economic growth.

The net effect of state activity during the transition to modern economic growth in Russia raises doubts about the very possibility of state-led, non-participatory institutional transition in general. The discrepancy in bargaining power between a leadership appointed on merits that are unchallengeable by the public (therefore lacking broad legitimacy and support) and disorganized individuals leads to arbitrary and discriminatory application of the law, much as prevailed under the Tsarist autocracy.

Theoretical Tools of Analysis: The New Institutional Economics (NIE)–Critical Realist (CR) Challenge and American Evolutionary Institutionalism (AEI)

The applicability of theories changes over time. In poorly informed illiterate populations that live under the strain of volatile agricultural yields, natural calamities, and perceived terror due to superstition, the Critical Realist (CR) paradigm, embodying American Evolutionary Institutionalism (AEI), as I defined and combined it with New Institutional Economics, NIE, in Chaps. 1 and 3, is the most applicable. This paradigm emphasizes the authoritarian long-term anxiety-controlling role of institutions; at the time and in the place of our analysis, this role was vested in the authority of the eldest. In AEI, institutions are conceptualized as temporally precedent to any individual decisions and transactions. New Institutional Economics augments AEI by inserting the premise that custom and codified legal statutes result from individual hedonistic rational utility maximization and explaining the formation of institutions by tracing it to relative scarcities and prices, and vice versa. NIE shares its hard core with the Neoclassical paradigm. I find the NIE paradigm the most applicable in the early-to-middle stage of civilization and beyond because it defines individuals' decision-making as boundedly rational. Finally, the Neoclassical explanatory framework of the revisionist Paul Gregory is applicable to the

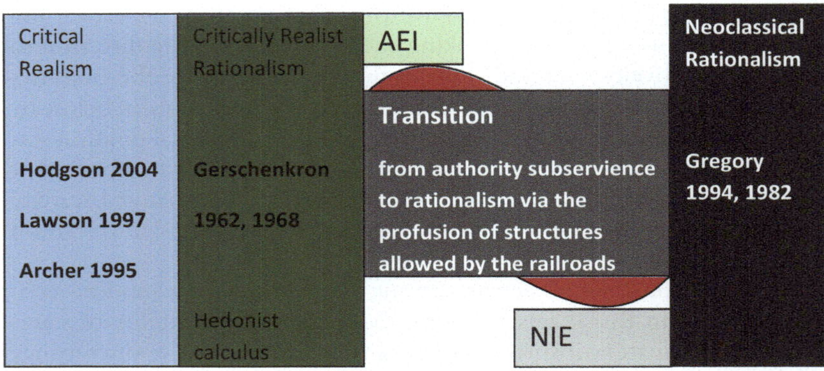

Fig. 2.6 Time axis—proportion of neoclassical utility maximization as a criterion of transition. *AEI* Structure Preconditions Individual Agency, *NIE* Individual Agency is the Source of Structure

microeconomic analysis of highly modernized industrialized societies characterized by anonymous economic interaction, close-to-ideal perfect competition, and full information, in which individual utility maximization is a realistic option. The long- and short-term hedonist evaluation is the common denominator (North, 1973; Vanberg, 1994) that makes these theories compatible.

As Gerschenkron's conception focuses on structure for the preconditioning of individual agency, I deem his work a rather good fit for the hybrid Critical Realist and NIE paradigm. Tsarist Russia's peasant society, modernizing in interaction with the railroads, may over time be successfully understood within North's New Institutional Economics framework. Finally, the peasantry's reaction to the Stolypin reform clearly reveals a rational individual-utility-maximizing calculus. Given that the turn-of-century rural population in Tsarist Russia made the transition to individualism and rationalism, it may be understood through the lenses of the Neoclassical Economics of Gregory, Simms (1977), and others.

Figure 2.6 summarizes the foregoing and introduces the next sequence.

The Historiographical Orientation

Conceptually and empirically, this part of the monograph, and the work at large, fills in the missing dimensions of the confrontation between Gerschenkron (1962, 1968) and the revisionist Gregory (1982, 1994) and Simms (1977) in their understanding of the standard of living and institutions of the post-emancipation Russian peasant. In response to Rostow (1960, pp. 6, 22), Gerschenkron emphasizes the retarding effects of rural collectivism[20] as the missing prerequisite for industrialization. His solution is encapsulated in the substitution of state entrepreneurship for the deficient formation of domestic markets. Gregory (1982, 1994) demurs, arguing that the ostensibly retarding custom gave way, de facto, to mutually beneficial habits (p. 52),[21] resulting in a neoclassically efficient resource allocation that protected the hereditary stability of land tenure, allowing productivity and peasant living standards to rise in Tsarism's last decades.

My argument accepts Gerschenkron's insights. It assumes that the mainstream Greek Orthodox structuring of wealth, the landed assets, and the fiscally responsible redistributive collectivist village commune survived during the post-emancipation period. The coercively consolidated *obshchina*, inherited from the serfdom era, encouraged risk-averse behaviors among the peasantry. Bridging from Gerschenkron to Gregory, however, I propose that the state-led construction of railroads unintentionally and irreversibly exposed the conventional hierarchies of coercion, based on personalized rule, to general collapse.

The process was composed of several key elements. The novel technology induced a transition to rational choice among numerous emergent institutional structures, raising the propensity to spiritual/intellectual choice.[22] This allowed the peasant household to assess and act on the declining probability of death occasioned by the diversification of subsistence risk between the rural and the urban economy (Johnson, 1979, pp. 40, 41).[23]

[20] Nafziger (2007, pp. 20, 22), measuring the impact of the redistributional commune on land productivity, finds a weak negative correlation between the number of repartitions and the yield per acre, verifying Gerschenkron's assumptions.

[21] Specifically, informal "side payments" compensated for the land rotation redistribution that was practiced, allowing households to manage land via long-term leases.

[22] For historical examples, see Burds (1998, p. 188) and Shevzov (2004, p. 45) on the emerging-structure plurality and democratization within the Church, and Worobec (2001, p. 58) on consideration of medical judgment in diagnosing *klikushestvo*-(demon possession) as cases of hysteria, anticipating the transition to rationalism.

[23] Johnson (1979, pp. 40, 41); see also Smurova (2003, p. 102), on the cultural transformation of young couples embodied in the transition to *otkhodnichestwo*—wage labor—in city centers. The source emphasizes that not only the amount but also the type of income, that is, agricultural versus industrial, was of significance.

I propose that the pace of transformation from land as a production factor burdened with tradition and "ceremonial knowledge" to a growing share of "matter of fact" industrial income-contingent knowledge in the national accounts should be seen as an indicator of a transition to rationality.[24] Estimates of the Gerschenkronian great spurt, bounded by the years 1883–1887 and 1897–1901, provide a numerical proxy for the pace of the transition to rationality, as the share of agriculture in national income increased by 2.55 percent per annum while that of industry surged by 5.45 percent—almost twice as fast (see Chap. 5).

The trend recurred at the micro level. The rapid proportional increase in household industrial income relative to agricultural income illustrates the pace of households' transition to rationality and the corresponding atrophy of authoritarian coercion relative to the calculus of utility maximization in members of households' decision-making. The emergent aggregate outcome of this process is assumed to be the voluntary dissolution of the collectivist custom. This premise is consistent with Atkinson's (1983, p. 74) finding that roughly 80 percent of European Russian households never rotated their land or did so less frequently than once every ten years during the late nineteenth century. This finding challenges Gerschenkron's assumptions of continuous instability of ownership, stability of collectivist redistribution, and the existence of a mobility barrier.

Railroad construction abetted the formation of a national grain market by encouraging price convergence (Metzer, 1972, p. 12), itself a proxy for a rising proportion of rational calculus. The ensuing increase in predictability and specialization (Smith, 1998, p. 19) initially pushed net transaction costs up. According to my application of Martens' model (Martens, 2004, p. 193), the division of labor facilitated by railroad construction boosted transaction costs and, in turn, gradually relaxed the practice of state-induced collectivism that had held the commune together. By deduction, Stolypin's 1906 reform was a Tsarist concession that granted title to land in response to the gradual upturn in transaction costs during the post-emancipation era in order to secure the tax base (see Chap. 3).

The nullification in 1903 of *krugovaya poruka*—the communal peasants' mutual responsibility for taxes and dues (Atkinson, 1983, p. 44)—improved the stability of ownership significantly. By implication, the Gerschenkronian description may remain valid *but with decreasing*

[24] These concepts are cited in a Veblenian context by Hodgson (2004, p. 209); on the Veblenian dichotomy, see Hodgson (2004, p. 367) and Gregory (1982, Table, pp. 133–134).

explanatory weight over time. Referring to the Revisionist school represented by Gregory, Simms (1977), and Bideleux (1990), I suggest that a virtuous cycle was at work: the growing de facto stability of land control and subsequent ownership raised land productivity and standards of living, making collectivist risk-sharing unnecessary (Gregory, 1994, p. 53; Nafziger, 2007, pp. 20, 22; Moon, 1999, p. 236; Scott, 1976, p. 4; Pallot, 1999, p. 75). Stolypin's speeches before the Duma, informed by eyewitness experience, envisaged and abetted the ensuing de facto voluntary exodus of peasants from the commune (Klimin, 2002, pp. 11, 12).

I propose here that the interaction between railroad technology and the landholding system, initiated in 1842, paved the way to an informal voluntary transition to hereditary household ownership of land that was subsequently codified in the Stolypin reform. Paradoxically, the assumption of voluntary peasant cooperation, according to Pallot (1999, p. 157), emphasizes rationalist peasant resistance to the 1906 reform, which aimed to formalize the property rights in land of the individual head of household. Still, the negligible number of peasant revolts related to land settlement in the course of the 1906 reform (Yaney, 1982, p. 187, points 1–2) renders challengeable Pallot's focus on the intensity of peasant resistance to the reform.

Either way, the costs of the Tsarist autocracy had been rising ahead of the 1906 reform, in tandem with the demand for public suffrage and a constitution that the Tsarist Ministry of the Interior addressed with pure oppression. The intensifying informal transition to individualism gave these costs another upward push (Mironov, 1999, p. 288). I therefore conceptualize the bloodshed and social displacement of the 1905 Revolution, pursuant to the peasantry's petition to the Tsar (Ascher, 1988, pp. 87–89), as the "costs of dictatorship"—all in relation to the properties of stable dictatorships, that my thesis, contrary to Gerschenkron (1968, p. 315), deems applicable to post-1890 Russia.

As noted, Gerschenkron (1962, p. 355) advises that, under conditions of deficient prerequisites for industrialization such as vagueness in the delineation of property rights in land, the state takes over as the source of capital formation and serves as a uni-directionally benevolent, progressive, and modernizing agent. Such, he says, was the case in the post-emancipation Tsarist Russia, explained by the deficient delineation of property rights (Barzel, 1989, p. 5), occasioned by the perpetuation of the village commune. Gerschenkron's concept of the village is congruent with that of the nineteenth-century Westernizers as defined by Boris Chicherin

(1828–1904). The commune's level of collectivism, says Gerschenkron, was continuous and stable over time. In his model, state entrepreneurship substituted for a domestic market for industrial goods. As railroad construction induced the formation of "development blocs" (Gerschenkron, 1962, p. 125), however, the risk inhering to the absorption of the novel technology was internalized via a guaranteed 5 percent return on government bonds, government fiat (Westwood, 1964, p. 43), deficient or sharply fluctuating demand, and full nationalization of the Tsarist railroads in 1880 due to risk of bankruptcy (Owen, 1995, p. 31).

The Gerschenkronian Proposal, the Revisionist Challenge, and My Argument: The Questions I Seek to Answer

The Railroads and the Metamorphoses of the Obshchina and the Tsarist Autocracy

My argument calls attention to the microeconomics of the institutions that constitute the Russian peasant village commune in its interaction with railroadization. I hypothesize that the railroads affected the conceptualization, temporal and spatial cognition, and mutual dependency for survival of Tsarist Russia's peasant constituency and its village-elder assemblies, staffed by peasant entrepreneurs and creditors. Inspired by Frierson (1990), I ask: Were mutual-dependence structures affected not solely within but also among extended families? How did peasants' access to urban industrializing economies and the cantonal and Imperial court system affect their dignity and willingness to take individual entrepreneurial risks? Which changes in belief systems and theories about the world did the culture of the railroad-using *otkhodniks* (urban wage laborers from the *soslovie*, the peasant estate) bring to the villages? Did the acquisition of literacy, contingent on spatial mobility, decisively affect the structures of those changes? If they did, in what way was the emerging modernization unique relative to that typical of the Petrine era? Finally, and in sum, did the Tsarist Russian village remain the stable bastion of patriarchal veneration *à la* "Batjushka the Tsar" that it had been, willingly relying on patriarchal experience to allocate its surpluses as an insurance premium vested in the eldest generation? Alternatively, did the *obshchina* evolve, contrary to Tsarist expectations, into a vehicle of pious and secularized subversion (Freeze, 1996)? Did the Russian peasants who rode the rails to *otkhod* (wage labor) with their newly acquired literacy and urban industrial skills remain obeisant, or did they begin to make personal utility choices, or at least satisfyingly bounded-rational choices, that were congruent with those endeavors (Burds, 1998; Nelson & Winter, 1982; Williamson, 1991)?

Population Increase and the Mobility Barrier
Against the background of population increase, was there a mobility barrier indicating that adherence to custom exceeded rational survival deliberations in institutional power, or did the elder assemblies adjust rationally to the growing abundance of labor and the declining relative scarcity of land?

Gerschenkronian State Entrepreneurship and Modernization
Is it reasonable to assume that the substitution of state entrepreneurship for the market, characterized by the importation of the novel railroad technology (Fig. 2.3), would be free of modern-dictatorship costs of going forward? Could Tsarist Russia, in the course of its belated industrialization, still be perceived as a stable, tradition-compliant monarchy based on consent to leadership under the anointed Tsar as the source of law? Did the mainstream Orthodox Church, the base of the autocracy's spiritual legitimacy, remain unchallenged by the role of the railroads as the core of the Tsarist industrialization? Did not the railroads affect peasants' standards of living and, in turn, the purchasing power of the domestic market, rendering the state entrepreneurship institution a wielder of politically rational control rather than an instrument of economic progress? Both Gregory and Simms note the increase in peasants' living standards as industrialization moved ahead. Thus, deficient purchasing power was not a static condition.

The State, the Railroad, and the Mir: From Compliance with Authority to Rational Calculus

Here and in this monograph at large, I fill in the micro dimension that the Gerschenkronian macro narrative leaves unclear. While Gerschenkron's work points to the inhibiting properties of village-commune collectivism as stable effects, it does not address the cumulatively intensifying effect of railroad technology on qualitative and quantitative changes in the collectivist structures. Specifically, it overlooks the discontinuity of the stultifying, coercion-structured collectivism in late Imperial Russia. Neither does it elaborate on how and why Russia's rural value systems changed and adapted to their European counterparts. In the Gerschenkronian reckoning, the Tsarist Russian entrepreneurs' adjustment to European standards of entrepreneurial honesty, encapsulating business trust, credit, ensuing the ability to foresee the returns on economic decisions in declining transaction costs and uncertainty environment, an institutional transition that embeds economic values is vaguely conceived of as the importation of value systems.

Applying Boyer and Orlean (1993, p. 22), I quantitatively define the "external invasion" of Tsarist Russia by thought systems that were prevalent in the democratized parliamentarian West. The superior and increasingly egalitarian and democratic land-management strategy, adapted to the exigencies of technological change and novel terms of survival, gradually attracted more and more households until they outnumbered those that adhered to the traditional way of life.

The crucial aspect—the core of this monograph—is that due to the industrialization process that centered on railroad construction, Tsarist Russia transformed its rule from an authoritarian, coercion-based system that meddled at every micro and macro level to a rationalist system predicated on individual utility calculus. Rationalism, in turn, heralded the transition to impersonalized constitutional rule that presupposed individually delineated rights. By presupposing the rationalist calculus unquestioningly, Gerschenkron overlooks this aspect. The Western standards of honesty that the Tsarist Russian entrepreneur absorbed, as Gerschenkron (1962, 1968) notes, resulted from rationalist competition over peasant labor. As the use of modern technology rendered peasant labor increasingly individualistic and human-capital-intensive, contrary to Gerschenkron's assumptions, demand for mobility and personal rights escalated. (See Chap. 7 on demand for internal passports and resort to the court system.) Rationalist competition concerns domestic as well as foreign creditors. Thus, as I emphasize in Chap. 4, the Tsarist Empire's debtor status vis-à-vis European financiers was an important factor in the harmonization of the two blocs' value systems.

Empirical Aspects, the Railroad, and the Landholding System

This monograph concretizes the beneficial role of state entrepreneurship by focusing on railroad construction. Its essence is the view of the landholding system in Tsarist Russia as a function of available technology. The main hypothesis states that the closer a village commune was to a railroad station, the less the inhabitants' subsistence was at risk and the less their dependency on mutual insurance would be. Taken to an extreme, railroadization should have caused the *obshchina*, the village commune, to disintegrate. More generally, the more available this particular dual-purpose technology was, the higher the degree of individualism and the less coercive and more voluntary the commune-village structure would become. I derive the latter prognosis from the notion that the strong collectivism prevalent in the pre-structuring serfdom era guaranteed serfs' lives and productivity as would mutual insurance—a guarantee that the serfs' superior in the hierarchy, the *pomeshchik* (landlord), encouraged by coercion. This ensured an adequate return on tax extraction efforts and reduced the ruler's surveillance costs (Ofer, personal communication, 1997; North, 1990, p. 51).

I propose several models to measure the transition to rationalism that the railroads induced:

- The ratio of household agricultural/industrial income = *f*(distance to railroad station).
- The proportion of peasants per village who defected to Old Belief or other sects/ideologies such as Molokane, Duchobory, Secularized Socialist Revolutionary = *f*(distance to railroad station).
  The latter model explains the decreasing propensity to repatriate agricultural income to the commune and, thereby, to influence the extent or pace of exodus from the land.[25] The emerging spiritual choice, induced by the railroad, challenged the mainstream orthodoxy that held the autocracy and the commune together.
- *Otchodnichestvo*—the number of wage laborers per village or the extent of *otkhod* (wage labor) = *f*(distance to railroad station).

To control for omitted variable bias in the extended model (not shown in this monograph), I propose the following:

Land category proxy for level of collectivism = *f*(distance to school, railroad station, number of dependents per household, yield per *desiacina* [an endogeneity issue], labor productivity, and agricultural/industrial income share [multicollinearity to distance]).

[25] For the history, see Matossian, in Vucinich (1968, pp. 81, 85), and Burds (1998, pp. 204, 205). As for the secularized movements, see Ascher (1988, p. 34).

For the nineteenth century (1842–1914), it would also be fruitful to test the following time-series models:

- Population annual increase in the region = *f*(annual length of rail increase in the region).
- Population density in the region (Atack et al., 2010) = *f*(distance to the railroad station).

And finally:

- The degree of commune-village collectivism proxy = *f*(population density, measured via Penza zemstvo [rural self-government] statistics for 1913).

Summarizing Remarks

Congruent with NIE and supplemented by the Regulationist paradigm and the Boserupian insights, I contend within a broader AEI framework that the change in conventions in the pre-revolutionary period was ultimately set in motion by population increase, which necessitated the absorption of technological innovations, specifically railroads. This, in turn, paved the way to the transition from anxiety-driven subservient obedience to authority (Lawson, 1997, pp. 180–182) to anonymous and rationalist rule compliance that rejected personalized interaction. The institutionally personalized hierarchies of coercion had proved inadequate in military rivalry with Western powers, forcing the initial Tsarist concession—the 1861 emancipation of the serfs—and the subsequent codification of the peasants' emancipation from compulsory collectivism in Stolypin's land reform.

Summary and Conclusion

The essence of Russia's historical personalized hierarchy of coercion is the metaphysically legitimized concept of main means of production in the pre-modern economy, land, in the form of the *votchina*—the ruler's patrimony—and the ruler him/herself as a high priest, the anointed intermediary between God and man (Pipes, 1995, p. 70; 1999, p. xii). I argue that the systematization of government and the importation of technology for strategic purposes during the Petrine era, which consolidated the autocracy, fostered over the following half-century a quest oriented in human plurality-challenging structures that until then had been conceptualized as metaphysically inspired. It also encouraged the formation of intellectual capital that conduced to intensified demand for egalitarian rights in land distribution—emerging in the coordinating principle of the 1773 Pugachev rebellion (Pipes, 1995, p. 155; Hughes, 1998, p. 457; Hartley, 1999, p. 110; Moon, 1999, p. 242). This uprising, challenging the throne of Catherine II in the name of the true Tsar, Peter III (Moon, 1999, p. 245), should be understood as Freeze (1996) would have understood it: as conceptualized by a "piously subversive" political disequilibrium that opposed a Tsardom nominally enlightened and inspired by Western philosophy. The post-Petrine demand for institutional egalitarianism and the acceptance of the Russian culture induced by peasant and Cossack xenophobia overshot the economic tipping point of their transaction costs. The rebellion itself should be defined in Gerschenkronian terms, even as his consensus conceptualization of Tsardom as lacking the cost of autocratic dictatorship should be challenged.

In the initial stage of the reform, involving the delegation of property rights, the de facto and de jure impersonalization of law was sought. By making concessions in view of the threat that this posed to political stability, the Tsarist throne secured the loyalty of the nobles for internal strategic purposes. Such had been the function of the 1785 Charter to the Nobility (Pipes, 1999, p. 192), which granted the nobility allodial property rights in land that countervailed and restricted the throne's despotic decrees (Sztern, 1994; Martens, 2004, p. 193; Pipes, 1999, p. xii). Thus, the transition from personalized privilege to rights allowed for the relative impersonalization of law through the enforceability of allodial property rights, albeit partial for broad population strata. The granting of land entitlements to the peasantry (Pipes, 1999, pp. 193, 194) was discussed in the eighteenth century but was not implemented due to the triumph of "political rationality" over economic (Hayek, 1944). The ultimate impersonalization of the law through the assurance of enforceable civil rights, including the right to landed property, took 121 years to achieve—in the Stolypin reform.

I offer the foregoing as a preface to the following investigation of the historical origins of liberalism in Russia, beginning with several questions:

- Was the modern transition from state to individual ownership of means of production—that is, from communism to capitalism in

1986[26]—the result of economically coercive institutional adaptation to the Western system for short-term strategic purposes?

- Was the process analogous to the 1921 Soviet New Economic Policy (NEP) (Boettke, 1993)? If it was, why was the Democratic Socialism formula swept away in the Perestroika thaw instituted by Gorbachev and the relaxation of private means of production and propaganda (*glasnost*), alien to Marxian theory, in 1986?
- Is Russia indeed historically collectivistic in its mindset, as the term is understood in the West (Ofer, personal communication, 1997)?
- Can Stolypin's 1906 land reform, imported from Bismarck's Germany, be regarded as the historical forerunner of the modern transition and should the socioeconomic costs of the implementation of the reform to rationalist–collectivist peasant Russia be emphasized, as Pallot (1999) suggests?
- Did the process have the structural capacity to allow the individualistic householder to stabilize the autocracy in perpetuity or to enhance the transition to constitutional monarchy?
- Are these historical transformations indicative of Russia's regression to an authoritarian system, or will the modern transition eventually bring on a Slavonian democracy?

In sum: the hypothesis advanced in this chapter and elsewhere in this monograph proposes that the 1906 Stolypin reform was driven by individual human-capital accumulation induced by spatial mobility, such as to pose a credible threat of a rurally organized rebellion. The latter was driven by surging popular demand to reduce the costs of dictatorship, accumulating in the fires of the industrialization that was structured atop railroad construction. The rising surveillance costs that had become typical of the

[26] Sztern (1994, pp. 4, 31, 57). I chose 1986 to mark the takeoff of the informal institutional disintegration of the Soviet Union. The series of reforms that structured this process started 1985 with Perestroika, which liberalized information flows. In 1986, the combination of the Chernobyl disaster and the transparency of information flows to Soviet citizens illuminated the grave deficiencies of the Communist Party's monopoly on governance—a structure that abetted quantitatively defined five-year production plans that induced deficient quality construction that had escaped public scrutiny due to censorship and propaganda. The formal privatization process dates to the July 1991 Privatization of State and Municipal Enterprises Law and marks the beginning of the formal dismantlement of collective ownership of means of production, the constitutive Marxist axiom of the Soviet system.

Tsarist dictatorship destabilized the metaphysically legitimized monarchic consensus that Gerschenkron envisaged.

References

Alexandrov Alexandrovich, V. (1990). Land re-allotment in the peasant communes of Late Feudal Russia. In R. Bartlett (Ed.), *Land commune and peasant community in Russia: Communal forms in imperial and early Soviet society*. Macmillan in Association with the School of Slavonic and East European Studies.

Ascher, A. (1988). *The revolution of 1905. Part I: Russia in disarray. Part II: Authority restored*. Stanford University Press.

Atkinson, D. (1983). *The end of the Russian land commune 1905–1930* Stanford University Press.

Atkinson, D. (1990). Egalitarianism and the commune. In R. Barlett (Ed.), *Land commune and peasant community in Russia; Communal forms in imperial and early Soviet society*. Macmillan in Association with the School of Slavonic and East European Studies.

Atack, J., Bateman, I. A., Haines, F. & Margo, M. (2010). Did railroads induce or follow economic growth? Urbanization and Population growth in the American Mid-West 1850–1960. 1850–1960. *Social Science History, 34*(2), 171–197.

Backhouse, R. (1985). *A history of modern economic analysis*. Blackwell.

Bakunin, M. (1970). *God and the state*. Dover Publications.

Bartlett, R. (1999). Liberty and property, land and freedom: Landownership and agriculture in imperial, Soviet and post-Soviet Russia. In G. Hosking & R. Service (Eds.), *Reinterpreting Russia*. Arnold.

Barzel, Y. (1989). *Economic analysis of property right*. Cambridge University Press.

Bideleux, R. (1990). Agricultural advance under the Russian village commune system. In R. Bartlett (Ed.), *Land commune and peasant community in Russia: Communal forms in imperial and early Soviet society*. Macmillan in Association with the School of Slavonic and East European Studies.

Boettke, P. J. (1993). *Why perestrojka failed: The politics and economics of socialist transformation*. Routledge.

Boyer, R., & Orlean, A. (1993). How do conventions evolve? In U. Witt (Ed.), *Evolution in markets and institutions*. Physica-Vlg.

Burds, J. (1998). *Peasant dreams and market politics: Labor migration and the Russian village 1861–1905*. University of Pittsburgh Press.

Coase, R. (1937). *The firm, the market and the law*. University of Chicago Press.

Crisp, O. (1989). Peasantland tenure and civil rights implications before 1906. In O. Crisp & L. Edmondson (Eds.), *Civil rights in imperial Russia*. Clarendon Press.

Eggertsson, T. (1990). *Economic behavior and institutions*. Cambridge University Press.

Ermolov, S.A. (1906). *Nash zemel'nyivopros.* SPB 1906 *Our land issue English Edition.*

Freeze, L. (1996). Subversive piety: Religion and the political crisis in late imperial Russia. *Journal of Modern History, 68*(2, June), 308–350.

Frierson, C. (1990). Land commune and peasant community in Russia: Communal forms in imperial and early Soviet society. In R. Bartlett (Ed.), *Land commune and peasant community in Russia: Communal forms in imperial and early Soviet society.* Macmillan in Association with the School of Slavonic and East European Studies, University of London.

Gerschenkron, A. (1962). *Economic backwardness in historical perspective.* The Belknap Press of Harvard University Press.

Gerschenkron, A. (1968). *Continuity in history and other essays.* The Belknap Press of Harvard University Press.

Gregory, P. R. (1982). *Russian national income 1885–1913.* Cambridge University Press.

Gregory, P. R. (1994). *Before command. An economic history of Russia from emancipation to the first five-year plan.* Princeton University Press.

Hartley, J. (1999). *A social history of the Russian empire 1650–1826.* Longman.

Hayek, F. A. (1944). *The road to serfdom.* Routledge.

Hodgson, G. M. (2004). *What are institutions? From orders to organizations.* Essay presented at the 6th International Workshop on Institutional Economics, University of Hertfordshire.

Hosking, G. (1997). *Russia: People and empire 1552–1917.* Harvard University Press.

Hughes, L. (1998). *Russia in the age of Peter the Great.* Yale University Press.

Johnson, R. (1979). *Peasant and proletarian: The working class of Moscow in the late nineteenth century.* Leicester University Press.

Klimin, I. I. (2002). *Stolypinskayaagrarnayareformaistanovleniekrestiansob stvennikov v Rossii.* Csentristoricheskichigumanitarnychissledovani 'Klio'.

Lawson, T. (1997). *Economics and reality.* Routledge.

Leonard, C. S. (1990). Landlords and the mir: Transaction costs and economic development in pre-emancipation Russia (Iaroslav Gubernia). In R. Bartlett (Ed.), *Land commune and peasant community in Russia: Communal forms in imperial and early Soviet society.* Macmillan in Association with the School of Slavonic and East European Studies.

Martens, B. (2004). *The cognitive mechanics of economic development and institutional change.* Routledge.

Matosian, M. (1968). The peasant way of life. In W. S. Vucinich (Ed.), *The peasant in nineteenth century Russia.* Stanford University Press.

Metzer, J. (1972). *Some economic aspects of railroad development in Tsarist Russia.* Unpublished doctoral dissertation, University of Chicago.

Mironov, B. N. (1999). *Socialnayaistoria Rossiiperioda Imperii (XVIII-nachalo XX v) genezislichnostidemokraticheskojsemiigrazhdanskogoobshchestvaipravovogogosudarstva: v dwuchtomach*. Dimitrij Bulanin.

Moon, D. (1999). *The Russian peasantry 1600–1930. The world the peasants made*. Longman.

Nafziger, S. (2007). *Land redistributions and the Russian peasant commune in the 19th century*. EHES, Department of Economics Williams College.

Nelson, R., & Winter, S. (1982). *An evolutionary theory of economic change*. The Belknap Press of Harvard University Press.

North, D. C. (1973). *Västerlandets Uppgång*. SNS.

North, D. C. (1990). *Institutions, institutional change and economic performance*. Cambridge University Press.

North, D. C. (1993). *Economic performance through time*. Prepared for Presentation as the Prize Lecture in Economic Science in Memory of Alfred Nobel.

North, D. C. (2005). *Understanding the process of economic change*. Princeton University Press.

Owen, T. (1995). *Russian corporate capitalism from Peter the Great to perestroika*. Oxford University Press.

Pallot, J. (1999). *Land reform in Russia 1906–1917. Peasant responses to Stolypin's project of rural transformation*. Clarendon Press.

Pipes, R. (1995). *Russia under the old regime*. Penguin Books.

Pipes, R. (1999). *Property and freedom*. Harvill Press.

Poznanski, K. (1985). *The environment for technological change in centrally planned economies*. World Bank Staff Working Papers.

Pravilova, E. (2014). *A public empire: Property and the quest for the common good in imperial Russia*. Princeton UP.

Raeff, M. (1966). Introduction to plan for political reform in Imperial Russia, 1730–1905. In M. Raeff (Ed.), *Political ideas and institutions in imperial Russia*. Westview Press.

Raeff, M. (1984). *Understanding imperial Russia*. Columbia University Press.

Rostow, W. W. (1960). *The Stages of Economic Growth: A Non Communist Manifesto*. Cambridge at the University Press.

Scott, J. (1976). *The moral economy of the peasant. Rebellion and subsistence in Southeast Asia*. Yale University Press.

Shevzov, V. (2004). *Russian orthodoxy on the eve of revolution*. Oxford University Press.

Simms, Y. J. (1977). The crisis in the Russian agriculture at the end of the nineteenth century: A different view. *Slavic Review, 36*(3), 377–398.

Smith, A. (1998). *An Inquiry into the Causes of the The Wealth of Nations. With the Classic Introduction by Ludvig von Mises*. Regnery publishing Inc.

Smurova, O. V. (2003). Niezemliedelcheskij otkhod krestian v stolitsu i jego vlejanie na transformacju kulturnoj tradicji. Izdanie Kostromskogo Gosudarstvennogo Technologicheskogo Universiteta.

Sztern, S. (1994). *Det socioekonomiska systemets institutionella desintegration och omvandling Sovjetunionen/Ryssland.* Unpublished Candidate Paper, Lund University, Department of Economic History.

Vanberg, V. (1994). *Rules and choice in economics.* Routledge.

Wagner, W. (1994). *Marriage property and law in late imperial Russia.* Clarendon Press.

Westwood, J. N. (1964). *A history of the Russian railways.* George Allen and Unwin.

Williamson, O. E. (1991). The logic of economic organization. In O. E. Williamson & S. G. Winter (Eds.), *The nature of the firm: Origins, evolution and development.* Oxford University Press.

Worobec, C. D. (1995). *Peasant Russia family and community in the post-emancipation period.* Northern Illinois University Press.

Worobec, C. D. (2001). *Possessed women, witches, and demons in imperial Russia.* Northern Illinois University Press.

Wortman, R. (1976). *The development of Russian legal consciousness.* University of Chicago Press.

Wortman, R. (1989). Property rights, populism and Russian political culture. In O. Crisp & L. Edmondson (Eds.), *Civil rights in imperial Russia.* Clarendon Press.

Yaney, G. (1982). *The urge to mobilize: Agrarian reform in Russia, 1861–1913.* University of Illinois Press.

CHAPTER 3

Through the Lenses of Theory: New Institutional Economics and American Evolutionary Institutionalism—Railroads, Specialization, and Democracy in Late Tsarist Russia

In this chapter, I investigate the applicability of two theoretical perspectives, mentioned in previous chapters without much elaboration, that I consider instrumental in addressing the following question: Who was the nineteenth-century Russian peasant, the representative of the majority of the Russian population?[1]

The New Institutional Economics (NIE) paradigm (North, 1981) universally sets forth a Homo Economicus who, hedonistically and rationally, seeks to maximize his or her personal utility. This conceptualized human calculates the payoff of cooperation while considering relative resource scarcities and historical and present opportunity-cost matrices. Interactions among such people generate utility equilibria that explain the resulting stable structures ("institutions") that determine relative scarcities. Critical

[1] Concerning the ongoing discussion on whether the classical assumptions are realistic (Hodgson, 1999; comments by Lawson, 1997), one may say that ever since Adam Smith—for well over two centuries—classical theory has been shaping the culture and institutions of Western societies as it did those of nineteenth-century Russia. Consequently, even if the hedonistic Homo Economicus assumption is unrealistic and faulty *ab initio*, an approximation of an agent endowed with such properties could have been generated through a process of "re-constitutive downward causation" (Hodgson, 2004, 105)—proving Lawson (1997) and Hodgson (2004) right and rendering the classical assumptions realistic.

S. Sztern, *Russia on the Move*, Studies in Economic Transition,
https://doi.org/10.1007/978-3-030-89285-2_3

Realists (CRs) challenge this "atomized" conception of the human, advising that individuals are born into preexisting structures that shape their preferences and goals, meaning that totally independent rational-utility-maximizing choice does not exist. American Evolutionary Institutionalism (AEI), in turn (Veblen, 1931; Hodgson, 2004), which I conceptualize in this monograph as complementary to NIE, explains that individual agency—choice—evolves through social interaction while being shaped and molded by temporally prior institutional structures. These structures, in turn, are the results of natural selection and adaptation of socially acquired "habits of thought," on the one hand, and conditions of life on the other (Veblen, 1931, 188).

In NIE, individual agency is the source of structures (institutions). In AEI, structures precondition individual agency. Again, I suggest that these theories are complementary.

The foregoing question should be answered as posed, within a time- and place-specific framework. Are there insights to gain from a theoretical approach that is neutral in time and place? Any theoretical framework, irrespective of its level of abstraction, inherently flows from time- and place-specific assumptions about human nature. Theories may be likened to institutions, by which I mean socially embedded systems of thought (Hodgson, 2004). Their viability varies as a contingency of their perceived instrumental value, the general stock of human knowledge, humankind's current dreams and aspirations, and research communities as repositories of the former.

How Railroad Construction in Tsarist Russia Demonstrates the Complementarity of NIE and AEI

Understood from the NIE perspective, railroads affect relative prices and scarcities, reducing the costs of transactions and uncertainty in spatial interaction while allowing anonymous trade to take place (North 1973; Martens, 2004; Metzer, 1972). By expanding the market in the manner predicted by Adam Smith, railroads facilitate skill accumulation, specialization, and exchange, paving the way to productivity increases, wealth, and the amassing of political bargaining power. At the crossroads of NIE and Evolutionary Institutionalism, Martens (2004, 193) explains that specialization causes transaction costs to rise, forcing rulers to delegate property rights to their subjects in order to secure their tax base. Thus, by allowing specialization, railroads lead to the transfer of property rights and, with them, civil rights, submitting rulers' decisions to the popular franchise. NIE's "bottom-up" interpretation, however, needs a supplement and finds it in AEI. Individual choice, AEI emphasizes, is not independent of the preconditioning institutional structure that predates all individual interaction. One part of such a structure is tradition, an essential for the control of anxiety (Lawson, 1997). By discontinuously expanding the spatial area and the spectrum of cultures that peasants could access, railroad technology revised the peasantry's perceived "conditions of life" (Veblen, 1931). Access to the new transport technology shrank cognitive distances (Shivelbusch, 1986) to urban economies and their non-agricultural sources of income and forced the imperial courts to adapt. Initially the perceived threat of natural calamity, promoting dependence on inherited structures and the powers embedded in them, profoundly affected the shaping and molding of habits of thought among those "fittest [to the emerging conditions]" (Veblen, 1931, 188). The ceremonial-tradition and authority-bound components of institutions were challenged by matter-of-fact knowledge acquired via the new spatial mastery. Institutions did not vanish but transmogrified by natural selection and adaptation amid the totality of social interaction. Made accessible by the railroads' novel ambiance, cultures and cultivation methods facilitated natural selection and adaptation congruent with institutions that shaped and molded the habits of thought of a new generation born into the structures of a railroad age created by the invasion of railroad technology. Viewed from my combined theoretical perspective, railroads make the institutions congruent and invest them with novel cognitive capacities and relative scarcities that condition levels of uncertainty, budgets, and, ultimately, the propensity among people to choose individualist structures instead of collectivistic and mutually insuring ones.

The Theoretical Angle: The Legitimacy of the NIE/AEI Combination—Critical Realism Challenges NIE

NIE: The Rationalist Explanation of Peasant Custom

The New Institutional Economics (NIE) school, represented in this discourse by North (1973, 1981, 1993, 2005; North et al., 2009), clearly acknowledges the merits and limitations of the Neoclassical approach

(North, 1981, 11). Throughout history, people have been observed to follow rules and unwritten, custom-based moral norms under circumstances that may render shirking, freeloading, and opportunism consistent with maximization of self-seeking benefit.

North's solution to this problem is an individual calculus, in which the premium over the opportunity cost of an illegal act reflects the measure of the value charged to the legitimacy of the institutional structure (1981, 11). This introduces a historical dimension to the Neoclassical core. According to North (1993, 3; 2005, 36), institutions, both in formal rules and in informal behavioral norms, embody a common cultural heritage, a belief structure inherited from past generations.[2] The institutional structure and its change constitute rational responses to an evolving environment—to relative price changes, for example, including changes in transaction costs that reflect the costs of measurement and of the coercion necessary for the enforcement of rights (North, 1973, 29; 1993, 53).

Contrary to the Neoclassical approach, which assumes perfect information and, consequently, no transaction cost, NIE (Williamson, 1985, *inter alia*) is grounded in Herbert Simon's assumption of "bounded rationality"—a limited capacity to gather and process relevant information—and focuses on the effects of information costs on organizational structures (Martens, 2004, 49).

Given NIE's commitment to methodological individualism, the logic consequent to it, and the claim to universality flowing from its Neoclassical foundations,[3] the nineteenth-century Russian peasant may be characterized as a version of Homo Economicus, albeit a "boundedly rational" (Williamson, 1985, 30) maximizer of utility or minimizer of maximal loss or a risk of death (Scott, 1976, 4) who, independently of others, hedonistically calculates his payoffs at each discrete moment and chooses to interrelate with his fellows to insure himself against starvation and other calamities (Eggertsson, 1990, 303). In the long run, it was the demand for insurance that gave rise to the collectivist peasant custom elaborated upon in Chap. 2. The observed peculiarities of the peasantry's institutional structure and its change over time may be understood as the products of rational deliberation among individuals who interacted in response to changes in

[2] For parallels between NIE and the "Old Institutional Economics" represented by Veblen's school, see below.

[3] For a critical review of these claims, see Hodgson (2001, 23). Hodgson strongly rejects the notion of a dimension of the Neoclassical approach that is valid across time and space.

relative prices/opportunity costs triggered by population changes (North & Thomas, 1973, 29). Viewed through this prism, any collectivist practice would atrophy if confronted by increased opportunities for stable income streams (Bates quoting Sahlins 1989, 42) that would mitigate the risks to individual survival (Sztern, 2000) and, more generally, make economic relations more predictable (lower transaction costs) by allowing uncertainty to be absorbed into the national, as opposed to the pre-modern, social unit (Sztern, Project Description). The systematization of governance would trigger such an absorption by formalizing the structures that governed peasant life (Mironov, 2000, 329, 328, *inter alia*).

Bounded Rationality: The NIE–AEI Bridge

As a point of departure, the assumption of bounded rationality[4] suggests the possibility of an intersection between NIE and the evolutionary approaches. An additional point of agreement between the two clusters of theories is the role of institutions as anthropogenic structures that aim to mitigate uncertainty in human interaction (North, 1993, 17). As "durable systems of established and embedded social rules that structure social interactions," institutions are viable because they can "usefully create stable expectations of the behavior of others," thus mitigating uncertainty in human interaction (Hodgson, 2004, 424, 425, 430). Insofar as social structures carry out their uncertainty-mitigating function, they remain viable over time (North, 1981, 11, 20; Hodgson 424, 425).

Unlike North (1993, 64, 78), who appears to view informal and formal institutions as restrictive of individuals' behavior, Hodgson emphasizes their enabling function. His school maintains that although institutions are contingent on individual intellectual and other activities, they are not explainable by such factors (Hodgson, 2004, 425).

Hodgson's interpretation of the AEI approach conceptualizes institutions, including formal rules, unwritten norms, and socially sanctioned conventions, as socially or culturally transmitted. *In this respect*, it conforms to the NIE conception of the phenomenon. AEI, however, views social structures as emergent entities that cannot be reduced to the interaction of its constituents (Hodgson, 2004, 425). Then, basing itself on

[4]Williamson (1991). The cognitive assumption based on Williamson (1991, 92), invoked by transaction-cost economics, is that human beings are "intendently" rational but only limitedly so.

Veblen's and Commons' tradition of Old Institutional Economics, it assumes that institutions have a causal effect on agents' preferences and aspirations (185, 291).

While NIE is understood as an example of what Hodgson (2001, 3) calls "downward conflation,"[5] namely, the reduction of structure to individual interaction, Hodgson's evolutionary approach focuses on the interaction between agency and structure, refuting any reductionism—including biological—as well as methodological individualism and collectivism.

The bridge between the two schools of thought is the concept of economics of cognition, exemplified in this discourse by Martens (2004) and the precursors of the Old Institutional Economics school that anticipated AEI (Hodgson, 2004). Specifically, Lewes defines civilization as an accumulation of experiences encapsulated in institutional structures (104, 105). Following Lewes, social institutions are considered "repositories of social knowledge" (105) that allow people to allocate rationally their cognitive capacity, thereby giving them an evolutionary advantage.

How Far Apart Are NIE and AEI in Distributing Determination of Action between Agency and Structure?

North (1993, 65) identifies cultural heritage as the source of informal institutions. Culture, he explains, provides the language-based conceptual framework through which information is gathered and processed. In a manner surprisingly reminiscent of an evolutionary approach, North, (1990, 37) quoting Johansson, proposes that the capacity of the human intellect to utilize information depends on the ability to acquire moral values, attitudes, and opinions encoded in the preconditioned language-learning process. Thus, learning capacity, in the sense of the ability to process information rationally and reflexively, is itself dependent on informal institutions such as language.

North also acknowledges the tendency of human preferences to change over time due to changes in value systems, meaning transformations of the institutional structure. This, in turn, affects the price of the convictions (North, 1981, 11, 53) that shape a society's ideological outlook, where an effect in the opposite direction may occur through the legitimization

[5] A methodological individualism in which structure is explained in terms of individual interaction. Hodgson (9) also speaks of "upward conflation"—a methodological collectivism in which individual interaction is explained in terms of structures.

process. In this example, then, although the source North does not say it in so many words, the price mechanism animates a process of "reconstitutive downward causation" (Hodgson, 2004, 105), embedded in the NIE conception of the role of institutions as anthropogenic information-handling phenomena.

Thus, it may be too simplistic to interpret NIE as an example of the explanation of institutional structure through ad hoc individual interactions among people now present. Not contrary to what Archer (1995) would have expressed (see below), cultural heritage, the Northian "collective memory reservoir" (North, 1993, 12, 14) embedded in institutional structures, can at best be only partly reducible to synchronic individual interaction among maximizing Homo Economicus agents. North, however, emphasizes individuals' subjective thought models, which cannot be fully explained by collectively determined structures that restrict the scope of available options (North 1990; 1993, 35). Given the parallels outlined above, the suggestion that these theories may be at least compatible with each other defies refutation.

Critical Realism

Critical Realism's challenge to the Neoclassical paradigm, in which NIE is regarded as an offshoot of "mainstream economics" (Hodgson, 2001, 248, 249), indicates that an evolutionary approach focusing on historically specific structures may complement NIE in its properties.

The commonality of all Critical Realist (CR) approaches is their emphasis on structure as a "generative" or causal mechanism (Hodgson, 2004, 53–73). Below, I select Tony Lawson's *Economics and Reality* (1997) and Margaret Archer's *Realist Social Theory: The Morphogenetic Approach* (1995) to represent these approaches.

When one says "critical," one acknowledges the dependency of social structure on human agency. "The sciences along with philosophy," says Lawson, "are themselves social structures and practices which are unavoidably susceptible to critique" (Lawson, 1997, 158; see also exposition above). By implication, all social structures, including theoretical ones, can be reproduced or transformed via thoroughgoing critical enquiry (Lawson 2003). Structures are dependent on individual human conceptions but cannot be reduced to them. CR thought may be applied as a tool for the evaluation of merits and the limitations of theories. Importantly, however, the tool itself has limitations, given ideologically determined abstractions that may favor one type of causal factor over another (Hodgson, 2004; March 68).

The next term in need of clarification in this context is "realism." Lawson (1997, 19) advocates a *transcendental realist* conception in social science as opposed to empirical realism. The latter adheres to the positivist tradition, which Lawson deems inadequate because "Objects of science are structured (irreducible to events) and intransitive (existing and acting independently of their being identified)" (28). There are structures, powers, and generative mechanisms and their tendencies (e.g., gravitation) that have a causal effect whether they are known or not (Lawson, 1997, 27–35; Lewis, 1999). The *causal criterion*, then, is applied in order to assign the term "reality" to social structures (Lawson, 1997, 31).

Transcendental realism encompasses three layers of reality: the empirical (experience and impression), the actual (actual events), and the real (structures, powers, mechanisms, and tendencies), in addition to actual events and experiences. The real cannot be reduced to the actual and the actual cannot be reduced to the empirical. These layers are unsynchronized; their mode of reasoning is neither inductive nor deductive but inferential—progressing from a "surface phenomenon" to an underlying causal one (Lawson, 1997, 31).

It is not the rationality or maximizing assumption per se that Lawson's critique targets. Rather, it is the view of such phenomena as actualities as opposed to capacities, which may be subjected to countervailing tendencies, that constitutes the core of the CR approach (Lawson, 1997, 106).

Since NIE grows from the foundations of the Neoclassical core while extending the framework to include an analysis of institutions oriented to transaction costs (North, 1981, 25), this critique also indirectly targets NIE.

Opposing the atomistic conception of social beings, Lawson emphasizes interdependencies. Social structures—"rules, relations, positions"—are contexts that shape human agency. Neither structure nor agency, however, is taken as given; the emphasis is on the unintended transformation of the former through the routinized action of the latter. Each layer presupposes the other but is irreducible to the other.

In Lawson's model, the keystones of social systems are internal relations that result in positions; the latter are construed as constitutive of the identity of the parts (Lawson, 1997, 164). Lawson does not deny that some interaction is defined from an atomistic perspective as externally related; randomly bypassing individuals who are unrelated to each other by any type of endeavor or emotion is an example. Within this construct, a social system is understood as a "structured process of interaction" (165) and as an institution. In Lawson's view, the latter term is relevant in reference to "those structured processes of interaction (collecting together rules, relations, and positions as well as habits and other practices) that are relatively enduring and identified as such" (318).

In defense of methodological individualism (as a useful simplification) and NIE, I argue that insofar as mainstream interaction in a society is characterized by external versus internal relations, is continuous (embodying both dimensions in various proportions over time), and is dependent on the type of society as regards its constitution and rule systems, it is related to material conditions. Seen from a different angle, the level of coercion in enforcing the rules (North, 1981, 21; 1993, 97; Martens, 2004, 190) determines the degree of voluntarism in relations, in turn affecting the degree to which said relations will be genuinely constitutive of the identities of the parts involved. In totalitarian states that do not recognize rights of association and are noted for acute distrust among individuals (due to repression), relations are said to be atomized, namely, external (Ticktin 1992, 24). In democratic societies, rights of association are codified in law and enforced but the association that is expected to "constitute identity" is not necessarily durable and, therefore, will remain ineffective in respect of this very expectation. Consequently, the constitutive role of relations–positions cannot be taken as a given; it is a factor that has to be explained in the context of the legitimacy issue (North, 1981, 11).

An additional example pertains to Tsarist Russia. The extent to which the relationship between a household head—a *bolshak*—and his grown sons would be constitutive of their identities hinged on the economic dependency of the former on the latter. Factors such as literacy, wage labor in an urban center, or a change in religious affiliation (Burds, 1998, Table 1.3, 23; 177; the information revolution [193], the allure of the Old Belief) might shift the balance of power in favor of the sons (in the extreme), making the relationship an external one. Moreover, internal relations may, in the course of reform processes that legally amplify sons' autonomy—restricting *bolshaks'* control of income streams—(Hesse, 1993), be transformed into external ones.[6] The same pertains to relations between seignior and serf, which may cease to exist as such.

[6] Emotions are disregarded in both cases.

The extent to which relations are formally internal[7] or external appears to be a matter of institutionalized dependency/domination and voluntarism. The extent to which a teacher–student relationship is constitutive of both identities is a function of custom, formal rules, and voluntary choice. By implication, every internal relation may have an atomistic dimension. Moreover, not all relations of the same type are identical. However, many commonalities they may have, each relation has a uniqueness that depends on the *individuals* involved.

The ability to engage in reflexive monitoring of, for example, adherence to social norms presupposes discursive as well as tacit consciousness (Lawson, 1997, 178). Thus, human agency guides itself by drawing on both discursive and tacit knowledge. Lawson recognizes the unconscious component of action; most human motives cannot be consciously identified (179). This scholar seeks the explanation of routinized behavior in this phenomenon.

Lawson (1997, 181, 182) traces rule-following behavior to the need for continuity and stability that were once satisfied within mutual-trust frameworks of parental relations. The predictability of routinized behavior serves as an anxiety-controlling device; so does some level of identification with authority. Thus, rule-following behavior is explained by psychological factors, which are implicitly evolutionary.

Archer (1995, 65) links structure and agency, focusing on time. Consistent with transcendental realism, she advises that "Structures … contain non observable emergent powers whose combination generate the further emergent properties …" (69).

Reflexive human agency has the power to cause unintended structural changes. Thus, structure, although predating any given individual, is transformed through reflected action, albeit unintentionally (75; see also Lawson, 1997).

Archer's main argument against treating structure as an epiphenomenon of interaction among people "now present" is the existence of structural properties that cannot be changed in the short run (Archer, 85). Thus, phenomena such as prevalent demographic structures or literacy levels in a population are inherited from past generations and have causal effects on the interaction, including the dispositions, of present actors.

[7] Internal by being anchored in a formal rule system as opposed to informal internal dependency relations.

Inferring from Archer, such effects have been abstracted from NIE, conflating structure with individual agency.

The Marxian Angle

One may identify the Marxian source of inspiration that permeates CR thought (Hodgson, 2004, 54) by pondering the following quotation:

> *In the social production of their life, men enter into definite relations that are indispensable and independent of their will, relations of production which correspond to a definite stage of development of their material productive forces. The sum total of these relations of production constitutes the economic structure of society, the real basis, on which rises a legal and political superstructure, and to which correspond definite forms of social consciousness. The mode of production of material life conditions the social, political and intellectual life process in general. It is not the consciousness of men that determines their being, but, on the contrary, their social being that determines their consciousness.* (Marx 1859, quoted in Cohen, 2000, 1)

The Austrian, the Marxian, and, for that matter, the Evolutionary Economics approaches, the last-mentioned including AEI, are conceived as consistent with the CR line of thought (Lawson, 1997, 247).

Archer (1995, 82) deems purely structural explanations an "oversocialized" or "overdetermined view of man," as would be relevant in the Marxian case but which cannot explain social change. In Archer's model, human agency at T2 is the source of the transformation that takes place as the inherited structure, T1, interacts with the present generation of agents.

Is NIE Incongruent with CR in Principle, Refuting the Temporal Priority of Structure?

The justification for applying NIE within a combined NIE/AIE framework is that the CR conception of NIE, the latter represented by North (1981, 1993), is too simplistic. Thus, NIE and AEI should not be deemed incompatible. The temporal precedence of structures over any given individual is implicitly acknowledged by North (1981) in his allusion to Hodgson's "reconstitutive downward causation." North's analysis of the effects of population increase (1981)—"initial conditions" within Archer's framework—may serve as an example. Unlike the results of deduction from the Neoclassical model, in which the adjustment on the margin would be instantaneous, implying simultaneous interaction, "in the context of institutions and positive transaction costs" (9), the adjustment to changes in relative prices depends on the size of the market (an initial structural condition) and the technology of information dissemination (an initial condition). Such factors, North admits, do not change in the short run: "The "thinner" the market and the more primitive the technology, the longer it takes for the adjustment process to unfold. Thus, structures predate interaction, creating initial conditions that determine the time lag until adjustment takes place and that dictate the pace of the adjustment. Informal institutions such as Tsarist Russia's "customary land agreements" introduce uncertainty in the nature of the adjustment process (9). North (1981, 13) states clearly that the construction of present-day institutions "does not occur in a vacuum but [is] the result of people's perceptions stemming from historically derived opportunities and values." If so, historical institutions are the source of present-day people's perceptions. Here, I believe, lie both the implied temporal priority of structures and the structural conditioning that Archer envisions in regard to people's perceptions and, in turn, their preferences and goals. Moreover, there is no indication of an assumption of an "institution-free state of nature"—CR theorists' most frequent argument against NIE.

The thing that we call "reality"—and, for that matter, that we call "necessity"—is relative to people's historically derived rationalizations of the world (North, 1981, 13). This line of thought is congruent with the Old Institutionalist tradition as understood by Hodgson (2004) and the Critical Realist perspective as per Lawson (1997).

My remark above on "reality" implies an additional dimension: a rational, calculative aspect of human nature that guides individual choice irrespective of time and place—albeit in varying proportions—as the urge to obey authority may restrict the number of available options. The utility-maximizing calculus of the historical and present costs of forgone opportunities constitutes the aspect of the evaluation that reflects the theory's Neoclassical insight. North incorporates into this insight the rationalist ad hoc adherence to values—rule-following that is only indirect by definition, through the maximization of reputation and other social rewards that are linked to economic utility maximization.

Should a Neoclassically Shaped NIE be Conceived of As Realistic in a Sense Other Than CR?

Arguably, the emphasis in North (1981, 48, 49) on the freeloader problem and the role of ideology in overcoming it is veristically absolute and abidingly realistic.[8] Uscali Mäki argues that Friedman's thesis is "a coherent combination of semantic[9] and axiological[10] essentialist realism" (1990, 41). As such, it is preoccupied with "deep" structure as opposed to surface phenomena (27). The same argument is true of the Neoclassically shaped dimension of NIE:

> *A fundamental hypothesis of science is that appearances are deceptive and that there is a way of looking at or interpreting or organizing the evidence that will reveal superficially disconnected and diverse phenomena to be manifestations of a more fundamental and relatively simple structure.*[11]

Thus, the concept of the rational—utility maximizing—Homo Economicus, shared by Neoclassical theory and NIE, is the result of essentialist isolation.[12] Friedman's "as if" formulation does not necessarily imply instrumentalism (Mäki, 1990, 41). Mäki presents a general formulation of theory in "as if" terms: "Entities behave as if the isolated conditions were realized under which only those real and fundamental forces that are mentioned in the theory are in fact acting." Following Mäki's outline of the versions of realism, there are forms of realism that require certain kinds of unrealisticness. Essentialist realism is such a form; in it, the notion of the "whole truth" is purportedly violated. Applying Mäki, I understand the Neoclassical dimension of NIE as committed to this type of realism.

As indicated at the beginning of this chapter the limitations of the Neoclassical model are well acknowledged by North (1981), emphasizing the commitment in NIE to explaining real-world phenomena. The idealization of "zero transaction costs," allowed for in Neoclassical economics,

[8] Mäki (1990, 25), Def. 31: a representation is veristically realistic iff it is true of features of its referent.

[9] Mäki (1990), Def. 11, Referential Realism; Def. 12, Representational Realism; Def. 13, Veristic Realism (20).

[10] Mäki (23), Def. 26: Axiological Realism (or Methodological Realism) is the thesis that true representations of what exists should be pursued.

[11] Friedman (1953), quoted in Mäki (1990, 41), in support of Mäki's derivation.

[12] Mäki (1990, 33), Def. 54: "Essentialist isolation is a purported isolation of the (at least objectively existing) essence of the object under study from its inessential features."

is annulled in NIE, which centers on transaction costs and the role of institutions.

Challenging the CR critique of NIE, North (1981, 17) provides an additional example that implies the shaping, reconstitutive role of institutions: "These rules spell out the system of incentives and disincentives that guide and shape economic activity," that is, those that guide and shape individual agents. An allusion to a multilayered analysis that distinguishes between the observable dimension, the "superficial manifestations" (35) of transactions, and a generative deeper structure is found in the following: "Underlying the transaction—making it possible—was a complex structure of law and its enforcement. Members of modern monetary economies accept pieces of paper as legitimate surrogates for a command over a certain amount of other resources and know that they can use it for that purpose" (35). Here North (1981) calls attention to what Searle (1995, 33) would define as the type of social fact that requires an institutional structure.[13] Contrary to Hodgson's critique of North, stating that the latter focuses on the constraining, restricting function of institutions (Hodgson, 2004, 424, 425), this quotation acknowledges the enabling role of institutions (425).

Ultimately, however, as Archer (1995, 71) emphasizes, NIE explains structures in terms of individual interaction. There is no explicit indication in NIE of structures possessing emergent properties that are irreducible to individual interaction, which is the essence of methodological individualism and the focus of the CR challenge.

One of the differences between NIE and Critical Realist Evolutionary theories is their different conceptions of human nature. While NIE sets out from the assumption of a rational-utility maximizer guided by hedonism, evolutionary approaches focus on instinct and habit (Hamilton, 1999, 29, 44, 45; Hodgson, 2004, 258) and emphasize tacit knowledge (Hodgson, 1999, 212), accepting the unconscious dimension of agency that dovetails with CR theory.

I argue that, by centering on different aspects of human nature, the NIE and Evolutionary schools of thought may be seen as complementary rather than substitutional.

[13] "For social facts, the attitude that we take toward the phenomenon is partly constitutive of the phenomenon."

American Evolutionary Institutionalism and Darwinian Economics: Adaptation of Peasant Customs to Conditions of Life through Natural Selection

American Evolutionary Institutionalism (AEI) puts forward a conception of institutional structures as historically selected in the context of communities that respond to time- and place-specific conditions of life through strategies of survival into which individuals are born. These structures must be understood as predating any given individual and, as to their nature, must be irreducible to individual choices and interaction (Lawson, 1997, 32). Following the Hodgsonian interpretation of AEI, institutional structure acts on any given individual in a process of "reconstitutive downward causation" that shapes his or her habits of thought and, thereby, his or her preferences and aspirations (Hodgson, 2004, 105, 106, 107). Following Hodgson (422, 423), human intentionality and rational deliberation cannot be accepted as an axiom, a cause in no need of explanation. These capacities, unique to humankind, hinge on innate instincts and acquired habits. Human rationality is the product of this evolution. An institutional transformation is an adaptation to a change in conditions following a process of selection and adaptation at the level of multiple and competing institutional structures (cf. Veblen, 1931, 188).

My Hypothesis of NIE/AEI Complementarity

I propose an instrumental explanatory value for AEI/NIE complementarity and suggest that these theories cannot be reduced to, but possess, a common denominator in the preference, assumed in the theory, of the life perpetuation of individuals. Given that AEI is derived from Darwinian evolutionary universalism, it does not recognize abstraction from time- and place-specific contexts (a historically unique structure). NIE, in turn, assigns heavier weight to a dimension of human nature that is absolutely universal across time and place. Thus, a combined framework may yield a holistic explanation of the changes in the institutional structure of the communal-village system in Tsarist Russia as it interacted with the Tsarist state.

Known Theory Combinations: Bridging NIE and AEI through the Economics of Cognition

An interesting example of a combination of sociological, Classical, and Neoclassical economic theories that yields a synergy (a theoretical dimension irreducible to its component parts) is offered by Vanberg (1994). This specific mating of theories also suggests that its main sources of inspiration, the NIE school and Evolutionary Economics, need not be mutually exclusive. Committed to methodological individualism and normative individualism, Vanberg (1994, 1) reconciles Homo Sociologicus—the being whose behavior is norm- or rule-guided—with Homo Economicus, the being who makes rational self-seeking choices (12). He explains the institutional structure and its change over time by a long-term-oriented rational calculus that addresses itself to the level of rational preference of compliance with rules.

Vanberg (17) identifies three ways in which the perceived advantages of compliance with rule (as opposed to case-by-case responses) affect behavioral dispositions—a strategy that encourages the search for complementarities between NIE and Evolutionary approaches. Thus, rule-following may be the product of (1) natural selection and genetic evolution, (2) non-reflective habitual learning, in which individuals adopt the strategy of following rules unconsciously, and (3) a diachronic rational calculus, in which individuals see that they gain more in the long term by following the rule than by making case-by-case adaptations. None of these ways excludes the other. In effect, Vanberg suggests the long-term rationality of custom. Transposing this reasoning to Tsarist Russia, the precarity of life in the pre-revolutionary peasant world may explain the strength and the viability of custom. The benefits of pre-commitment, in turn, relate to the social image of the agent. The essence of this combination of theories is its understanding of morality as conditional and contingent on the characteristics of the environment and its evolution and the long-term response to changes in it (24).

Martens combines Evolutionary theory, Adam Smith's Classical economics, and NIE in the following way: The search for a cognitive economy results in specialization, which leads to asymmetrical distribution of knowledge (Martens, 2004, 4, 51, 104). The role of institutions is to relax the constraint on individuals' limited cognitive capacity (113). Thus, in this sense, efficient institutions offer an evolutionary advantage. Given actors' limited capacity to process information, their motivation to follow rules (or reject institutional structures) may be seen as a strategy that maximizes their long-term probability of survival (1993, 10, Vanberg, 1994, 55). The enabling and constraining function of institutions is emphasized. Initially treating institutions as exogenous to the model, Martens states that knowledge embodied in exchangeable goods is evolutionarily superior to that conveyed in symbols because it results in trade and specialization. Specialization, in turn, diffuses asymmetrically distributed knowledge, causing transaction costs to rise. The tradeoff between *ex ante* transaction costs and ex post transaction costs is a function of the institutional structure (Martens, 2004, 112, 113). Thus, rule systems determine the degree of the division of labor and the accumulation of knowledge and, by so doing, the society's level of development (134).

Rational Choice/Atomist Universalism: NIE—Indispensable But Insufficient for Understanding the Russian Peasant's Transformation

The reason for deeming the NIE perspective insufficient per se centers on the Neoclassical paradigms that make up the core of this group of theories, the underlying metaphor in Newtonian physics. Neoclassical economics conceives of the human being as analogous to an atom, composed of protons and neutrons, who reacts to price signals in accordance with the principles of magnetism that govern nature (Hamilton, 1999, 22–24). I argue that Neoclassical theory and its offshoot, NIE, should be understood as universalistic. Contrary to the Neoclassical theory that bases itself on the Newtonian metaphor, Evolutionary theory, inspired by the "Old" Institutionalism, is predicated on Darwinism (Hodgson, 2004, 91; Hamilton, 1999, 22, 25). Inasmuch as the application of Darwinian ideas in social sciences is controversial for commendable ideological reasons, it is worth quoting Darwin himself ahead of the discussion:

> *As man advances in civilization, and small tribes are united into larger communities, the simplest reason would tell each individual that he ought to extend his social instincts and sympathies to all the members of the same nation, though personally unknown to him. This point being once reached, there is only an*

artificial boundary to prevent his sympathies extending to the men of all nations and races.[14,15]

The Darwinian framework of analysis yields a multidimensional understanding of institutional evolution that focuses on continuity and change and defines human intentionality and preferences as phenomena that can and must be explained. Importantly in this context, however, it rejects biological reductionism. Social sciences operate at an emergent level that is, by nature, irreducible to any knowledge of biotic matter. Still, biotic matter cannot be ignored in a realistic inquiry into human beings. Thus, the hypotheses posed must be consistent with biological insight (Hodgson, 2004, 95–97).

Additionally, the most abstract and general framework of analysis within Darwinian economics, represented here by Veblen (1931) and his Hodgsonian interpreters, emphasizes the time- and place-specific social contexts and dependencies of the emergent human social world.

Veblen (1931, 188) applies the Darwinian metaphor to social sciences while explaining the evolution of institutions through natural selection and adaptation of the socially fittest habits of thought. All dimensions of

[14] See also Hodgson (2004, 79), who convincingly challenges the distorted versions of Darwinism.

[15] Hodgson identifies seven philosophical pillars of Darwinism that valorize the theory for Realist social science:

1. Determinacy (universal causation)—there are no uncaused causes.
2. Emergentist materialism—for example, human intentions are regarded as emergent properties of materialist interactions within the human nervous system.
3. Population thinking—understanding the essence of something involves not only the singular entity but also its membership in a population composed of similar but non-identical entities. The essence of a type necessarily includes its potential to exhibit or create variety.
4. Continuity—complex outcomes are the result of accumulated incremental changes.
5. Cumulative causal explanation—one traces causal processes by focusing on their key processual algorithms.
6. Evolutionary explanation—social sciences must be consistent with acceptable versions of biology.
7. Consistency of sciences—any scientific assumption or principle at a specific ontological level must be consistent with a scientific understanding of all lower ontological levels.

institutions, he says, adapt to conditions of life. I apply Lawson's CR conception of the human's need to control anxiety by relying on structures that emulate or manifest a "parental bent" (Veblen, analyzed in Hodgson, 2001, 147; Lawson, 1997, 180, 181) even if this instinct, defined by Veblen, carries the scope for the instinct of "exploit" while coping with uncertainty.

In the context of the pre-modern peasant world—poorly informed, illiterate, dependent on physical experience, and subject to the precarious climatic and highly uncertain topographic conditions that characterized late Tsarist Russia (Engelgardt, 1993, 37; Chubarov, 2001, 4)—I deem Veblenian AEI, applied to my time- and place-specific environment, instrumental. This model emphasizes the experience of the generations of sages embodied in the leading authority of elites as the source of selection and adaptation of individual habits of thought. The latter justifies the inclusion of the AEI model (Veblen, 1931, 188) as conducive to the explanation of tacit-knowledge-bearing (Hodgson, 1999, 249) rural collectivism as a supplement to NIE. The latter theory flows from a rationalist utility-maximization axiom. Given its restricted information-processing capacity, the at-best "bounded rationality" of the pre-modern peasantry cannot be taken as a given (Hodgson, 2004, 423).

Evolutionary economics focuses on explaining and predicting "changes in elements of the institutional context; norms, values, (and) legal rules" (Groenewegen & Vromen, 1999, 1). Contrary to the atomized and isolated individual in Neoclassical economics, AEI views individual interaction as preconditioned on community and society. Following Hodgson (2004, 123–283), Veblenian institutionalism explicitly conforms to the CR school of thought in its conviction that social structures are dependent on individual interaction but cannot be reduced to it. Thus, it rejects methodological individualism. Furthermore, it sees individuals as dependent on social structures but denies the possibility of explaining their behavior in terms of structures alone. That is, it rejects methodological collectivism. Finally, the temporal precedence of society over any individual is one of its conceptual pillars. The end-state variant of Evolutionary theory selects the individual in interaction with the environment as the unit of analysis (Groenewegen & Vromen, 1999, 4). This paradigm encompasses competence-based theories of the firm rather than the contract-based approach of Transaction-Cost Economics. Combinations of these two theories, however, are both possible and fruitful.

Psychological and Sociological Perspectives

According to the hedonistic psychology that underlies the Neoclassical and Neo-Institutional paradigm, it is sensation and feelings that power action (Hamilton, 1999, 44). Hamilton's analysis distinguishes between more recent psychological doctrines—instinct, behaviorist, Freudian, and Gestalt—and hedonism, perceiving the human being as "a creature of motor impulses that result in a series of actions" merely accompanied by sensations. The sensations, in turn, are viewed as influencing further action rather than initially motivating it. Consequently, motive assumes secondary importance to action as an object of inquiry.

AEI anchors its conception of human nature in the findings of the more recent psychological schools listed above (Hamilton, 1999, 44). Thus, past activity gives rise to habits that further activity subjects to change and adaptation. This view of individuals as undergoing processes of cumulative change in interaction with their social milieus is the outcome of the Darwinian revolution in habits of thought (46).

It is widely believed that in principle, hedonism is obviously incompatible with evolutionary thinking. The question, however, is: Are sensations of pleasure and pain as *foci for the analysis* of human action inadequate from an evolutionary vantage point?

As regards the biochemistry of the Homo Sociologicus, the existence of a culture that embeds the time- and place-neutral dimension of human nature must be axiomatic because people can identify with others across time and space or, as Adam Smith says (2000, 4), "bring their case home to ourselves." This universalistic ability is—to quote reflections of North's hedonism-based Institutionalism—contingent on a specific collective memory reservoir (North, 1993, 12) and individuals' subjective thought models (North, 1993, 35; 2005, 38, 64).

The hedonistic dimension appears to be the common denominator of, and a *sine qua non* for, all human interaction. Therefore, hedonistic psychology conveys an understanding of the human that can be complemented, but not replaced, by other schools of thought.

According to the evolutionary-behaviorist schools, structures create an emergent source of causality for individuals' behavior, preferences, and choices by shaping habitual interaction among individuals (Hodgson, 2004, 14, 188). Thus, the hedonist evaluation cannot be cast aside in any quest to understand human behavior. Instead, it must be acknowledged as an element in the evolutionary analysis because causality in social structures concerning individual habit formation depends on subconscious and conscious hedonistic choices that determine compliance versus default. These choices, however, are not atomized phenomena; they are synergies of feedback mechanisms in social interaction.

Rizello (1999, 83), standing at the intersection of psychology and economics, criticizes the behaviorist conception of human nature, suggesting that it overlooks "retroactive round systems" that operate in individual–environment interaction. The concept of feedback in defining the improvement upon behaviorism, I suggest, is encapsulated in cognitivist theory of human nature.

In accordance with the cognitivist essence, every external impulse is subjected to a history-contingent "checking process." I suggest that this very process, ubiquitous in Hodgson's AEI-delineating "reconstitutive downward causation" view of enculturation—whereby institutions shape and mold individual habits of thought—includes hedonistic elements.

Referring to Soviet neurophysiology, Rizello (92) advises that action is the consequence of new data and past experience as well as prediction of events—a conception that, he says, is congruent with Hayek. Quoting Rizello (1999) I suggest that the hedonistic element of action is embedded in feedback, whereby:

> *[B]rain centers are constantly informed about the success or failure of an action. If necessary a correcting mechanism is starting. The correspondence between present state and pursued goal is constantly checked. Every time a discrepancy is revealed new steps are taken towards a new afferent synthesis.* (92)

Neo-Institutionalism

The inclusion of three time dimensions in the cognitivistic conception of human nature—present-time stimuli from the environment, historical experience embedded in the individual's enculturation within an institutional–organizational structure, historically shaped preferences, and future goals—broadens the scope of legitimacy of the AEI/NIE combination and the assumption of complementarity that underlies it. From Rizello (1999, 98), one may convincingly deduce that bounded rationality is the common denominator of North's Neo-Institutionalism, with its orthodox core and unorthodox economics including AEI. The reflection adduced from Rizello, crucial for my theoretical combination, is that the interaction of an individual with his/her environment is characterized neither by a reflex nor by an immediate ad hoc calculus. Instead, it includes a dimension of historical knowledge storage in the mind–brain dyad that renders each present phenomenon institutionally intelligible through the cognitive prism of experience. Moreover, each individual's subjective model of thinking (North, 2005, 38, 64) is shaped and molded by his or her reservoir of collective memory (North, 1993, 12). The insight offered by the socio-cognitive approach as interpreted by Rizello (1999, 86–92) legitimizes the assumption of compatibility and complementarity between NIE and AEI. I suggest that the feedback-to-experience decision-making process, ever-present due to the need, brought on by uncertainty, to economize on cognitive energy, includes the hedonist dimension that allows NIE and AEI to mate.

North (2005, 24) justifies my linking of the Old Institutionalism to the Neo-Institutionalist economic framework by saying, "Imperfect information and feedback underlie the ubiquitous character of uncertainty; in addition the rationality assumption fails to deal adequately with the relationship of the mind to the environment." Applying North's argument (23), I find that the more an environment is characterized by perfect competition, following one of the assumptions of the Neoclassical model, the more legitimate the Neoclassical psychological conceptions of human nature—"substantive rationality, self-interest, [and] perfect knowledge" (Rizello, 1999, 97)—become. Thus, these human traits are not taken for granted in North's more recent work, which is surprisingly redolent of and close to the Old Institutionalist tradition.

My thesis starts chronologically in the insulated, pious, and patriarchally structured peasant world of the nineteenth-century Russian subsistence economy. The historical conditions of life there were characterized by the suffocation of competition in the absence of alternative options. A protracted transition began in 1861: from adherence to routines of action enculturated by the patriarchal authority of heads of households and village-commune assemblies to the evolution of available options contingent on bounded rationality. The transition, intensifying in tandem with technological advances and enhanced by the ever-present cognitive-feedback process—approaching the substantive rationality of individual members of peasant households after Stolypin's reform—is most convincingly explained within the combined NIE/AEI framework that acknowledges the triple dimension of time (North, 2005, 23, 24; Sheshinski, 2010, 3; Gintis, 2009, 1, 2; Rizello, 1999, 86–98). Such a dimension is congruent with the CR approach.

One of the instruments of Hodgson's reconstitutive downward causation is precisely the association of perceptions of pleasure and pain with reward and punishment, fear and security, and inclusion versus exclusion. Thus, the process of cultural conditioning, shaping, and molding of individuals' preferences, emphasized by the Old Institutionalist tradition, presupposes an ongoing hedonistic calculus. This, in turn, suggests that NIE, also expressed via the proposed direct NIE/AEI combination by basing its assumptions about human nature on a hedonistic conception, may be understood as fully compatible with and, as I will argue presently, complementary to evolutionary approaches.

Before proceeding toward the proposal of complementarities, I wish to convey the essence of the Old Institutionalist conception of institutional change by quoting its most representative exponent, Veblen:

> *Social structure changes, develops, [and] adapts itself to an altered situation, only through a change in the habits of thought of the several classes of the community; or in the last analysis, through a change in the habits of thought of the individuals which make up the community. The evolution of society is substantially a process of mental adaptation on the part of individuals under the stress of circumstances which will no longer tolerate habits of thought formed under and conforming to a different set of circumstances in the past.* (Veblen, 1931, 192)

Thus, a prima facie parallel exists between NIE and Veblen's evolutionary approach, in that both schools of thought posit changes in conditions of life, or in relative scarcities/relative prices due to population changes (North 1973, 29), as the precipitants of institutional change. In both teachings, the path of causality seems to be circular or feedback-generating because the conditions of life/relative prices are somewhat traceable to the institutional framework.

In NIE, for example, the model implies a causal chain captured as follows:

> Institutional change ⇔ technological change ⇔
> change in relative prices ⇔ institutional change

Note that the arrows point in both directions. According to Veblen's theory of the leisure class, the predatory culture that shapes individuals' habits of thought creates a set of wants that determine the perceived conditions of life. A closer analysis, however, discloses that those schools diverge in their emphasis on the constitutive weight of individual agency relative to structure.

NIE and AEI Understood As Mutually Complementary

Figure 3.1, inspired by Hodgson (2004), describes the relation between structure and agency in NIE (right-hand side) and AEI (left-hand side) according to a "loop" of determinants of ultimate and proximate behavior (Vromen, 2001, 194).

Veblen's theory places greater weight than NIE on structure, which it construes as the result of the natural selection of institutions (Veblen, 1931, 188; Hodgson, 2004, 141) that molds individuals' preferences and goals (Vromen, 2001, 184; Hodgson, 2004, 105)—that is, shapes their habits of thought—through selection and adaptation. Thus, the theory emphasizes Hodgson's reconstitutive downward causation process, as shown by the red arrow in Fig. 3.1 and the thicker arrows in Fig. 3.3. As proximate causes are the effects of the ultimate causes, intentional human

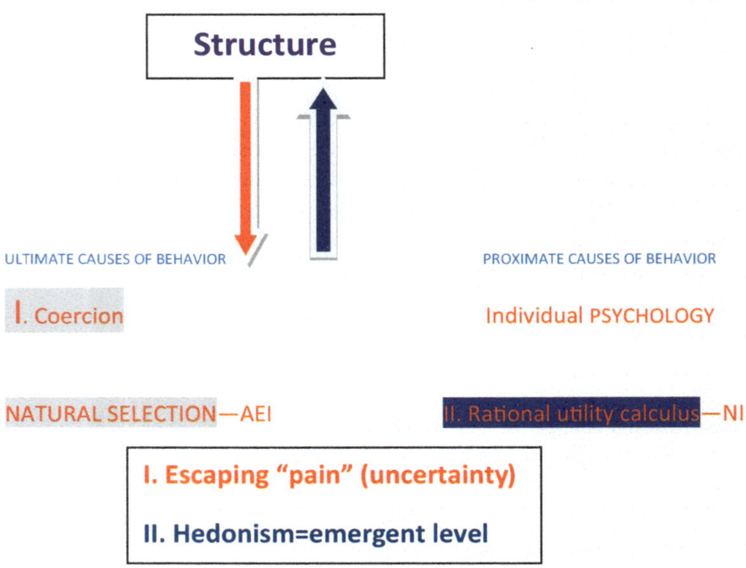

Fig. 3.1 The loop of behavioral determinants

agency is the product of evolution (Vromen, 2001, 194; Hodgson, 2004, 96).

In NIE, with its methodological-individualism orientation, the relative explanatory weight is assigned to interaction among rational-utility-maximizing individuals as the ultimate source of structure (Archer, 1995, 79, 80, on conflationary social theory): "Institutions are the creation of human beings. They evolve and are altered by human beings; hence our theory must begin with the individual" (North 1990, 5). Thus, the assumption about a Homo Economicus who is relatively independent of the institutional environment in his or her preferences and goals emphasizes the reconstitutive upward causation process (the blue arrow in Fig. 3.1 and the thicker arrows in Fig. 3.2 [Hodgson, 2004, 105]).

It is through organizations, which differ from institutions because they play the game while institutions constitute the rules of the game, that the set of strategic choices brings about institutional change by interacting with the institutional environment (North, 1993, 19, 23, 114; 2005, 59). The informal institutional dimension—for example, a custom that structures a historical pre-modern community or contemporaneous unwritten conventions enforced by social sanction—is often codified into, and legitimizes or provides ideological/cultural grounds for the rejection of, the formal rule.

That structure channels individual choices through a particular set of incentives is self-evident. The theory elaborates on this by presupposing an ongoing hedonistic calculus, in which relative scarcities, expressed as relative prices, give rise to particular problem-solving—uncertainty-reducing—devices, namely, institutional structures.

AEI proposes, given the dependency of the replication of habits on common institutional constraints, that common conventions may yield similar habits of thought (Hodgson & Knudsen, 2004, 10). Rationality is said to depend on "a complex foundation of habit, tacit knowledge and experience"; thus, reason is partly seen as a cultural phenomenon (20). This line of thought emphasizes reconstitutive downward causation. As argued above, it is the awareness of this process, accenting the temporal precedence of structure, that inspires CR evolutionary thought. At the organization level, knowledge is encapsulated in routines of action (Hodgson & Knudsen; 2004, 22; 2005, 14). At the society level, institutions constitute repositories of knowledge (Hodgson, 2004, 12, 168).

The argument concerning "downward causation" in the evolutionary approach may best be presented in Veblen's own words:

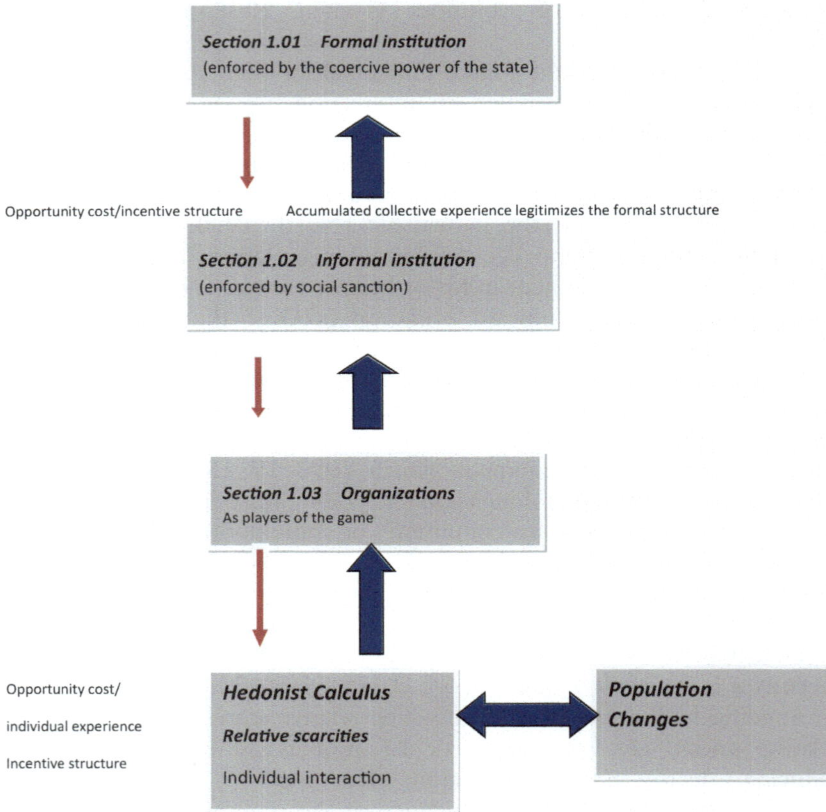

Fig. 3.2 NIE, based on North's emphasis on "upward causation" as the source of structure. (*Source*: North (1973, 1981, 1990, 2005); Sztern, with profound gratitude to Hodgson for personal communication)

> *The evolution of social structure has been a process of natural selection of institutions. The progress which has been and is being made in human institutions and in human character may be set down, broadly, to a natural selection of the fittest habits of thought and to a process of enforced adaptation of individuals to an environment which has progressively changed with the growth of the community and with the changing institutions under which men lived.* Institutions are not only themselves the result of a selective and adaptive process which shapes the prevailing or dominant types of spiritual attitude and aptitudes; they are at the same time special methods of life and human relations, and

are therefore in their turn efficient factors of selection. *So that the changing institutions in their turn make for a further selection of individuals endowed with the fittest temperament, and a further adaptation of individual temperament and habits to the changing environment through the formation of new institutions.* (Veblen, 1931, 188; emphasis added)

With the foregoing aspects taken into account, the theories may be seen as complementary.

Figure 3.3 summarizes the evolutionary approach as inspired by Veblen (1931), Hodgson (2004), Hodgson and Knudsen (March 2004), and

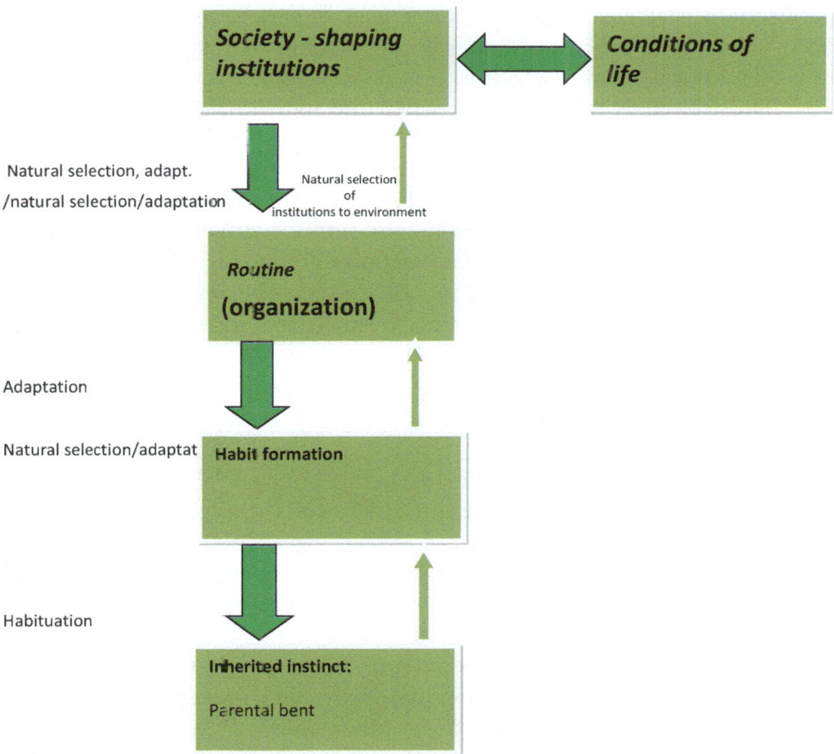

Fig. 3.3 The evolutionary approach, stressing reconstitutive downward causation. (*Source*: Sztern, with profound gratitude to Hodgson for personal communication)

Hodgson and Knudsen (2005). The emphasis in this approach is on reconstitutive downward causation that operates through a process of natural selection and adaptation.

Habits and Evolution

Following the evolutionary approach to the social sciences, with its focus on mechanisms of inheritance, variation, and selection, the repositories of knowledge that are ontologically specific, each level having emergent properties relative to the one below it, are replicators (Hodgson & Knudsen, 2005, 12; 2002 on routine as a replicator and repository of knowledge) that ensure continuity as well as variety over time. Variety occurs through a process of imperfect replication that is acted upon by a non-teleological natural selection process (Hodgson & Knudsen, 2005, 12). Thus, habit is the replicator when the individual is the interactor, routine is the replicator when organization is the interactor, and institution is the replicator when society is the interactor (14).

Instincts, in turn, are "inherited behavioral dispositions that, when triggered, give rise to reflexes, urges or emotions," with the sensory input necessary to arouse the instinctive reaction (Hodgson, 2004, 162). The notion of inherited predispositions clashes with the understanding of a newborn human as a *tabula rasa*, since instincts are vital to the structuring of incoming information (163). Hodgson, however, states emphatically that the human personality is shaped predominantly *after* birth; thus, socialization and acculturation assume higher weight in the model in Figs. 3.2 and 3.3.

It may be assumed that habit formation through social interaction plays an anxiety-controlling role (Lawson, 1997, 181), thereby conferring an evolutionary advantage.

The suggestion, and expressed in Fig. 3.3, is that at each of these levels, a process of natural selection (Veblen, 1931, 188) by higher-level structures and adaptation by lower-level structures takes place such that individual habits of thought are selected and/or adapted to routines within organizations that harbor the individual agent. Such units may be a household, a modern firm (Hodgson & Knudsen, 2005, 7), or a pre-modern collective of the *obshchina* type.

Ultimately, habits of thought adapt to institutional structures that meet the criteria of selection among a society's organizational forms by inducing/obstructing the replication of corresponding routines of behavior

(Rizello, 1999, 27). This model suggests that since competition is endemic to the institutional structure, it acquires the ultimate explanatory weight.

Although institutional change ultimately depends on change in individuals' habits of thought (Veblen, 1931, 192), the emphasis is on "top-down" causation because habits are largely shaped by the institutional environment. Thus, the effects of the systematization of Tsarist rule[16] and Stolypin's land reform (1906–1917) on the peasantry's habits of thought may be investigated from a "top-down" perspective.

Within this framework, both of these macro-level institutional transformation processes may be seen as adaptations by institutional structures to changed conditions of life in the empire as a whole, brought on by industrialization—itself the result of an institutional change that ultimately constituted a response to the empire's endangered geopolitical position and population increase. By emphasizing the "top-down" interpretation of the historical facts, however, I would leave the analysis incomplete. The propensity of institutions to shape individual activity in each particular situation is not limitless (Hodgson, 2004 and, focusing on individual motives, Goldhagen, 1996). There are ample examples of extremely individualistic behaviors in the face of severe stress conditions, as evidenced in survivors of the Nazi Holocaust (Wiesel, 1958, 86). It is plausible to assume that the individualistic dimension of mankind is ubiquitously universal across cultures and diachronic époques.

The NIE approach, again, is anchored in methodological individualism (Fig. 3.2) and endowed with a historical dimension focusing on the collective memory reservoir encapsulated in informal language belief systems inherited from past pre-modern communities—namely, custom—and formal institutions codified in laws and statutes and enforced by the modern state (North, 1993, 15; idem., 1990, 80). As such, it may very well have support in real-world phenomena.[17] This approach bathes the origin of institutions in the light of rational survival calculus. What people inherit today is the result of historical payoff matrices. An approach that emphasizes independent individual choice is needed to explain, at least partly, the process by which structures—routines of action—are legitimized and reproduced or refuted or transformed. The "bottom-up" perspective,

[16] See Yaney (1973, 15, 16, 17) on the predictability of peasant mutual dependence in a systematic versus a non-systematic society.

[17] This understanding of NIE counters Lawson's critique (Lawson, 1997, 168) of Neoclassical economics and NIE.

departing from the rational-utility-maximization assumption, is *instrumental* and complementary in this context. As argued above, the hedonistic conception of human nature, implicit in the evolutionary approaches, must be included in the model explicitly. The theories may be seen as complements rather than rivals.

NIE does not concern itself with the evolutionary processes that bring about intentional human agency; instead, it uses human agency as its point of departure. Therefore, one may also view the NIE model above as a special case of Evolutionary theory (Hodgson, 2004, 449, 450; personal communication, June 22, 2005). In this context, however, the focus is on the complementary properties of these theories. I suggest instead that Newtonian Neoclassical economics offers a dimension of higher and more universalistic abstraction.

Reflections on the Theory of Institutional Change

Let us reevaluate *da capo* our conceptualization of Tsarist Russia for a moment. Is it historically accurate to claim, as the Gerschenkronian school does, that the Tsarist state substituted for the market, making up the missing Rostowian prerequisites for industrialization? Viewed from a time- and place-specific perspective, it appears instead that the post-emancipation Tsarist state substituted for the serf economy of the feudal lords—the *pomeshchiks*, the serf-dependents' protectors of last resort. Acting in the manner of the Coasian–Gerschenkronian conceptualization, the post-emancipation Tsarist state took over all functions of the landed gentry while allowing a limited, intra-estate peasant market in land to exist by means of the Stolypin reform. Therefore, to attain a full understanding of Tsarist Russia, I propose the Boyer and Orlean (1993) model on the conditions for institutional transformation. In late Tsarist Russia, set on the move by the railroad technology that it imported, all conditions for a Boyer and Orlean institutional-cultural revolution—a challenge to an evolutionarily stable strategy (ESS)—are met.

Informal Institutional Change in a Path-Dependent Society

From the combined NIE/AEI perspective that I have formulated, society is a pioneering agent that seeks to shape and mold an institutional structure consistent with technology and population change. Below I add that any sanctions applied by society are based on prevalent conventions, otherwise known as informal rules of conduct.

Boyer and Orlean (1993, 19) define a convention as "a social arrangement which allows people to cooperate with each other ... The convention is self-sustaining, each agent will choose to follow it provided he expects his opponent to follow it. The quality of conventions is thus self-enforcing." The utility derived from choosing any strategy is a function of the number of individuals who previously chose the same strategy. Boyer and Orlean (1993, 22) envisage returns freighted with composite socio-economic reputation for the risks incurred by choosing the invading strategy that may be understood as a general source of the utility. Following convention delivers social returns in the form of good reputation or the feeling of belonging to a group. Thus, a convention is an informal institution that provides social incentives for compliance. The stability of conventions, however, does not ensure their Pareto efficiency (Boyer & Orlean, 1993, 19); this explains the viability of economically inefficient institutions and the inefficient organizations derived from them.

The transformation from a rationally inferior convention to a superior one can take place if a process of social differentiation exists that makes it possible to "localize the coordination effects" (Boyer & Orlean, 1993). In a totally individualistic or atomized society, this cannot happen because agents lack the links with which they may identify one another. To satisfy the conditions necessary for agents to coordinate, a micro-collective grounded in social or historical reference must organize to overcome the strategic uncertainty. One may relate this argument to the theorems of both Coase (1937) and North (1990). The costs of strategic uncertainty may be lowered if an informal institution socially legitimizes organizations that serve to internalize the transaction costs of a conventional transition.

Although informal restrictions are generally understood as impeding institutional innovation, it is plausible to suggest that all custom is formed in reference to its long-term objective of ensuring survival. Thus, an organization based on historical reference may abet the adjustment, namely, the revision of custom, by investing its *objective* with the dignity of principle. Conforming to Hodgson's analysis (1996, 249–269), the Boyer and Orlean (1993) model assumes that "coordination problems cannot be solved on the basis of individual rationality alone." A change in conventions is conditioned by the formation of "social filters" (Boyer & Orlean, 1993, 19), which, in turn, depend on the possibility of forming institutionally autonomous units.

An additional assumption inspires my thesis: the pre-revolutionary rural *obshchina* system, although seen by Gerschenkron (1968) and Atkinson

(1983) as an impediment to the transition to modern economic growth, actually abetted the diffusion of institutional novelty by providing historical reference ground for the formation of urban organizations. The process of novelty diffusion yielded a particular folklore-based type of trade-union activity. The challenge to authoritarian society was embedded in the potential for cooperation in units based on an internally homogeneous set of values, coupled with autonomization or anti-atomization, that allowed "strategic uncertainty" to be internalized. The existence of these units in micro-collectives that were subversive to the autarchy activated the demand for "corrective measures" in the form of institutional adjustment.

Action in the wake of an informal institution may, according to Boyer and Orlean (1993), be defined as an evolutionarily stable strategy (ESS) if *all* members of the population adopt the strategy so that no mutant strategy can invade.[18] Boyer and Orlean also define the concept of "path dependency" as follows: in quantifiable concepts, any choice oriented toward novelty will depend on the number of agents who have already chosen the innovative strategy. This definition is oxymoronic because the novelty will be chosen only after it ceases to be novel. Even so, the Boyer and Orlean taxonomy of conventional change defines four generalizable conditions under which an ESS may give way to an informal institutional innovation, namely, the adoption of an alternative convention: general collapse, external invasion, translation, and collective agreement.

General collapse occurs when an overall change in conditions gradually depletes the individual utility of an ESS and lasts until a non-frequent choice acquires an invasive property, meaning that it becomes dominant.[19] By implication, events such as war or internal upheaval diminish the ability of ESS-based organizations to fulfill their uncertainty-internalizing function, inducing a gradual increase in the population of individuals who

[18] Boyer and Orlean (1993, 21) define the equilibrium between two ESS conventions as follows; $p^* = UB/UA + UB$, where p^* is the equilibrium *frequency* at which the utility of strategy B for an individual equals the utility derived from choosing strategy A. For $p > p^*$, $U(A, p)$ is greater than $U(B, p)$ even if UA is less than UB because ***insufficient agents chose*** *B*. If convention A prevails, proportion of individuals d^*, equal to $(1-p^*)$, would have to change their behavior ***simultaneously*** for the system to converge to convention B. The greater UB is, the smaller is proportion d^*.

[19] Boyer and Orlean (1993, 22). As the utility of ESS falls, $d^* = 1-p^*$. That is, 1 (the equilibrium frequency at which both conventions, the new and the preceding, deliver equal utility) approaches 0 and a very non-frequent choice may gradually become an ESS.

choose an institutional strategy that has adjusted to the "environment change." The individual utility derived from an alternative convention of this kind rises in tandem with the frequency of its choice. General collapse is also defined as an overall fall in the utility of a path-bound strategy, so that a new convention is adopted simultaneously and, thereby, emerges as a new ESS. In the first case, a "small number of mutants" (Boyer & Orlean, 1993, 22), combined with the gradually declining utility of the ESS, both in response to changed conditions, triggers a change in the choice of an evolutionarily stable convention. In the second case, the previously ESS-based organization simultaneously perceives an alternative convention as an evolutionarily stable one as the environmental change obliterates the utility of the erstwhile ESS. If so, general collapse may be seen as society's counterpart of the political disequilibrium depicted in the Gerschenkronian–Hayekian model interpreted above.

In an *external invasion*, a convention that is new and competes with the old one in frequency of choice causes the remaining over-equilibrium frequency of adherents to the initial ESS—1-p* = d*—to convert to the novelty. Such a conversion is even more likely if the utility derived from the previous convention decreases in relative terms due to an extra-institutional change such as the infusion of a novel technology.

In *translation*, the prevailing convention, if it is compatible with the new one—meaning that the combined value expected from both conventions is in excess of null E(novelty, path dependent) > 0 as the choice frequency of the path-dependent convention—would not necessarily fall as the increase in choice frequency of the novelty translates into novelty. In this process, the more compatible the utility of the novelty is with the utility of the path-dependent convention—or, in Boyer and Orlean's terms, the smaller the difference between U path dependent and U novelty path dependent—the lower d* is. This represents a decrease in the proportion of conversions needed for the whole population to convert to the novelty, resulting in a systemic change in favor of the novelty.

Collective agreement signifies a change in path dependency in favor of a novelty because a collective exists that induces participating individuals to embrace the novelty. Such a pattern of institutional innovation is possible only under central government.

Applying the Boyer and Orlean Model to Russia, 1890–1906

Having explicated the Boyer and Orlean (1993) model, I now apply it to construct a partial framework for analysis of the change in conventions that is assumed to have occurred in 1890–1906, when late Tsarist Russia transitioned from a backward to a relatively modern and developed economy. I conceive the industrialization process, powered by imported technology and skills, as having exposed the previously rural population that now stratified itself in urban unions, as well as the local entrepreneurs and bankers, to an external invasion of individuals who were inclined to choose a novelty-oriented institutional structure. Thus, the informal custom shaped by personalized law gave way to growing demand by an autonomizing society for an objectivized legal infrastructure. The presentation that follows, applying North's (1973) paradigm, identifies society as the pioneering force in an innovative adaptation to changed scarcity conditions.

Notwithstanding historical evidence that characterizes the late Tsarist industrialization process as state-led, I postulate that it was the change in informal institutions and social sanctions—an external invasion that induced change in favor of a superior ESS, one adjusted to technology and concentration of production—that powered society's commitment to institutional "corrective measures." These measures, in turn, constituted an adjustment to the change in transaction costs that industrialization had brought about. The adjustment was effected amid escalating demand for civil and property rights embedded in an opposition movement of growing strength that demanded political decentralization. The centralized government, adhering to political rationality, erected a barrier against the "bottom-up" diffusion of novelty, oppressing autonomous organizations that based themselves on the new ESS. Consequently, the confrontation between society's innovative adaptability to population increase and industrialization and the autocracy's conservative inclinations and thirst for further centralization—with which it could monitor and impede this very development—toppled the previous ESS, which had been based on personalized rule. Thus, the personalized formal institutional infrastructure yielded to a relatively impersonalized one that was codified in 1906 in the Stolypin land reform. If so, Boyer and Orlean's (1993) model may be applied to the pre-revolutionary transition as follows:

> Industrialization—›› external invasion—›› **(political rationality = a barrier to innovation)**—›› the upheaval of 1905—›› **general collapse**—›› Δ ESS = institutional change

Furthermore, it may be assumed that by responding to population increase and launching an industrialization process enabled by imported

Western technology, the Tsarist government shifted the production possibility frontier (PPF) upward. However, by allowing political rationality to supersede economic rationality, it let the structural possibility frontier (Eggertsson, 1990) lag behind, resulting in rising transaction costs as the transition to modern economic growth proceeded. The 1906 reform, aimed at institutionalizing the individualization of all civil rights including property rights—applying the principle of equality before the law and promoting the objectivization of the law—would have as its goal greater synchronization of the structural and the technological PPFs by revising the incentive structure that the formal institutions would set forth.

By implication, Gerschenkron (1962) may be said to assume that the political structure "reformed itself"—took a corrective measure in response to the threat to internal stability posed by the rising industrialization-caused uncertainty, the defeat in the 1904 Russo-Japanese war, and the political destabilization itself. The idea behind the reform, according to Ascher (1988), was to base the continuing legitimacy of the Tsar's monopoly on political power and thus to sustain the autocracy. From this perspective, the late Tsarist transition is comparable with Russia's recent one in one sense only: It caused economic structural hardships resulting in political instability that triggered a formal, state-determined institutionalized adjustment. Like the recent transition, the late Tsarist one was only partly and formally a "top-down" institutional reform, engineered in this case in response to the widening gap between the technological PPF and the structural one. As for its results, the goal of preserving autocracy at the cost of increased oppression of autonomous organizations, such as the zemstvos, may be seen as an equivalent of the unsuccessful coup d'état that Russia experienced in 1991.

My objective here is to supplement Gerschenkron's position by tracking down the source of the novelty. As stated above, the development-promotive change was driven by society and not solely by the political superstructure. One may presume that the higher the level of participation, the faster the transition from structurally obsolete institutional systems to those conforming with the technological PPF will be. Whether the change in PPF (or, in Boyer and Orlean's terms, the material cause of an external institutional invasion) may itself be promoted by the decentralization of the political structure would depend on the novel property rights incentive function, contingent on the barrier to novelty encapsulated in the viability of the structural possibility frontier of the previous system. Viewed thus, one may "blame" Tsarist Russia's economic backwardness on its institutional backwardness, which ultimately traced to the Empire's climatic and geopolitical conditions. These, in turn, had been structured by an initially high land-to-labor ratio that, both during the Golden Horde and the Tsarist eras, inspired recourse to various degrees of bondage and degradation of subjects in relation to rulers.

Precipitants of Endogenous Change

Before proceeding, I wish to present additional models and definitions as components of the explanatory framework or perspectives on which I will elaborate in the following chapters.

Witt (1993, 1–15), examining the conditions for an endogenous institutional change, asks rhetorically: When is a system inclined to set out on a self-transformation process? The first condition to be met, he says, is *novelty*. The quest for novelty is triggered primarily by a preference for the kind of novelty that "would ensure a basic rate of innovativeness, the latter varying with the cultural or social acceptance of innovations" (4), namely, with the prevailing conventions. The process is a function of the availability of the skills and motivation that allow the search to take place (Witt, 1993, 3, 4). Witt then offers a satisficing hypothesis: the motive to discover an unprecedented solution also exists if "the best presently feasible action is inferior to the best one in the past" (4).[20] Thus, an assessment of an *inferior optimum* would generate motivation to discover novelty. The strength of this motivation to would be a function of the probability of success, the latter based on past record. In addition to the existence of a novelty, its transition into innovating behavior—its acceptance and utilization—is supremely important in assessing when an endogenously generated change in conventions will occur. In this context, Witt emphasizes frequency dependency (7)[21] and the selection effect (9).[22] Individuals'

[20] Witt offers a two-track prognosis: An adjustment to the best possible solution, even if it is inferior to the one desired, will occur if an *optimization* hypothesis is followed. If a *satisficing* model is verified, in contrast, the search for novelty will take place in an equivalent situation. According to the latter hypothesis, a crisis will trigger a quest for novelty.

[21] fa(t) = f (Fa(t)), the probability of a marginal "a" strategy choice at time "t" is the function of the frequency of "a" at time "t" in a population.

[22] w a = aa – 1. "The rate of change in the relative frequency of one alternative follows from the equation as a difference between the individual alternative's advantage and the average population advantage." For further proof, see the source. The *selection effect* is a special case of replicator dynamics, of which an example is given by the equation. "The process of com-

decision-making, be it innovative, imitative, or conservative, is said to affect the relative frequencies of behaviors in a population (5). Applying the Boyer and Orlean (1993) and Witt (1993) models in combination, I expect the "culturally learned interpretation patterns" and the choice frequency to be systematically interdependent. The selection effect may be the result of external pressures as well as "intra-group interactions" (Witt, 1993, 12). Witt, commenting on his model, rules that "Innovativeness creates the variety upon which selection effect operates" (10).[23] The satisficing hypothesis yields a cyclical pattern. The erosion of innovative variety through selection is said to threaten aspiration levels; this, by triggering the search for novelty and causing the rate of basic innovations to rise, sets a new cycle in motion.[24]

Below I apply these models to explain the endogenous change in values that is said to have occurred gradually ahead of the formal codification of the Stolypin reform. In the specific context of Tsarist Russia, the novelty was the transformation of *obshchina*-specific *egalitarianism in land-use rights* into the principle of *equality before the law*. Applying Boyer and Orlean's model, I contend that the diffusion of this unprecedented phenomenon in Russia's rural and urban labor-force constituencies was promoted by the unionization of the latter. Thus, the transition from a novelty to an institutional innovation occurred through a process of *stratification* and *translation*. It follows that state-led industrialization subjected the informal institutional paradigm to an endogenously generated change. Moreover, the Emancipation Act (February 19, 1861) raised the levels of aspiration or, alternatively, the probability of success in promoting egalitarianism, rendering obsolete the legislative "apartheid" that had been manifested in the collectivist peasant custom—an inferior optimum in these constituencies' own view. This may imply that the invasion of liberal ideology from the West and the land-tenure institutions shaped by the gentry's individual rights would penetrate the habitus of the Russian

petition constitutes a *selection device* which continually works to eliminate variants and thus, to reduce the variety of economic behavior in a population" (Witt, 1993, 12).

[23] The variance of profit distribution and also of productivity within an economy should be positively correlated with the intensity of innovative activities and negatively with the selection.

[24] "Variety eroding and generating activities reappear as coordinating and decoordinating tendencies and the dynamic balance between them produces a viable" and evolutionarily stable alternative (Witt. 1993, 11, 12). This postulate counters the Neoclassical general equilibrium hypotheses.

peasantry, creating a novelty that the village elders would select and transform into an institutional innovation within the erstwhile *obshchina* system. This, in turn, would tip the institutional frequency in favor of hereditary household land-use rights. This chain of inferences may explain the voluntary omission of *obshchina* repartitions in the late nineteenth century, preceding the 1906 land-rights reform, as well as the increase in labor mobility, namely, the ongoing equalization and individualization of property rights. The absorption of a novelty—the individualization and, therefore, the equalization of rights—may be seen as an innovative adaptation to the reduced risk of death in the serf economy since the perdurant change in population density since the eighteenth century (Hesse, 1993, 47–61), paving the way to state-led industrialization, railroad construction, and the stimulus of the latter for population increase during the nineteenth century. The last-mentioned process, additionally, strengthened the endogenous change in values in favor of institutional egalitarianism.

The emancipation and redemption Acts of 1861 and 1863, respectively, may be assumed to have intensified competition between the gentry and its former serfs for grain markets. From this perspective, the selection pressure would act to homogenize the rights of the peasants with those of the nobility, attenuating the initial institutional variety in favor of the institutional innovation absorbed by the peasantry. Increased demand for a property-rights reform endowed this strategy with ESS properties. As for the state, the strategy of suppressing the innovative process amid industrialization yielded an inferior optimum. The reforms introduced by political agents from Petrine times onward gradually broadened the set of available skills, stimulating the search for novelty. Each reform raised the levels of aspiration, providing additional motives for the translation of folk egalitarian conventions into de jure egalitarianism. It also facilitated the imitative absorption of Western ideologies, including liberalism and Marxism. Applying from left to right the combined models of Eggertsson (1990), Witt (1993), Boyer and Orlean (1993), Metzer (1972), Smith (1998), Martens (2004), Gintis (2009), and Sheshinski (2010), I would summarize the assumptions that structure my analysis as follows (Fig. 3.4).

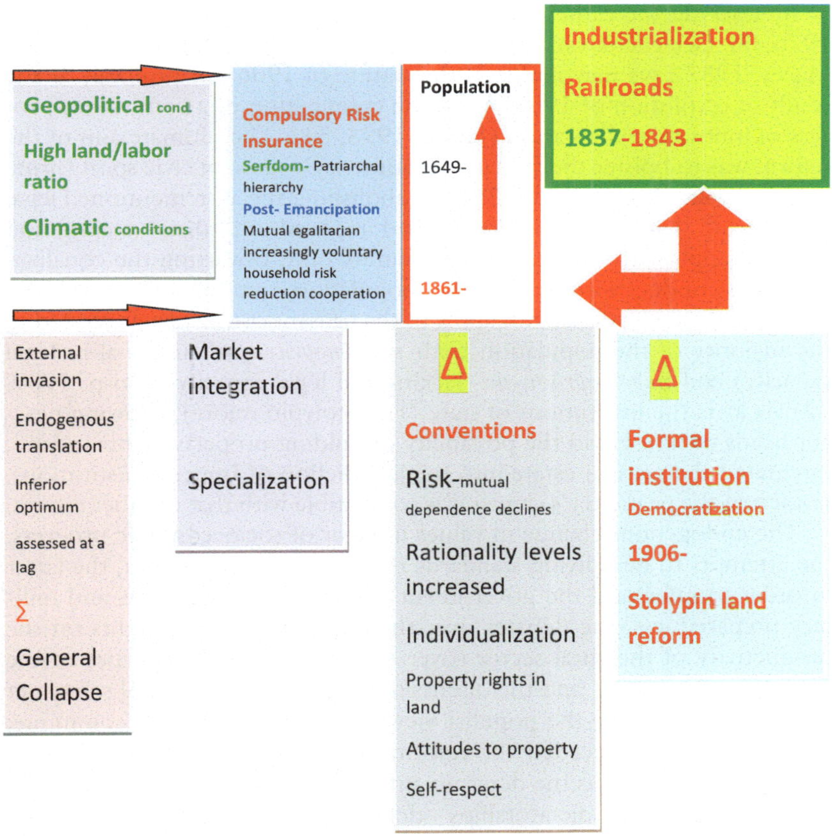

Fig. 3.4 The railroad-population conundrum—institutional "bottom-up" demand leading to general collapse of ESS in 1905

Lagged Institutional Adaptation: Stolypin's Land Reform (1906)

The "first emancipation" had one goal: the abolition of serfdom. The aim of the second reform, in contrast, was twofold: to institutionalize individual ownership of land—to "emancipate" its inhabitants from the formal boundaries of the commune—and to equalize the civil rights of peasants and non-peasants (Ascher, 1988, 269). Thus, the *obshchina*, the village commune, would constitute a totally voluntary form of land holding.

By tracking the earlier debates on civil and property rights (Wortman 1976, 5; Gerschenkron, 1968, 132, 133; Crisp, 1989, especially 42; Macey, 1987), we may construe the statute of 1906 not primarily as the result of revolution of 1905 but as the culmination of a continuous process of innovative adaptation (Hesse, 1993, 51). The ultimate aim of the reform was to bolster the peasant constituency's sense of civic spirit (*grazdanstvennost*) (Ascher, 1988, 268) by abolishing the aforementioned legal "apartheid" that the customary law had imposed until then—a condition that had applied to the peasant community only, thwarting the equalization of its conduct with that of other population strata. Before the reform, the imperial civil code did not apply to the peasant constituency, rendering the majority of the population both *neravnopravnymi* (unequal in legal capacity) and *nepolnopravnymi* (lacking full legal capacity—Crisp, 1989, 42) vis-à-vis the institutions of state. The Stolypin reform, allowing peasant heads of household the possibility of holding property rights in land, integrated the peasant estate into the jurisdiction of Imperial institutions, rendering the peasantry's civic status compatible with that of other estates.

The endogenous change in values in favor of socioeconomic progress, the attempts to raise living standards through industrialization, the latter in order to safeguard the government's reputation, legitimacy, and military preparedness, the debates over the effect of property rights on the productivity of the rural sector (over the instrumental properties of the ownership structure), and the discussions concerning the social safety net (which, according to the populist view, was provided by the commune; Wortman, 1967) preceded the reform. Therefore, the 1905 turmoil in itself cannot be seen as the determinant of the change. The options traditionally available to dictatorships—deflecting demands for institutional improvement by embarking on an extraterritorial military confrontation (in the Far East in this case) and mobilizing patriotic civic spirit on its behalf, or by selecting alleged internal enemies and provocateurs among the minorities, such as the Jews, for the same purpose—proved to be an inferior optimum (Witt, 1993, 4) relative to the political utility of such strategies in the past. Theoretically, the failure of the traditional pattern of governance could have strengthened the imperial government's motivation to "search for new choices" (Witt, 4), which, in the case at hand, would have meant accepting the demands for institutional innovation. While the contents of the reform cannot be seen as a novelty introduced top-down, the acceptance of the innovative adaptation process through an institutionalized adjustment may be seen as such. Still, it is worth noting that the "usual pattern" actually proved to be an inferior optimum that may be attributed to the pro-innovation skill set that had accumulated over time.

Since collective ownership was traditionally sanctioned by rural custom and became endemic in the imperial institutions merely by ex post acceptance (serving the interests of the state by securing its tax revenues, as is believed by the Westernizers school headed by Boris Chicherin [1828–1904]), the generalization of imperial law to include the peasants also implied the voluntary granting to the former *obshchina* dwellers of full, that is, individual, household head property rights as well as obligations. (On the limitations of estate-specific property rights, see Kotsonis, quoted in Chap. 10.)

Collective responsibility for taxes and dues had been repealed back in 1903 (Atkinson, 1983, 41). Redemption payments were reduced following the November Manifesto of 1905 and canceled in 1907 (44). The government's aim in taking these measures was to loosen the formal institutional ties that held the commune together (53). Under Stolypin's reform proposal to the Duma in June 1906, all peasant holders of allotment land would be able to claim it as their personal property and withdraw it from the commune at their will (53). Land purchases by peasant smallholders would be facilitated through credits granted by the Peasant Land Bank, established back in 1882 (44, 67), almost a decade before the first industrialization wave. This would expedite the peasantry's admission to the "club" of owners of property tradable within the peasant estate (45; Gaudin, 2007).

As a result of the reform, peasants could consolidate their holdings within commune boundaries by establishing one of two entities: an *otrub*—a smallholder's parcel within the voluntary cooperative of the commune—or a *khutor*, separate from the commune and outside its boundaries. Most *khutors* were established where groundwater was abundant; this was the favored mechanism of large extended multi-nucleus families, which had higher ratios of labor teams (*tyaglo*) per family than did others. The higher ratios are explained by the character of the landholdings as hereditary landed assets, which, in the case of *otkhod*, could better serve as insurance against urban-income volatility (Johnson, 1979, 38) than could *otrubs*. Literacy was also higher on *khutors* than on *otrubs*; consequently, *khutor* holders were seen as pioneers in the formation of an emerging class of peasant-entrepreneurs (94).

Table 3.1 itemizes personal appropriations of communal allotment land.

Table 3.1 Personal appropriation of communal allotment of land, 1907–1915 (39 provinces of European Russia and Stavropol Province)

Year	*Applications for appropriation*	*Appropriations completed*	*Land appropriated, desyatinas*[a]	*Avg. area appropriated, desyatinas*
1907	212	48	4316	7.7
1908	840	508		
1909	650	579	4115	7.1
1910	342	342	2303	6.7
1911	242	145	996	6.8
1912	152	122	785	6.4
1913	160	134	747	5.5
1914	120	98	594	6.1
1915	37	30	267	9.0
Total	2755	2008	14,123	7.0

Source: Atkinson (1983, 76)

[a]A desyatina is approximately 1.1 hectare, 2.27 acre

As noted, the Northian formal conversion of individual household heads' communal land into hereditarily owned private land was impeded by the need to execute agreements with the commune assembly. Thus, unconcluded negotiations explain the discrepancy between the number of applications and actual appropriations. Although the reform was theoretically based on voluntarism, hereditary tenure could as well be imposed against individuals' will. Given that the assembly had to sign off on any household-based collective conversion by a two-thirds majority, some individual preferences relative to collective ones may have been overruled (Atkinson, 1983, 76; Johnson, 1979, 76). The decline in conversion applications between 1909 and 1910 is explained by the institutionalization of de facto hereditary ownership under a statute passed on June 14, 1910, according to which all communes that had not effectuated a repartition since the initial land allotment stipulated in the Emancipation Act of 1861 would automatically be transformed into hereditary household-based villages. To sell land parcels, however, individual certificates of title were required. Therefore, so-called "land captains"—government officials appointed as aides in the field for the implementation of the reform—encouraged peasants to apply for appropriation. Nevertheless, the number of applications remained limited (77). Notably, fewer certificates of title were issued to communes between 1910 and 1911 than to individual heads of household (78, table 8). The smaller the unit of transition was, the lower the transaction costs were and the faster the adaptation to novel relative scarcities, resulting in novel institutions. General clauses concerning larger collectives as generic entities were costlier to change than specific economic institutions relating to individual or restricted collective interaction (North 1990). The Tsarist Russian village commune relative to individual households is a case in point.

The decline in applications for appropriation of communal allotment land after 1908 is also explained by changes in demand during the reform period. The initial dramatic increase in the number of applications (1907–1908) expressed demand for the codification of the erstwhile de facto practice of individual land cultivation. Once this requirement was met, the number of applications tapered off. The *rate* of applications for the consolidation of strips that were held in de facto hereditary tenure, however, rose steadily until World War I.

According to Atkinson (1983), the assumptions of an exodus from the commune in favor of individually owned land are exaggerated. By 1915, an estimated 61 percent of all peasant households remained in formal communal tenure as against 77 percent in 1905, the revolution year (Atkinson, 1983, 81). However, the pace of "privatization," as stated, exceeded that of peasant acquisition of gentry land (81). The steady increase in applications for consolidation indicates that the peasantry in principle responded enthusiastically to the reform (95), which aimed to strengthen individual households' control of land. Consolidation of landholdings also made the land more productive (81).

Unlike agrarian programs proposed by the Kadet Party, the Trudoviks, and the Social Revolutionary Party in the Duma (Ascher, 1988, 171–73), Stolypin advocated the inclusion of the peasantry in the inviolability of civil and property rights in the belief that this would secure internal stability. He also deemed the delineation of rights to be in the interest of the rural population.[25] The Social Revolutionaries were demanding immediate socialization, namely, compulsory expropriation without compensation for anyone, including the gentry, and the subsequent equal distribution of the land among male peasants (Ascher, 1988, Vol. 2, 270).[26] The Kadet

[25] See below and Ascher (1988, Vol. 2, 50), on the Tsarist government's response to its pledges on the general socialization of ownership through nationalization.

[26] Consider Stolypin's polemics in response to the Social Democratic proposals on the agrarian issue, which implicitly addressed the problem of the incentive structure: "Everything

Party and the Trudoviks agreed that expropriation was the way to proceed. The former, however, mulled full compensation for erstwhile owners while the latter proposed the creation of a "land fund" by nationalizing state, church, and landed possessions in areas where the norm was exceeded, with state compensation to the owners for the value lost (Atkinson, 1983, 49).

In view of the "political marketing effort" that attended the issue of land-distribution rights in 1906 (oratorical rhetoric in which every faction indulged, especially as the reform and political turmoil progressed), Stolypin expressed the gist of his attitude several times, first in a memorandum from 1904: "Private peasant ownership is a guarantee of order because each small owner represents a nucleus on which the stability of public order rests" (quoted in Ascher, 1988, 269). Thus, he emphasized the linkage between civil and property rights. As for the Kadet Party's expropriation proposals, he expressed himself in a speech on May 10, 1906, in a way that certainly addressed the nationalization question as well: "Compulsory expropriation also abrogates the *principle* of private ownership; *consequently, no one's land would be safe any longer*" (321, italics added). This may be interpreted as a shift toward the rule of impersonalized universal laws, an essential component of equality before the law. At long last the regime acknowledged the objectivization of the distribution and enforcement of property rights as the ubiquitous foundation of the predictability of social order and, in turn, a guarantee of political stability.

According to the sources, the reform had several aims: to reorient the peasants from customary law and collectivism (268 and Wortman, 1989, 31) toward individual property rights, to broaden the understanding of these institutions' public functions, and to diffuse respect for private ownership as an integral part of civil rights at large, namely, to provide the majority of the Russian rural population with a sense of institutionalized protection of life and property and public obligation. The concepts were clearly Western-inspired (Ascher, 1988, 269; Wortman, 13, 14).

I am going to argue, however, that this change in convention had been taking place through *general collapse* and *external invasion* at the formal and informal levels even before the statutes of 1906 codified it once and for all. General collapse, a discontinuous disruptive catastrophic event of the type of war or revolution—such as Bloody Sunday (January 9,

will be equalized—and one can make everyone equal only at the lowest level ...." For this and the Social Revolutionary Party's proposals, see Atkinson (1983, 50).

1905)—that renders the previously stable evolutionary strategy inapplicable while forcing the totality of the stricken population into institutional adaptations to unprecedented conditions (as defined by Boyer & Orlean, 1993, 22; Fig. 3.5 below), may have originated in the interaction of population increase and railroad technology. External invasion may have been the result of the industrialization of 1890, which by involving the importation of technology and skills may have diffused the sense of legitimacy of Western-style change. External invasion could have occurred within the *obshchina* as a consequence of strengthened interaction between the urban and the rural sectors. Thus, the government-provoked violence during the 1905 Revolution—specifically, the events of Bloody Sunday—may have merely accelerated the process that created the conditions for general collapse. If so, the impact of the railroads on the revolution may have catalyzed the change in conventions but was not its primary cause. How the combined change may have evolved is described in the following scheme:

The scheme combines three separate theoretical models and applies them to the Russian case: Witt (1993, 1–17) on the motivation to exploit novelty, the function of available skills, frequency dependency, and selection effect; Boyer and Orlean (1993) on the conditions for a change in

Railroad ⟷ Pop. ⟷	**Innovative adaptation‹—›**	**General collapse**
	Falling per-capita land allotment	**Continual endogenous Δ values**—frequency dependency upon the number of innovators adhering to unprecedented strategy
	Human capital accumulation	Bloody Sunday—› secularization, pious subversion human will and choice
	Intensification of land use ‹—› Fixed investments	**External invasion** The 1890 industrialization The import of technology *and values.* Rural–urban interaction

∑=Institutional Δ «—»∑ = Convention Δ

Objectivization of rights «—» Individualization of rights

Fig. 3.5 Back to theory: the Regulationist–Institutionalist summarizing loop

conventions; and Hesse (1993) on the process of innovative adaptation. *Applying the last-mentioned model, I find that population increase interacted with railroad technology to spur a process of innovative adaptation* for the purpose of accumulating human capital. The scarcity of land led to the intensification of its use. Necessary fixed investments induced institutional adjustment. By applying Boyer and Orlean's model, I uncover additional aspects of the process. An endogenous change in values interacted with, and was a part of, the aforementioned innovative adaptation. Demand for a novelty (equality before the law) gradually spread. The government's efforts to repress this development, ostensibly led by anointed Tsar, caused a massacre (Ascher, 1988, vol. I, 91). The massacre elevated the concept of secularizing the Tsar as the source of law, inducing the general collapse of prevailing conventions that legitimized a hierarchy of coercion—a development ultimately legitimized by the Greek Orthodox Church. Preceding this event, the industrialization of the 1890s allowed novelty-oriented ideologies to invade from without; it may also be seen as an interactive part of the innovative-adaptation process. From the perspective of Boyer and Orlean (1993, 22), general collapse and external invasion caused the change in conventions. From Hesse's perspective (1993, 51), the process of innovative adaptation culminated in the adjustment of institutions.

If the concept of institutional change is understood in this context as a shift toward the objectivization of rights (a shift to the right on the aforementioned time range), this scheme may be related to the one offered above. In the case of Stolypin's reform, the assessment of complementarity between the objectivization and the individualization of rights seems to be correct. Arguably, too, this interdependence can be generalized and applied to Russia's contemporaneous transition.

In a system of collectively assigned institutions, individuals' rights are enforceable on a personalized basis because the law generally subordinates them to those of the collective. The impersonalization/objectivization of law depends on the degree to which individual rights are delineated and hence enforceable, transferable, and predictable. Thus, the individualization of institutions leads to their objectivization. The latter determines the level of transaction costs and the incentives emanating from the structure of property rights, a matter of decisive importance for the pace of economic growth and development. In the Tsarist Russian case, I adduce the following: The industrialization process, with railroad construction at its core, abetted impersonalized interaction and specialization by offering wage-labor opportunities in industrial centers. This would have increased transaction costs unless these costs were internalized within the national unit. Indeed, residual uncertainty may be reduced—an institutional adjustment can be made—without raising transaction costs by effecting structural change (Martens, 2004). The transition from community to society (formalized structures) is assumed to be such an adjustment and is identified as having occurred in Russia by Mironov (2000, 286), who defines the institutions adjusted as composed of general laws, social and moral norms, normative beliefs and taboos, and private contracts.

Summarizing the Complementarity of Perspectives in This Chapter

c = Methodological Collective; i = Methodological Individualism

The analysis I offer now has three dimensions: formal law, which in late Tsarist Russia saw the national collective as the source of its objective reflection; conventions originating in the pre-modern kinship-based village commune; and individual motives within the household. With all these in mind, I propose that a mutually supplementing parallel between NIE and AEI congruent with Critical Realism is appropriate. North (1990, 78), adopting a methodologically individualistic view, proposes that general basic statutes constitutive of the social order statutes are the costliest to amend, while Archer (1995, 76), a Critical Realist who rejects all reductionism, rests her arguments on the temporal precedence of structures. Synthesizing the two, I suggest that the larger the collective that codifies the tradition to formal law and perpetuates the institutional structure over time, the less flexible the structure will become. Such a structure, preceding the current generation's micro-collectives, will precondition current decision-making in environments such as the village. Following the same argument, the traditional assembly of village elders will precondition the socioeconomic behavior of households. The households' patriarchal structure, in turn, will shape and mold individuals' behavior preferences and choices until the ultimate individual emancipation arrives—which does not constitute a Critical Realist condition of life. Boyer and Orlean's model, as I apply it, explains the metamorphosis of conventions and analyzes quantitatively the size of the collectives that adhere to the previously evolutionarily stable strategy (ESS) and the conditions under which they will change.

It follows from the foregoing that the mutual exclusion of methodological individualism and collectivism is not a feasible analytical option for the diachronic understanding of institutional transformations that take place amid inter-structural friction. It is the daily interaction among a multitude of structures, corresponding to the different sizes of their generative collectives, that makes institutional change possible. Therefore, methodological individualism and collectivism cannot be seen as mutually exclusive. Every decision outcome is contingent upon institutions of higher historical dignity. As advised by Hodgson (2004, 161, 252) and, in our specific historical context, by Bakunin (1970, 23), rational choice cannot be taken for granted and must be understood as a capability attained at a specific stage of development that is reached in an evolutionary process. Analyzing North (2005, 117) in Boyer's and Orlean's terms, I posit that the broader the scope of the institutional "translation" between novelty and tradition, the less costly the transition will be. The demand for materialist egalitarianism—redistribution of assets—and abstract egalitarianism—equality before the law—must be seen as endogenous to the Russian superstructure as well as to the country's informal conventions.

The reforms that entailed the individualization and privatization of property and the individualization of civil rights in Russia did not require violent revolt then or now (Yaney, 1982, 187). In the Russian case, the historically organic outcome should have been rationalist democracy and neither brutal crackdown nor authoritarian rule. See Chap. 9, "Was Stalin Necessary?"

The combination of theories on which this thesis is structured is summarized in the matrix below. Formal law is ontologically irreducible to individual rationality; therefore, methodological individualism cannot be adopted even as a merely instrumental option. Rational choice is at all times contingent on the prevalent hierarchies of institutional restrictions, congruent with the generative collectives; consequently, it is always "bounded" (Hodgson, 2004, 412; Lawson, 1997, 187). This adduction is the bridge between NIE and AEI. If so, I propose the construction of a cluster of complementary theories that will embody the complementary elements of methodological collectivism and individualism, each contributing different proportions of explanatory power over historical time. The processes of upward (NIE) and downward causations (AEI) are complementary (Figs. 3.6 and 3.7).

	Dynamic	Static	Σ (c+i)
I. State	Gerschenkron (1962) c	Coase (1937) i	
II. Society	Boyer and Orlean (1993) i|c	Gregory (1994,1982) i	
	Witt (1993) i|c		
	Hesse (1993) i|c		
Σ(I,II)	**Individual rationality |Conventions |Formal law**		**NIE |AEI**

Fig. 3.6 Complementarity of NIE and AEI, applied to selected sources. (*Sources*: Neoclassical core, Newtonian; Hamilton (1999), North (1973, 1990, 2005), Veblen (1931), Hodgson (2004), Lawson (1997))

Structural precondition (Archer, 1995): Serfdom and Petrine Modernization, 1709–1725

1861–1914

I. Serfdom-collectivism ——— Voluntary-collectivism —— -Libertarian individualism

II. Personalized rule ———— Pre-modern Custom ———— Impersonalized law

III Coercion ———————— Path Dependency ———— -Rational calculus

Fig. 3.7 Interdependent dimensions of cultural evolution in imperial Russia and applicable theories. (*Sources*: Hoch (1986), Gerschenkron (1962); Emancipation statutes (§165 vykup—redemption), 1906 Stolypin Reform, ukreplienie entitlement, zemstvo statistics for Penza Province 1913: Groman, Raeff (1984), North (1973, 1981, 1990, 2005), Williamson (1991), Veblen (1931), Hodgson (2004))

Historical Application: Linking the Railroads to Democracy

AEI (RDC) ———————— NIE (Rationalism)

The 1861–1914 Transition within Applicable Explanatory Frameworks

The foregoing theoretical discourse clarifies my argument and leads to the composite model that I apply in later chapters of this monograph to disclose the peculiarities of the transition triggered by the communal village's interaction with railroad technology. My assumption is that, in the course of this transition, the Russian peasant constituency relinquished authoritarian collectivism and endorsed individualism and voluntary cooperation. In the course of this process, the institutional structure transformed from a hierarchy of coercion to impersonalized objective law. The goal in this part of the chapter is to do the groundwork for a history-specific investigation based on primary sources. This inquiry will focus on the impact of railroad construction on the redistribution of property rights from the Tsarist patrimony to the peasantry, providing the latter with resources for the acquisition of economic and, therefore, political bargaining power—paving the way for the transformation of autocracy into constitutional monarchy, namely, democratization.

The Reforms and Their Political Aims

In the introduction to my theoretical discourse, I analyzed the institutional framework of peasant life in European Russia in 1861–1914 and its transformation from institutions that formally sanctioned peasant collectivism (1861–1906) to those that legitimized peasant individualism (1906–1917). The great reform era that began with the emancipation of the serfs in 1861, followed by judicial reform and legislation on rural self-government in 1864, triggered changes in the peasantry's habits of thought and set the stage for the Tsarist state-led industrialization spurts of the 1890s and 1907. This process, with railroad construction at its core, catalyzed the adaptation of peasant customs to population increase and previously launched reforms. To accommodate *otkhodnichestvo*—peasant wage labor in industrial centers—the Tsarist Russian communal village had to absorb urban culture in its theretofore insulated world (Smurova, 2003, 100, 101), additionally changing the rural value systems. The informal institutions of the peasantry, transformed endogenously and through external invasion, brought on the 1905 Revolution in confrontation with the autocracy's repressive response. The general strike in October 1905 forced Tsar Nicholas II to make a historical concession: allow the passage of legislation to depend on the approval of an elected parliament, the Duma. As it happened, he broke his promise, restoring the autocratic structure of governance in breach of the constitution. The initial concession, however, had irreversible implications: Tsarist Russia embarked on slow democratization.

Here my discourse departs from the formal abolition of serfdom in Russia (1861) and centers on the nature of Stolypin's land reform (1906–1914–1917). The declared objective of the reform was to free the peasant estate from the formal restrictions imposed on it by collective ownership[27] and its corollary, collective responsibility for taxes and dues under the communal-village system.

Stolypin's rural-transformation project (1906–1917), inspired by a German schema, would result in the formation of a peasant proprietor class (Klimin, 2002, 11). Following the Westernizers' school of thought, the intellectual elite that inspired the landowning nobility, led by the head of the Ministry of Agriculture and State Domains, S.A. Ermolov—selected by Plehve (the Minister of the Interior) in 1906 (Macey, 1987, 31)—by Nicholas II himself, and by his Prime Minister, P.A. Stolypin, thought that the transition from communal to hereditary household ownership[28] would unleash the nation's productive potential, enhancing Russia's socioeconomic development relative to the West European adversaries of the empire (13).

In his speeches before the Tsar and the Second Duma, when the peasant uprising and the revolution of 1905 clearly exposed the failure of the *obshchina* to deliver on the Tsarist expectations of social stability warranty (Gerschenkron 134, Macey xi), rendering his dissident address less controversial, Stolypin urged the government to satisfy two requisites for the successful implementation of the reforms: material aid in the form of government credit and educational institutions that would enhance literacy among the post-serfdom peasantry. The idea behind his project was to revise the incentive structure and provide resources for the accumulation of physical and human capital, stimulating peasant entrepreneurship.[29]

Historically, individual property rights in land, as well as exclusive rights to other material and intellectual property, are closely related to

[27] The abolition of serfdom led to the transformation of collective use rights into collective property rights through the submission of a "redemption payment" over a forty-nine-year period.

[28] Sztern (2000) and Mironov (2000, 344, 348, 349). According to the latter source, the government's abolition of mutual responsibility for taxes and dues gradually legitimized the spontaneous rise of individualism in the commune prior to Stolypin's land reform.

[29] Klimin (2002, 17, 22–23). Stolypin's emphasis on the voluntary exodus of the Russian peasantry from the commune, itself an element of choice and rationalism, prepared the ground for productivity-enhancing entrepreneurship. The reformers' focus on peasant education had the same effect.

parliamentary governance structures (Pipes, 1999, 116–17; Martens, 2004, 166, 168, 193). Pipes, adopting an evolutionary perspective, finds the acquisitiveness instinct universal in the biotic world and manifest among humans irrespective of age and cultural development, exposing as a myth the putative existence of pre-modern communities that lack consciousness of possession. The evolution of private property proceeds from inheritance is greatly intensified by commerce and urbanization, which give private property a relatively well-delineated form. The formation of states is the ultimate stage, heralding a transition from custom-sanctioned possession to legally enforceable ownership (117).

Property and Political Freedom: The Nexus

The principal axiom in this monograph is the positive correlation between individually delineated property rights in the context of civil rights and freedoms and factor productivity, enhanced by the accumulation of knowledge over time on the basis of diachronic insurance against the poverty pattern. I address myself to collectivist dependency within a hierarchical order in Chap. 5, making an effort to delineate and explain the optimal ratios of individualism to collectivism in terms of factor productivity and calamity insurance. In this chapter, I focused on the correlation between the infusion of railroads as a dual-purpose technology that had uncontrollable effects on the political structure—bringing on the formation of national commodity markets, in grain, for example (Metzer, 1972, 82), and property rights in material and intellectual assets—and democracy.

The crucial point is that the development of civil and political rights flows intrinsically from the evolution of property rights. In structures that allow property rights to emerge unsuppressed, an economically empowered citizenry democratically demands that the state protect them even as it protects them from itself, with law as the byproduct (Pipes, 1999, 116–117). Thus, according to Pipes, property rights are an effective bulwark against unlimited state power and arbitrary rule. Individual ownership of means of production gives citizens a power base that countervails the state, ensuring equality before the law in the long run. Martens (2004, 168) makes the same point: "When property rights are fully assigned and enforced by law, the autocrat's margin for discretionary behavior is reduced to zero and he becomes a civil servant without residual claim rights." Democratic parliamentary systems of governance generally correlate with higher levels of economic development (ibid.). Sen (1999, 150–51) also emphasizes the intrinsic, and not merely the instrumental, value of democracy. It follows that rights to material and intellectual assets are closely related to personal security, freedom, and prosperity.

The Tsarist land reform of 1906–1917 emphasized the instrumental characteristics of property rights. Stolypin's ultimate political objective was the perpetuation of the autocracy and the empire's internal stability by creating a new middle and affluent class of peasant proprietors, loyal to the Tsarist state. This "wager on the strong" (Klimin, 2002, 16; Ascher, 1988, 269)—the independent peasant-entrepreneur—was the essence of the autocracy's gamble with the revolutionary forces that had built up. The peasant upheaval in 1905 clearly challenged the regime's prevalent belief in the commune, based on an egalitarian ethos, as the barrier to a peasant insurgency (Gerschenkron, 1962, 131, 133).

Nevertheless, by granting the peasantry title to land, the reform drew a line between property and sovereignty controlling the latter, lest the reform led to the ultimate abolition of the patrimonial state structure that had shaped ruler–subject relations in Russia since the dawn of Muscovy. The Charter to the Nobility (1785) had set the precedent of ceding property rights to subjects without the latter's meeting the condition of state service. By enacting the Charter, Catherine, inspired by the Enlightenment and the Physiocrats, attempted to secure the nobles' support against the background of a recurrence of the Cossack-led peasant rebellion of 1773–1775 (Pipes, 1999, 191). Notably in this context, the idea of emancipating the peasantry and granting it title to land also traced its roots to eighteenth-century liberal thinking (192, 193). However, a totalitarian agent—the Tsarist autocracy in this case—always takes necessary corrective measures at a lag, reacting to external challenges to its territorial claims or its internal political control (Gerschenkron, 1962; Coase, 1937; North, 1981, 91; Hayek, 1944 81). This generalization is justified and necessary because centralized hierarchical systems, so I assume, are flexible and less prone to self-correcting marginal-utility responses to changed relative scarcities than are pluralist democracies. The Hayekian (1944) conception of political rather than economic rationality as the determining factor in transaction costs and uncertainty-adjusting structural reforms explains the belated, in terms of relative material scarcities, institutional adjustments in Tsarist Russia and the Soviet Union. It is this presence of structural preconditions, among the political institutional stability considerations, that makes my integrated NIE/AEI model a necessity.

Thus, the Russian serfs were emancipated six years after the Crimean War of 1855 and were allowed to own land after the 1905 Revolution, not as would have been economically rational in anticipation of the industrialization spurt of the mid-nineteenth century. The difference is this: while Catherine the Great, challenged by peasant unrest, "wagered" on the nobility, Nicholas II, challenged by the Liberation Union (representing a liberal intelligentsia that sought constitutional governance), placed his bet on the peasantry.

From the vantage point of a patrimonial state, reforms that decentralize property rights to subjects must be seen as concessions that indirectly affect potential insurgents' aspirations to success. Facing a credible grassroots threat as well as external challenges, the Russian autocracy moved toward a parliamentary structure of governance. As I argue below by applying Martens' (2004, 193) model, industrialization and railroad construction played a crucial role in the democratization of Tsarist Russia—a process that was interrupted by World War I.

Stolypin's Reforms: Intentions and Consequences

May Stolypin's land reform be understood as an imported Western innovation, introduced "from above" into a peasant community that had voluntarily and deliberately chosen to structure its life around a rationally reflective communal (*obshchina*) ethos (Pallot, 1999)? Pallot's analysis of peasant resistance to the Stolypin reform (1999, 166–68) unambiguously emphasizes peasant opposition to the historical shaping of peasant–state relations by the Tsarist authorities. Moreover, Pallot traces this resistance to the destruction of the commune to rational reflection rather than "primordial," "elemental," or "animal" rage, as liberal and Marxist historians contend (157). However, despite her mention of manifestations of "collective will," including peasant petitions against the coercive measures that were applied in the implementation of the reform, a Ministry of Internal Affairs survey in 1911, also cited by Pallot, reports a threefold increase in land-related lawsuits between 1908 and 1910. This, if supported by other findings (Chaps. 4, 5, and 7), would indicate growing differentiation and individualism within the peasant community.

Alternatively, should the land reform of 1906–1914–1917, intended de jure as a voluntary transition from a communal-based to a household-based land-tenure system, be seen as a Tsarist concession to the peasantry's genuine demands, thereby constituting an ex post codification of an ongoing individualization process? I answer in the affirmative.

Mironov's analysis of the pre- versus post-emancipation peasant institutions (2000, 349) clearly supports my argument. Mironov structures his analysis on Ferdinand Tönnies' two ideal types of social organization: the Gemeinschaft (the community—the *obshchina* in the case at hand) and the Gesellshaft (a society—*obshchestvo*) (286). In the former, interaction is spontaneous, personal, kinship-oriented, and traditionally (consciously) and emotionally (unconsciously) structured. The determinants of individual conduct are irrational, based on notions of morality and respect. In a community, the collectivist spirit is said to predominate and the economy is based on agriculture and crafts. A society, in contrast, is characterized by rational and relatively impersonalized interaction. The formal system of rules that determines social status leaves more room for the individual will. Trade and industry constitute the economic base of social organizations of this type.

One may array history- and space-specific social organizations along a continuum bounded by the relative predominance of the "community" properties or the "society" properties that structure peasant life. In Mironov's view (338, 349), social relations under serfdom in the peasant communes of European Russia, which were historically self-governing to varying extents, were structured by the characteristic principles of the community. The Emancipation Act of 1861 set in motion a gradual transition to social relations centering on shifts from collectivism to individualism in land tenure, family structure, and gender and intergenerational relations, while paradoxically bureaucratizing, and modernizing the oldest structure—the commune assembly (Mironov, 2000).

The differences in interpreting the viability of the communal-village system in pre-revolutionary Russia suggest that the rural institutions constituted historical units that exhibited, over time, changing degrees of collectivism versus individualism (Kingston-Mann, 1991, 45, 46). They may also imply ideological differences, namely, the impact of the sources' native cultures on the tendencies of their analyses (North, 1981, 55). They may even reflect the merits and limitations of the theoretical frameworks applied, each model allowing the focus to settle on different aspects of the object of inquiry (Bengtsson, 2004).

Railroad Construction and Its Unintended Consequences

Here I apply Martens' insights to explain the allocation of property or use-rights strategies for the likes of the *obshchina*, pre-emancipation Russian village commune—a relatively small social unit that exhibits little specialization in its agriculture-based economy, in which power is equally distributed and information on players/producers is shared.

For "anonymous trade"[30] to arrive successfully, three basic conditions must be met: Transaction costs must be reduced, the solution must be applied in large communities without raising transaction costs, and it must be effective under terms of information asymmetry (Martens, 2004, 162). These conditions may be partly fulfilled under non-violent third-party enforcement such as the threat of social and economic exclusion (164). Relevant examples include the heads of household (the *bolshaki*), religious sects of the Old Believers mold, and the communal-village assembly, the *skhod*. There is, however, a limit to such a sanction: its cost to the defaulting party must not exceed the benefits of membership (165). This statement is especially valid in the context of Russia's industrialization, which mitigated members' social and economic dependence on the agrarian commune organization.

In NIE, the ultimate condition for "anonymous trade" is said to be fulfilled through *violent* third-party enforcement, namely, the state's monopoly on violence. However, while such enforcement reduces transaction costs, it amplifies the power asymmetry in the distribution of benefits.

Applying insights from Martens' theory to the Tsarist Russian transition from coercive collectivism to voluntary individualist cooperation, I identify the following initial causal relation:

> **Railroad construction (reducing physical distance and indirectly [through increased interaction] reducing cognitive distance, expanding the market) ⇒ specialization (rising transaction costs) ⇒ institutional change**

[30] That is, long-distance trade in which the distance is both physical and cognitive and is reduced or eliminated through a structural adjustment that allows changes in perceptions. This type of trade expands the market, allowing economics of scale and specialization to come into play. Its inspiration from Adam Smith—"The division of labor is limited by the extent of the market"—is explicit (Smith, 1998, 19).

The essence of Martens' theory of institutions that are endogenous to society (2004, 190, 192) defines individuals' asymmetrically distributed knowledge as a variable exogenous to the economy and the political system. The evolution of political-institution-specific property rights is a function of a combination of asymmetrically distributed conflict technology (state monopoly on violence) and asymmetrically distributed production technology (high division of labor).

Martens' model (188, 190) departs from "stable anarchy," a condition of indecisive decentralized conflict technology and low division of labor. In such a society (pre-modern agrarian and "stateless" or self-governing), egalitarian sharing norms prevail, dictating weak incentives and low levels of development. As implied above, the "stable anarchy" developmental stage, in which communities are based on egalitarian sharing norms, approximates the Slavophile depiction of the *obshchina* system (Sztern, 2000). In the next step, asymmetry in conflict technology is introduced while the division of labor remains weak. The result is slavery or dictatorship. The only motive a ruler might have to cede property rights to subjects is his expectation of higher productivity and a larger extraction base, especially in view of rising surveillance costs. This model may be understood as a simplification of the early stages of Tsarism in fifteenth-century Russia. Finally, production technology asymmetry is introduced, inducing an acute division of labor and raising transaction costs. The state lacks the capacity to measure the properties of all traded goods and services. The decentralization of property rights, relying on intermediaries and independent third-party enforcers, self-protecting in mutually monitoring for successful competition "commitment devices" (Greif, 2006), incentivizes producers to reveal important information and increase productivity and, in turn, to broaden the ruler's tax base. Thus, the combination of acute division of labor and decisive, monopolized conflict technology results in democratic government (Martens, 2004, 193, 201).

Deducing from Martens' theory, I posit that in nineteenth-century Tsarist Russia the railroad expanded the market, widening the division of labor and, thereby, individuals' specific stock of knowledge. Production technology distribution became unequal, resulting in rising transaction costs. To improve the incentive structure and, in turn, enhance productivity[31]—including the disclosure of important information—the state, with

[31] Poznanski (1992), Sztern (1997). Consider the link between transaction costs and productivity: the lower the former is, the higher the latter because innovative investment

its monopoly on violence, decentralized and enforced property rights to ensure its tax base (Martens, 2004, 193).

The upshot of the foregoing deduction is that Stolypin's rural transformation project may be better understood from the perspective of Martens' integrated theory.[32] Thus, given the state's monopoly on violence and the asymmetric distribution of conflict technology, the link between industrialization and technological change—specifically, railroad construction, which aggravates asymmetry in production technology—and movement toward enforceable civil rights (including property rights) and democracy for the peasant population may be summarized as follows:

Railroad *⇒ division of labor ⇒ delegation of incentives in the form of property rights by the state ⇒* ***democratization***

It is essential in this context to note Metzer's (1972, 82) dissertation on the importance of railroad development for the creation of the national grain market and gains from trade in Tsarist Russia. Combining this purely Neoclassical model with North's, it may be suggested that railroad construction triggered institutional change by the convergence of grain prices and specialization in the spread (variance) of prices, transaction costs, allowing diversified portfolios to be built. If so, an elaboration of the effects of market integration on institutional change, specifically in property rights, would be the following:

Railroad *⇒ market integration (specialization) ⇒ Δ relative prices ⇒ Δ institutions (transition from inclusive to exclusive property rights)*

Notably, Martens implicitly combines aspects of Evolutionary theory, Classical economics, and NIE by putting forward a theory on the economics of cognition-endogenizing institutions while modeling the transition from "stable anarchy" to "democratic capitalism," inspiring a hypothesis that points in the same direction of change.[33] The integration of the three models—Metzer's, Martens', and North's (1973)—is obvious:

increases as the incentive function of property rights gathers strength. The relationship may also act inversely, depending on the institutional structure.

[32] See also the causal chain below.

[33] On the relation between property rights and democratic government, see Pipes (1995, xi, xii), and sequences above.

Railroad *⇒ market integration ⇒ specialization ⇒ Δ relative prices including transaction costs ⇒ tacit transition to excluding property rights ⇒ delegation of incentives in the formal redistributing of property rights by the state (Stolypin's rural-transformation project in 1906–1917)*

In general terms, I express this as follows:

NIE/AEI: (structural preconditions—Archer, 1995, 76; North, 1981)
The structure at t-1 preconditions the pace of the institutional adjustment at time t,
climatic volatility and topographic absence of natural barriers (Montesquieau, Chubarov, 2001, 4)

agricultural uncertainty coupled with Tatar invasions, and high land-to-labor ratio (Kolchin, 1987)

Clustering of population in collectivist mutually ensuring structures

Population increase, challenge to geopolitical stability: the 1855 Crimean War (Gerschenkron, 1962, 125, 131)

RAILROADS—ongoing transition to individualism and rationalism, 1861–1914, in accordance with the foregoing causal chains.

References

Archer, M. (1995). *Realist social theory: The morphogenetic approach.* The University of Hertfordshire: Chapter Presented at the 6th International Workshop on Institutional Economics.

Ascher, A. (1988). *The revolution of 1905. Part I: Russia in disarray. Part II: Authority restored.* Stanford University Press.

Atkinson, D. (1983). *The end of the Russian land commune 1905–1930.* Stanford University Press.

Bakunin, M. (1970). *God and the state.* Dover Publications.

Bates, R. (1989). *Beyond the Miracle of the Market - The Political Economy of Agrarian Development in Kenya.* Cambridge UP.

Bengtsson, T. (2004). *Living standards and economic stress.* Seminar, Department of Economic History, Lund University.

Boyer, R., & Orlean, A. (1993). How do conventions evolve? In U. Witt (Ed.), *Evolution in markets and institutions.* Physica-Vlg.

Burds, J. (1998). *Peasant dreams and market politics: Labor migration and the Russian village 1861–1905.* University of Pittsburgh Press.

Chubarov, A. (2001). *The fragile empire: A history of imperial Russia.* Continuum.

Coase, R. (1937). *The firm, the market and the law.* University of Chicago Press.

Cohen, G. A. (2000). *Karl Marx's theory of history: A defense.* Clarendon Press.

Crisp, O. (1989). Peasant land tenure and civil rights implications before 1906. In O. Crisp & L. Edmondson (Eds.), *Civil rights in imperial Russia.* Clarendon Press.

Eggertsson, T. (1990). *Economic behavior and institutions.* Cambridge University Press.

Engelgardt, P. N. (1993). In C. Frierson (Ed.), *Aleksandr Nikolaevich Engelgardt's Letters from the Country, 1872–1887.* Oxford University Press.

Gaudin, C. (2007). *Ruling peasants: Village and state in late imperial Russia.* University Press.

Gerschenkron, A. (1962). *Economic backwardness in historical perspective.* The Belknap Press of Harvard University Press.

Gerschenkron, A. (1968). *Continuity in history and other essays.* The Belknap Press of Harvard University Press.

Gintis, H. (2009). *The bounds of reason: Game theory and the unification of the behavioral sciences.* Princeton University Press.

Goldhagen, D. J. (1996). *Hitler's willing executioners. Ordinary Germans and the Holocaust.* Little Brown and Company.

Greif, A. (2006). *Institutions and the path to modern economy: Lessons from medieval trade.* Cambridge University Press.

Groenewegen, J., & Vromen, J. (1999). Implications of evolutionary economics: Theory, method and policies. In J. Groenewegen & J. Vromen (Eds.),

Institutions and the evolution of capitalism: Implications of evolutionary economics (European Association for Evolutionary Political Economy). Edward Elgar.

Hamilton, D. (1999). *Evolutionary economics: A study of change in economic thought*. Transaction Publishers.

Hayek, F. A. (1944). *The road to serfdom*. Routledge.

Hesse, G. (1993). Land use systems and property rights. Evolutionary versus institutional economics. In U. Witt (Ed.), *Evolution in markets and institutions*. Physica-Vlg.

Hoch, S. (1986). *Serfdom and social control in Russia. Petrovskoe, a village in Tambov*. University of Chicago Press.

Hodgson, G. M. (1996). Corporate culture and the nature of the firm. In J. Groenewegen (Ed.), *Transaction cost economics and beyond*. Academic Publishers.

Hodgson, G. M. (1999). *Evolution and institutions: On evolutionary economics and the evolution of economics*. Edward Elgar.

Hodgson, G. M. (2001). *How economics forgot history: The problem of historical specificity in social science*. Routledge.

Hodgson, G. M. (2004). *The evolution of institutional economics: Agency, structure and Darwinism in American institutionalism*. Routledge.

Hodgson, G. M., & Knudsen, T. (2004). *The replication of habits*. Paper presented at the 6th International Workshop on Institutional Economics, The University of Hertfordshire.

Hodgson, G. M., & Knudsen, T. (2005). The nature and units of social selection. *Papers on Economics & Evolution*. Max Planck Institute of Economics.

Johnson, R. (1979). *Peasant and proletarian: The working class of Moscow in the late nineteenth century*. Leicester University Press.

Kingston-Mann, E. (1991). Peasant communes and economic innovation: A preliminary inquiry. In E. Kingston-Mann, T. Mixter, & J. Burds (Eds.), *Peasant economy culture and politics of European Russia*. Princeton University Press.

Klimin, I. I. (2002). *Stolypinskaya agrarnaya reforma i stanovlenie krestian sobstvennikov v Rossii*. Csentristoricheskichigumanitarnychissledovani 'Klio'.

Kolchin, P (1987). *Unfree Labor, American Slavery and Russian Serfdom*. Harvard UP.

Lawson, T. (1997). *Economics and reality*. Routledge.

Lawson, T.(March 2003). Institutionalism: On The Need to Firm Up Nothions of Social Structure and the Human Subject. *Journal of Economic Issues* VolXXXVII No 1 March 2003.

Lewis, P. (1999). Metaphor and critical realism. In S. Fleetwood (Ed.), *Critical realism in economics: Development and debate*. Routledge.

Macey, D. (1987). *Government and peasant in Russia 1861–1906: The prehistory of the Stolypin reforms*. Northern Illinois University Press.

Mäki, U. (1990). *Studies in realism and explanation in economics.* SuomalainenTiedeakademia.
Martens, B. (2004). *The cognitive mechanics of economic development and institutional change.* Routledge.
Metzer, J. (1972). *Some economic aspects of railroad development in Tsarist Russia* [Unpublished doctoral dissertation]. University of Chicago.
Mironov, B. N. (2000). *A social history of imperial Russia, 1700–1917* (Vol. I). Westview Press.
North, D.C. (1973) *Vasterlandets uppgang.* SNS
North, D. C. (1981). *Structure and change in economic history.* WW Norton and Company.
North, D.C. (1990). *Institutions, Institutional Change and Economic Performance.* Political Economy of Institutions and Decisions. Cambridge UP.
North, D. C. (1993). *Economic performance through time.* Prepared for Presentation as the Prize Lecture in Economic Science in Memory of Alfred Nobel.
North, D. C. (2005). *Understanding the process of economic change.* Princeton University Press.
North, D. C., & Thomas, R. P. (1973). *VästerlandetsUppgång.* SNS.
North, D.C. & Wallis, J.J. & Weingast , B.R. (2009). *Violence and Social Orders - A Conceptual Framework for Interpreting Recorded Human History.* Cambridge U.P.
Pallot, J. (1999). *Land reform in Russia 1906–1917. Peasant responses to Stolypin's project of rural transformation.* Clarendon Press.
Pipes, R. (1995). *Russia under the old regime.* Penguin Books.
Pipes, R. (1999). *Property and Freedom.* Harvill UP, 191.
Poznanski, K. (1992). A property rights perspective on the evolution of communist-type economies. In K. Poznanski (Ed.), *Constructing capitalism. The re-emergence of civil society and liberal economy in the post-Communist world.* Westview Press.
Raeff, M. (1984). *Understanding imperial Russia.* Columbia University Press.
Rizello, S. (1999). *The economics of the mind.* Edvard Elgar.
Searle, J. (1995). *The Construction of Social Reality.* Pinguin Philosophy.
Sen, A. (1999). *Development and Freedom.* Oxford UP.
Scott, J. (1976). *The moral economy of the peasant. Rebellion and subsistence in Southeast Asia.* Yale University Press.
Sheshinski, E. (2010). *Limits in individual choice.* The Hebrew University of Jerusalem.
Shivelbusch, W. (1986). *The railway journey: The industrialization of time and space in the 19th century.* University of California Press.
Smith, A. (1998). *An inquiry into the nature and the causes of the wealth of nations.* Regnery Publishing.

Smith, A. (2000). *The theory of moral sentiments*. Prometheus Books.

Smurova, O. V. (2003). *Niezemledelcheski odkhod krestian v stolitsu I ego vlejanie na transformacjiu kulturnoj tradicji*. Kostroma: Izd-voKostromskogogos. technologich. Universiteta.

Sztern, S. (1997). *From Obshchina to the market an introduction- Russia's transition from plan to market in face of pre revolutionary transition*. Master Thesis Lund University.

Sztern, S. (2000). *The railroad and the mir. Project description*. Lund University and (1997) The Hebrew University of Jerusalem.

Ticktin, H (1992) "*Origins of the Crisis in The USSR, Essays on the Political Economy of a Disintegrating System*" Routledge.

Vanberg, V. (1994). *Rules and choice in economics*. Routledge.

Veblen, T. (1931). *The theory of the leisure class*. Viking.

Vromen, J. (2001). The human agent in evolutionary economics. In J. Laurent & J. Nightingale (Eds.), *Darwinism and evolutionary economics*. Edward Elgar.

Wiesel, E. (1958, 1960, 1961, 1986). *Natten, Gryningen, Dagen*. Översättning Arenander; B Halléen, K Forum.

Williamson, O.E. (1985). *The Economic Institutions of Capitalism*. The Free Press New York

Williamson, O.E.(1991). *The logic of economic organization*. In Williamsson, O.E. & Winter, S. G. Ed The nature of the firm -Origins Evolution and Development. Oxford UP.

Witt, U. (1993). *Evolution in markets and institutions*. Physica-Verlag.

Wortman, R. (1967). *The crises of Russian populism*. Cambridge University Press.

Wortman, R. (1976). *The Development of Russias Legal Consciousness*. The University of Chicago Press.

Wortman, R. (1989). Property rights, populism and Russian political culture. In O. Crisp & L. Edmondson (Eds.), *Civil rights in imperial Russia*. Clarendon Press.

Yaney, G. (1973). *The systematization of Russian government: Social evolution in the domestic administration of imperial Russia 1711–1905*. University of Illinois Press.

Yaney, G. (1982). *The urge to mobilize: Agrarian reform in Russia, 1861–1913*. University of Illinois Press.

CHAPTER 4

Industrialization as a Precipitant of Tensions Between Tsardom and Nascent Civil Society

The reigns of Peter the Great and Catherine were plagued by uprisings. Gerschenkronians may argue that the rebellious forces were united by veneration of the "true" Tsar, Peter III. The warriors who rose against Catherine's rule, however, questioned the very essence of Tsardom, the "sovereign" lands, and property rights in land that belonged to the anointed Tsar. In the mid-Volga Penza region, Pugachev's decrees promised the agricultural serfs land and freedom. Finally, the revolt of the heterogeneous (pious and secular) peasantry and elites in 1905 allows one to analyze Nicholas II's Russia as a stable dictatorship rather than a hereditary contract between rulers and the ruled.

What follows is an exposition on the Nicholaean modernization and its transformation of the erstwhile Russian peasant.

The Autocracy Tentatively Engages Its Citizens

In this chapter, I call attention to the challenges that egalitarianization and impersonalization of law presented to the Late Imperial Russian autocracy. The demand for institutional equality, elucidated in previous chapters, placed a question mark over the compulsory collectivism, encapsulated in the legacy of the pre-emancipation commune, that typified the takeoff conditions of the Tsarist industrialization. As before, I start the discussion with Gerschenkron, who distinguishes between a voluntarily endorsed hereditary monarchy that is legitimized through religious beliefs, as in his

S. Sztern, *Russia on the Move*, Studies in Economic Transition, https://doi.org/10.1007/978-3-030-89285-2_4

parlance was Russia of the Tsars, and a dictatorship legitimized by its actions, such as the one that emerged from the October Revolution and was manifested in the Soviet system (1968, pp. 314, 315). Russia in 1861–1906 was saddled with the towering costs of its dictatorship, embedded in hierarchies of coercion that came about when the state took over for individual entrepreneurship in its urge to industrialize under conditions of backwardness. The legitimacy of my challenge to Gerschenkron's distinction is found in the institutional emergence of elites in the Decembrist revolt of 1825, fueled by the egalitarian ideas of the French Revolution, and from Napoleon's invasion (1812) to the emancipation of the Russian peasantry four decades later and beyond. Abetting the process were the pious challenge to the autocracy, emerging from the seventeenth-century dissent of the Old Believers (Moon, 1999, p. 239) and the Masonic lodges that Catherine II persecuted (Chap. 2). To view Tsarist Russia as legitimized by a consensus among the pious surrounding the legitimacy of hereditary rule, a thoroughgoing explanation is needed.

Peter the Great's rein was plagued by the Bulavin rebellion (1707–1708), otherwise known as the "Don Cossack revolt" (Moon, 1999, p. 242; Anisimov, 1989), while that of Catherine II was terrorized by the Pugachev peasant and Yaik Cossack uprising (1773–1775) (Pipes, 1999, p. 192, and Chap. 2). Gerschenkronians may argue that the rebellious forces were united by veneration of the "true" Tsar, Peter III. Pugachev's warriors, however, questioned the very essence of Tsardom: the *votchina* ("sovereign" lands) and *gosudarevy zemli* (property rights in Russian lands that belonged to the anointed Tsar). In the mid-Volga Penza region, Pugachev's decrees of July 28 and 31, 1774, promised the agricultural serfs land and freedom (Moon, 1999, p. 245). Finally, the revolt of the heterogeneous (pious and secular) peasantry and elites in 1905—a repeated challenge to the monarch's perceived legitimacy as manifested in battle—suggests that Tsarist Russia should be seen as a stable dictatorship rather than as a hereditary contract between the rulers and the ruled.

I propose that the Nicholaean modernization transformed the former peasant inhabitants of the village commune (the *obshchina*), who migrated to wage labor while organizing along landsman ties, into members of urban workforce associations that could effectively pose a credible threat of upheaval in their demand for equality before the law. Stratifying in urban associations of peasant origin, *otkhodniks*—wage laborers originally from the peasantry—helped to diffuse Western value systems, which invaded along with Western technology, to the peasant commune. In so doing, they transformed rural material egalitarianism into egalitarian pious and secular ideologies that demanded predictability and rule of law.

The Tsarist State and the Costs of Dictatorship: The Gerschenkronian Conception and Imperial Self-Perpetuation

With Tsarist state entrepreneurship substituting for the market, the hierarchies of coercion were snared in a vicious cycle that retarded modernization. Consequently, in the long run, the Gerschenkronian "costs of dictatorship" (1968, p. 315) exceeded the intended beneficial effects of the substitution pattern and became increasingly burdensome to Tsarist Russia as the country's modernization process advanced. Gerschenkron's conception of the modern Soviet dictatorship, explaining the substitution theory of the state through the lenses of Coase's (1937) transaction-costs theory of the firm, is, I propose, applicable to Tsarist Russia. Applying this theory and the Hayekian conception of political rationality (Hayek, 1944, pp. 75, and 81 on the domination of politics over economics) to the absence of individual choice in an economy oriented to the supply of a common good—in the case of Tsarist Russia, the good that best fit the autocrats' plans and priorities—the real value of the state-for-entrepreneurship substitution should be deflated by the rising burden of transaction costs over equilibrium, a factor that burdens the state management function and therefore expands in a vicious cycle (Coase, 1937, p. 43) (Fig. 4.1).

As the following sequences show, it was the technological shift embodied in the application of railroad technology that catalyzed the transition between 1861 and 1914 from coercion-based pure collectivism, which had characterized the communal village system inherited from serfdom, to a voluntary individual calculus-based cooperation, effectively an individualist structure, as codified and implemented in Stolypin's 1906 land reform.

Industrialization Productivity and Income in the Russian Village Commune

The inherent long-term growth potential of the Tsarist economy was comparable to that of the industrialized countries in Europe and the U.S., and squares with the evidence of rising and not declining living standards

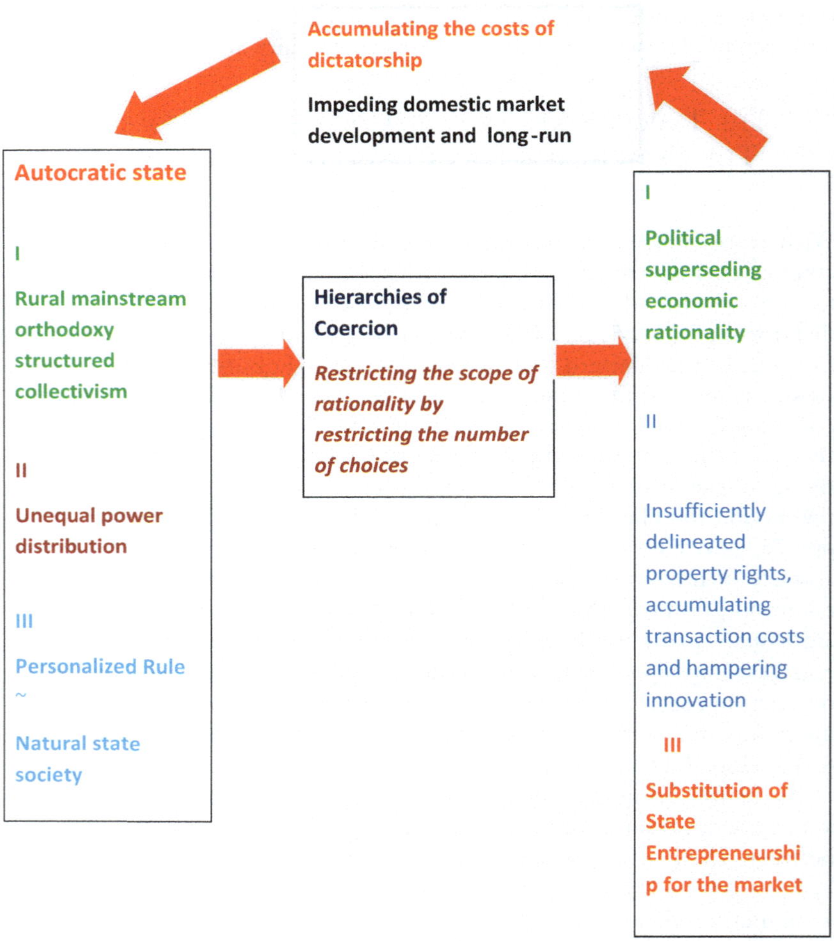

Fig. 4.1 Accumulation of Autocratic Dictatorship Costs, 1709–1914. (Sources: counterclockwise from center: Gerschenkron, 1962, pp. 122, 123, 1968, p. 315; Owen, 1995, p. 21; Hughes, 1998, p. 136; Ascher, 1988, p. 84, Burds, 1998, p. 188; Martens, 2004, p. 165; Raeff, 1984, pp. 82, 83; North et al., 2009, p. 2; Gintis, 2009, pp. 1, 2; Sheshinski, 2010, p. 3; Hayek, 1944, pp. 75, 81; Coase, 1937, p. 43; Poznanski, 1992, pp. 71–94; Barzel, 1989, pp. 7, 9, 65)

due to industrialization (Gregory, 1982, 1994; Bideleux, 1990). Given the conformity and comparability of Russian growth indicators with international ones, it can be argued that Russia's economic and institutional systems, in the aggregate were such, that qualify Imperial Russia in Tsarism's last quarter-century as a market economy (Gregory, 1982, 1994). That is, the compatibility of the average annual increase in product per worker with that of systems based on individual property rights indicates that the Russian commune village system had, de facto, evolved into a hereditary household ownership structure.

This reasoning, derived from Revisionist School descriptions viewed through international comparative lenses, challenges Gerschenkron's claim that the Tsarist commune village system, with its perennial instability in property rights, induced an industrialization-hindering stalemate in productivity increases. The extent of structural change in the industrializing Russian economy may provide additional indirect information about Russia's balance of rigidity versus flexibility, inherent in its agrarian and commercial institutions, relative to other countries. If we date Imperial Russia's entry to the era of modern economic growth in the 1880s, then thirty years later, the share of agriculture in its national product declined by 6 percentage points, that of national product attributed to industry increased by 8 percentage points, and the share of services declined by 3 percentage points (Gregory, 1982, p. 166, Table 7.3).

In Britain, the share of national product attributed to agriculture as estimated at the time of the country's industrialization (1786–1885) fell by 13 percentage points over the next thirty years, that of industry in national income climbed by 5 percentage points, and that of services increased by 8 percentage points—indicating more vigorous commercial activity in post-industrialization England than in post-industrialization Russia.[1] In Japan, where the relevant period ran from 1874–1879 to 1904–1909, the share of agriculture in national income fell by 24 percentage points, that of industry rose by 15 percentage points, and that of the services increased by 10 percentage points. In the U.S., the fraction of agriculture in national income declined by 14 percentage points between

[1] On the scope and importance of the service sector for the availability and, in turn, the costs of information—transaction costs—and the correlation between this sector's development and the overall level of economic development in the Soviet Union compared with other economies, see Ofer 1973. The signs of a restricted service sector already seemed to be present in the Tsarist period, implying that Gerschenkron's postulates on continuity between the Tsarist and the Soviet economic structures are indeed valid.

1834–1843 and 1864–1873, that of manufacturing surged by 15 percentage points, and that of the services was unchanged—approximately 10 percentage points higher than its Russian equivalent. The data on the extent of structural change between the onset of each country's great spurt of industrialization and a point in time thirty years later show that Russia underwent a larger structural change than France did, though the latter country experienced a 2-percentage-point increase in its share of services in national income. The extent of Russia's transformation resembled that in Germany, where the economy was based on individual households' property rights in land. In general, the decline in the share of agriculture in national income and the increase in that of industry was more gradual in Russia and France, although the extent of the structural transformation in Russia fit the average pattern of change in Western economies in the thirty years following their industrialization (Gregory, 1982, pp. 166–167 and Table 7.3)—clearly indicating the compatibility of the Western and the Russian institutional structures.

During the periods of Russia's industrialization spurts (1883–1887 to 1909–1913), agricultural labor productivity grew at a 1.35 percent annual pace, industrial labor productivity by 1.8 percent, and total productivity by 1.5 percent (Gregory, 1982, p. 168). The ratio of yearly agricultural productivity growth to the annual productivity increase in the economy at large was 0.9. Given the size of Russia's agricultural sector, this may indicate somewhat limited annual productivity growth in the rural sector. This, in turn, implies a potential increase in output that might have been realized had the formal institutional conditions been better suited to a transition to modern economic growth, namely, to industrialization. Even if Gerschenkron (1962, 1968) overstates the effect of formal rural institutions on economic performance, this effect cannot be entirely ignored where its continuity aspects are concerned. Considering the ratio of agricultural to industrial productivity growth, however, this structural component of economic development in Tsarist Russia cannot be deemed unusual by international standards. As for dynamic development, the 1.8 percent annual rate of industrial labor productivity growth indicates the rising profitability of industrial investment and the increasing availability of skilled labor, rather than the exploitation of a massively available but limitedly productive Marxian "reserve army." Given the characteristics of the Russian economy, in which rural proletarians seldom severed their ties with their native villages, the expectations of rising productivity in agriculture due to the infusion of skills through landsman networks, interacting with the correspondingly rising institutionalized individuation of returns to human and physical capital and investment (Hesse, 1993, p. 51), should have been legitimized.

Thus, the differentiating feature of Tsarist Russia's economic development relative to that in the West was its high level of domestic investment. Until the gold-standard era began (1897), it was domestic savings that financed development. The high share of government spending in NNP and the small proportion of private consumption for a low-income country explain the investment-driven growth (Gregory, 1982, p. 175). During the 1897–1901 period, 20.56 percent of net investment originated abroad.[2] Given the size of the Russian economy, a *derived industrialization* in the Gerschenkronian sense—an acceleration of economic growth induced by inflows of demand, capital, and technological knowledge (Gerschenkron, 1968, pp. 80–82)—should be seen as unusual. As the initial upturn in the growth rate of industrial output (1890) resulted from a political decision by the imperial government and as it was financed through domestic savings, the Russian process generally qualifies as autochthonous (Gerschenkron, 1962, p. 361, 1968).[3] However, considering the advances facilitated by the import of modern technology and skills from already-industrialized economies—the main advantage of backwardness that Gerschenkron (1962, 1968) emphasizes in the Russian case—and the importance of foreign demand as well as foreign capital inflow in the Tsarist-era industrialization, the process may be said to have both derived and autochthonous elements. What is more, the autochthonous contribution defined Russia's overall transition to modern economic growth through its identifiable "great spurts" of 1890 and 1907.

[2] Gregory 1982, p. 127, Table 6.1, from which the share of net foreign investment in total net investment is calculated.

[3] An autochthonous industrialization process is defined by the decisive role of the state. A derived process is said to emerge when industrialization is induced by a foreign market and knowledge available in a more advanced country; such industrialization is more gradual and lacks a "spurt" or a distinguishable takeoff phase. The transition to modern economic growth is promoted by interaction with domestic institutions, which are assumed to be highly adaptable to innovation. As a rule, derived industrialization is an exception and is likely to occur in a small country that has an appropriate geographic location and a well-developed or rapidly developing transportation system.

Industrialization and the Invasion of Modernity

The derived components of this state-induced autochthonous industrialization contributed to an invasion of prevalent Western thought habits, powering a change in conventions in favor of entrepreneurial integrity[4] and stronger popular demand for active participation in political and economic decision-making. The particular features of the Russian industrialization[5] evidently intensified the anti-atomization or autonomization

[4] Gerschenkron (1966, repr. in idem, 1968), pp. 128–139, initially challenges propositions about the emergence of entrepreneurial talents as a prerequisite for industrialization. The interdependence between entrepreneurial honesty and revulsion toward illicit conduct in commercial relations, prevailing rates of lending interest, and the development and fine-tuning of interest rates oriented to individual entrepreneurship and long-term investment are thought to be instrumental for the process of modern economic growth. The independence of the industrial decision-making process from the prevalent set of values, which in the Russian case were alien to industrialization, is implicitly assumed to be one of the requisite entrepreneurial qualities. The necessary entrepreneurial talents are said to develop often in the course of, and in, very backward countries due to an initial industrialization spurt; therefore, they cannot be viewed as prerequisites for industrialization. In Tsarist Russia, a country that Gerschenkron (1962, p. 138) classifies as utterly backward, "The importation from abroad of foreign entrepreneurial talent" in the course of industrialization substituted for the absence of such talent in the domestic economy. As a result of the initial spurt in the 1890s, the emergence of a domestically skilled entrepreneurial segment contributed to the renewed industrialization effort in 1907–1913. The active role of the Russian state in "substitution for missing prerequisites," something that Gerschenkron assumes to have occurred, is further addressed below.

[5] In this context, I emphasize the relatively high share of *government spending* and, especially, its distribution (see below), a relatively low level of private consumption for a low-income country, and the heightened importance, for an empire, of economic interaction with Western and previously industrialized economies. In this respect, Gregory's findings (1982, 1994) and Gerschenkron's postulates (1962, 1968), which assign the state the dominant role in the 1890 industrialization, do coincide. Moreover, Owen 1995, p. 19, provides evidence of an interventionist state policy that aimed to industrialize through concentration but in fact impeded progress. The policy was applied with special intensity in regard to incorporation concessions and selective granting of credit facilities to large companies that wished to set up shop in bureaucratic power centers. The specific feature of Russia's industrialization under this policy would have been the net effect of saving on transaction costs through concentration and state intervention, whereas such costs increase due to this process. It is the latter tendency that conforms to Gerschenkron's notion of continuity and the "Asian development pattern." Moreover, Gregory's assumptions on the limited role of the state in regard to subsides to preferred industries are countered by Owen 1995, pp. 16, 17, 19, 21. The Tsarist state, much like its Soviet successor, participated in principle, though not in scope, in the economic sphere by allocating funds to industries that it preferred on political or other non-economic grounds. Thus, the role of the state as an entrepreneur—or, to use

movement,[6] an innovative trend that was also novel in its opposition to the autarchy's aspiration to retain a total monopoly on political decision-making. The collision between this movement's demand for institutional change, in terms of public representation and the right of association, and the Tsarist state's oppression of it (launched in the name of "public order," in the conservative sense of this term) may *partly* explain the violent and socially costly aspects of the exodus from compulsory hierarchical collectivism. The village commune, expecting to serve as an extended control unit of the Tsarist state, petitioned the Tsar in protest while being shot at—effectively revolting, as manifested in the events following Bloody Sunday, January 9, 1905. Moreover, as mentioned above, the eighteenth- and nineteenth-century reforms that tilted in the direction of impersonalized law[7] (an innovative process that found formal expression in the

Gerschenkron's words, the substitution of state entrepreneurship for independent entrepreneurship—may be seen as a specific feature of the Russian transition to modern economic growth. The social anti-concentration movement, induced by the state's interventionist policies, and the costs of excess concentration, meaning those incurred when political rationality supersedes economic rationality, should be viewed similarly.

[6] Smith 1989, pp. 145–165. Following the industrialization (from 1899 onward), Russian workers as a collective repeatedly demanded civil and political rights. An interesting example of a policy transition that coincided with the industrialization spurt occurred in the activities of *zemstvos*, rural self-governments. Originally, the 1864 Law on Zemstvos stated that the zemstvo's decision-making power should be constrained by the landed gentry in that 42.1 percent of the elected deputies must be selected from the gentry's ranks, an additional 38.5 percent could be chosen among the peasants, and the remaining 19.3 percent should be recruited from the merchants and the clergy. In 1890, the state, wishing to strengthen the power of its bureaucracy (in Gerschenkronian terms: to broaden the base of its "surrogate" entrepreneurship), enlarged the prescribed share of the gentry. As a result of this measure, aimed at widening the scope of bureaucratic intervention, zemstvo activists—*zemtsy*—pivoted to the "left," assigning additional decision-making and agitation power to the so-called "third element"—technical experts employed by rural self-government. Thus professionals, including teachers, statisticians, and agronomists, were invited to transform their human capital into a political force. This transformation brought entire zemstvos, as autonomous units, into opposition with the bureaucracy, intensifying the commitment to political reform. This shift in zemstvo attitudes coincided with the industrialization effort.

[7] In addition to the foregoing discussion of the reforms introduced by Catherine the Great, the origins of liberalism in Russia can be traced to her reign (1762–1797). It took the movement until the late nineteenth and the beginning of the twentieth century to organize formally; in the eighteenth century, it was actively precluded from disseminating its ideology and becoming an oppositional political force. Still, the intelligentsia among the nobility, which held liberal views and adhered to the notions of rationalism, individualism, and patriotism during Catherine's reign, became increasingly active in various charitable and educational organizations. The Russian people labeled those constituencies *obshchestvennoe*

abolition of serfdom in 1861 and the judicial reform in 1864) contributed, through a "translation" process (Boyer & Orlean, 1993, p. 22), to an endogenous change of values: increased adaptivity to and a quest for institutional innovation, diffused at the informal level.[8]

Facing "bottom-up" demand for public representation and constitutional government (intensified by industrialization), the autarchy responded with unequivocal resistance, regressing to despotism and centralized and personalized totalitarianism. From 1864 (when the law creating the zemstvo—rural self-governments—was enacted) onward, the

dvizhene—a social movement. It may be of interest to note that the Russian word obshchina, a village commune, has a similar root as the adjective *obshchestvennoye*. The village commune in Russia may be assumed to have been a symbol of egalitarianism, majority rule, and social responsibility for its members. *Obshchestvennoe dvizhenie* under Catherine the Great was committed to moral and spiritual improvements and even advocated outright institutional change to bring about social progress. The movement is said to have been less concerned with improving material conditions per se than it was with demanding freedom of speech and association and raising the question of moral standards and the legitimacy of governance. During the 1860s, the obshchestvennoe dvizhene increasingly expanded to include *raznochintsy*—people, mostly intellectuals, of different and not necessarily noble ranks. Finally, the nineteenth-century liberals demanded fundamental institutional reform: equality before the law, specifically equal civil rights, and universally elected constitutional rule. The movement organized in 1904–1905 and became powerful enough to induce the Mensheviks to cooperate with them in their opposition to the absolutism of Tsarist rule.

Notably, too, the newly formed trade unions were greatly influenced by the original ideology of obshchestvennoe dvizhenie—Russian liberalism—in their demands of the autarchy for social and institutional improvements (Ascher, 1988, pp. 58, 59).

[8] The Liberation Union advocated universal suffrage for the election of a constitutional assembly that could influence the empire's future politics. In the course of their opposition to the autarchy, the Liberals became associated with the industrial workers movement and influenced the demands for institutional change that the nascent trade unions subsequently raised. Even the Slavophiles, who generally supported the Tsar's patriarchal rule, deeming it an organic form of governance suited to the Russian cultural model, favored the "introduction of a legal order" and went so far as to suggest the formation of a "consultative legislative body" composed of members chosen by zemstvos and municipal councils. The quest for popular participation in political decision-making was a direct response to the military disasters that the empire had sustained in the Russo-Japanese war of 1904. Nevertheless, one may argue that the demand for popular representation and a more conspicuous rethinking of the concept of legality developed tacitly as a complementary quality to the emergence of entrepreneurial integrity and the autonomization of decision-making induced by industrialization. In the 1890s (corresponding to the great spurt of industrialization), Russian liberalism is said to have attracted the support of sundry professionals. A decade and a half later, the ideas diffused by this constituency became the principal source of massive demand for constitutional reform and the right of association for industrial workers.

organized pluralistic and predominantly liberal opposition posed an increasingly credible challenge to the autocracy—a challenge that intensified during the industrial spurt of 1890–1905. The apex of the clash between this movement and the Tsarist Ministry of the Interior after the debacle of the Russo-Japanese War occurred with the government's repression of the zemstvo congress, which incentivized organized liberal demands for a constitution under the congress' forerunning but still constitute slogan *obshchestvennoe dvizhenie* (liberalism, patriotism, rationalism) (Ascher, 1988, pp. 31, 34, 65, 66–67). As the demand for a political-reform-oriented change in conventions collided with the formal inflexibility of totalitarian rule, the costs of dictatorship rose. One may state that by substituting bureaucratic supervision for the development of an adequate institutional infrastructure that would protect and induce independent entrepreneurship, the Russian state generated such social tensions as to incur surveillance costs that made autocracy economically irrational. Evidence in support of such a proposition is provided by Owen (1995, p. 19), who questions the applicability of the neoclassical theory of the state to the case of late Tsarist Russian development. According to Owen's theory, the formation of a nation-state abets economic development by reducing transaction costs through the guarantee of property rights. Gerschenkron's (1962) dynamism-oriented model also credits the state with a constructive function in the internalization of transaction costs.[9] Both approaches, however, seem refutable in the Russian case because the "strong state" environment there, by means of intervention, could contribute mainly to the arbitrariness of economic activity[10] due to the personalized nature of property rights as well as other civil rights—rendering predictability, probability of enforcement, and transferability low and transaction costs, including the state's surveillance costs, high (Fig. 4.2).

Basing myself on revisionist sources, I have argued thus far that Russia's industrialization process cannot be said to have impoverished the rural classes. The country's transition to modern economic growth did, however, centralize and concentrate a rural population that had been tied to its

[9] Incorporation of Coase (1937) into Gerschenkron's substitution theory of the entrepreneurial state.

[10] Owen 1995, pp. 25, 27, comments on selective concessions granted by the autocracy to formally illicit cartels and syndicates, which may be seen as parallels to the de facto personalized concessions on property rights that the Soviet-era *nomenklatura* received.

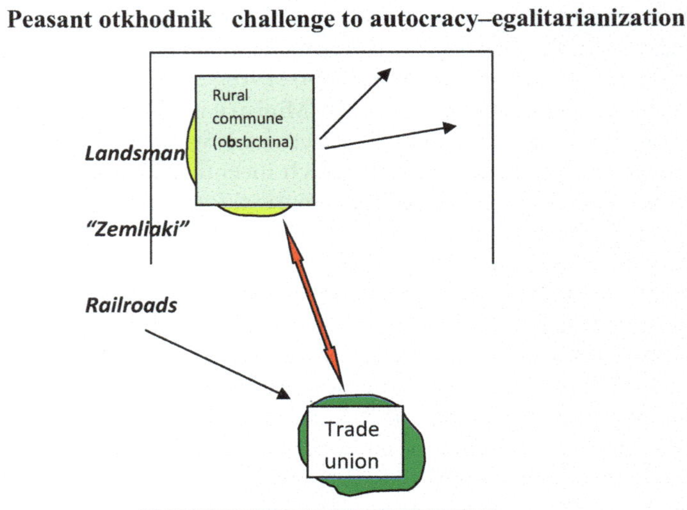

Fig. 4.2 Peasant trade unions, the Tsarist state, and innovative adaptation. (Source: Derived from Johnson, 1979, p. 68. Hesse, 1993)

villages by wage-repatriation obligations (Burds, 1998, p. 189) and landsman relations (Johnson, 1979, pp. 68, 69) in large urban industrial units, depriving it of the self-governing institutional environment that characterized the communes. The structures of this environment came to constitute an informal, in the Northian sense, institution that ultimately shaped the character of the urban industrial labor associations and, in their transformed version, imported urban tastes to the commune. This erstwhile peasant constituency went about its urban wage labor under state bureaucratic supervision on factory premises—a process that may in many respects be likened to the internalization of the self-sustaining and self-managing soldiers' artel in regimental economies (Bushnell, 1990, p. 389). A contemporary interview with Tsarist soldiers reveals that they valued their economic and social autonomy within their artel economy more than their fellows valued the post-centralization betterment of per capita economic conditions and the diminished responsibility occasioned by the inflow of treasury funds (pp. 390, 391). True to the Russian custom, even convicts punitively exiled to Siberia alleviated the hardships of punitive labor servitude (*katorga*) by forming artels or obshchinas.[11] These mechanisms of mutual social and economic responsibility appointed their eldest—the *starosta*—as representatives whose function it was to negotiate better conditions for the collective as Tsarist gendarmes escorted them down their "road of chains" (*kandal'naia doroga*) (Wood, 1990, p. 403). Seen against the background of this traditional institutional environment, the industrialization-induced transformation of former rural obshchina-dwellers into an industrial labor force and the centralization of this constituency in urban industries, as was specific to the process, resulted in the creation of a new and initially socially displaced stratum. By implication, the obshchina as a latent institution had been ubiquitous in the otkhodniks' urban environment, which, by facilitating the transfer of urban institutional pluralism to the village commune, transformed the Russian agrarian landscape.

The class consciousness of the Russian industrial proletariat during and after the industrialization period is moot. According to Lenin, such awareness must be taught, implying that it does not exist independently of political agitation, a.k.a. indoctrination. Nevertheless, considering Russia's deeply rooted folklore-based institutions, one would expect urbanization and centralization processes that placed the peasantry under state bureaucratic supervision and deprived it of its mediators/negotiators to be accompanied by demands for freedom of association and enhanced social security. Moreover, aware of the growing economic significance of their class, the better-informed peasant industrial workers undertook to translate their labor power into political power in coordination with their lesser-informed peers and non-peasant intellectuals. By so doing, industrial peasant workers emulated commune village traditions, in which the most industrious individuals were chosen as natural leaders, just as the most prominent rural-entrepreneur peasant heads of household were historically named to the communal-village assemblies. These assemblies, elected by village members, were expected to negotiate with the state bureaucracy on behalf of the communes. Internally, the *starosta*—elder-headed organizations—complied with traditional egalitarian norms while applying rural common law to land repartitions, transfers of immobile assets, and mediation in internal conflicts. By retaining their ties to the

[11] Dostojewski 1860, "Zapiski iz miertwego doma " published in Polish as "Wspomnienia z domu umarlych" by Panstwowy Instytut Wydawniczy (Warsaw, 1977) on the redistribution custom relating to *jalmuzna*—alms, charity.

obshchina, as most did, the urban peasant workers experienced the relative institutional autonomy that typified the rural sector (including participation in decision-making through the election of representatives) in the course of the industrialization, urbanization, and labor-force centralization that they were now undergoing. This experience evoked and shaped their demand for political reform. Instead of being requited, however, they were met with an increase in bureaucratic intervention in their daily lives through their foremen, who were puppets of the state. Considering the mounting demand for social services (including resources for the improvement of human capital) and the subsequent increase in dissatisfaction with the imperial government, the centralizing entrepreneurial role assigned to the Tsarist bureaucracy had a destabilizing effect.

Otkhodniks who had not yet melded into a disciplined industrial labor force were initially predisposed to establish associations functionally equivalent to artels/obshchinas for industrial workers. Their demands centered on freedom of association, freedom of coalition (through which employees could establish mutual-aid funds and engage employers in collective bargaining for working conditions), and the right to strike. The labor movement specific to Tsarist Russia, constituted of otkhodniks, intuitively strove to have the deficient state safety net replaced with a traditional type of net, the kind sustained by autonomous organizations.[12] By clearly promoting the autonomization of society, the movement confronted the autarchy's atomization strategies. Its ultimate goal was to increase public participation in political decisions, namely, to induce a "top-down" transfer of political power commensurate with the increasing economic significance of industrial labor.

The union apparently had the additional goal of protecting its constituencies from bureaucratic enserfment in the process of industrial centralization. In its entrepreneurial role, the imperial government, restricting the labor force's behavior by deploying its deficient judicial machinery, police, and army, ostensibly aimed to protect the transition to modern economic growth against the intrusion of hostile agrarian values. I propose that the endogenous autonomization of the otkhodnik industrial labor force,

[12] Ascher (1988, pp. 80, 81, 88, 89). In 1898, paralleling the industrialization and to a greater extent consolidating it—in a manifestation of what Lenin would call class consciousness—the St. Petersburg Union of Struggle for the Emancipation of the Working Class demanded civil rights as well as social improvements: "freedom to strike, freedom of speech, the press, assembly, freedom of conscience and religion, equal rights for all nationalities, an elected parliament and a statutory eight hour day."

effected by translocating the autonomy of the rural mutual-aid network to an urban industrial environment, was the direct product of the Tsarist industrialization. Contrary to Gerschenkron's proposition (1968, p. 138), *it enhanced the peasantry's rural–urban mobility and its amalgamation at the factory level.* Unlike obshchinas, urban labor associations specifically were formed under conditions of multiple institutional structures that had become available in tandem with peasant utilization of railroads, creating previously unexplored possibilities of choice. Thus, the propriety of distinguishing traditional rural associations from modernizing rural-urban ones was the belated result of an increasingly rational individual calculus rather than obedience to authority or pure peer pressure within the migrating landsman networks (Johnson, 1979, p. 69).

Tensions Between the Rigid Traditional Order and the Social Effects of Industrialization

Rephrasing my argument above, I propose here that the disharmony between informal and formal institutions increasingly saddled Russia's industrialization, under state entrepreneurship, with uncertainty that came at exorbitant cost.

Tellingly, the number of complaints to the Factory Inspectorate concerning maltreatment of workers by their foremen (*durnoe obrashchenie*) rose from 2136 to 21,873 between 1901 and 1913 (Smith 1989, 151), reflecting a per capita increase as well. Industrial workers repeatedly protested against *proizvol* (arbitrariness) and *bezpravie* (absence of rights). As events unfolded, the peasant perception of a linkage between bezpravie in the workplace and bezpravie in society at large would burden the Tsarist substitution of state entrepreneurship for private entrepreneurship with rising surveillance expenses. Importantly, the peasant-workers' protest movements were by no means the only, or even the most ideologically homogeneous and autonomous, vehicles of change. In 1905, the mining and metallurgical workers and entrepreneurs in the Ural region, protesting against the state's bureaucratic tutelage, demanded a permanent system of just law and independent courts (*pravovoi poriadok*) (Owen, 1995, p. 28). The zemstvo constitutionalists, serving constituencies that were concerned mainly with charity, education and health, roads and bridges, and improvements in agricultural productivity and statistical record-keeping in rural society (Ascher, 1988, p. 32), sought very limited suffrage and the participation of elected representatives in economic and political

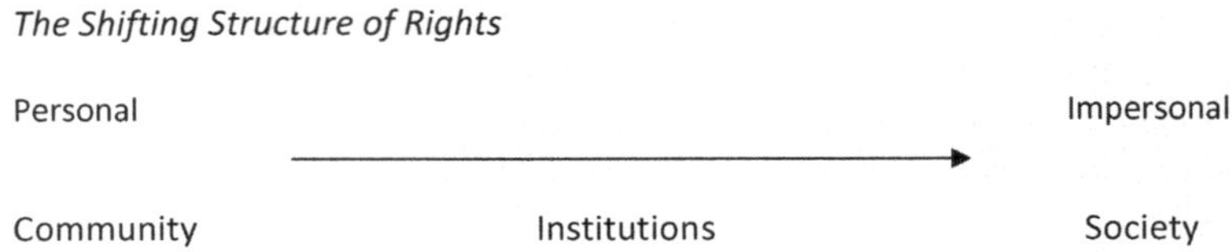

Fig. 4.3 The shifting structure of rights. (Source: Mironov, 2000, p. 286)

decisions (including the government's distributive praxis). What they got at first was persecution (p. 33). The constitutionalist campaign of 1904–1905 also enjoyed the active support of students (Fig. 4.3).

Let us bear in mind the assumed continuous transformability of socioeconomic institutions from regimes of personal entitlements to systems of impersonal rights (within the time frame sketched above) and the industrialization-induced autonomization of urban workers, following the rural-commune model, against government efforts to centralize surveillance of the labor force under the state's bureaucratic thumb. It was via this policy that the state conveyed its entrepreneurial function. The decreasing socioeconomic returns of this state practice as against the increasing internalization of this function (Coase, 1937) amplified the social potential of achieving, through stratification, a shift in the structure of the rights demanded (Witt, 1993). The direction of this shift at this particular time and place was determined by the liberal movements' demand for universal suffrage, civil and political rights, and, by implication, equality before the law irrespective of social rank, ethnicity, religion, and sex. Generally, equal civil and political rights—the impersonalization of law—leads to the individualization of ownership, as in egalitarian per capita distribution of property rights and vice versa. Only as an abstract idea could such rights be linked to the folklore-based agrarian egalitarianism specific to Russia. Unlike that concept of equity, "repartition" achieved via universal suffrage would address itself not to the material good itself but to the right to acquire and own it on equal terms. Thus, formal political liberalism could lead to economic liberalism, provided the informal institutions would not impede individuals in demanding optimum control over their property and its fruits.

The individualization of ownership from the family nexus on up, in turn, would herald society's transition from the principle of *violence* to the principle of *contract* (Mises, 1981 [1922], pp. 32–35) amid enfirming the rationalist reflexive challenge to patriarchal authority. An emerging institutionalized egalitarianism would necessitate the impersonalization of law because any political or civil action—be it of the king, the landlord, the factory owner, the intellectual, the industrial worker, or the peasant—would have to conform to the same set of basic restrictions. The autonomization of executive authority relative to legislative authority, reflected in the establishment of an autonomous judiciary, would secure the right to enforce compliance with a coherent set of norms. In this manner, the judiciary would cease to be merely an instrument of the ruler and formal law would evolve into a *socially enforceable* impersonalized system of higher dignity than anyone's command or decree.[13] The manifestation of liberalism described above may be conceptualized as aiming to achieve a rightward shift on the aforementioned time axis, theoretically leading to lower system-specific transaction costs and better economic performance.

External Invasion and an Endogenous Change of Values Topple ESS

Let us represent the intensified demand for such a shift by the expression IF, denoting innovative force in both the economic and social sense. The industrialization-induced autonomization that facilitated the endogenous change in conventions as well as the assimilation and diffusion of externally invading strategies through stratification is symbolically summarized as [End Δ + Ext. Inv.] Str, of which IF is the function. The conservative, concentrating, and centralizing force is symbolically expressed as CF

[13] Arguably, a social order based on a state religion might yield a socioeconomic system that submits to the restrictions of impersonalized law. If so, theoretically there was nothing wrong with the Tsarist order other than the monopolization of the right to interpret morality by the earthly ruler, an institutional power, and the subsequent distribution of this right as a tool of favor. A religion-based social order, however, can prevent injustice only if each individual is equally and identically conscientious and pious, answering to with a universal conscience—an unattainable outcome among humans. Attempts to attain social "purification" of this kind have repeatedly plunged humanity into bloodshed; the goal of "preventing injustice" has resulted in monstrous abuses of this very concept by any human norm of conduct. Even if a social order is based on Natural Law, for example, the French Code de Napoleon, which traces its ultimate source to the Judeo-Christian cognitive sphere of the Ten Commandments, a society as well as an international community can achieve internal peace only if it equilibrates political and economic power in a way that ensures non-discriminatory enforcement of the law. Such an equilibrium, in turn, depends on the unrestricted right to form associations in order to shape the de facto content of the civil and political institutions and their enforcement.

f[centralized state entrepreneurship/decentralized, independent entrepreneurship] atomization.

If so, the discrepancy of impact between the structural-institutional and technological production possibility frontier that caused surveillance costs to exceed transaction costs, including uncertainty saved through centralized state management of the socioeconomic fabric, may be summarized as follows (Fig. 4.4):

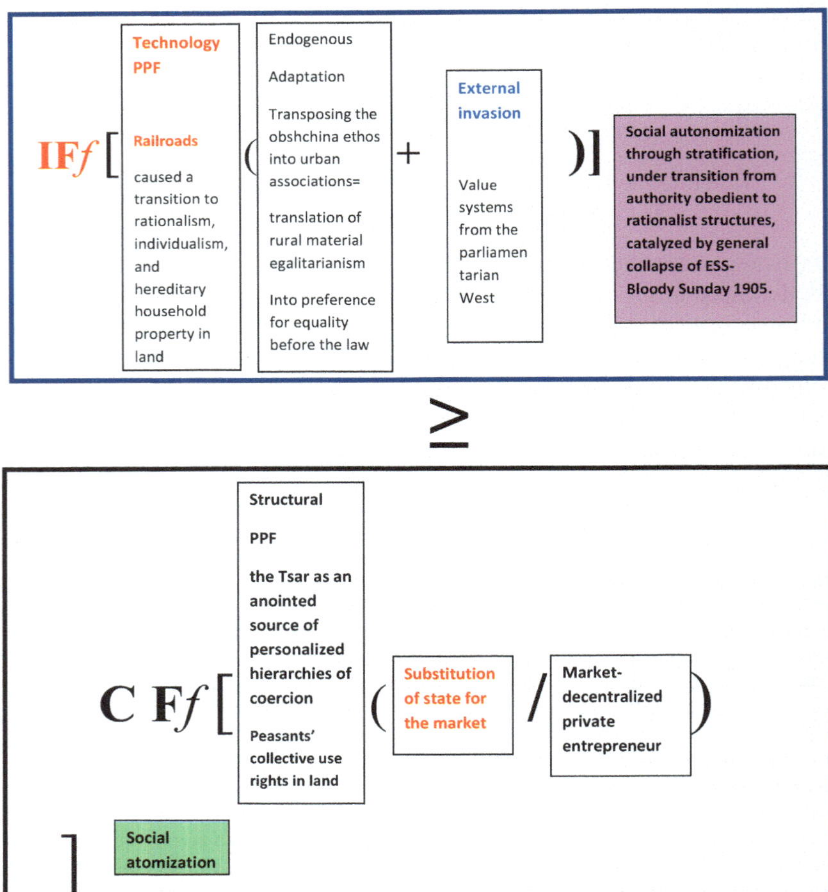

Fig. 4.4 Imported (Railroad) technology and the collapse of the ESS

The figure above summarizes the essence of the Tsarist Russian authoritarian Janus. IF is the consequence, unintended by the autocratic ruler, of state-led industrialization imported for military purposes. The missing aspect in Gerschenkron's analysis is the marginal microeconomic impact of the imported railroad technology on the landholding system and the peasants' attitude toward individual property as an aspect of civil rights, that is, the marginal institutional adaptation that the technology caused. Therefore, from a historical perspective, it is legitimate to suggest that the institutional backwardness in terms of personalized totalitarian hierarchies of coercion-breeding compulsory collectivism, as a means of uncertainty insurance against arbitrariness, was the source of economic poverty and not the other way around.

If so, the substitution of state entrepreneurship for individual entrepreneurship was but one element of a vicious cycle.

References

Anisimov, V. E. (1989). *Vremja Petrovskich reform*. Lenizdat.

Ascher, A. (1988). *The revolution of 1905. Part I: Russia in disarray. Part II: Authority restored*. Stanford University Press.

Barzel, Y. (1989). *Economic analysis of property right*. Cambridge University Press.

Bideleux, R. (1990). Agricultural advance under the Russian village commune system. In R. Bartlett (Ed.), *Land commune and peasant community in Russia: Communal forms in Imperial and early Soviet society*. Macmillan in Association with the School of Slavonic and East European Studies.

Boyer, R., & Orlean, A. (1993). How do conventions evolve? In U. Witt (Ed.), *Evolution in markets and institutions*. Physica-Vlg.

Burds, J. (1998). *Peasant dreams and market politics: Labor migration and the Russian village 1861–1905*. University of Pittsburgh Press.

Bushnell, J. (1990). The Russian soldiers' artel', 1700-1900-A history and interpretation. In Bartlett R, (1990) ed. Land Commune and Peasant Community in Russia -communal forms in Imperial and early Soviet society. Macmillan in Association with the School of Slavonic and East European Studies.

Coase, R. (1937). *The firm, the market and the law*. University of Chicago Press.

Dostojewski, F. (1977). *Wspomninenia z domu umarlych*. Panstwowy Instytut Wydawniczy.

Gerschenkron, A. (1962). *Economic backwardness in historical perspective*. The Belknap Press of Harvard University Press.

Gerschenkron, A. (1968). *Continuity in history and other essays*. The Belknap Press of Harvard University Press.

Gintis, H. (2009). *The bounds of reason: Game theory and the unification of the behavioral sciences.* Princeton University Press.
Gregory, P. R. (1982). *Russian national income 1885–1913.* Cambridge University Press.
Gregory, P. R. (1994). *Before command. An economic history of Russia from emancipation to the first five-year plan.* Princeton University Press.
Hayek, F. A. (1944). *The road to serfdom.* Routledge.
Hesse, G. (1993). Land use systems and property rights. Evolutionary versus institutional economics. In U. Witt (Ed.), *Evolution in markets and institutions.* Physica-Vlg.
Hughes, L. (1998). *Russia in the age of Peter the Great.* Yale University Press.
Johnson, R. (1979). *Peasant and proletarian: The working class of Moscow in the late nineteenth century.* Leicester University Press.
Martens, B. (2004). *The cognitive mechanics of economic development and institutional change.* Routledge.
Mironov, B. N. (2000). *A Social History of Imperial Russia, 1700–1917.* Westview Press.
Mises, L. v. (1981 [1922]). *Socialism.* Liberty Fund.
Moon, D. (1999). *The Russian peasantry 1600–1930. The world the peasants made.* Longman.
North, D. C., Wallis, J. J., & Weingast, B. R. (2009). *Violence and social orders: A conceptual framework for interpreting recorded human history.* Cambridge University Press.
Ofer (1973). The Service Sector in Soviet Economic Growth a Comparative study. Harvard UP.
Owen, T. (1995). *Russian corporate capitalism from Peter the Great to perestroika.* Oxford University Press.
Pipes, R. (1999). *Property and freedom.* Harvill Press.
Poznanski, K. (1992). Property rights perspective on evolution of communist-type economies. In Poznanski K (1992) ed. Constructing Capitalism - The Reemergence of Civil Society and Liberal Economy in Post -Communist World. Westview Press Inc.
Raeff, M. (1984). *Understanding imperial Russia.* Columbia University Press.
Sheshinski, E. (2010). *Limits in individual choice.* The Hebrew University of Jerusalem.
Smith, S. A. (1989). Workers and civil rights in Tsarist Russia 1899–1917. In O. Crisp & L. Edmondson (Eds.), *Civil rights in imperial Russia.* Clarendon Press.
Witt, U. (1993). Evolution in Markets and Institutions. Heildelberg: Physica-Verlag A Springer Verlag Company.
Wood, A. (1990). Administrative exile and criminals commune in Siberia. In Bartlett, R (1990) Land commune and peasant community in Russia - Communal Forms in Imperial and Early Soviet Society. Macmillan in Association with the School of Slavonic and East European Studies.

CHAPTER 5

Peasantry and Land in Industrializing Late Tsarist Russia

The challenge put forward in this chapter to the conception of the commune as the source of backwardness proposed by the Gerschenkronian school briefly mentioned in Chap. 4: the emergence of anti-atomization or the consolidation movements were politically unintended "battleships" that rode the waves of socioeconomic adaptation to the processes of urbanization and technological progress. This chapter explores the actual effects of industrialization on the late Tsarist Russian peasantry as opposed to those intended by the Tsarist government and traditionally assumed by those who study the Tsarist import of technology, with railroad construction at its heart. Did this process impoverish the peasant population while replenishing and strengthening the perceived legitimacy of the Tsarist autocracy? Or was it the other way around?

Here as before, the validity of the Gerschenkronian analysis, which sees the *obshchina*, the peasant communal village, as continuous in character from the emancipation of the serfdom to the Stolypin reform of 1906, is of great importance. According to Alexander Gerschenkron's conception, the commune, structured by the legacy of serfdom, was the primary cause of a mobility barrier that led to peasant impoverishment due to industrialization. If so, industrialization, in Gerschenkron's view, created a "dual economy"—backward agrarianism speckled with modern, state-led industrial enclaves. In this chapter, I challenge the conception of the commune as a stable and continuous post-serfdom institution, proposing instead that the interaction of population increase and railroad technology

S. Sztern, *Russia on the Move*, Studies in Economic Transition,
https://doi.org/10.1007/978-3-030-89285-2_5

rendered the commune marginally responsive to the initiation of market formation as the Tsarist industrialization proceeded.

Gerschenkron versus Gregory: Mobility Barriers and Transition from Extensive to Intensive Growth

I begin by presenting a paradox. The effect of state-led autochthonous industrialization in Tsarist Russia, conceptualized through Gerschenkron's lenses, was a coercive and authoritarian resource repartitioning process that nevertheless allowed external novel ideas to invade,[1] abetting change in conventions and weakening the informal foundations of autocratic rule. Industrialization created demand for institutional transformation. The validity of the Gerschenkronian analysis, which conceives of the commune village as continuous in character from the emancipation of the serfs to Stolypin's 1906 reform, is of great importance in this context. According to Gerschenkron's conception, the commune, structured by the legacy of serfdom, was the primary cause of a mobility barrier that impoverished the peasantry in the course of industrialization. If so, industrialization, in Gerschenkron's view, created a "dual economy"—of modern, state-led industrial enclaves against the background of primitive agrarianism.[2]

The challenge put forward in this chapter is briefly mentioned in Chap. 4: the emergence of anti-atomization or the consolidation movements were politically unintended "battleships" that rode the waves of socioeconomic adaptation to the processes of urbanization and technological progress. In this chapter, I explore the concrete effects of industrialization in late Tsarist Russia as opposed to those intended by the Tsarist government and traditionally assumed by scholars of the Tsarist import of technology, with railroad construction at their core. Did this process impoverish the peasant population while replenishing and strengthening the perceived legitimacy of the Tsarist autocracy? Or was it the other way around?

[1] Given the generally strong interdependence of the turn-of-the-century Russian economy on Western development, the intensified inflow of foreign capital, technology, and knowhow from 1897 onward presumably helped to overthrow conservative conventions by facilitating the invasion of ideas. The theoretical model depicted on this basis suggests that conventions may change if a group that follows conservative habits is "invaded" by a sufficient number of individuals who have chosen an alternative convention. Constitutional government and the impersonalization of law, for example, may be sought in this manner.

[2] Gerschenkron (1968, p. 229), Gregory (1994, p. 29).

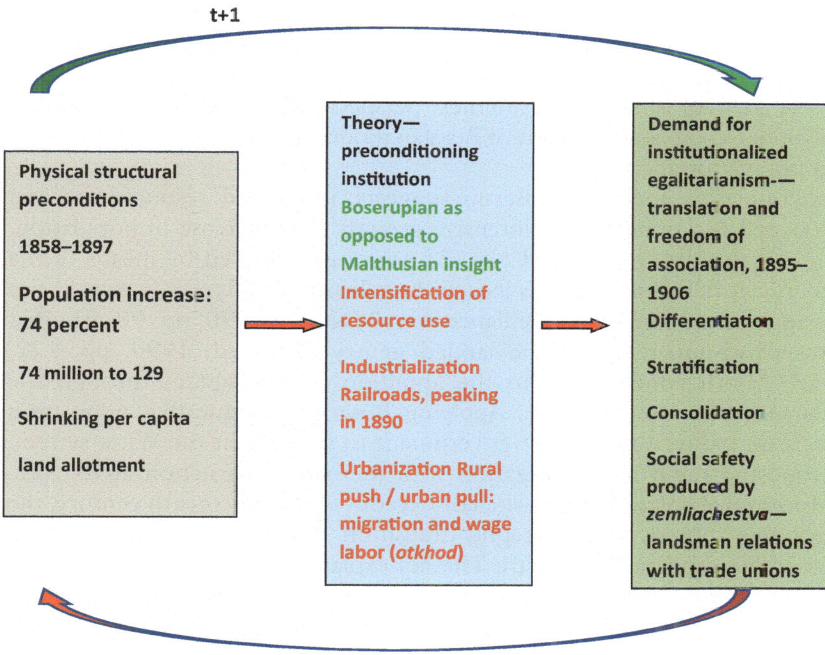

Fig. 5.1 Population increase and the Boserup versus Malthus insight. (*Sources*: Archer (1995, p. 76), Boserup (1965), Johnson (1979, p. 39), Hesse (1993, p. 51), Boyer and Orlean (1993, p. 22), Witt (1993), Atkinson (1983, p. 29), Johnson (1979), North (1973), Gatrell (1994))

Figure 5.1 assumes a partial[3] developmental scheme, a chain of phenomena that transformed institutions and represents the structure of this chapter. Soviet and post-Soviet scholars emphasize the agrarian-crisis hypothesis, by which severe overpopulation impoverished the peasant constituency as Malthusian thinking would have it. In the Tsarist Russian

[3] The scheme focuses primarily on the role of industrialization as an intensification of resource use, that is, an "innovative adaptation" (Hesse, 1993, p. 1) to population increase in the serfdom and post-emancipation era, cumulatively promoting technological and institutional change; and hence, its partial nature.

context, however, I find superior explanatory value in Boserup's (1965, p. 41) hypothesis of intensified resource use *in tandem* with and *occasioned by* population increase, along with the findings of Gregory's (1982, 1994) revisionist school. From these perspectives, industrialization should be understood as an element of Russian modernization that is endogenous to population increase.

Population increase, Boserup suggests, intensified resource use and powered the transition to intensive growth. The increase in population, viewed through the NIE (Chap. 3) prism, is explained by means of the safety net of serfdom and its legacy (Engelgardt, 1993, p. 37), as well as a change in the rate of "surveillance costs" (North, 1990, pp. 90, 91) that was disadvantageous to the landed gentry (Leonard, 1990, pp. 122, 123)—both contributing to the abolition of this system through the Emancipation Act of 1861. Applying Boserup, I argue that population increase induced the Tsarist government to implement the Witte system, proposing rapid industrialization with railroad construction at its core. Moreover, I suggest that in the last decades of the nineteenth century, the railroads caused a demographic transition that reduced mortality and raised life expectancy at birth. The net explanatory effect of the railroads on population increase and regional density is adduced by Atack et al. (2010, pp. 171–197) and is suggested for empirical test in Chap. 2.

The Hesse-Boserup Perspective: Railroads, Population Increase, and the End of Land Reallotment

Hesse and the Causes of Population Increase

From a dynamic perspective, the relation between land-ownership structure and population growth may be addressed within the framework of the investment theory of childrearing and, more specifically, the wealth-flow theory of population (Caldwell, 1982, quoted in Hesse, 1993, p. 52). Hesse emphasizes the importance of the level of income generated by offspring and the intensity of control, namely, the degree to which the parents' generation may, de facto, take possession of and/or exert control over income generated by the child. Turning to Tsarist Russia, let us bear in mind the principle of patriarchalism, the household-based tradition of land rights, and collective use rights until redemption and, subsequently, the implementation of redemption and property rights through control of ownership by the assembly of elders in the obshchina—an element inherent in the communal land-tenure system. These matters considered, the level of control must have been higher before Stolypin's reform than after (See below.) Consequently, the fertility rate before the 1906 reform must have been higher as well. If this hypothesis can be verified, one may establish the combined effect of collective and relatively individualized land rights on population growth, something that may well add knowledge to the attempts to test this assumption. The post-emancipation correlation between collective ownership and population increase, however, remains to be proven, whereas the aforementioned schools of thought define the pressure of population increase on available land resources as the cause of impoverishment.[4]

Incorporating the railroad function into this analysis, I suggest a testable hypothesis on this technology's attenuating effect on patriarchalism, collectivism and, in turn, the parental generation's control of income—an effect that reduced fertility while helping to alleviate famine and other calamities. The result would be an increase in life expectancy at birth, in effect causing a demographic transition that, in terms of its net effect, may be determined in purely empirical ways. Gerschenkron's analysis, argued in previous chapters, advises that mobility barriers and disincentives to innovation and capital investment in agriculture inherent in the institutional structure of peasant land tenure,[5] rendered unavoidable a decline in standards of living for the growing peasant masses, which were held hostage by the land. The great scholar's analysis, however, systematically omits the wealth- and insurance-generating role of the railroads, which incentivized innovative wealth-generating investments in land and

[4] The Malthusian model may initially be seen as instrumental in this context.

[5] Gerschenkron (1968, p. 219). The mandatory consent of the commune, reflected in a two-thirds vote of the assembly, created an exit barrier (p. 220). An amendment to Article 165 of the Redemption statute had a similar effect (p. 221), as did the passport statute (219–222, 224). The combination of population increase and these mobility barriers made less land available per capita and the effect of this was intensified by limited output capacity of soil and, in 1881–1891, falling prices of agricultural produce relative to industrial produce. The combination of these exit barriers and the strengthening effect of unfavorable market conditions resulted in a dearth of investment capital that was further aggravated by lack of credit, hampering the possibility of productivity increase through innovation (p. 218). Prior to the 1893 legislation that prohibited repartitions less than twelve years apart, the instability of household ownership within the commune is assumed to have created an investment barrier (Atkinson, 1983).

enhancements in the proximity of the rail lines. Contemporary opponents of collective land tenure, who wished to modernize and perhaps Westernize the Russian countryside, evaluated in this manner the effect of the legal and customary restrictions on economic performance in the rural sector. The development- and industrialization-oriented theoretician of our time, Gerschenkron, does the same. As I argue in Chaps. 1–8, however, this assessment did not go unchallenged.

An additional concept in this analytical toolkit is "innovative adaptation," a process that Hesse (1993) defines as the "recombination" of elements and the "introduction" of new ones as a creative adjustment to population changes. The population changes, in turn, interact with the marginal value product of labor to determine the land-use system (Hesse, 1993, p. 57). According to this model (p. 51), reproductive behavior adjusts human-capital accumulation as a result of cognitive creativity—"a cumulative variation/selection process" (p. 50). This innovative adaptation of human-capital endowment determines population density and vice versa. When the population grows, land must be used more intensively. Consequently, the adjustment of land- and resource-use systems is seen as an innovative adaptation to the increase in population density. It encourages immobile investments that trigger the subsequent adjustment of the property-rights structure in favor of exclusive access to landed assets. Thus, "Increasing population density, intensification of land use and more excluding property rights are all parts of one process of innovative adaptation to a few basic and invariable constraints" (p. 48).[6]

In the Russian context, the entire industrialization process was an adjustment of resource uses, an innovative adaptation to population increase. The importation of modern technology and the performance of the requisite domestic investments for the intensification of resource use were long-term-oriented input that set in motion an institutional transition from collectivism to individualism, meaning the exclusivity of property rights in land, in agriculture. Hereditary household ownership and its **de jure codification via the 1906 reform** represented an innovative adaptation by institutions to the population increase and precipitated the subsequent intensification of resource use.

Hesse's model, applied, indicates the crucial role of railroad technology in its selective ability to affect population density (Atack et al., 2010),

[6] The basic constraints are energy and information availability.

resource-use intensification, and, ultimately, the transition to exclusive access to land, attracting immobile investments, and vice versa. The paradigms that I apply as I continue—conforming to Neoclassical, Neo-institutional, and Evolutionary economics—are organized according to their explanatory function and are presented in the matrix section below. As an introductory step, my thesis supplements Gerschenkron's and serves as grounds for deduction in conjunction with North's insight (North, 1973, pp. 28–29). In the Northian model, population changes explain relative scarcities that cause institutional change. Practically speaking, the eighteenth-century increase in the Russian population (Kahan, 1985) that traced to the safety net provided by landlord patronage during serfdom, lowered land-to-labor ratios—ultimately resulting in the abolition of serfdom and the gradual individualization of peasant attitudes toward land. This integration of the Northian and the Gerschenkronian models reveals that during the 1890 industrialization spurt, the Russian peasant behaved in a way that is explicable on the basis of rational calculus, all of it within the limits of inherited custom. I assume that population increase and its outcome, shrinking per-capita land allotments, adapted and weakened the adherence to custom that epitomized the collectivist legacy of serfdom. Ultimately, it was the population increase that eroded the mobility barrier. Boserup, as well as Hesse (Fig. 5.2), affirms the relation of population increase to the de-collectivization of property rights in land. Rising population, according to Boserup, triggers the transition from extensive to intensive growth patterns. In my argument, railroad construction is understood as the catalyst of this process. Rising returns on investment in land near railroad lines, explained by the proximity of urban markets, abetted the individualization of land tenure and innovative investment control by exclusivizing property rights—initially de facto, through forgone land repartitions, and subsequently de jure with the implementation of the Stolypin reform and the choice of individualist land categories.

I will have more to say about this in this chapter below (Fig. 5.2). For now, I suggest that the railroads should be understood as the ultimate causal factor in the erosion of the mobility barrier during the post-emancipation era. This technology served to alleviate famines in cases of crop failures, constituting (along with the railroads' impact on literacy, education, and skill accumulation) an explanatory variable for the nineteenth-century net population increase (a greater decrease in mortality than in fertility). Concurrently, it mitigated households' mutual-insurance dependency on the village commune for protection against

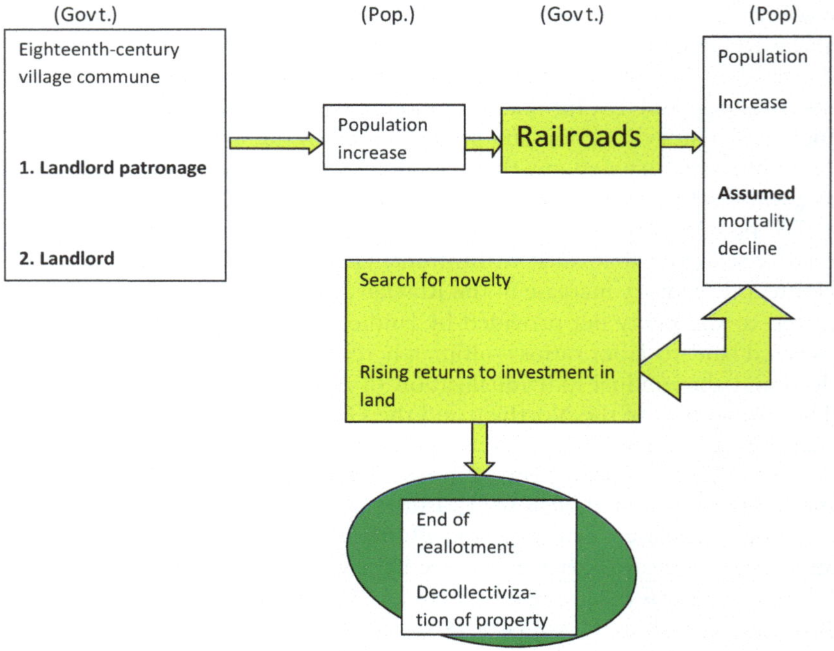

Fig. 5.2 Population increase, the railroads, and the end of land reallotment. (*Sources*: Boserup (1965, p. 41), Hesse (1993, p. 51), Witt (1993, p. 2), Atkinson (1983, p. 31), Worobec (1995, p. 93), Kahan (1985, p. 8, Table 1.1), Hoch (1986, pp. 84–89), Engelgardt (1993, p. 39), Gerschenkron (1962, pp. 125, 126), Kahan (1989, p. 3, Table 1))

other calamities and shortages. This gave households easier access to multiple earning and spiritual options, fueling the transition to rationalism (Sheshinski, 2010; Gintis, 2009) and encouraging the peasantry to form individual risk-diversifying portfolios of sources of income. This process entailed the presence of work, industrial, and agricultural sources that evolved in the direction of increasingly stable variance, namely, became increasingly predictable (Bates, 1989), and set in motion a self-enforcing virtuous cycle that culminated in cumulatively facilitated peasant mobility and migration.

Let us summarize the argument as follows:

Introducing Discontinuity in Compulsory Collectivism

Using the schema above as a framework, I propose to reexamine Gerschenkron's analysis of the coerciveness of barriers to labor mobility and the assumed impoverishment of the peasant population due to industrialization in order to emphasize the economic and historic complementarity of institutional and technologic factors and of institutional reforms. In so doing, I ask whether the Tsarist Russian institutional legacy is, as a matter of peasant legal and customary coercive enforcement, collectivist and homogenous in character, as advised by mainstream Western scholars (Ofer 1997, personal communication). Thus, the question is whether individualism and rationalism in the Russian context should be viewed as phenomena imported from the West in 1906 and 1991 and coercively implemented through privatization processes led by a "big bang" government rejection of collectivism. May the transaction costs of an institutional transformation be lowered solely through adherence to gradualism? (Keren, 1992, p. 90; North, 2005, p. 117). Alternatively, is there an organic source of individualism and rationalism in Russia that was catalyzed by the railroads and codified in the Stolypin reform? What happened in the era between the emancipation and the 1905 revolution? Did collectivism continue, or did the interaction of population increase with the railroad technology trigger spontaneous transitions to individualism and rationalism, bringing on discontinuity?

Here and throughout Chaps. 1–8, I focus on the assumed—not yet proved—discontinuities that occurred in Tsarist Russia's village-commune collectivism in 1861–1914 that were occasioned by the technological change. The Gerschenkronian conceptualization of the continuous village commune structure, as I understand it, is encapsulated in mutual insurance against famines and calamities, ostensibly mandating a mobility barrier that caused the severe poverty embodied in the redistribution of assets practice of the Russian village commune. Challenging this, I quote the findings of Gregory's (1982, 1994) revisionist school to ask three other questions about the depth of the peasantry's impoverishment: (1) Were peasants subjected to unusual consumption restrictions relative to their urban counterparts during the industrialization process (due to restricted labor mobility and oppressive taxation), contributing to a specifically "Asian" type of industrialization? (2) Was the Russian industrialization indeed autochthonous, as Gerschenkron (1968, pp. 80–81) insists? And (3) Were its sudden spurts in 1890 and 1907 exploitive/oppressive of the peasant as well as of entrepreneurs, the landed nobility, industrialists, intellectual constituencies, and the clergy?

Challenging Gerschenkron, Gregory identifies the industrialization process as derived from Europe and largely following global business cycles. Such a process inescapably created institutional harmonization in price structures between Russia and the industrialized, relatively politically pluralistic, and parliamentarian Europe. In this harmonization, the Tsarist state came to represent an obstacle to modernization rather than its vehicle (Owen, 1995, pp. 17, 19).

I claim that these two seemingly conflicting conceptions of the Tsarist Russian industrialization—the Gerschenkronian substitution of state entrepreneurship for a market that failed because of the poverty-stricken peasant constituency's insufficient purchasing power, and Gregory's assumption of a relatively market-led modernization process—are merely end points on a continuous scale. The transition from the initial point to its opposite leaves room for my explanation. Namely, the daily interaction between the imported railroad technology and the rural commune led to changes on the margin in the character of collectivism during the post-emancipation era (1861–1914). The crux of my argument is as follows: The underlying structures inherited from serfdom, such as the rate of population growth and the distribution of regional density, interacting with the ever-expanding railroad network, reduced the land-to-labor ratio. This raised land values along rail lines and attenuated peasant households' dependency on the mutual-insurance function of the collective in the event of famine or other calamities. This, in turn, relaxed the legitimacy and the grip of compulsory collectivism—affecting the frequency and purpose of land repartitioning and paving the way to the formation of a domestic market for industrial produce and a national grain market.

Generally speaking, uncertainty and the dependency on hierarchy did retreat, enhancing the creation of horizontal and increasingly egalitarian-democratic institutional development blocs (Gerschenkron, 1962)—which one may alternately call voluntary collective action networks (Barzel, 2002)—that evolved in complementarity to technological-material ones.

As this chapter continues, I will evaluate the plausibility of this hypothesis against the findings of Gregory (1982, 1994), Bideleux (1990), and their respective schools.

Tsarist Industrialization Interpreted: Gerschenkron versus Gregory

Gerschenkron and Gregory agree about the occurrence of an initial upsurge of industrialization in the 1890s.[7] Gregory identifies the percentage growth rate per annum of output, measured in 1913 prices, in five-year averages as spiking between 1889–1893 and 1893–1897 and between 1906–1909 and 1909–1913 (Gregory, 1982, p. 128, Table 6.1c) Over the entire 1885–1913 period, aggregate product grew by 3.25 percent and per-capita income by 1.7 percent, both annualized (182, Table 8.1). Aggregate product expanded more quickly, on average, before the turn of the century than after because political instability and the Russo-Japanese War caused a loss of output in 1904–1906. Per-capita income grew at an annual rate of 2.3 percent before 1900 and by barely 1 percent annually after; this is understood to be the combined effect of faster population growth and slower annual average output growth after the turn of the century (p. 126). Both schools conclude that the *relative* annual growth rates (measured for industrial and for aggregate output) were higher before the 1905 revolution than after.

During the great spurt of industrialization in the 1890s as periodized by Gerschenkron, the share of net investment in national income rose to 10.9 percent. Since net domestic savings amounted to 9.3 percent of national income (1.6 percent of GDP), 15 percent of net investment total had to be financed by net foreign investment, which is to say foreign savings. By the end of the decade, the share of net investment funded from

[7] Gerschenkron (1968, pp. 129, 133). During the 1890s, the average annual rate of industrial growth was estimated at 8 percent. From the 1905 revolution to the outbreak of World War I, it was estimated at 6 percent. The difference between Gerschenkron's estimates and .Gregory's traces to the components chosen, that is, the definition of industrial output (Gerschenkron) and of aggregate output . (Gregory), as well as the methods of calculation, the chosen base years, and the periodization and sub-periodization. Notably, too, .Gregory identifies two five-year periods of *negative per capita* and *zero absolute* growth—1885–1889 to 1889–1893 and 1901–1905 to 1905–1909—which he credits to declines in personal consumption expenditure and net investment. The first period may have contributed somewhat to Gerschenkron's different findings, that is, lower estimated average annual growth during the entire 1885–1913 period, measured in 1913 prices. At this point, this assumption is unsupported.

this source exceeded 20 percent (Gregory, 1982, p. 127, Table 6.1b).[8] Since this foreign capital was channeled primarily to industrial investment (physical plant, inventory accumulation, and railroad construction), it had more of an impact on the growth of industrial output than on that of aggregate output. Thus, according to both schools—the Gregorian revisionist and the Gerschenkronian—industrialization strengthened economic ties between Russia and the West. Gerschenkron maintains that the state-led industrialization, financed by foreign capital, created a dual economy. Indeed, by the onset of World War I, foreign savings were financing 40 percent of Russian industrial investment (Gerschenkron, 1962, p. 129). Moreover, the Russian price index and national output (the real GNP series), measured in 1913 prices, indicate that the Russian economy in 1885–1913 was strongly integrated into the world economy. Domestic prices were roughly determined by the world market and the index series of total output, especially before the turn of the century, followed Western business cycles, giving evidence of general interdependency in development between Russia and the countries that preceded it in industrialization. Therefore, the data presented thus far support Gerschenkron's periodization and the importance that he attributes to the role of foreign capital in the industrialization process. The industrialization decade was characterized by an especially rapid increase in the share of net fixed investment in national income, from 4.3 percent at its beginning to 8.2 percent at its end.[9] Those growth per decade rates data may even be mobilized in support of the Gerschenkronian and my application of Boyer and Orlean (1993)—external invasion conceptualization, expressed above, that the increased economic interaction between the Russian and Western economies, tracing to ongoing industrialization, allowed ideas from the latter to invade the former.

[8] During the period immediately preceding the "great spurt," net foreign investment accounted for barely 3.7 percent of net investment, suggesting that the initial industrialization effort was financed by domestic and not foreign savings. The breakthrough in attracting foreign capital occurred when the ruble became convertible, that is, when Russia adopted the gold standard in 1897.

[9] This finding is especially valuable in regard to the continuity aspects of Russian and Soviet industrialization. The tilting of resource allocation toward fixed investment was definitely characteristic of the Soviet era. (See previous essay, 1994, *Det socioekonomiska systemets institutionella desintegration och omvandling.Sovjetunionen/ Ryssland.*) Viewed in a Gerschenkronian context this particular aspect of .Gregory's findings does not allow the rejection of Gerschenkronian reflections on the continuity of allocation behavior that typifies a totalitarian state, the foregoing data provide interesting starting points for further elaboration.

Was the Peasant Standard of Living Sacrificed on the Altar of Industrialization? Gregory Challenges Gerschenkron

Central to Gerschenkron's analysis (1962, 1968) and Atkinson's (1983) Gerschenkronian evaluation (1983) is the assumption that the rural economy "financed" the industrialization of 1890 by sacrificing subjects' consumption (Chap. 2, Fig. 2.3). If so, the Gerschenkronian conception of continuity structurally links the Tsarist industrialization to the Soviet industrialization in terms of the priority that both gave to the urban industrial-military sector. In reference to the Tsarist era, the "common good" (Anisimov, 1989) of a successful territorial claim by the Empire justifies the involuntary sacrifice of individual rural households' living standards. In this case, should the Tsarist legacy be understood as compulsively coercively collectivistic at the national level? Gerschenkron conceptualizes the Tsarist Russian village commune as a player in a process of this nature: an instrument of tax collection and immiseration of the peasant economy for the sake of industrialization and social stability. Data presented by Gregory, reproduced in the following tables, challenge such a theory.

Table 5.1 shows that urban consumption expenditure grew slightly faster during this period, by 3.2 percent per annum on average, than rural consumption expenditure, which advanced at an annual pace of 2.7 percent, and that growth was fastest in "other" government expenditure plus investments, at 4.5 percent. The question is: To what extent was compulsory exploitation of the rural economy characteristic of the Tsarist industrialization? Generally speaking, the growth rates at that time imply the reapportionment of personal consumption expenditure from rural to urban sectors and attribute the fastest-growing resource flows to "other" government expenditure and investment. If the reapportionment of national income to "other" government expenditure and investment at the expense of consumption is proven to be *unusual* by international comparison, one may qualify the Russian industrialization of 1890th 4.5% growth rate at 1885–1889 to 1909–1913. industrialization period as "Asian."[10] Moreover, if the transfer of labor from rural to urban sectors

[10] State-led autochthonous industrialization is observable through an international comparison that shows an exceptionally high ratio of government to personal consumption in national income; see below. An increase in the annual growth rate of government investment in national income during the period from 1889–1893 to 1893–1897 (five-year averages calculated by Gregory, 1982) also illuminates the state's active role in the Russian industrialization.

Table 5.1 Personal consumption expenditure, "urban" and "rural" components 1885–1913, 1913 prices, five-year averages

	Personal consumption expenditure, "urban" proxy (retail sales, urban housing, services)		*Personal consumption expenditure, "rural," proxy (retained farm consumption, rural housing)*		*Other final expenditure (government, investment)*	
	Pct. of national income	*Annual growth rate*	*Pct. of national income*	*Annual growth rate*	*Pct. of national income*	*Annual growth rate*
1885–1889	45.6		37.9		16.5	
		1.2		**0.4**		**0.4**
1889–1893	46.5		37.3		16.3	
		5.7		**5.9**		**11.9**
1893–1897	45.3		36.2		18.3	
		5.7		**1.6**		**3.4**
1897–1901	49.0		33.9		17.1	
		2.9		**3.1**		**2.9**
1901–1905	47.9		33.6		18.5	
		0.1		**0.3**		**1.0**
1905–1909	47.8		33.8		18.4	
		3.0		**5.1**		**8.2**
1909–1913	46.5		34.0		19.5	
1885–1889 to 1909–1913		**3.2**		**2.7**		**4.5**
1885–1889 to 1897–1901		**4.2**		**2.6**		**5.0**
1897–1901 to 1909–1913		**2.3**		**2.9**		**4.0**

Source: Gregory (1982, p. 131, Table 6.2)

was indeed impeded, these data taken separately, given the population increase, may indicate a decrease in per-capita consumption in the rural sector, proving Gerschenkron right. The data for the period from 1893–1897 to 1901–1905 illustrate the effects of the turn-of-the-century recession and revolution: faster growth in rural consumption expenditure (the insuring sector) and slower growth in urban consumption expenditure as time passes. Even so, before one ventures any assumption about the alleged impoverishment of the peasant economy due to the ongoing industrialization process, the next table, again calculated and presented by Gregory (1982), should be studied.

Table 5.2 provides further evidence of structural change and verifies the occurrence of industrialization. Between 1883–1887 and 1897–1901, the share of agriculture in national income fell from 57.4 percent to 51.3 percent as the agricultural sector grew at a sluggish 2.55 percent annual rate, while industry ramped up from 23.4 percent to 30.6 percent driven by a 5.45 percent annual rate of growth. What is more, the industrial sector grew more rapidly than did total national income (3.4 percent per annum). The annual growth rate of the sector-specific labor force (Panel B.*) provides a case in point.[11] During the late nineteenth-century industrialization (1883–1887 to 1897–1901), the industrial labor force grew at an annual rate of 3.4 percent, while the agricultural labor force crept forward by a mere 1.1 percent per year, indicating *an exodus of labor from the rural to the urban sector*. Moreover, the meager differential between agriculture and industry in per-worker annual productivity growth (Panel C.*, first row)—0.6 percentage point—suggests that Gerschenkron's and Atkinson's assessment of unusually restricted consumption in agriculture due to impoverishment may be refutable. An international comparison of ratios of agricultural productivity to industrial productivity growth, shown in Table 5.3 below, does not indicate unusually depressed agricultural productivity growth in Russia, further challenging the dual-economy hypothesis implicit in Gerschenkron's depiction of the Russian industrialization.[12]

[11] Gregory (1982, p. 135). Gregory chose sector-specific labor force *growth rates* and not the sector-specific labor force shares in order to avoid arbitrary outcomes. For further elucidation of his methods of calculation, see pp. 134, 135.

[12] Gregory (1994, pp. 29–31). Russia in Tsarism's last thirty years was seen by both Lenin and Gerschenkron as an utterly backward ocean with an island-of-modernity industrial sector. The productivity increase in agriculture, Gerschenkronians say, was hampered by the remnants of feudal institutions; such increases in industrial productivity as took place were generated by inflows of foreign capital and knowhow. The ostensible discrepancy between the productivity rates of agriculture and of industry, intensified by the industrialization effort, resulted in a "dual economy" of stagnating agriculture and developing industry. The deficiencies of the domestic market hampered the latter but they were offset by the aforementioned substitution of government and foreign inputs for domestic demand. Whether the role of the state and foreign capital in Russian industrialization was indeed unusually large by international standards—that is, whether Russia's industrialization pattern qualifies as "Asian"—is discussed below. Table 5.2 provides at best a premise on which to question the dual-economy hypothesis.

Table 5.2 Composition of Russian national income by sector of origin, 1883–1913, 1913 prices

	Agriculture		*Industry, constr., transport, com.*		*Trade and services*		*National income*
	Pct. of national income	*Annual growth rate*	*Pct. of national income*	*Annual growth rate*	*Pct. of national income*	*Annual growth rate*	*Annual growth rate*
A. Sector output, structure, and annual growth rates							
1883–1887	57.4		23.4		19.2		
1883–1887 to 1897–1901		**2.55**		**5.45**		**2.5**	**3.4**
1897–1901	51.3		30.6		18.1		
1897–1901 to 1909–1913		3.0		3.6		2.75	3.1
1909–1913	50.7		32.3		17.1		
1883–1887 to 1909–1913		2.8		4.5		2.7	3.3
B. Sector labor-force growth rates							
1883–1887 to 1897–1901		**1.1**		**3.4**		**1.4**	**1.4**
1897–1901 to 1909–1913		1.7		2.0		2.0	1.8
1883–1897 to 1909–1913		1.4		2.7		1.7	1.6
C. Sector output-per-worker growth rates							
1883–1887 to 1897–1901		**1.45**		**2.05**		**1.1**	**2.0**
1897–1901 to 1909–1913		1.3		1.6		0.75	1.3
1883–1887 to 1909–1913		1.4		1.8		1.0	1.7

*A. Sector output, structure, and annual growth rates

*B. Sector labor-force growth rates

*C. Sector output-per-worker growth rates

Source: Gregory (1982, pp. 133–134, Table 6.3)

Table 5.3 Growth of agricultural labor productivity divided by growth of industrial labor productivity, Russia and select countries

Country	*Period*	*Relative growth rate*
Russia	**1883–1913**	**0.75**
Germany	1850–1909	0.67
France	1870–1911	0.99
United States	1870–1910	0.87
Japan	1880–1920	0.86
Norway	1875–1930	1.00
Canada	1880–1910	0.77
United Kingdom	**1801–1901**	**0.74**

Source: Gregory (1982, 169, Table 7.4, 1994, 31, Table 2.4)

This table, again reproduced from Gregory, shows that the ratio of agricultural to industrial productivity growth is comparable to its equivalents in non-dual Western economies, including post-enclosure England. The estimated growth rates of annual average product per worker in the late nineteenth and early Russian twentieth centuries also reveal comparability between Russia and England.

Gregory's (1982) findings on the pace of employment growth in Russian industry and positive labor productivity growth rates in agriculture, as well as his conclusions about the period from 1883–1887 to 1897–1901, cast reasonable doubt on Gerschenkron's evaluation of the adverse effects of the obshchina system on the mobility and productivity of agricultural labor during this period. Subsequently, Gregory (1994, pp. 37–54) refuted Gerschenkron's (1962, p. 49) hypothesis about severe impoverishment of the rural population due to industrialization amid a countrywide agrarian crisis. Emphasizing growth modes that diverge from Gregory's analysis (1994, p. 38), Russian agriculture developed on the basis of an extensive growth policy that allowed frontier or peripheral regions to achieve higher annual output growth rates than central black-earth regions. Therefore, countrywide aggregate agricultural production grew faster than the population, while traditionally cultivated regions suffered from an inverse relation between agricultural output and population growth. I provide additional evidence to Gregory's for this by noting the intensification of migration to peripheral regions, which, among other factors, shielded the rural population from general impoverishment (Treadgold, 1968, pp. 33–34, Tables 2 and 3). By implication, the railroad- intensifying migration averted a Malthusian crisis in the Black Earth regions while paving the way for aggregate Boserupian growth of output on par or in excess of the population increase.

Thus, amid an ostensibly intensifying agrarian crisis in 1883–1901 (Gregory, 1994, pp. 37, 44), agricultural output grew at a 2.55 percent annual rate, while the population expanded at a 1.3 percent pace.[13] *Moreover, an index of consumption goods output comprising grains, animal products, and textiles, deflated by 1913 prices, shows a 26.25 percent increase in real per-capita output of consumption goods between 1887 and 1904* (Gregory, 1994, p. 45).[14] Since 85 percent of Russia's population was rural, the general increase in output of consumption goods may be taken to reflect increasing per capita rural demand and consumption. Per capita agricultural output, in turn, grew at an annual pace of 1 percent, as stated.

Thus, Gregory (1994) counters the hypotheses emphasized by Atkinson (1983) about "hunger exports" of grain. He interprets the imperial government's shift from direct to indirect taxation as evidence of peasant accumulation of direct-tax arrears in a manner countercyclical to harvests, implying that peasants were able to improve their living standards by exchanging cash crops, thus freeing their grain for export, for imported manufactures.[15]

The annual growth rate of agricultural capital stock between 1890 and 1904 suggests that the estimate of a deficiency in fixed investment due to unstable ownership and impoverishment in agriculture, as depicted by Atkinson (1983) and Gerschenkron (1962), may have been the result of

[13] Indexes of agricultural production, factory production, and population, fifty European Provinces, 1870–1874, as estimated by Goldsmith:

Period	Crops	Factory production	Total population	Rural population
1870–1874	100	100	100	100
1883–1887	117	217	120	117
1900–1904	185	588	156	151

[14] Gregory's presentation of Varzar's index of output of consumption goods in 1913 prices follows

Period	Value of production (millions of rubles)	Per capita output
1887	4298	48
1904	7057	60.6

[15] Gregory (1994, p. 46). Peasants paid direct income taxes when harvests were good and accumulated tax arrears when they were bad, thus securing a stable income, that is, smoothing their income, by producing grain for export.

an overestimate by these scholars of the formal institutions' practical effect on economic performance. Agricultural capital stock is said to have grown more rapidly than population during this period (Gregory, 1994, pp. 46, 49–52)[16] and evidence of rising price value of grain products retained for consumption casts doubt on the rural impoverishment hypothesis. Indeed, while the rural population increased by 17 percent between 1885–1889 and 1897–1901, the real value of retained grain products was 51 percent higher by 1913, indicating rising and not falling per-capita income in agriculture and refuting the impoverishment hypothesis (47, 48). Given the migration of labor from rural to urban areas, the annual growth rate of rural consumption according to the foregoing data is consistent with the assumption of growing, not falling, annual consumption per capita. The 14 percent average real increase in the wages of rural hired farm workers between 1885–1887 and 1903–1905 gives further evidence of *rising living standards in agriculture* that squares with the data on the rising growth rate of per-capita consumption.

I recapitulate: Gregory supports Gerschenkron's periodization, which detects two waves of industrialization: the first in 1887–1901 and the second peaking shortly before World War I.[17] Reflecting on the first industrialization and weighing the shortcomings of his own statistical estimates, Gregory concludes that Gerschenkron's hypothesis about the mobility barrier imposed by institutionalized collective ownership and fiscal obligations during the period from the emancipation (1861) to the turn of the century, resulting in the impoverishment of the peasant economy and intensified by industrialization, *is not supported by the data* (Gregory, 1982, p. 136).

An examination of the formal law detached from actual economic performance, and deduction based on it, does suggest qualitatively that the

[16] Annual growth rate of agricultural capital stock 1890–1914, 1913 prices

1. Equipment and structure	2.7%
2. Equipment, structures, and livestock (Kahan's estimates)	1.8%
3. Equipment, structures, and livestock. (Gregory's estimates)	2.0%

Source: Gregory (1994, Table 3.4)

[17] Gregory (1982, p. 137) .notes with emphasis that Gerschenkron premised his periodization on changes in *industrial output* while his own calculations are extended to *aggregate output value*.

combination of mobility and investment barriers and population increase did intensify the peasants' pauperization. Particularly implicated is the institutionalized acceptance of collectively assigned land rights and the obshchina-specific egalitarianism manifested in the periodic redistribution of control over agricultural means of production as was inherent in the rural custom. The effect of the statutes was aggravated by the coerced financing of industrialization via tax increases, which dealt the rural population's living standards an additional blow.

Gerschenkron (1962, 1968) may have arrived at his foregoing conclusion, refuted by Gregory, by concentrating on the socioeconomic effects of formal institutions in Imperial Russia, inferring from the emancipation and redemption acts of the 1860s their effect on economic performance. Countervailing his deduction, Gregory (1994, pp. 50–52) proposes that informal rural habits seem to have neutralized the adverse effect of formal restrictions on economic performance, allowing agricultural output to increase more rapidly than the population and ensuring rising rural living standards during the industrialization decade. Gregory's argument is supported by Semyonova Tian-Shanskaya (1993, pp. 153, 154), who finds that according to the Tsarist state's hierarchy of responsibilities and coercion, the village elders guaranteed the tax debt payments of heads of household. By custom, the joint-responsibility norm that structured the village commune resulted in auctions of draft animals for the collective payment of tax arrears, affecting all villagers for the worse. It is important to acknowledge this practice because it created an informal substitution of chattels for land—the redistribution of movable assets—in repartition agreements that pertained to the common land pool. These *"informal contracts,"* which protected the stability of landholdings, were one example among many that neutralized the investment disincentive effects of the formally institutionalized and imposed land rotation in accordance with the tax-obligation custom.

Elasticity of Collectivist Land Repartitioning, Population Increase, and Risk of Poverty

The informal habit of mutual beneficence within the communes, with reapportionment of chattels substituting for reapportionment of land as a way to equilibrate taxpaying capacity, may have created a de facto hereditary family-based land-ownership structure throughout European Russia, rendering the differences in increases in land productivity explainable in

Table 5.4 Frequency of land redistribution

Never redivided their land	48%
No redistribution in more than 40 years	3%
No redistribution in more than 15–25 years	13%
No redistribution in more than 10 years	15%
Periodic repartition	21%

Source: Atkinson (1983, p. 74). Atkinson cautions that the aforementioned survey does not include a comparison with the pre-emancipation frequency of land redistribution. Moreover, communes had been customarily redistributing after each census, and no population census took place in 1858–1897

ways additional to the institutional restrictions recorded in the *Svod Zakonov*.[18] Indeed, a study by the Russian Ministry of Internal Affairs shows the following distribution of actual land repartitioning after the emancipation in 73,000 rural societies (Atkinson, 1983, p. 74).

It follows that turn-of-the-century Russia saw controversy over the de facto characteristics of the village commune. Kachorovsky points to the near ubiquity of redistributions during the 1880s, followed a decade later by peasant resistance to the procedure due to shrinking land allotments amid population growth. This notwithstanding, redistribution was practiced among peasant households that had small land allotments (Atkinson, 1983, p. 74). While the Ministry of Internal Affairs survey advised that 48 percent of the communes never really redivided their land (Table 5.4), a survey by the Free Economic Society in 1910 among ten central agricultural and mid-Volga provinces disclosed that 60 percent of the communes had redivided their land in 1895–1906, even though the 1893 statute imposed a twelve-year moratorium on this practice (p. 75).

As the Ministry of Internal Affairs assumed that the commune had lost its vitality by the time it conducted this survey, its aforementioned findings may be biased on this account. Table 5.4 implies that even though joint responsibility for taxes and dues was enshrined in formal law, land redistribution was not ubiquitous de facto. Thus, as Tian Shanskaya indicates, in

[18] The *Svod Zakonov Rossijskoi Imperii* was the legal code of Imperial Russia. Presumably, the state's incentive and power to tax and apply social control would be unequally distributed (Migdal, 1988, pp. 1–9; Sztern, 1994). Consequently, peripheral regions that were far from political centers, newly colonized, or "protected" by topography, although communally cultivated, would not be formally induced through a collectively assigned fiscal burden to enforce the obligations and rights attendant to repartition.

cases of accumulated tax arrears among poorer households, the redistribution of chattels substituted for land reapportionment—an outcome that additionally vindicates Gregory's findings. The data on the actual frequency of repartitions are highly self-contradictory. A Free Economic Society inquiry in 1910 and 1911 concerning ten central agricultural and mid-Volga provinces found that only 8 percent of 400 communes did not redistribute their land (Atkinson, 1983, p. 75). Roughly 60 percent did redivide their land in 1895–1906, after the introduction of the 1893 law that prohibited land repartition within a twelve-year interval. If so, the practice was widespread and the government, attempting to intensify land use, felt it necessary to legislate against doing it too frequently. Obviously, there was a discrepancy between de jure and de facto practice. Notably, although the letter of the law accepted the tenure of the obshchina including its egalitarian value system for taxation purposes, it did not prohibit the skipping of repartitions. On the contrary, periodic land redistributions were outlawed gradually (Atkinson, 1983, p. 30; Gerschenkron, 1968), increasing the de facto stability of household ownership (Loewe, 1990; Bideleux, 1990). Moreover, forgone repartitioning—de facto hereditary land ownership—was gradually applied de jure through the implementation of the 1893 and June 14, 1910, statutes. Under the latter act, lands of villages that had not redistributed since the original allotment in 1861 were placed under hereditary tenure automatically and in their entirety (Atkinson, 1983, p. 76). The informal substitution of chattels for land in repartition agreements, however, probably could be enforced by social sanctions only. Given the industrialization-induced increase in the mobility of the rural population—a trend that the commune assemblies presumably tolerated due to population pressure[19]—the assumed habitual exchange system, based on personal relations, became increasingly burdened with transaction costs. This led to greater adamancy in the demand for an adjustment of formal law (Eggertsson, 1990) that would institutionalize household as well as individual ownership and "emancipate" the peasants from the commune.

[19] Atkinson (1983, p. 74) verifies this assumption, maintaining that despite the formal mobility barrier ostensibly imposed by the obshchina system, "Communes were not unwilling to release members when there were opportunities for more profitable employment elsewhere," as their willingness to do this could spare them from impoverishment.

Having refuted Gerschenkron's emphasis on formal institutional constraints that gravely impeded development on the basis of Gregory's interpretations, I now turn to the alleged "great famine." Bideleux (1990, p. 216) explains that the excess of 280,000 deaths in 1892 relative to the average mortality rate in 1861–1890 cannot be explained by the crop failures of 1891–1892, which ostensibly dealt a *coup de grace* to the already exhausted rural population. Instead, Bideleux traces the heightened mortality to cholera epidemics that occurred in 1892 according to a periodically repeating pattern. The sixteen provinces that were struck by crop failures, Bideleux reports, accounted for barely one-third of cholera deaths recorded in 1892. Thus, the remaining two-thirds of deaths from cholera cannot be explained by a causal relationship between the crop failures and cholera, even though some scholars do put forward this theory. Importantly, cholera is water-borne and could have spread from Asia via the slow-moving waters of the Volga River. It has also been argued that the diffusion of the disease should be attributed to ignorance, poor education among the peasants, and deficient public sanitation in regard to water supplies, and not to a shortage of food (Bideleux, 1990, p. 207).

Thus, the evidence reported by Bideleux of sufficient and rising food production in the Russian countryside relative to other European countries—the crop failures notwithstanding—and of increased labor mobility lends further support to Gregory's (1982, 1994) conclusions concerning a rising rather than a declining standard of living among the Russian peasantry before and during the industrialization decade.

Gregory (1994) derives the existence of "informal habits" from a Neoclassical model based on the assumption that economic agents, including peasants, act as utility maximizers[20] that seek profit, that is, possibilities of survival, by downing barriers to economic activity imposed on them by formal restrictions or institutionalized custom. He suggests that "side payments" (Gregory, 1994, pp. 50–52) or their alternative—compensation in the form of draft animals or a share of the crop—substituted for the reassignment of land parcels at repartition times, leaving the long-term investment incentives unaffected by formal restrictions. Although the direct evidence of rationalist peasant response to population increase and

[20] Gregory (1994, p. 50). .The assumption according to Gregory .contradicts the position of Chayanov (1930).

shrinking per-capita land allotment (Atkinson, 1983, p. 30) is speculative and anecdotal at the very best, the quantitative indicators of structural transformation in favor of nascent industrial sectors and migration to peripheral regions indicate that the redistribution practice that related household land endowment to the number of adult males/work teams (*tyaglo*) per household was handled flexibly by the peasants, implying that movable capital compensation for land rotation was in place (Kingston-Mann, 1991, pp. 35, 37, 45; Nafziger, 2010).

Thus, an egalitarian practice of chattel redistribution substituted for the ubiquitous redistribution of land rights—the equity-maintaining repartitioning of immobile assets and fixed investments—within the obshchina. Informally practiced compensation habits of these kinds, .Gregory concludes, may have affected income redistribution within the commune without affecting the productivity of land and labor employed in agricultural production. In the long run, then, the equity-oriented obshchina spirit would not have impaired the growth of agricultural output. .Gregory's argument is corroborated empirically by Nafziger's (2010) studies on peasant response to mortality shocks and changes in the land-to-labor ratio.

Bideleux versus Gerschenkron—Mobility Barrier, Agrarian Property Rights, and Productivity

The possibility of questioning the assumption of peasant pauperization during and as a result of the industrialization is very valuable for those who wish to make room for a conceptualization of the character of collectivism brought about by the infusion of Western technology. The objective of such a conceptualization is to hypothesize about the institutional origin of the transfer of land rights from rulers' patrimony (*votchina*) to subjects—a practice codified in Stolypin's 1906 land reform. Did the reform merely emulate the agrarian structures of Bismarckian Germany in a quest to preserve the stability of the autocratic dictatorship (Ascher, 2001, p. 2)? Alternatively, did the individualization of land rights in Russia originate in changes in relative scarcities that were caused by the interaction of the post-serfdom agrarian institutions—still compulsorily collectivist—and the railroad technology, introducing rising predictability into transactions and thereby reducing the risk to subsistence? If the latter is the case, the Russian peasantry must be understood as having transitioned from obeying authority within a coercive collectivist hierarchy to individual household rationalism spontaneously, gradually, organically, and in tandem with the use of railroads. The legacy of the pre-revolution Late Tsarist institutions must then be understood as individualistic and not, as Western scholars commonly assume, collectivistic. My deduction from the Neoclassical model, above, has explanatory value in this direction provided the peasants actually were utility maximizers, as Neoclassical doctrines assume as a core proposition.

Even if the data-based calculations are valid, as presumably they are, they reflect a doctrinal mindset. Therefore, an additional source confirming the findings may provide at least the minimum necessary extent of "theoretical objectivization." It is with this in mind that I present the empirical findings of Bideleux (1990, pp. 196–217). Bideleux argues effectively against the proposition of the peasant population's severe impoverishment due to the first wave of industrialization in the last decade of the nineteenth century. As proponents of Gerschenkron's agrarian-crisis thesis suggest, the pauperization culminated in 1891 and 1892 in a disastrous famine that, according to analysts inspired by the Malthusian tradition, provided an additional and justifiable reason for the occurrence of a Malthusian crisis. Such conditions would intensify rural collectivism. According to the Soviet and Leninist tradition that piggybacked on the "agrarian crisis" hypothesis, the crop failures and the resulting famine were of political rather than economic origin. The assumption of an institutionally determined retention of labor by the rural economy is the core premise of the "dual economy" model. If agricultural productivity increased amid mobility barriers, the rural sector would generate a surfeit of labor relative to the needs of agriculture, a "reserve army" potentially available for capitalist exploitation. Only a challenge to the traditional institutions could unleash the productive forces of capitalism. Bideleux (1990) counters this position as well.

The Gerschenkronian analysis, compatible with the Malthusian tradition,[21] assigns the main blame for the peasantry's pauperization and backwardness to population increase, institutionally determined immobility, and, as a result, overpopulation in the rural sector. This, according to the Gerschenkronian conception championed by Atkinson (1983), among others, led to falling per-capita land allotments, intensified soil exploitation, and inadequacy of technological improvements in agricultural production—the last-mentioned outcome attributed to the conditions of poverty and unstable ownership that inhered to the communal land-tenure system.

[21] The analysis inspired by Malthusian tradition is represented by both Soviet and select Western scholars and was presumably adopted by Atkinson (1983), referenced above.

Strip farming, additionally induced by periodic repartitions, impeded the rationalization of land use and supposedly thwarted the requisite increases in food supply. These factors contributed to the incidence of Malthusian positive control—in this case, death from starvation. Thus, population increase is assumed to have outpaced agricultural production, making the countryside overpopulated in the Malthusian sense.

To strengthen the foregoing argument, I note that the immobility of rural labor would have caused a shortage of skilled labor. Against this background, the sluggishly increasing participation of craft and landsman worker cooperatives (*zemliaki artelii*) in industrial settings would have subjected the urban industrial labor force to exploitation in the short run, albeit not beyond—a phenomenon that industrialization would have intensified. Furthermore, insofar as these workers had an alternative source of subsistence, the restriction of labor supply could have rendered industrial wages susceptible to upward pressure.

Given the ostensibly poverty-stricken countryside, the insufficient competition for unskilled labor would have denied employers the necessary incentive to offer wage increases. With the possibility of substituting capital for working hands taken into account, the mobility impediment may indeed explain general impoverishment within a "dual economy" and, in turn, the crisis. The country-bound peasantry, which as a potential "reserve army" due to rural pauperization could have abetted capitalist exploitation of the urban workforce, would have rendered the rural sector definable as overpopulated in both the Malthusian and the Leninist senses. Moreover, even if the rural sector was not overpopulated in the Malthusian sense, it would have been perceived as such in the Leninist sense due to the irrationality of labor-force allocation caused by the mobility impediments, which would have triggered the crisis and necessitated political corrective measures.[22] The available Soviet literature, based on Tsarist-period statistics that support the Leninist as opposed to the Malthusian overpopulation concept, conforms to Bideleux's estimates in Bartlett, the Western source.

According to both the former and the latter, however, grain and potato output grew faster than the population in 1860–1890 (Table 5.5):

[22] Bideleux (1990, p. 198). Bartlett emphasizes the difference between the Malthusian concept of overpopulation and the Leninist one. Presumably, Gerschenkron's emphasis on the adverse effects on economic development of institutionally determined labor-mobility hindrances incorporates the concept of rural overpopulation in the Malthusian as well as the Leninist sense.

Table 5.5 Net grain and potato increase, European Russia, 1860–1890

	1860s	*1870s*	*1880s*	*1890s*	*Annual pct. increase*
European Russian population, millions	63.7	69.8	81.7	94.2	Total 1.3 Rural 1.2
Net grain + potato output (million chet-verts, grain equivalent)	158	187	228	290.5	2.00
—per inhabitant	2.48	2.68	2.79	3.08	
—per rural inhabitant	2.75	3.00	3.18	3.55	

Source: Bideleux (1990, p. 199)

Bideleux: A.S. Nifontov Zernovoe proizvodstvo Rossii vo vtoroi polovine XIX veka

The Marxist-Leninist allegations concerning the post-emancipation pauperization of the peasantry (poverty intensified by industrialization, providing a just cause for the eruption of a crisis) do not, in principle, contradict the acknowledged increase in per-capita agricultural output and income amid population growth. Bideleux's estimates, however, support. Gregory's in their refutation of the peasant-immiseration hypothesis.

The Ideologically Inspired Concept of Relative Poverty in Soviet Sources

The Soviet concept of relative poverty, derived from the Marxist-Leninist one, refers to an increase in differentiation within the rural class that impoverishes the poorly skilled relative to the rural entrepreneurship strata within the peasant community. Such a differentiation is said to be independent of the increase or decrease in per-capita agricultural output and may be interpreted as the result of skill inequalities—differences in peasants' relative industrial aptitudes that are subsequently reflected in income inequalities. Rising entrepreneurial skills combine with growing per-capita income, the latter providing certain farmers with opportunities to accumulate non-agricultural earnings and wealth—to create, according to Leninist thinking, class differentiation. Therefore, the critique of the Tsarist industrialization in Soviet sources concerns primarily the potential assault on the principles of equity and the viability of the commune, namely the prospect of the impoverishment of some that would eventually lead to the impoverishment of many. This ostensible class differentiation, it is argued, doomed the peasants to misery relative to their wealthier fellows, the kulaks, as well as to the landed nobles. This, along with the exploitation of the former by the latter two social strata, provides the Leninism-inspired sources with their mainstream analytical framework (e.g., Dubrovskij, 1963).

Unfortunately for the Leninist paradigm, the empirical evidence does not sustain the fears of *increasingly differentiated* opportunities to acquire means of production within the obshchina. The characteristic value system of the obshchina, probably manifested in the redistribution of chattels, actually assured the property interests of the majority, as noted.[23]

Wage Labor and Migration as Buffers against Impoverishment

Paradoxically, data conveying information that one may use to refute the hypothesis about the impoverishing effect of the Tsarist economy's "feudal institutions," showing an increase in de facto labor mobility during the 1861–1910 period, are also provided by Soviet historians, additionally verifying the assumptions that Western sources have expressed on this issue.[24]

[23] Bideleux (1990, p. 200). The average size of an average peasant *household* allotment in European Russia was 11.1 hectares/27.4 acres. In 1877, only 4.4 percent of peasant allotments were smaller than 2.2 hectares/5.4 acres. The percentage share of the smaller allotments rose to 4.7 by 1905. The share of farms smaller than 2.0 hectares was 1/3–2/3 in France, Germany, and southern and Eastern Europe. In Japan, 2/3 of all farms were smaller than 1.0 hectare. By international comparison, then, access to agricultural means of production seems to have been quite equally distributed in Tsarist Russia. Moreover, the hired agricultural labor force, presumably consisting of landless peasants, was only 5 percent of total agricultural labor at the turn of the century.

[24] Bideleux (1990, p. 199) confirms .Gregory's hypotheses (1994, p. 51) about an increase in labor mobility during the post-Emancipation era. The fact that Soviet sources, subjected to censorship, would contain information that could be interpreted in favor of the commune village as an "economically rational" institution is hardly surprising. The Marxism-inspired pre-revolutionary Russian intelligentsia, as well as the Populists, saw the "folklore-based" collective land-tenure system as a possible shortcut, at an interim bourgeois stage, to full-fledged socialism. Moreover, the Leninist concept of overpopulation notwithstanding, the issue on which both the Bolshevik leader and Count Witte actually agreed was the need to preserve the commune. While the former hoped for the commune to become a vehicle of the socialist revolution, the latter, until the upheaval of 1905, expressed the Tsarist government's expectations of the obshchina system as an assurance against such a development. It may be added that history proved Lenin right in this respect; the commune did become a very convenient forum for socialist revolutionary agitation. The reflection on the Marxists' position is based on Gerschenkron (1962, pp. 152–187); Lenin's and Witte's view of the obshchina and its role in the upheaval, among other topics, are analyzed by Ascher (1988, Part I).

Table 5.6 Internal passports issued, 1861–1910

	1881–1870	*1871–1880*	*1881–1890*	*1891–1900*	*1901–1910*	*1906–1910*
Millions	1.3	3.7	4.9	7.0	8.9	9.4

Source: Bideleux (1990, p. 199)

Table 5.7 Rural population according to Bechasnov

Social estate	*Number (thousands)*	*Percent of total population*
Peasantry	96,897	77.12
Cossacks	2929	2.33
Townspeople (half)	6693	5.33
Aliens	8298	6.60
Total	114,817	91.39

The empirical findings in the following table provide grounds for a challenge to Gerschenkron's assumptions about the ostensible labor-mobility barrier inherent in the post-emancipation Tsarist economy (Table 5.6).

The 1897 census defines roughly 13.4 million people as *meshchanie* (townspeople), of whom 5.9 million (44.4 percent) shared their livelihood with inhabitants of rural areas and shared customs with their peasant neighbors. Moreover, numerous rural villages had been defined as towns. In addition, 1.5 million inhabitants of urban areas described their vocation as agriculture or animal husbandry. Thus, it should be accepted, as Bechasnov estimated (see Table 5.7), that half of the townspeople were in fact rural.

Table 5.7 reproduces the composition of the rural population in European Russia according to Bechasnov (Moon, 1999, pp. 141–153).

Given the total population of European Russia according to the 1897 census (125.6 million), the urban population was the residual (approximately 10.8 million). According to Bideleux's data in the foregoing table, internal passports issued to members of the rural population in 1891–1910 covered only 6.9 percent of this population on average. Nevertheless, it is the dynamics of the urbanization process that should receive the main attention because they conduce to the indication of a mobility barrier.

Table 5.8 Internal passports of different time durations, 1861–1900 (thousands)

Years	*1–3 months*	*6 months*	*Yearly*	*Over 1 year*	*Total*
1861–1870	1869.6	5661.1	5332.9	59.2	12,913
1871–1880	17,258.5	10,169.8	9414.0	87.1	36,929
1881–1890	24,366.7	13,118.9	11,889.4	91.2	49,466
1891–1900	20,539.8	11,101.6	37,880.1	1844.7	71,366

Source: Reproduced from Kahan (1989, p. 4, Table 1.2)

Valuable data that support the assertion of dynamically rising labor mobility due to industrialization and railroad construction follow (Table 5.8).

The declining issuance of 1–3-month passports and the dramatic increase in issuance to terms of more than a year in the decade of the industrialization spurt indicate atrophy in ties to the village and the rising propensity of long-term migration. This, in turn, suggests growing individualism in households' decision-making on the rising marginal utility of wage labor and the unfavorable tradeoff with subsistence ethics of the household that had been anchored in the customary reliance on agricultural income and land redistribution in accordance with the number of males per household. Thus, the mutually enforcing combination of railroad construction and population increase, coupled with general industrialization, eroded the mobility barrier that rural custom, structured by the legacy of serfdom, had imposed. Thus, Gerschenkron's proposals concerning the existence of a stable and constant mobility barrier during the post-emancipation period is challenged.

Supplementing the foregoing statistics, the 1897 census reports that 15 percent of the Russian population changed residence permanently or on a long-term basis during the post-emancipation period—a "migration wave" by Russian standards.[25] ***Between 1860 and 1913, migration from rural to urban centers gave Russia's "industrial proletariat" an annual growth rate of 2.5 percent.*** This "proletariat" grew predominantly due to migration. It had no natural increase, as the peasant laborers kept their families in the village and repatriated their urban incomes to them

[25] Bideleux (1990, p. 199). The United States, however, boasted a very impressive level of mobility at this time, twice that of Russia.

Table 5.9 Peasant mobility by rail

Year	*Rail passenger traffic per year (millions of people)*
1871	21
1891	48
1912	245

Source: Bideleux (1990, p. 200)

(Johnson, 1979, p. 41). Industrial output grew by 5 percent per year during the same period. Data on rail passenger traffic (see Table 5.9) lend additional support to the claim that labor mobility *increased* during this time (Bideleux, 1990, p. 200) due to growing population and improved transport.

Considering the annual growth in the urban labor force—observed by two mutually independent sources—and the evidence of the generally increased mobility of the population, the rural *push* and urban *pull* assumption presented in the foregoing developmental scheme is justifiable.

How Coercive Was the Enforcement of Collectivist Custom in the Post-Emancipation Commune?

The obshchina, the pre-emancipation commune—the legacy of post-emancipation rural life—penalized peasants who wished to defect by saddling them with obligations and invoking informal sanctions such as damage to reputation and creditworthiness (Mironov, 2000, p. 306). Given the level of mutual dependence that the precarity of Russian agricultural conditions imposed on daily life in the peasant commune, the threat of ostracism, hostility, and neighbors' distrust were effective means of deterrence and enforcement of compliance. Deviance from agreed-upon norms posed real dangers to individuals' and households' subsistence and survival. Formal sanctions that were applied in the rare cases of breach of communal customary agreements on obligations, Mironov says, included "fines, flogging, confiscation of property and sale, detention, expulsion from the commune, recruitment into the army, exile, and imprisonment." In the infrequent cases of theft of draft animals or indispensable agricultural implements, the accused could be exposed to *samosud*, an extrajudicial compulsory collectivist spree of peasant violence that more often than not ended with the alleged offender's violent death (Mironov).

In its ruling structure, the commune emulated in microcosm the macro superstructure of the Russian Empire. The elder's position was analogous to that of the Tsar. The council of the eldest (the *stariki*) emulated the Boyar Council. The village assembly (the *skhod*) constituted the equivalent of the *Zemskij Sobor* and the patriarchs mirrored the ruling elites (Mironov, 2000, p. 314). Mironov defines the pre-emancipation communal structure as a "patriarchal egalitarian democracy" with a clear hierarchy of authority that subordinated to the patriarch's authority women, the young, and men who were not *bolshaks* (heads of household) or who belonged to minority groups. Example of the last-mentioned were peasant outsiders to the village *postoronnie*—who during the historical serfdom era had belonged to other villages and landlords, unlike the *pripisnoe*—registered as belonging to the village stable members, traditional particular village population (Penza region statistics collection, 1913). Following the 1861 emancipation, government regulations and decrees replaced the serf owners' edicts, codifying the custom that structured peasant life into written law (Mironov, 2000, p. 328). The emancipation statutes restricted the village assembly's prerogatives but allowed it to continue convening in order to manage land repartitions, allotment of taxes and expulsion of members from the commune. Peasants elected their police subject to communal and crown control. The laws of 1861 empowered the commune to serve as a first-instance "cantonal court" (p. 330). The post-emancipation commune became bureaucratized, the village elder (*starosta*) and the tax collector subordinated to state administration at the cantonal *(volost)* and district *(uezd)* levels (p. 330). In delineating the hierarchies of coercion, it is important to note that the peasant eldest, the *stariki*, were punished for peasant defections through arrests and fines. It was the disputes that resulted from this that ultimately made the commune the subject of state laws (p. 332).

In spite of bureaucratization, the traditional communal village court system—family courts, commune village courts, courts of the eldest (*starikov*), courts of neighbors, courts of village elders (*sud starosty*), and the village assembly (*skhod*) court—continued to serve after the emancipation (p. 336). The communes' policing functions, in turn, were broadened with responsibilities previously assigned to serf owners. The types of penalties that remained in effect accorded with tradition more or less, "ranging from admonition [to] arrest, [and] selling of tax delinquents' property" (p. 337). Nonconformists could still be exiled to Siberia. A regression for all of Russia on the occurrence of *samosud* (as adduced from police records) relative to distance from the nearest railroad station might disclose a positive correlation between the two. Thus, a plausible testable hypothesis would be: The closer to the railroads (the shorter the distance in kilometers), the more cantonal and imperial legality-compliant interaction there was, and the less the structure of rural ancient custom persisted. Contrary to (Worobec, 2001) assumption, the frequency of these extrajudicial compulsory collectivist sprees of peasant violence would be explained by physical and cognitive distance to the railroads, to the cantonal court, and to the imperial court.

Peasant conceptions of the legitimacy of mutual help/rescue (*pomoch*)—indispensable for the fulfillment of the survival obligation in the event of fire, floods, illness, other forms of breadwinner disability, and other calamities striking individuals and groups—in itself constituted a concealed system of penal sanction and rewards. Reliable, foreseeable, thrifty, trustworthy entrepreneurial peasants, heads of households who as a rule did not shirk their obligations, were assisted when temporarily disabled or stricken by calamity. Those whose reputations were impugned were allowed to fail, chased away, fined, jailed, dispossessed, and excluded from the commune's mutual-insurance frameworks. These attitudes in themselves shed light on the coercive enforcement mechanism that structured post-emancipation village life. Moreover, mutual insurance and pomoch were subject to individual utility evaluations rather than blind obedience of custom. It was of ultimate importance for assistance that the calamity-stricken household be temporarily disabled and could be counted on even while in need of neighbors' assistance (Worobec, 1995, pp. 23, 24).

Such communal cohesion mechanisms lost potency for two mutually contingent reasons: population increase and access to railroads, which eroded the effectiveness of coercive sanctions as a function of the probability of calamities, conflict, and mutual dependence in handling individual and household challenges to survival.

The peasants' moral code reveals the very long-term rationality of the custom itself, subject to natural selection and adaptation of rule systems (Vanberg, 1994; Veblen, 1931; Hodgson, 2004), in which the "collective memory" of famines (North, 1993) assumed a custom-perpetuating function. Such an interpretation of custom is supported by Vanberg (1994), who stresses that compliance with written and unwritten rules is the result of a perceived higher long-term payoff to rule-following than to noncompliance. The Russian peasant's experience and wisdom is encapsulated in two adages: "He who disregards tradition cannot live with others" and

"What the Mir ordains is what God has decreed" (Mironov, 2000, p. 322).[26] Thus, the rejection of custom embodied in defection triggered severely ostracizing formal and informal sanctions against the offender as a means of coercive enforcement. It is important to emphasize that labor mobility was allowed through the de facto implementation of a *teleological*, not a *semantic*, interpretation of custom by the village assembly, resulting in a two-thirds majority vote in favor of issuing the requisite internal passport or passports at that time of population increase (Atkinson, 1983, p. 74). Thus, I posit, peasant mobility occurred not in defiance of custom but precisely in adherence. The Gerschenkronian conceptualizations of peasant custom and mobility view the informal legal restrictions as rigid, while .Gregory seemingly relates to "side payments—" "informal habits of mutual beneficence"—as extra-customary, which they are not. The custom itself was flexible, adjusting to changing scarcity relations due to population increase and allowing migration and seasonal wage labor. The visible structural changes illuminated in Tables 3 and 4 above indicate that the mobility barrier to peasant labor was weak if not nil.

[26]Volyn (1970). The word *mir* denotes either a single commune (obshchina) or a group thereof. Its exact definitions are a function of local emancipation agreements and their legacy, and are not unproblematic (Atkinson, 1983). In Black Earth provinces, local historical conditions, volatility of yields, access to groundwater and the collective memory of Tatar riots, and the level of literacy shaped the proportions of *barshchina* (corvee labor at the demesne) versus *usadba* (own household garden labor) that delineated the agreements of which the commune was constitute. After the emancipation, such agreements among landlords left 80 percent of the land in the hands of the Tsarist state and the assembly of householders—the *skhod*—defined the levels of mutual dependency that constituted the post serfdom legacies (Atkinson, 1983; Hoch, 1986. The term pertains to the evolution of the commune from its *zadruga* (kinship) form, which emerged in the peasantry's transition from hunting and gathering to sedentary farming, and from the labor team that was appropriate for *podsega* (the slash-and-burn practice, in which the extended family clears the woods). Its organizing principle was risk diffusion or mutual household insurance (Eggertsson, 1990) and internal cohesion (Ma, 2006). The historical pre-serfdom commune was self-governing (Mironov, 2000). From the gradual encroachment of landlord economies and the imposition of serfdom (1549) onward, communes were enforced by landlords while maintaining their initial function and resorting to their assembly as the organized intermediary for communication about taxes, loans, allowances of last resort, and judicial, policing, and healthcare functions (Hoch, 1986) with the bailiffs of the estate. In Chap. 6 below, I dwell at length on the complementarity of the Slavophile concept of the commune and that of the Westernizers (Chicherin, 1904). In Chap. 9, I explain the delineation and structure of the commune in a selected region (Penza province), manifested in the statistical proportions of fifteen different aspects of emancipation and the legal agreement under the Stolypin reform, between the Tsarist state in lieu of the landlords and the communal assembly representing the householders.

To sum up, it is clear from .Gregory's tables that the communal mechanisms of coercion that were employed to enforce *krugovaya poruka*—mutual responsibility for taxes and dues, resulting land redistributions that aligned endowment with the fiscal obligations of adult labor teams, which, according to Gerschenkron, hindered the mobility of labor from the rural to the urban sector—must have been weak and elastically adaptable to the earning opportunities intrinsic to the industrialization that railroad construction was spearheading. This observation is important and is supported by Burds (1998) and Nafziger (2010). A detailed discussion of the approach in this monograph to Nafziger's explorations of the economic rationality behind factor flexibility within the communes is found in Chap. 9. .Gregory's data indicate that the communes' labor mobility adapted itself to the land-to-labor ratio, on the one hand, and to households' standard-of-living aspirations, on the other. From Burds (1998), I adduce that adult family members were not hindered by the elder structures in leaving the commune, provided they repatriate their *otkhodnik* (wage-labor) income for the upkeep and tax payments of kin who remained in the commune. Defection from the obligation to repatriate earnings to the communal pool resulted in criminal charges against wage-labor violators refusing to repatriate their wages otkhodniks (Burds, 1998, pp. 29, 211–215; Johnson, 1979, p. 30).

Burds' findings for the interval between the emancipation and the Stolypin land reform (1861–1910) disclose the growing proportion of internal passports issued to peasants, advising of the de facto absence of a mobility barrier and the rising proportion of the peasant population participating in *otkhod*—wage labor—and migration (Burds, 1998, p. 23, Table 1.3.). In decisions on issuing internal passports, the village assembly of heads of household was the enforcer of the customary restrictions. Burds, supplementing .Gregory, allows us to refute Gerschenkron's and Atkinson's static conceptualization of the effect of custom on actual peasant choices, decisions, and mobility norms.

Here it is important to call attention to evidence, and a side-outcome, of the upturn in peasant migration: a perceptible increase in criminal cases that were brought before the circuit courts, district assemblies, land captains, and volost' courts during the decade of peak industrialization and railroad construction, as reported for Riazan province in 1892–1908 (Frank, 1999, p. 56, Table 2.1). It was the bureaucratization of the commune that accounts for the upturn in documenting and recording criminal cases. Nevertheless, *the mitigation of mutual dependency due to greater use of railroads* and dwindling distances of communes from railroad lines may be expected to have attenuated the deterrent potency of the traditional sanctions depicted above. This, I posit, resulted in an upsurge of criminal, as well as innovative, activity. Frank (1999, p. 77, Graph 2.4) reports that rural felony convictions crested in tandem with the Stolypin reform and the crumbling of the commune, namely, with the erosion of coercion and enforcement of the compulsory collectivist custom. This allows me to formulate a testable hypothesis for future research: The frequency of criminal cases is explainable by the distance from railroads.

Formal Restrictions and the Head of Household's Decision Matrix

The formal restrictions that existed on paper empowered commune assemblies and heads of households to retain labor in the villages. In response to the increase in population, however, the motivation to enforce such a policy must have weakened. Generalizing from this example, one may depict formal laws as providing merely an incentive for a certain action; whether or not this action will actually take place depends on the motivation to undertake it when the exigency arises.[27]

The obvious conclusion is that compliance with formal and customary restrictions was attenuated by considerations of the village elders' assembly, which were informed by rational subsistence risks pertaining to time and region. It was in this assembly, which made its decisions by a two-thirds majority vote (Worobec, 1995, p. 3), that entrepreneurs among the heads of households effected their cooperation and coordination. Although the village administration—a legacy of serfdom—was variously composed, most such panels were headed by a headman (*burmistr*), a tax collector (*tseloval'nik*), and a *zemskii* (clerk), who may have been a priestly assistant from the parish church. The village administration often consisted of elders (*starosty*), foremen (*starchina*), selectmen (*vybornye*), overseers (*smotriteli*), and constables (*sotskie, pyatidesiatskie, desiatskie*). Its core was the village assembly (*skhod*), which elected the remaining functionaries unless the landlords performed this duty, as had been the case in serfdom times (Moon, 1999, p. 202).

[27] This statement is inspired by Goldhagen's (1996, p. 18) analytical frame.

Viewed through New Institutional Economics lenses, the component of individual motivation in village assembly heads' decisions may be conceived, in terms of its quality and time horizon, as ontologically different from the direct effect of the formal and customary legal structure. Consequently, the acknowledgment of motive as an additional condition for a human action makes motive the determining explanatory dimension in each case specified in the matrix below. The cases, aggregated diachronically, follow an ex post identifiable pattern that may disclose a collective phenomenon of knowledge or memory that is definable and useful for an ex ante analysis focusing on informal institutions, such as Veblen's "habits of thought," that determine behavior, and vice versa. The latter may reveal the long-term collectively defined objective of a custom. Such a perspective, however, is by necessity insufficient because custom predates individually motivated interaction.[28] Thus, I suggest the long-term objective of the repartition commune, namely, securing its members' social and material well-being. Applying Vanberg (1994) and Veblen (1931) in combination, I assume the long-term rationality of custom itself, manifested in the natural selection and adaptation of rule systems to the conditions of life of whole populations. From this perspective, an increase in the population of an obshchina would give its assemblies a long-term customary motive to insure against the historically estimated probability of Malthusian impoverishment by allowing those willing to migrate to do so. The motive in this case may be understood as the result of an individually perceived present necessity shaped and molded by the tacit long-term objective of the custom. The growing flexibility of the commune, coinciding with population increase and railroad construction and abetted by the institutionalization of informal cooperation, itself constituted insurance against a mechanism that would adjust impoverishment to novel scarcity conditions of life. The rationality of a custom and ultimately, in tandem with modernization, that of an individual are a theoretical expectation in this monograph, not the proof of the phenomenon. Chapter 9, however, corroborates by induction that the nineteenth-century Russian peasant was hedonistically and rationally motivated to evaluate the marginal utility of membership in the commune as against that of leaving it.

[28] Archer (1995, p. 76). The Critical Realist school shares this axiom.

A decision by village elders to "open the commune borders," however, may also be explained in terms of an emerging "deviant innovative spirit"[29] created by the need to ensure survival.

Gerschenkron (1968, p. 186) summarizes two institutions that were constitutive of the commune: periodic repartitions and joint responsibility (*krugovaya poruka*) of commune members for government taxes and dues. In practice, the method of land allocation was variegated. Village assemblies allocated land to households according to the number of census "souls" (male household members, irrespective of age), the number of workers per household, and the number of eaters per household—all household members. Worobec (1995, pp. 22–26) specifies the *tyaglo*—the married couple—as the labor team that constituted the basis for land allocation.

The Impact of the 1861 Emancipation Act

The Tsarist Russian obshchina was characterized by egalitarianism. In regard to the intersection of this feature and the mobility barrier created by joint responsibility for taxes and dues, two articles in the General Statute of the 1861 Emancipation Act deserve attention. The first is Article 36:

> *Each member of a village commune can demand that out of the landholdings acquired as communal property a quantity of land corresponding to his contribution to the acquisition of this land be separated out onto his individual ownership. If such a separation should appear impractical or impossible, the commune has the right to satisfy the peasant wishing to leave the commune by a sum of money arrived at by agreement or by an official evaluation.* (Gerschenkron, 1968, p. 186)

Article 36 prejudicates the acceptance of chattel reapportionment—monetary side-payments—as substitutes for the reapportionment of immobile assets stemming from joint fiscal liability. Such a substitution would attenuate the mobility barrier that Gerschenkron emphasizes and vindicate .Gregory's proposal about stable de facto use rights in land. Theoretically, the population increase in the second half of the nineteenth

[29] This assumption is inspired by Gerschenkron (1962, Essay 3).

century would compel rational heads of households to allow adult family members to secede from the household and the commune, thereby compensating the outgoing party for the monetary value of his contribution to communal land. This swap would facilitate the urbanization process as well as migration to sparsely populated regions such as Siberia.

The redemption procedure encapsulated in Article 165 of the Emancipation Act of 1861, however, reflects the mobility barrier—temporary and technology-contingent—that actually existed:

> *Until the redemption loan is repaid, the separation of land to individual householders out of lands acquired by the commune is not permissible except with the consent of the commune. However, if a householder desirous of separation should pay to the District Treasury the whole redemption debt falling on his land, the commune is obliged to separate out to a peasant who has made such payment a corresponding amount of land, if possible in one locality, that is consolidated at the discretion of the commune. Until the separation takes place, the peasant will continue to use the land he acquired as part of communal lands.* (Gerschenkron, 1968, p. 187)

Article 165 anticipates the Stolypin reform by allowing, in principle, individual household land to be separated from the commune as the result of a down payment on the redemption debt. The railroads allowed diversification in sources of income. This rendered income streams stable and predictable and elevated real income due to non-agricultural seasonal employment (Johnson, 1979), which, in turn, enhanced the transition to individualism and to nuclear as opposed to extended families (Frierson, 1993), the accumulation of savings, and withdrawal from the communal land allotment redistribution and reapportionment system—which freed adult family members in the next generation to leave the commune for industrial employment. The interaction of the population increase and the railroads, each enforcing the other, should be identified as the factor that weakened the mobility barriers imposed by formal statute.

The General Statute of the 1861 Emancipation Act allowed peasants to abandon the mir provided they:

1. irrevocably waived their right to the communal allotment and to the use of the commons;
2. discharged all tax payments to central and local authorities, including arrears pertaining to the current calendar year—not only for themselves but for their households as a whole;
3. obtained their parents' consent.

The third point clearly marks the extent of the authority of the head of household (*bolshak*) and the patriarchal head of household (*bolshukha*) in determining the outcome.

All three conditions of separation indicate the crucial role of the railroads. The more stable and predictable the access to urban economies was, the less dependent the peasants would be on the social and economic safety provided by the commune, the higher the probability of tax arrears payments, and the weaker the mobility barrier embodied in formal law.

Article 173 of the Redemption Act specifies the mobility barrier, on the one hand, and the extent of elders' authority in controlling individual peasants' movements, on the other:

> *When land is acquired from the pomeshchik by the village commune as a whole, the single members of said commune have the right to be dismissed from the commune upon payment of one-half of the principal debt on state redemption loan, falling upon the holding of the respective member*, provided that the village commune guarantees payment of the other half of the debt.

Thus, the commune elder's authority extended to controlling migration from the commune due to the role of the commune as the guarantor of individual peasant householders' debts to the Tsarist state. The more stable peasant income from non-agricultural employment through access to urban economies would be, the more likely it was that the elders would guarantee debt and the weaker the mobility barrier would become.

To sum up, railroad construction—the core of Tsarist industrialization—abetted an increase in pressure from the population on land available for cultivation and attenuated peasants' bonds to commune land by giving them access to alternative sources of income. From a dynamic perspective, state-led industrialization eroded the barriers that the Tsarist rural institutions had erected—challenging Gerschenkron's emphasis on the barrier to labor mobility created by the continuity of the commune.

After the emancipation, the authority of the commune elders replaced that of the landlords. Now, for example, the obshchina in it could compel a head of household who had amassed tax arrears to accept a wage-paying job away from the commune (*otkhod*) and submit his earnings to the obshchina in order to repay the accumulated tax debt. Until 1894, when the Passport Law went into effect, a statement from the elected head of obshchina had been necessary for participation in outside wage labor (Gerschenkron, 1968, p. 195). The Passport Act extended passport validity from one year to five years. Even this extension, however, as well as the issue of a passport ab initio, required the consent of the head of the household (p. 196).

Authority over the mir,[30] subject to a two-thirds majority vote of the members of the village commune at a time- and place-specific assembly (skhod) of the communal structures in the hierarchy, was wielded by the Tsarist government bureaucracy. Thus, a government official ratified the decisions of the commune in passport matters. In effect, then, the mobility barrier, if any, was imposed by the Tsarist government, which consolidated the mir's taxpaying capacity, and not by the pre-modern insurance unit, the obshchina. Ultimately and as a paradox in Russian industrialization, it was the substitution of state for private entrepreneurship, encapsulated in the autocracy's historical goal (since the pre-serfdom era) of controlling population movements (Blum, 1961, pp. 110, 219), that might have hindered peasant mobility, the pace of industrialization, and, to a lesser degree, the peasant mir per se.

The fundamental norm that inspired communal asset management was "maximal use of the land" (Petrovich, 1968, p. 217). As a case in point mentioned above, the mutual-help mechanisms (pomoch) were not expressions of altruism and ethical collectivism. Land redistribution to widows who did not belong to a productive labor unit (*tyaglo*) was restricted. Households that were disabled or not thrifty enough to participate in tax payments were dissolved and their members were expelled and exiled (Worobec, 1995, pp. 23, 24).

[30] An abstract definition of the *krestianskoe soslovie*, the peasant-estate ethos that engaged in the consensus-preserving practice of asset allocation for its optimal use (Petrovich, 1968).

In conclusion, the commune assembly's decision was a function of a multidimensional determinant. The matrix below captures the aspects commented on above, each adding an explanatory level to the riddle of decision and action that must be solved to understand the Russian village-commune system. The analytical dimensions that structure the matrix are applied from North's definitions of formal and informal institutions (North, 1990, p. 78 and p. 64, respectively). These dimensions, however, do not suffice to explain individual motives of decisions and actions. Incorporating into the analysis the Critical Realist school, I posit that not all aspects of a decision in a modernizing society are functions of pre-structuring. The conceptualization of provision of choices that cohere with the cost matrixes of "shared mental models" and "historical opportunity" (North, 2005, p. 21) leave a crucial dimension of decision-making unexplained. Albeit applied to a different set of historical questions, Goldhagen (1996) focuses on "individual motive" as the ultimate explanation of ad hoc decisions and actions. I find this dimension generalizable to every decision that a social being makes. Thus, even situations that are institutionally preconditioned contain an element of choice that may result in divergent action from the one deducible and inferred from formal (state-stipulated) and informal (custom-determined) institutions.

The village commune's assembly of elders was institutionally preconditioned to hinder migration against the background of shrinking per-capita land allotments and additional complementary factors such as the otkhodnik's good reputation (Burds, 1998, p. 188). Still, a passport application for the purpose of urban employment might result in a decision on passport issuance that deviates from the one set forth in formal law and custom. Goldhagen emphasizes the omnipresent element of choice, which makes every decision and action at least potentially rational and endowed with personal responsibility. Moreover, against the background of population increase, the teleological contents of customary restrictions meant to ensure individual and group survival (applying AEI in combination with NIE—see Chap. 3__) would allow those willing to migrate to do so (Table 5.10).

The Rationality of the Nineteenth-Century Russian Peasant

The economic disincentives to the departure of adult family members from the commune, embedded in the tyaglo-contingent distribution of land allotments as interpreted by Gerschenkron and Atkinson, are

Table 5.10 NIE matrix on the complementarity of theories

Collective—C, C'/ Individual—I, Action determining Factors	*C Formal restriction*	*C' Informal restriction*	*I Motive*
C **Formal restrictions** **Σ(C) = *f*(A.,B.,D)=›**	A. Gerschenkron's model: mobility barrier State action—formally institutionalizing custom.	B. Gregory's frame: "informal habits" *Utility maximization* in response to formal restrictions.	D. Goldhagen's frame: state-supported human action, legal individual action.
C' **Informal restriction** **Σ(C') = *f*(E.,F.,G)=›**	E. North's model: institutional Δ in response to population increase, combining custom, culture, and state action.	F. Long-term informal objective of the collective, restricting the scope of what would be perceived as a necessity.	G. Goldhagen's frame: determinant of human action not supported by the state; socially sanctioned individual action.
I **Motives** **Σ(I) = *f*(H.,J.,K.)=›**	H. Goldhagen's frame: determining factor of individual human action supported by formal law.	J. Goldhagen's frame: determining factor of individual human action, obtaining legitimacy through a cultural pattern.	K. Gerschenkron's model: assumption of a deviant innovative decision.
Σ (CCI) => *f*(inst.det. incentive, motive)	Σ C—collective and individual determinants of individual action in political unit.	Σ C'—collective and individual determinants of individual action in social unit.	Σ I—individually perceived determinants of individual action.

Sources: North (1990), Goldhagen (1996)

presumed to have created a barrier to labor mobility. In this aspect of the analysis, Gerschenkron and Atkinson conform to. Gregory by imputing full economic rationality, that is, Neoclassical utility maximization, to the Tsarist Russian peasant constituency. Assuming that the peasantry of European Russia reached such a stage of rationality by the concluding decade of the nineteenth century, labor mobility and migration may be reexamined within a Neoclassical utility maximization model. Such a hypothesis, which I set out to prove empirically in Chap. 9, is justified in view of the use of railroads in 1843–1890 and the increasing participation in the emerging anonymous extra-village exchange, namely, a market economy, by the peasantry of European Russia as migrants and wage laborers. It is further justified by the multitude of institutional-selection adaptations and the widening spectrum of individual choice that were congruent with this novel means of transport.

By inference, then, an additional condition needs to be met for migration hindrance to occur: The present value of lifetime extra earnings from the increase in land allotment should exceed the discounted value of lifetime earnings outside the commune.

The observed migration of labor from the rural to the urban sector suggests, *inter alia*, that the rationalist payoff conditions for the customary mobility barrier had not been met, making the formal mobility restrictions questionable in their explanatory value. Furthermore, the village elders' economic incentive to "penalize" successful, income-generating households through land redistribution is assumed to be weak when analyzed from a Neoclassical perspective. The collectively assigned tax obligation would create a free-rider problem, which the elected assembly would recognize and try to neutralize by agreeing on compensatory" side payments—reapportionment of mobiliers—rather than the customary land repartition. Generally, the commune, understood within the Neoclassical model, is assumed to be a more flexible unit than may seem plausible if one fixates on its formal restrictions as definitive devices for the prediction of its economic performance. An attempt to inductively prove the evolving peasant rationality that was manifest at the turn of the century is made in Chap. 9. Here I consider the emerging Neoclassical rationality solely as an aspect of—a cell in—the decision-making matrix presented above, which is assumed by the Gerschenkronians, in self-contradiction, as well as by the revisionist schools.

As for the ostensible burden of oppressive taxation,. Gregory argues that the post-emancipation redistribution of land ownership between peasantry and gentry shifted in favor of the former. Changes in land prices correlated positively with changes in agricultural-produce prices. .Gregory interprets the increase in land prices, which exceeded redemption payments as early as 1879, as evidence of rising demand, which, in turn, implies rising net income, the latter supported by the data. Rising prices and incomes in agriculture, .Gregory concludes, are incompatible with the hypothesis of impoverishment and oppressive-taxation. Furthermore, he says, the accumulation of tax arrears is evidence of "countercyclical household policies." Such policies were rationalist in character. That is, households priced themselves for the income loss occasioned by the decrease in agricultural-produce prices that eventually occurred by delaying payments of direct taxes, leaving their net income unchanged. That direct taxes accounted for barely 6 percent of peasant income at the turn of the century is an additional reason to question the oppressive-taxation assumption . (Gregory, 1994, pp. 52–54; Simms, 1977, p. 382).

Refuting the dual-economy, the hunger-export, and, more generally, the agrarian-crises hypotheses, .Gregory suggests instead that peasant households and householders' assemblies engaged spontaneously and increasingly in rationalistic, individualistic calculations. Thus, postulates based on empirical material and deductions from a Neoclassical model premised on the assumption of agents' utility-maximizing behavior, such as .Gregory's, cast reasonable doubt on the existence of labor-mobility barriers and grave impoverishment in the Tsarist peasant economy in the last decade of the nineteenth century.

Moreover, the very applicability of the Neoclassical paradigm begs two questions: How collectivistic and authoritarian was the Russian countryside after the industrialization spurt of the 1890s? and Is Gerschenkron's conception of the stable continuity of Russia's de facto agrarian institutions legitimate in respect of the closing decades of Tsarism? Before these questions can be conclusively answered, additional investigation of Gerschenkron's hypothesis on the peasant mobility barrier is necessary.

As for the decisions and actions of individual peasants, 20–25 million people are said to have colonized Siberia and the southern steppes in the late nineteenth century and the first decade of the twentieth (Bideleux, 1990, p. 199). This flow undoubtedly supports Gregory's (1994) .hypothesis of migration from cultivated to peripheral regions in search of means of subsistence. If so, the observed migration wave may have been a response to a temporal or anticipated reduction in the standard of living—an ever-present circumstance in the peasantry's collective memory—that, from a dynamic perspective, helped to protect the peasant population from impoverishment. The adverse economic effect of the rural overpopulation, I suggest, was at least partly neutralized by the increasing mobility of labor. The barrier imposed by formal restrictions was destroyed by the long-term objective of informal constraints that were manifested in the motivation to ensure survival.

Returning to the foregoing developmental figure, I believe it necessary to justify the "intensification of land use" hypothesis. This aspect of countering Atkinson's (1983, pp. 32, 33) assumption of severe impoverishment is instrumental for analysis of the causes of the crisis. The scheme perceives the nation as the analytical unit and categorizes the industrialization process in regard to its function as a means of increasing subsistence and an effort to intensify resource use in response to population growth. The decision to embark on rapid industrialization in the 1890s was taken by the imperial government. Following Gerschenkron's (1962, pp. 120, 121) thinking, one may state that the process lacked complementary correspondence within the rural economy. The volatile ownership structure is said by Gerschenkron to have disincentivized technological improvements in *land cultivation*, which were economically impossible to begin with due to deteriorating material conditions, crimping domestic demand for industrial produce.

Peasant Allotment, Private Land, and Productivity Increase in Rural Russia: Indications of Innovative Investment in Agriculture

With Gerschenkron's (1968, p. 187) proposal on the investment disincentive and the economic deficiency assumption borne in mind, the increase in yields (measured in tons of grain per hectare) in post-emancipation European Russia comes as a surprise. According to Bideleux's estimates, the increase was slower in communal land than in privately held land at about a ten-year lag. By international comparison, however, land that was allotted to peasants notwithstanding *formally* collective ownership delivered steadily growing yields over time, allowing the productivity gap relative to privately held land in Europe, Japan, America, and Australia to narrow.[31] The following table provides the evidence.

[31] Bideleux (1990, p. 201) traces this productivity gap to several determinants: (1) the continental climate in the communally cultivated regions, verifying the Slavophiles' hypothesis about the communes "organic" origins and refuting the "state school" assumption; (2) relatively scanty education among the Russian peasants; and (3) the landed gentry's ability to retain the most fertile soil while selling off the less-productive land to the peasants, as guaranteed under the provisions of the Emancipation and Redemption acts—a legal inequity emphasized by Gerschenkron (1968).

Countering Gerschenkron's proposal, Bideleux (1990, p. 202) infers from the increasing productivity of land between 1860 and 1913 that "technical advances must have taken place." The increasing productivity of communally cultivated peasant land during this period, the narrowing of the productivity gap relative to some privately cultivated areas elsewhere, and the productivity lag behind traditionally privately cultivated land in Russia may be explained in a way that calls attention to the incentive function of ownership rights (Poznanski, 1992).

Due to forgone repartitions of regionally varied land, the emerging *de facto hereditary household property right* may, on average, have provided stronger incentives for productivity increases that facilitated innovative investment relative to the collectively assigned use rights of the serfs and of the newly (post-1861) emancipated peasants. Moreover, the formal legal structure gradually adjusted and even promoted a holding establishment that resembled a family farm within the formal boundaries of the obshchina system (Leonard, 1990, p. 121). In 1906, this informal transition toward hereditary household ownership would culminate in formal acknowledgment of individual ownership. The rising productivity of communally held land, observed in Table 5.11 above, expresses the increase in innovative investment in agriculture and it may be interpreted as reflecting a shift in the incentive function due to the informal privatization process that developed tacitly amid formally communal cultivated holdings. The gradual privatization of peasant allotment land marked an additional principal evolution of the challenge to the Tsarist *votchina* (patrimony) as a cultural historic axiom embedded in the ever-present right to a *usadba* (a household plot), which had extended from serfdom to the emancipation period and onward to the Soviet period even though the applied Soviet sociopolitical system affirmed collective ownership of means of production as an all-encompassing dogma. This system was also extremely tolerant of an illegal landholding practice whereby the *dvor* (urban household) cultivated a household garden plot for own subsistence and/or the urban market. Historically, the continuity of *usadba* rights indicates that a limited degree of risk insurance, creating institutional pluralism, was continuously accepted within the autocratic and totalitarian monolith, creating a precedent for the Soviet and post-Soviet "household plots" (Pallot & Nefedova, 2007; such plots are also mentioned by Ofer & Vinokur, 1992, p. 44).

Comparing peasant land yields diachronically, I find that the increase in land yields was most pronounced in 1880–1900 (a time that included the

Table 5.11 Annual yields of European and major world grain producers, 1860–1913

Annual			*Grain yields (tons/ hectare)*			*Compound annual rates of increase, percent*		
European Russia	*1860s*	*1870s*	*1880s*	*1890s*	*1900s*	*1911–1913*	*1860s with 1911–1913*	*1880s with 1911–1913*
Peasant communal allotments	**0.44**	**0.47**	*0.51*	*0.59*	*0.71*	*0.86*	**1.52**	**1.76**
(+6 percent) (W)				**(0.63)**	**(0.76)**	**(0.91)**		
Private land	**0.50**	**0.56**	**0.63**	**0.71**	**0.89**	**1.23**	**2.0**	**2.6**
(+6 percent) (W)				**(0.76)**	**(0.94)**	**(1.30)**		
Italy	(0.86)	(1.02)	(0.86)	0.84	1.10	1.24	(0.8)	(1.4)
Spain	(0.61)	–	–	**0.63m**	0.96	0.96	(1.0)	–
Portugal	–	–	–	**0.65m**	(0.65)	0.60e	–	–
Greece	–	–	–	0.75m	(0.80)	0.89f	–	–
Bulgaria	–	–	–	(0.89)	0.97	1.11	–	–
Romania	0.93	0.84a	0.95b	0.96	1.07	1.29	0.7	1.2
Serbia	–	–	–	(1.10)	0.96	1.12	–	–
Hungary	–	–	1.06	1.25	1.25	1.41	–	1.1
Austria	–	0.98	0.97	1.05	1.19	1.36	–	1.4
Germany	1.13	1.20	1.28	1.48	1.73	1.94	1.2	1.6
France	1.06	1.06	1.15	1.17	1.26	1.29	0.4	0.4
Ireland	1.53	1.68	1.74	1.92	2.12	2.24	0.8	1.0
Denmark	–	1.52d	1.60	1.71	1.85	2.01	–	0.9
Sweden	1.33	1.37	1.36	1.39	1.45	1.68	0.5	0.8
Neth.	1.54	1.55	1.62	1.75	2.02	2.08	0.65	0.95
Belgium	–	–	–	1.8	2.30	2.35	–	–
Britain	–	–	1.91c	1.95	1.98	1.88	–	0.0
Japan	–	–	1.74	1.80	2.02	2.22	–	0.9
USA	**1.23h**	1.29	1.32	1.31	1.38	**1.30**	0.1	0.0
Canada	–	–	–	1.16m	(1.27)	1.33	–	–
Argentina	–	–	–	1.07	0.98	0.98	–	–
Australia	0.83	0.83	0.68	0.61	0.74	0.79	0.0	0.3

Source: Bideleux (1990, p. 210)

Notes: a. 1870–1876; b. 1886–1889; c. 1884–1889; d. 1875–1879; e. 1918–1922, f. 1911, 1914, 1915; g. 1911–1915, h. 1865–1869; (m) 1892–1895. Brackets denote tentative estimates. Wheatcroft suggests that the Central Statistical Committee data understated grain yields by 6–7 percent (Bideleux, 1990). The computations are based on Soviet as well as Western sources

first industrialization spurt, 1890–1900) and in 1900–1913 (overlapping the second industrialization, 1907–1913), suggesting the intensification of land use[32] and implying the evolution of complementarity of demand between the industrial and the agrarian sectors. *Both sectors responded to the increase in population.*

Technical advances, although assessed by Bideleux (1990) as small in scale, included

> *newish crops (potatoes, maize, new wheats, sunflower, tobacco), improved livestock breeds [...], increasing specialization with cattle and sheep rearing, iron parts for wooden ploughs, carts, wheelbarrows, spades, forks, hoes and seed drills [...], cheaper and mass produced scythes, iron horse shoes, harrows, galvanized iron buckets, storage jars and bottles, wheels, axes, nails, screws, bolts, fencing (barbed wire), roofing iron, bricks, cement, fossil fuels, rope and sacking.* (Bideleux, 1990, p. 202)

Between 1890 (the beginning of the first industrialization) and 1913, agricultural equipment stock is said to have trebled. In the wake of the great spurt, Bideleux (1990, p. 202) reports, "Agriculture consumed more of Russia's booming iron output than the concurrent railway-building bonanza did."

Thus, the transfer of labor from agriculture to industry may be construed as a response to the rising demand for labor in the latter sector. The demand for industrial produce in agriculture presumably did create a small domestic market for industry. The complementarity of demand and the migration of labor from the rural sector to the urban in response to industrialization induced push and pull factors, and the general intensification of resource use through large- and small-scale technological progress (that is, the industrialization process itself, instigated for political reasons in response to the population increase) followed the assumed causal scheme described above.

The reported annual grain output per inhabitant in the period immediately preceding the 1890 industrialization indicates that the Russian peasants could not have been so impoverished as to verge on famine unless their counterparts in other European countries were in much the same

[32] The concept in this context does not allude to destructive overexploitation of the soil; on the contrary, it is assumed that the land became intensively cultivated in a manner oriented to the long term.

state.[33] The data on Russia's annual grain and potato output per inhabitant for the period including the industrialization decades and one of the years of the ostensible famine (1891/92) compare rather favorably with corresponding estimates in most European countries, which were found neither severely impoverished nor on the verge of a Malthusian catastrophe.[34]

The aforementioned postulates of Atkinson (1983) and Gerschenkron (1968) imply a generally valid inverse relation between the degree of formal communal land tenure (the obshchina-specific repartition practice)

[33] Annual grain output per inhabitant, Russia and other European countries 1885–1889 (hectolitres):

Russia	Italy	Austria-Hungary	Germany	France	Netherlands	Sweden	Denmark
6.75	2.67	6.22	5.36	6.66	3.08	7.49	14.04

Source: Bideleux (1990, p. 203), from Chuprov and Posnikov, eds., *Vliianie urozhaev i khlebnikh tsen na nektoriia storony russkogo narodnogo khoziaistva, I* (St. Petersburg, 1897)

[34] The following table, calculated by Bideleux (1990, pp. 203, 204) and reproduced here, may provide an illustration: *Annual Grain and Potato Output per Inhabitant, Russia and Other Countries, 1892–1913.* The data represent kilogram-grain equivalents. As potatoes are 78 percent water and contain only one quarter as many calories per kilogram as grain, four kilograms of potatoes are treated as equivalent to one kilogram of grain.

	Russia	Europe excl. Russia	Southern Europe	Italy	Portugal	Greece	Spain	Japan	Austria-Hungary	Bulgaria
1892–1895	534	415	260	221	174	209	350	225	507	-
1909–1913	555	411	276	274	160a	130b	400	240	508	545
	Serbia	Romania	Denmark	France	Germany.	Ireland	U.S.A.	Canada	Argentina	
1892–1895	–	780	1006	555	479	526	1291	1043	–	
1909–1913	470	880	852	514	595	633	1160c	1693c	1540	

a. 1918–1922; b. 1925–1929; c. 1911–1913

Source: Bideleux (1990, p. 204). Bideleux acknowledges that in 1891, at the beginning of the alleged famine, "Grain and potato output were respectively 19.5 percent and 3 percent below the 1881–1890 average [...]. In 1892, grain and potato output were respectively 93 percent and 155 percent of the 1881–1890 average." Furthermore, the changes in livestock holdings between 1888 and 1892 (ibid., Table 12.7, p. 205) indicate that livestock itself constituted a buffer against starvation. The slaughtering of farm animals, especially pigs, in 1888–1892 made coarse grain and meat available for human consumption. On the aggregate and notwithstanding the changes in livestock holdings, 44 million farm animals are said to have survived the "famine years" in the twenty-two provinces affected by the crop failures, an area populated by approximately as many people. Consequently, Bideleux finds it questionable that the people died of starvation while the animals were fed and survived.

and land productivity, the increase in the latter constrained by the scarcity of savings and the institutionally imposed disincentive to innovative investments. Although convincing, such an argument cannot be supported by Bideleux's findings in reference to regional data on Russia. The following estimates, reproduced below from the source, may provide a basis for challenging these assumptions.

The increases in grain yields per hectare between 1883–1887 and 1909–1913 in the communally cultivated northwest region were hardly different from those in the non-communal Baltic region. The most pronounced upturn during this period took place in the communal Ekaterinoslav area (southern region), while in roughly equally communal Jaroslavl (Central Podzols region), the increase per hectare was the lowest. In this context, it must be borne in mind that the data on de facto collectivism in both regions that are formally characterized as having communal holdings are insufficient. The de facto frequency of land redistributions, explained by the technological proprieties of each region, may render the actual degree of communality in land holding different in Ekaterinoslav as compared to Jaroslavl, explaining the differences in the land-productivity data.

The changes in per-hectare yields varied between the non-communal Baltic area and the West region, the increase in the former area being approximately half that in the latter. If so, the assumption of a generally valid inverse relation between the formally communal land-tenure system and land productivity cannot be verified. By implication, the tenure system in itself, as well as the land productivity that it should have brought about, ultimately are dependent variables relative to Veblenian conditions of life such as soil quality, climatic conditions, access to groundwater, and last but not least, the available railroad technology that would influence the region-specific level of agricultural technology, as in differences in the use of fertilizers.

The Gerschenkronian hypothesis of the impoverishment of the rural population due to the communal land-tenure system may be reexamined by testing it in an additional aspect. If collective ownership within the obshchina system indeed resulted in a Malthusian-overpopulated countryside and impeded investment and depressed the standard of living, one would expect per-capita property and output value to be lower, generally, in regions that had higher shares of communally held allotment land or higher shares of households belonging to communes. Below I reproduce data on per-capita property and output on peasant farms by region and the share of communal land tenure in these regions during the post-emancipation era by combining selected estimates from the two last columns of Table 5.11 above with statistics on per-capita regional property holdings in the 1880s (Table 5.12).

Per-capita land and arable land areas, measured in desyatinas (each of which is roughly equal to 1.1 hectare), were largest in the roughly communally cultivated region of the southeast and smallest in the Baltic region, where cultivation took place in privately owned family farms. Per-capita endowments of land and arable land were relatively high even in the southern steppes region, which was 85 percent communally held, and relatively low in the mostly privately held southwest. A possible explanation for the observed positive correlation between per-capita land endowment and degree of communal land tenure in these regions would be that the communes were established in areas of abundance in land but of scarcity in another resource, such as groundwater (Atkinson, 1983, p. 4), rendering communal land cultivation rational. The latter exemplifies the hypothesis that underpins my argument: as the risk to survival mounts, so does mutual dependency on cooperation. Access to a vital resource inspired communal management as a means of containing conflict and ensuring egalitarian survival probability. This type of egalitarianism, I believe, was a material forerunner to the demand for equality before the law (Table 5.13).

Serfdom and Its Relevance

Below is an additional and purely institutional explanation: The regions that had high land-to-labor ratios had also been the core the serf economy in the pre-emancipation era. Following Hoch (1986), one may argue that communal landholding reduced the surveillance costs of the peasantry against the bailiffs of the estate. Thus, the positive correlation between ample land endowment and the high percentage share of communal tenure indicates a strong legacy and viability of the institutions of serfdom.

Considering the perspectives reflected in the matrix above, one might assume that in areas where land was abundant, household elders would be less motivated to coercively retain labor in the villages in excess of the needs of agriculture. With mobility on the rise, the per-capita land endowment of those remaining in the commune would be quite high

Table 5.12 Regional changes in grain yields and degree of communal land tenure, European Russia, 1861–1913 (select regions)

Region/ province	*Regional changes in 1861–1870 to 1891–1900 (seed yields) (%)*	*Δ in yields between 1883–1887 to 1909–1913 (yields/hectare) (%)*	*Communal land as pct. of peasant land allotment (%)*	*Communal tenure as pct. of all peasant households (%)*
North	+22	–	–	–
Archangel	–	+27	96	98
Vologda	–	+17	99	97
Olonets	–	+22	100	97
Northwest	+37	–	–	–
Petersburg	–	*+28*	*99*	*100*
Novgorod	–	*+18*	*100*	*100*
Pskov	–	*+24*	*100*	*100*
Baltic	+11	–	–	–
Courland	–	*+23*	*N*	*N*
Lifland	–	*+16*	*N*	*N*
Estland	–	*+30*	*N*	*N*
West	+38	–	–	–
Vilno	–	+59	1	N
Minsk	–	+67	N	N
Grodno	–	+70	N	N
Kovno	–	+49	N	N
Vitebsk	–	+28	45	53
Mogilev	–	+51	79	81
Smolensk	–	+38	99	99
Central Podzols	+26	–	–	–
Moscow	–	+24	100	100
Vladimir	–	+23	98	97
Kaluga	–	*+26*	*100*	*100*
Kostroma	–	*+26*	*100*	*100*
Nizhni-Novgorod	–	+14	100	100
Tver	–	*+19*	*99*	*99*
Jaroslavl	–	*+5*	*99*	*100*
Left-bank Ukraine	+63	–	–	–
Kharkov	–	*+93*	*94*	*93*
Chernigov	–	+64	54	52

(*continued*)

Table 5.12 (continued)

Region/ province	*Regional changes in 1861–1870 to 1891–1900 (seed yields) (%)*	*Δ in yields between 1883–1887 to 1909–1913 (yields/hectare) (%)*	*Communal land as pct. of peasant land allotment (%)*	*Communal tenure as pct. of all peasant households (%)*
Poltava	–	*+76*	*15*	*18*
Right-bank Ukraine	+54	–	–	–
Kiev	–	+69	7	9
Podolia	–	+79	N	N
Volhynia	–	+70	3	2
South	+76	–	–	–
Bessarabia	–	+54	41	28
Don Oblast'	–	+47	100	100
Ekaterinoslav	–	*+120*	*99*	*99*
Tauride	–	+84	79	92
Kherson	–	+95	87	93
Southeast	+18	–	–	–
Astrahan	–	+24 (+44)*	100	100
Orenburg	–	-18 (+1)*	100	100
Ufa	–	+25 (+48)*	99	98
Total European Russia	+41	+40	83	77

Source: Bideleux, 1990, pp. 212, 213). * Omitting the 1911 harvest (which was worse than that in 1891)
N = negligible

permanently, notwithstanding the population increase.[35] If so, these areas would become overpopulated neither in the Leninist nor in the Malthusian sense. The eastern regions had long belonged to the Russian Empire and the obshchina tradition; in the typical manner of Slavonic tribes, they had not been challenged by other cultivation methods.

[35] This assumption can be only partly and superficially supported by data that imply the generally increasing mobility of labor. Whether the migration of labor *from* those regions ever occurred would depend on local labor demand, the possibility of hiring seasonal labor, the opportunity to earn an income outside the region, the techniques employed and the organization of production, and the distribution of duties between men and women. Importantly, only 5 percent of all agricultural labor in 1900 was hired labor (Bideleux, 1990), implying that migration streams headed toward peripheral regions where land was abundant or, alternatively, toward urban industrial centers. This assumption is supported by information on the colonization of the southern steppes and rural–urban migration, summarized above.

Table 5.13 Per-capita property and per-capita output on peasant farms, by region, European Russia, 1880s and degree of communal land tenure, European Russia 1861–1913

Property, c. 1890 value of output, 1883–1887 Rubles per an. Com. L.T.

	Land (des.)	*Arable (des.)*	*Cattle (head)*	*Grain*	*Fruit and veg.*	*Livestock prod.*	*Industries*	*Misc.*	*Total*	*Grain% of total*	*Com.t% of allt.*	*Com.t% of peas.h*
Southern steppe	2.95	1.53	0.84	24.49	4.65	12.60	5.20	18.71	65.65	37	84	85
South West	*1.07*	*0.74*	*0.71*	*13.59*	*4.72*	*10.75*	*10.40*	*12.43*	*51.89*	*26*	*16*	*16*
Centr.Chern.	1.35	1.00	0.52	17.26	3.58	7.90	9.55	12.69	50.98	34	75	78
South East	*3.17*	*1.74*	*0.95*	*20.44*	*1.45*	*14.35*	*5.50*	*16.12*	*57.86*	*35*	*98*	*99*
West	1.66	0.87	0.68	16.04	2.00	10.30	10.03	15.92	54.29	30	41	42
Semi Ind.	1.30	0.89	0.40	17.02	1.56	6.00	11.05	14.65	50.28	34	95	96
East	2.06	1.29	0.67	17.48	1.24	10.05	10.20	15.21	54.18	32	100	100
Baltic	*1.77*	*0.54*	*0.50*	*18.64*	*1.20*	*7.50*	*11.20*	*17.65*	*56.19*	*33*	*0*	*0*
Indust	*1.96*	*0.92*	*0.55*	*19.86*	*1.85*	*8.21*	*14.00*	*17.54*	*61.46*	*32*	*99*	*99*
Cap. Gub.	1.62	0.70	0.31	19.01	2.24	4.65	17.60	16.46	59.96	32	100	100
North	2.68	0.70	0.70	16.33	1.96	10.50	10.20	19.89	58.88	28	99	98
Eur. Russia	1.96	1.10	–	18.12	2.63	9.99	9.47	15.42	55.63	33	73	74

Source: Bideleux (1990, pp. 212–214). The last two columns, averaging the percentage shares of communal land tenure for each region, are calculated from the total of the table in Bideleux (1990, pp. 212–213). The regions are available in original form in Bideleux 214. Example: North: Novgorod, Olonets—names of averaged regions

In the Central Chernozem (Central Black Soil) region, where the communally held household share was somewhat lower than that in the South East region, the per-capita land endowment was less than half as large as in the latter region and per-capita arable land was 0.74 desyatinas smaller. Black soil is generally considered more fertile than other soil and was probably in greater demand for this reason. Therefore, this region could have become overpopulated in both the Malthusian and the Leninist senses. Although the total ruble value of output per capita and per year was considerably lower there than in the whole of European Russia, indicating poverty, the yield-per-hectare data for the region (defined as in Tables 5–12) indicate that land productivity kept increasing between 1883–1887 and 1909–1913, rendering the disincentive to innovative investment and the long-term impoverishment hypothesis debatable. Total output value per capita, measured in rubles per year, was highest in the southern steppes, where roughly 85 percent of households belonged to communes, and high in the industrial region, where 99 percent of households belonged to communes. The same estimate in the mostly non-communally held Southwestern region (where 84 percent of households produced in privately owned farms) was below that for European Russia as a whole. Taking the per-capita land endowment and the total per-capita and per-year value of output into consideration, an interesting observation may be made: restricted arable land or land endowment does not necessarily imply that the region would be impoverished.

For example, the communally held Capital Gubernia region attained the highest per-capita and per-year industrial output values in the 1880s—a decade before the great spurt augmented the total per-capita value of the region's output—exceeding the estimate for European Russia. Moreover, only 33 percent of total per-capita annual output value in the European part of the empire traced to grain production. Grain exports in 1892–1913, a period that overlapped the industrialization spurts, constituted 13.5 percent of total grain production on average.[36] If one assumes that the share of the total annual per-capita output value attributed to grain production did not change much between the 1880s and 1892–1913, one may estimate the per-capita output value of grain exports at 4.46 percent, hardly worthy of the conceited description of severely impoverishing " "hunger exports."

If labor had been truly free to choose between industrial and agricultural production (the latter including peripheral areas that had abundant land, the landless "rural proletariat" constituting only 5 percent of the rural labor force) and assuming that (1) migration streams generally would not tend toward lower per-capita income and (2) the wage in urban industry would equal the value of marginal product of labor, then the wage could not fall below the value of income of an additional adult in agriculture. Since migration from the rural to the urban sector did take place, the agricultural sector could not have been severely overpopulated in the Leninist sense. Whether the newly established industrial sector could have absorbed more labor and maintain rising productivity is moot.

.Gregory, the main source for the counterargument to Gerschenkron's emphasis on an institutionalized mobility barrier as the reason for the rural crisis, clearly argues that the Tsarist economy performed fairly well by

[36] Bideleux (1990, p. 215), average percentage share calculated from Table 12.12.

international standards, displaying long-term growth potential *despite* the formal impediments imposed upon it by the institutionalized collective ownership that prevailed in much of the rural sector and low per-capita income, relative to other countries, due to population increase.

An additional aspect, taken into account below (Chap. 6), is the changing properties of the obshchina over time against the background of Russia's specific climatic conditions and available technology. Following Gerschenkron's conception which corresponds to the view of the Westernizer Boris Chicherin (1828–1904), the obshchina was the product of Tsarist state coercion rather than what the Slavophiles would call as an organic unit and what NIE would characterize as a mutual-insurance and risk-diversification unit.[37] The latter was embedded in an increasingly voluntary cooperative practice that originated in chosen adherence to custom by individual households on the basis of the long-term rational calculus on which the village commune was constituted (Vanberg, 1994, c55).

Conclusions

The ostensible relative decline in living standards among most of the rural population in 1860–1905 (intensified by the 1890 industrialization) remains unsupported. The urban labor force could not have been severely exploited materially and thus driven to taking up arms in the 1905 upheaval. Relative to the serfdom era, material equity—defined in this context as per-capita access to means of subsistence—had been improving, the rural sector included, despite the increase in population. The discrepancy between Gerschenkron's understandings of the effects of the communal-village system and .Gregory's grasp of the same suggests weak verification of Gerschenkron's deduction from the direction of formal legal restrictions and strong verification of the deduction from the perspective of Neoclassical rationalism. The deduction from Gerschenkron in tandem with railroads construction historically legitimized the emphasis on substitution of personalized hierarchies of coercion embedded in formal legal structures for the rationalist-individualist utility maximizing

[37] See Moon (1999, p. 214), Mironov (2000, p. 297), and Kingston-Mann (1991, p. 45), on compensation for individual households' land investments at times of repartitioning that recognized aspects of individual property rights in land. On the flexibility of the Russian village commune, see Nafziger (2006), Summary.

calculus that had actually been taking place within the peasant constituency during the post-emancipation era. Consequently, .Gregory's application of Neoclassical theory to the historical facts acquires higher explanatory value. The village commune structure inherited from the serfdom era, in which assemblies of elders interacting with state bureaucracy replaces the function of the landed gentry (*pomeshchik*) in managing land and maintaining order, underwent a metamorphosis that resulted in the granting of de facto hereditary household use rights in land. In Chap. 8, it will be my dual task to design a theoretical framework that will allow the reader to conceptualize this transition and to dwell on the role of the primary force behind the industrialization, the railroad technology. My thesis does not disprove Gerschenkron's analysis. On the contrary, it demonstrates its validity, in terms of the continuity of the aspiration to control, like the Imperator (Peter I), of the monolithic Communist Party.[38] I do propose, however, that the typology of the Gerschenkronian school overlooks the micro-level changes that took place in the course of the industrialization process. Nafziger (2006) shows that the village commune was a more flexible structure than the Gerschenkronians assume. The explanation for this flexibility, I propose, lies in the interaction of the landholding system with the railroad technology. With reference to Chap. 3 and in Chaps. 4, 5, 6, through 11 below, I will investigate the structure of state expenditure to verify the assumption about the atrophying of hierarchical social structures and the strengthening of egalitarian (horizontal) ones. Did the industrialization expand the scope within which individualistic identities and voluntary associations could form?

In sum, land productivity increased during the post-emancipation era and the innovations introduced in 1860–1913 deserve the credit. Thus, the upturn in land productivity was the economic result of increases in knowledge combined with growing investment in agricultural equipment, intensified by the industrialization spurt of the 1890s. The escalating productivity of agriculture was also manifested in rising grain and potato output per inhabitant and per year in 1892–1913, a period also noted for growing labor mobility. The migration oriented itself from industrial

[38] Stalin's progress from 1928 onward should be deflated by its costs in socioeconomic human capital and suffering via the coercive (*nassilstvennyj*) method of enhancing resource allocation in Russia (Anisimov, 1993).

centers to peripheral regions, the latter providing additional land endowment. To determine whether the agricultural sector was overpopulated in the Leninist sense by international comparison, I reexamined the annual grain yields of European and major world producers in 1860–1913 and found increases in the productivity of Russian land, agricultural output per inhabitant (implying an increase in labor productivity), and per-capita income in agriculture. In this context, it is of interest to emphasize the 5 percent annual growth rate of industrial output during the period between the emancipation and the year preceding World War I[39] and the migration wave. All factors considered, I believe I have refuted the assumptions of severe impoverishment and Malthusian overpopulation in the Russian countryside.

References

Anisimov, V. E. (1989). *Vremja Petrovskich reform*. Lenizdat.

Anisimov. (1993). *The Reforms of Peter the Great -Progress through coercion in Russia*. M E Sharpe.

Archer, M. (1995). *Realist social theory: The morphogenetic approach*. Chapter presented at the 6th International Workshop on Institutional Economics, The University of Hertfordshire.

Ascher, A. (1988). *The Revolution of 1905. Part I Russia in Disserray*. Stanford UP.

Ascher, A. (2001). *P.A. Stolypin: The search for stability in late imperial Russia*. Stanford University Press.

Atack, J., Bateman, I. A., Haines, F., & Margo, M. (2010). Did railroads induce or follow economic growth? Urbanization and population growth in the American Midwest 1850–1960. *Social Science History, 34*(2, June). 171–197.

Atkinson, D. (1983). *The end of the Russian land commune 1905–1930*. Stanford University Press.

Barzel, Y. (2002). *The theory of the State -economic rights, legal rights, and the scope of state*. Cambridge UP.

Bates, R. (1989). *Beyond the miracle of the market: The political economy of agrarian development in Kenya*. Cambridge University Press.

Bideleux, R. (1990). Agricultural advance under the Russian village commune system. In R. Bartlett (Ed.), *Land commune and peasant community in Russia:*

[39] Gregory (1982, p. 133, Table 6.3).

Communal forms in Imperial and early Soviet society. Macmillan in Association with the School of Slavonic and East European Studies.

Blum, J. (1961). *Lord and peasant in Russia from the ninth to the nineteenth century*. Princeton University Press.

Boserup, E. (1965). *The conditions of agricultural growth: The economics of agrarian change under population pressure*. Allen & Unwin.

Boyer, R., & Orlean, A. (1993). How do conventions evolve? In U. Witt (Ed.), *Evolution in markets and institutions*. Physica-Vlg.

Burds, J. (1998). *Peasant dreams and market politics: Labor migration and the Russian village 1861–1905*. University of Pittsburgh Press.

Chayanov, A. V. (1930) *The theory of peasant economy with new introduction by Theodor Shanin*. University of Wisconsin. UP.

Dubrovskij, S. M. (1963). *Stolypinskaya zemel'naya reforma*. Iz istorii sel'skogo khozyaistva i krest'yanstva Rossii v nachale XX veka.

Eggertsson, T. (1990). *Economic behavior and institutions*. Cambridge University Press.

Engelgardt, P. N. (1993). In C. Frierson (Trans. and Ed.), *Aleksandr Nikolaevich Engelgardt's letters from the country, 1872–1887*. Oxford University Press.

Frank, S. (1999). *Crime, cultural conflict and justice in rural Russia 1856–1914*. University of California Press.

Frierson, C. A. (1993). *Peasant Icons-Representations of Rural People in Late 19th Century Russia*. Oxford University Press.

Gatrell, P. (1994). *Government, industry and rearmament in Russia, 1900–1914: The last argument of tsarism*. Cambridge University Press.

Gerschenkron, A. (1962). *Economic backwardness in historical perspective*. The Belknap Press of Harvard University Press.

Gerschenkron, A. (1968). *Continuity in history and other essays*. The Belknap Press of Harvard University Press.

Gintis, H. (2009). *The bounds of reason: Game theory and the unification of the behavioral sciences*. Princeton University Press.

Goldhagen, D. J. (1996). *Hitler's willing executioners. Ordinary Germans and the Holocaust*. Little Brown and Company.

Gregory, P. R. (1982). *Russian national income 1885–1913*. Cambridge University Press.

Gregory, P. R. (1994). *Before command. An economic history of Russia from emancipation to the first five-year plan*. Princeton University Press.

Hesse, G. (1993). Land use systems and property rights. Evolutionary versus institutional economics. In U. Witt (Ed.), *Evolution in markets and institutions*. Physica-Vlg.

Hoch, S. (1986). *Serfdom and social control in Russia. Petrovskoe, a village in Tambov*. University of Chicago Press.

Hodgson, G. M. (2004). What are institutions? From orders to organizations. Essay presented at the 6th International Workshop on Institutional Economics, University of Hertfordshire.

Johnson, R. (1979). *Peasant and proletarian: The working class of Moscow in the late nineteenth century*. Leicester University Press.

Kahan, A. (1985). *The plow, the hammer and the knout: An economic history of eighteenth-century Russia*. University of Chicago Press.

Kahan, A. (1989). In R. Weiss (Ed.), *Russian economic history: The nineteenth century*. University of Chicago Press.

Keren, M. (1992). The socialist firm, the value of capital and transition to capitalism. In M. Keren & G. Ofer (Eds.), *Trials of transition: Economic reform in the former communist bloc*. Westview Press.

Kingston-Mann, E. (1991). Peasant communes and economic innovation: A preliminary inquiry. In E. Kingston-Mann, T. Mixter, & J. Burds (Eds.), *Peasant economy culture and politics of European Russia*. Princeton University Press.

Leonard, C. S. (1990). Landlords and the mir: Transaction costs and economic development in pre-emancipation Russia (Iaroslav Gubernia). In R. Bartlett (Ed.), *Land commune and peasant community in Russia: Communal forms in imperial and early Soviet society*. Macmillan in Association with the School of Slavonic and East European Studies.

Loewe, H. D. (1990). Differentiation in Russian peasant society: Causes and trends, 1880–1905. In R. Bartlett (Ed.), *Land commune and peasant community in Russia: Communal forms in imperial and early Soviet society*. Macmillan in Association with the School of Slavonic and East European Studies.

Ma, D. (2006). Law and commerce in traditional China. An institutional perspective on the "Great Divergence." Seminar Paper, Department of Economic History, Lund University.

Migdal, J. (1988). *Strong societies and weak states. State–society relations and state capabilities in the Third World*. Princeton University Press.

Mironov, B. N. (2000). *A social history of imperial Russia, 1700–1917*. Vol. I. Westview Press.

Moon, D. (1999) *The Russian peasantry 1600–1930. The world the peasants made*. Longman.

Nafziger, S. (2006). Communal institutions, resource allocation, and Russian economic development. Unpublished doctoral dissertation, summary. Yale University.

Nafziger, S. (2010). Peasant communes and factor markets in late-nineteenth-century Russia. *Explorations in Economic History, 47*(4), 381–402.

North, D. C. (1973). *Västerlandets Uppgång*. SNS.

North, D. C. (1990). *Institutions, institutional change and economic performance*. Cambridge University Press.

North, D. C. (1993). Nobel Lecture 1993.

North, D. C. (2005). *Understanding the process of economic change*. Princeton University Press.

Ofer, G., & Vinokur, A. (1992). *The Soviet household under the old regime: Economic conditions and behavior in the 1970*. Cambridge UP.

Owen, T. (1995). *Russian corporate capitalism from Peter the Great to perestroika*. Oxford University Press.

Pallot, J., & Nefedova, T. (2007). *Russia's unknown agriculture: Household production in post socialist rural Russia*. Oxford UP.

Petrovich, M. B. (1968). The peasant in nineteenth century historiography. In W. Vucinich (Ed.), *The peasant in nineteenth-century Russia*. Stanford University Press.

Poznanski, K. (1992). "*Property Right Perspective on Evolution of Communist-Type Economies*". In Poznanski K 1992 ed. Constructing Capitalism - The Re-Emergence of Civil Society and Liberal Economy on Post Communist World. Westwiev Press.

Sheshinski, E. (2010). *Limits in individual choice*. The Hebrew University of Jerusalem.

Simms, Y. J. (1977). The crisis in the Russian agriculture at the end of the nineteenth century: A different view. *Slavic Review, 36*(3), 377–398.

Sztern, S. (1994). Det socioekonomiska systemets institutionella desintegration och omvandling Sovjetunionen/Ryssland. Unpublished candidate paper. Lund University, Department of Economic History.

Tian-Shanskaya, O. S. (1863–1906) Ed. by Ransel, D. L. (1993). *Village life in late tsarist Russia*. Indiana UP.

Treadgold, D. W. (1968). The peasant and religion. In W. S. Vucinich (Ed.), *The peasant in nineteenth-century Russia*. Stanford University Press.

Vanberg, V. (1994). *Rules and choice in economics*. Routledge.

Veblen, T. (1931). *The theory of the leisure class*. Viking.

Volyn. (1970). *A Century of Russian Agriculture from Alexander II to Khrushchev*. Harvard UP.

Witt, U. (1993). *Evolution in markets and institutions*. Physica-Verlag.

Worobec, C. D. (1995). *Peasant Russia family and community in the post-emancipation period*. Northern Illinois University Press.

Worobec, C. D. (2001). *Possessed women, witches, and demons in imperial Russia*. Northern Illinois University Press.

CHAPTER 6

The Railroads and the Metamorphoses of the *Mir*: Westernizer and Slavophile Conceptions Revisited

The NIE/AEI model suggests complementarity between the Slavophile and Westernizers' conception of the commune. The founder of the latter school, Boris Chicherin (1828–1904), emphasized the nineteenth-century bureaucratic origins of this institution. I suggest that the evolutionary advantage of the ever-present kinship-based organic collectivism conceived by the Slavophile school was transformed as it integrated into the Tsarist bureaucracy with its internalization of risk to subsistence (Mironov, 2000, p. 328). In this process, the kinship character of the *zadruga* commune "translated" (Boyer & Orlean, 1993, p. 22; Blum, 1961) into the structure of the skills and trades cooperative, the territorial *verv-artel* (Troyat, 1961, p. 98), and the territorial verv -*obshchina* (Blum, 1961). The latter, within the AEI framework, are assumed to have structured and mobilized migrating *zemliachestva* (landsman networks) that conduce toward the urbanization process (Johnson, 1979, p. 76). The voluntary formation of "institutionalized commitment" (Greif, 2006, p. 101) units of these kinds, legally recognized by the Tsarist bureaucracy, presented the autocracy with a "credible threat" from below that, paradoxically, challenged and weakened state-imposed hierarchical collectivism (Barzel, 2002). The artel ethos evolved endogenously into forerunners of labor unions. Below I propose that the Tsarist Russian "commitment devices" were of rural and kinship origin rather than of Marxian class rootedness.

In this chapter, I fit the Russian peasant custom and its change into a paradigm of developmental stages. According to the paradigm, general

S. Sztern, *Russia on the Move*, Studies in Economic Transition, https://doi.org/10.1007/978-3-030-89285-2_6

institutional conditions will determine whether a peasant will be a rational maximizer of utility—in this case, a minimizer of the risk of going under in a premodern economy (Shanin, 1985, Vol. 1, xi; Scott, 1976, p. 4)—or an obedient worshipper of patriarchal authority that embodies the tacit knowledge reservoir (Hodgson, 1999, p. 247; Rizello, 1999, p. 33, in reference to Hayek 1967) of previous generations, as encapsulated in institutions. The discussion that follows links the prevailing level of Tsarist peasant collectivism and authority obedience to the level of industrialization—and institutional modernization—in Russian society at large.

Scott (1976), in his Neoclassical utility maximization assumption, presupposes individual access to information that allows choice. Such an assumption is contingent upon the evolved cognitive spectra of action of the individual peasant vis-à-vis the household, the commune, and the community. My analysis begins prior to the Tsarist industrialization, at the advent of the railroads during serfdom. Inspired by Martens (2004), I select the level of peasant individual cognitive mastery over his physical and the natural environment (North, 2005, p. 87) as an exogenous explanatory variable. I identify and define the developmental stages by the level of mutual dependency and dependency on the experience and authority of the elder—the superior on the hierarchy—as the source of information that allows the peasant to choose among Evolutionary Stable Strategies of Survival.

Our peasant is born into an environment structured by prior custom, in which ceremonial and historical matter-of-fact knowledge is accumulated by and stored in inherited institutions that operate under patriarchal authority. Peasant learning entails the worship and obedience of the patriarchal sources of wisdom. Such knowledge is challenged when the peasant acquires literacy and other skills, as he may according to our analysis by using the railroads. Industrialization, with railroad construction at its core, elevated the Russian peasantry to a novel and unprecedented developmental stage of cognitive mastery of its environment. As the advent of railroads allowed individuals to diversify their existential risks, the level of mutual and hierarchical dependence declined. The emerging choice allowed peasants to transition to individualism and rationalism in a developmental stage congruent with modernization.

Was it the delay in Russia's industrialization relative to its European counterparts—a matter explained by the geographical dispersion of its natural resources, which made its modernization dependent on railroad construction (Baykov, 1954, p. 143)—to blame or to be credited for the greater persistence of peasant collectivism in that country than elsewhere?

Although Gerschenkron emphasizes Russia's geopolitical vulnerability rather than the geographical dispersion of its production factors across the imperial territory, such a dispersion could have affected the Tsarist government's perception of strategic comparative disadvantages, making railroad construction imperative for a strategic purpose in addition to the debacle that it had experienced in the Crimean War. This interpretation is consistent with Gerschenkron's theory of relative backwardness, discussed in previous chapters. As stated in Chap. 4, state activity in the Russian case promoted but also impeded the transition to modernity.

I argue that Russia's techno-economic backwardness is traced to its institutional backwardness and not the other way around. To establish the direction of causality, I need to address the following questions:

- Was Russia's state-structured peasant collectivism, stipulated by the autocracy with its historical accommodation of the landed gentry and its enforcement of the reduction of its surveillance costs (Hoch, 1986; North, 1990), partly responsible for the empire's slow transition to modernity in the nineteenth century, as Gerschenkron (1962, 1968) proposes?
- To what extent and from what time perspective do relative resource scarcities (North, 1973, p. 29) matter in determining a population's "habits of thought" (Veblen, 1931, p. 188) and the institutional structures that grow atop them?
- In the Russian case, did the "double weight of the past" (Hodgson, 2004, p. 168, quoting Veblen) of the informal institutions (North, 1990, p. 64), inherited from the serfdom era, matter in determining the pace of the nineteenth-century transition to modernity?
- What impact did these institutions have on nineteenth-century peasant custom?

To investigate these points, in this chapter I apply the integrated NIE/AEI framework set forth in Chap. 3 and propose (in the condensed diachronic flow chart below) that serfdom in the 1597–1861 period was reinforced and solidified in the *obshchina*, the village commune (Mironov, 2000, p. 297; North, 1990, p. 78). This institutional mechanism not only sowed the seeds of its own eradication but also, by interacting with state-led spurts of industrialization, created relatively persistent long-term vehicles for the destruction of totalitarian, autocratic governance in Russia, even as it atrophied in so doing. In effect, the January 9, 1905, petition to the Tsar, expressing peasant demands for universal suffrage, equality before the law, and a constitution, foreshadowed the end of the patrimonial state and announced the dawn of gradually increasing peasant individualism. The latter process may be inferred, however indirectly and inconclusively, from the changing images of the peasant in the ranks of the Russian intelligentsia (Frierson, 1993, pp. 76, 151). Viewed from this perspective, Stolypin's land reform in 1906 should be seen as the ex-post codification of the ongoing voluntary individualization of landholding rights (Klimin, 2002, p. 11, contrary to Pallot's proposal (1999, p. 159) during and due to the industrialization spurts in 1890 and 1907 (Gerschenkron, 1962, p. 124).

Marx

Structure

Karl Marx (1859)

"It is not the consciousness of men that determines their being, but, on the contrary, their social being that determines their consciousness."

Thus, the structure—the relations of production on which the legal structures of societies rest—is the source of human consciousness and agency: reconstitutive downward causation-relative to the extreme point.

The Interactionists—the Critical Realist School

Remarks by Hodgson (2004 , 2007), Hodgson and Knudsen (2005)), Lawson (1997)), and Archer (1995).

(*continued*)

American Evolutionary Institutionalism (Critical Realism)
Veblen (1931)), Hodgson (2004)) and Lawson (1997)).
Agency and structure interact. However, the relative explanatory weight is vested in structure—a generative causal mechanism, adapted to the conditions of life, that shapes individuals' habits of thought.
NIE (North, 1973, 1981, 1990, 2005)
Individual and hedonistic calculus of relative prices/opportunity costs, motivating interaction between the utility-maximizing Homo Economicus as the source of structure and its longitudinal change.
NIE—methodological individualism
Sztern: American Evolutionary Institutionalism points *relatively* to "reconstitutive downward causation" (Hodgson, 2004) while NIE points *relatively* to "upward causation" (ibid.); the theories are seen as having complementary elements.
Applications in this chapter:
This quartile emphasizes the synergy of my theoretical NIE/AEI combination.
Neoclassical Economics Agency
Neoclassical Economics
Scott (1976)
Institutions, technology, and transaction costs are exogenous to the model.
Methodological individualism: reconstitutive upward causation—relative to the extreme point.
In subsistence economies, the individual minimizes his/her risk of going under.
The "moral economy of the peasant" (Scott, 1976) is mutual insurance against the risk of going under, based on the individual's hedonistic calculus.

Collectivism versus Individualism

Before proceeding, I think it useful to define collectivism versus individualism for the purpose of this discourse. In general, the application of an exclusionary New Institutional Economics (NIE) perspective to explain a consensual or commonly pursued action is evidence of ongoing individualism rather than of collectivism, because the rational utility-maximizing calculus under the theoretical assumptions of NIE is carried out on an individual basis.

In the analysis below, an action taken collectively is seen as emanating from collective intentionality—"we-attitudes" that are shared—and must therefore be understood as social (Tuomela, 2002, pp. 2, 18, 22). Thus, collective action in this discourse is tantamount to social action. As my aim in this chapter is to explain a social action, however, below I view elements of collective action motivated by "I-intentionality" (Tuomela 2) as necessary but insufficient aspects of social action.

The concept of "collectivism" in this chapter implies neither an irrational collectivist "mentality" on the part of the Russian peasant nor the homogeneous continuity of collectivism in Russia (Ofer, personal communication 1997), as Western scholars often conceptualize it. By combining NIE and AEI, the discourse seeks to explain the changing degrees and quality of collectivism over time in view of changing conditions of life (Veblen, 1931, p. 188).[1] that encapsulate changing relative scarcities (North, 1973, p. 29).

I suggest that the Russian peasant calculated the maximum probability of his survival in both the long (Vanberg, 1994, p. 55) and the short terms. Ultimately, the discussion that follows will portray him as increasingly rational and individualistic within the limits of individual preferences that are shaped and molded by the institutional structure, namely, the "reconstitutive downward causation" process delineated by Hodgson (2004, p. 105). By including AEI in the model, I focus attention on this process.

By applying the combined model, I perceive the rational utility-maximizing calculus and its complement, the calculus that minimizes the risk of going under (Scott, 1976, p. 4), as implemented with growing frequency within the structural boundaries of an individual's birth (Hodgson, 2004, p. 10).[2] These boundaries affect the pace of marginal adjustment of prevalent "habits of thought" (Veblen, 1931, p. 188; North, 1981, p. 9; Archer, 1995, pp. 76, 77)[3] to changes in riskiness, relative opportunity costs or, in Veblenian parlance; "conditions of life."

[1] The term "environment" used in the source implies conditions of life.

[2] Introducing reconstitutive downward causation, Hodgson implies the temporal priority of structures over any given individual).

[3] Initial structural conditions determine the pace of adaptation.

Compulsory versus Voluntary Collectivism: Pre-Modern Risk Insurance

Seen through the prism of Western scholarship, Russian historical institutions are burdened with a legacy of collectivism. Explaining this view of the matter is to additionally clarify the foregoing cluster of theories while focusing on two distinguishable types of collectivism, between which I propose that the Tsarist Russian village commune fluctuated in metamorphosis as it emerged from serfdom during the nineteenth century. The common denominator of these types of collectivism is risk insurance through sharing while participating in the redivision of the use of, and proprietary rights to, assets within the extended family and the obshchina structure.[4] The dimension that distinguishes among these types answers the question about the origins of the impulse that entails subconscious imitation of collectivist sharing structured by a hierarchy of authority,[5] versus a rationalist decision in the neoclassical sense, that is, an independent or strategic one (Scott, 1976, p. 4; Rizello, 1999, pp. 4, 5), to share as a way to mitigate the individual household's risk. I denote these types as vertical-hierarchical and the horizontal-egalitarian types of collectivist and cooperative (respectively) risk management. This distinction is analogous to the Hayekian distinction between "cosmos" and "taxis" or Polanyi's distinction between the monocentric and the polycentric (Rizello, 1999, p. 33) in this paradigm.

In the premodern historical environment, the surplus allocation for the upkeep of patriarchs in accordance with the community norms of respect (Mironov, 2000, p. 286) is conceived in my model as a risk-insurance premium (North, 1981, p. 11). Retired patriarchs derived their income from those less endowed with historical experience and knowledge in handling the new-generation labor teams that dealt with agricultural crises (Hoch,

[4] The NIE explanation that links cooperation and the formation of premodern collectives to risk insurance in precarious environments, noted for high probability of crop failure, is provided by Eggertsson (1990, pp. 303, 304). Eggertsson does not distinguish among types of collectivism subject to the history-specific scope of rationalist choice and decision-making (Moon, 1999, p. 216). On the need to explain rationalist decision-making, see Hodgson (2001, p. 23, 2004, pp. 132, 133).

[5] See Rizello (1999, p. 30) and Hoch (1986, p. 117) in reference to egalitarian redistribution imposed by landlords.

1986, p. 105). The example of strategies such as "crust seeking,"[6] advised by the elderly, is anecdotally presented below.[7] Such a vertical-hierarchical collectivism is characterized by compliance to authority as risk insurance amid precarious, life-threatening uncertainty—an environment characterized by low predictability (Lawson, 1997, pp. 181, 182, in reference to Giddens). Eighteenth- and early nineteenth-century Russian agriculture was such an environment (Chubarov, 2001, p. 4). I assume that the reservoir of life-preserving tacit knowledge (Hodgson, 1999, p. 247) is asymmetrically distributed between ruler and subjects (Hodgson, 2004, p. 105).[8] In my history-specific model, the knowledge used to manage the risk of calamity is distributed between the elder structure, led by the chieftain in a *zadruga*, the patriarch in an extended family, the landlord, and the enserfed verv (Petrovich, 1968), after emancipation, the bureaucratized assembly of elders. Ultimately, the risk-mitigating knowledge is asymmetrically ascribed to the Tsar as an institution, meaning a personally anointed prophetic mediator between God and human (de Madariaga, 1998, pp. 43, 79; Blum, 1961, p. 25; Hoch, 1986, p. 117; Mironov, 2000, p. 328, inspired by Raeff 1984, pp. 98, 103, 107). An evolutionary stable projection (Boyer & Orlean, 1993, p. 22) of divine wisdom—the accumulated experience of generations (Bakunin, 1970, p. 24; Hodgson, 2004, p. 136)—was laid upon this structure. For the subconscious mitigation of their risk, the profane subjects, the peasantry, complied and obeyed the patriarch, concurrently sustaining him.

I suggest that peasant compliance, ultimately manifested in the relative absence of revolt against the authority of the ruler as such (Pipes, 1995, pp. 155, 156),[9] is explained by cognitive economics, related to anxiety economics (Martens, 2004, p. 104; Lawson, 1997, pp. 181, 182), among the relatively less informed strata—the members of the peasant household.

[6] See Mironov (2000, Vol. 1, p. 324) Engelgardt (1993, p. 28) in reference to redistributive famine relief.

[7] For additional examples, see Hoch (1986, p. 33) on healing, 37–38 on landlord credit, and 64 on agricultural hazards.

[8] In the above model, the person of the ruler is assumed to be a repository of [past] knowledge"—a personalized institution who embodies the historical experiences of the collective. The distribution of knowledge, encapsulated in his experience between the authority of the ruler-patriarch and the profane peasant subjects in my history-specific model, will perforce be asymmetrical (Martens, 2004, pp. 4, 51, 104).

[9] The Pugachev revolt of 1773 was characterized by veneration of the true Tsar, Peter III, as a mobilizing force, and challenged the perceived imposter to the throne rather than rejecting Tsarist authority per se.

Through my history-specific prism, I propose that the population increase in eighteenth-century Russia (Kahan, 1985, p. 8) should be explained by the insurance that the commune provided serfs against the effects of calamities such as climatic catastrophes, crop failures, and epidemics. Aid under conditions of calamity was coordinated and consolidated by historical agricultural experience within the coercively collectivist patriarchal elder structures of the commune. These institutions symbiotically shared their managing and risk-mitigating powers with the bailiffs of the estate, by which I mean the institution of the landlord (Hoch, 1986, pp. 117, 118). Evidence of such a process may be found in the reliance on the landlord as the lender of last resort in the initial post-emancipation decades, subject to reconstitutive downwards causation (Engelgardt, 1993, in Frierson 1993, p. 39; Hodgson, 2004, p. 105).

In my simplified model below (strongly inspired by Hesse, 1993, pp. 47–61), I assume the concurrence of three processes in response to population growth: decline in Ricardian-marginal productivity of land and labor factors, necessitating conquest of and migration to newly colonized regions (conforming to the extensive growth formula) and a process encapsulated in the Boserupian (1965) urge to innovate and implement novel technology for the intensification of resource use. The latter process stimulates proto-industrialization and industrialization in response to a population increase.

Although conquest may intensify obedience to authority, the urge to migrate and implement novel technology renders the knowledge reservoir vested in the patriarchal authority, rooted in historical experience, obsolete and challengeable by the knowledge horizontally acquired by heads of successively smaller kinship units, foretelling the dissolution of the extended family. Through Veblenian idle curiosity and Hayekian learning-by-doing, discontinuous strategies of knowledge acquisition adapt to novel conditions of life until atrophy besets the patriarchal capacity to insure against the hazards of calamities in an environment of low probability of prediction.

I suggest that in tandem with population growth—which, in accordance with Boserupian predictions, stimulates the application of novel technology—the emerging choice among multiple strategies brought about a relative increase in voluntary rationalist cooperation (Sheshinski, 2010, p. 3; Gintis, 2009, pp. 1, 2) and a corresponding decline in compliance with authority as a risk-insurance strategy. In the course of this process, serfdom would lose its raison d'être.

Thus, in tandem with population growth, technological progress (specifically in the context of railroads), interacting with the transition to anonymous trade in integrated and specialized commodity markets (Martens, 2004, pp. 104, 105, 193; Metzer, 1972, p. 82; Smith, 1998, p. 19), allowed boundedly rational cooperative contracts to be concluded among units that were increasingly endowed with material and intellectual property rights, such as crafts skills.

While the Veblenian, Hodgsonian, and Lawsonian explanatory frameworks are the most effective up to the bounded rationality equilibrium point, I deem it legitimate to resort to an NIE rationalist cost-benefit analysis that concerns risk reduction through horizontal cooperation. I undertake this analysis with a modification suggested by Ostrom (1990, p. 37) that establishes a context-specific conception of "boundedly rational" choice. According to this modification, "internal norms," in the late Tsarist Russian case, convey intergenerational "inequality aversion" including the unequal exposure to risk and "strong reciprocity" preconditioned by the ethical predisposition of Greek Orthodoxy/Old Believers and other sects to "conditional altruist cooperation" (Gintis, 2009, p. 56) due to the historical habit of resource redivision (Veblen, 1931, p. 188). Thus, applying my NIE/AEI combination to the case of the Tsarist Russian historical experience, I find that the reservoir of tacit knowledge,[10] encapsulated in "internal norms," passes the test of equilibrium substitution for the institution of personalized authority that existed in the serfdom era, while leaving room for voluntary cooperation—either fully horizontal or ceding a varying share of the risk-handling capacity to a rationally selected entrepreneur (Ostrom, 1990, p. 40; Coase, 1937).

Cooperation and Mutual Assistance through Peasant Collectivism

Khozhdenie v Kusochki—"Crust-Seeking"

Alexandr Nikolaevich Engelgardt's *Letters from the Country, 1872–1887* (1993) is an invaluable primary source on peasant customs in the decade preceding the industrialization spurts of 1890 and 1907 (Sztern, 1997). Living among peasants during his political exile (Engelgardt, 1993, p. 3) at his landed-gentry estate in Batishchevo (Smolensk Province), Engelgardt

[10] See Hodgson (1999, p. 247), for the competence-based theory of the firm, facilitating the integration of contractual conceptions.

observed the practice of redistributing baked bread at times of harvest failure or to indigent households:

> *On my place, the old woman simply gives out [to fellow peasants who temporarily run out of bread and or seed crop, becoming vulnerable to famine] "crusts" in the dining hall, just as crusts are given out in every peasant household where there is bread—as long as a peasant has his own grain or grain he has bought, he will give out crusts to the last loaf. I did not offer any instructions, I did not know anything about these crusts. The old woman herself decided that "we" must give out crusts, and she does so.* (Engelgardt, 1993, p. 29)

Interpreted through an NIE and Neoclassical prism, the "crust-giving" custom was a reciprocity-based premodern insurance system against famine (Eggertsson, 1990, pp. 33, 304). I infer that the individual household must have gained more in the long run by adhering to this custom than by eschewing the communal redistribution system. The eventual social sanction enforced this long-term rational calculus even more (Vanberg, 1994, p. 55).

The question, however, is whether the individual peasant household really had a choice in calculating its long- and short-run opportunity costs. A critical realist (CR) interpretation would advise that the household, and the individual peasant within it, had been born into and conditioned by a crust-seeking structure (Archer, 1995, pp. 76, 77) derived from the collective memory reservoir of relative poverty and recurrent famines (Kahan, 1985, p. 11). Habits of thought that had survived from generation to generation were inputs for the institutional structure of the present. The custom itself was a pool of experience and knowledge (Hodgson, 2004, p. 168). Routine compliance with the custom by submitting to elders' authority economized on the household's cognitive capacity, saving energy and lending an evolutionary advantage not only to the household but also to the entire commune (Martens, 2004, p. 145). Generally speaking, assuming that the group is necessary for the individual's survival, this type of cooperative behavior, following the AEI framework, ultimately traces to individual selection (Vromen, 2001, p. 194). Insofar as the custom survives the evolutionary transition to rationalism, I apply the NIE prisoner's dilemma and find that the sanction of social pressure (denial of insurance) leads to the optimal choice: adherence to custom.

Crucially for the purpose of this chapter, I argue that the NIE and AEI ways of interpreting the phenomenon of "crust-giving" are not alternative but complementary. The rational utility-maximizer assumption that underlies the NIE and Neoclassical approaches emphasizes, albeit in an oversimplified manner, the conscious survival calculus that is performed on an individual basis (North, 1973, p. 29, 1981, p. 9, 1990, p. 38, 2005, p. 47). The evolutionary approach focuses on subconscious determining mechanisms, such as moral sentiments, that bring about the life-preserving result.[11] While NIE emphasizes the economic motivation to follow the customary way of life, evolutionary institutionalism, set within a historically determined cultural context, calls attention to the social sanction and reward mechanism as a motivating factor. The result is an integrated socio-economic perspective (Greif, 2006, p. 101).

I argue that both systems of problem-solving, the conscious and the subconscious (Rizello, 1999, p. 25), are activated in a process of structure legitimization through which the custom is imprecisely replicated (Hodgson & Knudsen, 2005, p. 10) and, for this reason, gradually changes on the margin—adapts to changing conditions—or is transformed in a cumulative re-evaluation (Lawson, 1997, p. 192).

Before addressing the core subject of the chapter, the transformation of the structure of property rights in late Tsarist Russia, I present additional examples of cooperative behavior in the post-emancipation village commune.

***Pomoch*—mutual aid**: Mironov (2000, p. 338) and Engelgardt, among other sources, [12] speak of *pomoch*, a form of customary aid to the needy that was codified in law in 1860. Until the codification, this obligation was considered a moral one, deeply rooted in the communal peasant practice, rarely shirked, and addressed by social sanction in the rare cases of its transgression. Pomoch included rebuilding homes that had been stricken by fire, completing agricultural work, paying hospital bills, organizing and subsidizing funerals, and more. Although this type of mutual aid was sometimes spontaneous, decisions to aid calamity-stricken households were routinely made by village assemblies as well (Mironov, 2000, p. 338).

This type of institution, founded on the moral sentiment that my analysis, anchored in Mironov's, emphasizes, is essential for the survival of a group and, ultimately, the individual within it, and may be explained

[11] Hodgson (2004, p. 361). Hodgson's conception of tacit knowledge implies the unconscious dimensions of learning. See also Smith (2000, p. 3), and Vromen (2001, pp. 187, 188).

[12] Frierson (1990, p. 55) speaks of this particular type of help—*pomoch*—that a peasant extends to a wealthier peasant or a landlord "out of respect."

within a Darwinian evolutionary framework as well as by Adam Smith (2000) in an analysis of the subconscious psychological mechanisms that underlie the methodological individualism of classical economics. Neoclassical analysis, in contrast, would explain this reciprocal practice as the minimization, by rational utility-maximizing heads of household, of the risk. Funeral services, after all, do not save a person from death or prohibitive costs resulting from calamities and tragedies (Scott, 1976, p. 4). North (2005), implicitly acknowledging AEI and extending the traditional NIE approach in evolutionary directions,[13] would identify pomoch as an institution designed to deal with the hardships of the physical environment. Its codification in law, however, heralded two transitions: from personalized to impersonalized institutions or from community to society (Mironov, 2000, p. 286) and from the stage of uncertainty generated by the physical environment to that in which it is the human environment that brings uncertainty about (North, 2005, p. 127).

As suggested above, combining Darwinian evolutionary approaches with NIE and selected sources in Neoclassical analysis brings the integrated framework closer to a holistic state.

As argued in Chap. 3, NIE, with its roots in hedonistic psychology and its emphasis on a rationalist incentive structure, cannot be excluded from the model. Neither can one ignore the critical-realist AEI theory because human beings act in a cultural context that emphasizes the role of structures in molding individual preferences and goals, providing social motivation (Greif, 2006, p. 101) for their actions. The pomoch institution, a mutual household insurance arrangement in the face of calamity, offered the possibility of aid to temporally disabled households that were otherwise thrifty and fully able to reciprocate (Worobec, 1990). We may infer from Worobec's findings that the NIE framework is applicable: namely, peasants engaging in pomoch may be understood as cooperating in rationalist calamity insurance.

***Bratchiny*—communal feasts**: Celebrations related to Christian and local religious festivals, centering on offerings and giving of vows to various saints, were ritual vestiges of the villages' pagan past. Some feasts were organized for different age groups; others brought the entire village to the communal table. The eating and drinking were accompanied by door-to-door singing parties and the *khorovod*, a round dance. Peasants donated

[13] North, May 12, 2005. He did not fully verify my supposition.

food, money, and specially brewed beer to these celebrations (Mironov, 2000, pp. 324, 325).

Obviously, like the wedding parties, the dowry (the *kladka* described by Hoch, 1986, p. 95) and the *bratchiny* (derived from *brat*, brother, meaning expressions of brotherhood) were in part premodern mechanisms of wealth redistribution that had a leveling effect (Mironov, 2000, pp. 325, 326, 327; Hoch, 1986, p. 96) by feeding the poor and insuring the well-to-do against future calamities such as hunger. They also deterred internal conflict (ibid.; Eggertsson, 1990, p. 291) and dissuaded serf owners from encroaching on peasant communities in view of the genuine coherence and continuity that they radiated.[14]

Evolutionary institutionalist thinking interprets vows to and praise of saints, as well as togetherness per se, as having an anxiety-mitigating effect (Lawson, 1997, p. 181); as such, they gave the serfs an evolutionary institutional advantage (Martens, 2004, p. 145) over their owners and, after the emancipation, over the state's aspirations to control and exploit them.[15]

***Krugovaya poruka*—collective responsibility, the land-repartition practice, and peasants' attitudes toward landedness**: Ever since medieval times, the Russian land-tenure system in entire village communities rested on the principle of collective responsibility for obligations to the state—*krugovaya poruka* as state-centered Westernizers express it (Moon, 1999, p. 207; Worobec, 1990, p. 23). During the serfdom era, collective responsibility was enforced by landlords and included seigniorial obligations. The state peasant category, like the seigniorial serf population, was collectively responsible for taxes and dues. Collective responsibility was thought instrumental for the reduction of landlord and state surveillance costs (North, 1990, pp. 90, 95) and, after the 1861 Emancipation, expanded to include redemption payments to the state.[16]

[14] Kolchin (1987, p. 269) emphasizes the collective nature of the Russian serfs' resistance in contrast to that of American slaves.

[15] See Kolchin (1987, p. 269) and Moon (1999, pp. 242, 243) on peasant revolts. Although most such uprisings were perpetrated by border-region Cossacks who demanded autonomy, the Razin and Pugachev risings engaged conspicuous peasant populations that protested infringements by the Tsarist state on, for example, the relative autonomy that had been granted through *obrok*—quitrent—as opposed to *barshchina*—corvée labor obligations and the curtailment of peasant prerogatives by means of conscription and tax increases.

[16] See Gerschenkron (1962, p. 131) on the commune's joint responsibility for tax payments; Worobec (1990, pp. 3, 20, 24, 40), on the paid share of redemption payments that burdened the collectively liable village; and Pallot (1982, p. 5).

The Westernizers' school, represented by Boris Chicherin (1828–1904), finds a causal relation between top-down collective responsibility for obligations to landlord and state and the periodic land-redistribution practice in nineteenth-century repartitional Tsarist Russian village communes (Worobec, 1990, pp. 17, 21, 22). Since the commune apportioned its obligations among households on an egalitarian basis,[17] the amount of land awarded, a measure related to the household's ability to cultivate it, had to be distributed in accordance with the tax burden per household (Moon, 1999, pp. 165, 208; Worobec, 1990, pp. 22, 23). This, in turn, was determined in many communes by the number of *tyagla* (sing.: *tyaglo*)—labor teams, each composed of husband and wife plus one horse per household (Moon, 1999, p. 211; Worobec, 1990, p. 22; Hoch, 1986, p. 61, Table 12).[18]

Until the late seventeenth century, every household in a commune was entitled to a share of communal land in exchange for the commensurate fulfillment of communal obligations. Disabled peasants often remained landless due to their inability to work; widows who were not considered a *tyaglo* frequently joined them (Moon, 1999, p. 211; Worobec, 1990, pp. 22, 23). Thus, the egalitarian principle was linked to the ability to work and participate in meeting tax obligations and, after the emancipation, redemption payments.

In the eighteenth and nineteenth centuries, communal land was periodically redivided to take account not only of household divisions but also of changes in the number of *tyagla* among existing households (Worobec, 1990, p. 23). Thus, as the population increased and the land/labor ratio fell, repartitions grew in frequency and land tenure became increasingly unstable (Gerschenkron, 1962, p. 122).

Contrary to the Slavophile and, later, the Populist belief in the communal and egalitarian spirit of the Slavonic people—depicting the obshchina as a primordial Russian institution—the Russian peasantry of the fifteenth and sixteenth centuries is said to have held its land, including house and garden plots, arable land, and even meadows, in individual

[17] Mediated by the poll or "soul" tax, the *podushnaya podat'*, introduced in 1724, it most probably contributed to the motivation behind egalitarian land redistribution (Keren, 2000, personal communication).

[18] Although mean household size had been declining from the last quarter of the eighteenth century onward, it is evident from the table that the prevailing family structure was the extended multigenerational household, at least until the last decades of the nineteenth century.

household hereditary tenure, allowing differentiation (Moon, 1999, p. 212). During the serfdom era, attempts to hinder stratification among the Russian peasantry by enforcing egalitarian practices in land and wealth redistribution were effectuated through the seigniorial system (Hoch, 1986, pp. 94, 95, 96) and, in this sense, may be seen as initially involuntary. By the late nineteenth century, in contrast, only the farmstead (*usadba*) was held in hereditary tenure; arable land was periodically repartitioned (Worobec, 1990, p. 20). Thus, state-induced collectivism increasingly encroached upon what the Westernizers termed a landholding system initially predicated on the individual peasant. Communes throughout European Russia increasingly set aside 50–60 desyatinas of arable land for welfare functions such as aiding poor households and landless widows, hiring doctors and other rural employees, and repairing churches, bridges, and roads (Worobec, 1995, p. 21). This process may have been the result of the combination of population increase and onerous redemption payments, which increased perceived risks to the peasantry's subsistence. It may also have been the consequence of growing collectivism, manifested in the shaping and molding of peasant preferences by the Tsarist taxation system, namely, the Hodgsonian process of reconstitutive downward causation.

In support of the latter thesis, I should note that on "black" peasant land (Blum, 1961, p. 95; Moon, 1999, p. 219)—areas excluded from the allotment land redistributed for rotation among households—hereditary tenure persisted until 1829, at which time the state compelled the villages to enhance poorer households' taxpaying capacity by introducing repartition and equalization. Wealthier households opposed these reforms, showing that they objected due to individualism rather than voluntary communal spirit among the Russian peasantry. In all land other than "black" peasant land (not belonging to landlords), communal and repartitional tenure spread from the center to border regions, starting with the intensification of redistribution during the eighteenth and nineteenth centuries through the atrophy of this practice from the late nineteenth century to the codification of individualized landholding in Stolypin's 1906 reform. This reveals the state's growing extractive pressure as the cause of this process (ibid.) and demonstrates a causal relation between collective responsibility for tax payments and the land-tenure system (Worobec, 1995, p. 17).

By comparing the land-redistribution practice toward Russia's peasant villages with prevalent landholding systems in the areas that the empire had annexed in the late seventeenth and eighteenth centuries—Ukraine, Belarus, Lithuania, and the other Baltic provinces, where the land had been held in individual hereditary tenure—I find that the egalitarian practice in Russia's equalizing repartitional commune may have been related to the imposition of the egalitarian poll tax/soul tax, the *podushnaya podat'*. This impost, first collected in 1724 under Peter the Great (Hughes, 1998, p. 137), was introduced in the "new" areas in the late eighteenth century, following Russia by half a century (Moon, 1999, p. 214).

Communal and repartitional tenure also spread from seigneurial barshchina (corvée labor estates) to obrok, money-dues estates (Moon, 1999, p. 212). Moon traces the later repartition and equalization movement to the approximate equality of able-bodied men in their capacity to work. Thus, equalization in the provision of land for subsistence allowed surpluses to be transferred from the peasant household to the demesne (Moon, 1999, p. 218). On obrok estates, well-off households could be charged higher dues and the seignior would have less of an incentive to equalize households' land endowments.

Following Hodgson's reconstitutive downward causation reasoning, the patrimonial state structure inherited within the informal institutions (North, 1990, p. 64) combined with the seigniorial system to maximize the state's and the landholding gentry's tax revenue and to minimize its surveillance costs (North, 1990, p. 90). By imposing sanctions for noncompliance and selecting collectivist-minded individuals, the state and gentry authorities that lurked behind the collective-responsibility schemes fostered Russian peasant collectivism (Veblen, 1931, p. 188) and transformed these schemes into an evolutionarily superior strategy. As the Regulationist school posits, the rewards of any survival strategy are related to the number of individuals who followed it previously. The self-reenforcing mechanism that this creates—collective responsibility, in this case—delivers a superior outcome in the individual household's cost/benefit calculus. Through the extractive objectives of the Tsarist state and the landlord that had authoritatively established and encouraged collective responsibility for taxes and dues, the Russian peasantry's habits of thought were shaped and replicated in a communal collectivist spirit that outlived serfdom.

The combination of the egalitarianism-enforcing poll tax, collective responsibility for obligations to landlord and state, and periodic redistribution of land (equalizing the tax burden) abetted the emergence of egalitarian ideas among the Russian peasantry (Worobec, 1995, pp. 26, 27, 29,

40)—an estate that had been diffused by migration from the center of the empire to regions as far away as Siberia (Moon, 1999, pp. 64, 213). However, this evolutionary perspective (considering the initially high land/labor ratios in the empire as a whole as having induced the gradual tying of labor to land [Kolchin, 1987, p. 2] and imposed collective responsibility for obligations), combined with the insinuation that both the state and the seignior applied a rational, utility-maximizing calculus, offers only a partial explanation.

Even if wealthier peasants initially adhered to the collective-responsibility formula involuntarily, the NIE perspective suggests that egalitarian redistribution reduced the risk of conflict within the peasant village commune. Given the initially high land/labor ratios, the opportunity cost of labor employed in conflict must have been higher than that of labor employed in tilling the soil (Eggertsson, 1990, p. 291). It being axiomatic that informal institutional structures change very slowly, the egalitarian land-redistribution custom may have outlived the initial abundance of land relative to labor. Moreover, the prevention of intra-commune conflict or the preservation of social harmony (Ma, 2006, p. 11) amplified the voluntarily cooperative bargaining power (North, 1973, p. 29) of heads of household vis-à-vis the commune assembly, which was increasingly infiltrated by the seigniorial system, and ultimately vis-à-vis the landlord and the Tsarist state. From an evolutionary perspective, the peasant community must have regarded the historical preconditioning antagonism and distrust between itself and the Tsarist state, which kept the Tsarist gendarmes away by maintaining social harmony (Ma, 2006, p. 11), as a superior survival strategy.[19]

Another way to explain the peasant communal spirit, the periodic land redistribution, the three-field system that made it necessary to coordinate agricultural tasks, the strip farming that mitigated the effects of uneven soil quality, and the pomoch form of mutual assistance that implied a long-term rational calculus (Vanberg, 1994, p. 55) by the peasantry is to understand this practice as a premodern case of risk-sharing (Moon, 1999, p. 226; Pallot, 1999, p. 75). Thus, NIE complements evolutionary approaches in explaining the viability and, as I argue below, the

[19] See Frank (1999, p. 7) on the autocolonization condition of the Tsarist Russian peasant estate (*soslovie*) and Engelgardt (1993, p. 44) on peasant distrust of the imperial legal system. See also below on peasants' attitudes toward the Tsarist legal system.

universality of the type of collectivist practice that emanated from the collective-responsibility formula.

Moreover, given the manpower advantage of the Russian peasantry over the Tsarist bureaucracy (Kolchin, 1987, p. 366, Table 11; Mironov, 2000, p. 247), one cannot discredit the Slavophile understanding of the obshchina as an organic institution voluntarily based on egalitarianism and collective resource management as an reflection of long term survival orientated moral sentiment Smith (2000). Since the Russian peasants practiced *krugovaya poruka* and egalitarian redistribution in additional contexts,[20] and given evidence that some communes continued to invoke the serfdom practice of repartitioning all land, including garden plots, even after the emancipation (Worobec, 1995, p. 20), the implication of the reconstitutive downward causation process provides a necessary but insufficient explanation of the occurrence of collectivism in the landholding system, one that may conclusively be explained by the Russian peasant's living conditions during serfdom (Veblen, 1931, p. 188).

It is plausible to assume a degree of initial, environment-induced voluntarism in applying the mutual-aid collectivist practice[21]—as would happen if adverse climatic events shortened the growing season (Chubarov, 2001, p. 4)—that would credit the NIE explanations of the particular cooperative collectivist peasant custom. Thus, by combining the AEI approach with NIE, the aspects of the obshchina delineated by the Westernizers' and Slavophile schools may be disclosed and reconciled.

The combination of these two theories, NIE and AEI, implies that that the obshchina, especially during the serfdom era, had been the consequence of an authoritarian hierarchy of coercion, itself an institutional response to the conditions of life as conceived by Veblen. In the post-serfdom structure, the rational calculus of heads of household increasingly prevailed over obedience. The Slavophile notion of the obshchina as an organic institution that had structured the life of the Russian peasant since time immemorial cannot be refuted even though the Tsarist state, viewed from an NIE perspective, sought to lower the transaction costs of

[20] See Moon (1999, p. 338) on *pomoch* and *toloka* as the egalitarian redistribution of risk of death. See below on peasant *arteli*.

[21] Moon (1999, p. 338). Pomoch was sometimes spontaneous and at other times obligatory through a democratic decision of the village assembly. Worobec (1995, p. 40) finds that assistance was sometimes determined voluntarily by mutual dependence, as when calamitous conditions affected individual households; the sanction for non-compliance was exclusion from the communal mutual-help insurance mechanisms.

autocratic rule by legally enforcing the collectivist mechanisms of this structure. Thus, an understanding of the perspectives as reinforcing rather than the alternative is warranted and congruent with Critical Realism, while exclusive reliance on the neoclassical conception of rational-calculus explanation does not hold given the implausibility of atomism in the real world (Lawson, 1997, p. 129). In the context of dependency on experience, as encapsulated in the institutionalized patriarchal authority under the precarious conditions of premodern Russian agriculture, the manifestation of hedonistic individualist rationalism, as NIE assumes, and its rising explanatory weight at a time of technological change need to be explained. Peasant "procedural rationality" as an aspect of "bounded rationality" (Rizello, 1999, p. 48) must be conceptualized within the temporal priority of structure (Archer, 1995, p. 76).

Redistribution of Movable Capital

It may be adduced from Gregory (1994, p. 52) that the redistribution of movable capital, replaced and compensated for by "side payments" (Gregory) for refraining from land repartitions, rendered the land-tenure system more stable in practice than Gerschenkron would have it. Although Gregory offers no conclusive proof for this thesis, he implies an individual household property consciousness on the part of the peasantry, a phenomenon that cannot but have historical roots and that contradicts the accepted understanding of the Russian peasant as unconscious of property (Crisp, 1989, p. 36). This suggests voluntary intra-village cooperation by individual households in view of the land-tenure restrictions that had been imposed from above historically and up to the decades preceding Stolypin's 1906 land reform.

The existence of voluntary cooperation in movable capital redistribution implies that the Russian peasant community addressed the "hardships of the human environment" in the same manner as it had historically addressed the "hardships of the physical environment" (North, 2005, pp. 100, 101). The habits of mutual assistance and insurance must be understood as the result of a combination of rational short- and long-term calculus (NIE; Vanberg, 1994) and the predisposition to specific strategies that would resolve historical labor-shortage problems (AEI), fostered by the collectivist practice that had been authoritatively imposed during serfdom.[22]

Generally speaking, I propose that the more voluntarism there is, the more individual rational deliberation and the less subservience to coercive authority one encounters. The stronger the genuine cooperation is, the less shirking takes place, the weaker the freeloader problem becomes, and the stronger is the subversive capacity of the cooperative, in this case the agrarian collective (Barzel, 2002, p. 61). Thus, I maintain that the collective as formed in the manner conceived by the Westernizers—by the Tsarist state's endorsement of the organic obshchina practice (as the Slavophiles, referring to the Regulationist concept, propose)—"translates" the redistribution mechanism into subversive cooperation. This resulted in the formation of a "commitment device" (Greif, 2006, p. 101) that challenged autocratic rule in the rural and, subsequently, the urban institutional environment.

The Serfdom Commune Legacy in Nineteenth-Century Rural Custom

In this subchapter, I discuss reconstitutive downward causation as the source of collectivism as against individualism in property and labor relations within the peasant community. Through this process, the hierarchies of coercion and dependency on the patriarch and the landlord for the internalization of risks to living standards and life shaped under serfdom welded the village commune *mir*, paradoxically, into a collective action unit (Barzel, 2002, p. 61) that constituted a vehicle of subversion and the credible threat from below as well as tacit knowledge reservoir (Greif, 2006, p. 101, Hodgson, 1999) to the autocratic authority of the Tsarist government. The increasingly voluntary consolidation of post-emancipation obshchinas that demanded landholding reforms congruent with the peasant transition from community to society (Mironov, 2000, pp. 286, 287) afforded by the railroads, resulted in the codification of landholding individualization in Stolypin's 1906 reform.

[22] See Hodgson (2004, p. 105) on the shaping of individuals' "habits of thoughts" by reconstitutive downward causation.

Serfdom, introduced in Tsarist Russia in 1597,[23] shared basic commonalities with other forms of institutionalized bondage such as American slavery (Kolchin, 1987, p. 1). The patriarchal system (Hoch, 1986, pp. 117, 118)[24] was the playground of the exploitive instinct and the habits of thought that were fostered in two hierarchies of coercion: within the serf community and between landlord and serfs (Hoch, 1986, p. 91). Through natural selection and adaptation, the institutions of the *pomeshchik*—the Tsarist serviceman—and, ultimately, of the autocracy preconditioned the peasant to submission.

The dominant characteristic of the incentive structure of unfree labor systems, in which corporal punishment is applied for undersupply of skill and labor and for transgressions of rules of conduct defined and enforced by the master, is fear.[25] It follows that the bondsman's survival strategy, institutionalized through custom in the long term (Vanberg, 1994, p. 55), is risk-averse (Poznanski, 1985, p. 19; Hoch, 1986, p. 164) and guided by his assessment of the probability of direct danger to life posed by the omnipresent expectation and occurrence of corporal punishment. Hypothetically, the frequency as well as the predictability of the serf owner's corporal-punishment sanction should have affected the extent of innovation in the serf socioeconomy relative to the serfs' adherence to routine and custom.[26] In this supposition, I generalize from Poznanski's and Winicki's analysis (Poznanski, 1985, p. 45; Winicki, 1988, p. 18) of the reasons for the absence of innovating risk-taking in the Soviet five-year production plans. The institutionalization of the draconian penal system that proposed to discipline the managing boards of the Soviet state-owned enterprise discouraged industrial risk-taking due to the fear of underfulfillment. Considering the innovation-enhancing long learning curves in the mix of experimentation on new processes/products, the quantitatively

[23] See Blum (1961, p. 30) on the restriction of unmonitored peasant movement and Blum (1961, pp. 254, 256, 275, 276) on the gradual curtailment of peasants' right to move and the effective introduction of serfdom.

[24] As egalitarianism lowered landlords' surveillance costs (North, 1990, p. 90) while enhancing village cohesion, both the peasant patriarchs and the bailiffs of the estate had an interest in carrying out redistribution in a way that would have a leveling effect.

[25] Sztern (1994, unpublished doctoral course paper, Department of Philosophy, Lund University), Hoch (1986, p. 164).

[26] Here I apply, analogously, Winicki's argument (1988, pp. 17, 18) that producers in the Soviet era chose a risk-averse strategy due to heavy penalties for failure to meet quotas in the quantitatively defined five-year plans.

defined targets of the plan were met due to compliance to customary routine in all aspects of production.

Generalizing a model derived from the Soviet-type economy (Winicki, 1988, pp. 17, 18.) to the serf community, one may define the socioeconomic degree of innovation as a function of the frequency of corporal punishment or of a prohibitive penalty for non-fulfillment. Thus, compliance with authority as a risk-management system is not cost-free; it imposes paternalistic penalties for non-compliance that discourage experimentation with novelties and risk-taking. The Tsarist railroads, by entailing the transition to rationalism, limited the costs of coercion in the service of the risk-reducing authority.

Moreover, the frequency and predictability of corporal punishment should, again hypothetically, affect the *voluntary* elements of the extent of collectivism and egalitarianism in the village commune. This hypothesis is justified by NIE's disclosure (Eggertsson, 1990, pp. 291, 303, 304) of the function of the egalitarian and collectivist peasant practice in preserving internal harmony and cohesion (Ma, 2006, p. 11). This function, observed in the rural community as late as the nineteenth century,[27] may have been perceived historically as crucial for individual survival amid the reality of corporal abuse that attended to serfdom.

Serfdom—Cohesion versus Atomization in the Long-Term Post-Emancipation Imprint

I argue in this subchapter that through reconstitutive downward causation, the characteristic institutional system of serfdom including the corporal-punishment sanction affected the prevalent habits of thought of the Tsarist Russian peasantry at the time of and long after the Emancipation Act of 1861. Here, Gerschenkron's assessment of the detrimental effect of collective responsibility and the egalitarian land-redistribution practice adopted by the peasantry and enforced by the Tsarist state, rendering ownership unpredictable and thereby distorting the incentive structure, needs additional qualifications.

The crucial question is this: Was the peasants' involuntary and voluntary collectivism *in itself* to blame for their suboptimal agricultural performance, or should the fault be assigned to the heavy burden (Hodgson, 2004) of the institutions of serfdom, including the risk-survival strategies

[27] See Atkinson (1983, p. 21) for the Slavophile view of the peasant commune.

that the peasants invoked due to the threat or reality of corporal punishment in that era of unfree labor?

Communal Tenure and Innovation

Contrary to Gerschenkron's analysis, Kingston-Mann finds communal tenure compatible with innovative behavior. Individual potential innovators depended on the acceptance and the related social pressure of the commune to engage the majority of heads of households in the implementation of the novel ideas. Once applied, this pressure abetted an extent of innovation diffusion that the hereditary household tenure system could not have allowed (Kingston-Mann, 1991, p. 43).

Kingston-Mann repeatedly suggests, as does Pallot (1999), that the main function of the nineteenth-century commune was internalizing the risk of death and or pauperization by dispersing and sharing it.[28] The exploitive characteristic of the system toward individual property rights, effected by the over-hierarchization of patriarchal structures in which these rights were redistributed from the younger to the older generation,[29] had been extended during the serfdom era to include the landlord. This obviously amplified the perceived risk of death, which presumably was additionally aggravated by the phenomenon of corporal punishment that permeated serfdom as a total institution (Hoch, 1986, p. 184). Thus, I infer from Kingston-Mann that under conditions of serfdom beyond those of the post-emancipation nineteenth century, the village commune abetted the adoption and diffusion of innovation within a risk-averse environment of high risk of impoverishment and death.

Assuming the applicability of Winicki's (1988) and Poznanski's (1985) Soviet-type economy model—the predisposition to risk aversion that corporal punishment instilled in the peasantry under serfdom—the reconstitutive downward causation process revitalized and perpetuated peasant dependency on the commune as an insulating barrier to additional encroachment of the peasantry by the landlord and the Tsarist gendarmes (Mironov, 2000, p. 297)—a risk-internalization unit (Kolchin, 1987, p. 195) that the Emancipation Act of 1861 could not attenuate in the short run.

[28] Moon (1999, pp. 222, 223) gives examples of the role of risk-sharing cooperation in enhancing the commune.

[29] See Hoch (1986, p. 207) on oppressive dependencies within "familism" networks.

Gerschenkron's description (Gerschenkron, 1962, 1968) of the state-supported perpetuation of the repartitional commune as an impediment to increases in innovation and productivity cannot be rejected insofar as it focuses on the formal institutional dimension (North, 1990, p. 78). Under the institutional conditions of serfdom, however, the reconstitution of habits of thought after the emancipation and the formal and informal (North, 1990, pp. 64, 78) aspects of the risk-sharing custom (including the three-field system, the land-redistribution practice, and foremost the collective land-management mechanism established through the village assembly[30]) may have had a net enhancing effect on innovation (Kingston-Mann, 1991, pp. 39–41). Kingston-Mann's account of the cultivation of grass including clover by the collective, coordinated by the village commune assembly (Kingston-Mann, 1991, pp. 35, 38); the use of fertilizers in pre- and post-emancipation agriculture[31]—a risk-taking innovation that, due to individual peasants' conservative attitudes, would have been rejected from the outset (Engelgardt, 1993, p. 64)—serves as a case in point. Agricultural innovation had been infused into the communes by *zemstvo* (local government) agronomists who belonged to the so-called "third element," that is, professionals (Bucher, 2008, pp. 75, 76). These organizations included members of the peasant estate, whose share in the population declined from roughly half following the 1890 legislation (Atkinson, 1983, p. 29) but was of reconstitutive importance during the post-emancipation period. These institutions exposed even the most conservative peasant household heads to the progressive element among the urban professionals. The source of innovation was usually extra-rural but its diffusion was abetted by the communal mechanisms of cooperation (Kingston-Mann, 1991, p. 37).

An additional comment warranted by Kingston-Mann's study concerns the genuine actual level of collectivism in the nineteenth-century commune as a legacy of the serfdom era (Archer, 1995, pp. 76, 77; Hodgson, 2004, p. 14). As Kingston-Mann explains, elements of collectivism and, more conspicuously, of individualism intermingled within the flexible village-commune structure. Thus, as stated above, individual households owned garden plots or farmsteads (*usadba*) and individual married peasant

[30] See Moon (1999, pp. 211, 212) on land management and 227 on compulsory peasant compliance with decisions of the village assembly.

[31] See Kingston-Mann (1991, p. 41) on compulsory use of fertilizer to meet commune requirements.

women had a "women's box"[32] that was strictly theirs by tradition. Sophisticated reward mechanisms for individual labor and investment had been developed to compensate and provide these peasants with an additional incentive to supply labor and skills, increasing the value of their land allotment subject to its periodic redistribution (Kingston-Mann, 1991, pp. 44, 45).

The Legacy of Serfdom and Kinship

Serfdom left decisive imprints on nineteenth-century custom in its attention to family structure. According to Blum (1961), the pattern of early and universal marriage (Worobec, 1995, p. 42; Hoch, 1986, p. 77) and the custom of clustering in extended multigenerational family units had been prevalent among Russian peasants from the pre-serfdom era of *podsega*—slash-burn tillage—among the Slavonic tribes, which had formed kinship-based extended family communes that constituted labor teams (Blum, 1961, pp. 22, 25; Weber, 1981, p. 12). This survival strategy constituted an adaptation to the initially high land/labor ratios. However, serfdom additionally bolstered the long-term legitimacy of these structures as perceived by both the serf owner and the peasants (Vanberg, 1994, p. 55).

Universal early marriage—an inter-household contract of wealth, labor, and rights to the communally distributed allotment of land rather than the romantic formation of a couple—increased the total number of tyaglas (labor units) that worked on an estate in a way that benefited the landlord. By periodically redistributing land commensurate with the number of such units per household, this system assured each extended household enough land to survive and meet its tax obligations to the landlord. It also established the tyagla as a mutual-insurance unit that guaranteed individual household members' survival, amplified the power of the patriarch (*bolshak*), and strengthened the hierarchical symbiosis of exploitation that seized the surpluses generated by the sons for the upkeep of the parents'

[32] Kingston-Mann (1991, p. 35) refers to the "woman's box" as an inalienable right to the products of her labor, such as poultry raising and weaving. See Worobec (1995, p. 63) on net income from the sale of mushrooms, fruits, and knitwear as a wife's private property. Engelgardt (1993, p. 164) remarks on work performed by women not for the household but for the accumulation of their own resources in terms of individual property.

generation, which had retired from working the land, and divided them between bolshak and landlord.[33]

The Legitimacy of the Malthusian-Trap Assumption

This legacy resulted in structural preconditions (Archer, 1995, p. 76) that, during the nineteenth-century population increase that it animated, could have snared the Russian countryside in a Malthusian trap. Following Gerschenkron (1962, 1968) and Pallot (1999, p. 75, on the commune as a land-rotation mechanism and Scott's view of the institution as a forerunner of household insurance against maximum loss, respectively), the overpopulation of the countryside occasioned by these preconditions would necessitate and perpetuate intensified collectivism and wealth redistribution.[34] The mutual-assistance and -insurance function of the serfdom-enhanced extended family would gather strength in tandem with population increase. Thus, in an inference from Gerschenkron's argument, the effect of collectivist mechanisms of cooperation would trigger the long-term vicious cycle of collectivism, causing population to increase at the rate exceeding food production. This would entail a high probability of death, in turn breeding poverty and an even greater risk of death. Had such a chain of causality remained unchallenged, the Gerschenkronian and materialist explanation of the 1905 revolution would gain additional credibility. In other words, paradoxically, collectivism in terms of mutual household insurance raised life expectancy at birth but the demographic transition that would adjust fertility habits failed to take place in the short run. The resulting rate of population increase (Kahan, 1985, p. 16, and Table 15 below), driven by constant technology improvements, land endowments, and the allocation of bonded labor to the demesne, would

[33] Hoch (1986, p. 119) comments on the exploitive distribution of income from younger to older generation that estate bailiffs and patriarchs in concert.

[34] Hoch (1986, p. 95). The practice of *kladka*—"bride-price"—attenuated the redistribution of wealth somewhat by having the groom's family compensate a bride's household for the loss of a worker and a labor unit in the coin of an additional land endowment due to the formation of a new labor unit. Thus, movable capital was redistributed from the groom's household to the bride's while the land, theoretically, moved in the opposite direction. While dowries had been customary in the relatively more individualistic obrok regions and were observed in Western custom—keeping wealth in the household—kladka was customary in the barshchina regions under serfdom as a way of redistributing wealth and insuring the individual against poverty and its consequent inability to pay tax.

outpace food production, raising the probability of malnutrition, sensitivity to epidemics such as water-borne cholera (Bideleux, 1990, p. 207), and, therefore, death. These conditions would trigger a compensatory mechanism that would mutually ensure against impoverishment. This, coupled with excess childrearing (Atkinson, 1983, Table 2, p. 31, and Appendix, pp. 383, 384) as old-age insurance (Hesse, 1993, p. 52), would unleash a Malthusian vicious cycle.

Changing Types of Collectivism

Here I show with emphasis that neither the particular combination of risk nor the type of collectivism was diachronically constant over time. Historically, cooperation was meant to insure against a different set of risks. In the course of the nineteenth century, the population increase that reduced the land/labor ratio perforce necessitated more intensive resource use in regard to land. During the eighteenth and early nineteenth centuries, the high land/labor ratio enhanced egalitarian land redistribution, internal cohesion, cooperation, and harmony, the purpose of which was to increase the aggregate opportunity cost of labor employed in conflict instead of agriculture while enforcing commune autonomy vis-à-vis the landed gentry, the *pomeshchiks* (Eggertsson, 1990, pp. 291, 303, 304; Ma, 2006, p. 11).

Cooperation in the Late Post-Emancipation Era

Cooperation amid rising population in the late nineteenth century, after the emancipation, concerned itself with growing numbers of dependents (elderly and minor children) per tyaglo and shrinking per capita land allotments (Gerschenkron, 1962, p. 120; Atkinson, 1983, p. 30), making mutual insurance against pauperization crucially important. Mutual assistance and cooperation persisted but changed in character, in tandem with the growing availability of railroad technology and the bureaucratization of the commune assembly in the second half of the nineteenth century (Westwood, 1964, p. 31, 2000, p. 334). Whereas the precarity of the physical and the human environment had burdened eighteenth-century agriculture (North, 2005, p. 7), enforcing submission to the landlord and the patriarchal elder authority (Lawson, 1997, pp. 181, 182) as a risk-reduction strategy, the industrial spurt of 1890 allowed heads of household to subject the worth of cooperation to rationalist evaluation as one of many options. This took place within the framework of a relatively more predictable institutional environment and novel technology, both facilitated by the systematization of government (Yaney, 1973, p. 230). Thus, in the last quarter of the nineteenth century, the character of collectivism changed from a hierarchy of coercion to voluntary cooperation.

The exploitation of serf by serf and peasant by peasant via the customary clan hierarchy, additionally legitimized by serfdom's patriarchal structures, continued into the post-emancipation and industrialization era.[35] The same hierarchies of patriarchal coercion set police measures in motion by invoking internal-passport restrictions that redistributed the supplementary incomes of the *otkhodniks*—wage laborers—from the young generation to the older (Burds, 1998, pp. 57, 58; Hoch, 1986, p. 119). Such an expropriation must have stirred strong individualistic sentiments among the young peasantry, creating a countervailing force that kept the Malthusian trap from snapping shut. Moreover, the reliance on peasant "informers" and the prohibitive intensity of estate-management coercion during serfdom (Hoch, 1986, pp. 160, 167) thwarted the formation of genuine internal relations, congruent with Lawson's conceptualization (Lawson, 1997, p. 166), by fomenting a deep mutual distrust that also hindered the coalescence of class solidarity and cohesion within the peasant community at large.

Peasant Collectivism versus Marxist Class Cohesion

Peasant collectivism, before and especially after emancipation, was structured rather strongly on *zemliachestvo*, peasant cultural micro-collectives from the same province (Johnson, 1979, p. 68) and *pomestie*, state service as a quid pro quo for title to land. Both were geographically and institutionally restricted affinities that originated in compliance with a common landlord authority and reciprocal aid, rather than an abstract peasant class structured by a shared ideology. The valorization of mutual dependency versus individualist prerogatives caused the character of the village commune structure to vary over time. The phenomenon of "peasant informers" during serfdom bred individualism in its most atomized forms and

[35] Hoch (1986, pp. 132, 133) implies that the commune embodied aspects of intergenerational exploitation and conflict. See Worobec (1995, pp. 140, 151) on the punitive and oppressive attitude toward women, who were seen foremost as an addition to household labor in double-standard patriarchal societies such as Russia's.

explains the dearth of violent revolt during the serfdom era.[36] Peasant intra-village cooperation was a bilateral and heterogeneous risk-insurance strategy (coordinated through village assemblies) rather than a matter of homogenous stratification, independent of regional conditions, within the peasant estate. An additional short-term impact of serfdom on post-emancipation institutional structures was the risk aversion flowing from the younger generation's initial economic dependence on its elders[37] and the elders' vested interests in the hierarchies established by the patrimonial state, all permeated by traditional thinking. Patriarchs protected their privilege while the Tsarist bureaucracy, having replaced the landlords, reduced its transaction costs by ruling via the authority of the bolshak.[38]

Intergenerational Shift of Power to the Young

A contrasting process from the middle of the nineteenth century onward deserves emphasis: *otkhodnichestvo*—wage labor in city centers—which abetted increased literacy and, as a consequence, mitigated sons' dependency on fathers in the long run. This shifted the balance of power in the *skhod* (the village commune assembly) in favor of the former, forcing the latter to apply majority rule in order to diffuse innovation (Kingston-Mann, 1991, p. 43; Burds, 1998, pp. 151, 176, 177). Indeed, following Hodgson's reconstitutive downward causation argument and North's assumption of very slow change among informal institutions, the tension between the vestigial patriarchal authority and the growing rationalist individualism turned the village commune into a vehicle of innovation diffusion rather than an obstacle to such development. This process included not only novel agricultural techniques but also the importation of subversive ideology from urban centers. Paradoxically, patriarch-entrepreneurs

[36] Hoch (1986, p. 163) notes the violent revolt in 1841 as an exception. See 175, Table 35, on passive resistance as reflected in the incidence of labor offenses, and 187–188 on the absence of class cohesion.

[37] See Burds (1998, p. 45) on the *volost* court ruling in 1860. According to Hoch (1986, p. 109), extended family households headed by patriarchs enjoyed higher capital/worker ratios than did others. The higher dependency ratio that this allowed created a tradeoff between risk internalization and the leveling mechanism powered by egalitarian redistribution.

[38] Hoch (1986, p. 119), Burds (1998, p. 43), Leonard (1990, p. 136). The emancipation, triggered by surveillance costs (North, 1990, p. 90), transferred these costs from the landlords to the mir.

could overcome minority opposition in the skhod ruling, becoming triggers of institutional challenge to the assemblies' very authority.[39]

An analogous argument may be applied to further our understanding of the long-term institutional effect of the egalitarian ethos as fostered during serfdom (Hoch, 1986, p. 117; Worobec, 1995, p. 20; Atkinson, 1983, p. 9). In an attempt to secure its broad and stable tax base, the *pomestie* system[40] in effect during that era became institutionalized, transforming the redistribution of wealth via kladka (bride price) and land redistribution into custom. Thus, households could not default on their collectively assigned tax and dues obligations because each household could control sufficient resources to pay its share (Hoch, 1986, p. 95). The resulting leveling effect, preventing class stratification and limiting the ultimate destitution and proletarianization of the peasantry, ensured a stability that suited the landowner and the post-emancipation Tsarist state in the short run even though it was incongruent with voluntarism-based incentive structures (Poznanski, 1992, p. 72). Low but stable levels of productivity (Martens, 2004, p. 187; Kahan, 1985, p. 13) could be maintained by applying the disciplinary measures that serfdom allowed—a condition that seemingly became self-enforcing (Hoch, 1986, pp. 117, 118).

Diffusion of Egalitarianism and Subversion

The fostering of egalitarianism within the bounds of an institution that had its own effective diffusion mechanisms, such as the obshchina (Hodgson, 2004), had the opposite long-term results of those intended. It stimulated material egalitarianism in conjunction with a libertarian ideology that the peasant world imported via occasional interaction with landlords during serfdom[41] and in the post-emancipation industrialization spurts. This easily "translated" into a demand for equality under the law, something incongruent with serfdom, autocracy, and the power hierarchies that these systems supported. Thus, by fostering material

[39] See North (1990) and Boyer and Orlean (1993, p. 22) on the "external invasion" of urban ideology.

[40] Before the 1785 Charter to the Nobility, land and serfs had been allotted to the landed nobility—the *pomeshchiki*—by the Tsar on condition of state service. See Blum (1961, p. 182) and Pipes (1995, p. 52).

[41] For the case of resident as opposed to absentee landlords—pomeshchiks, carrying on in the Decembrist spirit, see Figes (2002, p. 72).

egalitarianism, serfdom may be said to have created the mechanisms of its own abolition.

The Commune: A Vehicle of Organized Subversion after the Emancipation

Serfdom, as long as it persisted, faced a quandary: The less serfdom could depend on economic incentives for the growth of its aggregate output as it strove to curb stratification and differentiation, ensuring a stable tax base, the more it had to rely on discipline alone, breeding fear and antagonism toward its beneficiaries, the pomeshchiki. Indeed, during the serfdom-era peasant uprising that the Tsarist system had most dreaded—the Pugachev rebellion of 1773–1774—the leaders' call to "kill the pomeshchiki" (Kolchin, 1987, p. 246) is unlikely to have fallen on deaf ears as far as the peasant-warriors were concerned.

Peasant resistance to serfdom and its attendant exploitation escalated steadily—from "silent sabotage" to flight toward border regions, petitions, and recurrent *volneniia Krest'an*—peasant unrest—up to outright war (Kolchin, 1987, pp. 243–244). With each escalation, the instances and costs of surveillance to the Tsarist state and the seigniorial system grew (Leonard, 1990, p. 121). Kolchin's comparison of the peasants' resistance patterns with those of the American slaves (Kolchin, 1987, p. 253) emphasizes the differentiating role of the Russian serfs' communal organization, additionally invigorated by the institutions of serfdom, as against the American slaves' largely individual, atomized doings. It was this that made the Russian serfs' threat from below increasingly credible (Greif, 2006, p. 441) and, in selected cases, effective.

Importantly, the post-emancipation Tsarist state's motive for the transfer of landlords' rights and obligations (e.g., the collection of taxes) to the obshchina, additionally empowering the latter, still envisaged the village commune and its array of leveling mechanisms as a guarantor of political stability (Gerschenkron, 1962, pp. 131, 132). During the 1905 revolution, however, the Tsarist government realized that this unit of agrarian collective action (Kolchin, 1987, p. 441) had become a vehicle of revolutionary subversion that was making the demand for a constitution and equality before the law effective. This outcome could easily have been predicted had the government given the obshchina's mobilizing and coordinating role in the peasant resistance to serfdom, strengthened by serfdom itself, due attention (Kolchin, 1987, p. 441; Hodgson, 2004, p. 105).

Although the landlord had de jure power to restrict peasants' freedom of movement severely, the unrestricted peasant mobility had been a universal phenomenon in old Russia until the end of the sixteenth century (Chicherin 1858, cited by Blum, 1961, p. 249). By 1724, according to legislation enacted that year, a serf who wished to leave his village needed a permit from his lord, the lord's agent, or the local priest to do so. Any walking distance that exceeded thirty versts from home, or departure for any period of time exceeding six months, necessitated a government passport, for which the serf had to pay (Blum, 1961, p. 452). Serfs found away from home without this document were treated—and punished—as fugitives. The formal juridical legacy of the serfdom era and the legislation hindering peasants' freedom of movement survived the implementation of the Emancipation Act of 1861. This is well commented upon by Gerschenkron (1962, 1968), who notes that the legal requirement of permission from the head of household and the commune assembly to engage in seasonal wage labor—*otkhod* or urban migration—posed another de jure obstacle to labor mobility (Gerschenkron, 1968, p. 195).

Unintended Consolidation

It is not implausible to assume, however, that the severe restrictions on peasant freedom of movement that characterized serfdom contributed, through the Hodgsonian process of reconstitutive downward causation, to the phenomenon of *zemliachestva*, networks that cultivated strong rural ties, regional loyalties, and associations among migrant workers of peasant origin (Johnson, 1979, pp. 68, 69). These networks must have greatly facilitated the rural-to-urban information flows, enhancing cognitive economics (Martens, 2004, pp. 4, 51, 104) and raising the cumulative probability of success of any decision to migrate and assimilate into the urban factory environment, intensifying the peasants' rural-to-urban migration during the industrialization spurts of 1890 and 1907. Also, by facilitating the import and diffusion of urban ideology and tastes to the rural community (Smurova, 2003, p. 100), they irreversibly transformed this community into a unit of subversion that challenged the autocratic order itself (Pipes, 1995, p. 314).

Thus, the legacy (in the Hodgsonian sense of the concept) of the institutions that implied the concept of organizations as institutions of serfdom, such as landsman ties (Johnson, 1979, p. 69), had the unintended consequence of facilitating and, thereby, amplifying the peasants' de facto freedom of movement before and after the emancipation. The unintended consequence of the peasantry's collective-action institutions, inherited from the serfdom era and embedding the authority vested in the village commune, evolved into an effective "bottom-up" threat to the stability of the Tsarist state. This became manifest in the course of the 1905 revolution, heralding the gradual democratization of Tsarist Russia.

Structural Preconditions—Structural Preconditioning versus Individualism in Property Relations

Here I focus on conditions of life (the subject matter of AEI) that embody perceived relative scarcities (the concern of NIE) as the ultimate explanation of institutional structures. Two questions are asked: Why is the sole conception of the village commune among the Westernizers, led by Chicherin, implausible? and: Is it necessary to view the obshchina not solely as an expression of peasant compliance with the state-imposed institutions but also as an organic rational response to the time- and place-specific perceived risk of death?

Natural Calamities and the Origins of the Commune

Using Kahan's (1985) data on natural calamities that directly affected grain yields and, in turn, the peasantry's food supply during the eighteenth century, I infer that the perceived risk of death at that time and place must have been exceptionally high. As Table 6.1 below shows, life-threatening calamities befell the rural population more than once every ten years, meaning that an adult would experience at least five of them on average.

By introducing the NIE/AEI theory combination above, I emphasize that the individual household head's ad hoc calculus, envisaged in NIE and stemming from the rationalist assessment of the relative probability of an *i*-household's being stricken by calamity, is a necessary but insufficient explanation for the collective coordinating custom that insured against the effects of crop failures. The application of NIE proposes that a high-uncertainty environment makes cooperative agreements among household heads the option that best maximizes utility. Applying this in combination with Veblenian AEI, I propose that the risk- and uncertainty-mitigating commune, constituted by the custom of collective

Table 6.1 Natural calamities affecting grain yields in eighteenth-century Russia

Year	*Type of calamity*	*Location*	*Intensity*
1704	Cold winter	Moscow and Central Russia	Relatively mild; killed the winter crop; grain supplies brought from southern provinces
1709	Severe winter and spring floods	Most of Russia	Severe; coincided with a plague epidemic
1716	Excessive rainfall and floods	Moscow Province	Relatively mild; casualties more from floods than from starvation
1721–1724	Excessive rainfalls and cold	Moscow, Smolensk, and most of central Russia	Crop failures for four successive years in a large area. Famine conditions, food shortages, high grain prices, human casualties
1729	Extremely cold winter	All of Russia	Interrupted communications, winter kill
1732–1736	Early frosts	All of Russia, especially Nizhnii Novogorod province and Ukraine	Crop failures for successive years in the upper Volga and Ukraine; famine conditions
1735	Floods	Northern and central Russia	Severe floods and famine
1739	Very cold winter	All of Russia	Winter crops affected, food shortages
1740	Lack of precipitation in the winter; excessive rainfall in the summer	Southern Russia	Winter crops froze; spring crops did not sprout; "very hungry summer"
1747–1749	Drought and locusts	All of Russia	Famine in Belgorod province; low yields in many provinces
1757			Low yields
1767	July hail storm followed by drought		Primarily spring grains suffered
1774	Drought	Left-Bank Ukraine	Crop losses and low yields in adjacent provinces
1780	Drought	Central and southern Russia	Low yields crop losses
1781	Low yields	Same	Famine-like conditions due to cumulative effect of previous year
1786	Drought	Central and southern Russia	Crop losses leading to high grain prices and import of grain to St. Petersburg in 1787
1788	Drought	Western and central Russia	

Source: Kahan (1985, p. 13)

responsibility, should be attributed to the hierarchy of group and individual natural selection and the adaptation of institutions to the precarious, unpredictable, and harsh climatic conditions of life in European Russia. Historically, the hierarchy of dependence of peasants, peasant households, and entire communes on insurance against the effects of the region's frequent natural disasters, the tribal chieftains' experience, and the authority of princes, landlords, and patriarchal elders, was an evolutionarily stable strategy (ESS) (Boyer & Orlean, 1993, p. 22). In tandem with the choice afforded by increased access to railroad technology, however, this ESS was further enforced by the additional mechanism of the rational calculus of household heads and members, paving the way to voluntary, individualistic bilateral and reciprocal insurance agreements. Against this background, the proposition raised by Chicherin and the Westernizers—that the nineteenth-century repartitional commune, which embodied the elements of collectivism outlined above, was *solely* the consequence of the Tsarist government's outstretched hand and the seigniorial system for tax-extraction purposes—cannot withstand a realistic inquiry that accommodates the truth (Mäki, 1990, p. 25[42]).

It is in this context that Vanberg's (1994) conception of the "rule-following economic man," the implicit intermediary dimension of my NIE/AEI theory combination, deserves elaboration. Against the background of severely adverse and unpredictable climatic conditions, the collectivist mutual-responsibility norm of which the village commune was constituted should be understood as a long-term mutual-insurance practice applied by entire peasant communities as well as individual peasant households through their retention of village membership. This institution reflects the long-term rationality of a peasant custom (Vanberg, 1994, p. 55) that is assumed to have been evolutionarily selected and, through adaptation, applied in response to the high frequency of natural calamities on the Russian plain (North, 2005, p. 7; Chubarov, 2001, p. 4).

Average adults in eighteenth-century Russia endured a non-anthropogenic famine or famine-like conditions twice in their lives. This must have left a heavy imprint on their habits of thought and the institutions emanating from them. It was these institutions, once solidifying into established institutional structures, that created the structural conditions into which nineteenth-century people were born (Hodgson, 2004, p. 105). Moreover, given the place-specific historical conditions, the

[42] The relevant concept in Mäki is "veristic inquiry."

process of natural selection and adaptation of institutions would, in the Russian case, favor an institutional solution to the very high probability or risk of starving to death. It is for this reason that, given the frequency of famines, I assign a function of mutual insurance against starvation to the "crusts of bread" redistribution custom that I noted above. This custom, however, was only one of many elements of collectivist, cooperative, and *redistributive* practice among the peasantry. As stated above, the peasants also redistributed wealth through the mechanism of the bride price (Hoch, 1986, p. 97) and did the same with food via the bratchiny (Mironov, 2000, pp. 324, 325). Ever since the population increase and the imposition of *Krepastnoye Pravo* (serfdom) in the seventeenth century, land had been periodically redistributed to adjust for the changing numbers of tyagla and the varying tax burden per household (Gerschenkron, 1962, p. 120; idem, Gerschenkron, 1968, p. 190; Moon, 1999, p. 220). Even among convicts, alms (although not earnings) were redistributed in accordance with egalitarian principles (Dostoyewskij, 1977, p. 25) as a manifestation of the general peasant concept of the equal right to life nurtured in the Greek Orthodox- Nicholean, and Old Believers structures.

As Kolchin (1987, p. 52, Table 3) implies, given the decisively high and rising ratio of serfs to landowners (Kahan, 1985, p. 8, Table 1.1) and the flaccidity of the Tsarist bureaucracy, the redistribution practice could not have been superimposed during serfdom by coercion alone. It is likely, instead, that the obshchina came into being as an insurance instrument against the risk of starvation or other calamities (Eggertsson, 1990, pp. 303, 304). Moreover, the Slavophile understanding of the commune as an organic Russian institution that adapts over time to local conditions of life deserves more credit to evolutionary economics than scholarship has given it.

Serfdom as a Historical Calamity?

In an era of railroads, it is unrealistic to assume the "institutional purity of regions." Nevertheless, a time factor exists in the adaptation to diverse levels of risk in a given region, caused by diverse regional climatic and institutional conditions. The diversity of institutions, in turn, is determined by institutional barriers *inter alia*. The institutions of the Kingdom of Finland and the Polish Kingdom within the Tsarist Empire would have been relatively diverse irrespective of railroads, at least in the short term, due to linguistic and other cultural-historical barriers. Generally, the regional risk-coping strategies that determine the intensity of collectivism adapt to pre-structuring physical and institutionally determined relative scarcities (North, 2005, p. 7) that are akin to conditions of life. If so, Table 6.1 above should be amended to add conditions such as longitudinal land-to-labor ratios (Kolchin, 1987, p. 2), access to groundwater (Atkinson, 1983, p. 4), susceptibility to epidemics due to sanitary habits (Bideleux, 1990, p. 207), and the ever-present determining factor in risk levels: available technologies. It is these, along with the extent of cultural insularity, that determine evolutionarily stable survival strategies, namely, the degree of institutionalized collectivism versus individualism in the rural structures.

In this context, the determining variable for institutional adaptation and natural selection of institutions (Hodgson, 2004, XV; Veblen, 1931, p. 188) is the frequency of natural calamities in European Russia generally and during the previous century particularly.

Serfdom, I argue, should be regarded as an *institutional* calamity that befell the peasant population and had a long-term structural impact; as such, it should be seen as a structural precondition (Archer, 1995, p. 76) for any inquiry pertaining to the nineteenth century. In the future, it should be subjected to quantitative analysis through variables such as the degree of exploitation during the *previous* century, measured in terms of the share of the burden in the peasant's household budget. These are the aspects that, hypothetically, determine the viability of the mutual-insurance custom. The larger the share of quitrent—in the household budget or the share of weekdays devoted to day labor at the landlord's demesne, the more mutually dependent households are on insurance against impoverishment in terms of the precarity of their survival.

Nafziger's proposal (EHES, June 2007) of "the percentage of (former) serfs in the population" as an explanatory variable for the dependent variable, the number of repartitions per commune in 1858–1878 (EHES, Table 5, p. 34) is very perceptive and may capture some of the structural aspects. Ultimately, Nafziger's test of the Gerschenkronian hypothesis advises that the share of serfs in the population is positively correlated with the frequency of repartitions and negatively with yields per acre (EHES, Table 4, p. 23). Although the correlation is weak, it squares with the Gerschenkronian implication. That is, the village commune, structured by serfdom, thwarted a pace of productivity growth that would have kept up with population growth, causing peasant poverty to increase in the industrialization era and slowing industrialization as well. Nafziger's research indicates, however, that the obshchina was more flexible than Gerschenkron predicted (Nafziger 2006, dissertation, Summary, 573).

Chapter 9 focuses on the role of technological innovation, intrinsic to the railroads, in the level of collectivism—defined in the original model (2000) that precurses Chap. 9 as the number of land repartitions over a fifty-year period and, in the tested model, as the share of the relatively individualistic category in total peasant land, adjusted to the data model and explained by distance to the nearest railroad station. Relating Nafziger's findings to mine, I propose that the closer to the nearest railroad station a peasant village was, the less collectivistic its landholdings were. One may surmise that in regions where the share of former serfs had been relatively large at the outset, peasant mobility and migration, measured in terms of the number of migrant wage workers per household, would correlate negatively with the distance to the nearest railroad station, positively to the share of former serfs in the peasant population and the number of repartitions per village, and negatively to the yield per acre generated by a peasantry increasingly untethered from the commune. The negative yield correlation would reduce the number of dependents per household and increase the level of individualism in relation to personal dignity (as yet untested) and property (Gaudin, 2007, pp. 103, 104, 108). If this is the case, our findings would supplement Nafziger's. The institutional impact of serfdom, however, transcended the population directly affected. For example, the frequency of corporal punishment in one region may have affected habits of thought in adjacent regions where the population was not directly affected. Therefore, I propose to use data on life expectancy at birth in past decades during serfdom to capture the real risk of death *under the institutional conditions now prevailing*. The subjectively perceived risk of death is assumed to correlate positively with the real risk of death.

What Brought Serfdom Down?

According to Gerschenkron (1962, 1968), the durability of serfdom and coercive rural collectivism was eroded by the debacle of the Crimean War and the need, as perceived by the Tsarist state, to modernize the rural economy. The aim of the Emancipation Act of 1861, which unintentionally unleashed a transition to voluntary cooperation and subjected repartition frequency to rationalistic calculus, had been to improve Russia's performance on the battlefield. My analysis, focusing on the Critical

Realist critique, supplements the NIE perspective, which finds agricultural productivity to be positively correlated with the delineation of property rights in land (Barzel, 1989).

The structural precondition (Nafziger; EHES, June Nafziger, 2007) that shaped power relations between landowners and peasants in the nineteenth century, thereby influencing the institutional structures and leading to the abolition of serfdom in 1861, was population growth during the eighteenth century. Data on the growth of the male population follow (Table 6.2).

Thus, despite epidemics, famines, war, the lethal depredations of the penal system, and the colonization of additional cultivated areas, population growth—especially in the Central Agricultural region—caused per capita land allotments to drop. The highest share of planted area among all land allotted to peasants in use rights per male "soul" contracted from 3.50 *desyatinas* in 1725 to 3.19 in 1763 and 3.04 in 1796 (Kahan, 1985, p. 45). Despite roughly 75 percent population growth in the Central Agricultural region in 1719–1795, planted area per male individual contracted by only 10 percent. This condition traces to the rising share of the peasantry that was "assigned" to mines and factories, serfs hired for factory work (Kahan, 1985, p. 83; Anisimov, 1993, p. 176), and collective resettlement (Vladimirskaya, 1997, personal communication) in newly colonized regions where land was abundant.

Deducing from the NIE model, the shrinking per capita land allotment in densely populated black-soil areas increased serfs' economic dependency on landowners (Engelgardt, 1993, pp. 37, 38). Concurrently, the rising peasants-to-nobles ratio, in a population inspired by an egalitarian ideology, amplified the risk of rebellion (Kolchin, 1987, p. 52, Table 3), making such a threat from below credible.[43] This, in turn, raised landlords' surveillance costs (Leonard, 1990, p. 136; North, 1990, pp. 90, 91) and undermined the rationale for serfdom itself, namely, the initial high land/labor ratio.[44]

Against this background, I suggest that the structural precondition (Archer, 1995, p. 76)—population growth during the eighteenth century, itself probably the result of collectivist mutual insurance and mutual help as well as landlords' mandatory care of their serfs (Hoch, 1986)—abetted

[43] See Greif (2006, p. 441), on shirking as a freeloader problem that is overcome by voluntary peasant cooperation.

[44] Kolchin (1987, p. 2), remarks on the shortage of labor.

Table 6.2 Population growth (males) in various regions of Russia

Date	*Comparable territory a*	*North and Northwest b*	*Central industrial c*	*Central agricultural d*	*Total "Old Territory" e*	*Areas of colonization f*
1 reviziia 1719	6,345,101	834,484	2,278,535	1,443,349	**6,740,183**	**832,330**
2 reviziia 1744	7,399,546	983,157	2,275,275	1,633,099	7,640,762	1,308,804
Yearly % change	0.6	0.7	0.0	0.5	0.5	1.8
3 reviziia 1762	8,436,779	1,040,143	2,540,465	1,819,897	9,014,287	1,928,525
Yearly % change	0.7	0.3	0.6	0.6	0.9	2.2
4 reviziia 1782	10,469,767	1,235,293	2,938,056	2,315,110	10,209,797	2,836,327
Yearly % change	1.1	0.9	0.7	1.2	0.6	1.9
5 reviziia 1795	11,352,774	1,304,398	3,036,913	2,515,612	10,685,352	3,519,486
Yearly % change	0.6	0.4	0.3	0.6	0.4	1.7
Yearly % increase 1719–1795	–	–	–	–	0.58	2.0

a. Territory of the first population census

b. Includes Arkhangelsk, Vologda, St. Petersburg, Novgorod, Olonets, and Pskov Districts

c. Includes Moscow, Vladimir, Kaluga, Iaroslav, Kostroma, Nizhnii Novgorod, and Tver

d. Includes Riazan, Tambov, Orel, Kursk, and Tula

e. Includes the sum of North and Northwest, Central Industrial, and Central Agricultural E=a+c+d

f. Includes Voronezh District, Novorossiya, Lower Volga, the Urals, and Siberia

e+f All of Russia, the Old Territory and areas of colonization with their various revisions

Sources: Kahan (1985, Kabuzans data, 16); regional map of Russia: Hosking (1997), "Russia People and Empire," Map: x–xi "Expansion of the Russian Empire in the eighteenth century"

the abolition of the unfree labor system between 1861 and 1866. The institutions fostered by serfdom also did their share. The debacle of the Crimean War may have been explained by rising surveillance costs and the irrationality of serfdom which catalyzed the transition but was not its primary cause.[45]

The Village Commune, Dependence on the Landlord, and Individualism of the Emancipation Era—The Determinants of Serfdom

According to Heinz-Dietrich Löwe, there is evidence of leveling processes in which the intermediate household stratum expanded on account of small and large farmsteads, the *dvory* (Löwe, 1990, p. 181). This is consistent with the foregoing depiction of the obshchina, the village commune, as a redistributive cooperation network. There is no evidence, however, of a bidirectional "capitalist" differentiation, in which the percent share of both the large and the small strata, especially landless households, grows (Löwe, 1990, p. 181). Thus, as the nineteenth-century Tsarist bureaucrats expected, the collectivist practice of the obshchina and the egalitarian ethos spared the peasantry from pauperization and proletarianization.

The following table illustrates the long-term leveling effect of the post-emancipation peasant custom as it interacted with the inherited institutions of serfdom (Table 6.3).

Löwe concludes that the limited differentiation actually observed must trace to additional economic/political factors, such as the terms of the emancipation agreement, and not only by the economic forces at work

Table 6.3 Long-term changes in household stratification by land ownership, 1765–1900

	Gorodinsk district, Chernigov Gubernia farms, in desyatiny (pct.)					
	Up to 1	*1–5*	*5–15*	*15–25*	*Over 25*	
1765/1768	17.3	8.4	28.4	15.6	30.0	100
1883	10.0	***29.0***	***38.2***	11.9	10.9	100

Source: Löwe (1990, p. 181 [italics and emphasis added])

[45] Contrary to Gerschenkron (1968, p. 143).

Table 6.4 Longitudinal ownership of serf categories (percent)

Categories of peasants—percent changes, 1719–1857					
Year	*Landlord (%)*	*State (Tsarist) (%)*	*Church (%)*	*Court (Tsarist) (%)*	*All peasants (%)*
1719	55.80	21.46	13.84	8.90	100.00
1744	56.46	23.72	13.42	6.41	100.00
1762	55.47	25.46	12.88	6.19	100.00
1782	53.16	40.61		6.23	100.00
1795	54.47	40.79		4.74	100.00
1811	52.44	42.75		4.81	100.00
1815	51.01	42.58		6.41	100.00
1833	48.18	45.53		6.29	100.00
1850	43.53	50.85		5.62	100.00
1857	41.84	52.26		5.90	100.00

Source: Moon (1999, p. 99)

Table 6.4. Moreover, says Löwe, landless wage labor seems to have become rarer instead of more common, actually indicating increasing dependency on the complementarity of industrial and agricultural production, rather than industrial work alone.

According to Field, stratification in the peasant community due to economic factors alone had been inhibited by the leveling mechanisms inherent in the village commune structure (Field, 1990, pp. 143, 160, Table 10, p. 8 A).[46] Field's findings, below, suggest that the weaker the structural serfdom legacy, expressed in terms of its proxy—the percentage in the population of individuals who had been serfs before the emancipation—due to peasant mobility, migration, and the contingent intergenerational structural shifts (power transfers from fathers to sons), the stronger become individualism and stratification along income and urban versus rural cultural affinities in the village commune.

The table 6.4 above illustrates the structure of types of enserfment of the peasant constituency during the 1719–1857 period.

[46] Field finds a positive correlation between the percent of ex-serfs in a district and the number of households in the in-between class. This is consistent with my assumption about the uneven post-emancipation survival of the serfdom structures, characterized by the leveling redistribution.

According to Archer's (1995, p. 76) structural-preconditions concept, the immediate post-emancipation structure of the peasant community was subject to reconstitutive downward causation brought on by centuries of serfdom. Bondage at the hands of the landed gentry, the pomeshchiks, was most common in the agricultural black-soil belt (Moon, 1999, p. 70) and entailed barshchina (day service labor) on the landlord's demesne. Serfdom at the hands of pomeshchiks had been the most onerous form of bondage in peasant eyes.

In non-black-soil regions, quitrent as well as state taxes (Moon, 1999, p. 70; Mironov, 2000, p. 302) burdened the peasants. Serfs ("seigniorial peasants"), unlike other members of the peasant estate, were directly bound to the person of the landowner on a hereditary basis and were subject to the landed gentry's administrative and judicial authority (Moon, 1999, p. 66). This peasant category had been subjected to physical, climatic, and anthropogenic institutional hardships (North, 2005, p. 7). Therefore, it is assumed here that this type of bonded labor was motivated by the strongest peasant dependencies on landlords (Engelgardt, 1993, p. 38), mutual responsibility and mutual assistance (Worobec, 1995, p. 24), and work done "out of respect" at the landlords and former landlords demesne and for well-to-do fellow peasants household as well as famine insurance of the "crust seeking" kind (Engelgardt, 1993, pp. 28, 52). All these strategies inspired the redistribution of landed and movable assets, namely, collectivism. One would expect the structural impact of the railroads to be stronger in these areas than in areas that had been populated by the state—those owned by the Tsarist State (Moon, 1999, p. 99)—with peasants and other peasant categories before emancipation. The empirical tests in Chap. 9 concern the Penza region, the northern black-soil area.

Here I address the regional conditions that explain the variance in the percentages of serfs. Viatka Province is located in the western *tajga* (forested) regions near the natural barrier, the Ural Mountains, that protected the village population from armed intrusion. One would expect crafts related to hunting to have generated a relatively high share of household income in this region (Figes, 2002, Map 3—European Russia, xviii; Gatrell, 1994, ix). Landlords in such regions would derive higher revenue from obrok than from barshchina (Moon, 1999, p. 76) and the utility of serfdom to the landed nobility would be relatively lower. The percentage of former serfs in the population is the lowest, a dependency of the ratio of low-sedentary agricultural land endowments to labor. In 1850–1917, Iaroslav, Kostroma, and Vladimir together constituted the Central Industrial region, located in semi-desert areas and mixed forests along the Volga River (Figes, 2002, Map 3—European Russia, xviii: Gatrell, 1994, ix). River-related transport and haulage, identified by Gerschenkron (1970, p. 19) as the preferred and chosen sources of livelihood among the subversive Old Believer (*starovery*) sects, motivated serfdom at the hands of the Tsars for social-control purposes. This, in turn, made it necessary to preserve commune internal harmony by smoothing redistribution among the serfs (Ma, 2006, p. 11). Well-to-do and piously subversive Old Believer peasant entrepreneurs posed a challenge to the autocracy, which was supported by mainstream Greek Orthodoxy.

In the forested Viatka region, the low percentage of former serfs in the population may also be explained by the relatively high independence of the peasantry from landlord protection and famine insurance because crafts, hunting, gathering, and natural barriers to intruders insured against calamities on their own. Semi-desert regions with unpredictable precipitation—such as Iaroslav, Kostroma, and Vladimir—were prone to crop failure, making peasants there dependent on the demesnes of technologically more advanced landlords, "assigned" industrial income, hired labor, and mutual insurance. These abetted serfdom and rendered the share of former serfs relatively high. (See table below.)

Table 6.5 below shows the positive correlation between the share of serfs in the population and that of middle households, reflecting the intensity of the leveling effect determined by redistribution. The lower the percentage of former serfs, the higher the individualism expressed in differentiation.

Table 6.5 Percent distribution of village resources for allotment in Vladimir and other provinces, 1905

	0–1	*1–3*	*3–5*	*5–10*	*10–15*	*15+*	*Percent of former serfs*
Iaroslav	0.5	4.4	15.9	**65.9**	12.0	1.3	**76.4**
Kostroma	0.6	3.4	8.5	**57.6**	23.3	6.6	**63.7**
Viatka	0.0	0.1	1.9	**12.9**	**28.1**	**56.5**	**10.4**
Vladimir	5.9	4.2	7.8	**49.8**	23.3	9.1	**64.3**

Intervals in *desyatinas*, four provinces: Iaroslav, Kostroma, Viatka, Vladimir

Source: Field (1990, Table 10.8, p. 160)

Thus, Viatka Province serves as a case in point: It has the lowest percentage of former serfs in the population (10.4 percent as against ≤ 50 percent in Iaroslav, Kostroma, and Vladimir provinces) and the highest differentiation (56.5 percent of the households controlled fifteen or more *desyatinas* of land per household, as against 1.3 percent in Iaroslav, 6.6 percent in Kostroma, and 9.1 percent in Vladimir), indicating weakness in smoothing land repartitions—a reflection of redistributive collectivism. It must be acknowledged, however, that the share of poor households (those controlling less than five *desyatinas* of land per household) is also the lowest among the provinces. Nevertheless, the span between 12.9 percent of households controlling five to ten *desyatinas* of land per household and 56.5 percent controlling more than fifteen *desyatinas* per household is indicative not of collectivist land redistribution but of individualism. Some 98 percent of households' landholdings exceeded five *desyatinas* per household and 2 percent were smaller, indirectly indicating acute dependence on agrarian income, relatively stable living standards, and relatively lower leveling effects, namely, weakening of collectivism.

Table 6.5 implies, contrary to Gerschenkron's proposition and in support of my argument, that the nineteenth-century obshchina was not a homogeneous and stable structure during the post-emancipation period. The technological change embodied in the construction of railroads, which enhanced peasant mobility and, in turn, migration intensity, inexorably eroded the viability of the structures of serfdom, attenuating their reconstitutive downward causation. Presumably, then, the degree of compulsory collectivism that was constitutive of serfdom, manifested in the leveling effects of the post-emancipation peasant commune, weakened over time and atrophied at the dawn of Stolypin's reform, which constituted an ex-post codification of the de facto transition to voluntary cooperation (individualism). The industrialization spurt in 1890 should be tested for a structural shift from compulsory elder-authority–structured collectivism to rationalistic voluntary cooperation between individualistic householders (*bolshaki*). Such a shift may be measured as the "income-control intensity" (Hesse, 1993, p. 52) of the patriarchs' generation—a proxy for the long-term share of wage laborers, seasonal and urban industrial wage income coercively repatriated to the commune for the support of kin. Field's findings are consistent with Löwe's.

Worobec notes regional differentiation by soil quality. In the infertile non–black-soil regions where land had to be manured, even partial redistributions were less frequent than elsewhere because households wished to protect their investment (Worobec, 1990, p. 96). As land repartitions in these regions were less frequent, the degree of differentiation could have been higher. In the central black-soil area bordering the Chernigov region in the southwest Gorodinsk district (Gatrell, 1994, pp. ix, 37), the share of middle households had been the highest (Table 6.3 above). Land in these regions needed no manure, while collectivist redistribution was the result of declining land-to-labor ratios in an area that historically had been burdened with labor shortages—a typical feature of "seigniorial servitude" in the black-soil belt. The leveling effect, however, could have been caused by differential obrok payments in those regions (Moon, 1999, p. 218).

Communalism or Individualism and Strife in the Final Phases of the Commune?

Would it be correct, in the absence of "capitalist" differentiation (Lenin, 1974) under variegating regionally communal leveling,[47] to conclude that the communal redistributive action and the accompanying spirit permeated peasant daily life to such a degree as to rule out egoism, individualism, and individual entrepreneurship? Qualitative anecdotal evidence suggests that individualism within the formally collectivist structure of the village commune actually increased and flourished. As stated above, the peasantry adhered to the principle of individually valuing and remunerating individuals' labor. Labor constituted the rationale for the peasantry's concept of possession and, ultimately, its understanding of property rights (Pipes, 1999, p. 87). It was usually apportioned such that each worker was rewarded commensurate with his or her input and the difficulty of the task performed (Engelgardt in Frierson, 1993, pp. 115, 116, 158, 160). As the following quotation from Engelgardt may illustrate, the meticulous division of labor commensurate with the burden of debt of each member of the labor team to the landowner, gives unambiguous evidence of individualism:

[47] Löwe (1990, p. 173). Lenin's renowned book, *The Development of Capitalism in Russia* (1974) and its calculations concerning the question of differentiation in the Russian peasantry, deserve a separate discourse due to their theoretical and ideological framework and are not discussed in this chapter.

> *[...] To cultivate rye or spring wheat, the peasants would come primarily to divide the land into half desyatinas, quarter desyatinas, or eighths,* corresponding to who borrowed how much money. *There is the most horrible shouting and cursing during this division; it seems as if a brawl is about to break out at any minute [...] but as soon as the division is finished, everyone gets quiet and you will see how accurately all the shares are cut.* (Engelgardt in Frierson, 1993, p. 116, emphasis added)

One presumes that the alignment of land apportionment with the tax burden also had an individualistic aspect. Furthermore, this principle of individualism guided every egalitarian obshchina formation inasmuch as heads of household who had invested in allotted land were compensated at the time of repartition (Kingston-Mann, 1991, pp. 44, 45). Mutual compensation arrangements of this type should be regarded as short-term adjustments to technological infusions that allowed individualization to take place and constituted intermediary forms of landed-asset control. The decision-making authority had been vested in the commune assembly of heads of household (Worobec, 1995, p. 21), a middle-management organ, positioned between the self-governing commune and the Tsarist government institutions, that resolved repartition disputes by a two-thirds majority in accordance with the principle of joint responsibility for taxes and dues (Gaudin, 2007, p. 17). Therefore, compensating investing parties at times of repartitions cannot be understood as substituting for the formation of *otrubs* (consolidated hereditary household plots) or *khutors*, in which, upon the implementation of the Stolypin reform (1906–1917), heads of household obtained hereditary and exclusive allodial property rights to landed assets (Gaudin, 2007, pp. 43, 44; Pallot, 1982, p. 19).

Worobec (1995, pp. 23–29) and Pallot (1982, p. 14) provide a systematized account of the practice of repartitions. Land was assigned in accordance with the number of husband-and-wife labor teams, assuring the most productive use of this asset and egalitarian distribution of the tax burden among households (Worobec, 1995, p. 23). A general or "basic" repartition"—*korennoi peredel* (Pallot, 1982, p. 14)—pertained to all households and took into consideration differences in soil quality, moisture, and distance from the village (Worobec, 1995, p. 24). After the heads of the labor units chose one three fields in a given year, they grouped themselves in tens to divide it into strips. The soils that were the richest and the closest to farmsteads were divided by lot. The next-best lands were divided the same way. Household heads then divided this group of lands in accordance with the number of labor units or the number of "eaters" per household. The strips of arable land assigned to each household were demarcated by passages for plows and animals or by boundary markings. Such repartitions took place at intervals of three to twenty-five years. Given unchanged technology, such variation was explained by soil quality, the need to apply manure, and land values. In Northern and Central Russia, heavily manured land allotments were excluded from the redistribution process. In 1880, with the decrease in redemption dues and the increase of land values (in response to peasant use of the railroads, as explained in this monograph), repartition adjustments meant to equalize the tax burden became more frequent (Pallot, 1982). In view of Atkinson's findings (1983, p. 74) however, this cannot be proven as a general trend. The impact of the railroads on the stability of use and property rights in land among the Late Tsarist Russian peasantry is ultimately an empirical question, in which acute regional variation is expected. Not only were soil quality and climatic conditions diverse, but so were incremental population densities and systems of rule in their interaction with ethnicities and cultures in the areas successively conquered by and incorporated into the Tsarist Empire.

Pallot (1982, p. 14) illuminates two additional repartition practices applied by the peasantry: *zhereberka*, "partition by lot," and *pereverstka*, "re-ordering repartition." Here the physical arable land remained the same but title was adjusted to reflect change in the number of labor units or eaters per household. Similarly, Dostoyewskij (1977, p. 25) shows that any remuneration owed to convicts on account of labor performed was remitted individually; only alms for prisoners were redistributed by egalitarian calculus.

The principle of retaining remuneration for labor performed was strongly related to the peasant conception of property (Engelgardt in Frierson, 1993, p. 160; Pipes, 1999, p. 87). As stated above, the house and garden plot had been retained by the household in hereditary tenure at all times. A woman's dowry was her inalienable property (Worobec, 1995, p. 42). In general, too, as Engelgardt lamented in reference to the 1872–1887 period:

> *The peasants live in separate households and every household has its own separate farm that it also manages through its own supervision [...]. Every year, the independence of peasants' actions grows and grows, so that many tasks that were still done together several years ago by the whole village are now done separately*

> *by each household. I think that the peasants will soon divide even the land by household and destroy communal landholding.* (Engelgardt in Frierson, 1993, p. 87)

Thus, Engelgardt's eyewitness account reports rising individualism among the peasantry even before the 1890 industrialization spurt. The spurt, powered by intensified urban wage labor (Johnson, 1979, p. 12), merely made the younger generation even more independent of the decisions of the patriarch and the commune (Burds, 1998, p. 29), allowing the more individualistic urban culture to penetrate the rural habitus with greater ease (Smurova, 2003, p. 100). If so, individualism had always been present but had been suppressed by the reinforcement of the hierarchy of exploitation among household heads, the commune, the landlord, and ultimately the Tsarist state in the serfdom era (Hoch, 1986, p. 160) and, before the emancipation, by the state's pitting of serf against serf for information and, ultimately, for control in order to reduce its surveillance costs (North, 1990, p. 91; Leonard, 1990, p. 136).

In his tenth letter, Engelgardt notes the peasants' very strong sense of wealth despite their inexperience in hereditary land tenure:

> *I have stated more than once that individualism, egoism, and the urge to exploit are very much developed amongst the peasantry. Envy, the mistrust of each other, scheming against each other, the humiliation of weak before the strong, the arrogance of the strong, the worship of wealth (landed and movable property)—all of this is highly developed in the peasant milieu.* (Engelgardt in Frierson, Engelgardt, 1993, p. 223)

Notably, Engelgardt nurtured populist sentiment, praising the commune and denouncing individualism. The most telling element in his account is based on the peasant distinction between a "real *kulak*" (a "fist," namely, an individualist, exploiter, and usurer) and a "not-real *kulak*," a peasant-entrepreneur. One who works and amasses a fortune by his own labor, even if employing others as well, and who says "I love the land, I love the work" (Engelgardt in Frierson, 224) is regarded by the peasantry not as a real kulak but as an entrepreneur who deserves respect and admiration; he who works with capital and says "labor loves fools" is taken by the peasantry to be a true kulak and a *miroed*, one unworthy of respect (Shanin, 1985, pp. 156, 157). Thus, peasant hostility gravitated not to individualistic agrarian entrepreneurs but to those whom the community perceived as usurers—a way of thinking much supported by the Church and its admirers. Moreover, the link between agricultural labor invested and the perception of legitimate property is ubiquitous in Russian peasant conceptions.

Shanin (1985) describes the peasants' differentiation similarly. The "real" kulaks in Engelgardt's account, the usurers who did not live off their own agricultural labor, earned the following derogative epithets from the contemporary peasantry: *skryaga*—niggard, *miroed—mir* eater, *maklak*—go-between, *and vorotila*—a shady wheeler and dealer. A 1903 etymological dictionary defined all these sobriquets as synonyms for "kulak" (Shanin, 1985, p. 156). Thus, the nineteenth-century peasant did not resent but rather admired those whom he perceived as successful individualist agrarian entrepreneurs. This, as noted above, cannot be said about noble intellectuals of populist inclinations such as Engelgardt, who were bowled over by the rational logic of the village commune.

Before concluding this overview on peasant collectivism versus individualism, some references to peasant attitudes toward the process that formalized the individualization of rights—Stolypin's land reform—are warranted:

Macey (1990) focuses attention on endemic conflicts among peasants and peasant communities due to poorly defined property rights in land. Before 1906, the courts throughout the empire, *including the peasantry*, were "clogged with lawsuits over property rights." Given the morass of faulty deeds and lack of written documents concerning what belonged to whom, possession was nine-tenths of the law (Macey, 1990, p. 221). Macey refutes the notion that the peasants had no sense of individual private property. The commune, he says, was a major arena of conflict over property rights in land, making repartition the most difficult point in what North would call the life cycle of the relevant organizations (Macey, 1990, p. 222). Macey depicts the nineteenth-century peasant commune not as an egalitarian social unit but as a hotbed of deep-rooted peasant egoism. Taking into account the "extreme competitiveness, individualism, [and] self-interestedness" of the heads of household, he says, the function of the periodic land redistribution must have been simply conflict resolution.

Thus, according to Macey's account, the antagonism and peasant violence that accompanied the implementation of Stolypin's rural transformation project in 1906 (as depicted by Pallot, 1999, p. 166) could not have reflected the defense of the communal organization and spirit, an act that targeted individualism among fellow peasants as such. Rather, the climate of conflict manifested the peasants' historical deep-rooted antipathy to any type of imperial encroachment on their autonomy, risk aversion in view of the rumor-mongering that accompanied major institutional changes in premodern communities (Moon, 1999, p. 240), and the previously somnolent but now unleashed intra- and inter-village conflict over the use of and property rights in land (Macey, 1990, p. 221; Pallot, 1999, p. 166; Frank, 1999, pp. 105, 108).

If so, Stolypin may have been right (Klimin, 2002, p. 11) in assuming that the rural commune had exhausted its life-preserving role and had begun to atrophy in its interaction with industrialization, including railroadization, while peasant individualism—always present but latent due to the prevalent conditions of life—was becoming increasingly manifest. Worobec, for example, cites statisticians who note that after the emancipation, even in black-soil regions (where land redistribution had traditionally been more frequent because the soil did not require costly fertilization), a "significant lobby among peasants" (Worobec, 1995, p. 96) existed that opposed repartition, guarding their right to use land that was becoming scarcer and more valuable due to the interaction of population increase and railroad construction.

Theoretical Interpretation

As for theoretical interpretation, AEI explains individualism in terms of individual selection whereas NIE sets out from an individualist and hedonistic understanding of human nature. Within an ahistorical framework, there would be little to explain about individualism, let alone peasant individualism. Both schools, however, prescribe the study of history-specific conditions and past legacies. Thus, according to Chicherin's and the Westernizers' understanding of the commune, serfdom *forced* collectivism and communal practice while suppressing and thwarting individual initiative. From the combined AEI/NIE perspective, in contrast, serfdom *enforced* formally organic peasant institutions (as in the Slavophile understanding of the commune), additionally necessitating and therefore fostering rational reflexive collectivism (Pallot, 1999, p. 157) while exploiting peasant individual initiative for both tax extraction and control purposes, respectively. Thus, it lowered the surveillance costs incurred by landlords and, ultimately, the state (Hoch, 1986, p. 128; Leonard, 1990, p. 136). Within a temporally and topographically specific framework, it is obvious that the proportions of collectivism versus individualism, institutionalized over time, generally are continuous, non-discrete, and mutually exclusive. The overview above implies that microlevel institutions—peasant custom in our case—are functions of a supra-institutional structure as well as physical conditions of life and that these two are partly interdependent. Ultimately, institutions are explainable by relative scarcities or physical conditions of life (North, 1973, p. 29, 2005, pp. 100, 101). Against the foregoing account, can any optimal proportion of collectivism versus individualism be derived from the perspective offered by the combination of the schools applied? The discussion that follows will attempt to answer in the affirmative.

According to my combined model, the optimal mix of collectivism and individualism, hierarchy and egalitarianism, and exploitation and workmanship coincides with Stolypin's land reform. An additional push to defend and enforce all property rights aspects may inhibit cooperation and risk-sharing, impairing productivity. Additional collectivism weakens the incentive structure, leading to the same result (Poznanski, 1992, p. 71) (Fig. 6.1).

Summarizing Remarks

Congruent with North's NIE (North, 1973) and supplemented by the Regulationist paradigm, I contend within a broader AEI framework that the change in conventions in the pre-revolutionary period was ultimately set in motion by population increase that necessitated the absorption of technological innovations, specifically railroads. This, in turn, paved the way to the transition from anxiety-driven subservient centripetal authority obedience (Lawson, 1997, p. 180–182) to centrifugal anonymous and rationalist rule compliance that rejected personalized coercion. The institutionally personalized hierarchies of coercion had proved inadequate in military rivalry with Western powers, forcing the initial Tsarist concession—the 1861 emancipation of the serfs—and the subsequent codification of the peasants' emancipation from compulsory collectivism in Stolypin's land reform. The centrifugal challenge paved the way to participatory rules.

In sum, the cost-benefit analysis of the delineation of property rights—the full exodus from communal structures that aimed to reduce transaction costs and enhance the incentive structure, as proposed in the 1906

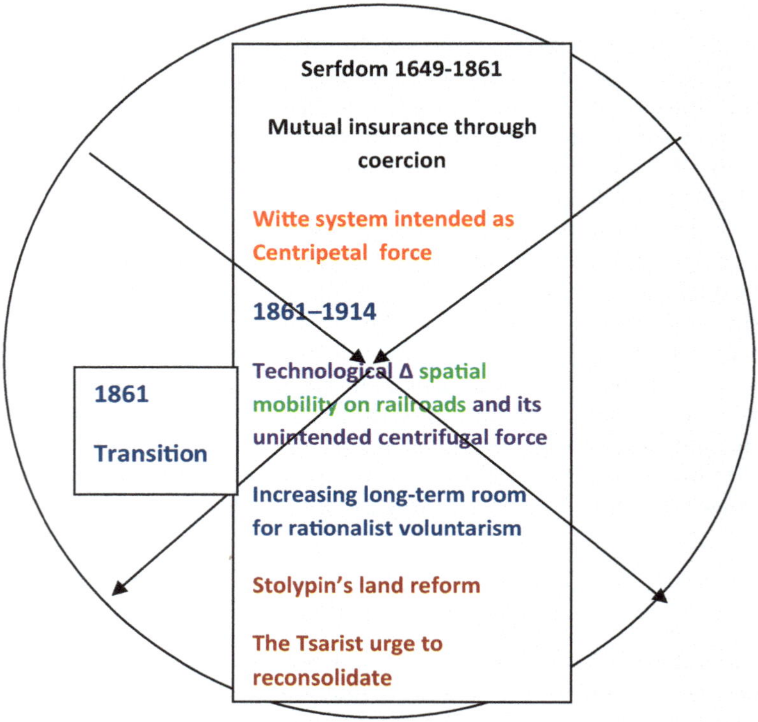

Fig. 6.1 The railroad and the transformation of the Mir—summary. (*Sources*: Migdal [Migdal, 1988, p. 268], Sheshinski, 2010, p. 3], Gintis, 2009, pp. 1, 2], and Hoch, 1986 on the institutionalization of mutual insurance in collective responsibility for taxes and dues and the landlord's role as lender of last resort during the serfdom era)

Stolypin reform—must entail the opportunity costs of forgone tacit knowledge, encapsulated in this case in the obshchina, the increasingly voluntary commune-village structure (Barzel, 1989, pp. 10, 11; Hodgson, 1999, p. 247). The obshchina was the wheel of subversion that was unintentionally spun off from the serfdom structure that, after the emancipation, was driven by the railroads' techno-cultural revolution. Thus, it was transformed into a voluntary collective action unit that eroded the heritage of serfdom and would soon reform the autocracy, atrophying in the process (Barzel, 2002, p. 61).

Figure 6.2 summarizes the transformation of the obshchina and its precipitants.

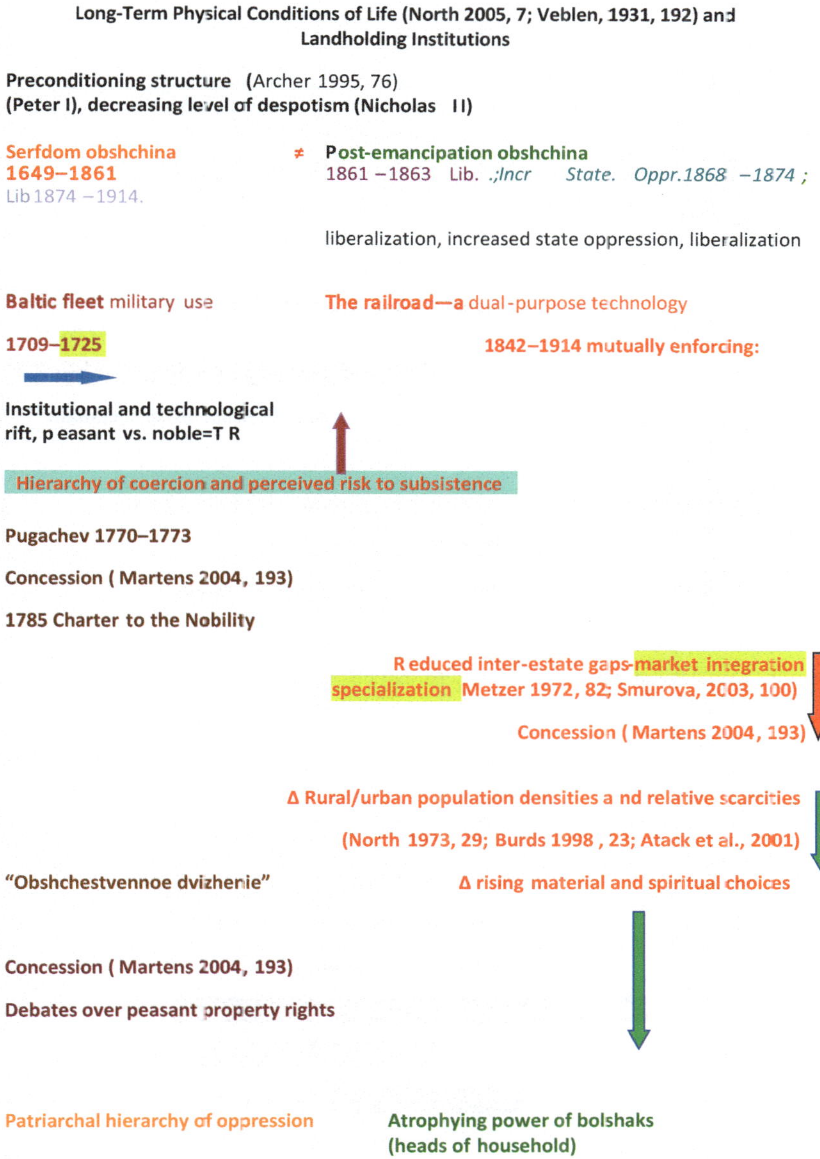

Fig. 6.2 The railroad and the unintended metamorphosis of Mir and autocracy. (Examples from Ascher [1988, p. 34], Burds [1998, pp. 204, 205], and Matosian in Vucinich [1968, pp. 81, 85], Legitimized by Sheshinski [2010, p. 3] and Gintis [2009, pp. 1, 2], NIE [Hodgson, 2004, pp. 14, 105], Poznanski [1985, p. 45, 1992, pp. 71–94])

(continued)

Fig. 6.2 (continued)

References

Anisimov, V. E. (1993). The reforms of Peter the Great -Progress through coercion in Russia. M.E. Sharpe.

Archer, M. (1995). Realist social theory: The morphogenetic approach. Chapter presented at the 6th International Workshop on Institutional Economics, The University of Hertfordshire.

Ascher, A. (1988). *The Revolution of 1905- Part I Russia in Disarray*. Stanford UP.

Atkinson, D. (1983). *The end of the Russian land commune 1905–1930*. Stanford University Press.

Bakunin, M. (1970). *God and the state*. Dover Publications.

Barzel, Y. (1989). *Economic analysis of property rights*. Cambridge University Press.

Barzel, Y. (2002). *The theory of the state: Economic rights, legal rights and the scope of the state*. Cambridge University Press.

Baykov, A. (1954). The economic development of Russia. *Economic History Review, 7*(2), 137–149.

Bideleux, R. (1990). Agricultural advance under the Russian village commune system. In R. Bartlett (Ed.), *Land commune and peasant community in Russia: Communal forms in Imperial and early Soviet society* (Macmillan in Association with the School of Slavonic and East European Studies). University of London.

Blum, J. (1961). *Lord and peasant in Russia from the ninth to the nineteenth century*. Princeton University Press.

Boserup, E. (1965). *The conditions of agricultural growth the economics of agrarian change under population pressure*. Allen Unwin LDT.

Boyer, R., & Orlean, A. (1993). How do conventions evolve? In U. Witt (Ed.), *Evolution in markets and institutions*. Physica-Vlg.

Bucher, G. (2008). *Daily life in imperial Russia*. Greenwood Press.

Burds, J. (1998). *Peasant dreams and market politics: Labor migration and the Russian village 1861–1905*. University of Pittsburgh Press.

Chubarov, A. (2001). *The fragile empire: A history of imperial Russia*. Continuum.

Coase, R. (1937). *The firm, the market and the law*. University of Chicago Press.

Crisp, O. (1989). Peasant land tenure and civil rights implications before 1906. In O. Crisp & L. Edmondson (Eds.), *Civil rights in imperial Russia*. Clarendon Press.

de Madariaga, I. (1998). *Politics and culture in eighteenth century Russia*. Longman.

Dostoyewskij, F. (1977). *Wspomninenia z domu umarlych*. Panstwowy Instytut Wydawniczy.

Eggertsson, T. (1990). *Economic behavior and institutions*. Cambridge University Press.

Engelgardt, P. N. (1993). In C. Frierson (Tr. and Ed.). *Aleksandr Nikolaevich Engelgardt's Letters from the Country, 1872–1887*. Oxford University Press.

Field, D. (1990). Stratification and the Russian peasant commune: A statistical inquiry. In R. Bartlett (Ed.), *Land commune and peasant community in Russia-communal forms in imperial and early Soviet Society* (Macmillan in Association with the School of Slavonic and East European Studies). University of London.
Figes, O. (2002). *Natasha's dance: A cultural history of Russia*. Allen Lane, an Imprint of Penguin Books.
Frank, S. (1999). *Crime, cultural conflict and justice in rural Russia 1856–1914*. University of California Press.
Frierson, C. (1993). Land commune and peasant community in Russia: Communal forms in imperial and early Soviet Society. In R. Bartlett (Ed.), *Land commune and peasant community in Russia: Communal forms in imperial and early Soviet Society* (Macmillan in Association with the School of Slavonic and East European Studies). University of London.
Gatrell, P. (1994). *Government, industry and rearmament in Russia, 1900–1914: The Last argument of Tsarism*. Cambridge University Press.
Gaudin, C. (2007). *Ruling peasants: Village and state in late imperial Russia*. Northern Illinois University Press.
Gerschenkron, A. (1962). *Economic backwardness in historical perspective*. The Belknap Press of Harvard University Press.
Gerschenkron, A. (1968). *Continuity in history and other essays*. The Belknap Press of Harvard University Press.
Gerschenkron, A. (1970). *Europe in Russian Mirror*. Cambridge UP.
Gintis, H. (2009). *The bounds of reason: Game theory and the unification of the behavioral sciences*. Princeton University Press.
Gregory, P. R. (1994). *Before command. An economic history of Russia from emancipation to the first five-year plan*. Princeton University Press.
Greif, A. (2006). *Institutions and the path to modern economy: Lessons from medieval trade*. Cambridge University Press.
Hayek FAv. (1967). *Philosophy, Politics and Economics*. Chicago UP.
Hesse, G. (1993). Land use systems and property rights. Evolutionary versus institutional economics. In U. Witt (Ed.), *Evolution in markets and institutions*. Physica-Vlg.
Hoch, S. (1986). *Serfdom and social control in Russia. Petrovskoe, a village in Tambov*. University of Chicago Press.
Hodgson. (2007). Personal communication.
Hodgson, G. M. (1999). *Evolution and institutions: On evolutionary economics and the evolution of economics*. Edward Elgar.
Hodgson, G. M. (2001). *How Economics Forgot History*. How Economics Forgot History. The Problem of Historical Specificity in Social Science. Routledge.
Hodgson, G. M. (2004). What are institutions? From orders to organizations. Essay presented at the 6th International Workshop on Institutional Economics, University of Hertfordshire.

Hodgson, G. M., & Knudsen, T. (2005). The nature and units of social selection. *Papers on Economics & Evolution*. Max Planck Institute of Economics.

Hosking, G. (1997). *Russia: People and empire 1552–1917*. Harvard University Press.

Hughes, L. (1998). *Russia in the age of Peter the Great*. Yale University Press.

Johnson, R. (1979). *Peasant and proletarian: The working class of Moscow in the late nineteenth century*. Leicester University Press.

Kahan, A. (1985). *The plow, the hammer and the knout: An economic history of eighteenth-century Russia*. University of Chicago Press.

Keren, M. (2006). personal communication.

Kingston-Mann, E. (1991). Peasant communes and economic innovation: A preliminary inquiry. In E. Kingston-Mann, T. Mixter, & J. Burds (Eds.), *Peasant economy culture and politics of European Russia*. Princeton University Press.

Klimin, I. I. (2002). *Stolypinskaya agrarnaya reforma i stanovlenie krestian sobstvennikov v Rossii*. Csentr istoricheskich i gumanitarnych issledovani 'Klio'.

Kolchin, P. (1987). *Unfree labour, American slavery and Russian Serfdom*. The Belknap Press of Harvard University Press.

Lawson, T. (1997). *Economics and Reality*. Routledge.

Lenin, V. I. (1974). *The development of capitalism in Russia*. Progress Publishers.

Leonard, C. S. (1990). Landlords and the mir: Transaction costs and economic development in pre-emancipation Russia (Iaroslav Gubernia). In R. Bartlett (Ed.), *Land commune and peasant community in Russia: Communal forms in imperial and early Soviet society* (Macmillan in Association with the School of Slavonic and East European Studies). University of London.

Löwe, H. D. (1990). Differentiation in Russian peasant society: causes and trends. In R. Bartlett (Ed.), *Land commune and peasant community in Russia: Communal forms in imperial and early Soviet society* (Macmillan in Association with the School of Slavonic and East European Studies) (pp. 1880–1905). University of London.

Ma, D. (2006). Law and commerce in traditional China. An institutional perspective on the "Great Divergence." Seminar Paper, Department of Economic History, Lund University.

Macey, D. (1990). The peasant commune and the Stolypin reforms: Peasant attitudes, 1906–1914. In R. Bartlett (Ed.), *Land commune and peasant community in Russia: Communal forms in imperial and early Soviet society* (Macmillan in Association with the School of Slavonic and East European Studies). University of London.

Mäki, U. (1990). *Studies in realism and explanation in economics*. Suomalainen Tiedeakademia.

Martens, B. (2004). *The cognitive mechanics of economic development and institutional change*. Routledge.

Matosian, M. (1968). The peasant way of life. In W. S. Vucinich (Ed.), *The peasant in nineteenth century Russia*. Stanford University Press.
Metzer, J. (1972). *Some economic aspects of railroad development in Tsarist Russia* [Unpublished doctoral dissertation]. University of Chicago.
Migdal, J. (1988). *Strong societies and weak states. State–society relations and state capabilities in the Third World*. Princeton University Press.
Mironov, B. N. (2000). *A social history of imperial Russia, 1700–1917* (Vol. I). Westview Press.
Moon, D. (1999). *The Russian peasantry 1600–1930*. Longman.
Nafziger, S. (2006). Communal institutions, resource allocations and Russian economic development. Dissertation summery.
Nafziger, S. (2007). Land redistributions and the Russian peasant commune in the 19th century. EHES, Lund and Department of Economics Williams College.
North, D. C. (1973). *Västerlandets Uppgång*. SNS.
North, D. C. (1981). *Structure and change in economic history*. WW Norton and Company.
North, D. C. (1990). *Institutions, institutional change and economic performance*. Cambridge University Press.
North, D. C. (2005). *Understanding the process of economic change*. Princeton University Press.
Ostrom, E. (1990). *Governing the commons: The evolution of institutions for collective action*. Cambridge University Press.
Pallot, J. (1982). *Social change and peasant landholding in pre-revolutionary Russia*. Research Paper 30, School of Geography, Oxford University.
Pallot, J. (1999). *Land reform in Russia 1906–1917: Peasant responses to Stolypin's project of rural transformation*. Clarendon Press.
Petrovich. (1968). The peasant in nineteenth century historiography. In Vucinich W ED. (1968) *The peasant in nineteenth century Russia*. Stanford UP.
Pipes, R. (1995). *Russia under the old regime*. Penguin Books.
Pipes, R. (1999). *Property and freedom*. Harvill Press.
Poznanski, K. (1985). *The environment for technological change in centrally planned economies*. World Bank Staff Working Papers.
Poznanski, K. (1992). A property rights perspective on the evolution of communist-type economies. In K. Poznanski (Ed.), *Constructing capitalism. The re-emergence of civil society and liberal economy in the post-communist world*. Westview Press.
Raeff, M. (1984). *Understanding Imperial Russia*. Columbina UP.
Rizello, S. (1999). *The Economics of the mind*. Edvard Elgar.
Scott, J. (1976). *The moral economy of the peasant. Rebellion and subsistence in Southeast Asia*. Yale University Press.
Shanin, T. (1985). *Russia as a developing society*. Macmillan.

Sheshinski, E. (2010). *Limits in individual choice*. The Hebrew University of Jerusalem.

Shevzov, V. (2004). *Russian Orthodoxy on the eve of revolution*. Oxford University Press.

Smith, A. (1998) *An inquiry into the nature and the causes of the wealth of nations*. Regnery Publishing.

Smith, A. (2000). *The theory of moral sentiments*. Prometheus Books

Smurova, O. V. (2003). Niezemliedelcheski otkhod krestian v stolitzu I ego vlejanie na transformacjiu kulturnoj tradicji. Izd-vo Kostromskogo gosudarstvennogo technologicheskogo universiteta.

Sztern, S. (1994). [Unpublished doctoral course paper], Department of Philosophy, Lund University.

Sztern, S. (1997). *From obshchina to the market: An introduction. Russia's transition from plan to market economy in face of pre revolution transitions 1861–1914*. Lund University.

Troyat, H. (1961). *Daily life in Russia under the last Tsar*. Stanford University Press.

Tuomela, R. (2002). *The philosophy of social practices*. Cambridge University Press.

Vanberg, V. (1994). *Rules and choice in economics*. Routledge.

Veblen, T. (1931). *The theory of the leisure class*. Viking.

Vladimirskaya, I. (1997). personal communication.

Vromen, J. (2001). The human agent in evolutionary economics. In J. Laurent & J. Nightingale (Eds.), *Darwinism and Evolutionary Economics*. Edward Elgar.

Weber, M. (1981). *General economic history*. Transaction Books.

Westwood, J. N. (1964). *A history of the Russian railways*. George Allen and Unwin.

Winicki, J. (1988). *The distorted world of Soviet-type economies*. Routledge.

Worobec, C. (1990). The Post-Emancipation Russian peasant commune in Orel province 1861–90. In Bartlett, R (1990) Ed. Land commune and peasant community in Russia - Communal forms in Imperial and Early Soviet Society. Macmillan in Association with the School of Slavonic and East European Studies.

Worobec, C. D. (1995). *Peasant Russia: Family and community in the post-emancipation period*. Northern Illinois University Press.

Yaney, G. (1973). *The systematization of Russian government: Social evolution in the domestic administration of imperial Russia 1711–1905*. University of Illinois Press.

CHAPTER 7

Secularization and Pious Subversion: To the Constitution by Rail

Here I investigate the crucial role of railroads in Russian modernization from by focusing on additional aspects of the institutional change that technological innovation brought about in nineteenth-century Russia. Supplementing tangible aspects of modernization, I argue that the new technology challenged the Greek Orthodox legitimacy of Tsarism by thrusting Russia's spiritual cultures into a state of flux. Massive canonization gatherings, defection to the revolutionary Old Belief (*Starovery*), and retreat to other piously subversive sects, as well as secularization, destabilized the empire's spiritual base. The emerging institutional competition caused the intra-ecclesiastical structure of the parish to transition from hierarchical-authoritarian to egalitarian and participatory. The Russo-Japanese War, instigated to distract discontent, ended in a debacle in 1904, destabilizing the army. By launching allodial reform in 1906, Tsar Nicholas II sought to re-legitimize the empire by improving the peasantry's living standards. Bearing in mind the incongruence of individual property rights and autocratic rule, I find that the railroads paved the way to the Constitution.

Railroads and Pious Subversion

Building on the theoretical and historical foundations established in previous chapters, here I emphasize three interdependent phenomena associated with the institutional change that technological innovation brought about

S. Sztern, *Russia on the Move*, Studies in Economic Transition, https://doi.org/10.1007/978-3-030-89285-2_7

in nineteenth-century Russia: choice, transition to rationalism, and democratization. The transition to rationalistic thinking was occasioned by a choice that individuals felt compelled to make—between pious subversion triggered by peasant flight to the Old Belief, and a form of secularization—in a synergy that forced the mainstream Orthodox Church to democratize in response to the competitive challenge (Worobec, 2001, p. 121; Freeze, June 1996, p. 311; Shevzov, 2004, p. 36). These factors together gravely subverted the legitimacy of autocratic government in *fin de siècle* Russia. Above (Chap. 5) I asked, Why did the collectivist custom inherited from the serfdom era not erect a mobility barrier and impoverish the peasantry, as Gerschenkron predicted, due to the state-financed spurts of industrialization in the 1890s and 1907? I propose the following answer: the infusion and proliferation of dual-purpose technology by means of the state-led industrialization process unintentionally introduced ***multiple institutional structures*** that triggered a transition from authoritarian coercion to rationally structured agrarian collectives, reducing uncertainty, and transaction costs. Such processes would strengthen the incentive function of any set of property rights (Barzel, 1989, pp. 7, 9, 65; Poznanski, 1992, pp. 71–94; Hesse, 1993, p. 51; Bates, 1989, p. 42). *Under such conditions, growth of productivity outpaces that of population*, allowing the Malthusian trap to be avoided. The Boserupian (Boserup, 1965) transition from extensive to intensive growth triggered by population increase additionally explains this evolution. Indeed, rising and predictable peasant living standards caused the mutual dependency frameworks that constituted the ***obshchina,*** the collective village commune (Bartlett, 1990), to atrophy, paving the way to individualism. The railroads, in turn, determined the nature of the national-market formation and specialization that set democratization in motion.

My immediate task at hand is to explain the impact of the railroad technology on the level of rationalism that determines subsistence risk and the peasant community's habits of thought. The resulting chain of argumentation (Smith, 1998, p. 19; Metzer, 1972, p. 82; Martens, 2004, p. 193; Pipes, 1999, XII, XIII), filling in the missing dimensions of Gerschenkron's theory, is captured in Fig. 7.1:

The question elaborated upon here is how the technological revolution launched in 1890 influenced the religious institutions—namely, the Orthodox Church—that structured Russian society as an institution that held the Tsarist Empire together.

The Orthodox Church played a crucial, nay foundational, role in the Tsarist autocracy's legitimacy (Freeze, 1996, p. 309). Apart from backing the military defense of the empire's territorial claims, Greek Orthodoxy

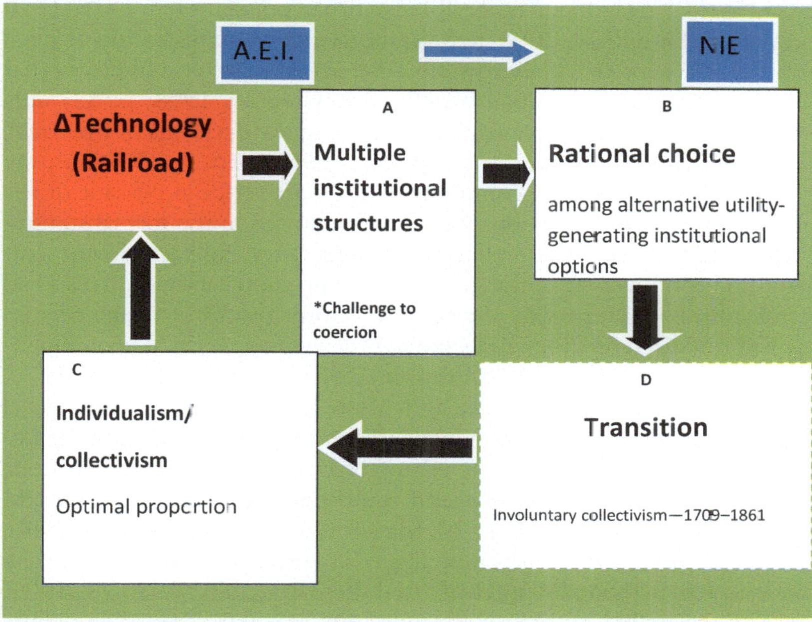

Fig. 7.1 The role of technological change in value-system adaptation: thesis and model. (Sources: (a) Nelson and Winter (1982, p. 35) on "bounded rationality" and North (1990, pp. 93, 94), on its consequences; (b) Sheshinski (2010, p. 3); Gintis (2009, pp. 1, 2); (c) the property-rights incentive function: Poznanski (1992, pp. 71–94); Mokyr (1990, pp. 176, 177); invention innovation: Mokyr (1990, p. 155); collectivism vs. individualism—remuneration for individual householders in the next repartition for investments in land: Kingston-Mann (1991), in Kingston-Mann et al. (1991, pp. 35, 45, 46))

was the most reliable pillar of rural collectivism (Burds, 1998, p. 189), its institutions collaborating with rural collectivism itself to lower the Tsarist regime's surveillance costs (North, 1990, pp. 90, 91; Freeze, 1996, p. 311).

In the second half of the nineteenth century, the dramatic increase in the number of *otkhodniks*—farmers who augmented their income by performing industrial wage labor—implies that railroad construction helped to enhance the mobility of the Russian peasantry. The acceleration of urbanization toward the end of that century suggests the same. The 3.12

percent annual growth rate of the Russian urban population in 1870–1890 (Leonard & Ljungberg, 2008, p. 33) reflects increasing migration of labor toward urban centers.[1] The growing incidence of migration indicates that the informal habits of mutual beneficence (Gregory, 1994, p. 52) outweighed the formal legal constraints in guiding the decisions of the *skhod*, the communal-village assembly (Worobec, 1995, pp. 6, 7, 17). Thus, the de facto ties to the village commune of the post-serfdom peasant of the railroad era were more flexible than those indicated in the formal statutes of 1861–1863 were. The technological innovation inherent in the railroads did more than make the great Russian peasantry mobile. It also had an individualizing impact on the communal dimensions of village custom that had outlasted serfdom and survived the emancipation. These dimensions were captured in the institution of the obshchina (Volyn, 1970, p. 78)[2] that characterized Russian agriculture as the heritage of patriarchal and tribal institutions. By the nineteenth century, the repartitional commune, a customary setting in the central black soil (*czernozem*) provinces, inhered to wealth-redistributing and mutual-aid structures (Engelgardt, 1993, p. 29; Worobec, 1995, p. 24; Mironov, 2000, p. 338; Moon, 1999, p. 216). By reconstituting, enforcing, and fostering communal village cohesion, the Orthodox Church abetted these functions (Worobec, 1995, p. 175; Burds, 1998, p. 188; Hodgson, 2004, pp. 105, 185). The regime considered this institution a labor organization on the one hand and a customary way of life practiced for generations, on the other. Although changing conditions were transforming this way of life, the Church remained a bulwark against revolutionary movements and, for this reason, was seen by the regime as yet another prop for its political stability. The regime was wrong; by the turn of the twentieth century, the obshchina had become a major vehicle of subversion.

The *otchod* process—the practice of wage labor—intensified in tandem with the development of the railroad network (Westwood, 1964, p. 8; Kahan, 1989, p. 30; Gatrell, 1994, p. 14), making peasant households and individual peasants increasingly independent of each other (Sztern, 2000). Concurrently, the importance of the commune's welfare functions fell into

[1] See Chapters 2 and 5 above concerning Gerschenkron's opposing view: that mobility barriers persisted de facto and de jure until Stolypin's reform (1906).

[2] The word *Mir* denotes "the world" and "peace." In the nineteenth century, it defined a community of former serfs or state peasants who, as a rule, were settled in a single village or, at times, in a village that comprised more than one mir or a single mir comprised of several villages.

decline, enhancing the migration of individual members and entire nuclear families while providing with migrant family members a social safety net (Burds, 1998, p. 125).

The Railroads: A Challenge to Orthodox Enforcement of Mutual Insurance

Increased opportunities for wage labor lowered the peasants' dependency ratio and, in turn, the economic significance of the extended family and other forms of rural collectivism. Intensified railroad construction gave peasant populations greater access to towns by shortening travel times. This tended to raise the share of non-agricultural income in the peasant budget and, by implication, to reduce family size. By inducing a transition from extended family units toward nuclear ones (Frierson, 1990), railroad-building instigated a full-fledged movement toward the individualization of property and other personal rights. As individualism ascended pursuant to emancipation and railroad construction, pre-mortem household divisions—partitioning of an extended family unit's assets before the death of the head of household—became more and more frequent (Worobec, 1995, p. 12). The rural-to-urban mobility of nuclear families, in contrast to extended-family counterparts with their higher dependency ratio, reduced migrating households' long-term dependency on the commune. While extended families left behind on the commune became dependent on income repatriation of otkhodniks—proletarianized peasants—nuclear households on the move experienced a multitude of choices. Although they returned to their native villages when disabled by ill health or old age, thus activating the aforementioned safety net,[3] the avalanche of rural–urban migration (Burds, 1998, p. 23, Table 1.3) implies a net decrease in dependence on communal welfare. The peasantry's rising living standards at this time reinforce this point.[4]

[3] Johnson (1979, p. 38); Burds (1998, p. 125). The social safety nets that were unfurled by relations between otkhodniks and their villages facilitated migration decisions by making them less risky. They also enhanced cohesion among those who remained in the village because the repatriated wages helped to maintain the institution's social security. Importantly, however, the farther from the village the urban employment was, the smaller the amount of wages repatriated.

[4] So indicated by an increase in indirect-tax receipts between 1886 and 1899 (Simms, 1977, p. 382, Table 1) and by Gregory (1994, pp. 44, 45, Tables 3.1, 3.3).

The intensity of migration streams varied inversely with the distance from industrial and the administrative centers. The Central Industrial region, comprised of Moscow at its apex and six surrounding provinces, accounted for the largest number and proportion of internal passports issued (Burds, 1998, p. 21). If so, the railroads obviously abetted more and more migration by reducing distances from periphery to center and among central points, both cognitively and in opportunity cost in terms of the returns on forgone agricultural labor and travel expenses (in money and in time lost during travel) (Engelgardt, 1993, p. 44).

Table 7.1 presents my proxy for the increase in migration intensity: the growing issuance of internal passports for wage work otkhod or migration to villagers in the post-emancipation decades.

The non-agricultural industrial and central industrial regions, the ones most dependent on urban wage labor, showed a conspicuous increase in the proportion of village population carrying internal passports between 1861–1870 and 1871–1880. It was exactly then that railroad construction in the empire gained momentum. During the 1865–1875 decade, the length of the Russian railway network grew from 3845 to 19,029 kilometers and the volume of freight doubled (Kahan, 1989, p. 30, Table 1.14).[5] The correlation between the intensity of the urban wage-labor migration, measured in millions of peasant passengers per kilometer, and the annual pace of railway construction, measured in kilometers, is unmistakably positive.[6] As for the direction of causality and the endogeneity problem, it is more plausible, given the time range and the short time span—less than half a century—to assume that the railroads, initially built to serve military purposes and enhance bureaucratic control of the imperial population, unintentionally stimulated the peasantry's wage-labor migration than the other way around.[7] Growth of industry, in contrast, was caused by strategic geopolitical considerations exogenous to the consequent parallel increase in the population of wage-earning peasants.

Between 1861–1870 and 1906–1910, the proportion of villagers issued with internal passports at the consent 2/3 majority of the village skhod increased threefold in Moscow. It is especially interesting to note that Penza Province, located in the Central Volga region, an agricultural area, displays a similar proportion of passport-carrying peasants and a

[5] Volume of freight is expressed in millions of metric tons per kilometer.

[6] Adduced from ibid.

[7] L.J. Borodkin, personal communication, Moscow (2008).

Table 7.1 Peasant labor migration as proportion of village population, 1861–1910

	Proportion of peasant population holding passports					
Regions and provinces	*1861–1870*	*1871–1880*	*1881–1890*	*1891–1900*	*1902*	*1906–1910*
Nonagricultural/Industrial North and Northwest						
Arkhangel	5.9	13.0	11.3	12.6	14.7	13.8
Vologda	1.8	6.1	6.0	8.2	10.4	10.7
Olonets	3.2	9.1	9.6	12.4	13.4	13.2
St. Petersburg	8.6	17.9	21.8	28.9	27.6	23.0
Novgorod	4.5	11.6	10.5	13.1	13.4	14.2
Pskov	2.0	3.3	3.6	6.2	8.7	10.4
Smolensk	6.3	11.2	10.3	11.2	12.6	13.0
Tver	8.0	14.6	14.4	16.7	22.6	23.0
Central Industrial Region						
Iaroslavl	9.1	17.0	16.4	18.9	24.1	23.1
Moscow	10.0	18.0	20.4	29.9	33.9	34.2
Vladimir	4.8	16.0	16.7	19.1	26.1	24.2
Kostroma	3.9	12.3	13.8	13.1	7.6	20.0
Kaluga	8.8	17.2	18.3	20.5	25.8	25.4
Nizhnii Novgorod	**3.1**	**8.8**	9.6	11.0	13.1	12.0
Tula	4.2	8.8	9.9	14.3	20.1	20.0
Riazan	5.4	12.7	14.3	17.5	22.7	20.5
Belorussia						
Vitebsk	3.5	5.0	6.0	8.3	10.8	10.9
Minsk	1.1	2.8	4.6	4.9	10.0	4.1
Mogilev	1.6	4.5	5.0	6.0	6.5	9.1
II Southern Agricultural Ukraine						
Poltava	1.4	4.2	5.9	7.0	8.2	6.3
Kharkov	1.2	3.6	5.9	7.2	9.9	9.2
Chernigov	1.4	4.2	5.7	6.9	8.3	8.0
Kiev	0.6	2.5	6.1	8.5	7.2	7.8
Volynia	0.6	2.0	3.2	3.7	0.5	3.2
Podolia	0.4	1.7	3.6	4.2	3.9	4.1
Kherson	1.2	3.3	4.4	4.8	4.8	5.0
Ekaterinoslav	1.2	2.4	3.7	3.9	6.3	3.2
Taurida	1.4	4.2	4.8	4.9	3.8	5.0
North Caucasus						
Don Oblast	0.1	0.5	1.1	2.3	3.7	4.0
III Central Agricultural Central Chernozem						
Voronezh	1.3	5.7	6.1	7.4	8.5	8.0
Kursk	1.8	5.3	7.0	9.2	11.9	10.0

(*continued*)

Table 7.1 (continued)

	Proportion of peasant population holding passports					
Regions and provinces	*1861–1870*	*1871–1880*	*1881–1890*	*1891–1900*	*1902*	*1906–1910*
Orel	2.6	5.3	6.7	9.2	11.6	12.2
Tambov	1.9	4.2	4.7	5.9	8.8	8.2
Volga						
Astrakhan	1.9	10.8	15.9	17.6	8.3	9.0
Saratov	0.9	3.8	5.2	6.1	7.7	6.0
Samara	0.4	1.6	1.5	1.9	4.6	3.4
Penza	**2.1**	**6.1**	6.2	7.6	10.6	10.0
Simbirsk	1.4	7.5	9.3	8.6	10.8	10.0
Kazan	1.0	5.3	5.6	6.7	9.2	9.2
Viatka	1.5	5.8	6.1	6.9	8.5	8
Ufa	0.5	1.7	3.2	3.0	3.9	4.3
IV Eastern Agricultural Ural						
Perm	0.6	3.2	4.3	6.1	7.5	7.0
Orenburg	1.2	5.6	4.9	4.1	3.9	4.3

Source: Burds (1998, Table 1.3, p. 23); Treadgold (1968, pp. 208–09, 264–65); and maps in the Appendix

Note: The numbers are not cumulative; the flows do not add horizontally because the migrating peasant population at time t and the corresponding population at t1 are not the same

The bold values refer to the case study Chap. 9 regions—Povolzhe-Nizhnij Novogorod and Penza

similar growth pattern to that in the industrial regions, indicating inadequate agricultural productivity. In Penza Province, reached by the railroad in 1874, the proportion of village population carrying internal passports tripled between 1861–1870 and 1871–1880. In several other Volga region provinces, this population quadrupled. By implication, this indicates greater dependency on wage labor in Penza than in other *chernozem* (black earth) agricultural regions located farther away from the canal system. I assume that the proximity of this province to the Volga River and the canal system stimulated *custar*—proto-industrial crafts production—and other industries, allowing local sources of industrial income to develop and making further use of internal passports superfluous. The markedly steep increase in the number of peasants who carried internal passports in Penza at precisely this time, coinciding with the advent of the railroad in the area, points to the crucial role of the railroads in the intensity of the peasantry's migration and travel to wage labor. Although the proximity of this province to the Volga River and the canal system abetted the peasantry's growing wage-labor mobility, the Penza statistics leave no doubt that the contribution of the newly constructed railroad was decidedly greater.

These statistics also challenge the hypothesis, advanced by Nefedov and other Soviet historians, that the central provinces were stricken by a Malthusian crisis during the industrialization decades. Plainly, Gerschenkron (1962, p. 120) overestimates the effect of control by habit and custom, as well as the weight of the Tsarist legal restrictions, on the communal village assembly's boundedly rational calculus (Nelson & Winter, 1982, pp. 66, 67) and underestimates the effect of population increase on the outcome of such a calculus. The growing weight of rational calculus in itself indicates that the railroads metamorphosed the commune in the direction of voluntary rationalist cooperation rather than perpetuation of patriarchal obedience networks. Gerschenkron derives his theory on low labor mobility from the rationally expected outcome of the land-rotation custom known as *peredely,* the redistribution of land commensurate with the number of labor teams per household. According to Gerschenkron, this rule, entailing the consent of the head of household and a two-thirds majority of members of the village assembly for the migration of an adult son to wage labor (Gerschenkron, 1962, p. 120; Burds, 1998, pp. 12, 18, 19), chained peasants' labor to the land. My source thus assumes the use of a rational decision-making process in the application of the formal rule system (Gerschenkron, 1962, p. 120). If they are prompted by an NIE assumption, an industrious *bolshak* (paterfamilias) and *skhod* (communal-village assembly of entrepreneurial patriarchal heads of household) would apply a rational-survival calculus amid population increase, causing the per-capita land allotment to contract and, in turn, triggering an increase in the number of wage-labor passports issued. Although the individual *bolshak* and the assembly's interests might have different interests, each dispute resolved by the assembly created a precedent for the settlement of future disputes. Therefore, if population increase entailed the curtailment of land allotment at the next repartition, the opportunity cost of labor employed in urban wage work could be reduced and compliance with patriarchal rules by the individual *bolshak* and, by extension, the assembly might become more flexible (Burbank, 2004, p. 47). In fact, the number of passports issued grew more often than not in all forty-three provinces of European Russia (Burds, 1998, p. 23, Table 1.2), indicating the importance of "informal habits" in relation to formal law (Gregory, 1994, p. 52) as well as the high level of rationality, in the Neoclassical sense, that guided the decisions of the late-nineteenth-century elder-based peasant constituency.

The Railroads Abet Peasant Individualism: The Rational Peasant, the Church

By applying my combined Veblenian Evolutionary Institutionalist/Northian NIE theory (see Chap. 3), I find that peasant proletarians' applications for title to their land allotments in the village commune, which burgeoned as Stolypin's land reform was being implemented (Gaudin, 1998, p. 754), reflected a "boundedly rational" calculus on the individual applicant's part, one that spanned his life cycle. Importantly, however, even if peasant proletarians intended by applying for land title to insure themselves against poverty and old-age destitution (Gaudin, 1998, p. 754), their act carried the long-term potential of turning them and their offspring into agrarian entrepreneurs. Therefore, an application to become a householder-owner of a land allotment should not be misconstrued as nostalgia or a predisposition to collectivism.

Paradoxically, by acting on behalf of the Tsarist state and enhancing the repatriation of *otkhodnik* income to the commune—thereby abetting the legal enforcement of the rural collectivist custom, tying the *otkhodnik* to the commune and ostensibly promoting political stability—the mainstream Greek Orthodox Church in fact increased the transaction costs of the Tsarist modernization. This, in turn, magnified the transaction and surveillance costs of tax extraction in the short run (Leonard, 1990, p. 136; North, 1990, pp. 90, 91; Martens, 2004, p. 193; Barzel, 2002, p. 61), weakening the Tsarist state and, with it, the involuntary component of the collectivist rural structure.

In sum, the technological innovation imported from Europe, the railroad, increased the mobility and migration of labor and facilitated the flight of peasants to the Old Belief, with its attendant doctrine of *razkol* (Schismaticism) (Burds, 1998, pp. 193, 203, 205), and to secularization. Both choices, heralding the transition to rationalism, weakened a crucial pillar of stability in Tsarist rule, the Church (to which I devote extensive discussion in a separate subchapter below). The consequent erosion of the Tsarist government's spiritual base of legitimacy made territorial conquest all the more important. Against this background, the debacles of the Crimean and the Russo-Japanese wars marked the beginning of institutional transformation and challenge to unquestioned Tsarist authority (Freeze, 1996, p. 309; Ascher, 1988, p. 43)—placing the Tsarist Empire aboard a train to constitutional monarchy.

Culture Clash—*Otkhod* Urban Freedom vs. Rural Safety The Railroads Abet Peasant Individualism

As demonstrated above, the novel railroad technology encouraged the diversification of the risk to subsistence by creating greater dependency on non-agricultural wage labor and sharply lowering the transaction costs (including the uncertainty) of rural–urban migration. Thus, the introduction of this technology allowed individuals to choose among multiple institutional structures, challenging the patriarchal institutions on which the communal village was based and arguably rendering the village, conceptualized as a transaction-cost internalization unit, redundant (Coase, 1937, p. 42). As the technology advanced, the costs of collectivism increasingly outweighed the benefits in both the short and the long terms (Vanberg, 1994, p. 55).

As population growth in the communes necessitated greater recourse to opportunities for wage labor, and as the industrialization effort made this recourse possible, more and more commune households opted for permanent urban settlement. As the increased tax burden on households remaining in the villages bred dissatisfaction (Burds, 1998, p. 29), commune assemblies increasingly attempted to hinder peasants and households from engaging in rural–urban migration, exacerbating internal conflicts and fomenting general discontent with the communal organization (Gaudin, 1998, p. 104, Table 3.4). Concurrently, the government's growing commitment and ability to provide social security and other welfare services eroded the rational raison d'être of the collectivist communal form of organization.

Paradoxically, the escalation of internal peasant conflict in the villages during the implementation of the Stolypin reform (Macey, 1990, p. 222: 1998), although unambiguously indicative of the rise of individualism, made the remaining households in the village even more dependent on the communal and reciprocal communal-help mechanisms in the short run. The peasants' observable resistance to the Tsarist government's encroachment on their relatively strong rural autonomy as the Stolypin reform went ahead (Mironov, 2000, pp. 290, 347) elicited peasant fears of the erosion of these mechanisms (Pallot, 1999, pp. 156, 157)—a development consistent with the intensified transition from rural collectivism to rural–urban individualism. After having survived 200 years both due to and despite these state-supported collectivist rural structures, some of the European Russian peasantry had indeed become dependent on mutual insurance and mutual assistance, retarding its development and discouraging entrepreneurial risk-taking.[8] The agency effect of the opportunities introduced by the new technology, embedded in industrialization, is cumulative in the long run. Thus, while individual entrepreneurial risk-takers seized the opportunity presented by the novel technology and broke away, others placed their trust in the tried-and-true communal structures. However, as the proportion of risk-takers in the village population who invoked novel survival strategies climbed, these strategies granted the marginal risk-taker greater and greater utility, making it increasingly likely that the proportion of the population choosing the novel strategy would grow even more, as indeed happened (Boyer & Orlean, 1993, p. 22). Thus, the process of exodus from the village, set in motion by the railroads, became self-enforcing.

The changes in kinship-structured habits of thought in favor of the individual risk-taker—the *otkhodnik*—are clearly manifested in the *smena ideala yunoshy*, the transformation of the ideal husband, that occurred in the villages as industrialization, railroad construction, and urban wage-labor progressed. Traditional agrarianism, bound to the family-and-village structure, was increasingly perceived by the peasantry as an inferior choice. The refrain of a folk song confirms this voluntary transition to an urban and more individualistic culture: *"Krestianskij syn durashen, on mnogo pashni pashet"*—The peasant son is an imbecile; he ploughs a lot of ploughland."[9] Traditional peasants who remained in the villages received the derogatory nickname *domoleg*, "idle homebody," and were increasingly associated with vulgarity and inflexibility.

Still, the changes in preferences and prejudices in favor of the *Petershchiki*—peasant *otkhodniks* who worked in the capital, dressed in worldly attire, and increasingly embraced secularization or the Old Belief—cannot always be explained by the material opportunities presented by wage labor. The domoleg could offer his young bride

[8] See Chap. 6 above, discussion of Hodgson's reconstitutive downward causation of historical institutions.

[9] Folk song transcribed by D. Zhvankov in Soligalicheskij canton, Kostroma Province (Smurova, 2003, p. 100).

membership in an established household. The Petershchik's wage income was incomparably less certain, at least in the short run, and his bride might have to remain behind in the village alone for quite some time until her husband could save up enough to establish an urban household (Smurova, 2003, p. 101).

It is legitimate to suggest that the main attractiveness of the urban wage laborer relative to the domoleg—the obshchina-bound young peasant who becomes a paterfamilias and the husband of a young village bride[10]—was the former's individualistic experience of interaction in the city and, in turn, his increasingly less hierarchical-patriarchal-authoritarian and more democratically egalitarian conception of family relations. This supposition is reinforced by growing demand for personal rights during the industrialization spurt, itself a product of the transition to individualism (Mironov, 1999, p. 476). This new tendency recurred in the villages as well, as evidenced in the rising incidence of criminal cases in Moscow, Vladimir, and Riazan provinces from 1890 to the beginning of World War I, in which personal insult was an increasingly frequent charge. The growing propensity to litigation in the villages suggests an escalating transition to individualism among the peasantry, manifested in an increasingly powerful sense of personal dignity (Gaudin, 2007, p. 103, Table 3.3; Mironov, 1999, Vol. I, 475, 476, 477). I venture that the demand for personal dignity and freedom on the part of the transplanted villager gathered strength not only because his additional wage income gave him the means to instigate lawsuits but also due to the inevitable importation of multiple institutional structures, which presented a hitherto unknown challenge to the traditional rural collectivist habits of thought. The very fact of being able to choose among these structures added a novel element—an individualistic experience—to the decision-making process. I suggest that the complementarity of the 1861 emancipation statute and the railroad technology in their effect on habits of thought, both of which intensifying the *otkhod* process, amplified the demand for individual freedom, as manifested in the transformation of the "ideal husband" notion from the traditional, patriarchal, collectivist domoleg to the Petershchik, the urbanized individual risk-taker, be he entrepreneurial or proletarian.

[10]There was also a smaller population of female *otkhodniks* (Johnson, 1979, p. 58, Table 3.3).

Rejecting the Hierarchy—Herzen, Bakunin, Emancipation, and the Iron Horse

These twin complementarities—emancipation from serfdom and the novel technology—enhanced ongoing processes of cultural transformation among the Russian intelligentsia, which emerged as a social force in the mid-nineteenth century as it launched, absorbed, and legitimized Saint-Simonian ideology (Kimball, 1992; Herzen, 1985, p. 120). Alexander Herzen's memoirs, "Past and Thoughts," published after 1855 in the popular *Poliarnaia zvezda*, although cultivating the romantic conception of going to the *narod*—the people—criticized the path propagated by the populists, Kimball said were inspired by Slavophile beliefs (p. 117). Stressing the property of irreversibility in history, Herzen lamented the propensity among intelligent young men after the emancipation to regard service in the Tsarist bureaucracy, the military, or a commercial enterprise as occupationally superior options. His social critique totally omitted vocations such as "landowner," "peasant," or even "industrial laborer," which he understood as obsolete (pp. 117, 120). Indeed, Herzen deemed the shackles of all aspects of the social order known thus far, including the estate system with its anchor in birthrights, class-related occupations, and the peasant estate in itself, as belonging to Russia's past. Although the technological revolution embodied in the introduction of the railroad in 1842 is not mentioned in his writings, Herzen's "concern for the freedom and dignity of human individuals" (Herzen, 1985, p. xxii) should be understood as ***anticipating the atrophy of the brutality of cognitive barriers, namely restrictions on choice, that had been imposed by estate- and class-related occupations earlier in history.*** "The old world was crumbling visibly and deserved to fall" (xxvii). The antagonism between Herzen and Marx (p. 677) additionally suggests that his insight allowed him to anticipate individual choice formally unhampered by the historical adherence to class estate.

Following the Saint-Simonian way of thinking, Herzen envisioned the future Russia as being guided by an elite of savants—*uchenych*—who would derive their authority neither from a hereditary birthright estate (*soslovie*) nor from a hierarchy rank enforced by the autocratic state (*chin*). According to Herzen, Russia's future depended on its society's ability to attain a higher stage of development, to make "a transition from aristocratism and militarism to egalitarian humanism and peaceful productivity" (Kimball, 1992, p. 122).

Thus, this leading revolutionary intellectual rejected all the aforementioned occupations—the historical as well as the currently preferred—on the grounds that all had been derived from the externally bestowed, privilege-based formation of either religious or secular hierarchies, implying by definition individual degradation and obedience of the superior. By so professing, Herzen drew somewhat closer to the ideas of the anarchist leader Prince M.A. Bakunin (1814–1876), as evidenced in the title of the latter's work, *God and the State*. However, Herzen's belief in the superiority of government by the learned, much contrary to Bakunin, legitimized in principle the legal domination of people by people, provided the domineers obtain their authority and its consequence, their elite status, through their own creativity and effort. In Herzen's Simonian vision of post-Revolution Russia, universities would replace churches as "networks of communication" (p. 123; Timberlake in Timberlake, 1992, p. 10) between rulers and ruled. The idea of the government by a "scientific academy," however, met its mocking nemesis in Bakunin's radical egalitarianism:

> *It is the characteristic of privilege and of every privileged position to kill the mind and the heart of men. That is the social law which admits no exception and is applicable to entire nations as to classes, corporations and individuals. It is the law of equality the supreme condition of liberty and humanity.* (Bakunin, 1970, p. 31)

The peasant's cultural transformation (Smurova, 2003, p. 100)—facilitated by the railroad and the commuting *otkhod wage labor*, intensified by urban interaction, and manifested in the rejection of the inherited rural, hierarchical, and patriarchal structures that historically redistributed the entitlement to surpluses and the power to rule to the paterfamilias (Hoch, 1986, p. 128)—was congruent with the ideas and the sentiments nurtured by the Russian intelligentsia. In both Herzen's and Bakunin's writings, the idea of ultimate humanism was captured succinctly in the egalitarian perception of human ability and value.

Rule of Law and Industrialization—The Individuation of the Peasant

According to Lenin's application of Marx to the social conditions of Tsarist Russia, it was the intensification of economic differentiation and class struggle, occasioned by the development of capitalist structures in the home market (contrary to the

Narodniks' expectations), that ultimately doomed the Tsarist state (Lenin, 1974, pp. 588, 589). By this reasoning, the Tsarist effort to modernize Russia, which enhanced the development of capitalist structures only ambivalently (Kahan, 1989, p. 91; Owen, 1995, p. 39, 1995, p. 19), toppled the pillars of autocracy. I stipulate that the post-Emancipation modernization process, with its unintended consequences, was inconsistent with autocracy. I propose, however, that the factors that weakened and transformed the autocratic structures were different from those identified by the Marxist-Leninist school.

Relations between peasants and former landlords were symbiotic more often than not (Engelgardt, 1993, p. 82). The literature that explains the 1905 revolution solely in terms of class antagonisms oversimplifies the specificities of peasant life in Tsarist Russia; in particular, it overlooks the historical intra- and inter-class dependencies brought on by harsh and unstable climatic conditions (Milov, 2001, note 128 and pp. 1, 2; Kahan, 1985, p. 13, 1989, pp. 139, 140, 141, Table 3A on the frequency of natural calamities). Moreover, the perception of the late nineteenth-century Russian peasantry as monolithic in its antagonism to the Tsarist governmental institutions must be revised (Gaudin, 2007, p. 7).

Worobec (1990, pp. 103, 104) and Engelgardt (1993, p. 87) report rising individualism and its consequence, greater heterogeneity of values, in the peasant environment. Engelgardt and Frank (1999, pp. 87) emphasize the historically established peasant preference of the rural community's internal conflict-resolution mechanisms, such as reconciliation and compensation, over formal penalties. Even the custom-based peasant *volost'*—township courts—were seen by the rural constituency as instances of last resort that were fit to use only when the informal conflict-resolution mechanisms failed (p. 97).

This condition of life changed dramatically during the industrialization decades. The direction of the institutional change, unambiguously pointing to the growing individualism of the Russian peasant, was, according to the model underlying this thesis, consistent with the rising living standards that typified the modernization decades, as verified by the upward trend in indirect-tax receipts during the post-emancipation period. Studies on institutional conditions in the last decades of the nineteenth century report the increasing litigiousness of the Russian peasantry (Gaudin, 2007, p. 103, Table 3.3).[11] Formal litigation rates, defined as *volost* court cases

[11] The rate of intra-communal lawsuits over insults increased until World War I, giving evidence of greater independence in communal mutual-risk insurance that permitted an increase in individualism and the perception of personal dignity. The kink in the curve in

per 1000 rural inhabitants, steadily increased in 1891–1911 in the provinces of Central European Russia: Moscow, Novogorod, Riazan, and Kursk (p. 89, Table 3.1). This clearly points to the weakening of collectivist dependence and practice in the peasant village and a commensurably stronger propensity to the enforcement of individual rights.

The escalation of litigiousness among individuals in both the affluent and the impoverished classes is inconsistent with a state of conflict stratified along class boundaries or among peasant classes that are ostensibly more and more differentiated by material possessions,[12] as Marxist scholars would have it. The upturn in litigiousness clearly indicates the disintegration of the commune as well as the absence of Marxist class cohesion. Thus, I suggest that the pre-modern risk internalization unit, the *mir*, crumbled with the increase in peasants' trust in Tsarist jurisprudence, as evidenced through the proxy of the litigation rate. This line of reasoning conforms to Stolypin's observations (Klimin, 2002, pp. 10, 11) and those that Engelgardt formed as he lived among the Russian peasantry. Both eyewitness accounts stress rising individualism ahead of the 1906 land reform.

The rise of individualism suggests, in turn, that during the late nineteenth-century industrialization the Tsarist state began to internalize the transaction costs, including uncertainty, that had previously been checked by the pre-modern obshchina community. The upturn in litigiousness, representing escalating individualism, gives evidence of the ongoing transition from community to society (Mironov, 2000, p. 286). By implication, the Tsarist Empire had tacitly embarked on the transition from personalized to impersonalized institutions, reducing system transaction costs in the long run while increasingly including the peasants of European Russia in imperial state structures.[13]

1908, following the second industrialization spurt (1907), supports this argument. Until then, dependency on mutual insurance had been expressed in a declining rate of litigants over insults per 1000 inhabitants. The dip in 1908 suggests that industrialization exacerbated rural uncertainty in the short run. From then on, the curve rises steeply until 1914, indicating the rebound of individualism.

[12] Löwe (1990, p. 167, Table 11.1a) offers evidence to the contrary. The share of medium-sized farms was highest in those villages where the share of colonists, who held their land in personal tenure, was the lowest. Thus, the village commune had a long-term leveling effect, reflected in the absence of Marxist differentiation, which eroded on the margin due to households' reduced dependency on the mutual risk-insurance role of the commune.

[13] See Raeff (1984, pp. 178, 179), on the introduction of universal compulsory military service in 1874, which irreversibly integrated the peasantry into the imperial structure on equal footing with other classes.

Thus, the turn-of-century peasant constituency was characterized by weakening estate and class cohesion and growing intra-class conflict (Gaudin, 2007, pp. 103, 104, 108). This conclusion is vindicated by Macey (1990, p. 222), who ultimately challenges the Marxist interpretations, and by Freeze (1996, p. 312), who analyzes the widening schism between the Church and the Tsarist state. The declining authority of mainstream Orthodoxy paved the way to a future participatory government structure.

Formally, the legislation that was passed on November 9, 1906, allowed heads of households to claim their *nadel*—their share of the communal land—as personal property and/or to enclose it in a single parcel (Gaudin, 1998, p. 747). This novel institution granted applicants for title legal autonomy vis-à-vis the decisions of the village assembly, which until then had shaped households' use rights in land by adjusting land allotments to the number of labor teams per household. Thus, after Stolypin's reform, one would expect the subsequent desultory adjustment of habits of thought to cause land rotations during redistributions to decline gradually. Moreover, departing households' land would no longer revert to the commune. Thus, the paterfamilias' title to land constituted the formal foundation of a transition to a hereditary family-farm system. Since the paterfamilias could claim conditional land allotments as his personal property at any time, the application for title—*ukreplenie*—formalized the transition of the household away from the collectivist risk-sharing and mutual-aid system of the village commune to the individualism of a hereditary family farm (Gaudin, 1998, p. 751). The main restriction that distinguished erstwhile allotment land from the gentry's private property was the injunction against selling the parcel to a non-peasant. Legislation passed on June 14, 1910, however, allowed any head of household to purchase up to six parcels. The new statute specified that the acquisition of allotment land also included transactions in common village resources such as pasture and wood lands. Thus, the village assembly's control over the redistribution of common resources weakened, additionally heralding the transition to individualism in the landholding system.

The peasants responded to the 1906 reform in a way that belied their characterization as a timid mass, as Gerschenkron's analysis would have it, or as a "property unconscious" population in the Kantian sense (Crisp, 1989, pp. 34, 36) that had been manipulated and exploited by the Tsarist state. Instead, the peasants brought a sophisticated, landed-property-conscious, opportunistic attitude to the choice between imperial institutions based on a civil code and the more custom-based rulings of the township courts in resolving conflicts over title to land.[14] Again, the increase in peasant recourse to the Tsarist judicial system shows that the peasants increasingly trusted these institutions (Wortman, 1976, 1989; Yaney, 1973). Thus, the rural constituency's *grazhdanstvennost*—perception of citizenship—evolved gradually in accordance with the objectives and ethos of the 1906 land reform.

The steady increase in civil complaints per 1000 inhabitants between 1891–1913 (Gaudin, 2007, p. 104, Table 3.4) and 1903–1913 raised the proportion of land-related suits in the total caseload (p. 108, Table 3.5), clearly demonstrating that the informal institutional transition from collective use rights in land to household-head property predated by at least a decade and a half the formal transition to individualism in landholding institutions codified in the Stolypin land reform (North, 1990, p. 78).

Gaudin's (2007) findings are fully consistent with Mironov's analysis. Mironov emphasizes the intensified demand for personal rights and the newly acquired sense of personal dignity among the European Russian peasantry. Gaudin as well as Worobec (1995), the latter demonstrating the increased frequency of pre-mortem household divisions, imply that Tsarism's last decades saw rising demand for individually delineated rights in movable as well as landed property, as manifested in the proportion of such cases in the total caseload (p. 108, Table 3.5). In four central Russian provinces (Riazan, Moscow, Tver, and Vladimir), the proportion of suits pertaining to land increased markedly. Suits concerning family divisions and inheritance did the same.

As the 1906 land reform went ahead, the transformation of governmental judicial institutions affected peasant attitudes and vice versa. Interpreted from this perspective, the individualization of rights to land title could not have been alien to the traditional institutions of the Great Russian peasant. Kingston-Mann (1991, pp. 43, 44), focusing on inter-household transactions that compensated individual households for investments in land at times of repartitions, indicates that the nineteenth-century obshchina metamorphosed increasingly into a unit of voluntary

[14] See Gaudin (1998, pp. 750, 751, 754, 755) on the rationality of peasant ties to the land and Gaudin (2007, pp. 114–17, Table 3–8). The increase in appeals of volost court rulings to district congresses was steeper in civil cases than in criminal cases. The volost court, a custom-structured and tradition-bound instance, took a common-law view of property while the district congress, structured by the imperial code, was less predictable in its verdicts and better adapted to codifying new relations in property rights, albeit with higher risks of loss.

cooperation between independent and individualistic agrarian entrepreneurs. Engelgardt's eyewitness accounts verify this.

Thus, following Gaudin's (2007) empirical research, I find Stolypin's reform fully consistent with the peasants' genuine demand for the universal individualization of civil rights, including rights to landed property, as opposed to a process imported from Germany to the Eurasian Empire and implemented vis-à-vis the peasant commune by sheer coercion (Pallot, 1999, pp. 158, 159). Such a demand, I propose, was manifested before and during the 1905 revolution, reflecting an unambiguously positive attitude toward land ownership (Zakharova, 1992). Against this background, the transition from collective-communal rotating and redeemable use rights in land, set in motion in the emancipation, to personal property rights under Stolypin's reform may be perceived as a predominantly voluntary process, as Stolypin himself envisioned it (Klimin, 2002, pp. 11, 15). The Soviet scholar Dubrovskij (1963, p. 241, Table 29) reports a steep increase in peasant petitions for land title in the provinces of European Russia—from 219,332 in 1907 to 380,691 in 1908 and 704,964 in 1909, receding to 650,347 in 1910. As proposed above, Evolutionary Institutionalist reasoning suggests that the conspicuous interest in personal landed property reveals the historically present individualistic dimensions of the village commune structure (Kingston-Mann, 1991, pp. 43, 44) that reconstituted and predisposed the peasant (Hodgson, 2004, pp. 105, 185), enabling the individual farmer to seize the opportunity presented by the novel legislation and to acquire title. Thus, the assumption about the continuity of the Russian peasant's collectivist mentality, a notion nurtured in the Western debate, is unambiguously challenged.

Challenging the Perception of the Slavonic Collectivist (Muzhik) Mentality—The Railroads Transfer Life-Risk Insurance from the Commune to the Imperial State

Ultimately, too, the observable rationalism of the peasant constituency challenges proposals flowing from the pervasive assumption of the existence of a collectivist Slavonic mentality, as evidenced in nineteenth-century Slavophile writing. The peasantry's rational individualistic inclination in the second half of the nineteenth century is explained by the rural landholding institutions' interaction with the industrialization spurt in the 1890s and the resulting increase in urban wage labor and reliance on non-agricultural income, which ensured against the risk of starvation due to crop failure. Moreover, the Tsarist government was increasingly able to employ railroads as instruments of famine relief. Thus, the Tsarist railroads insured against starvation at times of famine by assuring access to industrial and agricultural regions that were not stricken by crop failure; they also facilitated access to wages, lowered transaction costs, increased the predictability of income by facilitating the formation of a price-converging national grain market (Metzer, 1972, p. 82), made stored grain more accessible (Robbins Jr., 1975, pp. 22, 33), and mitigated dependency on the communal mutual-insurance custom.

The positive correlation between peasant economic household independence and the railroads is composed of the following elements:

- Reversal of the undersupply of seasonal labor to industry. The shortage, occasioned by a preference for agricultural income on the basis of "ceremonial knowledge" (Hodgson, 2001), was engineered historically by inducement structures in industrial employment—including strict coercive binding of labor to industry by employers, keeping otkhodniks' wages down despite the scarcity of non-agricultural labor except in the metalworking industries, in which a pecuniary incentive structure did allow for wage increases (Johnson, 1979, p. 36, note 41). Access to railroads facilitated the accumulation of literacy and industrial skills while shortening the cognitive distance from countryside to city. (See Chaps. 9, 10, and 11___ for an extensive econometric analysis.) Given the costs of coercion to employers, the growing supply of skilled labor allowed the marginal value product of labor, rather than coercion, to determine otkhodniks' wages. Amid the escalating demand for labor and the relatively sluggish adjustment of supply, wages rose and households' mutual dependence subsided.
- The interaction of railroads with the 1866 food supply statutes institutionalized a famine-relief system that created an empire-wide capital fund (Robbins, 1975, pp. 22, 23), causing grain prices to converge (Metzer, 1972, p. 82). The decline in transaction costs, including those related to uncertainty mitigation, had a decisively abetting effect on households' individual ability to cope with famine, making mutual insurance within the village commune redundant.

By reducing the risk of death, the railroads allowed rational choices and demands to be made with greater ease than before. The escalating number of civil lawsuits—individualistic acts par excellence—demonstrating empirically that a transition to rationalism and individualism actually occurred. The rising proportion of criminal cases also (Gaudin, 2007, p. 103, Table 3.3; see also Frierson, 1987) also signals the development of a more nuanced definition of what was perceived as a criminal offense and how such an offense should be countered. Future empirical research may also reveal a slow but steady decrease in the incidence of *samosud* (violent extrajudicial collective penalization parties), an often grotesquely brutal social sanction in Russian villages, in Tsarism's last decades. Although the frequency of samosud was essentially unaffected by the closer proximity of villages to railroad stations (Worobec, 2001, p. 87), it stands to reason that the shrinking distance to the railroad and, in turn, the intensified rural–urban cognitive exchange (Martens, 2004, p. 101) would have a slow and enduring long-term effect.

This universal quality of the transition to rationalism and individualism challenges the Marxist interpretation of the 1905 revolution. Heads of household who petitioned mainly for separation of allotment land from the commune in order to establish a farm on personal property were anything but a homogeneous group of well-to-do individuals. They actually belonged to marginalized groups: widowed female heads of household and absentees (wage laborers in urban industries) who risked the loss of their right to an allotment in the commune upon the next repartition. Their purpose in petitioning was to secure their access to landed property at all junctures of their life cycle (Gaudin, 1998).

The implementation of Stolypin's reform touched off escalating intra-commune conflicts among individuals over the newly available right to title, sundering the previously enforced collectivist cohesion of the village. This again challenges the Marxist assumptions about class formation within the peasant estate, the transformation of this estate into a class, and populist postulates about the impossibility of individual capitalist institutions in Russia (Macey, 1990, p. 222; Gaudin, 1998, p. 750, 2007, p. 108, Table 3.5; Atkinson, 1983, p. 76).

As for cultural differences among the estates in recourse to governmental judicial institutions, the relation between peasant custom and the civil code may be understood as continuous rather than discrete and dichotomous (Burbank, 2004, p. 10). Due to the railroads, inter-class (-estate) cultural boundaries became increasingly blurred and the differences narrowed over time (Crafts, 2007; Martens, 2004, p. 101). The surge in general peasant litigiousness, the dramatic increase in the proportion of landholding cases in the civil caseload in 1901–1913 (Gaudin, 2007, p. 108, Table 3.5), and the growing proportion of cases concerning family divisions and legacies give unambiguous evidence of the escalation of private-property consciousness growing trust in governmental institutions among Russian peasants.

Importantly, the timing of the process vindicates the hypothesis that the peasants' intensifying property consciousness and transition to individualism predates the November 1906 codification of these changes in Stolypin's reform.[15] Thus, the reform may be seen as an ex post codification of a process already under way. Several factors abetted this institutional transformation:

- The judicial reform of 1864 and the consequent professionalization of the judiciary made law enforcement more predictable, paving the way to greater social reliance on governmental justice (Gaudin, 2007, p. 117, Table 3.8).[16]
- The establishment of a representative public organ, the first Duma (1906), channeled the public discourse into a formal forum that both the state and the society accepted. This, in turn, mitigated repression and enhanced citizens' trust in the state, lowering the transaction costs of law enforcement.

  The introduction of railroads decisively reduced interdependent physical and cognitive distances between the peasant and the custom-based volost court. It also shortened distances between peasants and the civil-code-based imperial court institutions that had until then given them a powerful motive to settle conflicts informally and within their communities, invoking their intricate mechanisms of reciprocal agreements and compensation for grievances that had the further advantage of developing social consciousness (Engelgardt, 1993, p. 36; Frank, 1999, p. 92). Before the railroads, fear of discriminatory and degrading treatment by governmental institutions, coupled with the perceived opportunity cost of working time spent in travel to and from the courtroom, deterred both plaintiffs and witnesses from engaging the Tsarist judicial system. The technologi-

[15] An additional argument for this hypothesis is advanced by Mironov (2000, p. 349).

[16] On the increase in appeals of volost court cases to district congresses, see Hodgson (2004, pp. 105, 185) and Burbank (2004, p. 31).

cal innovation intrinsic to the railroads reduced the opportunity-cost hazards and uncertainties of traveling, making litigation less fraught with transaction costs and more predictable in whatever instance—the cantonal volost courts, structured by peasant custom applied as common law (Gaudin, 2007, p. 4; Engelgardt, 1993, p. 44), or the imperial courts (Svod Zakonov Rossijskoj Imperii), which applied the imperial statutes of 1832. Thus, repeated interaction alleviated the insecurity of arbitrary law enforcement and encouraged more peasants to rely on Tsarist governmental institutions. The process transformed these institutions as well. By giving the peasantry recourse to the judiciary, the railroads allowed witnesses to be heard at length, abetting equality before the law and encouraging additional engagement. The railroads cumulatively promoted the institutional transformation of the peasant estate as well as that of the elites, abolishing cultural-estate boundaries before the October Revolution and the Bolshevik takeover.

Landownership and Freedom The Peasantry's Share in the Ancestral Russian Legacy

Under the November 9, 1906, statute, the central government guaranteed the household head the right to transfer his strips of land from communal to personal ownership:

> *The actual fulfillment of this right [to leave the commune ... meets practical obstacles in most rural communities. ... Therefore ... it is necessary now to eliminate existing legal obstacles to the practical fulfillment of the peasants' right to their land allotment.* (quoted in Yaney, 1982, p. 260)

The legal transformation of the entire system of peasant rights, which at least formally allowed the commune to be exited, freed the individual householder from the daily imperative of submitting to the authority of the elder-based communal structure, namely, the Tsarist bureaucracy and, ultimately, the autocracy. The November 1906 legislation did more than encourage a transition from landholding collectivism to individualism from a static perspective. It also amplified the effects of urban industrial wage labor under the still-extant village commune system, facilitating the de jure emancipation of young heads of household from their fathers'

Table 7.2 Motives for land sales by households in the 1913 government survey, percent distribution

Reasons for sale	*Households that sold all their land*	*Households that sold part of their land*
Migration beyond Urals	**12.6**	2.3
Land purchase elsewhere in European Russia	**30.0**	12.1
Work in industry or services	**26.4**	14.9
Labor shortage	11.1	22.1
Harvest failure, famine, alcoholism	9.6	24.9
Other reasons	10.3	23.7
Total	**100.0**	**100.0**

Source: Pallot (1982, p. 27)

The bold values refer to the case study Chap. 9 regions—Povolzhe-Nizhnij Novogorod and Penza

patriarchal authority. This intensified the transition from extended to nuclear household units and, in turn, enhanced peasant mobility and migration.[17] The ability to sell the acquired land, albeit only to other members of the peasantry (Yaney, 1982, pp. 265, 260), precipitated structural changes. Table 7.2 illustrates the peasants' response to this institutional novelty.

Thus, the interaction of land reform and industrialization allowed individual householders to escape from the perils of disadvantageous agricultural conditions by migrating and taking up industrial labor. This, from a dynamic long-term perspective, mitigated individual economic dependency and challenged the organic rationality of peasant collectivism, which was motivated by necessity. Concurrently, the utility of the individualistic strategy increased not only due to the formal institutional transformation, which shaped and molded peasant preferences in its favor (Hodgson, 2004, pp. 105, 185, Boyer & Orlean, 1993, p. 22; Institutional Economics University of Hertfordshire Workshop 2001), but also by enhancing the returns on individual decision-making in tandem with the proliferation of

[17]Worobec (1995, p. 102, Table 3.3) indicates that the frequency of fissions was positively correlated with the accumulation of household assets—which, in turn, was enhanced by seasonal rural and urban wage labor (p. 98). The peasants' most frequent response to the famines in 1891–1892, merger, clearly indicates that they considered extended households a risk to the insurance unit that was meant to fend off hunger in the event of a calamity (Eggertsson, 1990, p. 303; Scott, 1976; Burds, 1998, p. 29).

individualism, which contributed to the popular legitimization of the reform and strengthened the effects of the reconstitutive downward causation process. The reform instigated a rapid (6–7-year) peasant response in spatial and occupational mobility that altered the social structure of the countryside. If so, the peasant village commune must have been ripe for destruction by the time the novel institutional reforms went into effect. This is why various aspects of Stolypin's reform may be understood as the ex post codification of an ongoing individualization process. The process had been formally acknowledged in the June 14, 1910, legislation that allowed former repartitional communes that had not conducted a general land redistribution since 1861 to acquire title to allotment land that had been managed in de facto hereditary tenure. The assumption that the commune disintegrated squares with Stolypin's personal perceptions and expectations (Klimin, 2002, p. 14).[18]

The frequency of peasant petitions for land settlement under the November 9, 1906, law points to the formal novelty of the institution, inspiring the peasants to move cautiously at first despite unambiguous enthusiasm about consolidation and household land ownership. Thus, in 1906 only 600 petitions for settlements relating to village land reached the agencies that administered the reform. Just one year later, however, the same agencies were flooded with 220,000 petitions, of which 81,000 proposed the full individualization of landholding by forming either an *otrub* (a consolidated parcel within the commune) or a *khutor* (a consolidated piece of household land outside of the commune). In 1908, 386,000 peasant petitions were filed, prompting the Ministry of Internal Affairs (MVD) to remark about the popularity of the process (Yaney, 1982, p. 275). It follows that the traditional pre-reform commune left enough room for individualism within its institutional framework to informally familiarize the peasant community with the advantages of individual entrepreneurial risk-taking and returns on investments in land (Kingston-Mann, 1991, p. 43; Gregory, 1994, p. 52; Nafziger, 2010).

The escalating use of the petition privilege counters Pallot's (1999) emphasis on the coercive character of the Stolypin reform as implemented and suggests instead that the peasants were genuinely interested in owning land. Yaney's findings indicate a high degree of voluntarism (Klimin, 2002, p. 14) that accompanied, and determined, the outcome of the process. The implementation of the Stolypin reform caused almost no

[18] Stolypin's emphasis on the voluntary character of the reform indicates his belief that the commune was dysfunctional at that time.

revolutionary violence on the part of the peasant constituency (Yaney, 1982, p. 187). As for non-violent coercion, the main cause of peasant fears had been the expected enforcement of individualistic risk-takers' land rights by government agencies, necessitating costly adaptations by such communal peasants as remained (Yaney, 1982). These fears may have motivated the petitions for the consolidation of the entire communes. The adversaries in these conflicts, however, were some peasant household heads against others, rather than peasants versus government agencies (Yaney, 1982, p. 296; Macey, 1990, p. 222).

The Transformation of the Orthodox Church-Railroad Technology Challenges the Pillar of Political Stability

Gerschenkron (1962, p. 133) posits that the Tsarist state revitalized the village commune structure after the emancipation. To repeat briefly, functions previously performed by the landlord such as tax collection, control of family structure, and responsibility for law and order were transferred to the jurisdiction of the village commune assembly, the *skhod*, in the Tsarist belief that this would enhance political stability. This analysis, however, is incomplete. Since the peasants constituted roughly 80 percent of the Tsarist Russian population, the commune could not have been consolidated by government coercion alone. The collectivist organizational structure of the nineteenth-century village commune, with its mutual-assistance properties, needed further backing and obtained it from one of the empire's mainstays of support, the Byzantine (Greek Orthodox) Church (Burds, 1998, p. 97).

The Church as the Pillar of Tsardom

Since Petrine times, relations between the Tsarist state and the Church had been typified by a tightly knit symbiosis. The state subventioned the Church and protected its monopoly on proselytizing. Most important, state organs including the police were obliged by law to prosecute any subject who challenged Greek Orthodoxy "by word or by deed." Legally, the Tsar was "the supreme defender and preserver of the dogmas of the ruling faith and protector of the purity of belief and the decorum of the holy Church" (Timberlake, quoting Curtiss). In exchange for this protection, the Church legitimized the imperial structure by proclaiming the Tsar "divinely anointed." The coronation of each new monarch, including Nicholas II in 1894, centered on an anointment ceremony at the Uspenskii Cathedral. Thus, the Tsar was conceived as an intermediary between God and man, his rule to be accepted by all subjects as a divine agency—rendering any discourse or opposition a sacrilege. The Orthodox clergy was obliged to report on any conspiracy against the autocracy, even if discovered during confession. Since governmental decrees and statutes were announced by the clergy in the course of religious services (the clergy being more literate than the peasantry), the Church also served de facto as a communication medium for the Tsar and his government (Timberlake, 1992, p. 11).

The implications of this institutionalized dependence of an autocratic regime—the Tsarist *samoderzhavie* (de Madariaga, 1998, p. 43)—on an ecclesiastical authority cannot be fully understood without reference to the work of one of Russia's most dynamic intellectuals, Prince Mikhail Bakunin's *God and the State*. Applying the essence of his pan-humanitarian analysis to specific conditions in Tsarist Russia, Bakunin claims that the Orthodox Church's consecration of the oppressive and despotic state structure is the source of the ultimate human degradation and retardation that Gerschenkron calls institutional "backwardness":

> *Christianity is precisely the religion par excellence because it exhibits and manifests, to the fullest extent, the very nature and* essence of every religious system, which is the impoverishment, enslavement, and annihilation of humanity for the benefit of divinity. ... *God being master man is the slave. ... Whoever says revelation says revealers, messiahs, prophets, priests, and legislators inspired by God himself; and these once recognized as the representatives of divinity on earth as the holy instructors of humanity, chosen by God himself to direct in the path of salvation,* necessarily exercise absolute power. *All men owe them passive and unlimited obedience, for against divine reason there is no human reason and against the justice of God no terrestrial justice.* Slaves of God men must also be slaves of the Church and State insofar as the State is consecrated by the Church .... (Bakunin, 1970, p. 24, emphasis added)

This radical rhetoric notwithstanding, elsewhere in *God and the State* Bakunin neither rejects nor denies the insight that the history of religious beliefs reflects "the development of collective intelligence and conscience of mankind" (p. 23). Thus, religiosity as such is a necessary stage in human development, an enterprise ultimately aimed at the attainment of individual dignity and liberty. Bakunin's vision of the ultimate rebellion—the rejection of all hierarchy, all domination of men by men, and the demand for absolute egalitarianism—reflects an aspect of the general sentiment that, albeit to a notably different degree, inspired other movements in nineteenth-century Russia, including radical clerical ones (Freeze, 1999, p. 281).

The interaction between the modernization process launched by the Tsarist autocracy, entailing technological change, and the Tsarist institutions' ongoing dependency on ecclesiastical structures paradoxically and unintentionally radicalized the religious base of the regime's legitimacy and instigated an institutional change in the direction of egalitarianism (Shevzov, 2004, pp. 36, 51, 52; Freeze, 1999, p. 280, 281). These mechanisms induced the gradual movement of the autocracy toward monarchy.

Bakunin, the true leader of the anarchist intelligentsia (as opposed to Karl Marx; after all, the landless proletariat constituted 5 percent of the Russian population), illuminated and defined the type of heterogeneous rebellious force, individualistic in character, that was being directed at the secular hierarchy, which itself was embedded in the religious mainstream. It was this that propelled the institutional transformation of both the Orthodox Church and the autocratic state toward the modernized pluralist Russian society that took shape with growing celerity before World War I. The technological innovation that set the whole country in motion—railroad construction, the core of the state-led industrialization process—contributed a condition of irreversibility to the process of democratizing social change.

The weaker the secularized base of the autocratic governance system's legitimacy became, the more the Tsarist state strove to lean on the pillar of spiritual legitimacy provided by the Church. The government-launched industrialization under Nicholas II, creating new wants, tumbled the peasantry into a self-perceived (relative) economic plight in the short run. The famine of 1891 and the economic depression of 1901–1903 bred dissatisfaction with the ruler just as the twin debacles of the Crimean War and the Russo-Japanese campaign of 1904 severely diminished the empire's power in international affairs. That the last Russian monarch was totally devoid of charisma only made things worse. Thus, by the end of the nineteenth century, the secularized bastions of Tsarism's stability—the persona of the ruler, the appearance of prosperity, and the relative projection of power in international affairs—no longer sufficed to ensure the political stability of the empire. This, in turn, amplified the importance of the regime's ecclesiastical and spiritual base of legitimacy (Freeze, 1996, p. 309).

Here it is important to elaborate on the vicious cycle, the consequences of conquest, and the reliability of the Greek Orthodox base of legitimacy for the perpetuation of the autocracy. Historically, the Empire's secularized "power in international relations" (p. 309), growing at this time and manifested in the imperial army's ability to secure territorial claims (due to technology imported from Western Europe), brought a host of non-Orthodox populations under the wings of the Tsarist autocracy. This accumulation of populations, although ostensibly strengthening the empire's secularized base of legitimacy, menaced the long-term stability of the autocratic regime by posing a spiritual challenge to the Tsar's ally, the Orthodox Church, as the conquered peoples practiced Islam or different forms of Christianity and owed no national and political loyalties to the crown. A long-term vicious cycle ensued: territorial conquest eroded the spiritual base of Tsarist legitimacy, making it necessary to bolster the secularized base of legitimacy even more by means of conquest. In graphic form, the cycle looks like this (Fig. 7.2):

To break the cycle, the Tsarist state appears to have attempted to "resacralize" autocratic rule (Freeze, 1996, p. 311), as may be judged by the marked increase of canonizations in the second half of the nineteenth century, in which the imperial family played an active if not an initiating role. Freeze (1996) proposes that the Tsarist attempt to hitch religious rites to the political wagon had the unintended consequence of consolidating pious subversion within the ranks of the mainstream Orthodox Church. Thus viewed, contrary to the implications of Gerschenkron's analysis and the expectations suggested by Marxist theory, the Church was not necessarily a reactionary force and the Tsarist state was not necessarily a progressive modernizer in all respects.

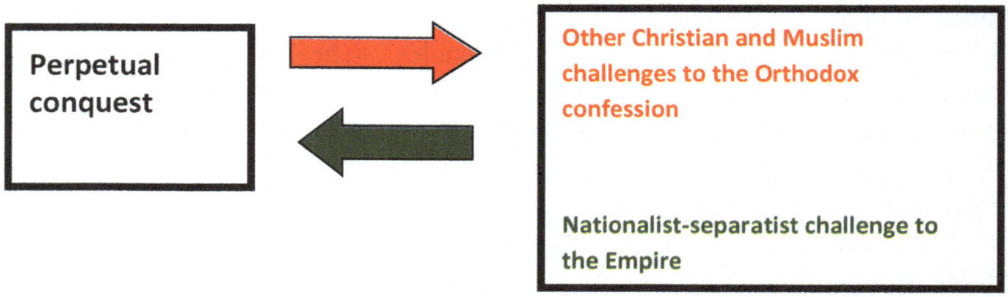

Fig. 7.2 Endemic necessity of conquest for the preservation of autocracy

The canonization in 1902 of Serafim of Sarov (Serafim Sarovskii, 1760–1833) is a case in point. Serafim, an obscure, humble, egalitarian monk, renounced the Church hierarchy and proclaimed a bright future for the Romanov dynasty. Although Nicholas II was born more than three decades after the pious preacher went to his eternal reward, the posthumous legacy of Serafim's teachings envisaged and predicted the perpetuation of autocracy under the Romanov rule that Nicholas II piously applied to his court. Thus, despite the skepticism of the Holy Synod, the imperial family initiated Serafim's canonization to enhance "unity between the Tsar and the people" (Freeze, 1996, pp. 315, 317, 318, 323). At the ceremony that solemnized the event, the imperial court, having organized masses of religious pilgrims, unintentionally revealed its value systems and thus overtly exacerbated the cultural and material rift between the pilgrims and the ruling elites. Exactly as the Tsarists had neither intended nor expected, Serafim's canonization revealed and aggravated the estrangement that prevailed between the Tsar and the people. The Tsarist court's attention to materialist splendor, the nobles' extravagant dressing and dining habits accompanied by extensive reliance on servants, and their worship of physical well-being, all manifested at this gathering in order to kindle the devotion of the timid masses, alienated the pious pilgrims, for whom asceticism, rejection of worldly matters, and elevation over daily deprivations of the body were a metaphysical creed. Influenced by the radicalization of its constituency, the mainstream Church increasingly fomented pious dissent and subversion rather than obedience to the crown (Freeze, 1996, pp. 317, 321, 324, 325, 329, 1999, p. 280).

Institutional Pluralism, Schisms in Orthodoxy, and the Impact of the Rails

The railroad technology allowed popular pious dissent to express itself on a scale theretofore unknown by allowing lengthy pilgrimages and unprecedentedly massive gatherings at canonization events. The latter inevitably posed a credible grassroots threat (Greif, 2006, p. 440) that prodded and pressured the Tsarist government toward democratizing concessions.

Given the weight of religious beliefs in the peasant way of life, any analysis of the vitality of nineteenth-century peasant collectivism (Veblen, 1931; Gerschenkron, 1968) entails a closer look at the institutional transitions within the Church that initially consolidated the communes (Burds, 1998, p. 97). These internal reevaluations were prompted by the challenge to the mainstream Orthodox hegemony presented by the Schismatics and other sectarians as well as the accelerating secularization that typified Tsarism's last decades (Treadgold, 1968, pp. 81–91).

The tensions within mainstream Orthodoxy coincided with the industrialization spurt of the 1890s and its consequences: intensified railroad construction, more peasant migration to urban centers for wage labor, and religious pilgrimages to remote and obscure monasteries. Attractive secular ideologies such as those of the Union of Liberation and the Socialist Revolutionaries, as well as an intensified peasant flight to the Old Belief *(staraya vera and razkol)*—a movement that was more often than not antagonist toward the Tsarist state—combined to pose a credible (and subsequently realized) threat of an uprising against the mainstream Church.

Importantly, none of these harbingers of progressive future development took place at the village level; they were individual-level processes. It is of great interest in this context that Archimandrite Theodore, the Bishop of Volokolamsk and the dean of the Moscow Theological Academy, expressing his concerns in the revolutionary year of 1905—before the land reforms—observed, "One of the most characteristic traits of our time is that the individual *lichnost* [personality], previously strongly suppressed, now unreservedly strives forward in his or her development and self-expression" (Shevzov, 2004, p. 13).

The ascendancy during this period of *beztserkovnoe khristianstvo* or "churchless Christianity"—the belief that the larger ecclesiastical order and community were no longer essential for salvation—constituted an additional challenge to traditional Orthodoxy (Shevzov, 2004, p. 13). Therefore, the pious dissent expressed by the Schismatics and, especially, the Old Believers should be seen as causally related to the growing revival of egalitarian doctrine that had earlier concerned small parishes and to the large-scale transition to democratic piety within the mainstream ecclesiastical system (Shevzov; Burds, 1998, p. 193). The depth of the institutional transformation set in motion by industrialization and its corollary, *otkhod*, cannot be overestimated. Neither can the shaping and molding effect of the democratization of the ecclesiastical system and its corollary, the individualization of customary peasant structures (Shevzov, 2004, p. 36; Hodgson, 2004, pp. 105, 185).

The hierarchical ecclesiastical system that legitimized the autocratic Tsarist state, structured on the authority of both clerical and civil officials' and preaching to and monitoring the obedient laity's religious habits, was established under Peter the Great and codified in the Spiritual Regulation of 1721 (Shevzov, 2004, p. 18).[19] Formally, the Spiritual Regulation constituted the institutional foundation that legitimized the Tsarist Empire from Petrine times to the October Revolution of 1917. The following quotation from the Regulation shows that the state tolerated neither autonomous ecclesiastical authority nor any formal institutional recognition of a faith community:

> ... *Common people do not understand how the spiritual authority is distinguishable from the autocratic. ... They imagine that such an administrator is a second Sovereign, a power equal to that of the Autocrat, or even greater than he ....* (Shevzov, 2004, p. 16)

In the last decades of the nineteenth century, however, the Tsarist state of Nicholas II and the Church increasingly parted ways (Freeze, 1996, p. 312). The Byzantine structure had identified the laity with the profane—matters belonging to "this world"—and likened the peasantry to the "dark masses," in contrast to the ordained, spiritually superior, and leading clergy, represented by the supreme procurator of the Holy Synod, K.P. Pobedonostsev. Now, informally and through an emerging internal debate influenced by the older egalitarian concept of *sobornost*—literally a "church-community gathering"—the parish laity as well as the clergy were seen as the "People of God," namely, equals before God (Shevzov, 2004, p. 33). All of this coincided with, and was occasioned by, the 1890 industrialization spurt and the peasants' growing propensity to wage-labor migration.

The laws of April 17, 1905, and October 17, 1906, which established religious tolerance and legalized the Old Belief and other "sectarian" practices, marked the advent of an emerging pluralist society in Tsarist Russia (Treadgold, 1968, p. 85). These late-Tsarist concessions, geared to the restoration of law and order, also suggest that the 1905 revolution did not find its main motive in material impoverishment. The common denominator of Stolypin's reform and the establishment of freedom of religious belief a year earlier is the acknowledgment of all individual civil rights that Tsarist Russia had never known before.

[19] In the context of relations between clergy and laity, the Spiritual Regulation was heavily influenced by the thinking of Bishop Feofan Prokopovich (1681–1736), trained at the Kievan Academy, which was strongly influenced by Roman Catholic Jesuit teachings.

The intra-ecclesiastical debates that ensued in 1905 and persisted until 1917 concerned the very identity of Orthodoxy. Countering the Marxist intuition, the competing visions crossed both social and ecclesiastical class lines. Liberalizing reforms were often proposed by bishops while the laity represented the conservative adversary. Thus, the Orthodox establishment, perceiving the spiritual challenge posed by the individual choices that industrialization allowed and fearing rootlessness in its own constituency, competed for hearts and minds—so its conservative adversaries charged—by absorbing "republican" ideas (Shevzov, 2004, p. 14).

While organs of the contemporary secular press such as *Ruskii Vestnik* and *Moskovskie Vedomosti* defended conservative positions, two ecclesiastical journals, *Bogoslovskii Vestnik* and *Tserkovnyi Vestnik,* were accurately accused by the conservative laity of injecting into the Tsarist Empire the very ideas that had fueled the French Revolution (Shevzov, 2004, p. 14). Indeed, the ecclesiastic reformers considered the transition to an egalitarian conception of the parish as urgent as the Emancipation Act of 1861 had been (p. 16).

The mainstream religious authority was additionally challenged in the closing decades of the nineteenth century by a sharp turn to the Left—toward rationalism from the perspective of scientific enlightenment—in Orthodox attitudes toward superstition.[20] This liberalization may explain the paradox among the peasants of *klikushestvo*—the perception of being possessed by a demon, a being of sinister black magic, and its consequence: samosud, *the extrajudicial peasant system of punishment and vengeance aimed at alleged witches and sorcerers.* These states of mind seemed immune to the effects of modernization, specifically the call of urban culture that peasants could now heed due to the increasingly proximate railroad station (see Chaps. 9, 10, and 11). As both the ecclesiastical and the imperial systems became more and more tolerant of pious dissent practices, peasants had less of an incentive to conceal klikushestvo. Consequently, the number of reported cases increased, possibly also fueled by the improvement in peasants' ability to visit remote monasteries for exorcism.

It is of interest that the industrialization process, with railroad construction at its core, also abetted the transition to pious rationalism in the modernizing and democratizing Church.[21] Challenged by the seculariza-

[20] Shevzov (2004, p. 209) remarks: "The bishop was subordinate to the icon not the icon to the bishop."

[21] On the rationalist definition of klikushestvo as hysteria and on the multiple structures that enabled rationalist reform, see Shevzov (2004, p. 39).

tion that the urban culture inspired, Orthodox clerics increasingly regarded cases of klikushestvo as attacks of hysteria, hesitantly opening the door to the acceptance of the possibility of recovery through medical treatment. This progressive gesture notwithstanding, the Church perceived itself as the miracle cure that it offered as one of its main functions (Worobec, 2001, pp. 40, 41).

Railroads Allow Choice: Mainstream Orthodoxy or Dissent? The Advent of Peasant Rationalism

The choices newly afforded by the railroads included not only movement toward religion but gravitation away from it, as in secularization (Mironov, 2000, p. 500, Table 7.18). Another option was flight from the moral economic obligations that the mainstream Orthodox Church imposed on kin who remained on the commune by embracing the Old Belief (*staraya vera*) movement and its doctrine of *razkol.* Unlike mainstream Orthodoxy, the *staraya vera* consolidated during the seventeenth century and was deeply antagonistic to the perpetuation of unchallenged Tsarist authority—a characteristic that it shared with the secularized urban ideologies. The Tsarist government persecuted Old Believers more harshly than it did any other community of dissenters because it viewed secession from the official state religion as both apostasy and treason (Lieven, 2000, p. 257).

The mainstream Orthodox village priesthood, in turn, legitimized the sanctity of the patriarchal hierarchy (Hoch, 1986, p. 183; Burds, 1998, pp. 76, 84, 189), helping the Tsarist police to enforce the peasants' customary obligation to repatriate income earned from wage labor in support of their families in the commune, tying the urban proletarian to his native village. Thus, by invoking rural social-sanction mechanisms and collaborating with the formal penal system, mainstream Orthodoxy tightened controls over the income of peasants generally and of peasant workers particularly (Burds, 1998, pp. 29, 83). If so, the popular and ostensibly voluntary peasant conception of the village commune as an unemployment and old-age "insurance company" (Johnson, 1979, p. 38) was anchored in and shaped by Orthodox worldviews (North, 2005, p. 23). The peasantry's newfound mobility for wage work and migration, enhanced by the railroads, created potential exposure to sectarianism and to piously subversive and secularized dissent. This introduction to rationalistic choice irreversibly challenged the hierarchies of coercion that mainstream Greek Orthodoxy had constructed at the level of the autocracy and in the village commune. By facilitating the challenge to the spiritual pillars of the autocracy's legitimacy, the railroads brought about the democratization of the Church and the autocracy, paving the way to the individualization of landholding in Stolypin reform and ultimately heralding the advent of constitutional monarchy in Russia (Fig. 7.3).

The Peaceful Monarchy—Autocracy, Peasant Individualism, and Stolypin's Reform

The idea of modernizing Tsarist Russian agriculture by dissolving the village commune through the reassignment of land rights to heads of household was an institutional novelty. This reform, forever identified with Prime Minister Pyotr Arkadyevich Stolypin, was congruent, I maintain, with the civil-rights-oriented spirit of the 1905 laws on personal freedom of faith and the growing egalitarianism and consequent democratization "from within" that transformed late nineteenth-century Russian Orthodoxy. The long-term objective of the November 9, 1906, statute that allowed heads of household to obtain title to obshchina land was to free these individuals from the bureaucratized paternalism of the elder-dominated communal-village structure (Mironov, 2000, p. 330). Thus, the Tsarist concession embodied in the reform presaged the future retreat of state bureaucracy from the countryside in what Atkinson (1983, pp. 41, 42) calls the "second Emancipation" of the Russian peasantry.

At the government level, the Stolypin reform was motivated by two dominant concerns relating to political stability. It aspired to inculcate a sense of citizenship, *grazhdanstvennost* (Ascher, 1988, pp. 268, 269), in the peasant paterfamilias by persuading the masses that loyalty to the Tsarist crown was economically rational. It was thought, in accordance with agricultural doctrines promoted in the nineteenth century, the individualization of control and ownership of landed resources would pave the way to greater productivity and, ultimately, eliminate peasant poverty (Yaney, 1982, p. 164, 165, 166, 174). In the long run, the reform would do away with the periodic land redistribution schemes that the European Russian peasant had practiced to regionally varying degrees—frequently until 1893 and afterwards, under a new law, at a minimum interval of twelve years. Abolishing this practice, it was thought, would enhance the transition from extensive to intensive land use (Atkinson, 1983, pp. 29, 174; Nafziger, 2007, pp. 12, 14, Table 2, 15; Hesse, 1993, pp. 51; Gerschenkron, 1962, pp. 120).

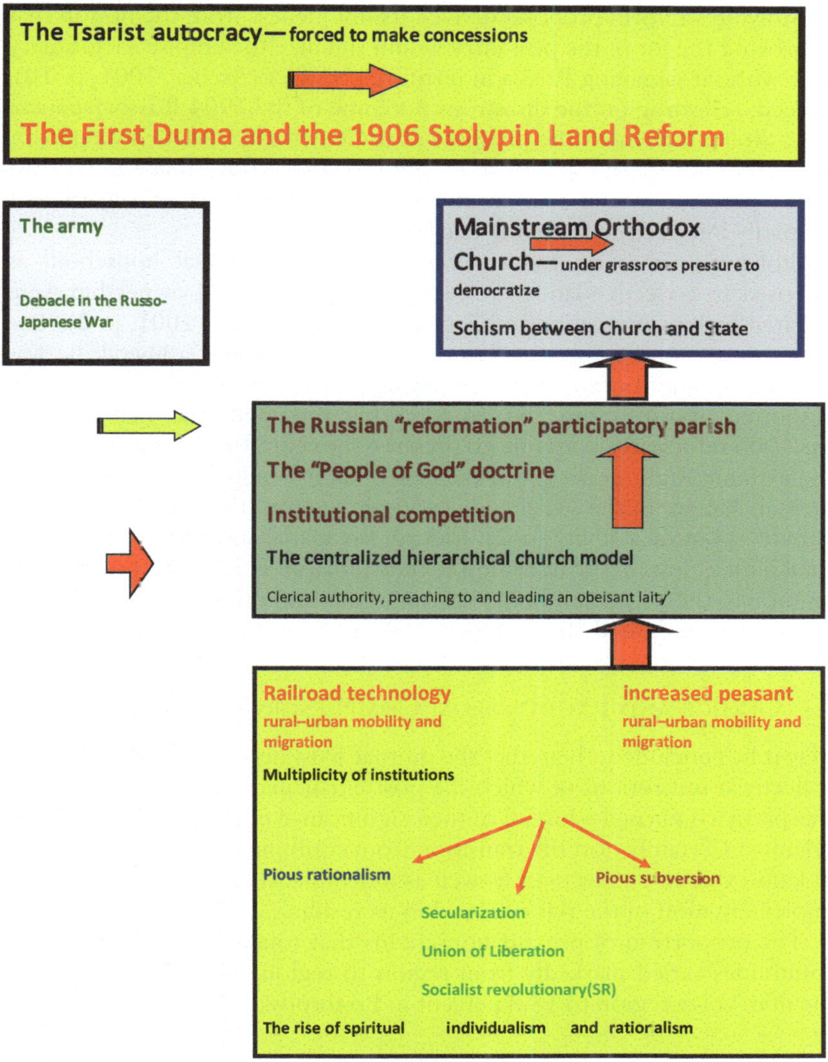

Fig. 7.3 The Transition from Hierarchy to Egalitarianism by Rail. (Sources: Ascher (1988, pp. 50, Vol. I, 93–96, 165–183, 194, Vol. II, 269), Freeze (1996, pp. 309, 312), Shevzov (2004, pp. 32–41), Burds (1998, p. 23, Table 1.3, 188), Worobec (2001, pp. 41, 55), Treadgold (1968, pp. 80, 81), Sheshinski (2010), Gintis (2009), Gaudin (2007), Martens (2004))

Stolypin's reform proposal derived its uniqueness from the notion that improving the lot of the peasantry would stabilize the empire's legitimacy base without engaging Russia in territorial conflict (Ascher, 2001, p. 10). Indeed, reflecting on the disastrous outcome of the 1904 Russo-Japanese War, Stolypin deemed the prospect of armed conflict decidedly unfavorable to the future of the monarchy (pp. 10, 11). Thus, unlike the Tsarist state's previous modernization initiatives, the 1906 land reform was not primarily intended to serve the needs of war.

Stolypin's views on the superiority of the individual household as opposed to collective landed resource management and ownership were inspired by his observations of German farming (Ascher, 2001, p. 2). The Tsar's prime minister was neither a constitutionalist nor a liberal; he was devoted to the Tsarist monarchy as well as to the Orthodox Church, authoritarian institutions both (p. 9). While the intellectual Left opposed the 1906 reform as an attempt to preserve the centralized autocratic order, the extreme Right decried it in the belief that it would bring about fundamental changes in the social and economic systems, thus endangering the empire's political stability (p. 2). Indeed, the spatial and, in turn, the structural implications of the transition to individualism in landed property were inimical to the perpetuation of autocratic rule, and the Stolypin reform did indeed have unintended consequences for the Tsar's government.

Choice and Exodus from Compulsory Collectivism

May it be concluded, then, that the mutual-trust networks—the voluntary collectivist institutions of which the post-emancipation communal village was partly composed—lost all of their significance in the peasants' survival calculus? Certainly not: the transition from communal to individual rights in land exhibited collectivist as well as individualist elements, both in the implementation of the reform[22] and in its results.

The proportion of peasant households that totally seceded from their communes varied markedly from region to region—from 3.7 percent in the mid-Volga region to 18.3 percent in Bogorodskii District, part of Tula

[22] Yaney (1982, pp. 277, 280, 357, 358) identifies the conversion of entire communes to hereditary household-head ownership under the statute enacted on June 14, 1910. The path to such conversion had been paved by household and individual secessions and group land settlements, both entailing corresponding levels of communal cooperation (Atkinson, 1983, p. 61).

Province in the central black-soil belt. A 1913 government survey of 17,567 households set the average share of household withdrawal from communes at 7.4 percent (Pallot, 1982, p. 25) (Table 7.3).

Bogorodskii District, however, was not typical; it boasted an unusually high share of industrial labor. "No specified employment" might include farming for a wage; so could "migration beyond Urals." To determine what became of the missing 14.6 percent, comparisons with other regions are needed.

Pallot's definition of the consolidation process (1982, p. 19; 1984) speaks of the transfer of title to household land and property rights in chattels to the paterfamilias. Household land was consolidated in accordance with two methods:

- The establishment of a *khutor* (a consolidated piece of household land outside of the commune), causing the settlement to "disperse" (1982, p. 18) as heads of household withdrew consolidated strips, dwellings, and outbuildings from the commune's common pool.
- The aggregation of allotment land into an *otrub* (a consolidated parcel within the commune), characterized by ongoing cohesion of the communal village. Each household's consolidated parcels and the adjoining household dwellings could be combined to form a hamlet.

The propensity to cooperate voluntarily after making a choice based on individual utility increased. Since authoritarian and autocratic rule in the

Table 7.3 Activity of households in Bogorodskii District before and after consolidation of land strips into one household parcel that receives rights to title (Pct. Distribution), 1913 survey

Activity	*Before consolidation*	*After consolidation*	*Change*
Farming	22.6	9.5	**-57.8%**
Migration beyond Urals	6.6	9.2	**+40.0%**
Industrial labor	41.6	46.6	**+11.8%**
No specified employment	14.4	23.3	**+61.4%**
Unknown	14.6	11.4	-22.2%
Total	100.0	100.0	-

Source: Pallot (1982, p. 27).

Note: The percent share of all peasants specifically in Bogorodskii District who remained agrarian after consolidation dropped from 22.6 percent to 9.5 percent—a 57.8 percent decline

The bold values refer to the case study Chap. 9 regions—Povolzhe-Nizhnij Novogorod and Penza

Tsarist Empire rested on pre-modern tribal institutions at the grassroots level (de Madariaga, 1998, p. 79; Hoch, 1986, p. 183), Stolypin's reform also increased the surveillance costs of authoritarian control over implementing the reform (North, 1990, pp. 90, 91). Peasants who remained in agriculture gained more long-term bargaining power vis-à-vis the ruler now that they held title to land, augmenting these costs even more (Pipes, 1999, p. xii; Martens, 2004, p. 193; North, 1973, p. 29). Stolypin's reform transferred the monitoring capacity in regard to conscripts, tax remittances, and compliance with the Autocrats Law, as set forth in the Russian Imperial Statutes, from the peasant village officialdom (the assembly) to the Tsarist bureaucracy. This centralized modality, alien to the peasantry, exacerbated surveillance costs even more. Moreover, title to land created a peasantry that, in the aggregate, enjoyed increasing alternative spiritual options and was therefore less likely to homogeneously choose the mainstream and support Tsarist autocracy. The peasant followers of the schismatics including Old Believers community engaged in pious subversion as a spiritual option. Given the totalitarian control aspirations of an autocracy, the expansion of choice options pushed transaction costs up. Importantly, then, the 1906 legalization of peasant individualism did not result in an atomized peasantry.

Freedom through Cooperation

It did the opposite: As the reform moved ahead, the communal rural cooperation mechanisms adjusted to the challenge of land settlement (Yaney, 1982, p. 366). Individual household governance allowed and enforced withdrawal from the communes, necessitating the correction of land redistributions and communal land consolidations on the basis of formal acknowledgement of individuals' rights. This, in turn, strengthened the evolution of the voluntary mechanisms of collective action among communal and formerly communal peasants (p. 280).

By strengthening peasant migration to urban areas as well as to other rural locations, the reform helped to reinforce the necessary *zemliachestvo* (landsman) ties that characterized relations among the wage laborers (Johnson, 1979, p. 69).

The Stolypin Reform: Shifting Rule from the Tsar's Patrimony to Peasants' Countervailing Negotiating Power

The institutionally legalized peasant individualism codified in Stolypin's 1906 reform had both spiritual and material aspects. Peasants' participation in the reform was characterized by informal spontaneous and voluntary individualization of landholding within the communal village. Due to increasingly rationalistic cooperation, the benefits of the process were evaluated through refined mechanisms of collective action within the commune that sometimes led as far as dissolution (Barzel, 2002, p. 61). Labor and peasant entrepreneur voluntary associations came together in these mechanisms, resulting in the gradual emergence of a peaceful element of organized credible demand for the transfer of political power from ruler to subjects. Craftsman and soldiers arteli cooperatives constitute cases in point (Troyat, 1961; Bushnell, 1990). Stolypin's reform marked the end of the Tsarist *votchina* (patrimony) (Pipes, 1995, p. 70)—as the new landed property holders, the *bolshaki*, acquired political power. This exposed the autocracy to a two-edged challenge: the transfer of property rights in land to a newly institutionalized citizen community that constituted 80 percent of the population *and* the ability of this constituency to organize in both rural and the industrializing urban environments. *Zemliachestvo* ties, strengthened by rural cooperation mechanisms, easily transitioned into modern urban trade-union activity and pious opposition (Martens, 2004, p. 193; Pipes, 1999, p. xii; North, 1973, p. 29; Freeze, 1996, p. 311; Boyer & Orlean, 1993, p. 22; Troyat, 1961, Bushnell, 1990). The challenge to the autocracy posed by the emerging civil society was an unintended consequence of the reform.

State-led industrialization, with railroad construction at its heart, promoted ideological and religious heterogeneity in Tsarist Russian society, forcing and facilitating the legalization of individual household property rights in land and, in turn, triggering the formation of voluntary collective action units (Barzel, 2002, p. 61). None of this was consistent with the perpetuation of autocratic governance. By acting as it did, the Tsarist Russian Empire embarked on the road to constitutional monarchy.

Paradoxically, the technological change effectuated by Tsarist railroad construction and its effect—democratization, meaning the dissolution of the pious hierarchy and, in turn, the weakening of interdependencies between the state and the Orthodox Church—amplified the significance of the debacle of the 1904 Russo-Japanese War. Finding both the ecclesiastical *and* the military bases of its legitimacy eroded, the Tsarist state had to make institutional concessions in an attempt to create an alternative secularized base of legitimacy to conquest. In the eyes of Stolypin's government, the land reform and its aim—rallying the loyal citizen-landowner behind the crown—seemed an adequate solution to this problem. In fact, it was not. Against the background of technological change, the Stolypin reform was inconsistent with the preservation of autocratic privileges and prerogatives because these phenomena emanated from Muscovy's founding principle of land as the ruler's personal patrimony. The very process that Stolypin had intended to assure the stability and perpetuation of autocracy weakened and would ultimately demolish this structure. The secularized base of legitimacy in the Tsars' gradually democratizing empire would be provided by a prosperous peasantry. Such an outcome represented a historical discontinuity because it was conditioned on perpetuating peace instead of preparing for conquest as tradition would have had it (Ascher, 2001, pp. 9, 10, 11).

By participating in World War I, Russia would breach this condition in a manner disastrous to the possibility of peaceful democratization (Fig. 7.4).

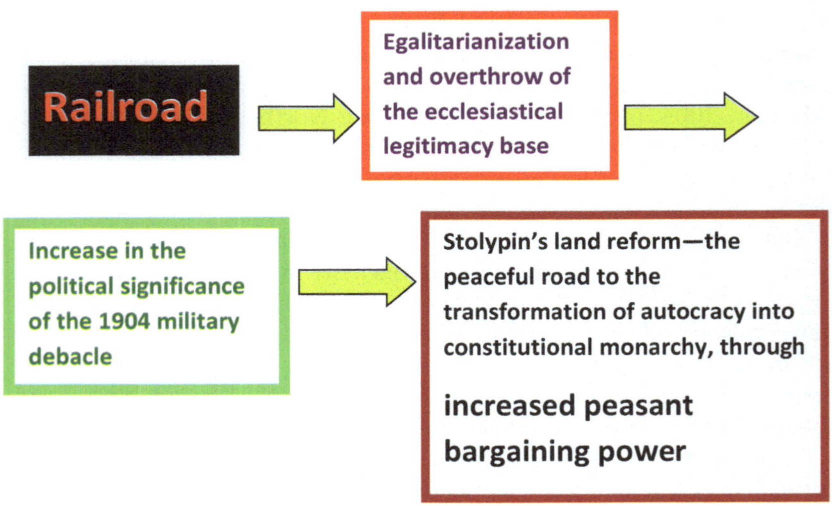

Fig. 7.4 Railroads and the emergence of collective action units. (Sources: See sources in Fig. 7.3 above, as well as Shevzov (2004, p. 36); Freeze (1996, p. 309); Ascher (2001, pp. 9–11); North (1973, p. 29); Martens (2004, p. 193); Pipes (1999, p. xii); Barzel (2002, p. 61))

References

Ascher, A. (1988). *The revolution of 1905. Part I Russia in disarray. Part II Authority restored*. Stanford University Press.

Ascher, A. (2001). *P.A. Stolypin. The search for stability in Late Imperial Russia*. Stanford University Press.

Atkinson, D. (1983). *The end of the Russian land commune 1905–1930*. Stanford University Press.

Bakunin, M. (1970). *God and the state*. With a New Introduction and Index of Persons by Paul Avrich Dover Publications.

Bartlett, R. (1990). *Land commune and peasant community in Russia: Communal forms in imperial and early Soviet society*. Macmillan in Association with the School of Slavonic and East European Studies, University of London.

Barzel, Y. (1989). *Economic analysis of property right*. Cambridge University Press.

Barzel, Y. (2002). *The theory of the state: Economic rights, legal rights and the scope of the state*. Cambridge University Press.

Bates, R. (1989). *Beyond the miracle of the market: The political economy of agrarian development in Kenya*. Cambridge University Press.

Borodkin, L. I. (2008). *Discussion*.

Boserup, E. (1965). *The conditions of agricultural growth the economics of agrarian change under population pressure*. Allen Unwin.

Boyer, R., & Orlean, A. (1993). How do Conventions Evolve? In U. Witt (Ed.), *Evolution in markets and institutions*. Physica-Vlg.

Burbank, J. (2004). *Russian Peasants go to Court-Legal Culture in the Country Side 1905–1917*. Indiana UP.

Burds, J. (1998). *Peasant dreams and market politics-Labor migration and the Russian village 1861–1905*. University of Pittsburgh Press.

Bushnell, J. (1990). The Russian soldiers' artel', 1700 -1900-A history and interpretation. In J. Burbank (Ed.), *Russian peasants go to court: Legal culture in the countryside, 1905–1917*. Indiana University Press.

Coase, R. (1937). *The firm the market and the law*. University of Chicago Press.

Crafts, N. (2007). *Lecture*. Lund: EHES conference.

Crisp, O. (1989). Peasant land tenure and civil rights implications before 1906. In O. Crisp & L. Edmondson (Eds.), *Civil rights in imperial Russia*. Clarendon Press.

de Madariaga, I. (1998). *Politics and culture in eighteenth century Russia*. Longman.

Dubrovski, S. M. (1963). Stolypinskayazemel'nayareforma.

Eggertsson, T. (1990). *Economic behavior and institutions*. Cambridge University Press.

Engelgardt, N. (1993). *Letters from the Country, 1872–1887* (C. Frierson, Trans. & Ed.). Oxford University Press.

Frank, S. (1999). *Crime, cultural conflict and justice in rural Russia 1856–1914*. University of California Press.

Freeze, L. (1996). Subversive piety: religion and the political crisis in late Imperial Russia. *Journal of Modern History, 68*(2), (June), 308–350.
Freeze, L. G. (1999). Church and politics in Late Imperial Russia: Crisis and radicalization of the clergy. In A. Geifman (Ed.), *Russia under the last Tsar: Opposition and subversion 1894–1914.* Blackwell Publishers.
Frierson, C. (1987). Crime and punishment in the Russian village: Rural concepts of criminality at the end of the nineteenth century. *Slavic Review, 46*(1), 55–69.
Frierson, C. (1990). Land commune and peasant community in Russia: Communal forms in imperial and early Soviet Society. In R. Bartlett (Ed.), *Land commune and peasant community in Russia: Communal forms in imperial and early Soviet Society.* Macmillan in Association with the School of Slavonic and East European Studies, University of London.
Gatrell, P. (1994). *Government, industry and rearmament in Russia, 1900–1914: The Last argument of Tsarism.* Cambridge University Press.
Gaudin, C. (1998). No place to lay my head: Marginalisation and the right to land during the Stolypin reforms. *Slavic Review, 57*(Winter), 747–773.
Gaudin, C. (2007). *Ruling peasants: Village and state in late imperial Russia.* Northern Illinois University Press.
Gerschenkron, A. (1962). *Economic backwardness in historical perspective.* The Belknap Press of Harvard University Press.
Gerschenkron, A. (1968). *Continuity in history and other essays.* The Belknap Press of Harvard University Press.
Gintis, H. (2009). *The bounds of reason: Game theory and the unification of the behavioral sciences.* Princeton University Press.
Gregory, P. R. (1994). *Before command. An economic history of Russia from emancipation to the first five-year plan.* Princeton University Press.
Greif, A. (2006). *Institutions and the path to modern economy: Lessons from medieval trade.* Cambridge University Press.
Herzen, A. (1985). *My past and thoughts: The memoirs of Alexander Herzen.* University of California Press.
Hesse, G. (1993). Land use systems and property rights. Evolutionary versus institutional economics. In U. Witt (Ed.), *Evolution in markets and institutions.* Physica-Vlg.
Hoch, S. (1986). *Serfdom and social control in Russia. Petrovskoe, a village in Tambov.* University of Chicago Press.
Hodgson, G. M. (2001). *How economics forgot history: The problem of historical specificity in social science.* Routledge.
Hodgson, G. M. (2004). *What are institutions? From orders to organizations.* Essay presented at the 6th International Workshop on Institutional Economics, University of Hertfordshire.
Johnson, R. (1979). *Peasant and proletarian: The working class of Moscow in the late nineteenth century.* Leicester University Press.

Kahan, A. (1985). *The Plow the Hammer and the Knout.* An Economic History of Eighteenth Century Russia. The University of Chigaco Press.

Kahan, A. (1989). *Russian economic history: The nineteenth century* (R. Weiss, Ed.). University of Chicago Press.

Kimball, A. (1992). Alexander Herzen and the native lineage of the Russian revolution. In C. E. Timberlake (Ed.), *Religious and secular forces in Late Tsarist Russia.* University of Washington Press.

Kingston-Mann, E. (1991). Peasant communes and economic innovation: A preliminary inquiry. In E. Kingston-Mann, T. Mixter, & J. Burds (Eds.), *Peasant economy culture and politics of European Russia.* Princeton University Press.

Klimin, I. I. (2002). *Stolypinskaya agrarnaya reforma i stanovlenie krestian sobstvennikov v Rossii.* Csentristoricheskichigumanitarnychissledovani 'Klio'.

Lenin, V. I. (1974). *The development of capitalism in Russia.* Progress Publishers.

Leonard, C., & Ljungberg, J. (2008). Vol. 2, Chapter 5: *Population and living standards.* Unpublished draft. Department of Economic History, Lund University.

Leonard, C. S. (1990). Landlords and the mir: Transaction costs and economic development in pre-emancipation Russia (Iaroslav Gubernia). In R. Bartlett (Ed.), *Land commune and peasant community in Russia: Communal forms in imperial and early Soviet society.* Macmillan in Association with the School of Slavonic and East European Studies, University of London.

Lieven, D. (2000). *Empire: The Russian empire and its rivals.* John Murray Albermarle Street.

Löve, H. D. (1990). Differentiation in Russian peasant society: causes and trends, 1880–1905. In R. Bartlett (Ed.), *Land commune and peasant community in Russia: Communal forms in imperial and early Soviet Society.* Macmillan in Association with the School of Slavonic and East European Studies, University of London.

Macey, D. (1990). The peasant commune and the Stolypin reforms: Peasant attitudes, 1906–14. In R. Bartlett (Ed.), *Land commune and peasant community in Russia. Communal forms in imperial and early Soviet society.* University of London, London: Macmillan in Association with the School of Slavonic and East European Studies, University of London.

Macey, D. (1998). A wager on history: The Stolypin agrarian reforms as a process. In J. Pallot (Ed.), *Transforming peasants: Society, state and the peasantry, 1861–1930.* Selected Papers From the Fifth World Congress of Central and East European Studies, Warsaw, 1995.

Martens, B. (2004). *The cognitive mechanics of economic development and institutional change.* Routledge.

Metzer, J. (1972). *Some economic aspects of railroad development in Tsarist Russia.* Unpublished doctoral dissertation. University of Chicago.

Milov, L. (2001). Velikorusskiipakhariosobennostirossijskogoistoricheskogo protsessa. BibliotekaGumer-istoria. http://www.gumer.info/bibliotek_Buks/History/milov/01.php
Mironov, B. N. (1999). SocialnayaistoriaRossiiperiodaImperii (XVIII-nachaloXXv) genesislichnostidemokraticheskojsemiigrazhdanskogoobshchestvaipravo-vogogposudarstva: v dvuchtomach.DimitrijBulanin.
Mironov, B. N. (2000). *A social history of imperial Russia, 1700–1917* (Vol. I). Westview Press.
Mokyr, J. (1990). *Lever of riches: Technological creativity and economic progress.* Oxford University Press.
Moon, D. (1999). *The Russian peasantry 1600–1930. The world the peasants made.* Longman.
Nafziger, S. (2007). *Land redistributions and the Russian peasant commune in the 19th century.* EHES, Lund and Department of Economics Williams College.
Nafziger, S. (2010). Peasant communes and factor markets in late nineteenth century Russia. *Explorations in Economic History, 47*(4) 381–402.
Nelson, R., & Winter, S. (1982). *An evolutionary theory of economic change.* The Belknap Press of Harvard University Press.
North, D. C. (1973). *Västerlandets Uppgång.* SNS.
North, D. C. (1990). *Institutions, institutional change and economic performance.* Cambridge University Press.
North, D. C. (2005). *Understanding the process of economic change.* Princeton University Press.
Owen, T. (1995). *Russian corporate capitalism from Peter the Great to perestroika.* Oxford University Press.
Pallot, J. (1982). *Social change and peasant landholding in pre-revolutionary Russia.* Research Paper 30, School of Geography, Oxford University.
Pallot, J. (1984). Khutora and otruba in Stolypins program of farm individualization. *Slavic Review, 43*(2, Summer), 242–256.
Pallot, J. (1999). *Land reform in Russia 1906–1917: Peasant responses to Stolypin's project of rural transformation.* Clarendon Press.
Pipes, R. (1995). *Russia under the old regime.* Penguin Books.
Pipes, R. (1999). *Property and freedom.* Harvill Press.
Poznanski, K. (1992). A property rights perspective on the evolution of communist-type economies. In K. Poznanski (Ed.), *Constructing capitalism. The re-emergence of civil society and liberal economy in the post-Communist world.* Westview Press.
Raeff, M. (1984). *Understanding imperial Russia.* Columbia University Press.
Robbins, R. G., Jr. (1975). *Famine in Russia 1891–1892: The Imperial government responds to a crisis.* Columbia University Press.
Scott, J. (1976). *The moral economy of the peasant. Rebellion and subsistence in Southeast Asia.* Yale University Press.

SemenovaTjan-Sanskaja, O. (1863–1906). In D. L. Ransel (Ed., 1993), *Village life in Late Tsarist Russia*. Indiana University Press.
Sheshinski, E. (2010). *Limits in individual choice*. The Hebrew University of Jerusalem.
Shevzov, V. (2004). *Russian Orthodoxy on the eve of revolution*. Oxford University Press.
Simms, Y. J. (1977). The crisis in the Russian agriculture at the end of the nineteenth century: A different view. *Slavic Review, 36*(3), 377–398.
Smith, A. (1998). *An inquiry into the nature and the causes of the wealth of nations*. Regnery Publishing.
Smurova, O. V. (2003). *Niezemledelcheski odkhod krestian v stolitsu I ego vlejanie na transformacjiu kulturnoj tradicji*. Izd-voKostromskogogos. technologich. Universiteta.
Sztern, S. (2000). *The Russian commune-village, the obshchina: Its origins, function and character*. Paper presented at the Economic History Seminar, Lund University.
Timberlake, C. E. (1992). Introduction: Religious pluralism, the spread of revolutionary ideas, and the church state relationship in Tsarist Russia. In C. E. Timberlake (Ed.), *Religious and secular forces in Late Tsarist Russia*. University of Washington Press.
Treadgold, D. W. (1968). The peasant and religion. In W. S. Vucinich (Ed.), *The peasant in nineteenth-century Russia*. Stanford University Press.
Troyat, H. (1961). *Daily life in Russia under the last Tsar*. Stanford University Press.
Vanberg, V. (1994). *Rules and choice in economics*. Routledge.
Veblen, T. (1931). *The theory of the leisure class*. Viking.
Volyn, L. (1970). *A century of Russian agriculture: From Alexander II to Khrushchev*. Harvard University Press.
Westwood. (1964). *A History of the Russian Railway*. Georges Allen and Unvin Ltd.
Williamson, O. E. (1985). *The economic institutions of capitalism: Firms, markets, relational contracting*. The Free Press.
Workshop on Institutional Economics, University of Hertfordshire. (2001–2010). Discussions.
Worobec, C. D. (1990). The post-emancipation Russian peasant commune in Orel province 1861–90. In R. Bartlett, (Ed.), *Land commune and peasant community in Russia: Communal forms in imperial and early Soviet Society*. Macmillan in Association with the School of Slavonic and East European Studies, University of London.
Worobec, C. D. (1995). *Peasant Russia family and community in the post-emancipation period*. Northern Illinois University Press.
Worobec, C. D. (2001). *Possessed women, witches, and demons in imperial Russia*. Northern Illinois University Press.

Wortman, R. (1976). *The development of Russian legal consciousness.* University of Chicago Press.

Wortman, R. (1989). Property rights, populism and Russian political culture. In O. Crisp & L. Edmondson (Eds.), *Civil rights in imperial Russia.* Clarendon Press.

Yaney, G. (1973). *The systematization of Russian government: Social evolution in the domestic administration of imperial Russia 1711–1905.* University of Illinois Press.

Yaney, G. (1982). *The urge to mobilize: Agrarian reform in Russia, 1861–1913.* University of Illinois Press.

Zakharova, L. G. (1992). Samoderzhavie i reformy v Rossii 1861–1874. In L. G. V Zakharova, B. Eklöf, & D. Z. Bushnell (Eds.), *Velikie reformy v rossii 1856–1874.* Izdatelstvo Moskovskogo Universiteta.

CHAPTER 8

From Janus to Janus: Peter I, Nicholas II, and Industrialization

Institutions and Their Evolution: The Tsarist Case

According to Evolutionary Institutionalism, institutions do not vanish; instead, their structures transform. In this chapter, I apply this theory to ask why Tsarist Russia became an importer of technology via a war-induced crisis. I also continue the discourse in Chap. 6 about the role of technology in the modernization of Tsardom including its democratization, all of which were unintended by the rulers. The aim is to call attention to the structural continuity that extended from Peter I to Nicholas II and to juxtapose it with discontinuous, revolutionizing institutional progress.

Since time immemorial, those living on the Russian plain have been exposed to hazards of nature that result in volatile harvests amid high land-to-labor ratios. Given the scarcity of historically acquired collective knowledge, those who amassed the kind of agrarian experience that conduced to survival attained a level of authority so unchallenged as to have been invested with divine legitimacy. Tsar-Imperators commanded similar obedience, as did their emulators in the elder-dominated hierarchy of the peasant estate. The Tsar's authority constantly depended on the military success that ensured vigorous growth and stability as well as their outgrowths, subjects' survival, and labor. While the hierarchies of oppression and coercion discouraged the search for novelty and risk-taking in innovation, success in battle could be ensured through spurts of autochthonous modernization effectuated by the importation of technology. If so, a

S. Sztern, *Russia on the Move*, Studies in Economic Transition,
https://doi.org/10.1007/978-3-030-89285-2_8

temporally continuous and systematically prioritized norm of *obshchego blaga*, "common good" (Anisimov, 1993) surfaces in Russia—victory in battle and conquest that entail the ubiquitous sacrifice of civilian services such as healthcare and education. This norm saw its origins with Peter I, continued under the enlightened Catherine II, and moved onward under Nicholas II and beyond. Two major clusters of technology give structure to the reign of the Tsar-Imperators:[1] the imports of the Baltic fleet and related arts and sciences under Peter I, and railroads during the reign of Nicholas II. This conceptualization of "common good" continuity may be challenged on the grounds that each of these technologies was imported for a military purpose. Each of them also, however, helped to improve the civilian economy, and civilians' survival options, in novel and multiple ways. The technology imported by both Tsars, as a subset of a general infusion of technology, evoked new demands, promoted the urge to associate in new constellations, and instigated cognitive cultural revolutions that increasingly posed a credible threat from below, forcing the ruler to concede to his subjects by delegating rights. The thesis of this chapter is that the railroads, due to their dual-purpose (military/civilian) function—unlike their modernizing eighteenth-century predecessor, the navy—brought about the delegation of property rights in land to the Russian peasantry that constituted 80 percent of the population. In this manner, the railroads carried, passenger-style, Russia's transition to rationalism individualism and constitutional monarchy.

By reducing cognitive distance through intensified *otkhodnikhestvo*—peasant wage labor as a side pursuit—the railroad contributed to the rural–urban institutional exchange in Tsarist Russia, enhancing the creation of urban cooperation and collective action units (Barzel, 2002, p. 61) that emulated the agricultural commune-village system on the basis of *krugovaya poruka* (shared liability)—initially by means of a kinship unit that metamorphosed into a territorial unit, the *verv* (Petrovich, 1968, p. 215). Through this transformation, the railroad promoted the formation of urban trade unions anchored in *arteli* crafts cooperatives wondering in *zemliachestva* (landsman networks structured by mutual solidarity in

[1] De Madariaga (1998, p. 50). As this chapter deals with the continuities vs. discontinuities among the eighteenth and nineteenth centuries modernizations, I included an understanding of the institution of the Tsar-Imperator, which bears in mind the Catherinian-era Nakaz (decree) that promulgated the shedding of despotism. Chapter II, Article 9, of the Nakaz, concerning the fundamental laws states "*Quis imperat est monarca*"—legally defining *samoderzhavie* (sovereignty).

responsibility for all obligations (de Madariaga, 1998, p. 79; Johnson, 1979, p. 69; Hodgson, 2004, pp. 105, 185; Troyat, 1961, p. 98). The labor-commitment devices (Greif, 2006, p. 101) that were created in this manner evolved into a successful mechanism of subversion that amplified the ruler's surveillance costs, enhancing democratization. Thus, the imported railroad technology, the most successful of the Tsarist ventures in state entrepreneurship, abetted the disintegration of the ancién régime.

The Baltic fleet technology of Petrine times and, to a greater extent, Nicholas' railroads sowed elements of modernization and introduced a discontinuous but progressive demand for equality under the law—all of which were unintended by the Tsars.

The Baltic Fleet Technology of Petrine times: "Progress Despite Coercion"

The modern Russian historian Evgenii V. Anisimov (1989) subtitled the English translation of his book, *Vremia Petrovskich Reform* (the era of the Petrine reforms), "the era of the Petrine reforms." Studying selected Western and modern Russian sources, one senses that this title captures the Janus-faced character of the Tsarist industrialization. Namely, this very infusion of novel technology triggered an unintended institutional transformation that weakened the coercive hierarchy and fueled the transition to egalitarian rationalism in Late Imperial Russian society.

Anisimov's title, however, captures more than the Petrine époque. The transition to modernity under the last Tsar, Nicholas II, long after the emancipation of the serfs (1861–1863), was burdened with the collective violation of individual rights (albeit to a much smaller extent than under its eighteenth-century predecessor).

Gerschenkron's substitution theory (Gerschenkron, 1962), according to which state entrepreneurship fills in missing "prerequisites" for industrialization (Rostow, 1960, pp. 6, 22), analyzes the crucial role of the *samoderzhavia*—the autocratic regime (de Madariaga, 1998, pp. 43–45)—in the modernization of Russia. Importantly, such a pattern of substitution is not costless to society. Coercion is profoundly costly, not least in the coin of invention and innovation forgone due to the degrading treatment of the individual by the absolutist state structure (Hughes, 1998, p. 129; Poznanski, 1992, pp. 85, 88, 93; Mokyr, 1990, pp. 176–177). The loss is aggravated by a hierarchy of values (Mokyr, 1990, p. 173) that prioritizes common over individual welfare and defines the former according to the requisites of war. As I argue below, the appropriate way to characterize the spurts of industrialization under Peter I and Nicholas II is *progress despite coercion*. Both spurts were characterized by massive importation of skills and accompanying value systems that modernized the domestic production of new technology (Boyer & Orlean, 1993, p. 22). The absorption of European value systems abetted an institutional revolution, of which cultural revolution was an aspect (Cracraft, 2004, p. 24), that fueled the demand for civil rights and its unintended consequence, democratization.

Much of this has been discussed above. In this chapter, I trace the unbroken thread of this dualism in Tsarist Russia's transition to modernity. The eighteenth century saw the progressive systematization of government and the reform of the taxation system, the military statutes, and the education and welfare systems (Yaney, 1973, p. 7; Cracraft, 2004, p. 57; Hartley, 1999, p. 135; Kahan, 1985, p. 4) and the equalization of servicemen's *pomest'ie* (service landholding) with allodial property in 1714 (Bartlett, 1999, p. 76). These reforms and the Table of Ranks (1722)[2] presaged the growing tendency to allocate political posts on the basis of achievement rather than ascription (Cracraft, 2004, p. 14). Since this legislation, however, coexisted with reliance on bonded serf labor, the supply of labor and skills was coerced rather than induced (Anisimov, 1989, p. 122).

My objective here is to stress the social cost of the transition to modernity within the reconstituting structure (Hodgson, 2004) of militarized Russian absolutism, focusing on the cost of pledging a large and shackled labor force to a Tsarist industrial system that prioritized production for military purposes. The analysis emphasizes the cost to society of the loss of invention and innovation due to disabling restrictions anchored in an ethos of bondage and corporal punishment (Mokyr, 1990, pp. 177, 180, 181; Poznanski, 1985, pp. 45, 46; Hoch, 1986, p. 182; Hughes, 1998, p. 129). I take it as axiomatic that these phenomena retarded human-capital accumulation and entrepreneurial risk-taking in the eighteenth and nineteenth centuries and burdened the post-emancipation era with the

[2] Hosking (1997, p. 154). The 1722 Petrine Table of Ranks institution replaced family status, rights, and status functions acquired by geniture, with merit. Henceforth, "education, personal achievement, and experience" would define the rank that one might attain in the service of the Tsar.

long-term legacies of serfdom. Given that structures shape the preferences and goals of individuals for generations to come, the newly emancipated nineteenth-century population still carried the imprint of serfdom institutions in its Veblenian habits of thought (Hodgson, 2004, pp. 105, 185; Hoch, 1986, p. 182).

By criteria such as levels of government involvement and centralization of government functions, Petrine Russia was indeed a rapidly modernizing society (Cracraft, 2004, p. 14). Nevertheless, deficiencies in other criteria of modernization, such as what Cracraft calls the "impersonalized rule of law" and the "level of individualization" in rural structures[3]—which are interdependent (Frank, 1999, pp. 100, 101; Sztern, project description)—imply that uncertainty of life and property remained very high in Petrine Russia, indicating backwardness relative what Western European reforms achieved in Western Europe.

It is true that the Russian estate most affected by the Petrine cultural revolution, the nobility, acquired the French language, internalized Western habits of thought, diet, and dress, and cultivated ties with Western philosophers, engineers, and other specialists. Society at large, however, remained modeled on hierarchies of patriarchal structures (Hoch, 1986, p. 182) and was permeated by the degrading practice of corporal punishment (Hughes, 1998, pp. 129–130, Hartley, 1999, p. 67). It was corporal punishment, by fostering risk aversion, that retarded invention and innovation and made the domestic stock of knowledge dependent on imported technologies (North, 1981, p. 4; Mokyr, 1990, p. 177; Poznanski, 1985, pp. 45, 46). If so, most Russian technological improvements and their congruent institutional innovations were initially foreign and alien to the greater part of society (Raeff, 1984, pp. 32, 50, 51). The resulting shortage of skilled labor led to the enserfment of skilled workers (Kahan, 1985, p. 89), creating short-term disincentives to the acquisition of new skills and triggering a vicious cycle.

Although Peter's Europeanization of Russian governmental institutions, norms, and values merit the term "modernization process" in a narrow sense, the endemic social burden of bondage, aggravated by an inter-estate cultural gap and intra-estate authoritarian rifts that widened due to the nobility's Western orientation (Frank, 1999, pp. 5–7; Raeff,

[3]Cracraft (2004, pp. 15–16), Yaney (1973, p. 16) on personalized structures and pp. 28–29 on Peter's attempts to systematize and depersonalize the law; Raeff (1984, pp. 64, 80, 84).

1984, pp. 50, 51), justifies Gerschenkron's conception of the Russian peasant constituency, a hundred years later, as backward relative to the West European empires and the United States. Applying additional criteria of modernity (such as that proposed by Cracraft: "mass popular interest and involvement in the political system"), one may clearly distinguish the Russian Empire, with its burden of serfdom and absolutism, from its European counterparts.

Until Stolypin's land reform, the issue of the peasantry's *grazhdanstvennost* (civil status) as relating to the principle of equality before the law was not addressed. Living under customary law (Yaney, 1973, pp. 18–19), which rested on different institutional foundations from those guiding the Imperial Code, peasants could neither take an interest nor be involved in the political system of the empire due to lack of transparency and widespread illiteracy. Instead, the participation of the peasants—roughly 80 percent of the Tsarist Russian population—was characterized by passive and active resistance to the yoke of serfdom and the obligations of post-emancipation life, manifested in armed uprisings, responses to violations of collective rights (Kolchin, 1987, pp. 244–250, 303, 311), petitions, and emigration (Gerschenkron, 1962, p. 133).

At the time of Napoleon's invasion of Russia (1812), the thing most feared by the conservative leaders of the Tsarist empire was the importation of the value-system adaptations that the French Revolution had set in motion (Tolstoy, 1953, Vol. 1–2, p. 407). This is why I stated above that Peter's modernization drive was dictated by the needs of war. The prominent Russian historians Vasily Kliuchevski and Pavel Miliukov concur. It was war, Kliuchevski states, that "determined the order of reform, set its pace and its very methods. Reforming measures followed one another in the order dictated by the requirements imposed by the war" (Hughes, 1998, p. 63). Even if organized belligerency (particularly the Northern War with Sweden) was not the sole motive for the Russian empire's importation of European institutions under Peter, as Raeff (1984) argues, the aftermath of the Crimean War and the timing of the great reforms starting with the Emancipation Act of 1861 justify treating the eighteenth-century reforms, too, as expressions of the continuous longitudinal geopolitical rationality of a totalitarian state structure (Hayek, 1944, p. 80). In such a structure, three dominant motives for concession and reform exist: improving surplus extraction, securing a territorial claim including conquests, and attaining internal stability (Gerschenkron, 1962, p. 134; Ascher, 1988, Vol. 1, p. 177). If so, war (the Northern War in respect of the Petrine period) is treated as an organizing principle in conceiving the Europeanization and modernization of Tsarist Russia.

The Petrine projects relating to "development blocs" (Gerschenkron, 1962, p. 125)[4] such as the Baltic fleet, the core of which created vertical and horizontal supply and undersupply transactions among industries in the ascending order of complexity of production, all of which conspicuously driven by government demand, were the Arsenal in Moscow and the fortress and the Admiralty in St. Petersburg (Kahan, 1985, pp. 86, 99; Hughes, 1998, p. 63). Under the post-reform government (1717–1718), the Colleges of War, the Admiralty, and foreign affairs received larger shares of state revenues than did any other cause (Hughes; Yaney, 1973, p. 28). The 1722 Table of Ranks placed the social standing of the military above that of any civilian endeavor (Hughes 63; Hartley, 1999, p. 53). In a letter of congratulation to Alexander Menshikov upon the birth of a son, Peter wrote, "God has given him to you as a recruit" (Hughes 63)—a blessing that clearly indicates a hierarchy of values in the structuring of Russian society in which war came first.

Reputable Western historians attribute to Peter the transformation of the Russian army "from an Asiatic horde into a professional force" (64) such as that maintained by Sweden, France, and Prussia. Russia's victories in the seventeenth-century Thirteen Years War against Poland challenge this view by demonstrating the pre-Petrine professionalization of Russian troops (64). It is unchallengeable, however, that the Russian defeat at Narva in the war against Sweden in 1700 lent urgency to Peter's drive to modernize the Russian army and, while he was at it, the government (150).

Traditionally initiated by the reign of Ivan III (1461–1505), Russian imperial modernization entailed the importation of weapons and ammunition and the hiring of foreign military specialists (71). Peter the Great's modernization of the army and society followed this tradition. His imports of technology, however, included European structures that conceptualized military organization as a preconditioning institution (Hodgson, 2004, p. 181), a fact that itself indicates Russia's relative geopolitical techno-institutional backwardness.

[4] "Development blocs," to use Erik Dahmén's phrase, are "the component elements of growth in individual industrial branches."

Inventiveness Lost: The Cost of Corporal Punishment

This raises two important questions: Why did Tsarist Russia import foreign technology and foreign expertise on a massive scale for defense purposes as a matter of *historical continuity*, and why were Britain, France, and Germany the leading countries of origin in this respect? The figure below proposes an answer.

In Petrine times, the Russian peasant was subjected to institutionalized serfdom, based on ownership of man and fear of corporal punishment as an incentive for the supply of labor and skills (Hoch, 1986, pp. 185, 186; de Madariaga, 1998, pp. 101, 102). He had no allodial property rights, if only because such did not exist, even for nobles, until 1714 (Bartlett, 1999, pp. 76, 77).

The degrading treatment of the individual peasant in Tsarist Russia, I propose, should be understood as a causal factor that, while continuous, strongly weakened over time. Nevertheless, the risk aversion occasioned by the high frequency of corporal punishment may explain the low long-term propensity to invent (Mokyr, 1990, p. 177; Poznanski, 1985, p. 45; Hoch, 1986, p. 188; Hodgson, 2004, pp. 105, 185). Indeed, the reconstitutive downward causation process would prolong the adverse effect of corporal punishment inflicted during serfdom (Hodgson, 2004, pp. 105, 185; Hoch, 1986, p. 188).

The Instructions of Catherine II included a general condemnation of cruelty (de Madariaga, 1998, p. 199). The 1785 Charter to the Nobility awarded the nobles property rights irrespective of state service (Bartlett, 1999, p. 76; Hartley, 1999, p. 17). These reforms and, of course, the emancipation of the serfs were codified long before the modernization spurts of Nicholas II. Nevertheless, until the Stolypin reform, the peasant was continuously subjected to the coercive collectivist elements of village custom. More often than not, this system continued to curb individual initiative, lowering the transaction costs of Tsarist tax extraction by strengthening the grip of *krugovaya poruka* (kinship-based collective liability for all obligations) (Chaps. 2, 4, 5, 6 above). This structure offered, at best, collective use rights in land (Gerschenkron, 1962, p. 120; Moon, 1999, p. 120; Worobec, 1995, p. 27). The village assembly could designate undesired commune members for military conscription or exile to Siberia by administrative order (*w administrativnom poriadke*), namely, without trial (Worobec, 1995, p. 24; de Madariaga, 1998, p. 119; Wood, 1990, p. 395). The institutionalized hegemony of collective judgment, including instances of *samosud* (vicious organized punishment of social undesirables) with their cachet of arbitrariness, abetted the all-pervasive violation of individual rights, inhibiting domestic technological invention and innovation.

At times of armed conflict, the dependency of the Tsarist state on the international technology market relative to domestic technology producers weakened the bargaining power of the latter as well as that of home entrepreneurs of whatever class (Paltseva lecture, 2008). Instituting the importation of technology as an Anisimovian "common good" primarily for military use instead of entrepreneurial progress in peacetime also hindered the transition to delineated property rights in two ways: by retarding voluntary socioeconomic progress in Russia (Anisimov, 1989, pp. 121–125) and by establishing the hierarchy of coercion, rather than the acquisition of individual human and physical capital, as the basis for knowledge and skills allocation. Moreover, with each victory on the battlefield, the totalitarian state consolidated and centralized its powers, enhancing its extractive capacity and control of people (Hobson & Weiss, 1995). By weakening civil society in this manner, the state hobbled the domestic production of new technology, exacerbating the country's historical dependence on imported technology.

Despite these obstacles to modernization, I suggest that the continuous "top-down" reform effort did plant the seeds of transformation (Fig. 8.2). Paradoxically, the continuity of reforms (even amid internal revolt and war) that entailed technology imports raised literacy levels and expanded the available skill set. As more and more individuals were able to read the Tsarist ukases to the peasants, fueling rumors of change (Moon, 1999, p. 240; Burds, 1998, pp. 176, 177; Mokyr, 1990; EHES, 2007), the regime's surveillance costs escalated. As the peasant constituency amassed human capital, the balance of power shifted from the patriarchate-based autocratic-agent structure to a society predicated on the redistribution of earnings from the younger (nineteenth-century peasant otkhodniks, who commuted by rail to employment in the emerging industries, to the still-illiterate elder bolshak-domoleg generation (Martens, 2004, p. 193; Burds, 1998, p. 29; Hoch, 1986, p. 128) (Chap. 6 above; Sztern, 2018; Chaps. 10 and 11). The modernization spurt and the technology imports that it entailed, motivated by the Imperial territorial claims and secured at a heavy social cost, ultimately enhanced the credibility of a threat from below, forcing concessionary reforms. During the two centuries overviewed, this is assumed to have abetted the transformation of the rule of serfs by autocratic agents into a constitutional monarchy increasingly ruled by free people. The following figure summarizes the argument.

The secondary sources show that Tsarist Russia was a long-term net importer not only of technological innovation but of institutional innovation as well. The question, then, is which endogenous factor made the empire's conquests, expansion, and viability possible. The answer, as a working hypothesis, is the autocratic system of governance anchored in Greek Orthodoxy—a source of relative strength and weakness, historically an asset to the Russian rulers and a liability to the Russian people. The combination of pagan and Christian folk wisdom (Treadgold, 1968, pp. 78, 79) embodied in the peasants' kinship-based egalitarian custom (de Madariaga, 1998, p. 79) made obshchina-dwellers highly responsive to the importation of egalitarian and libertarian ideas from the West (Boyer & Orlean, 1993, p. 22). By absorbing the imported innovations, the peasants reformed the empire.

Thus, I claim, the vicious cycle depicted in Fig. 8.1 retarded but did not ultimately hinder Tsarist Russia's post-emancipation modernization, including the peasant transition from collectivism to individualism.

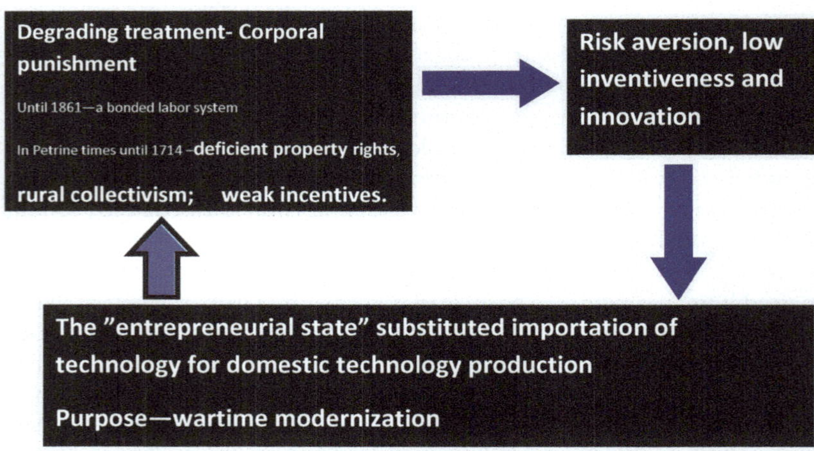

Fig. 8.1 Accumulated social costs of state entrepreneurship—a vicious cycle. (Sources: Hughes, 1998, pp. 129–130; Bartlett, 1999, pp. 76, 77; Mokyr, 1990, pp. 173, 177; Poznanski, 1985, p. 45; North, 1981, p. 4, 1990, p. 64, 78; 1973, p. 29; Anisimov, 1989, p. 122; Hughes, 1998, p. 63, Gerschenkron, 1968, p. 315)

Transaction Costs, Including the Uncertainty Implications of Tsarist Government Centralization

Formally, the principles of law and administration in Russia were much the same as in the West. Not so, however, were the role of the system in society and its place in the individual's sense of values (Yaney, 1973, p. 21). The origins of the empire's legal and administrative order date back to 1240 CE when the Tatar (Mongol) horde held sway. The Russian princes, manifesting their Greek Orthodox affiliation and unity, operated an organized tribute-collecting network to provide the Tatars with recruits and protection money (22). The reconstitutive downward causation process, in which the institutional superstructure shapes prevalent habits of thought in a way that abets their replication (Hodgson, 2004, pp. 105, 185; Hodgson and Knudsen Mars, 10, 11, 12.), ensured the survival of forced tax collection and military induction after the dissolution of the horde (Yaney, 1973, p. 22; Hodgson, 2004, pp. 105, 185).

Thus, the coercion and cruelty that typified the raising of tribute and the mobilization of recruits characterized the Tsarist state from its inception. Frank's account of the nineteenth-century legal and cultural rift between the Tsarist state institutions and their peasant subjects (Frank, 1999) suggests that the quasi-colonization condition of the state–citizen relationship persisted throughout the period reviewed, that is, the late Tsarist era. Moreover, in the de facto absence of a functioning legal system, the hierarchy of personal dependencies imposed structural restrictions on behavior (23; North, 1990, p. 64). Under these conditions, the Tsar, who as the ultimate superior was vastly empowered to act arbitrarily, actually had very little control over his subordinates' doings (Yaney, 1973, p. 24).

In pre-Petrine Russia, state power was distributed from the center to forty separate offices in a way that made local "strongmen"—*gubnye starosti*, territorial chiefs (*voevodas* or *starchiny*, elders)—more potent than the state (Migdal, 1988, p. 40; Yaney, 1973, p. 28). The exercise of arbitrary state power was obstructed only by pervasive awe of the superior, which served as the basic motive for the supply of labor and skills, and by bribery (26, 27). The long-term imprint of Veblenian habits of thought on these structures hindered Peter's efforts to create a well-functioning Western-style governmental apparatus (20, 21).

In the realm of the rural village commune, serfs faced steep transaction costs including uncertainty about life and use rights in land. This reinforced all the premodern networks—mutual trust, mutual insurance, and mutual aid—that were based on shared responsibility for obligations (de Madariaga, 1998, p. 79). Thus, these structures proved viable over time, as Pallot's analysis of peasant responses to Stolypin's land reform indicates (Pallot, 1999, p. 172)—albeit with decreasing intensity (Mironov, 2000, p. 344).

Peter imported several institutional innovations. The introduction of the Senate, the Procuracy, and central colleges represented attempts to centralize and systematize the Tsarist government, reducing transaction costs and bureaucratic uncertainty. Due to the reconstitutive imprint of centuries of personalized rule, however, people who had been sufficiently and arbitrarily empowered by the Tsar could tip Senate rulings in their favor. Although de facto the Senate became the Tsar's ill-tempered clavier, both ordinary people and statesmen increasingly resorted to it to solve their problems. This indicates the existence of powerful and ideology-driven demand for the impersonalized rule of law, a desideratum that gained intensity in the course of the eighteenth century (Yaney, 1973, p. 29; Raeff, 1984, p. 48).

Peter's reign, a clearly distinguishable term due to the weight of imported technological and institutional innovations in it (Raeff, 1984, pp. 50–52), instigated a deepening rift in Russian society between the increasingly West-oriented elite; intelligentsia, and nobility, and the introverted and xenophobic peasantry (Owen, 1995, p. 10). The incongruence of the formal institutions' Imperial Code, which structured the daily lives of the elite and non-peasant town dwellers, and the informal customary law that structured the daily lives of the peasantry[5] resulted in a system endemically burdened with high transaction costs (Nee, 1998 85; North, 1990, pp. 64, 78; Yaney, 1973, p. 29; Hartley, 1999, pp. 1–3) that were only exacerbated by the Mongol horde's long-lasting legacy of personalized and arbitrary rule. Since high transaction costs weaken the incentive structure of property rights (Poznanski, 1992, p. 72), the level of innovation in an environment of high transaction costs is assumed to be low. Thus, the transaction-cost aspect of property-rights theory may additionally explain why, historically, Russia had been a net importer of technological innovation. Moreover, due to private entrepreneurs' weakened incentive structure, it is more than likely that the importation of

[5] See Hartley (1999, pp. 1, 2, 3, 52, 78) on the dichotomy of privilege/non-privilege and Figes (2002, pp. 15–18, 100) on the peasant commune.

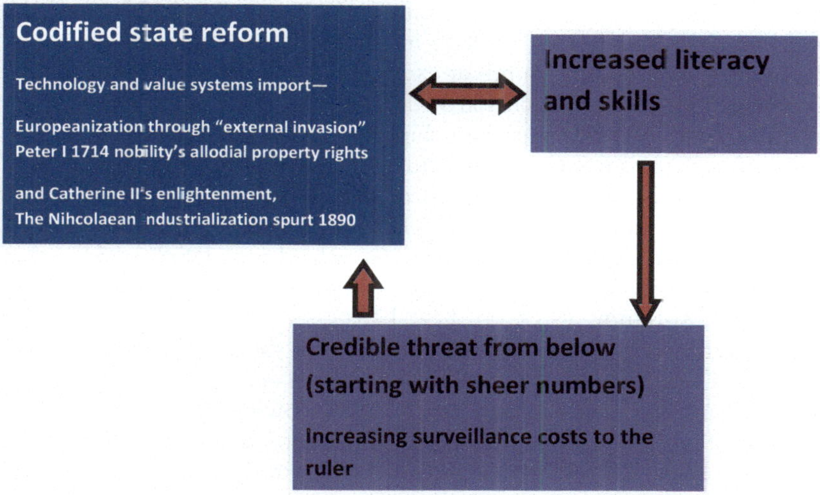

Fig. 8.2 Unintended consequences of Tsarist modernization—a virtuous cycle. (Sources: Greif, 2006, p. 441; North, 1990, pp. 90, 91; Burds, 1998, pp. 176, 177; Gerschenkron, 1962, pp. 127, 128; Kahan, 1989, pp. 188–189, Tables 8.3 and 8.4; Barzel, 2002, p. 61; Boyer & Orlean, 1993, p. 22; Lal, 1998, p. 12; de Madariaga, 1998, p. 173)

technology in a high-transaction-cost environment would be state-led (Coase, 1937, pp. 38, 39; Gerschenkron, 1962, pp. 126–131). Indeed, a crucially important commonality of Peter's eighteenth-century techno-institutional revolution and the modernization spurt under Nicholas II is the state-led importation of technology that subjected Russia to an "external invasion" (Boyer & Orlean, 1993, p. 22; Cracraft, 2004, pp. 58, 69) of European value systems (Fig. 8.2).

Given the peasantry's linkage of technological innovation with the force-feeding of foreign culture (Hughes, 1998, pp. 107, 108) and the imposition and implementation of formal foreign institutions (North, 1990, p. 78; Cracraft, 2004, pp. 57, 60, 61), the peasant folklore linked imported technology with non-Christian values. This nexus induced a short-term increase in transaction costs, necessitating the expansion of state entrepreneurship to achieve technological modernization. In the mindset of peasant Russia, Peter the Great was the embodiment of the

Antichrist (Raeff, 1984, p. 53; Anisimov, 1993, pp. 208, 215)[6] and the importation of railroad technology in the nineteenth century was much the same in the peasants' minds at its inception (Westwood, 1964, p. 32). Following Hayek and Gerschenkron combined with Coase, I note that the substitution of state entrepreneurship for private initiative due to high transaction costs is not cost-free. Thus, in addition to the growing risk of mistakes (transaction costs) due to excess centralization (Coase, 1937, p. 44), the autocracy—contrary to Gerschenkron's conceptualizations—was burdened with dictatorship costs (Gerschenkron, 1968, p. 315) that entailed resource allocation guided by battlefield priorities (Winicki, 1988, pp. 74, 78; Anisimov, 1989, pp. 122, 123).

An additional vicious cycle that powered a short-term widening rift between the tax-exempt elites and the non-privileged population strata—the taxpaying peasants—is illustrated in the following figure.

Figure 8.2 summarizes an aspect of state entrepreneurship that, in the Russian context, represented a historically continuous vicious cycle until the nineteenth-century railroads homogenized the rural customary and imperial institutions. The institutions of backwardness that Russia had inherited from the Mongol horde thrust the backward regions into a characteristic substitution of state initiative for private entrepreneurship that raised transaction costs due to excess centralization and dictatorship, all of which exacerbated by incoherence between formal and informal institutions (see also Chap. 4).

This institutional incongruence is best specified by the historical position of the Old Belief (*razkol*). It is plausible to argue that the Old Believers' position within the body social of the country and their antagonistic relationship with the state (Gerschenkron, 1970, p. 21) prompted them to develop alternative ways to alleviate the transaction costs through the mutual-trust networks and the stringent moral discipline that held their communities together (19).

Paradoxically, state entrepreneurship and its outcome, increased uncertainty, strengthened the premodern mechanisms, based on shared belief systems, kinship ties, and identity-by-negation that mitigated structural risk and uncertainty. This resulted in the formation of commitment devices such as those described by Greif (2006, p. 101) and unintentionally yielded one of the most prominent manifestations of domestic

[6] See also Westwood (1964, p. 33) for a discussion of nineteenth-century railway construction via serf labor under the most degrading conditions.

entrepreneurship, one that enhanced the transition to modernity. The accumulation of fortunes within the ranks of "merchant dynasties" (19) of peasant origin, formed by Old Believers, was one of the few autonomous sources of capital in the Tsarist Empire that could be invested in modernization (19; Gregory, 1982, pp. 56, 57). Indeed, in Russia's high-transaction-cost environment, the Old Believers' mutual-trust networks were the vehicles of growth in pre-industrialization eighteenth-century textiles as well as in the pre-nationalization nineteenth-century railroad industries (20).

Generally speaking, the elitist and coercive character of Peter's cultural revolution proved to be one of its main weaknesses, as the very social groups that were sympathetic to entrepreneurship were also the most severely alienated by the rule of the centralizing, West-imitating government and the increasingly militarizing society (Hughes, 1998, p. 63; Raeff, 1984, pp. 50, 51; Gerschenkron, 1970, p. 20). The Old Believers community is a case in point.

The Tsarist Motive for Industrialization to Perpetuate the Coercive Hierarchy or to Make Progress?

In Petrine times, only state service offered a path to social mobility (Raeff, 1984, p. 41). Among the mechanisms of state service, the Imperators' institutional innovation, the 1722 Table of Ranks, granted military service a higher status than any civilian vocation (Hughes, 1998, p. 63). This condition, beyond clearly sketching the hierarchy of values that characterized the Petrine institutional environment, proved persistent over time If so, Raeff's proposal, challenging the "reform for the needs of war" understanding of the eighteenth-century modernization drive, must be seen as controversial and refutable. Peter's observation on economic affairs may be summarized in a quotation from the monarch himself: "Money is the artery of war" (Raeff, 1984, pp. 36, 135).

By studying the institutional structures, particularly the distribution of allodial property rights within the empire—established in 1714 under Peter and sustained until Stolypin's land reform in the early twentieth century—it is easy to trace the hierarchy of exploitation that was designed to serve the priorities of warfare. In view of a historical narrative that spanned centuries, Gerschenkron deserves credit for observing implicitly that the source of money and conscripts for Tsarist Russia's wars, in general, was the indigenous peasantry (Hughes, 1998, p. 135; Gerschenkron, 1962, p. 125). The Petrine drive to modernize Tsarist Russia entailed the institutional colonization (Frank, 1999, p. 19) of the peasant estate, additionally strengthening the institutions of backwardness, foremost serfdom, in the name of progress (Hoch, 1986, p. 189).

To judge whether resource allocation during Peter's reign prioritized the exigencies of war, one need only look at the distribution of state expenditure (Table 8.1). In 1704, the fourth year of the Northern War with Sweden, it is evident that Peter I, unlike Nicholas II, envisaged a relatively secularized state (Cracraft, 2004, p. 7; Hughes, 1998, p. 136) that would anchor the legitimacy of absolutist rule primarily in the empire's ability to secure its territorial claims and exercise bureaucratic control rather than in a system of religious beliefs centering on the anointed

Table 8.1 Imperial government expenditure, 1913 prices recalculated

	Administration expenditure (% share)	*Expenditure for education and health (% share)*	*Defense expenditure (% share)*	*Total (%)*
1885	**44%**	5%	**51%**	100
Δ	+5.2%	-7.7%	+3.8%	+3.8
1888	**44.6%**	4.4%	**51%**	100
Δ	*+25%*	*+26.9%*	*+19%*	*+22.2%*
1891	**45.8%**	4.6%	**49.6%**	100
Δ	+3.9%	+18.18%	+16%	+10.5%
1894	**43%**	4.9%	52%	100
Δ	+16.6%	+2.5%	+4.8%	+9.8%
1896	**45.7%**	4.6%	**49.7%**	100
Δ	*+2.2%*	*+45%*	*+20.9%*	*+13.5%*
1900	**41.2%**	5.9%	**52.9%**	100
Δ	+24.5%	+25.8%	+7.8%	+15.7%
1903	**44.3%**	6.4%	**49.3%**	100
Δ	*−6.7*	*−15.9*	*+6*	*−0.7%*
1907	**41.8%**	5.5%	**52.7%**	100
Δ	*+22.4*	*+74.6%*	*+/−0%*	*+13.5%*
1910	**45%**	8.6%	**46.4%**	100
Δ	*+/−0%*	*+40%*	*+61.6*	*+32%*
1913	**34.%**	9.2%	**56.8%**	100

Source: Gregory (1982, Appendix F, Table F.4, p. 256) and my recomputations. Rows in boldface are shares of absolute totals; rows marked with "Δ" are calculated by comparing absolute ruble values vertically so that each period relates to the preceding one. Italics are used for emphasis

person of the Tsar (North, 2005, p. 83; Freeze, 1996, p. 309). This proposed construct is consistent with the efforts made at this time to establish *zakonnosc*, the rule of impersonalized law, in Russia.[7]

Progressive aspects notwithstanding, the distribution of government expenditure (Tables 8.1 and 8.2) challenges the idea that Peter's objective was to modernize Russia rather than to win the war with Sweden, which Russia could have accomplished anyway due to its advantages in manpower and harsh climate (Raeff, 1984, pp. 36, 37, 50, 51). Government expenditure on education and healthcare was negligible compared with military spending (Table 8.2). Moreover, education in Petrine Russia centered on forcing the nobility to acquire skills in navigation, navigational astronomy, geography, arithmetic, geometry, and trigonometry, all conducive to the development of the navy and the installation of Russian officers as its commanders, displacing the foreign experts (Hartley, 1999, p. 126; Cracraft, 2004, pp. 82, 83). Therefore, defensive and offensive warfare should be seen as the major and continuous motive for the modernization that characterized the Tsarist endeavor under Peter and beyond.

An additional indication of the establishment of a war economy, induced by the Northern War, is the degree of centralization in the ownership of industries constitutive of development blocs (Gerschenkron (1962, p. 125). The Admiralty's shipbuilding complex in St: Petersburg, for

Table 8.2 Approximate proportions of expenditure in 1704, the fourth year of the Northern War

	Hughes (1998) (rubles)	*Hughes (1998) (pct.)*	*Sztern's calculation, based on Hughes' absolute numbers*
Military expenditure	1,439,832	40.9%	47.5%
State apparatus	1,313,200	37.6%	43.3%
Royal household	156,843	4.4%	5.2%
Diplomacy	75,042	2.1%	2.5%
The Church	29,777	0.8%	0.98%
Education, healthcare, postal services	17,388	0.5%	0.57%
Grand total	3,032,082	~100%	~100%

Source: Hughes (1998, p. 136). The table is constructed from the percentage shares in the text

[7]Yaney (1973, p. 7). See also de Madariaga (1998, p. 122), on attempts to introduce systemic predictability. Namely, the rule of law was reinforced under Catherine II.

example, was state-owned and -operated (Kahan, 1985, p. 86). Peter was much less concerned about the merchant fleet than about the navy (Hughes, 1998, p. 63; Cracraft, 2004, p. 56).

Kahan (1985, p. 80) offers a useful way to gauge the extent of state intervention: "Intensity of demand on the part of the government, for the output of a particular industry, measured by relative shares of output purchased or otherwise acquired by the government." Thus, throughout the eighteenth century the Tsarist government purchased the largest shares of output in precious metals, armaments, and woolen cloth, an in-between share of output in copper and ironworks, and the smallest share of linen, cordage, silk, and cotton—civilian and dual-purpose industries. Consequently, war was a preferred government sector in the long term, one that structured and preconditioned economic activity in the empire (Hodgson, 2004, pp. 105, 185; Archer, 1995, p. 76).

The Tsarist government's Western orientation was also structured to serve the needs of war. Its most significant and viable tax reform had as its main objective "shorten[ing] the route of the money from the pockets of the peasants into the regimental cash boxes" (Hughes, 1998, p. 138). The *podushnaya podat'*—the poll or "soul" tax imposed on each male head of household instead of the household at large—was modeled after the Swedish system of levying taxes to support the troops (ibid.). The population census (*revisia*) of 1722–1723, preceding and anticipating the tax reform, was carried out by military commanders. The tax was first collected in 1724 at 74 kopeks per head. At this rate and given the state of military technology, it took forty-seven peasants to maintain one infantryman and fifty-seven to sustain one cavalryman (Hughes, 1998, p. 138; North, 1981, p. 137). Centralized tax record-keeping and tax liability itself determined the social status of various population strata within the empire (Hughes, 1998, p. 138; Hartley, 1999, p. 52). As the direct result of the census, previously free people were enserfed to new masters. The imposition of the tax created new strata of taxpayers (Kahan, 1985, p. 331). As for the actual economic burden that the measure foisted on the peasant population, calculations differ. According to Miliukov, the imposition of the poll tax raised the tax burden on the taxpaying population by 61 percent (Kahan; Hughes, 1998, p. 138). In Kahan's estimation, most of the increase in budget revenue due to the poll tax traced to an upturn in the number of taxpayers rather than a heavier tax burden on pre-reform individuals.

I argue that even if, contrary to Gerschenkron's and Miliukov's estimates, the transition from household tax to soul tax actually mitigated the direct economic burden on the peasant population (Kahan, 1985, p. 331), the improved efficiency of the Tsarist government in collecting direct taxes and mobilizing conscripts after recurrent censuses inevitably exacerbated the economic hardships of the peasant population even if taxation eventually became lower and more predictable.[8] Moreover, the material egalitarianism inspired by the tax structure may have contributed to a higher level of *perceived* discrimination among the peasant estate. Kahan terms the increase in burden due to the imposition of the poll tax a "myth" and traces it to the coincidence of the reform with a natural calamity known as the Little Ice Age, a period of severe winters that induced famine. The introduction of the poll tax, he adds, also coincided with hardships related to money-supply restrictions due to compensation payments to Sweden (Kahan, 1985, pp. 332, 11). Mironov challenges these conclusions, citing the inflation that occurred in the early eighteenth century and advising that the tax "restored the peasant obligation in real terms" (Hughes, 1998, p. 139). The imposition of a stable and predictable tax in the highly volatile environment of Russian grain yields, however, implies a de facto increase in the economic burden at times of crop failure.[9] Either way, the Petrine poll tax created a dominating institutional continuity that structured the peasant economy in the eighteenth and nineteenth centuries until it was abolished in 1887 (Hughes, 1998, p. 139).

Russia's foreign trade increased fifteen-fold during the eighteenth century, linking the empire to Europe and the New World and demonstrating the developmental capabilities of the country's commercial sectors. Part of this was due to favorable terms of trade. Additional to this was government intervention in trade, ranging from the creation of trading monopolies in exports and imports to the formation of state-run companies. True to the principles of mercantilism, the government sought to stimulate exports, limit the importation of manufactures, and protect domestic import substitutes by means of tariffs and direct subsidies (Kahan, 1985, p. 163). The heavy imprint of state control was indeed a reconstituting "habits of

[8] See Hobson and Weiss (1995, p. 6) on the magnitude of the state's invasive power.

[9] Scott (1976, p. 11), Milov (2001, pp. 1, 2). The *zemledelcheskaya obshchina*—the customary redistribution of land endowments commensurate with the household unit's tax burden—was an institutionalized risk-internalization strategy that enhanced predictability even amid unpredictable grain yields under volatile climate conditions.

thought" continuity that characterized the Tsarist institutions, resulting in structures that expanded, centralized, militarized, and, more often than not, expropriated[10]—all of which imposed with an arbitrariness that inhibited the long-term development of foreign and internal trade for civilian purposes (Owen, 1995, p. 19). Although Peter ostensibly sought to promote the foreign-trade sector, the credit institutions that such trade requires, and insurance, shipping, and brokerage, he did not allow them to develop sufficiently. Foreign merchants are said to have commented on the excessive state interest in trade and the pervasive insecurity in society as to its rights to immovable property, hampering capital accumulation. The Tsar, Hughes reports (Hughes, 1998, p. 149), coveted aristocrats' property and aristocrats coveted landed merchants' property, creating a hierarchy of expropriation. "The picture is of a hierarchical society with checks downward on the amassment of power and wealth," he concludes. Even as the Moscow-based *Pomernaia izba* (Chamber of Commerce), operating under the Tsarist states' regulation of internal trade, reduced transaction costs and enhanced internal trade during the Petrine era by standardizing weights and measures (North, 1990, p. 53), the state in its net effect restricted the development of domestic markets by regulating internal trade, for example, charging duties on grain sales (Hughes, 1998, p. 149).

Owen (1995, p. 19) implies that the substitution of state entrepreneurship for the private initiative under conditions of socioeconomic backwardness, as in Gerschenkron's model, underestimates the costs of state entrepreneurship in terms of private entrepreneurship forgone due to excessive control and expropriation through taxes by a centralizing and politically rational, as opposed to economically rational, state structure. The Tsarist state is said to have erected barriers to corporate entrepreneurship instead of promoting it (Owen, 1995, p. 16). Additionally, the adverse effects of state entrepreneurship were very long-lasting because nothing is more costly than changing a general structure that determines the nature of economic institutions (North, 1990, p. 79), meaning that institutions of a given nature determine the economic behavior of agents for generations to come (Hodgson, 2004, pp. 105, 185).

Nine companies were founded during the reign of Peter the Great. One was the Spanish Trade Company, chartered in 1724 to implement the Tsarist plan that proposed to transform Russia into a significant maritime power. The

[10] See Kahan (1985, pp. 2–4; 1989, p. 94), concerning confiscatory taxation. Owen (1995, p. 17) comments on the immaturity and institutional weakness of Tsarist Russian corporate capitalism.

company failed shortly after receiving its charter, giving clear evidence of an institutional environment inimical to private entrepreneurship, the government's declared objectives notwithstanding. Private entrepreneurship was constrained by the Emperor's arbitrary conduct in signing charters. The enlightened Catherine, for example, signed only four private company charters. The lack of success of the Russian-American company that had been founded in 1797 to exploit Alaskan fish and animal resources, relative to the company's British counterpart, which had been incorporated by English royal charter in 1670, is explained by the institutional differences between the British and Russian entrepreneurial structures. Unlike Hudson's Bay Company, which operated in a similar geographic environment in Canada, the Russian firm did not offer its investors limited liability until 1821 and operated under strict government control, both factors inhibiting its expansion and long-term viability (Owen, 1995, pp. 18, 19).

Corporate growth in the Russian Empire remained unimpressive until the Crimean War (1853–1856). Fifteen corporate charters arbitrarily approved by the Tsarist bureaucracy in 1821–1830 did represent an increase relative to the thirty-three that had been granted from 1700 to that time. Most of these companies, however, proved short-lived, clearly indicating institutional environment deficiencies, namely, the long-term cost of state entrepreneurship. Only one of them survived until World War II: the First Russian Insurance Company, founded in 1827, which branched from fire insurance into transport and accident coverage (Owen, p. 19).

Owen (1995) identifies two recurrent patterns in Russian corporate development: geographical concentration of corporations in St. Petersburg and relative success of insurance and textile manufacturing companies as against private ventures in metallurgy and transport. The concentration of corporations (approved corporate charters) in the vicinity of administrative centers and ports of exit indicates the Tsarist government's preparedness to apply bureaucratic control, Owen advises. As for metallurgy and transport, the paucity of success shows the inability of the state-controlled institutional infrastructure to enable these industries to develop in a corporate form. Against the background of the Tsarist government's acknowledgment of the vitality of the railroads for national economic development and their strategic importance in wartime, the turn-of-the-century volatility of profit in these industries resulted in the nationalization of railroad construction and maintenance, given the failure of the institutional infrastructure to provide sufficient incentives for the success of high-risk ventures in a private corporate form (Owen, 1991, p. 39).

Thus, the substitution of state entrepreneurship for private entrepreneurship as a way to internalize the burden of transaction costs in a backward society indeed came at a cost. In the long run, this strategy may have proved self-defeating as it inevitably led to state–society conflicts and vicious cycles (Figs. 8.1 and 8.3), retarding progress. In addition to this deleterious effect of the omnipresence of state intervention, the languid pace of Tsarist Russia's top-down reforms triggered an increasingly credible threat from below and transformed the autocratic entrepreneur into an interactive political entity (Fig. 8.2).

Industrialization under Peter the Great and Nicholas II: Continuity in Numbers

Here I call attention to the coercive nature of the militarized modernizations that the Tsarist autocracy set in motion under Peter the Great and Nicholas II. Instead of concentrating on the unique aspects of each period as a historian would (Confino, 1997), I focus on the institutional structure imposed by the rule of the Tsar-Imperator and the self-perpetuating mechanism that sustained it over time. It was in this manner that Peter I's

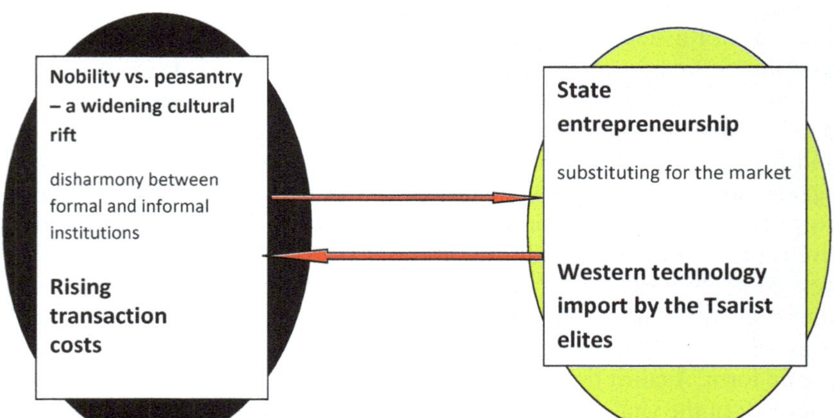

Fig. 8.3 Stratified modernization—the short-term vicious cycle of state intervention and rising transaction costs. (Sources: Raeff, 1984, pp. 50, 51; North, 1990, pp. 64, 78, 2005, p. 117; Nee, 1998, p. 85; Gerschenkron, 1962, p. 123, 1968, p. 315; Coase, 1937, p. 40; Hayek, 1944, pp. 69, 70)

"Big Bang" modernization and Europeanization preceded Nicholas II's modernization, including its spurts of industrialization.[11]

The great formal institutional divide between these processes (North, 1990, p. 78) was, of course, the emancipation of the serfs in 1861–1863. As for the intensity of the autocracy's economic intervention, structural continuity is evident from 1700 to 1721, due to and during warfare, specifically the Northern War. The modernization spurts of the eighteenth and the nineteenth centuries were dictated by war requisites (the Crimean War in the case of Nicholas II), which structured priorities in resource allocation.

The endogeneity of autocratic, totalitarian government and territorial conflict, which if successful would grant these structures their main basis of legitimacy, resulted in a perpetual war economy. The share of military purposes in state expenditure during and between Nicholas' and Peter's industrialization spurts implies as much.

Calculations based on absolute numbers show even more emphatically that the Tsarist state devoted the largest share of its expenditure to the military and administration, leaving education and healthcare with a residual share of less than 1 percent after the royal household, diplomacy, and the church received their allotments.

Notwithstanding the pecuniary and computational differences between the sources referenced, the institutional structure that determined the *proportions* of state expenditure on defense and state administration must have been roughly consistent over time. Under both Peter I and Nicholas II, at least 40 percent of sources originating in tax collection were allocated to the military and a similar share went to state administration (Tables 8.1, 8.2, 8.3). Table 8.3, covering a longer period in the eighteenth century during the reign of the enlightened Catherine the Great, is reproduced for comparison. Kahan (1985, p. 339), cautions that the lack of data on construction, communication, and other uses make the estimates of administrative outlays "tenuous indeed." Again, however, the military accounted for about 40 percent of gross expenditure on average during this and exceeded that proportion during the Pugachev revolt (1770–1773), the French Revolution, and the First Turkish War. Given

[11]Anisimov (1989, p. 121) maintains that, during the first quarter of the eighteenth century, Russia experienced an economic upswing comparable to the industrialization spurt of the Soviet era. Thus, in 1695–1725, 200 new factories were constructed, raising their numbers to ten times those in the previous century.

Table 8.3 Military budget expenditure under Catherine the Great, 1762–1796 (,000 rubles)

Year	*Army*	*Navy*	*Special war appropriation*	*Total military*	*Pct. of gross expenditure*	*Pct. of net revenues*
1762	9.219	1.200		10.419	63.15	
1763	7.920	1.200		9.120	52.92	62.75
1764	8.723	1.230		9.935	46.12	56.09
1765	9.676	1.508		11.184	49.44	58.77
1766	9.806	1.309		11.115	46.14	55.17
1767	9.828	1.263		11.191	47.60	52.22
1768	10.13	1.313	1.300	12.626	50.61	60.53
1769	10.000	1.400	1.800	13.200	49.48	65.16
1770	9.904	1.445	7.600	18.949	*54.11*	76.69
1771	10.282	2.578	9000	21.860	*56.62*	82.82
1772	10.508	1.378	7.700	19.586	*49.85*	76.12
1773	10.812	1.433	7.355	19.600	*50.27*	76.40
1774						
1780	n.a.	n.a.	n.a.	n.a.		
1781	10.600	3.250		13.850	33.81	48.18
1782	10.800	3.270		14.070	34.39	44.49
1783	13.720	3.820		17.540	36.40	55.54
1784	14.320	3.930		18.250	36.65	45.04
1785	16.400	4.130		20.530	36.36	51.22
1786	19.110	8.40		27.750	44.28	67.25
1787	21.060	4.640	5000	30.700	46.00	68.66
1788	18.690	4.350	16.000	39.040	*51.29*	89.41
1789	20.170	5.310	16.000	41.480	*52.38*	93.57
1790	21.620	5.470	16.000	43.090	*52.10*	94.28
1791	24.590	5.470	15.000	45.060	53.09	101.47
1792	23.100	6.200		29.300	40.55	67.94
1793	23.300	5.430		28.730	37.59	69.51
1794	21.600	5.670		27.270	37.71	63.87
1795	22.200	7000		29.200	36.87	52.98
1796	21.000	6.680		27.680	35.41	49.96

The italic values refer to the Pugachev revolt era that extorted higher social stability government outlays on the Catherinian government French revolution and government fear of its spread
Source*:* Kahan (1985, p. 337)

this allocation structure—a continuous dimension of the institutional structure—the economies under Peter I and Nicholas II may be thought to have had the commonality of being war economies, which, in terms of their elements, may be seen as precursors of the subsequent Soviet war economy (Anisimov, 1989, pp. 122, 123). What matters, in particular, is the steady share of the military in state expenditure in wartime and peacetime alike (Kahan, 1985, p. 337).

Characteristic of a war economy is the voluntary and involuntary collectivist ethos that takes over at times of national conflict. In the Petrine era, the industries developed were chosen according to national necessities and the "*common good*" as the Tsarist government perceived them. The consequent classification of industries as *nuzhnye*—"needed"—or *nienuzhnye*—"superfluous"—was dictated by the prerequisites of the Northern War (Anisimov, 1989, p. 121). Moreover, the ideas of mercantilism and protectionism that inspired this period in Russian history were congruent, in terms of involuntary collectivism and antipathy to freedom, with the idea of *nasil'stvennogo progressa*—"progress through coercion" (122)—that Peter nurtured. It should be emphasized in this context that the idea of state-controlled, bureaucratically shaped economic development was exceptionally long-lived in the Russian and Soviet superstructures, structuring individuals' habits of thought for decades upon decades to come.

It was the Russian defeat at Narva (1700) that ultimately determined the type and pace of the Petrine industrialization, which aimed to bolster the combat performance of the Russian army and navy (Anisimov, 1989, p. 122). The industries prioritized were those that manufactured armaments and clothing for military institutions (Anisimov, 1989, p. 122.). The formation of development blocs (Gerschenkron, 1962, p. 125), the Ural ironworks, and the St. Petersburg Admiralty (Kahan, 1985, p. 86), all for the purpose of supplying the Russian navy (Anisimov, 1989, p. 124), rested at the core of the war-structured industrialization and modernization process. The textile industries in the Moscow region were also developed to supply the combat forces (Kahan, 1985, p. 88; Anisimov, 1989, pp. 125, 127; de Madariaga, 1998), 51, 81, 82; Raeff, 1984, pp. 50, 51). This modernization for the sake of military victory had a byproduct: it allowed the Russian elites to compete culturally with their British, French, and Prussian counterparts for international acknowledgment of their empire's status (Raeff, 1984, p. 62).

One of the pillars of Russia's eighteenth-century Europeanization and modernization effort was the government-sponsored reorientation of commerce and the merchant fleet from Archangelsk port to the newly built St. Petersburg (Anisimov, 1989, p. 129). This process inflicted a dire cost on the Russian merchant class, whose traditional trust networks were destroyed in the short run, and had to be backed by heavy penalties for noncompliance. The destruction of the networks and the interventionist policy of the Tsarist government, which ruled through monopoly, taxation, and licensure, resulted during the Petrine era in drastic attrition among the *gosti,* the wealthiest merchant strata (Hartley, 1999, p. 168; Anisimov, 1989, pp. 129, 131, 132; Owen, 1995, p. 19).

The economic and social sacrifices demanded of the population make it evident that the involuntary, collectively mobilized war economy had been put in place not to produce a thriving individualist capitalist entity but to transform Muscovy into a major European military superpower. The price (social cost) of state entrepreneurship in the case of the Tsarist autocracy was the continuous reallocation of physical and human resources from the civilian to the military sector of the economy.

The coercive character of the Petrine Europeanization was manifest in the practice of *prinuditelnye pereselenia,* forced resettlement (Anisimov, 1989, p. 131)—a long-term policy meant to bring skills and labor to the purposes and centers of modernization, trampling on individual rights in the process. Under a series of ukases in 1711, the most successful merchants were forcefully resettled in St. Petersburg, the new capital that had been built by the 40,000 peasants who had been resettled in such a manner each year. Undernourished and housed in mud huts, they perished en masse while constructing the "pyramids" of Imperial splendor with half their bodies buried in the muck. Their living conditions were replicated among the serfs who built Russia's first railway lines under Nicholas I. To eliminate the possibility of their rising up, the Tsarist overseers plied them with alcohol (Westwood, 1964, p. 33).

According to Anisimov (1989), Peter secured his victory in the Northern War by increasing the fiscal burden on the peasant population. The structure of *krugovaya poruka* (collective liabilities) included supplying the state with soldiers, labor, horses, undertakings in natura, and monetary dues (Anisimov, 1989, p. 134). The Bulavin revolt that plagued Peter's reign (1707) was linked to the dire exploitation, degradation, and virtual enslavement of the peasantry as the Northern War was being fought (139). A commonality of Peter's and Nicholas' modernization spurts was the role of foreign human capital, in addition to imported technology, in the institutional revolution. The development of the Baltic fleet, a chief component of the Russian navy (Cracraft, 2004, p. 80), in the Petrine modernization and the initial construction of railroads in the nineteenth century were core activities in the development blocs. The role of British expertise in establishing the prestigious Russian School of Mathematical and Navigational Sciences, which abetted the eighteenth-century "cultural revolution" related to the navy, is comparable to that of the Viennese Professor Franz von Gerstner in Russia's importation of railway technology (1834) (Westwood, 1964, p. 22). The Petrine-era importation of maritime technology institutions and organizations,[12] although easily applicable to peacetime activities, did not augment the capacity of the Russian commercial fleet very much.[13] Thus, technology diffusion from the military to the civilian sector could not be taken for granted in the case of the Tsarist autocracy. In fact, the opposite continuously proved true. In this context, then, the emphasis belongs to Gerschenkron's (1968) identification of the "costs of dictatorship" rather than the positive long-term effects of state entrepreneurship, on which the great economic historians focus. These effects proved too deficient to foster the requisite value systems and skills for increased industrial production (Gerschenkron, 1968, p. 315) for civilian purposes.

The Tsarist enthusiasm for von Gerstner's suggestion to link by rail the "two capitals to the Volga system" (Westwood, 1964, p. 23) stemmed from military considerations. Once implemented, it would allow Russia to compete with Britain for access to the Persian Gulf; what is more, by facilitating swift troop movement, it would deter future Polish uprisings. The military purpose notwithstanding, one cannot but agree with Gerschenkron that the state-led importation of technology brought progressive institutional adaptations in train. Although they were unintended more often than not (Lal, 1998, p. 5), the Tsarist autocracy retarded but did not preclude institutional and economic civilian progress.

"Top-Down" Reform and Railroads to Progress

In view of the context established above, the question now is whether the most progressive of the Tsarist reforms, the emancipation of the serfs in 1861, was motivated by the increased transaction costs of the serfdom system (Leonard, 1990, p. 136). These costs, I surmise, accumulated amid population increase (Kahan, 1985, p. 8, Tables 1.1 and 1.2), even as the

[12] Cracraft (2004, pp. 61, 62), Statutes: "Ustav Morskoi," the 1720 Naval Statute, and the 1722 Admiralty Regulation, Reglament o Upravlenii Admiralteistva i Verfi—Regulation of the Administration of the Admiralty and Wharves, which codified naval innovations going back to 1680 and provided for maintenance of the navy.

[13] Cracraft (2004, pp. 55, 56). In Kahan's estimation, however, Russian maritime trade increased fifteen-fold between 1730 and the end of the century. The role of civilian maritime trade in terms of the cultural impact of the construction of the Baltic fleet was incomparably smaller (Hughes, 1998, p. 148). Plainly, the coercive insistence on rerouting trade through St. Petersburg as against other ports was strategically rather than commercially motivated

Crimean War debacle incentivized the import of spatial mobility technology that necessitated progressive institutional adaptations. Emancipation of the state peasantry with land had been considered amid the absorption of Enlightenment ideas under Catherine the Great. These eighteenth-century debates were precursors to what was institutionalized a century later as an accommodation to the intensifying rejection among the historically spiritual intellectual elites of the ownership of man by man and the conception of serfdom as socially costly amid the falling land-to-labor ratio (Kolchin, 1987, p. 2). The Emancipation Act of 1861, I suggest, encapsulated all these factors combined.

The perceived relative urgency of the reform clearly validates Gerschenkron's (1968) analysis. The debacle of the Crimean War showed Alexander II that the reform could be postponed no longer, for two reasons; geopolitical competition with Western rivals that had abandoned recourse to un-free labor and soldiering, and the risk of internal upheaval, ever-present but intensified by the Crimean defeat. Radzinskij (2008, p. 116) quotes the Tsar-Liberator as explaining that the Great Reform was actually an unavoidable preemptive measure: "If freedom will not be given the peasants from above, they will take it from below." This quotation demonstrates the legitimacy of the points made in Fig. 8.2 above. Alexander Herzen, a leading contemporary intellectual, urged Alexander II to spare the peasants from the agony that their otherwise ineluctable revolt would inflict on them: "*Smoite pozornoe piatno z Rossii. Zalechte rubcy ot platei na spinach vashych bratev. Izbavte krestian ot krovi kotoruju im nepremenno prijdiotsja prolic…*"—"Wash out the shameful stain of Russia. Heal the traces of the knout on your brothers' backs. Save the peasants from the blood that they will inevitably be compelled to spill […]" (Radzinskij 2007, p. 145, 2008, p. 116).

Denunciation of the degrading treatment of the individual, including the injunction against torture, is incorporated into Catherine's instructions, the Nakaz. The Pugachev revolt (1770–1773), which made the Tsarist empire exceptionally dependent on the nobles' loyalty,[14] led in 1785 to the enactment of the Charter to the Nobility, freeing the Russian elite from degrading corporal punishment, sparing it from compulsory state service, and guaranteeing it allodial property rights in land (Bartlett in Hosking and Service; Hartley, 1999, p. 76). The same dependence

[14] Pipes (1999, p. 192, 1995, p. 180). The Pugachev rebellion actualized the symbiotic relationship between the autocracy and the nobles.

retarded the liberation of the serfs, limiting the issue to social debate until the second half of the nineteenth century (de Madariaga, 1998, p. 86; Pipes, 1995, p. 255).

In face of the Enlightenment-inspired reforms "from above" and the Judeo-Christian values that had been disseminated continuously since the ninth century,[15] the peasants' attitude toward equal individual rights could not have been entirely ambivalent. As regards land ownership rights, 85 percent of the peasants agreed with the redemption (*vykup*) of land previously put to collective use from their creditor, the Tsarist state. The large proportion of peasants who voluntarily participated in the redemption process implies that the peasantry viewed land ownership enthusiastically, albeit on a village-commune basis, as early as 1881—twenty-five years before the Stolypin land reform (Zakharova, 1992, p. 36).

Zakharova (1992) advises that the institutionalized preservation of the village commune, including its collective control mechanisms, did not originate in the ranks of the peasantry. The empowerment of the commune assembly with legal capacities previously held by the landlord (Atkinson, 1983, p. 22), including enforcement of the formal restrictions on freedom of movement (North, 1990, p. 78; Gerschenkron, 1962, pp. 120, 121), may be understood as a Russian manifestation of the disadvantages of institutional backwardness.[16] Studying the Western experience and ideologies (Marxism), Tsardom feared a massive exodus from the rural sector and its corollaries, proletarianization, and revolution.

Contrary to Pallot's analysis (Pallot, 1999, pp. 75, 171) and consistent with Gerschenkron's, Zakharova maintains that the nineteenth-century collectivist village-commune control was imposed from above and supported by the Tsarist state. If so, the historical viability of the obshchina can be only partly explained by noting the climatic conditions of Russian agriculture (Milov, 2001, pp. 1, 2). Although the foundation of the commune and the ethos of Tsarist Russian collectivism—*krugovaya poruka* (mutual liability)—was kinship-based (de Madariaga, 1998, p. 79), the viability of the commune cannot be sufficiently understood without giving due account to Russia's institutional backwardness relative to West European empires such as Britain, as an interdependency of Russia's historically high land-to-labor ratio (Kolchin, 1987, p. 2) and its geopolitical vulnerability, manifested by frequent invasions from the West.

[15] Blum (1961, p. 36). Prince Vladimir accepted baptism in 988 CE.

[16] The mirror expression, "advantages of backwardness," also traces to Gerschenkron (1962).

The historical kinship-based obshchina was an organic unit. Its consolidation during serfdom and its viability in the interlude between the emancipation of the serfs (1861) and Stolypin's land reform (1906) may be explained as tracing to a state initiative that aimed to reduce the transaction and surveillance costs of Tsarist tax extraction.

After the Crimean debacle, Russia manifested its vulnerability in growing internal concern about European public opinion—*zabota o Evropeiskom obshchestvennom mneni* (Zakharova, 1992, p. 25)—and its government turned keener attention to the plight of the peasants. "[The] humiliation that autocratic Russia endured at the hands of the democracies England and France during the Crimean war" (Gatrell, 1994, p. 13) and the empire's debtor position stressed the need for libertarian reforms in general and peasant emancipation in particular. Consequently, the Russian defeat at Narva intensified the importation of Swedish, Dutch, and British institutions into the Euroasian Empire (Hughes, 1998, p. 138).[17] The unfavorable (for Russia) terms of the Paris peace settlement that concluded the Crimean War had much the same effect, including the importation of European disapproval of the ownership of man by man.

The Russo-Japanese War (1904), meant to placate and divert internal discontent with deficient civil rights, including the undelineated right of association, ended with Russia's shameful rout, further intensifying civil society's demand for institutional transformation (Ascher, 1988, pp. 47–50; Borodkin, 2008, Discussion). In this context, the 1905 revolution may be understood as an epitomic cost of dictatorship in the Gerschenkronian sense—one that could have been avoided had the autocracy made the concession demanded: the constitutional delegation of decision-making power to a publicly elected body, the Duma (Ascher, 1988, p. 2).

Paradoxically, then, I argue that preparations for the clash of powers on the battlefield and Russia's lost wars triggered imports of technology and progressive institutional adaptations, while victories consistently consolidated the autocracy, having a retarding effect. It is true that the Petrine economy was restructured after the victory in the Northern War, allowing private initiative, encouraging private commerce, and freeing private enterprise from state monopolies in what Anisimov (1989, p. 279) calls the historical NEP. This tolerance of private entrepreneurship, however, was temporary; the economy was subsequently placed under the

[17] On the Swedish origin of the poll tax, see Cracraft (2004, pp. 58, 69).

domination of government-dominated industry (Gerschenkron, 1962, p. 143). As autocratic control of production processes under consolidated governmental power intensified, resources were channeled to the achievement, in Gerschenkronian terms, of autochthonous modernization in supplying the army and the state with manufacturers (Anisimov, 1989, p. 279). Thus, the flow of resources from the civilian to the military sector of the economy under state entrepreneurship did not cease in peacetime. The idea behind the "commercial company," an imitation of the Western model, was to supply the state with manufactures for military use. The economy remained under full bureaucratic control. Then the railroad arrived.

Thus, Russia solved the problem of integrating industrialism with imperialism by keeping industry under intensive direct and indirect state control (Gatrell, 1994, p. 15) in self-perpetuating continuity. Importantly, the costs of imperialism were manifested neither exclusively nor primarily in higher taxes and recruitment obligations but in the dashed expectations of the internal upheaval that had induced the reforms.[18] If so, what animated the industrialization spurt of the 1890s? It was France, which after the Crimean War considered the Russian Empire a strategic interest, allowing Russia to benefit immensely from peacetime French capital flows. The growth of nineteenth-century industrial production, however, centered on the railroadization program that was induced and financed by the Tsarist government, allowing track length to grow from 30,600 kilometers to 56,500 between 1880 and 1900 (Gatrell, 1994, p. 16) (Table 8.4).

Focusing on the dramatic 51 percent increase in ridership during the last five years of the nineteenth century (verified by the increase in the sale of tickets and passports—Kahan, 1989, p. 4, Table 1.2), one may argue that the railways were the most progressive, peacetime-applicable, and freedom-enhancing of all the Tsarist government's initiatives. Unlike Peter's massive investments in developing the Baltic fleet, undertaken for solely military purposes (the technology, acquired from Britain, was not diffused to civilian commercial endeavors), the railways were dual-purpose from the outset: political (including military) and economic. Indirectly, by guaranteeing the railroad bonds at an unprecedented 5 percent rate (Kahan, 1989, p. 29; Westwood, 1964, pp. 43, 44; Borodkin, 2008, Discussion), thereby attracting massive foreign direct investment, the

[18] Gregory (1994, p. 53). The revolution occurred under conditions of rising standards of living.

Table 8.4 Growth of the Russian Rail Network 1860–1916

Year	*Length (km.)*	*Freight (million tons–km)*	*Ridership (millions–km)*	*Headcount (yearly average, ,000)*
1860	1,626	–	–	–
1865	3,843	0.571	–	–
1870	10,731	2.404	–	–
1875	19,029	5.146	–	–
1880	22,865	8.000	–	–
1885	26,024	11.238	3.929	213
1890	30,596	14.925	5.013	248
1895	37,058	22.615	***7.581***	344
1900	53,234	38.869	***13.003***	554
1905	61,085	45.109	19.467	751
1910	66,581	60.594	23.229	772
1913	70,156	69.731	29.312	815
1916	80,139			

The bold-italic values refer to the structural discontinuity in ridership and head count
Source: Kahan (1989, p. 30)

autocratic government set in motion an invasion of libertarian value systems that were prevalent in the West, creating multiple institutional structures. Concurrently, rural-to-urban migration and the cultural exchange associated with it weakened the rural institutions of collective patriarchal control and replaced them with *otkhodnikhestvo*—rural peasants' wage labor in urban industrial centers—as the core of the process (Smurova, 2003, p. 100).

Without the railroads, the commercialization of Russian agriculture would have advanced much more slowly, as would have GNP. The rising productivity among the gentry and the agrarian peasantry, raising the living standards of the latter (Kahan, 1989, pp. 31, 69, Table 1.36, p. 128, 3.7; Gregory, 1994, p. 53), can be explained partly by the direct and indirect stimulation that railroad construction provided for the expansion of the ferrous and machine industries (Kahan, 1989, pp. 19–21). The growth of rail abetted structural—and, in turn, institutional—changes in entire regions. From the mid-1860s onward, for example, mechanized construction industries began to expand due to structural transformation in parts of the Povolzhe region.

The railroad construction boom in the 1890s revived a large cohort of engineering industries (Gatrell, 1994, p. 53), not least through skills training, including downstream activities such as extraction of raw materials

Table 8.5 Gross output of machinery, 1900–1908

	1900			*1908*		
	Units	*Output (million rubles)*	*Percent share*	*Units*	*Output (million rubles)*	*Percent share*
Rolling stock	14	92.0	46	18	85.3	41
Vessels	32	6.1	3	18	4.6	2
Boilers	52	24.6	12	56	11.7	5
Agricultural machinery	**162**	**12.1**	**6**	**216**	**26.5**	**13**
Other	279	67.1	33	244	83.3	39
Total	539	201.9	100	552	211.5	100

The bold values refer to the agricultural machinery use and access which is important as an estate-specific trade
Source: Gatrell (1994, p. 55)

(iron, lumber), textile production, and the machine industry that abetted farming. Production for the railway transport sector explains the 9.7 percent annual rate of increase in the market for Russian-built machinery between 1885 and 1900 (Gatrell, 1994, Table 1.6.). The falling labor–capital ratio in larger and more capital-intensive production units (consistent with Gerschenkron's predictions) and the rising productivity of labor is reflected in the structural changes in the engineering industry depicted in Table 8.5.

That the share of agricultural machinery in gross machine-building output doubled may indicate that the growing mechanization of agriculture and the ensuing rising productivity of land and labor explain the upturn in peasant living standards (Gregory, 1994, p. 53) ahead of the 1905 revolution. It stands to reason that the railroads contributed to the sharp rise in land prices along rail lines, making investment and therefore de facto individually delineated property right in land profitable (Hesse, 1993, p. 51). By implication, the railroads abetted the transition from collectivism to individualism in the landholding system.

Thus, in terms of the risk of dying of starvation—which according to the rationalist model is assumed to have induced rural collectivism—the railroads had a triple hypothetical impact. At the indirect and direct institutional level, they powered the agricultural machine-building industry, improving factor productivity and the peasantry's living standards; they mitigated rural collectivism, opening up access to the urban market; and they created opportunities for wage labor in industrial centers. If so, existential risk and collectivist dependency declined in tandem. Finally, the rising return on investment in land occasioned by railroadization encouraged individualism, spurring a stronger and faster exodus from collectivist obshchina structures.

The 283 percent growth rate of the labor force in rail-transport services (Kahan, 1989, p. 30, Table 1.14) between 1885 and 1913 reflected the acquisition and dissemination of skills vital to the institutional development of the economy as a whole (Chandler, 1977). By making extensive use of the telegraph and improving the national postal service, the railroads helped to intensify information flows, raising the cultural level of the population (Kahan, 1989, p. 35, Table 1.18). By launching the industrialization process and, in particular, by building railroads—setting cultural-cognitive exchange in motion (Smurova, 2003, p. 100; Boyer & Orlean, 1993, p. 22; Martens, 2004, p. 101) and creating multiple institutional structures—the autocratic government unintentionally triggered democratization, causing an upturn in demand for parliamentary structures that made itself present in the 1905 revolution (Ascher, 1988, pp. 87–89; Martens, 2004, p. 193). Thus, the preemptive top-down libertarian reform, interacting with state-led technological innovation, enhanced the credibility of the bottom-up threat and forced additional top-down concessions and reforms (Fig. 8.4). Although the state entrepreneurship manifested in rail construction was meant partly for military purposes, it triggered the formation of progressive civilian institutions as an unintended epiphenomenon. In a nutshell, the effect of the virtuous cycle (Fig. 8.2), depicting the long-term unintended consequences of state entrepreneurship, was more decisive than the continuity of the vicious cycle of the costs of dictatorship that burdened state entrepreneurship. Thus, the credible threat from below constituted the vehicle of progress even as the self-perpetuation of autocracy promoted progress, via lagged reforms from above, and retarded it by burdening the institutional innovations with dictatorship costs.

From Collectivism to Individualism in Illustration

Figure 8.4, focusing on the transition from collectivism to individualism during the nineteenth century, summarizes the identifiable progressive mechanism in the interaction among the climate, the state (as the effectuator of technological innovation), and the mir, leading to advances in individual rights including the right to immovable property.

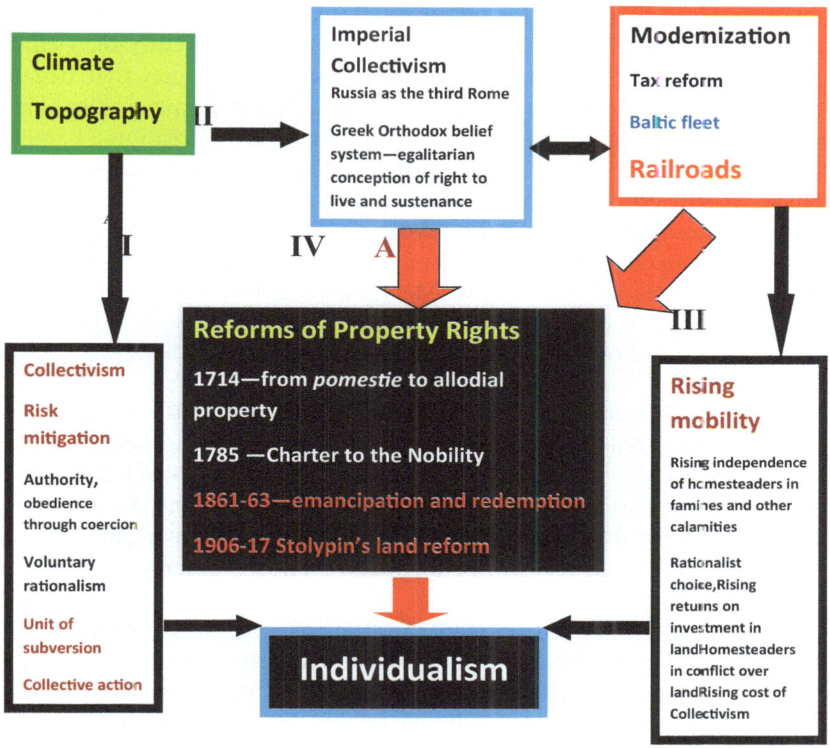

Fig. 8.4 The Tsarist state and the mir—four complementary roads to progress in late Tsarist Russia. (Volyn, 1970, p. 78. The term *mir* has two meanings: "the world" and "peace." In the nineteenth century, it denoted a community of former serfs or state peasants who, as a rule, settled in a single village, although sometimes a village included more than one mir and conversely several villages could combine into a single mir. Burds (1998, p. 18). The obshchina is a composite juridical person composed of the aggregate of the community's juridical persons—the *domokhoziaistvo*. Sources (left to right): Chubarov, 2001, p. 4; Milov, 2001, pp. 1, 2; Blum, 1961, pp. 21, 22; Montesquieau in Durkheim, 1960, pp. 26, 31; Anisimov, 1989, pp. 122, 123; Gerschenkron, 1968, p. 315, 1962, pp. 120, 123–124; Cracraft, 2004, p. 57; Kahan, 1989, p. 28; Bartlett, 1999, p. 76; Pipes, 1995, p. 70, 1999, p. xii; Gaudin, 2007, p. 43; Pallot, 1999, p. 113; Kingston-Mann, 1991, p. 43; Barzel, 2002, p. 61; Greif, 2006, p. 103; Burds, 1998, Table 1.3, p. 23; Hesse, 1993, p. 51; Sheshinski, 2010, p. 3; Gintis, 2009, pp. 1, 2; Macey, 1990, p. 222; North, 1990, pp. 90, 91, 1981; Kolchin, 1987)

Since time immemorial, Russia had exhibited a high land-to-labor ratio, a harsh climate that kept yield-to-seed ratios low, and unpredictable yields. These factors had long fostered collective survival strategies that began with kinship-based risk-sharing that had mutual-insurance properties. The unit of collective control—the mir—was an organic creation (Barzel, 2002, p. 61; Blum, 1961, p. 22) that had the potential of becoming a vehicle of subversion against the Tsars' despotic sway over the Russian plain (Montesquieu in Durkheim, 1960, pp. 26, 31). More benignly, the risk-sharing mechanism that structured the mir facilitated innovation (Kingston-Mann, 1991, p. 43; McCloskey, 2009; Hodgson, 2004, pp. 257, 414) that helped to instigate a long-term increase in household independence and transition to individualism (left-hand side of the figure, **Road I**).

The combination of harsh climate and frequent natural calamities necessitated landlord and ultimately state intervention in the form of loans, grain storage, and various modalities of famine relief. The last-mentioned had also been effectuated indirectly by the Tsarist government in the form of public works for peasants and injunctions against grain exports in famine years (Kahan, 1985, p. 136). These measures, by enhancing centralization and sheer peasant dependence on the Tsarist state, broadened the state's encroachment into the economic sphere of the peasantry, consolidating autocratic rule. Combined with Judeo-Christian values, they produced collectivist state structures in the short run (Milov, 2001, pp. 1, 2). In the long run, however, the ever-present credible threat from below, interacting in the nineteenth century with the imported technologies and value systems embodied in railroad construction, would prompt the government to codify the individualization processes ex post, launching the land reform that carries Stolypin's name (**Road IV**).

Railroad construction, the core of the Tsarist industrialization drive in 1890–1907, was yet another dual-purpose activity. As an instrument of warfare (simplifying troop transport, the railroad may have encouraged collectivism at both the state and village levels in the short run by making recruited soldiers' families dependent on the commune (Worobec, 1995, p. 64) and strengthening the mechanisms of state control over society at large (Hobson & Weiss, 1995, p. 6). In the long run, however, due to the improved transportation technology and the systemization of government that it facilitated (Yaney, 1973, p. 7), the bottom-up demand for individualizing reforms made upward progress easier to attain (**Arrow A, Road IV**).

The Tsarist taxation system, with its heavy reliance on collective responsibility for the liabilities of the village commune, unintentionally strengthened the unit of subversion, intensifying the credibility of the threat from below (Greif, 2006, p. 441; Barzel, 2002, p. 61) and challenging the Tsarist autocracy (**Road III**). In the communes, well-to-do households and individuals fumed at the collectives' violations of individual rights and regarded the commune as an obstacle to innovation, spurring the transition to individualism. The Westernizing Russian intelligentsia saw matters the same way. Such views were congruent with Stolypin's conceptualization of the commune as an obsolete institution that impeded agrarian modernization. (Hoch, 1986, p. 189; Worobec, 1995, pp. 79, 80; Boyer & Orlean, 1993, p. 22) (**Road III**). Individuals' expectations in this regard were justified in view of the civilian development afforded by the railroads, with their ability to transport grain and people alike. By instrumentalizing famine relief, the railroad made households independent of each other. Insensitive to climatic conditions unlike water transport, the railroads weakened the collectivist strategies of the mir in the long run, rendering them redundant (**Arrow A**).

The rows in the following figure are marked in chronological order. **Road I**, the village commune as an innovation-"enabling" institution (Hodgson, 2004 257, 414; McCloskey, 2009; Kingston-Mann, 1991, pp. 38, 43), is assumed to have dissolved due to skill accumulation (Hesse, 1993, p. 51) facilitated by risk-sharing (Moon, 1999, p. 216), leading in the long run to greater independence among householders. The interaction of the communal institutions with the state-led industrialization process, centered on railroad construction (**Road II**), catalyzed the atrophy of the collectivist practice. In this interaction, the railroads—the long hand of the Tsarist government—would ensure the peasant household against starvation, replacing the premodern collective risk-insurance and -sharing mechanism of the commune.

Concurrently, the inhibiting control mechanisms inherent in the commune alienated well-to-do households that wished to rid themselves of collective liability for their poorer fellows.[19] The wealth accumulation made possible by the mechanization and commercialization of agriculture,

[19]Worobec (1990, p. 97). In communes that practiced effective manure investment in land, mutual insurance through land repartitions was less necessary. Thus, land repartitioning was a function of the extent of economic dependency.

induced by railroad construction, intensified the exodus from the commune (Hesse, 1993, p. 51; Boyer & Orlean, 1993, p. 22) (**Road III**).

Given the interaction between these mechanisms and the intensity of the obligations (pecuniary and non-pecuniary) and the coercion, the top-down reforms should be seen as ex post codifications of ongoing processes and concessions to Russian society's demand for institutions of civil control (**Road IV**).

Was Stolypin Right or Wrong in Assuming that the Peasant Mir Had Atrophied? Mironov vs. Nefedov

It is of the utmost importance to call attention to explanations of the institutional discontinuity—namely, the institutional innovations implemented—that followed the 1905 revolution. Is there sufficient reason to assume that the First Duma and Stolypin's land reform, both occurring in 1906 and involving the individualization of the right to land tenure and the transformation of communal use rights in land to the property rights of heads of household, were indeed the concessions that the peasantry, the intelligentsia, and the urbanized peasant workers had demanded? (Johnson, 1979, pp. 123, 124; Ascher, 1988, Vol. II, pp. 268, 269)

If the peasant revolt in 1905—the torching of landlords' demesne due to the alleged excessive exploitation through the fiscal system that financed the industrialization drive (Gerschenkron, 1962, pp. 121, 122)—resulted in pauperization, logic would advise that collectivist practice within the realm of the village commune would have intensified during the post-emancipation period. The peasantry would then attempt by all means to resist Stolypin's pro-individualization land reform. The peasants' dependence on the mutual safety mechanisms of the commune would grow, prompting the Tsarist state to implement the reform by coercion. If so, the effect of the interaction of industrialization and population increase on the peasantry's standard of living would vindicate Pallot's (1999) analysis of the 1906–1917 land reform, which emphasizes peasant resistance to the individualization measures.

Contrary to Pallot's proposition, Klimin (2002) reveals that Stolypin himself lived among the peasantry and watched the collectivist practices atrophy. The peasant mir, Stolypin concluded, had played itself out, the peasants preferring to work for their own households' prosperity rather than to ensure that of others. Engelgardt's eyewitness account also notes ever-present and growing individualism in the peasant milieu in the post-emancipation period.

These observations, as well as Worobec's (1990, p. 97), are indicative of escalating peasant living standards and, consequently, the growing independence of peasant households as leading determinants of the rural constituency's conduct in the post-emancipation era. This being the case, the 1905 revolution should be understood as a battle for civil rights, including property rights in land, rather than a desperate peasant protest against pauperization and hunger. Consequently, Stolypin's land reform should be considered a Tsarist concession that the peasantry demanded (Ascher, 2001, pp. 7, 11, 12; Klimin, 2002, pp. 11–15) as opposed to a measure implemented through sheer administrative coercion to create a well-to-do peasant stratum loyal to the crown. This interpretation squares with the expectations of the model in the figure above, in which the railroad, by mitigating the risk of starvation, intensifies peasant demand for the legalization and enforcement of household heads' property rights, dooming the village commune to disintegration.

Here I contrast the work of two modern Russian scholars, B.N. Mironov and M.A. Davydov (2003), complementing the findings of Gregory and Simms, with Nefedov's traditional work. Nefedov emphasizes the interaction of a Malthusian crisis and the Tsarist aspiration to industrialize backward Russia as the cause of the peasantry's impoverishment. Thus, Nefedov explains the 1905 revolution in materialist terms.

Mironov writes that, in Soviet historiography, the peasant movement and the revolutionary situation in 1905 are matters of tradition that are explained by the pauperization of the peasantry due to severe exploitation by the Tsarist state. He quotes Druzhynin 1946 (Mironov, 2008), who saw the accumulation of peasant tax arrears as evidence of this constituency's deepening immiseration, brought on by an increase in the burden of obligations and declining agricultural entrepreneurship (Mironov, 2008, p. 2)

Other modern Russian sources quoted by Mironov lay the ultimate blame for the peasants' pauperization at the foot of the Russian climate, which left surpluses that were chronically smaller than those in Western Europe (Milov, 2001, pp. 1, 2). As for the reform that terminated serfdom in Russia, Mironov, citing the traditional historian B.G. Litvak 1972 (Mironov, 2008), notes the belief that the exploitation of the peasantry continued even after the Emancipation Act (1861), but now under the Tsarist state instead of the landlords.

Soviet and, in part, post-Soviet sources draw their inspiration from the notion of "hunger exports" of grain (*golodnyj export*) and press their point by quoting Finance Minister Ivan Vyshnegradzky (1887–1892): "*Sami neoedim a vyvezem*"—We'll starve but we'll go on exporting (Mironov, 2008, p. 4). This inspiration diffused to Western sources as well (e.g., Atkinson, 1983, p. 34). Conforming to the traditional interpretations, Nefedov focuses on demographical-structural conditions and maintains that the peasant constituency had been impoverished throughout the Imperial period.[20] Ryndzjunski summarizes the traditional Soviet interpretation of the post-reform period: "*Utverzhdenie kapitalisticheskogo stroja dostigaetsia cenoj razorenia i poraboshchenia naroda*"—The establishment of the capitalist system was achieved at the price of the people's bankruptcy and enserfment (Ryndzjunski, 1978, pp. 6, 7).

In the West, Simms (1977), Gregory (1982, 1994), and Bideleux (1990) challenge the agrarian-crisis hypothesis. Simms (1977, p. 382, Table 1), implying peasant rationality as a general principle, argues convincingly that the peasants of Tsarist Russia amassed tax arrears due to *unwillingness* rather than the inability to pay. By implication, the accumulation of arrears is more indicative of the low legitimacy of the autocratic government than of peasant poverty. In support of this conclusion, it is noted that indirect-tax receipts rose at that time. Thus, the increase in peasant consumption of indirectly taxed items such as tea, vodka, matches, and kerosene, proxied by rising indirect-tax receipts, shows that the peasantry's purchasing power and standard of living were rising. Publications of the Ministry of Agriculture in 1894 and zemstvo (rural government) publications in 1894 and 1895 (Simms, 1977) also document improvements in the rural sector. A correspondent in Korochansk District reported during this period that "*The bread the peasants eat is pure and in abundance*" (Simms, 1977, p. 394).

Among modern Russian economic historians, Davydov (2003, pp. 49–51) challenges the thesis of "hunger exports" of grain, demonstrating convincingly that internal Russian grain shipments grew faster than did export grain shipments, indicating an expanding national grain market.

The available data suggest that the peasants' tax burden in real terms had been falling during the 1801–1850 period relative to the eighteenth century (Mironov, 2008, pp. 7, 11). Thus, while the Bulavin revolt during

[20] Mironov (Mironov, 2008, pp. 1, 2, 3; the reference to Nefedov is on p. 5).

Peter's reign may have been set in motion partly by peasant material impoverishment (Anisimov, 1989, pp. 139, 140), other reasons for mass discontent should be sought for the peasant war of 1905. The emancipation statutes (1861–1863) merely created a liminal stage ahead of full civic status for the peasantry, paving the way for additional discussions within the ranks of the Russian nobility on the equalization of nobles' and peasants' rights to landed property (Macey, 1987, p. 46). The Great Reform simultaneously heightened the expectations of success, triggering resistance to the old order among the peasantry (Mironov, 1999, Vol. 1, p. 476). The emancipation reform, freeing the peasant from serfdom, rendered patriarchalism, which supported and had been supported by serfdom, badly weakened. Individual peasants were increasingly conscious of their personal rights vis-à-vis other family members, powering more and more intra-family egalitarianism in rights (Burds, 1998, p. 29; Mironov, 1999, Vol. 1, p. 477).

The crucial factor that enhanced the dissolution of the extended patriarchal family structure, the individualization process,[21] had been the peasants' rural–urban migration for "side earnings" (Burds, 1998, p. 34). The growing frequency of household divisions (*semeinye rozdely*) indicates a "cultural crisis" triggered by the waves of migrant workers who commuted between the urban and the rural milieus (Burds, 1998, p. 34; Smurova, 2003, p. 100). Data gathered by the Ministry of Internal Affairs in 1861–1882 show 116,229 household divisions in European Russia on an annual average. In 1874–1884, this number increased to 140,355. By the end of the period investigated (1884), more than half of the households in thirty-seven provinces of European Russia had made the transition from an extended to a nuclear structure (Burds, 1998, p. 34, 35; Worobec, 1995, p. 88).

It is of special interest to note in this context that Frierson (1990, p. 313) traces the upturn in family divisions to the individualism-abetting availability of non-agricultural income. By implication, proximity to railroad stations would have the same effect. If so, the growing prevalence of family divisions may be explained by intensified otkhod, facilitated by proximity to railroad stations (Sztern, 2008). While the first generation of *otkhodniki* had to be forced by their parents to leave in order to "moonlight," its successor generation flowed to capitals and other cities in a

[21] For Worobec (1995, p. 88), the escalation of intra-family tensions and pre-mortem fissions in the post-emancipation era is indicative of rising individualism.

"huge wave" (Burds, 1998, p. 38). Smurova investigated the clash between the rural culture and the sartorial and worship habits of the secularized *Pitershchiki,* rural peasants who thronged to St: Petersburg for work. These people, as noted above, were considered more attractive marriage partners than were their introverted rural brethren (Smurova, 2003, pp. 100, 101)—auguring the future dissolution of the mainstream Greek Orthodox patriarchy-structured village commune.

As argued with emphasis above, the Greek Orthodoxy that gave the Tsarist autocracy its spiritual legitimacy faced revolutionizing challenges not only from *secularization* but also from *otkhodnikhestvo.* The flight from the Church-based obshchina structure toward *razkol*—the Old Belief—may be seen as the result of the "side jobs" that the state-sponsored railroad construction made possible. Thus, paradoxically, the Tsarist state introduced the elements of its own transformation into its constitutional monarchy. As proposed in Chap. 7, peasants' spiritual choice among religious institutions—the Orthodox Church and the Old Belief—and their secularized adherence to leftist ideologies entailed an individualization process, something incongruent with the obedience of authority on which the Orthodox empire was based. The flight to the Old Belief allowed fugitive peasants to escape the requirement, sanctioned by mainstream Orthodoxy, that otkhodniki repatriate their industrial earnings to their village communes (Burds, 1998, p. 188). Thus, the adherence of most of the peasantry to the mainstream Orthodox Church, eschewing the Old Belief, temporarily strengthened and perpetuated rural–urban ties.

By legitimizing the communes' claim to the wage laborers' earnings, mainstream Orthodoxy effectively inhibited the formation of a genuine proletariat in pre-revolutionary Russia (Burds, 1998; Johnson, 1979). Thus, not only secularization but also the increasing adherence to Old Belief had an individualizing effect on the commune village structure and enhanced peasant mobility. Notably, however, the growing prevalence of otkhod, and *a fortiori* the resettlement of entire families in city centers, foisted a heavier fiscal burden on the remaining commune members. After all, their obligations were collectively defined and the *krugovaya poruka* practice held them collectively liable for their fulfillment. Thus, while commune members who left enjoyed a higher level of personal rights, those left behind were more dependent, in the short run, on the risk-sharing mechanisms of the commune. This dependency may have retarded the transition to rationalism and individualism. Moreover, the commune offered a form of old-age insurance for those "peasant proletarians"

(Johnson, 1979, p. 38) who returned to their native rural villages when they reached age forty (Burds, 1998, p. 188, 193). An explanation for this particular cohort's repatriation to the village is the following: The competitiveness of the peasant otkhodniki in the urban labor market appears to have declined at this age, whereas in agriculture their experience might still be a socioeconomic asset. This incentive may not have inhibited—it may have even enhanced—rational calculus among competing choices (Sheshinski, 2010, p. 3; Gintis, 2009, pp. 1, 2). Nevertheless, research (Burds, 1998; Frierson, 1990; Mironov, 1999, 2000; and others) clearly indicates that Stolypin was right (Klimin, 2002, pp. 11–15) in assuming that the commune had exhausted its utility as a survival strategy in the peasants' own judgment. Wage labor in industrial centers weakened the authority of the head of household, in turn vitiating the authority of the commune assembly and causing the commune's collectivist mechanisms of coordination and, at times, repression, to atrophy.

The last link in the causal chain—the Tsarist state's preemptive top-down emancipation of the serfs, a precondition for genuine modernization (Rostow, 1960, pp. 6, 7; Cracraft, 2004, p. 12)—is presented in the figure below. The process of reconstitutive downward causation (Hodgson, 2004) ensured change in the Veblenian habits of thought of a peasant population that increasingly demanded personal rights.[22] Moreover, the Gerschenkronian state entrepreneurship manifested in railroad construction set the entire nation on the move. The growing numbers of internal passports issued mirror the upturn in labor mobility, formal restrictions (Gerschenkron, 1962, p. 120; North, 1990, p. 78) notwithstanding. The mass migration that occurred at this time (Burds, 1998, Tables 1.2 and 1.3, pp. 22, 23), explaining and following the legal logic, is itself an indication of the weakening of patriarchal authority (Gerschenkron, 1962, p. 120). The dissolution of the extended family structure carried with it the atrophy of the historically kinship-based village commune (de Madariaga, 1998, p. 79), depriving the autocracy of its tribal and spiritual fundament. Ultimately, the state-led railroad construction triggered a transition from compulsory collectivism to voluntary cooperation, heralding the democratization of Tsarist Russia (Ascher, 1988, p. 1) (Fig. 8.5).

[22] Burds (1998, p. 29), Mironov (1999, Vol. I, p. 477), Frank (1999, p. 74, Table 2.3). In 1874–1913, the average increase in felonies was lowest in personal injury and property crimes and highest in assaults on state authority.

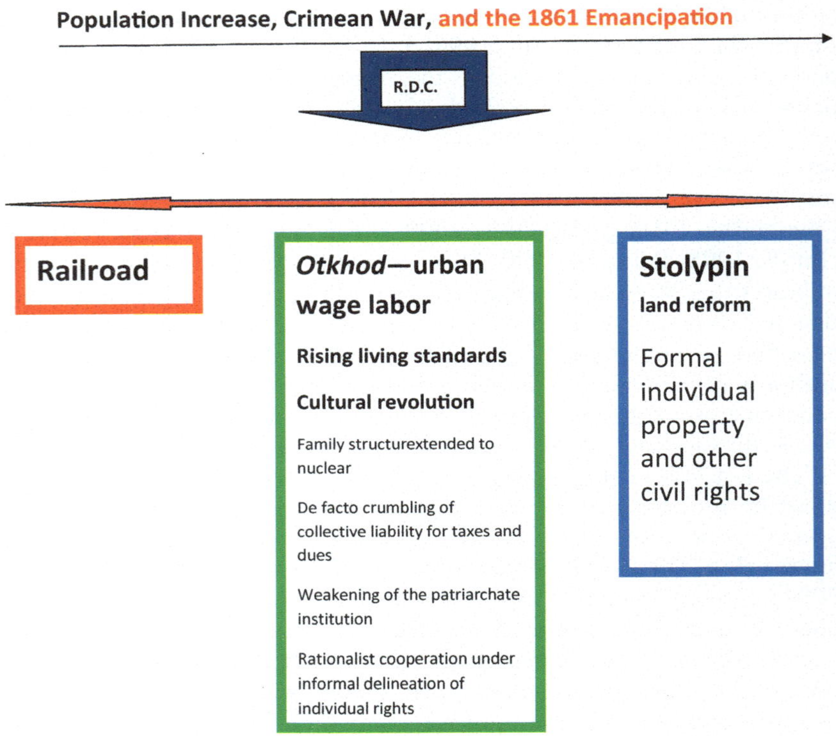

Fig. 8.5 Railroads and the individualization of rights to land. (Sources: Gerschenkron, 1962, p. 131, 1968, p. 159; Leonard, 1990, p. 136; Boyer & Orlean, 1993, p. 22; North, 2005, p. 83; Hodgson, 2004, pp. 105, 185; Kahan, 1985, 1989, pp. 28, 35; Cracraft, 2004, p. 12; Burds, 1998, Table 1.3, p. 23; Frierson, 1990, p. 313; Worobec, 1995, p. 88; Smurova, 2003, p. 100, Mironov, 1999, Vol. 1, p. 477; Atkinson, 1983, p. 41). On the 1903 abolition of collective liability: Gaudin (2007, p. 43))

Concluding Remarks

The combined "top-down"/"bottom-up" perspective, allowed by the complementarity of New Institutional Economics and American Evolutionary Institutionalism that I demonstrated in Chaps. 2, 3, fills important lacunae in the concept of state entrepreneurship as a substitute for the deficient market mechanism in backward economies, that is, Gerschenkron's thesis.

In the foregoing overview, focusing on the long-lasting institutional properties of the Tsarist Russian state, I proposed that state entrepreneurship in the hands of an autocratic, totalitarian government inflicts immense social costs in the long run. Gerschenkron's "costs of dictatorship" concept (Gerschenkron, 1968, p. 315) (relating to the stability of a dictatorship, which I propose is applicable to late imperial Russia, revealing the social costs of these structures) is crucial in this context. The institutions of a totalitarian state, structured to prioritize the collective's interests at all levels of the hierarchy while repressing individuals' claims to inalienable rights to life and property, are the ultimate sources of the institutionalized degradation and oppression of the individual and her or his resulting backwardness and impoverishment.

The pattern followed by a political superstructure is determined by political rationality in the Hayekian sense of the term (Hayek, 1944, pp. 69, 70). A totalitarian state aspires to maximize its control of social and economic activity to further its goal, namely, the perpetuity of its rule. The scope of its intervention in the economy systematically distorts its equilibrium level. Reform for modernization and development purposes is a lagged response to geopolitical vulnerability manifested in a military debacle; it also constitutes a concession induced by an internal revolt along with a credible bottom-up threat of more of the same in the future (Greif, 2006, p. 441). The case of Tsarist Russia emphatically illustrates this general principle among totalitarian regimes. Absent any base of legitimacy other than a set of religious beliefs that depicts the ruler as an intermediary between God and man and as the nation's anointed patriarch, success on the battlefield becomes the second factor that legitimizes autocratic rule (Freeze, 1996, p. 309)—again manifested epitomically in Tsardom.

Since the reign of Peter the Great, the steady vitiation of the Orthodox Church's political influence[23]—a structuring and preconditioning factor in Russian society (Hodgson, 2004, pp. 105, 185)—made territorial defense and conquest a cardinal foundation of legitimacy for the perpetuation of autocracy (Freeze, 1996, pp. 309, 311). Typically, among totalitarian structures, the Tsarist Empire engaged in endemic territorial conflicts, kept the economy on a war footing (Tables 7.1, 7.2, 7.3), and deemed

[23] Hartley (1999, pp. 229–231). On the pious subversion dissent put forward by the Old Believers, see Hughes (1998, p. 337).

national collective rights superior to individual claims. If so, the Tsarist autocracy burdened the civilian economy with costs of dictatorship, identified in this thesis as the long-run invention and innovation forgone due to degrading treatment of the individual, inducing extreme risk aversion (Poznanski, 1992, p. 72, 1985, p. 45; Mokyr, 1990, pp. 153, 173; North, 1981, p. 4, 1990, pp. 64, 78; Hodgson, 2004, pp. 105, 185).

By repressing individual creativity and talent over time in order to consolidate its totalitarian state structure, Tsarist Russia made itself historically dependent on imports of technology (Fig. 8.2). Owen (1995) defines the cost to Russia of excess centralization of economic activity—the substitution of state entrepreneurship for the market—as the private entrepreneurship forgone due to the Tsarist state's encroachment on, and its despotic and arbitrary intervention in, the economic sphere. By enforcing rural collective liability for all obligations, the autocratic state structure fostered habits of thought that were inimical to the cultivation of divergent behaviors such as "preference for novelty" (Witt, 1993, p. 3) and private risk-taking and entrepreneurship.

Unintentionally, however, by pursuing military-strategic and geopolitical objectives, the Tsarist autocracy brought about genuine modernization (Fig. 8.2). Its top-down importation of technology-led implicitly to the importation of politically pluralistic and increasingly democratic social institutions, that is, structures. In the short run, this process widened the inter-estate cultural rift, thereby increasing transaction costs including uncertainty in the Tsarist economy—necessitating additional state encroachment. The resulting vicious cycle (Fig. 8.3) continually retarded socioeconomic progress. The longitudinal effect of the importation of Western institutions, however, hastened the "translation" (Boyer & Orlean, 1993, p. 22) of the material egalitarianization of the rural sector into an effective demand for the implementation of the principle of abstract equality before the law, heralding the gradual transfer of power from the state to civil society and the long-term reduction of transaction costs.

By enforcing the obshchina, the autocracy unwittingly strengthened this organic entity, initially based on collective liability, into a unit of subversion and a practical vehicle of modernization in Tsarist Russia.

During the nineteenth century, the institutional structure set in place in the Petrine era was transformed under the pressure of institutional and technological change occasioned by population increase and the subsequent emancipation of the serfs, paving the way to industrialization spurt of the 1890s. Both of these modernizing processes—the Petrine and the

Nicholaian—as a matter of historical continuity, were Tsarist responses to Russia's military debacles at Narva in 1709 and in the Crimea in 1855, respectively.

Railroad construction lay at the core of Tsarist industrialization efforts from 1837 on. The "iron horse" (Fogel, 1964) facilitated not only troop transfer but also famine relief. In its latter capacity, it played a decisive role in the transition from collectivism to individualism at all levels of the hierarchy.

By absorbing into the Eurasian Empire a technology already applied in Europe—the railroad—the Tsarist state mitigated the rural population's risk of starvation at times of crop failure and created additional opportunities for wage labor in the industrial centers. Both processes attenuated peasant households' existential risk and facilitated cognitive cultural exchange between the rural and the urban milieus. As households became increasingly independent of each other, the communal village's mutual-insurance mechanism had been attenuated. This transition, defined by the North as "informal," anticipated the formal individualization of peasant landholdings—the Stolypin reform—which, in turn, enhanced democratization in the Euroasian Empire.

References

Anisimov, V. E. (1989). *Vremja Petrovskich reform*. Lenizdat.

Anisimov, V. E. (1993). *The reforms of Peter the Great: Progress through coercion in Russia*. Sharpe.

Archer, M. (1995). Realist social theory: The morphogenetic approach. In *Chapter presented at the 6th International Workshop on Institutional Economics*. The University of Hertfordshire.

Ascher, A. (1988). *The revolution of 1905. Part I: Russia in disarray. Part II: Authority restored*. Stanford University Press.

Ascher, A. (2001). P.A. Stolypin. In *The search for stability in Late Imperial Russia*. Stanford University Press.

Atkinson, D. (1983). *The end of the Russian land commune 1905–1930*. Stanford University Press.

Bartlett, R. (1999). Liberty and property, land and freedom: Landownership and agriculture in imperial, Soviet and post-Soviet Russia. In G. Hosking & R. Service (Eds.), *Reinterpreting Russia*. Arnold.

Barzel, Y. (2002). *The theory of the state: Economic rights, legal rights and the scope of the state*. Cambridge University Press.

Bideleux, R. (1990). Agricultural advance under the Russian village commune system. In R. Bartlett (Ed.), *Land commune and peasant community in Russia: Communal forms in Imperial and early Soviet society*. Macmillan in Association with the School of Slavonic and East European Studies, University of London.

Blum, J. (1961). *Lord and peasant in Russia from the ninth to the nineteenth century*. Princeton University Press.

Borodkin, L. J. (2008). Discussion.

Boyer, R., & Orlean, A. (1993). How do conventions evolve? In U. Witt (Ed.), *Evolution in markets and institutions*. Physica-Vlg.

Burds, J. (1998). *Peasant dreams and market politics: Labor migration and the Russian village 1861–1905*. University of Pittsburgh Press.

Chandler, A. (1977). *The visible hand: The managerial revolution in American business*. Belknap Press of Harvard University Press.

Chubarov. (2001). *The fragile empire the History of Imperial Russia*. Continuum.

Coase, R. (1937). *The firm, the market and the law*. University of Chicago Press.

Confino, M. (1997). *Personal communication.*.

Cracraft, P. (2004). *The Petrine revolution in Russian culture*. The Belknap Press of Harvard University Press.

Davydov, M. A. (2003). *Ocherki agrarnoj istorii Rossii v konce XIX-nachale XX VV*. Rossijskij Gosudarstvennyj Gumanitarnyj Universitet.

de Madariaga, I. (1998). *Politics and culture in eighteenth century Russia*. Longman.

Durkheim, E. (1960). *Montesquieu and Rousseau forerunners of sociology*. University of Michigan Press.

EHES conference. (2007). Lund.

Figes, O. (2002). *Natasha's dance: A cultural history of Russia*. Allen Lane, an Imprint of Penguin Books.

Fogel, R. (1964). *Railroads and American economic growth*. Johns Hopkins University Press.

Frank, S. (1999). *Crime, cultural conflict and justice in rural Russia 1856–1914*. University of California Press.

Freeze, L. (1996, June). Subversive piety: Religion and the political crisis in Late Imperial Russia. *Journal of Modern History, 68*(2), 308–350.

Frierson, C. (1990). Land commune and peasant community in Russia: Communal forms in imperial and early Soviet Society. In R. Bartlett (Ed.), *Land commune and peasant community in Russia: Communal forms in imperial and early Soviet Society*. Macmillan in Association with the School of Slavonic and East European Studies, University of London.

Gatrell, P. (1994). *Government, industry and rearmament in Russia, 1900–1914: The Last argument of Tsarism*. Cambridge University Press.

Gaudin, C. (2007). *Ruling peasants: Village and state in Late Imperial Russia*. University Press.

Gerschenkron, A. (1962). *Economic backwardness in historical perspective*. The Belknap Press of Harvard University Press.

Gerschenkron, A. (1968). *Continuity in history and other essays*. The Belknap Press of Harvard University Press.

Gerschenkron, A. (1970). *Europe in the Russian mirror*. Cambridge University Press.

Gintis. (2009). *The Bounds of Reason and the Unification of Behavioural Sciences*. Princeton UP.

Gregory, P. R. (1982). *Russian national income 1885–1913*. Cambridge University Press.

Gregory, P. R. (1994). *Before command. An economic history of Russia from emancipation to the first five-year plan*. Princeton University Press.

Greif, A. (2006). *Institutions and the path to modern economy: Lessons from medieval trade*. Cambridge University Press.

Hartley, J. M. (1999). *A social history of the Russian Empire 1650–1826*. Longman.

Hayek, F. A. (1944). *The road to serfdom*. Routledge.

Hesse, G. (1993). Land use systems and property rights. Evolutionary versus institutional economics. In U. Witt (Ed.), *Evolution in markets and institutions*. Physica-Vlg.

Hobson, J. M., & Weiss, L. (1995). *States and economic development: A comparative historical analysis*. Polity Press.

Hoch, S. (1986). *Serfdom and social control in Russia. Petrovskoe, a village in Tambov*. University of Chicago Press.

Hodgson, G. M. (2004). What are institutions? From orders to organizations. In *Essay presented at the 6th International Workshop on Institutional Economics*. University of Hertfordshire.

Hosking, G. (1997). *Russia: People and empire 1552–1917*. Harvard University Press.

Hughes, L. (1998). *Russia in the age of Peter the Great*. Yale University Press.

Johnson, R. (1979). *Peasant and proletarian: The working class of Moscow in the late nineteenth century*. Leicester University Press.

Kahan, A. (1985). *The plow, the hammer and the knout: An economic history of eighteenth-century Russia*. University of Chicago Press.

Kahan, A. (1989). *Russian economic history: The nineteenth century* (R. Weiss, Ed.). University of Chicago Press.

Kingston-Mann, E. (1991). Peasant communes and economic innovation: A preliminary inquiry. In E. Kingston-Mann, T. Mixter, & J. Burds (Eds.), *Peasant economy culture and politics of European Russia*. Princeton University Press.

Klimin, I. I. (2002). *Stolypinskaya agrarnaya reforma i stanovlenie krestian sobstvennikov v Rossii*. Csentr istoricheskich i gumanitarnych issledovani 'Klio'.

Kolchin, P. (1987). *Unfree labour, American slavery and Russian Serfdom*. The Belknap Press of Harvard University Press.

Lal, D. (1998). *Unintended consequences: The impact of actor endowments, culture, and politics on long run economic performance*. MIT Press.
Leonard, C. S. (1990). Landlords and the mir: Transaction costs and economic development in pre-emancipation Russia (Iaroslav Gubernia). In R. Bartlett (Ed.), *Land commune and peasant community in Russia: Communal forms in imperial and early Soviet society*. Macmillan in Association with the School of Slavonic and East European Studies, University of London.
Macey, D. (1987). *Government and peasant in Russia 1861–1906: The prehistory of the Stolypin reforms*. Northern Illinois University Press.
Macey, D. (1990). The peasant commune and the Stolypin reforms: Peasant attitudes, 1906–14. In R. Bartlett (Ed.), *Land commune and peasant community in Russia: Communal forms in imperial and early Soviet society*. Macmillan in Association with the School of Slavonic and East European Studies, University of London.
Martens, B. (2004). *The cognitive mechanics of economic development and institutional change*. Routledge.
McCloskey, D. (2009). *Talk on bourgeois ethics*. Economic History Seminar, Lund University, February 23.
Migdal, J. (1988). *Strong societies and weak states. State–society relations and state capabilities in the Third World*. Princeton University Press.
Milov, L. (2001). *Velikorusskii pakhar i osobennosti rossijskogo istoricheskogo protsessa*. Biblioteka Gumer-istoria. http://www.gumer.info/bibliotek_Buks/History/milov/01.php
Mironov, B. N. (1999). *Socialnaya istoria Rossii perioda Imperii (XVIII-nachalo XX v) genezis lichnosti demokraticheskoj semii grazhdanskogo obshchestva i pravovogo gosudarstva: v dwuch tomach*. Dimitrij Bulanin.
Mironov, B. N. (2000). *A social history of imperial Russia, 1700–1917* (Vol. I). Westview Press.
Mironov, B. N. (2008). Nablijudalsia li v pozdnie imperskoj Rossii Malthusianskij krizis; Dochody i povinnosti Rossijskogo krestianstva, v 1801–1914. Given by LJ Borodkin.
Mokyr, J. (1990). *Lever of riches. Technological creativity and economic progress*. Oxford University Press.
Moon, D. (1999). *The Russian peasantry 1600–1930. The world the peasants made*. Longman.
Nee, V. (1998). Norms and networks in economic and organisational performance. *The American Economic Review, 8*(2), 85–89.
Nefedov, C. A. (2008). Ob prichinach Russkoj revolutsii. Given by LJ Borodkin.
North, D. C. (1973). *Västerlandets Uppgång*. SNS.
North, D. C. (1981). *Structure and change in economic history*. WW Norton and Company.

North, D. C. (1990). *Institutions, institutional change and economic performance*. Cambridge University Press.
North, D. C. (2005). *Understanding the process of economic change*. Princeton University Press.
Owen. (1991). *The Corporation Under the Russian Law1800–1917*. Cambridge UP.
Owen, T. (1995). *Russian corporate capitalism from Peter the Great to perestroika*. Oxford University Press.
Pallot, J. (1999). *Land reform in Russia 1906–1917: Peasant responses to Stolypin's project of rural transformation*. Clarendon Press.
Paltseva. (2008). *Lecture on Post Soviet absence of democratization financed by the nationalized export of natural commodity*. Lund university.
Petrovich, M. B. (1968). The peasant in nineteenth century historiography. In W. Vucinich (Ed.), *The peasant in nineteenth-century Russia*. Stanford University Press.
Pipes, R. (1995). *Russia under the old regime*. Penguin Books.
Pipes, R. (1999). *Property and freedom*. Harvill Press.
Poznanski, K. (1985). *The environment for technological change in centrally planned economies*. World Bank Staff Working Papers.
Poznanski, K. (1992). A property rights perspective on the evolution of communist-type economies. In K. Poznanski (Ed.), *Constructing capitalism. The re-emergence of civil society and liberal economy in the post-Communist world*. Westview Press.
Radzinskij, E. (2007). *Alexander II Zhyzn I Smert*. Act Izdatelstvo.
Radzinskij, E. (2008). *Alexander II-den siste store Tsaren*. Nordsteds.
Raeff, M. (1984). *Understanding Imperial Russia*. Columbia University Press.
Rostow, W. W. (1960). *The stages of economic growth: A non-communist manifesto*. Cambridge University Press.
Scott. (1976). *The Moral Economy of the Peasant-Rebellion and Subsistence in Southeast Asia*. Yale UP.
Sheshinski. (2010). *Limits in Individual Choice*. The Hebrew University of Jerusalem Department of Economics and the Center for the Study of Rationality.
Simms, Y. J. (1977). The crisis in the Russian agriculture at the end of the nineteenth century: A different view. *Slavic Review, 36*(3), 377–398.
Smurova, O. V. (2003). *Niezemledelcheski odkhod krestian v stolitsu I ego vlejanie na transformacjiu kulturnoj tradicji*. Izd-vo Kostromskogo gos. technologich. Universiteta.
Sztern, S. (1994). *Soviet War Economy and Economy According to the Neoclassical Assumptions*. Paper for a seminar in the theory of science, PhD students Course. Departmernt of philosophy Lund university.
Sztern, S. (2008). *A transaction-costs perspective on the nationalization of the Tsarist Russian versus the American railways*. Paper prepared for NIE course, Lund University, Department of Economics.

Sztern, S. (2018). *Steam engine on the rail and landholding system in-nineteenth century Russia*. Lomonosov State University Economic History Seminar, Moscow (in Russian).

Tolstoy, L. (1953). *Voina I Mir*. Goslitizdat.

Treadgold, D. W. (1968). The peasant and religion. In W. S. Vucinich (Ed.), *The peasant in nineteenth century Russia*. Stanford University Press.

Troyat, H. (1961). *Daily life in Russia under the last Tsar*. Stanford University Press.

Volyn. (1970). *A century of Russian Agriculture -From Alexander II to Khrushchev*. Harvard UP.

Westwood, J. N. (1964). *A history of the Russian railways*. George Allen and Unwin.

Winicki, J. (1988). *The distorted world of Soviet-type economies*. Routledge.

Witt. (1993). *Evolution in Markets and Institutions*. Physica-Verlag A Springer Verlag-Company.

Wood, A. (1990). Administrative exile and criminals' commune in Siberia. In R. Bartlett (Ed.), *Land commune and peasant community in Russia: Communal forms in Imperial and early Soviet society*. Macmillan in Association with the School of Slavonic and East European Studies, University of London.

Worobec, C. D. (1990). The post-emancipation Russian peasant commune in Orel province 1861–90. In R. Bartlett (Ed.), *Land commune and peasant community in Russia: Communal forms in imperial and early Soviet society*. Macmillan in Association with the School of Slavonic and East European Studies, University of London.

Worobec, C. D. (1995). *Peasant Russia: Family and community in the post-emancipation period*. Northern Illinois University Press.

Yaney, G. (1973). *The systematization of Russian government: Social evolution in the domestic administration of imperial Russia 1711–1905*. University of Illinois Press.

Zakharova, L. G. (1992). Samoderzhavie i reformy v Rossii 1861–1874. In L. G. Zakharova, B. Eklöf, & D. Z. Bushnell (Eds.), *Velikie reformy v rossii 1856–1874*. Izdatelstvo Moskovskogo Universiteta.

CHAPTER 9

Was Stalin Necessary? Railroads and the Crumbling of the Obshchina in Tsarist Russia

Russian agriculture in Tsarist times was a stagnant, ossified enterprise and its practitioner, the *muzhik* (peasant), was listless, indolent, driven by prejudices, and beholden to the Tsar and the church. As a result, agriculture was trapped with the productivity of the Middle Ages. Only a serious jolt could set the peasant on the way to a more modern way of life and to the adoption of the new technologies that were drifting in from the West. The jolt was administered by Stalin. It may have been harder than it had to have been, even unnecessarily cruel, yet the jolt itself was inescapable. This is a widely accepted view that we propose to refute in this chapter.

The jolt, we contend, was provided by the invasion of modernity, of new technology and industry from the West, in particular the railroad construction that began in the middle of the nineteenth century: the ceremonial farewell to the pre-railroad era in 1837, the first train to the Tsars' summer residence at Tsarskoe Selo, and then the magnificent Moscow–St: Petersburg Nikoljajev Railway. The entry of railroads had a transformative effect on rural society in those parts of Tsardom that it reached, linking the village, which used to be isolated, to the rapidly changing outside world. It showed the peasant that he could improve his miserable life and incentivized him to take his fortune into his own hands. In particular, it

Co-authored with Professor Emeritus Michael Keren, the Hebrew University of Jerusalem

S. Sztern, *Russia on the Move*, Studies in Economic Transition, https://doi.org/10.1007/978-3-030-89285-2_9

sowed the seeds of the wish to be freed from the bonds to the ***obshchina***,[1] the village commune, and the desire for individual landholding in European Russia. We support our claim with evidence from socio-historical sources as well as econometric tests on data that I found and recorded in the course of my graduate research.[2]

The latter material, comprised of ***zemstvo*** (rural self-government) statistics for the Penza Black Earth region in 1913, documents the end of the process that started with the Emancipation and Redemption acts of 1861–1863 and transformed the peasant's mere right to usufruct, inherited from the serfdom era, into gradually expanding private land ownership. By continuing to enforce ***krugovaya poruka***—the mutual liability for taxes, dues, and redemption payments on which the commune was based (Gerschenkron, 1968)—the Tsarist state unintentionally allowed a commitment device (Greif, 2006) to be formed, paving the way to the peasant's exodus from the shackles of the obshchina even before the Stolypin reform of November 9, 1906. The process of privatizing the commune, if I may anticipate the use of that term—was permitted in this context and accelerated after this reform. Thus, significant shares of commune land were converted into privately owned and cultivated plots by the eve of the World War I. Tellingly, the process proceeded most quickly in communes that were close to the newly constructed rail lines.

The important element of insurance in Tsarist-era communal landholding bears repeating. The continental Russian climate—characterized by spells of extreme cold and heat, long dry seasons, and precipitation unpredictable in time and place, with much greater micro-climatic variations among contiguous plots than in the regions to its west—subjected peasants to sharp fluctuations in yields and income. The mir provided them with some promise of assistance in hard times. Peasants needed a reliable substitute before daring to leave the communal home and forgo the accustomed mutual help. The advent of the railroad and the national grain market that it abetted provided this alternative and did much to mitigate the underlying risk. A crop failure in any region still reduced local incomes but made food from other regions available at prices that did not have to skyrocket, mitigating the danger of death from starvation and epidemics.

[1] Below, we also use the term *mir* to denote the village commune that was the primary form of rural organization during the Tsarist period.

[2] Here and below, I use the first-person plural to denote my collaboration with Professor Keren and the first-person singular otherwise.

The peasants noticed the change (Scott, 1976) and felt the community's mutual insurance less and less necessary (Eggertsson, 1990, p. 303; Robbins, 1975, p. 80, map on, p. 89).

The new and affordable means of transport did much more than alleviate hunger. It reduced dependence on risky agriculture by linking the peasantry to the industrializing economy and its possibilities of non-agricultural and urban income, diversifying their budget sources.

Gerschenkron (1962, pp. 120, 121; 1968, p. 196) postulates that the practice of redistributing land and liabilities for variegation in the course of the household's life cycle, based on the inventory of male working hands, prevented adult household members from participating in the industrializing urban economies. We challenge this view, arguing that the new means of transport triggered a change in the peasant's view of the world. His environment was no longer the old unchanging scene of his ancestors. Choice entered his life; he could now question the patriarchal authority that underlay the inherited village-commune structure and shift from blind obedience to authority to rational deliberation (Gintis, 2009, p. 1ff; Sheshinski, 2010, p. 3). The decline in travel time reduced the cognitive distance between the rural periphery and the strange urban life and its divergent spiritual and legal cultures, allowing peasants to resort to the *volost'* (cantonal) court system for dispute resolution. This enhanced peasants' self-esteem and dignity and strengthened their property rights, both real and perceived (Gaudin, 2007, p. 103fff, Tables 3.3, 3.4; Burbank, 2004, p. 18ff). It also enabled them to acquire literacy and new skills. The gains in productivity brought on by the acquisition of these novel endowments (Burds, 1998, p. 177) and the accompanying reduction of transaction costs enhanced returns on investments in land and human capital. This, in a virtuous cycle, insured against starvation during famines and other calamities and expedited the transition to hereditary household property.

By enhancing national market formation and price convergence, the railroads fostered specialization in grain and other commodities. In the short run, this disruptive innovation raised transaction costs; in the longer term, however, it mitigated the uncertainty of these costs and ultimately lowered them due to the regime's consent to delegate tangible and intangible property rights to its subjects, as codified in the Stolypin reform (Martens, 2004, p. 193). This transfer of property rights—entailing the shift of political rights to citizens and making them subjects no longer (Pipes, 1999, p. xiii)—abetted the transformation of Tsarist Russia into a constitutional monarchy. Furthermore, the new technology weakened the veneration of the Tsar and the Church, the two institutions that had done the most to hold the Russian empire together and that used to have an unshakable grip on the countryside. This catalyzed the dissolution of the personalized hierarchies of coercion that had cantilevered on the anointed Tsar's authority.

These fundamental social and economic changes could not but leave their imprint on the Russian polity; they are likely to have contributed to the events of 1905 and even 1917. Here, however, we concern ourselves with a more limited sphere—the Russian village commune and its social organization, as embodied in the evolving forms of landholding.

If our contention is correct, we would expect the effects of the railroads to be most salient in the regions that benefited the most from them, namely, those most accessible to them. Fortunately, I found a dataset for a northern *czernozem* (Black Earth) region (Moon, 1999, Map 41, Lomonosov State University 2008 Seminar): the Penza Province; the set includes information on the distance from railway stations of clusters of villages and the distribution of fifteen landholding types that emerged between the emancipation (1861) and 1913, seven years after the Stolypin reform began. To our surprise, we found that the newly introduced ownership forms had taken root in many places there. A simple regression analysis establishes that the distance of a village from the rail station is a significant explanatory variable. It is quite remarkable that fundamental long-term social and economic changes that required statutory revisions for their implementation could be observed in such a brief span of time.

These findings run counter to accepted views of Russian agrarian development among historians, including such venerated names as Gerschenkron. And they touch upon a greater topic in Soviet economic development: Was Stalin necessary? This question was first asked by Nove in 1964, and following him, we have first to clarify exactly what it means. We are not interested at any kind of logical or circumstantial necessity; we are not asking whether the Soviets had no choice in adopting their development policies. Nor are we interested in the question that Nove (1992) debated extensively: Given the internal party politics and external Russian situation that he faced in the second half of the 1920s, did Stalin have any choice? Our question, rather, is whether, without his ruthless policies, Russian conservative rural society would not have remained dormant and stuck in the social rut of the technological practices and economic organization inherited from its feudal past. What our findings show is that, given the opportunity, Russian muzhiks, or at least a considerable number of their class, were ready to give up their traditional attachments and to adopt with gusto new institutions and invest in growth. In other words, there would have been progress without Stalin. He was not necessary.

Our research complements that of Cheremukhin et al. (2013) who, relying on macroeconomic data, find that up to 1940, given Tsarist growth trends, Soviet policies impeded growth and slowed the immanent economic advance. They believe that Tsarist agricultural development was held up by the shackles imposed by the institutions of the obshchina. We show, however, that these obstacles tended to melt away in those regions that were served by rail. In other words, with the spread of new means of transport agrarian growth would have accelerated.

We come back to this problem in the concluding section of this chapter. Here we proceed to alternative readings of Russian rural history and then describe the evolution of landholdings during the Tsarist period and present statistical evidence for the social influences of the new means of transport. Once this is done, we elaborate on the data from Penza Province that allowed us to test the hypothesis and then move on to the econometric regressions. We wind up by summarizing the findings and expanding on the problem of "Stalin's necessity".

Alternative and Complementary Theories of Russian Rural History

Alexander Gerschenkron, in his seminal work (1962, 1968), posits that for latecomers, the periphery—the peasantry in our case—is unable to initiate development; only the state can start the engine of growth. His conceptualization of the Tsarist village commune, the obshchina, depicts this institution as set in its ways throughout the post-emancipation period. In his view, the commune was shaped by a Tsarist tax extraction method. To simplify collection, a poll tax was imposed on the whole village and divided among households whose payment ability was "homogenized" by periodic repartitioning of the commune's land. The peasant was bound to this commune by habit, even after emancipation (Gerschenkron, 1968, pp. 271, 276). Yet our findings show that the peasant was not tied to the obshchina by shackles that could be broken only by a central authority. His bonds, hallowed by tradition though they were, derived their utility from the environment of their time and could therefore change with circumstances. The commune offered him mutual insurance and "fair" fiscal liabilities in exchange for unstable use rights and tenuous landownership. The real cost of these utilities was low productivity and immobility. We show that the post-emancipation commune was irreversibly transformed by its interaction with the railroads, into an increasingly individualist hereditary household farm system. This encouraged investment in land and human capital, raising peasant productivity and providing peasants with mobility to benefit from employment in the nascent industrial sector. This also adds doubt to the thesis that the Tsarist tax extraction that financed industrialization impoverished the peasantry and triggered the 1905 upheaval (see Chap. 8). Our empirical tests indicate clearly that Stolypin's reform (1906–1917) must have codified a spontaneous and voluntary, if hardly noticed, adaptation to the opportunities and choices that had been going on among the European Russian peasantry since the railroads began their inroads.

Pallot (1999) claims that Stolypin's reform was imported from Bismarck's Germany (Ascher, 2001, p. 2) and implemented by a coercive bureaucracy in expectation of increasing productivity through the dissolution of the commune. The negative correlation that we found between distance to railroads and individual peasant landholdings, however, shows that economic factors unrelated to the bureaucracy were at play. This squares with the findings of Gregory (1994, 1982) and Simms (1977), who call attention to informal peasants' transactions within the formal framework of the commune (Gregory, p. 52) that accompanied the rising agricultural standards of living and labor mobility that industrialization facilitated. The transformation is observable in the upward movement labor mobility, the decline of the share of agriculture in NNP, and the corresponding proportional growth of industry (Gregory, 1982, pp. 133, 134). Yet Gregory, Simms, and Gerschenkron all disregard the impact of the railroads on the Tsarist landholding system. We introduce this missing link in our explanation of the modernization of post-emancipation Tsarist Russia.

Nafziger (2007, p. 22), regressing yield per acre on land repartitions, finds a negative correlation between the frequency of land rotation, namely, instability in land ownership, and productivity. That is, the more frequently the land was redistributed, the lower was the yield per acre. We show that proximity to the railroads made land rotation less frequent. By mating the two findings, we infer that increased access to railroads led to a rise in land productivity in the form of larger yields per acre. Nafziger

(2010, pp. 390, 391, 393, Table 4) also finds support for Gregory's and Simms's observation that, despite constraints imposed by the commune, peasant households reacted to mortality shocks by conducting transactions inside the village but outside the communal system. These dealings involved leasing land (reallocating allotment land when the commune failed to do so), hiring labor, and looking for work outside the commune and even outside agriculture. By revealing significant flexibility in the communal collectivism in this manner, Nafziger's regressions cast doubt on Gerschenkron's claim of inertia in the commune's practice that supposedly impeded industrialization. Our findings complement Nafziger's by revealing the factor that ultimately attenuated the grip of collectivist custom that was the backbone of the commune: the railroads.

Burbank (2004, pp. 18, 19) highlights an upturn in peasant attendance in courtrooms in locations near railroads. This dovetails with our thesis. Her work does, however, lack a satisfactory explanation of the mechanisms behind the peasants' growing demand for and access to the law for the protection of their property and the enforcement of their personal rights. We attribute this, too, to the effect of peasants' exposure to the wider environment through the socially disruptive medium of the rails.

Russian Landholding Modalities from Peter to Stolypin

Until 1714, all landownership among nobles was conditioned on service to the state (*pomestie*). Peter's reform transformed this practice into the Tsarist concession of the *votchina* (patrimonium), which benefitted the nobles by granting them allodial property. Until the emancipation, in contrast, peasants needed their landlords' authorization even to take a walk in excess of thirty versts, approx. Thirty-three kilometers (Blum, 1961); what is more, their labor was subject to obligations that in effect sent them back to serfdom (Hughes, 1998, p. 161, quoting Kahan). Thus, serfs in Tambov, a black-earth province close to Penza—a region that we showcase below—and in other communities were tied to the person of the landlord (Hoch, 1986, pp. 91, 133). As for peasants' land, until the emancipation it was all allotment land that belonged to the *votchinnik pomeshchik* (landlord) (Hoch, 1986, p. 16). This preceded Peter and his reform. The 1714 reform concerned the holdings of the nobility. Although peasant households (*dvor*) held farmsteads and buildings (*usad'ba*) in perpetuity (Hoch and Worobec, 1995, p. 21), their hereditary property rights were limited to the "residential and storage portion" of the farmstead (Hoch, 1986, pp. 16, 117; Hughes, 1998, p. 138; North, 1990, p. 91).[3] Arable allotment land conferred temporary use rights and was periodically redistributed commensurate with changes in the number of *tyagla* (labor units) per household, usually meaning an extended household[4]; harvests from redistributed allotment land belonged to the household (Hoch, 1986, p. 16). The average peasant landholding was 60 *desyatinas* (1 desyatina = 1.092 hectares) or 15 *desyatinas* per head of population (1766 Survey Instructions; Bartlett, 1999 in Service & Hosking, 1999, p. 76). Landlords also gave members of peasant communes equal access to pastures, meadows, and estate woodlands. In return, serfs commonly had to remit dues in cash (*obrok*) (Hughes, 1998, p. 168) or, alternatively, in *barshchina* (corvée labor) in the demesne for the right to work an allotment of arable land. In *chernozem* (black-earth) areas that were oriented to agriculture, barshchina had been customary; in non-black-earth provinces oriented to crafts, *obrok* (quitrent) constituted the customary obligation (Moon, 1999, p. 8). In 1722–1880, a flat-rate poll tax (*podushnaya podac*) was levied against each male and against the household (Hughes, 1998, p. 138; Bartlett, 1999 in Service & Hosking, 1999, p. 77). To enhance the peasantry's taxpaying capacity while reducing their own surveillance costs, landlords enforced the egalitarian ethos of the commune by imposing the aforementioned mutual liability for taxes and dues.

Catherine II's era brought further changes. That period of time was characterized by two countervailing tendencies: territorial expansion that increased the land–labor ratio and the share of serfs in the population, and the influx of Enlightenment ideas. After the 1773–1774 Pugachev rebellion, Catherine promulgated the Charter to the Nobles (1785), thereby acknowledging her dependence on their loyalty (Pipes, 1999, p. 192). The transfer of authority from state to landlords under the Charter intensified the depth and extent of serfdom (de Madariaga, 1998, p. 124). An additional charter, pertaining to a limited category of state peasants, did reflect Enlightenment ideas imported from the West, including recognition of a form of peasant property rights, the right to "travel freely in and

[3] Keren (2007) suggests that this practice constituted an adaptation to the poll tax.

[4] Comprising an able-bodied male, his wife, and, at times, a draft animal (Worobec, 1995, 22).

out of town" for even the meanest of villagers (*poselyane*), and immunity from dispossession without a trial by peers (the *nizhnyj zemskij sud*) (de Madariaga, 1998, p. 87). This charter, however, was a draft that was informally debated but never promulgated.

We have already discussed the impact of the introduction of railroads by the Tsarist state, which started in 1837. Recapitulating, the novelty reduced, inter alia, risks of mass starvation due to famine and peasant vulnerability to catastrophes; provided peasants with an alternative means of insurance that could replace the serfs' mutual insurance, with landlords as lenders of last resort (Engelgardt in Frierson, 1993, p. 39); and induced population increase due to lower mortality occasioned by the railroad-facilitated control of the lethal effects of famines and epidemics. Under these structural conditions, the Russian debacle in the Crimean War (1855) laid bare the irrationality of serfdom to landlords and tenants alike, paving the way to the Emancipation and Redemption statutes of 1861–1863 (Gerschenkron, 1962, p. 131; Leonard in Bartlett, 1990, p. 317). This reform established peasants' theoretical equality before the law, abolished bondage, and made landownership contingent on local arrangements that allowed peasants to redeem their allotments (Gerschenkron, 1968, pp. 153, 154, 175; Leonard, 2011, pp. 38, 39). The new statutes also allowed the peasant to purchase *vykup* (allotment land). In the initial stage of the reform, the *ustavnye gramoty* (charters) created a *nadel* allotment—a subsistence quantity of pasture, arable land, and meadows for perpetual use—to peasant households (Leonard, 2011, p. 40; Gerschenkron, 1968, p. 172). Next, landlords were to sign agreements (*vykupnye zdelki*) with former serf tenants concerning 20–25 percent of the land, usually the farmstead. The remaining 75–80 percent, comprising arable land, was usually purchased from landlords by the state for redemption by the peasantry over a forty-nine-year period at 6 percent quitrent value (Leonard, 2011, pp. 40, 41; Gerschenkron, 1968, pp. 174, 176).

The obshchina constituted an administrative unit that required a two-thirds majority vote for decisions on land redistribution or on a household's exit from the commune (Gerschenkron, 1968, p. 188). According to Article 165 of the Redemption statute, a peasant household could obtain such permission only after it had paid all redemption arrears (p. 187). This arrangement allowed communes to perpetuate their jurisdiction over household landholdings for another forty-nine years.

The Stolypin reforms, legislated on November 9, 1906, put an end to redemption payments in 1907 and restructured the privatization of landholdings until it was stopped by World War I (Atkinson, 1983, p. 44). The law codified the privatization of land holdings by turning it into the hereditary ownership of the *bolshak* (head of household). Such holdings included previously allotted land that entered the process of *ukreplienie*—establishment of the head of household's entitlement to property rights in land; tradable within the peasant estate, that could serve as collateral for loans from the Peasant Land Bank. By legalizing individual household heads' right of title to their allotted landholdings, the Stolypin reform further mitigated the risk that an individual peasant assumed by leaving the village commune and effectively dissolved the commune (Gaudin, 2007, p. 43). It is noteworthy that titled land was the personal property of the *bolshak* and not of the household members at large. Insofar as the household left land fallow due to changes in land–labor ratios, the Stolypin ukase allowed the head of household to sell it instead of returning it to the commune as theretofore. Requests for land consolidation—the merger of scattered strips into a single parcel at the time of a general repartition—could not be rejected by the commune. In a subsequent decree (June 14, 1910), communes that had not repartitioned since the emancipation were allowed to convert members' holdings into hereditary household ownership by simple majority vote. The Stolypin reform allowed the formation of *otruba* (individual household farms within existing obshchina settlements) and *khutora* (the same but outside the village boundaries) (Pallot, 1999, p. 62). As explained above, titled land restricted the peasantry's relative property rights because it could not be sold outside of the peasant estate and could be mortgaged only at the Peasant Land Bank.

Table 9.1 shows the structure of land holdings in 1913, just before the outbreak of World War I. It includes only those ownership forms that represent more than 5 percent of total land area in my sample of the Penza dataset (below) but cover all but 5 percent of the total land area, showing they were the only forms that proved attractive to a significant share of the peasantry. (See Appendix for the full table.) Nearly two-thirds of the cultivated area were still repartitioned allotment land. Nearly 10 percent were allotment land, redeemed under the Emancipation and Redemption acts, and nearly 16 percent were acquired under the Stolypin reforms, but much of this was strip land, tilled collectively. The remaining 13 percent were individually owned under the Stolypin reforms and individually cultivated.

Table 9.1 Land categories, 1913

Major category	*Designation, Russian*	*Meaning*	*Year of origin*	*Legal origin*	*% in total area, 1913*	*Total*
Allotment land	Nadelnaya razverstannaya, razpredelonnaya	Allotment rotating, periodically repartitioned	1649	Serfdom	69.0	80.3
	Nadel ukreplienie 9 November Czerezpolositsa razpredelonnaya	Entitled allotment. Redistributed stripfarmed land	1906	Stolypin reform	7.3	
Non allotment land	Vnenadelnaya kollektivnaya	Non-allotment collectively managed land	1906–1917	Stolypin reform onwards	10.2	19.7
	Vnenadelnyj Yedinolichnyj Otrub	Non-allotment individually owned consolidated parcel	1906–1917	Stolypin reform onwards	7.7	

Source: Appendix Table 10.1. Only categories that account for more than 1 percent of land area are included

In sum, fifteen types of landholdings existed in 1913. Only one (allotted land) predated the emancipation. Emancipation and redemption introduced the redemption of allotment land. The Stolypin reform (1906) established the concept of individual entitlement to non-allotted and previously allotted land. Property rights, which in 1785 were transferred from the Tsarist votchina to the nobles, were handed to heads of household in 1906.

Evidence of the Socioeconomic Effects of the Railroads

Although comprehensive time-series data are not available, shorter-term tables in Atkinson (1983) reveal changes in the structure of holdings during the Stolypin reform (1907–1913) and indicate that the reform must have been preceded by spontaneous informal individualization, in consequence of changes in the environment, such as the arrival of railroads.

The tables below provide selected examples. We see from the data on personal appropriations of communal allotment land in 1907–1915 that the mass applications for land title and completed household land appropriations took place in the early stages of the Stolypin reform (1908–1909) (Tables 9.2 and 9.3). The mass applications for land title—the documented swarm-like demand for exodus from the commune—indicate that commune members had made up their minds before, namely, that their habits of thoughts had been changing before 1906. Our cross-section results for the Penza region (below) indicate that the most extreme changes occurred in locations most susceptible to the inroads of the railroads.

The median household allotment in 1765–1900 was 5–15 desyatins (Loewe in Bartlett, 1990, p. 181). According to Atkinson (1983, p. 28), the post-emancipation subsistence allotment was 5–6 desyatins (5.5–6.5 hectares) per male soul. The average per-soul allotment at the time of the emancipation to seigniorial serfs (40 percent of the total) was 3.3 desyatins (about 3.5 hectares). Peasants cultivating state lands were in better condition, holding 5.6 desyatins on average; appanage peasants belonging to the imperial family held 4.1 desyatins (Moon, 1999, p. 22). Therefore, the average appropriation corresponds to the average allotments, since most households had more than one male soul.

Table 9.2 Personal appropriation of communal allotment land 1907–1915 (thirty-nine provinces of European Russia and Stavropol Province)

Year	*Applications for appropriation ('000)*	*Appropriations completed ('000)*	*Land appropriated ('000 desyatins[a])*	*Average land per appropriation (desyatins)*
1907	212	48	4316	7.7
1908	840	508		
1909	650	579	4115	7.1
1910	342	342	2303	6.7
1911	242	145	996	6.8
1912	152	122	785	6.4
1913	160	134	1907	5.5
1914	120	98	594	6.1
1915	37	30	267	9.0
Total	2755	2008	14,123	7.0

Source: Atkinson (1983, Table 7, p. 76)

[a]1 desyatina = 1.092 hectares

Table 9.3 Certifications of personal ownership of communal allotment land, 1910–1915 (thirty-nine provinces of European Russia and Stavropol)

	Issued to communes				*Issued to individual heads of household*		
Year	*Number*	*Number of households*	*Land ('000 desyatins)*	*Avg. land certificate per household*	*Number*	*Land ('000 desyatins)*	*Avg. land certificate per household*
1910	69	1429	12	8.5	6787	45	6.6
1911	2623	75,356	460	6.1	91,894	526	5.7
1912	1626	36,756	248	6.7	71,920	424	5.9
1913	571	26,367	176	6.7	71,392	390	5.5
1914	432	10,368	65	6.3	54,915	287	5.2
1915	84	2627	28	10.5	19,981	135	6.7
Total	5405	152,903	989	6.5	316,889	1.807	5.7

Source: Atkinson (1983, p. 78; Table 8)

It seems to have been the pre-reform codification of landholdings, the de facto transition to hereditary household ownership, that gave rise to the massive appropriation of communal allotment land in 1907–1909. This process petered out in 1910–1914 (Table 9.3). Thus, all land that had been used de facto in hereditary tenure before the Stolypin reform became entitlement land once the reform began. The process slowed because the remaining land was less valuable and its potential purchasers, hereditary households, preferred land rotation for fiscal-insurance purposes (Burds, 1998, pp. 125, 133, Table 5.2).

Table 9.3 documents the issuance of land titles in response to applications (*ukreplenie*) submitted by communes by means of their assembly (left-hand side) or submitted personally by individual heads of household (right-hand side). The communes' applications indicate that there had been such a "majority aspiration in waiting during the post-Emancipation era" (Macey, 1998, p. 162) that had been legalized and released through the Stolypin reform, which explains the clustering of title issues in the second stage of the reform (1911–1912) (Macey, 1998, p. 162). The individualization process was disrupted by World War I, applications and title issues plummeting by 64 percent among heads of household and 81 percent among communes. In wartime, evidently, the communal resource pool and mutual insurance delivered greater marginal utility than the entitlement that commune members might claim upon their return from conscription (Johnson, 1979, p. 37ff; Burds, 1998, pp. 125, 133, Table 5.2).

These arguments are corroborated by the data on changes in peasant landholdings in 1905–1915—between the 1905 revolution and the formal inception of the reform in 1906 and the first full year of World War I (Table 9.4). During this decade, the share of allotment (periodically rotating) land held by communes in total peasant land declined by 15 percent while that held by individuals rose by over a quarter. Thus, the commune initially served as a risk internalization device, allowing greater risk-taking in the transition to individual household tenure in the 60 percent share of peasant land that was held in communal tenure. The share of peasant land

Table 9.4 Changes in peasant landholding, 1905–1915

	All peasant land		*Land held by communes*	
Category and date	*Amount (million desyatins)*	*Percent of total*	*Amount (million desyatins)*	*Percent of all peasant land*
1905				
Allotment land	138.8	85%	115.4	83%
Private land, owned by:				
Communes	3.7	2	3.7	
Associations	7.6	5	–	–
Individuals	13.2	8	–	–
Total	163.3	100%	119.1	73%
1915				
Allotment land	138.8	80%	99.0	71%
Private land, owned by:				
Communes	4.6	3	4.6	100
Associations	12.9	7	–	–
Individuals	16.8	10	–	–
Total	173.1	100%	103.6	60%

Source: Atkinson (1983, p. 83, Table 9)

held by associations and individuals rose by 40 percent during that decade, another indication of flexibility of peasant landholding arrangements (Eggertsson, 1990, p. 303). These data may challenge Pallot's conception (1999, p. 75) of the commune as an obstacle to land-tenure individualization. Paradoxically, the risk-internalizing functions of the commune, on which Pallot focuses, served as an institutional novelty diffusion mechanism (Kingston-Mann, 1991, pp. 43, 44–45). Once the commune assembly decided by a two-thirds majority (Worobec, 1995; Moon, 1999) to transform communally held allotment land into hereditary tenure or privately held communal land, clusters of households turned to achieving mutual insurance via cooperative cultivation rather than risking going it alone by leaving the commune altogether.

The share of total peasant land held by communes declined by 15 percentage points in 1905–1915. This downturn is explained by the acquisition of land title by associations and individuals and the transition to privately held communal land.

Table 9.5 reveals a shift in ownership of privately held gentry land to the peasantry. Individually and collectively held private peasant land increased by some 40 percent. This shift is explained by peasants' acquisition of gentry landholdings, rendering the total share of privately held land unchanged. It is evident from this source that the peasants, privatization notwithstanding, still preferred to cultivate much of their privately owned land collectively. This may be due to the prevalence of small strip-farmed plots that can be best cultivated collectively. This observation is corroborated by the higher frequency of collective cultivation than of individual cultivation in modern privately held non-allotment land, as the share of total land in our Penza data from 1913 shows.

Table 9.6 shows the relation between the price of land and the percentage of households that appropriated their plots. It is easily seen that the

Table 9.5 Private landholding, 1905–1915 (million desyatins)

Type of land	*1905*	*1915*
All privately owned land	97.9	97.9
Private land held by peasants thereof:	24.6	34.4
Individually	13.2	16.8
Collectively	11.4	17.5

Source: Atkinson (1983, p. 84, Table 10)

Table 9.6 Regional land prices and appropriations of communal land, 1906–1914

Great Russian communal provinces	*Size of average holding (desyatins)*	*Average price of land per desyatin in 1806–1808 (rubles)*	*Percent of households appropriating by 1914*
I southern steppe	8.5	172	40%
II Volga central agricultural	7.7	122	22%
III central industrial and North west	9.4	76	17%
IV border provinces	18.5	33	7%

Source: Atkinson (1983, p. 86, Table 11)

higher the price of land, the larger was the proportion going private. Unfortunately, we have just four items; therefore, this information cannot be generalized. Yet it does give an indication that the more productive the land, the more likely were peasants to leave the embrace of the commune. Proximity to railroads was not the only factor that may have raised land prices, but it was a strong one.

Finally, can we see any economic results of this social upheaval? Recent estimates of growth in agricultural inputs and outputs by Leonard (2011) show a remarkable jump in both inputs and outputs during the first decade of the nineteenth century, which indicate an increase of close to 3.5 percent in total factor productivity following decades of negative productivity growth (Table 9.7). "TFP grows positive in the era just before World War I and revolution," Leonard (2011, p. 30) remarks, "suggesting continuous growth involving structural change rather than simply additions to inputs." It may be hasty to extrapolate for a single decade, but it does seem that the changes taking place under the surface had started to have serious economic results at last.

The Data

The source of our data is the rural self-government statistics for the Penza Province in 1913, which professional statisticians regard as the most reliably gathered source of its kind (Davydov, 2008, personal communication). This type of collection, compiled annually since the adoption of the

Table 9.7 Average annual growth rate (%) of output and per-capita output per agricultural worker (labor productivity and total factor productivity, 1870–1913), 1913 prices

	Average annual growth (%)			
Period	*Gross agricultural production*	*Gross production per capita*	*Gross production per worker*	*Total factor productivity*
(1)	*(2)*	*(3)*	*(4)*	*(5)*
1861–1871	0.22	-0.4	-0.4	-0.28
1871–1881	3.26	1.68	1.81	0.42
1881–1891	2.55	1.03	1.11	-2.75
1891–1901	3.25	1.45	1.56	-3.54
1901–1911	4.8	3.13	3.34	3.46

Source: Columns (1)–(4): Leonard (2011, p. 20, Table 1), Keren. Column (5): calculated from Table 5 in Leonard (2011, p. 29. Table 5). Caption retained from source, Table 1 (Bb, the agreement regarding the period between the caption and the table is not complete

zemstvo law in 1864, should be available for all fifty *gubernias* (regions) in European Russia. The dataset, which I found on the advice of Davydov, contains, inter alia, records of land ownership in 1913 and distances to railroad stations. It is not clear to us whether the annual zemstvo statistics for other provinces also report these statistics.

My Penza dataset includes data for groups of obshchinas (village communes) aggregated in a *selenie*, an administrative unit that we abbreviate as *selo*. Villages in a selo had several common facilities, one of which is a railroad station. Thus, in the file of the Archangelskaya *volost* (canton), part of the Kerenskii *uezd* (district), we find, under the subtitle "*Spravochnaya Svedenia o Seleniach*" ("Certified witnessed data") that the railroad station closest to the Alexieevka *selenie* is 30 kilometers away. Apart from the distance, the dataset includes many other details that do not concern us at the present stage, such as the name of the closest township, the distance, and the number of windmills in the selo.

For each selo, we have data on the obshchinas that belong to it. These include statistics on the types of landholdings in each obshchina, as well as communal village tables that document the peasants' living conditions, the number of "souls" of both genders, and so on. Since the distance from the railroad station is given per selo while the data on the *zemlevladenie* (landholding system) is given per obshchina, we aggregated all the land areas by landholding type in *a selo*. We used the percentage of each land type in each selo observation as the dependent variable and the distance as the explanatory variable.

We registered our data in two steps. First, I registered a sample of two randomly selected cantons (*volosti*) in each of the nine districts (*uezds*) that account for 90 percent of the *uezds* in the Penza region. This sample contains about 100 pairs of randomly chosen obshchinas for each volost and adds up to 2202 obshchinas grouped in selo observations, around 10 percent of the dataset. On this basis we hoped to determine whether our hypothesis, that the structure of ownership is influenced by distance from rail transport, finds support in these data. To our surprise, it did.[5] We then continued by recording the full set; the outcome of our tests on it is reported below. This two-step method absolved us from the accusation charge of data mining: Our first step served as exploratory analysis and the second one, which used the simple equations of the first, as the confirmatory stage.

Table 9.8 uses the Alexieevka selo to illustrate how the data were aggregated. In this case, only four types of landholding were common enough to merit econometric testing.[6] Three of these types are allotment land: rotating allotment land (Type 1 in the Appendix Table), Stolypin allotment land in scattered strips distributed to the village (Type 7 in the Appendix Table), and Stolypin allotment land in scattered strips bought by the village (Type 8 in the Appendix Table).

The fourth type is a form of non-allotment land: individual scattered strips. Examining the percent share of the total area of non-allotment land and comparing it with the share of non-allotment scattered strips (Type 14 in the Appendix Table), we find a slight discrepancy of less than 0.01 desyatinas, indicating the existence of another type of individual non-allotment land: the non-allotment individual consolidated parcel (Type 15 in the Appendix Table). In other words, *for this selo*, the share of the land types missing in the table is insignificant.

[5] The results of this exploratory stage were reported in the biannual EACES congress in Budapest and the First International Conference on Comparative Economics in Rome in 2015.

[6] Our full dataset also includes only four non-identical types of prevalent ownership.

Table 9.8 Example—aggregation of villages into *Selo* data performed by Professor Michael Keren

Column 1	*Village 1*	*Village 2*	*Village 3*	*Village 4*	*Village 5*	*Village 6*	*Selo, total*
Households holding rotating allotment land	18	4	47	99	9	159	336
Area of rotating allotment land	96.46	0.17	134.44	737.35	139.44	1011.4	2119.26
% of total area of *selo*							91.08
Households holding Stolypin allotment land scattered strips, distributed to village	4	0	6	8	1	15	34
Area of Stolypin allotment land scattered strips, distributed to village	27.82	0	17.16	36.87	22.46	76.49	180.8
% of total area of *selo*							7.77
Households holding Stolypin allotment land scattered strips, bought by village	1	0	0	1	0	1	3
Area of Stolypin allotment land scattered strips, bought by village	4.8	0	0	8.57	0	8.57	21.94
% of total area of *selo*							0.94
Households holding allotment land, total	21	4	53	105	10	172	365
Total area of allotment land held	129.08	0.17	151.6	782.79	161.9	1096.46	2322
% of total area of *selo*							**99.79**

(*continued*)

Table 9.8 (continued)

Column 1	*Village 1*	*Village 2*	*Village 3*	*Village 4*	*Village 5*	*Village 6*	*Selo, total*
Households holding non-allotment individually scattered strips	0	0	0	2	0	2	4
Area of non-allotment individually scattered strips	0	0	0	2.43	0	2.43	4.86
% of total area of *selo*							0.21
Households holding non-allotment individually scattered strips, total	0	0	0	2	0	2	4
Total area of non-allotment individually scattered strips	0	0	0	2.43	0	2.44	4.87
% of total area of *selo*							0.21
Total land held in village	129.08	0.17	151.6	785.22	161.9	1098.89	2326.86

Econometric Tests

The independent explanatory variable in all the regressions that follow is the distance between a selo and a railway station. The dependent variable is the percent share of selected landholding categories in the total land area of the obshchinas grouped in the selo in 1913. We include only representative forms of landholding, those that account for at least 2 percent of the total land area in the Penza district. Rarer forms do not appear in many selos; the many zeroes their inclusion would create distort the statistics. The forms of main interest are rotated allotment land (the most communal form) and non-allotment consolidated individual holdings (the most individualistic).

Before the results of the regression are shown, a brief note regarding two econometric problems is in place. Most of the regressions exhibited serial correlation and heteroscedasticity—conditions that, untreated, would lead to inefficient estimates and unreliable measures of goodness of fit. The former problem is common in time series. Here it indicates that adjacent points are not independent or that villages are influenced in their choice of land forms by neighbors' decisions; it is either local conventions or local soil and climate conditions that might be the root of common decisions. This is obviated by running AR(1) routines. To deal with heteroscedasticity—non-constant variances—we employed the Generalized Least Squares (GLS) method.

Table 9.9 presents the results of the regressions for those forms of ownership that represent more than 2 percent of total Penza land. These regressions explain between 13–43 percent of the R square of the regressions. In non-allotment land, this is a remarkably high proportion, given the small window of opportunity for this process of change and the myriad other factors that must have influenced the choice. As stated above, only four landholding forms account for more than 2 percent of the total land area in the dataset. Two are types of allotment land: rotated allotment land (Type 1 in the Appendix Table) and stripfarmed allotment land (Type 7 in Appendix Table 9.10). The former is the traditional communal holding; its periodic rotation was an important equalizing tool that, however, weakened individual incentives to invest in land improvement. The proportion of land held in this form decreases as we near the railroad, as expected, namely, given that all land used to be allotment land, the closer peasants were to the railroad the faster they converted their allotments into other forms of ownership. The latter, strip farmed plot (Type 7 in the table), an entitlement to land that accommodates the variegation in soil quality introduced by the Stolypin reforms, retains some of the mutual insurance provided by cooperation within the commune and is selected by peasants who are closer to the rails.

The two other land types are all non-allotment land. The revolutionizing finding is that the share of consolidated individual plots (Type 15 in Appendix Table 9.10), the most individualistic type, increases as we near the rails, as expected. Non-allotment collectively farmed land (Type 13 in the Appendix Table, as distinct from Type 14, narrow strips that result from attempts at a fair distribution when land quality differs) entailed voluntary coordination and cooperation in land betterment among household heads. Non-allotment collectively farmed land and stripfarmed

Table 9.9 Regression results

Landholding type	*Allotment land*			*Non-allotment land*		
	Rotating	*Stripfarmed Stolypin*	*Allotment*	*Collectively farmed*	*Consolidated individual*	*Non-allotment*
# of type in Appendix Table	*1*	*7*	*Total*	*13*	*15*	*Total*
C	0.511***	0.116***	0.674***	0.133***	0.178***	0.326***
	0.018	*13.071*	*42.645*	*0.132*	*10.999*	*20.637*
DIST	0.0034***	-0.0007**	0.003***	0.133***	-0.0020***	-0.003***
	6.018	*−2.547*	*5.682*	*0.132*	*−4.472*	*−5.682*
AR(1)	0.520***	0.446***	0.521***	0.133***	0.655***	0.521***
	33.870	*16.705*	*29.576*	*0.132*	*30.141*	*29.576*
R-squared	0.293	0.204	0.012	0.133	0.439	0.288
Adjusted R^2	0.292	0.203	0.012	0.132	0.439	0.287
Durbin-Watson statistic	2.194	2.140	2.008	2.063	2.244	2.167
Schwarz criterion	0.520	-0.576	2.048	-0.414	-0.279	0.285
Observations number	3369	3369	3369	3369	3369	3369
Share of total land area	68.98%	7.29%	80.29%	10.22%	7.69%	19.71%

Note: Italicized numbers are t-values. Significance: *** = <1%; ** = <5; * = <10%

land—*cherezpolositza*—are economical to farm collectively and harvest individually; therefore, they still leave the fruit of any investment in the owner's hands. The farther peasants were from modern means of transport, the more they opted for this form. This is either because they opted for more remunerative contiguous land as against higher-quality strips for land closer to the rails, or because in regard to strips farther from the rails, where proximity to markets did not alleviate the risks, they preferred the cooperation that they chose to forgo where transport was cheaper and more reliable.

Thus, all the regressions support our hypothesis that the age of affordable and more reliable transport did start to relax existing communal bonds. The direction of influence of the new transport is easiest to explain in the case of the two extremes, rotating allotment land and consolidated private land; these regressions account for close to 30 percent and over 40 percent of the variance. The choices of the other two forms, strip plots, are also explicable on economic grounds. The Russian muzhik was clearly not stuck in any rut; he proved to be an agile decision-maker who took seriously the economic opportunities that he encountered.

It is remarkable how quickly the effect was manifested. Even if all that had to be accomplished was to formalize changes that had been taking place informally and gradually since the advent of rail and the beginning of industrialization, the change in the land-ownership regime, a tedious and time-consuming operation—especially given the slow and sleazy Russian bureaucracy— became visible after only six years of life under the new law.

Concluding Discussion

The thesis that early twentieth-century rural Russia was dormant and ossified in its traditional commune organization has strong roots. To change and awaken the peasantry, says this thesis, strong, nay, violent external forces were necessary, and these were applied by Stalin. His collectivization was cruel, possibly disproportionate in its bloodshed, but necessary. So it is said. The evidence we presented in this chapter disproves the thesis. Radical changes were taking place in the fields of late Tsarist Russia and the obshchina, the village commune, was disintegrating as its peasants transmogrified into independent farmers, individual or freely cooperating, driven by market forces. The strong influence of proximity to rail lines in our regressions indicates that railroad construction influenced this trend.

Yet the speed of changes in land registration, by a bureaucracy not known for its efficiency, is surprising. Formally, too, the changes in landholding were possible only since the Stolypin reforms of 1906 onwards, while the invasion of the rails started in the middle of the nineteenth century. This leads us to conjecture that the final registry changes—possibly even the laws themselves—came to formalize changes that had been taking place informally since the last decades of the nineteenth century. In other words, the peasantry was not blind to the transitions that were taking place around it and that were brought home by the new technologies, particularly the means of transport that converted the village into a part of the larger society around it. The unexpected and unforeseen result of the thirty-nine-year-long Tsarist-led industrialization drive (1874–1913) was that the rails attracted peasants to growing urban centers and integrated them into a society of which they had hardly been aware before. We posit that a gradual, though unrecorded, adaptation of the landholding system was taking place. If so, the railroads as the harbingers of the new economy determined the pace of transition to a hereditary household farm system and the dissolution of the commune. The Stolypin reform and the legalization of household-head property rights in land were merely responses to real changes that were occurring in the fields.

Stalin, clearly, was not necessary. But did he accelerate change? Or did he hold it up? This seems to be the right place to mesh our results with the masterly estimates of Cheremukhin et al. (2013). Leonard's estimates of a strong acceleration of productivity growth during the first decade of the nineteenth century (Table 9.7) indicate that the changes that we documented above were just starting to influence output in the fields, and it is very likely that they would have accelerated had the trends at the start of the twentieth century continued. Absent the three cataclysmic events that intervened—the Great War, the Revolution, and collectivization—we would therefore expect the high estimate of Cheremukhin et al. (2013) as the more likely one. After the war and even after the Revolution, Russia should have returned to its previous path. After collectivization, this was no longer conceivable. Stalin must have slowed down or even frozen rural development.

So Stalin was plainly the problem, not the solution. The Russian village, as we leave it behind the eve of the terrible war that would overturn Europe and prepare it for a second and even more terrible one, was in the throes of a wide-ranging upheaval. In Stalin's absence, the process would have accelerated, bringing Russian agriculture closer in shape to that of Western Europe. As it happened, Stalin destroyed the enterprising element in the village and converted the potential entrepreneurial farmer into a passive state employee. Even today, more than a quarter century after the end of communism in Russia, the country's agriculture has not awakened from the torpor that Stalin imposed on it.

Table 9.10 Land categories, 1913

	Major category	*Designation, Russian*	*English translation*	*Meaning*	*Year of origin*	*Law*	*Share of total area, %, 1913*	*Total*
1	Allotment land	Nadelnaya razverstannaya, razpredelonnaya	Allotment rotating, redistributed	Periodically repartitioned	1649	Serfdom 4	69.0	
2		Nadelnaya razversttannaya kupplennaya	Allotment rotating purchased, redistributed	Periodically repartitioned	1861	Emancipation	0.3	
3		Nadelnaya vykup statia165. Czerezpolositsa razpredelonnaya	Allotment redeemed paragraph 165, stripfarming, redistributed	Allotment stripfarmed land, redistributed, redeemed after § 165	1861	Redemption Statute, §165	0.1	
4		Nadelnaya vykup statia § 165 Czerezpolositsa kuplennaya	Allotment redeemed, stripfarm, purchased	Allotment household redemption of stripfarmed redistributed land	1861	Redemption Statute, §165	0.0	
5		Nadelnaya vykup § 165 Otrub razpredelonnaya	Allotment redeemed#165 consolidated redistributed	Redistributed allotment consolidated and redeemed after § 165	1861	Redemption Statute, §165	0.2	
6		Nadel vykup 165 § Otrub Kuplennyj	Allotment redeemed, consolidated, purchased	Redeemed allotment after §165 consolidated plot purchased	1861	Redemption Statute, §165	0.1	
7		Nadel ukreplienie 9 November, Czerezpolositsa razpredelonnaya	Allotment entitlement of redistributed stripfarmed land, Stolypin reform	Allotment entitlement of redistributed stripfarmed land, Stolypin reform	1906	Stolypin reform	8.3	
8		Nadelnaya ukreplennie 9 November, Czerezpolositsa kupllennaya	Allotment entitlement 9 November Stolypin stripfarming purchased	Allotment, entitlement strip farmed land, purchased by commune	1906	Stolypin reform	0.8	
9		Nadelnaya ukreplenie 9 November, Otrub razpredelonnaya	Entitlement to consolidated redistributed allotment land after Stolypin reform of 9 November	Entitlement allotment land, consolidated, redistributed	1906	Stolypin reform	1.4	
10		Nadelnaya ukreplenie 9 November, Otrub kupplennaya	Entitlement to consolidated purchased allotment land after Stolypin reform of 9 November	Entitlement allotment land, consolidated, purchased	1906	Stolypin reform	0.4	
11		Nadel v Drugoi obshchinie razpredelonnaya	Allotted land in other villages redistributed by the commune	Allotted redistributed land in other villages	1906–1917	Stolypin reform	0.4	
12		Nadel v Drugoi obshchinie purchased	Allotted land in other villages purchased by the commune	Allotted purchased land in other villages	1906–1917	Stolypin reform	0.0	80.3

(*continued*)

Table 9.10 continued

	Major category	*Designation, Russian*	*English translation*	*Meaning*	*Year of origin*	*Law*	*Share of total area, %, 1913*	*Total*
13	Non-allotment land	Vnenadelnaya kollektivnaya	Non-allotment collective	Non-allotment collectively managed land	1906–1917	Stolypin reform onward	10.2	
14		Vnenadelnaya yedinolichnaya cherezpolositsa	Non-allotment individual scattered strips	Non-allotment, individual, stripfarmed	1906–1917	Stolypin reform onward	1.8	
15		Vnenadelnyj yedinolichnyj Otrub	Non-allotment individual consolidated parcel	Non-allotment, individual, consolidated parcels	1906–1917	Stolypin reform onward	7.7	19.7

Table 9.11 Full regression results

Landholding type	*Allotment land*							
	Rotating	*Rotating, purchased*	*Redeemed, 165§ strip*	*Redeemed, purchased*	*Redeemed, consolidated, §165 redistributed*	*Redeemed, consolidated, purchased*	*November 9 Stolypin reform, redistributed, stripfarmed*	*November 9 Stolypin reform, stripfarmed, purchased*
# of type in Appendix Table 10.1	*1*	*2*	*3*	*4*	*5*	*6*	*7*	*8*
C	0.511***	0.002**	0.002***	0.001***	0.003***	0.003***	0.116***	0.009***
	28.987	2.368	3.257	3.110	3.153	2.690	13.071	5.861
DIST	0.0034***	0.000	0.000	0.000	0.000**	0.000*	-0.0007**	0.000
	6.018	1.105	1.223	-1.526	-1.683	-2.278	-2.547	-0.647
AR(1)	0.520***	0.032	0.134*	0.274***	0.256***	0.426***	0.446***	0.209***
	33.870	1.521	1.917	7.046	1.834	3.674	16.705	3.227
R-squared	0.293	0.001	0.018	0.076	0.067	0.183	0.204	0.04414
Adjusted *R*-squared	0.292	0.001	0.018	0.075	0.067	0.183	0.20315	0.04357
Durbin-Watson statistic	2.194	2.003	2.004	1.997	2.050	2.258	2.14002	2.05759
Schwarz criterion	0.520	-4.429	-4.562	-7.532	-4.785	-5.282	-0.576	-3.9439
# of observations	3369	3369	3369	3369	3369	3369	3369	3369
Share of total land	68.98%	0.17%	0.31%	0.06%	0.19%	0.12%	7.29%	0.76%

Landholding type						*Non-allotment land*			
	November 9 Stolypin, consolidated, redistributed	*November 9 Stolypin, consolidated purchased*	*Redistributed commune land in other villages*	*Purchased commune land in other villages*	*Total allotment land*	*Collective, farmed*	*Individual scattered strips*	*Consolidated individual*	*Total non-allotment*
# of type in Appendix Table	*9*	*10*	*11*	*12*		*13*	*14*	*15*	
C	0.016***	0.001	0.010***	0.003***	0.674***	0.128***	0.019***	0.178***	0.326***
	5.408	1.051	5.119	4.903	42.645	13.978	5.708	10.999	20.637
DIST	0.000	0.000	0.000	0.000*	0.003*	-0.001***	0.000	-0.0020***	-0.003***
	-0.949	1.243	0.301	0.298	5.682	-3.303	1.677	-4.472	-5.682
AR(1)	0.142***	0.117*	0.222***	0.034***	0.521***	0.357***	0.185***	0.655***	0.521***
	3.052	2.117	4.363	1.499	29.576	13.856	5.192	30.141	29.576
R-squared	0.021	0.017	0.049	0.001	0.012	0.133	0.036	0.439	0.288
Adjusted *R*-squared	0.020	0.016	0.048	0.001	0.012	0.132	0.035	0.439	0.287
Durbin-Watson statistic	2.012	2.016	2.034	1.968	2.008	2.063	2.026	2.244	2.167
Schwarz criterion	-2.006	-5.700	-3.304	-4.723	2.048	-0.414	-2.032	-0.279	0.285
# of observations	3369	3369	3369	3369	3369	3369	3369	3369	3369
Share of total land	1.44%	0.35%	0.42%	0.002	80.29%	10.22%	1.80%	7.69%	19.71%

References

Ascher, A. (2001). *P.A. Stolypin: The search for stability in late imperial Russia*. Stanford University Press.

Atkinson, D. (1983). *The end of the Russian land commune 1905–1930*. Stanford University Press.

Bartlett, R. (1999). Liberty and property, land and freedom: Landownership and agriculture in imperial, Soviet and post-Soviet Russia. In G. Hosking & R. Service (Eds.), *Reinterpreting Russia*. Arnold.

Blum, J. (1961). *Lord and peasant in Russia from the ninth to the nineteenth century*. Princeton University Press.

Burbank, J. (2004). *Russian peasants go to court: Legal culture in the countryside, 1905–1917*. Indiana University Press.

Burds, J. (1998). *Peasant dreams and market politics: Labor migration and the Russian village 1861–1905*. University of Pittsburgh Press.

Cheremukhin, A., Golosov, M., Guriev, S., & Tsyvinski, A. (2013). Was Stalin necessary for Russia's economic development? http://economics.mit.edu/files/8702

de Madariaga, I. (1998). *Politics and culture in eighteenth century Russia*. Longman.

Eggertsson, T. (1990). *Economic behavior and institutions*. Cambridge University Press.

Engelgardt, P. N. (1993). *Aleksandr Nikolaevich Engelgardt's letters from the country, 1872–1887* (C. Frierson, Tr. & Ed.). Oxford University Press.

Gaudin, C. (2007). *Ruling peasants: Village and state in late imperial Russia*. Northern Illinois University Press.

Gerschenkron, A. (1962). *Economic backwardness in historical perspective*. The Belknap Press of Harvard University Press.

Gerschenkron, A. (1968). *Continuity in history and other essays*. The Belknap Press of Harvard University Press.

Gintis, H. (2009). *The bounds of reason: Game theory and the unification of the behavioral sciences*. Princeton University Press.

Gregory, P. R. (1982). *Russian national income 1885–1913*. Cambridge University Press.

Gregory, P. R. (1994). *Before command. An economic history of Russia from emancipation to the first five-year plan*. Princeton University Press.

Greif, A. (2006). *Institutions and the Path to Modern Economy -Lessons from Midieval Trade*. Cambridge UP.

Hoch, S. (1986). *Serfdom and social control in Russia. Petrovskoe, a village in Tambov*. University of Chicago Press.

Hughes, L. (1998). *Russia in the age of Peter the Great*. Yale University Press.

Johnson, R. (1979). *Peasant and proletarian: The working class of Moscow in the late nineteenth century*. Leicester University Press.

Keren, M. (2007). Personal communication.

Kingston-Mann, E. (1991). Peasant communes and economic innovation: A preliminary inquiry. In E. Kingston-Mann, T. Mixter, & J. Burds (Eds.), *Peasant economy culture and politics of European Russia*. Princeton University Press.

Leonard, C. S. (1990). Landlords and the mir: Transaction costs and economic development in pre-emancipation Russia (Iaroslav Gubernia). In R. Bartlett (Ed.). *Land commune and peasant community in Russia: Communal forms in imperial and early Soviet society*. Macmillan in Association with the School of Slavonic and East European Studies, University of London.

Leonard, C. S. (2011). *Agrarian reform in Russia: The road from serfdom*. Cambridge University Press.

Loewe, H. D. (1990). Differentiation in Russian peasant society: Causes and trends, 1880–1905. In R. Bartlett (Ed.), *Land commune and peasant community in Russia: Communal forms in Imperial and early Soviet society*. Macmillan in Association with the School of Slavonic and East European Studies, University of London.

Leonard, C., & Ljungberg, J. (2008). Population and living standards, Vol. 2, Chapter 5. [Unpublished draft]. Department of Economic History, Lund University.

Macey, D. (1998). A wager on history: The Stolypin agrarian reforms as a process. In J. Pallot (Ed.), *Christ Church Oxford, transforming peasants. Society, state and the peasantry, 1861–1930*. Selected Papers From the Fifth World Congress of Central and East European Studies, Warsaw, 1995.

Martens, B. (2004). *The Cognitive Mechanics of Economic Development and Institutional Change*. Routledge.

Moon, D. (1999). *The Russian peasantry 1600–1930. The world the peasants made*. Longman.

Nafziger, S. (2007). *Land redistributions and the Russian peasant commune in the 19th century*. EHES, Lund and Department of Economics, Williams College.

Nafziger, S. (2010). Peasant communes and factor markets in late-nineteenth-century Russia. *Explorations in Economic History, 47*(4), 381–402.

North, D. C. (1990). *Institutions, institutional change and economic performance*. Cambridge University Press.

Nove, A. (1992). *An economic history of the USSR 1917–1991*. Penguin Books.

Pallot, J. (1999). *Land reform in Russia 1906–1917: Peasant responses to Stolypin's project of rural transformation*. Clarendon Press.

Pipes, R. (1999). *Property and freedom*. Harvill Press.

Robbins, R. G., Jr. (1975). *Famine in Russia 1891–1892: The Imperial government responds to a crisis*. Columbia University Press.

Scott, J. (1976). *The moral economy of the peasant. Rebellion and subsistence in Southeast Asia*. Yale University Press.

Sheshinski, E. (2010). *Limits in individual choice*. The Hebrew University of Jerusalem.
Simms, Y. J. (1977). The crisis in the Russian agriculture at the end of the nineteenth century: A different view. *Slavic Review, 36*(3), 377–398.
Worobec, C. D. (1995). *Peasant Russia: Family and community in the post-emancipation period*. Northern Illinois University Press.

CHAPTER 10

Individualism and Collectivism: Measuring the Transition to Modernity in Tsarist Russian Peasant Society, Penza Province, 1913

Here I introduce an often-overlooked production factor, a vital one at that—human dignity as the determinant of human performance. The aspect of perceived personal human dignity that unleashes creative productive performance is a socioeconomic choice driven by the individual's access to information and her or his ability to communicate and voluntarily organize. In a peasant society, spatial mastery and the acquisition of literacy and education are the means to the perception of human dignity, manifesting a structural change that heralds the transition to modernity. I support my argument empirically by presenting regressions of literate wage labor in relation to the population of Russian peasants in the post-emancipation transition of landholding (the dependent variable) from the collectivistic to individualistic. The changeover to individualism is a conceptual proxy for creative risk-taking that indicates a measure of reduced degradation. My data originate in the 1913 statistics of the *zemstvo* (rural self-government) of Russia's Penza Province.

Unlike Robert Schumann, who sensed that human creative performance thrives mushroom-like "in humidity and darkness," I propose in this chapter that productive performance, delineated as a declining input-to-output ratio amid rising quality of production—resulting in rising standards of living and quality of life—is dependent on personal dignity. Applying the insight of Kazimierz Poznanski (1985, 1992), I argue that Imperial Russia's dependence on technology imports (Sztern, 2017) was occasioned by individual degradation, restrictions on freedom of thought

S. Sztern, *Russia on the Move*, Studies in Economic Transition, https://doi.org/10.1007/978-3-030-89285-2_10

and movement, growing risk of poverty, and analphabetism. I disclose two sets of conditions: those under which collectivism insulates against individual degradation and those that render collectivism the source of that dire personal outcome (Fig. 10.1).

In this chapter I call attention to the confluence of spatial mobility, literacy, and demand for education, catalyzed by railroads, as the levers that gave peasant households and their members the ability to shake off the yoke of pre-modern insurance that had been imposed under the Tsarist hierarchy of coercion. The historical long-term legacy of this hierarchy is assumed to have occasioned servility and individual degradation in compulsorily collectivist structures, encouraging uninspired production under tried-and-true methods as opposed to risk-taking in the search and the application of novelty (Poznanski, 1985, p. 45). The railroad-contingent creation of multiple information-exchange forums, peasant access to production agglomerations in urban centers, and the knowledge spillover afforded by peasants' integration into urban economies incentivized the acquisition of, and the returns on, literacy and education—footloose human-capital accumulation—among the peasant population (Fujita et al.,

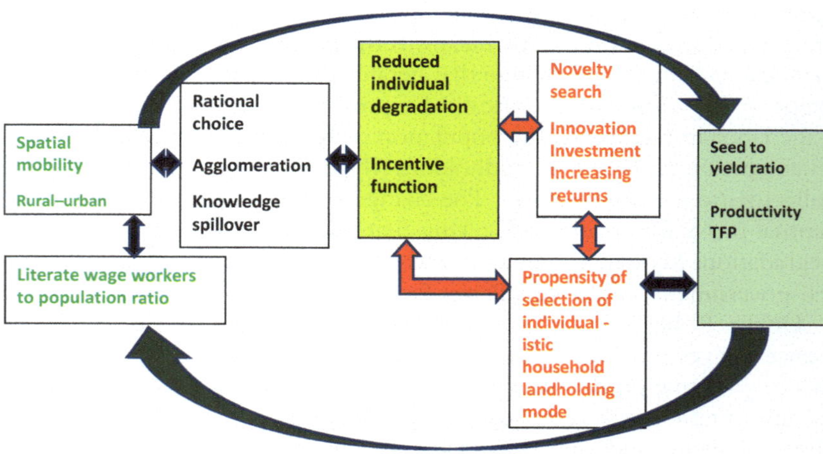

Fig. 10.1 Proposed development and modernization loop: late nineteenth-century Russia. (Sources: Kahan (1989, 1913 Penza self-government statistics), Sheshinski (2010), Gintis (2009), Fujita (2001), Hesse (1993), Mokyr (1990), Poznanski (1985, 1992), Brooks (2003), Leonard (2011), Gregory (1994), Bideleux (1990), and Nafziger (2007))

2001; Brooks, 2003). A modernizing developmental engine of tacit and contractual knowledge transmission (Hodgson, 1999) came into being as peasants commuted between the urban and the rural economies. Its sources of fuel were two: the increase in wage labor of literate peasants relative to the entire peasant population and relative to that of working peasants, and the share of peasant children who learned to read relative to the population at large. As I show below, the share of literate *otkhodniks* (peasant wage laborers) in the population explains roughly 34 percent of the muzhik's ability to take risks by choosing an individualistic landholding modality despite population increase and migration toward places served by railroads (Atack et al., 2010). The emerging rural individualism forced peasants to adopt a future-oriented strategy. Thus, parents increasingly preferred to enroll their children in school rather than to send them to work in the fields, increasing the share of literate youngsters in the total population. Interestingly, the gender distribution of the responsibility for household well-being gave females the task of preserving the pre-modern insurance system in the village; conversely, males explored the future-oriented individualistic options and engaged in urban economies to an incompatibly greater extent. The gender difference in literacy rates in Imperial Russia's closing decades attests to the existential beneficence of aspects of the collectivist redistribution practice in view of the acute unpredictability and volatility of agricultural earnings on the Russian plain. The same difference definitely links spatial mobility to literacy—thereby establishing an association between literacy and peasants' use of the railroads. This pre-Revolution development not only brought about a temporal change but also sowed dynamic seeds of long-term modernization. On the heels of Chap. 9, I ask again whether Stalinism should be seen as was indispensable for Russia's modernization—and again I answer in the negative. The acquisition of literacy, as required for spatial mobility, results in individual novelty-seeking choice, mitigates individual degradation, and strengthens the perception of self-dignity. It incentivizes subversion and the quest for political novelty and innovation; it also allows productivity to increase and absolves society of the spell of diminishing returns. Challenging the Malthusian-crisis conceptualization of upheavals in Late Imperial Russia, which Gerschenkronians credit with precipitating the revolutions of 1905 and 1917, here I reference Mironov (2012), who discloses that these revolutionary upheavals erupted under conditions of rising and not declining living standards—establishing the coincidence of rising factor productivity and subversion. My contribution in this chapter illuminates the nexus of knowledge and economy created by the peasantry's rural-to-urban mobility, a migration that in the longer run mitigated degradation by reducing individuals' uncertainty and transaction costs. It also empowered idle curiosity, search for novelty, and innovation (Witt, 1993), paving the way to the exclusivization of property rights and individualism in landholding and vice versa, raising land productivity in terms of the seed-to-yield ratio and Total Factor Productivity. Under such conditions, population increase results not in the Malthusian preventive and positive check but rather in the transition envisaged by Boserup, from extensive to intensive resource use.

Enter the "Iron Horse": The Discontinuance of Collectivist Dependency—Famine and Analphabetism Contained

Until the advent of the railroads from the mid-nineteenth century onward, movement of heavy commodities such as grain and flour in Tsarist Russia was determined by the availability of navigable waterways.

> *Great distances and severe climate with long frigid winters and summer droughts made water transport in Russia quantitatively and qualitatively different from water transport in western and central Europe. Nature set the terms: Russians could only hope to modify them.* (Jones, 2013, p. 148; author's emphasis)

Robbins (1975) emphasizes the crucial role of the railroads in famine relief, explaining that the causes of this type of disaster were meteorological. As late as 1891, the Minister of the Imperial Household called His Majesty's attention to the indispensability of emergency measures, reporting from Tambov Province: "Here we are, getting ready to go hungry" (Robbins, 1975, p. 1).

Alexander Gerschenkron, relying on the Westernizers school headed by Boris Chicherin, viewed the *obshchina*, the nineteenth-century village commune, as a Tsarist instrument of taxation that was continuous over time. In contrast, roughly conforming to the Slavophile tradition, I conceptualize this collectivist redistributive Russian village commune as a collectivist ESS—Evolutionary Stable Strategy of survival—the result, not the cause, of the evil. The Tsarist bureaucracy used the commune to reduce transaction costs associated with the goal of tax extraction. The village commune constituted a pre-modern resource redistribution mechanism aimed at diversification and mitigation of the risk of perishing in famines, epidemics, and other mass catastrophes caused by natural calamities, as were typical of Russian agriculture (Milov, 2001). Kingston-Mann (1991) maintains that the *shkod* (the village assembly), the coordination mechanism that evolved within the network of communal-resource management, was used by the peasantry to attenuate risk to individual households in the implementation of agricultural innovations such as fertilizer use and planting clover in fallow third fields in order to sustain claims to marginal lands and head off Ricardian-Malthusian impoverishment traps. The tradeoff between individuals' demand for a return on their investments and their dependency on the safety net established by the commune, emerging in the late nineteenth century, allowed new agronomic knowledge to be implemented.[1] My emphasis in this chapter is on the acute individual degradation caused by traditional patriarchal structures in the pre-railroad age. This degradation, emanating from faulty recognition and delineation of individuals' rights versus the collective, had the secondary effect of hampering productivity enhancement, the search for novelty, invention, and innovation (Mokyr, 1990; Poznanski, 1985; Atkinson, 1983).

The terrifying aspects of the "speed and sheer intensity of deprivation and the unexpectedness of disasters" in famine-causing natural calamities (Sen, 1999, p. 161), which were different from poverty, along with the frequency of natural calamities in Russia, brought about hierarchical dependencies (on the landlord during serfdom) and horizontal dependencies (of paupers on peer and relatively well-to-do peasant households, *krugovaya poruka*—mutual-insurance serfdom legacies perpetuated after the emancipation). The collectivistic structures of famine relief, which paternalized, degraded, and oppressed the individual, discouraged individual risk-taking (Frierson, 1993, pp. 37, 29; Poznanski, 1985). A vicious cycle was set in motion as individual risk aversion legitimized collectivist coercion. Obeisance of authority, servility, and at best passive resistance to the yoke of the superior in the hierarchy constituted the naturally selected responses, adapted to the conditions of life, to agricultural vicissitudes occasioned by the weather (Sztern, 2017, in reference to Veblen's American Evolutionary Institutionalism) (Tables 10.1–10.3).

Interpreting the tables above, one may plausibly surmise that the synergy of mutually contingent technological factors and the railroads, which

[1] Kingston-Mann (1991); see also Nafziger (2010) on the flexibility of the nineteenth-century commune.

Table 10.1 Population growth (percent) and years of natural calamities

	1719–1744	*1833–1850*	*1719–1857*
Average yearly rate of population growth	0.66	0.64	0.81[a]
Number of years of natural calamities	12	7	38
Frequency of natural calamities	0.48	0.41	0.275

Population data from Kabuzan (164–165). Years of natural calamities: from the catalogue

Source: Kahan (1989, p. 138)

[a]On a comparable territory

Table 10.2 Coincidence of epidemics and natural calamities in Russia (twelfth to nineteenth centuries)

Century	*Total natural calamities*	*Total epidemics*	*Epidemics following or coinciding with natural calamities*
Twelfth	14	5	3
Thirteenth	17	6	4
Fourteenth	14	19	5
Fifteenth	15	10	7
Sixteenth	16	6	5
Seventeenth	15	2	
Eighteenth	15	11	
Nineteenth	26	13	8

Source: Kahan (1989, p. 138)

Table 10.3 Mortality and population growth: deaths and births per 1000 of population in European Russia, 1861–1913

Years	*Deaths*	*Births*	*Excess of births over deaths*
1861–1870	38.7	51.9	13.2
1871–1880	35.5	49.1	13.6
1881–1890	34.2	48.7	14.5
1891–1900	32.8	48.7	15.9
1901–1905	31.0	47.7	16.7
1906–1910	29.2	45.3	16.1
1911–1913	27.7	44.1	16.9

Source: Kahan (1989, p. 3)

facilitated peasant mobility and incentivized literacy in a manner that intensified discontinuously in the mid-nineteenth century, dramatically diminished the perceived meteorological hazard to the population's well-being. Indeed, twenty-six natural calamities that coincided with eight out of thirteen epidemics did not trigger mortality shocks so severe as to have arrested the population increase. The individual degradation intrinsic to the Tsarist Russian collectivist redistributive hierarchies of coercion (the patriarchal household and the commune), caused by the perceived risk of morbid starvation and mortality, presumably waned. The "impact of wars, famines, and epidemics" was contained. Kahan (1989, p. 3) interprets the excess births over deaths in the post-emancipation era as the result of "spatial mobility of the population." Due to and in spite of improved transportation, the population stricken by crop failure was able to avoid the worst of the famine; thus, too, migrants carrying contagious diseases were freed from spatial control. As for the net effect, the population of Imperial Russia experienced declining mortality during the post-emancipation period and underwent a sluggish demographic transition in the form of declining fertility, challenging net population growth (Kahan, 1989, p. 139).

Now I juxtapose the foregoing with two proxies for peasant spatial mobility during the post-emancipation era (Table 10.4).

A discontinuous increase is observed in 1861–1871, the initial post-emancipation decade, in the issuance of short-term (1–3 month) and six-month passports and in one-year migrant passports, as individuals overcame travel risk aversion. In tandem with the rising frequency of travel, a discontinuous cumulative increase in annual passports is observed during the transition to the decades of the gold standard and the industrialization spurt, while the demand for shorter-term passports declined. The

Table 10.4 Railroad ticket sales and internal passport issuance to different time durations, 1861–1900 (in 1000s)

Years	*1–3 months*	*6 months*	*1 year*	*Over 1 year*	*Total*
1861–1870	1869.6	5661.1	5332.9	59.2	12,913
1871–1880	17,258.5	10,169.8	9414.0	87.1	36,929
1881–1890	24,366.7	13,118.9	11,889.4	91.2	49,466
1891–1900	20,539.8	11,101.6	37,880.1	1844.7	71,366

Source: Kahan (1989, p. 4)

revolutionizing increase in one-year passports in the closing decades of the nineteenth century indicates declining household dependency on agricultural income.

One may surmise that, despite long-term wage labor in urban economies, written communication between *otkhodnik* males and kin back in the village did assure *bolshaks* (heads of household) enough control of repatriated income to allow those willing to work in the urban economies to acquire their internal passports (Gerschenkron, 1962, 1968). The table sustains a challenge to the Gerschenkronian analysis of the ever-present and institutionally caused mobility barrier that ostensibly hindered the industrializing modernization of Russia. The grand scholar failed to acknowledge that increasing literacy among the peasants catalyzed their spatial rural–urban mobility and vice versa. Heads of household could easily do the math: As the population grew, the value of the additional land parcel obtained upon repartition was falling behind the industrial wage that the *otkhodnik* was repatriating, which was on the rise commensurate with the *otkhodnik*'s skill accumulation (Atkinson, 1983; Mironov, 2012; Kahan, 1989).

I hypothesize that the manifest increase in demand for long-term passports reflects the improvement in risk-taking ability due to the reduced hazards of travel. It also presumably mirrors the improvement in communication capabilities among spatially dispersed locations, explained by improved literacy, education, and information-exchange capacities that allowed cognitive distances between the village and urban economies, including the court system, to decline amid increasing contractual trust (Brooks, 2003; Yokoyama, 2008; Shivelbusch, 1986). These factors, taken together, allowed utility-maximizing choices to be made, resulting in a mutually enforcing decline in degradation and an increase in factor productivity. Cumulatively declining long-term transaction costs and uncertainty explain rising factor productivity, says Poznanski (1985, 1992), as such process strengthens the incentive function of every set of property rights, unleashing idle curiosity (Veblen, 1931), search for novelty, and innovation (Witt, 1993; Mokyr, 1990). The result was a modernization-enhancing cycle, in which interaction among spatial mobility and literacy-promotive rising returns to and demand for education allowed and incentivized the individualization of landed, movable, physical, and intellectual property holdings amid expanding rational choice (Sheshinski, 2010; Gintis, 2009), allowing factor productivity to grow.

Below I marshal a formidable arsenal of archive-based research findings to challenge the Gerschenkronians' hypothesis of declining peasant living standards that allegedly took the place after the emancipation, additionally aggravated by state-led industrialization. The latter, according to this renowned scholar and the school he inspired, came to precipitate the revolution of 1905. One source that deserves particular attention is Nafziger and Dennisson's discourse, *Micro-Perspectives on Living Standards in Nineteenth-Century Russia* (November 2007). Quoting Hoch (1986), this source argues that high fertility rates and constant or falling mortality reflected improved standards of living after the emancipation. Interestingly, Nafziger and Dennisson conceptualize literacy as one of several reflections of improvement in a population's well-being, namely, its standard of living. They reference Mironov's (2012) estimates, which show that the literacy rate for males over nine years of age rose from 19.1 percent to 42.2 percent between 1857 and 1907. The increase in female literacy was less pronounced, from 9.5 to 17 percent (Nafziger & Dennisson, 2011, p. 40). As women were less mobile than men, the gender difference in the proportion of literate individuals clearly indicates a link between spatial mobility and literacy.

Rising Living Standards: The Immaterial Aspects of Degradation—Nineteenth-Century Peasant Manifestations of Improving Self-Dignity

Mironov (2012, p. 396) uses anthropometric data to show that the Russian peasant standard of living moved upward during the nineteenth and early twentieth centuries. Much in line with the revisionist writings of Gregory (1982, 1994), he calls attention to the growth of per-capita food production, rising household income derived from crafts and agriculture, the declining real share of taxes and dues in the peasant budget, upward-slanting grain prices after 1815, peasants' southward migration toward affluence-generating fertile land and a milder, agriculture-friendly climate, governmental efforts to improve the peasantry's socioeconomic condition, and moves toward the intensification of resource use. It is the seventh factor in this discourse that deserves attention: "a rise in the cultural level of the population, especially in the post-reform era, when a phenomenal increase in literacy contributed to a rise in labor productivity and the corresponding rise in wages and income" (Mironov, 2012, p. 396).

The following table supports the above postulate (Table 10.5).

Table 10.5 Population and Human Development Index (HDI), Russia, 1851–1913 (excluding Finland)

Years	*Population (millions)*	*Per-capita GDP*[a]		*Education*[b]			*Average life expectancy*		*HDI*
		Amount	*Index*	*Years*	*Enrollment (percent)*	*Index*	*Years*	*Index*	
1851–1860	73.5	701.0	0.381	14	1.4	0.098	27.1	0.035	0.171
1861–1870	78.4	675.9	0.374	17	1.9	0.120	27.9	0.048	0.181
1871–1880	91.7	666.4	0.372	19	2.3	0.134	28.8	0.063	0.190
1881–1890	110.6	679.9	0.375	22	2.5	0.155	29.7	0.078	0.203
1891–1900	125.8	790.7	0.402	28	3.5	0.198	31.2	0.103	0.234
1901–1910	147.6	928.1	0.430	33	5.5	0.250	32.9	0.132	0.271
1913	171.0	1036.1	0.449	40	7.9	0.293	36.0	0.183	0.308

Source: Mironov (2012, p. 400)

[a]Expressed in 1989 US dollars

[b]Excluding Finland and Poland

The index in the foregoing table is Human Development Index (HDI), a metric that the United Nations has used since 1990 to quantitatively conceptualize the quality of life in a defined area. Indeed, it corroborates his analysis, which postulates an increase in living standards ahead of the 1905 and 1917 revolutions (Mironov, 2012, p. 399). The HDI embeds life expectancy at birth, education—*indicating the proportion of literate individuals in the population and the proportion of school-age children who attend school*—and productivity or income in terms of per-capita Gross Domestic Product (GDP). Each index has a value from 0 to 1 and is calculated as an average of the three indicators that also accommodate values of 0–1 (author emphasis). This makes it clear that the Gerschenkronian state-led industrialization spurt of 1890, with railroad construction as its developmental building block, catalyzed a discontinuous, quantity-turned-to-quality increase in all three indicators of economic and cultural well-being of the population of Late Imperial Russia, of which the peasantry accounted for 80 percent. The table indicates a Boserupian rather than a Malthusian evolution. Growing population correlates positively with upward trends in life expectancy at birth, education, per-capita GDP, and the Human Development Index.

An additional table presented by Mironov is of importance in our context (Table 10.6):

The table links the discontinuous growth in the industrial labor force during the decade of the state-led spurt to the dramatically rising indicators of spatial mobility—internal passports per 100 people and the average growth rate of passport issuance. Russia really was on the move. The table sustains the following summarizing assumptions:

1. The railroads facilitated the spatial mobility of the peasantry from the emancipation onward, allowing it to participate voluntarily and increasingly in the industrial labor force.
2. The quality and quantity of oral and written communication between fathers and sons enhanced the spatial mobility of the latter, implying an impact of rising literacy on the pace of industrialization.
3. The Gerschenkronian postulate concerning the mobility barrier imposed by peasant custom structures inherited from serfdom is challengeable. The positive correlation between growth in number of passports and the growth of the industrial workforce clearly indicates that the peasantry acted rationally in seizing the economic and social opportunities offered by the industrialization process. The peasants assumed their complementary roles as proletarians.

Table 10.6 Workers employed in heavy industry and passports (per 100 males and females) in fifty provinces of European Russia, 1770–1913

Years	*Average annual number of workers (thousands)*	*Interval*	*Average rate of growth in the number of workers (percent)*	*Passports per 100 people*	*Average rate of growth in the number of passports (percent)*
1770	70.0[a]	–	–	–	–
1799	81.7[a]	1770–1799	0.53	–	–
1804	95.2[a]	1799–1804	3.11	–	–
1811–1820	167.7[a]	1804–1815	5.05	–	–
1821–1830	208.0[a]	1815–1825	2.18	–	–
1831–1840	338.3[a]	1825–1835	4.98	–	–
1841–1850	485.0[a]	1835–1845	3.67	–	–
1851–1860	521.8[a]	1845–1855	0.73	–	–
1861–1870	451.9[a]	1855–1865	-1.45	–	–
1861–1870	799.7[a]	–	–	1.4	
1871–1880	945.6[b]	1865–1875	1.69	2.7	6.79
1881–1890	1160.1[b]	1875–1885	2.07	3.0	1.06
1891–1900	1637.6[b]	1885–1895	3.51	5.3	5.86
1900–1913[c]	2564.3[b]	1895–1907	3.81	6.0	1.04

Source: Mironov (2012, p. 323)
[a]Industrial enterprises
[b]Industry and mining
[c]All of Russia

4. *Bolshaks* found it advantageous, in a sum exceeding the value of forgone land-redistribution benefits, to let adult family members participate in the industrial economy by maintaining control of the income through efficient bureaucratic measures (Burds, 1998) that forced sons to comply in repatriating income. Kin remaining in the village provided a social safety net and insurance for peasant-proletarians (Johnson, 1979), encouraging an increase in the latter's marginal participation in the labor force and touching off a fast-moving industrialization-and-modernization avalanche.
5. The industrial wages rationalistically repatriated by the *otkhodnik* contained a premium to accommodate the risk of non-compliance or deferment by the wage-earning peasant.

6. The authority of ***bolshaks*** and ***domolegs*** (*bolshaks*' immobile sons back in the village—see Chap. 7) shifted to sons and siblings who participated in the industrial workforce due to the increasingly asymmetrical redistribution of access to and accumulation of practical knowledge between the former and the *otkhodniks*.
7. Crucially, the transport costs and transaction costs that encapsulated the declining uncertainty of travel (the passport requirement) were equal to or smaller than the de facto increases in land values derived from the declining cognitive distance to the urban industrial economies (Fujita, 2001), creating political demand for the universalization of property rights in land (peasant petitions: Freeze, 1988).
8. As peasant spatial mobility incentivized a rising share of literate male workers in the population, the spillover of knowledge from the urban industrial agglomeration that became accessible to peasants for this reason allowed peasants to make a rationalistic transition to individualism in thinking and landholding, improving their perception of self-dignity, risk-taking ability, attraction to novelty and innovation, and the resulting increasing productivity ofland and labor (Mokyr, 1990; Poznanski, 1992).

Point 8 brings me to a conundrum that I encounter in the model of Late Imperial Russia's developmental modernization. Here I promote the following interpretation of the transition that took place in rural Russia: The upturn in perceived self-dignity, in tandem with individual command of the economies of knowledge, transformed the demand for equal access to physical assets into an abstract demand for egalitarian and impersonalized access to rights to these assets. Ostensibly, I demonstrated all of this in my 2017 dissertation. That account, however, omitted a crucial link in the chain—between peasant spatial mobility afforded by the railroads and access to the agglomeration of knowledge in an industrial environment, made possible by the acquisition of literacy and participation in the multiple networks of written and oral information exchange. The latter mitigated uncertainty and transaction costs in the long run, strengthening the incentive function of property rights and catalyzing an increase in factor productivity. This combination of complementary developmental phenomena explains why population increase did not bring about a Malthusian catastrophe in Late Imperial Russia. Quite the contrary: the increases in seed-to-yield ratios in agriculture and factor productivity outpaced the rate of population growth, allowing standards of living to rise. They also abetted the acceleration of pro-subversion factors such as demand for a constitution and universal suffrage (Leonard, 2011; Mironov, 2012; Kahan, 1989) (Table 10.7).

Two phenomena can be learned from Kahan (1989, p. 128). First, Russia had a low output–seed ratio by international standards, indicating acute vulnerability to calamities. However, the ratio had been rising steadily since Russia's transition to the gold standard in the decade after 1897, through two industrialization spurts—1890 and 1907. The latter provides a case in point for my argument.

I now examine the development of Total Factor Productivity in post-emancipation Russia (Table 10.8):

Thus, Total Factor Productivity plainly had been on the rise during the post-emancipation and railroad era, with a kink during the 1880s and under the austerity policies occasioned by the Tsarist Government's determination to achieve international credibility ahead of its transition to the gold standard in the following decade.

Table 10.7 Output–seed ratio of grains, Russia, 1800–1914 (eight-year averages)

Term	*Ratio*	*Term*	*Ratio*
1801–1806	3.49	1863–1870	3.47
1807–1814	3.47	1871–1878	3.95
1815–1822	3.50	1879–1886	4.09
1823–1830	3.47	1887–1894	4.49
1831–1838	3.49	1895–1902	4.90
1839–1846	3.29	1903–1910	5.30
1847–1854	3.52	1911–1915	5.78
1855–1862	3.45		

Source: Kahan (1989, p. 128)

Table 10.8 Total factor productivity in Russian agriculture by period (annual percent rate of growth), 1801–2007[a] (Table excerpt, graphic change)

Regime	*Pre-1861*	*1860*	*1870*	*1880*	*1890*	*1900*
Servile Russia	NA					
Post-emancipation Russia		-0.35[b]	1.40			
Industrialization Russia				0.803	1.41	1.97

Source: Leonard (2011, p. 254)

[a]Output=Gross production (see Appendix one for Tsarist Russia) minus intermediate inputs unless otherwise indicated

[b]Negative Total Factor Productivity is not an unusual result in estimates for developing countries

Schools, Literacy, Individual Information Access, and Perception of Dignity

Here I turn the spotlight on literate, male, spatially mobile breadwinning wage-earners as the cause *and* the effect of the increase in peasants' self-dignity and, ultimately, as part of the explanation of the upturn in living standards achieved by increasing factor productivity during the railroad-construction era (Leonard, 2011). Before doing so, I nod to Engel's (1996) perceptive claim that male migration and seasonal out-work improved the complementary status of women in ways not readily measurable. Marriage to migrant laborers offered women a theretofore unknown level of mastery over their own lives and dignity, differentiating them from their village-culture-anchored peers (Engel, 1996, p. 50). A similar line of argumentation is advanced by Smurova (2003) in her analysis of change in favor of urban wage laborers as ideal marriage partners among brides back in the village notwithstanding the relatively secure income flows of grooms in their surroundings. Wage laborers introduced their brides to previously unexplored options of individual choice while enjoying personal liberty and its consequence: rejection of and escape from the yoke of the patriarchal household's domination in *domoleg* households. From these scholars' arguments, with a nod to Mironov (1999), I infer that industrial wage labor reduced dependence and degradation not only among households but also within them, allowing the potential search for novelty, with its productivity-increasing propensity for the individual, to become real. The table below illustrates the cultural mutation that took place in rural Russia when illiterate mothers' daughters became literate. Although the literacy rate of the peasantry's immobile female populations fell short of that of male peasants, the later into the railroad age a female was born, the more probable it was that she would cast off the yoke of analphabetism and backwardness. Thus, male workers' spatial labor mobility became an engine of general enlightenment in terms of the urge to acquire literacy and education among both men and women (Table 10.9).

Between the 1863 emancipation and the second stage of the 1906 land reform (1913), the population of Late Imperial Russia grew 2.3 times over. The number of high-quality intellectual laborers, writes Mironov (2012)—those in education, medicine, culture, and science—grew eight-to ten-fold. It is obvious that the cultural and knowledge revolution occasioned by the railroads explains the avoidance of Malthusian catastrophes during this time despite the population growth. The next table yields a

Table 10.9 Peasant literacy by age group (in percent), 1897 (sixty years into the railroad era)

Location	*Men*	*Women*		
		All	*10–19*	*20–29*
Kostroma Province	36.0	9.3	20.8	15.2
Galich	41.7	12.9	31.2	22.3
Soligalich	41.0	12.3	31.2	22.3
Chukhloma	50.0	21.7	46.4	36.7
Tver'	36.7	8.1	21.8	11.8
Iaroslavl'	48.9	21.6	46.8	34.1
Rural Russia	25.2	9.8	17.1	14.7

Source: Engel (1996, p. 51)

quantitative assessment of the levers of the transition from extensive to intensive growth models, applying Boserup's theories (Table 10.10).

The table above is instructive of the quality, extent, and multidimensionality of the post-emancipation social modernization, a progressive demarche that intensified in step with industrialization led by railroad construction. This process receives special emphasis here in respect of the harbingers of means of knowledge accumulation that propelled modernization and enhanced personal dignity. It not only mitigated the morbid and mortal threat of famine and other natural-calamity-related disasters to the population but also, as I show below, created a much more abstract demand for political rights and a constitution. The data that deserve particular attention in the context of literate wage labor are the numbers of primary schools, reflecting the demand for literacy. According to Mironov (2012), primary-school attendance increased more than sixfold during the decades preceding the 1890s' industrialization spurt, indicating the fulfillment of at least one of the prerequisites for industrialization—allowing proto-industrialization and effectuation of the process driven by railroad construction as envisaged by Count Witte. In line with Brooks (2003, p. 8), Mironov (2012, p. 414) argues that the institutions established in the course of the Great Reforms, such as the court system, rural self-government, and municipal councils, created demand for literate, better educated, and better informed personnel. The increase in the returns on, and the cumulatively generated demand for, literacy and education elevated the acquisition and possession of reading skill to the status of a craft in peasants' eyes. The wage-earning peasantry perceived reading skill as a vehicle of social mobility and an increasingly available path to "clean work" (Brooks, 2003), meaning a vocation that society considered more

Table 10.10 Population, educational, medical, and cultural indicators in Russia (excluding Poland and Finland)[a]

	1830–1860s	*1880–1890s*	*1913–1914*
Population (millions)	70 (1863)	84 (1880)	159 (1913)
Primary schools (thousands)	**17.2 (1856)**	**131.2 (1894)**	119.4
Secondary schools (thousands)	**0.116 (1856)**[b]	**0.645 (1894)**	**4.3**
Numbers attending all education institutions (thousands)	**1156 (1863)**	**4013 (1894)**	**9656**
Teachers (thousands)	**33.5 (1863)**[b]	–	**280**
Public libraries (thousands)	0.012 (1848)	–	143.9
Doctors practicing medicine, excluding dentists (thousands)	–	7.2 (1885)	23.2
Other medical personnel (thousands)	–	13.0 (1885)	46.0
Hospitals (thousands)	0.350 (1850)	–	5.3
Newspapers and magazines (number of titles)	204 (1840)	667 (1890)	2915
Books and brochure (thousands of titles)	0.764 (1832)	7.3 (1889)	34.0
Students in higher education (thousands)	**8.5 (1860)**	**25.6 (1894)**	**127.4**

Source: Mironov (2012, p. 415)

[a]The year of the relevant data appears in parentheses

[b]Excluding religious seminaries, Diocesan schools, and military schools

[c]Estimate, based on the ratio of teachers and pupils in 1914

The bold letters signify the discontinuous , and the chronological increase in the enrol ment in primary schools, secondary schools and students from the Emancipation to WWI.

It is especially interesting to note that this evolution in the varieties of human capital acquisition proceeds in tandem with the railroads construction. This chapter advises that the railroads allowing spatial mobility, incentivized the peasantry towards literacy and education acquisition (see also Brooks 2003). The latter had been indispensable for information exchange including orientation and selection among spatially divergent choice options, allowing rationally evaluated returns (Sheshinski 2010; Gintis 2009)

dignifying than agricultural labor. Mironov (2012, p. 414) argues that the emerging centers of culture—theatres, mass media, publishers, banks, and industry—incentivized the acquisition of literacy, contributing to the cumulatively rising returns to education. It is obvious that in the course of the industrialization under Nicholas II, the discontinuously increasing spatial mobility and the novel opportunities available to peasants on the move made the exodus from analphabetism a sine qua non for success in wage labor. Indeed, migrants to cities did not leave home until after school age (Brooks, 2003, p. 36).

In the first post-emancipation decades, some peasant communities satisfied their demand for literacy and education by establishing *shkoly gramoty* ("literacy schools") throughout Russia. Estimates of the phenomenon, available from 1894, speak of 15,000–20,000 such schools that accommodated 300,000–400,000 pupils (Brooks, 2003, p. 36). The following table documents the supply of primary education and the increase in enrollment in post-emancipation Russia. I call readers' attention to the revolutionizing upturn in enrollment in primary Education Ministry schools, which coincided with the approximate second stage of the Stolypin reform, that of 1911–1914.

Table 10.11 above indicates the presence of the pioneering autonomous, risk-reducing, spontaneous, and communally coordinated elements that paved the way to Russia's nineteenth-century modernization. Thus, countering the Gerschenkronian conception of the commune, not all aspects of the collective farming community were determinants of backwardness that hindered productivity. The new knowledge disseminated by literacy acquisition proved instrumental in the de facto individualization of land holding and the subsequent increases in productivity that allowed agricultural productivity to outpace population growth. The spontaneous communal urge to acquire reading skill, generated by the peasants' literacy schools, was institutionalized under rural self-government in the course of two decades and subsequently fit into the Imperial ministerial framework of literacy and education acquisition. Thus, it is important to note that the urge to self-emancipate from the yoke of analphabetism and backwardness was "bottom-up" rather than "top-down." It illuminates the peasantry's

Table 10.11 Number of rural primary schools

Year	*Zemstvo*	*Commune*	*Church*	*Literacy*	*Ministry*	*Other*	*Total*
1879–1884[a]	9108	?	4213	?	?	?	22,770
1894	13,129	8014	11,197	16,799	964	4333	54,436
1911	27,944	11,051	31,202	4291	5752	9478	89,718
1914	44,879	4893	34,341	2171	21,996	?	108,280

Source: Brooks (2003, p. 38)

[a]The statistics for 1879–1884 pertain to European Russia only. All data are for rural schools except in the case of the 1914 Church schools, for which the statistics relate to one-class schools, nearly all of which were rural

post-emancipation use of railroad technology for wage labor as the explanatory factor in the future process of literacy acquisition among children (Sztern, 2018).

Despite the absence of data for the first half of the 1880s, the table allows me to postulate a salient discontinuity in the number of peasant literacy schools that coincides with the industrialization spurt. Given the sluggish adaptation of institutions to relative price changes (North, 1973, 1990), it must be assumed that the peasants' demand for literacy preceded, anticipated, and possibly even facilitated the spurt. This, in its cultural context, counters the Gerschenkronian conception because in this case the spurt cannot be understood as entirely state-led. The state-driven infusion of railroad technology, although preserving ceremonial social appearances, had been inaugurated roughly sixty years earlier, in 1837, when the state first demonstrated the results of its investment in railroad construction, and it is plausible that cognitive-distance perceptions had been adapting commensurate with the introduction of this transport novelty. The new technology, I propose, destabilized previously Evolutionarily Stable Survival strategies, changing and reducing the alternative costs of tilling the land while increasing the perceived benefits to the peasant household of the acquisition of literacy. The inauguration of lines such as the Nikoljajev, connecting St. Petersburg with Moscow (1843), the trans-Siberian railroad (1891), and the track that traversed Penza Province (1874) incentivized the accumulation of reading skills by their very presence, boosting demand for literacy as a means of communication and information acquisition across increasingly vast distances. This caused literacy and education to spread from the geographical center to remote areas through the "grapevine" mechanism that typified communication and information dissemination in the pre-modern world (Moon, 1999).

As they established the aforementioned "literacy schools," peasant communes hired members to impart these skills and augmented their services with those of itinerant teachers (former conscripts and other literate laborers) who had an outsider status equivalent to that of other hired workers in the commune. It goes without saying that the railroads introduced the peasant commune to this pool of literate tutors. Importantly, literate instructors who were members of the village enjoyed higher social rank than did the itinerant tutors, bringing a "cottage industry" of literacy providers into being (Brooks, 2003, p. 37). These schools, "like tailors' and joiners' workshops" (Brooks, quoting Tolstoy 1862), predated the industrialization spurt by thirty years. Thus, one of the aspects of the proto-industrialization was an evolving future-oriented market of human-capital acquisition encapsulated in the peasants' proto-industrial exodus from analphabetism, leaving behind their degrading and asymmetrical dependency on the structures of elders, a prerequisite of traditional knowledge acquisition by experience. As for the spatial mobility of the literate laborers who educated the local cadres of tutors amid dwindling cognitive distances, the railroads linked the peasant communes' literacy schools to spatial dissemination and agglomeration of knowledge in urbanities.

Let us look at two tables. One plots the downward trend, of more than 20 percentage points, in the illiteracy rate of declining age cohorts commensurate with age of railroads (Mironov, 2012, p. 421). The other is an indicative anecdotal table that yields a first-glance correlation between literacy percentage share and internal passports, namely, between literacy and demand for spatial mobility (Kahan, 1989, p. 188) (Table 10.12).

Since the code of the Petrine reforms required the nobility to be literate, illiteracy was an indication of downward social mobility within the nobles' estate. The Great Reforms brought about a percent increase in the *déclassé* illiterate nobility, which had settled mainly in the countryside. The impoverishment and loss of rank and property holdings among the nobility, with its declining literacy rate, were invigorated by the future-oriented dynamism that infected also the cohorts of the children of civil servants (Mironov, 2012, pp. 420, 421). The table above and Mironov's analysis demonstrate that the peasantry, which constituted 80 percent of the population, was enjoying an upturn in literacy along with the other social estates. By implication, the interaction of the Great Reforms and the dawn of the railroad age had brought about a "pre-Revolution" and a nonviolent social transformation of a magnitude that has been neither studied nor assessed thus far.

Table 10.12 Illiteracy rates, various age cohorts, 1897

Age	*Year of birth*	*Percent illiterate*
10–19	1878–1887	54.5
20–29	1868–1877	55.1
30–39	1858–1867	60.5
40–49	1848–1857	66.8
50–59	1838–1847	73.5
60–69	1828–1837	77.6

Source: Mironov (2012, p. 421)

The nobility, clinging to the constitutive Veblenian habits of thought of the previously stable and effectively protective insulated hierarchies of service and coercion, lost out in the face of the multiple rational-utility-maximizing opportunities that evolved in tandem with spatial mobility, setting in motion a long-term reduction in transaction costs and uncertainty. Uncertainty was also falling from a long-term perspective due to the increasingly non-collectivistic attitude toward property rights amid market integration and specialization (Metzer, 1972). These processes were catalyzed by knowledge spillover from the urban agglomerations of production. The tradeoff of transport costs in their multidimensional sense (declining) and land rents (rising) favored risk-taking individualism in landholding. The declining physical and cognitive distances between the countryside and the cantonal and municipal systems of the judiciary and industry also promoted the individualistic state of mind. As urban markets became closer, the reading-skills workshops delivered steadily rising returns. Peasant Russia was on the move—a mass intellectual and physical move.

The transfer of property-ownership rights from landed gentry to purchasing peasantry reflects the shifts under way (Table 10.13).

By easy implication, the younger the cohort, the less locally bound, the more mobile, and the more literate it was. Kahan's table above reveals the positive correlation between internal-passport acquisition and literacy, namely, between spatial mobility and the exodus from analphabetism and, thereby, from degradation.

Table 10.13 Literacy among draftees in 1887–1889 and internal passports obtained by peasants in 1887 (several counties in Kostroma District[a]), in percent

Rank by percent of passports	*Counties*	*Passports per 100 males in 1887 (percent)*	*Literacy among draftees (percent)*
1	Chuchlomski	29.1	84.0
2	Soligalichskii	22.4	69.8
3	Galichskii	20.8	64.3
4	Kologrivskii	9.2	53.0
5	Buiskii	8.9	49.2
12	Vetluzhskii	0.4	33.3

Source: Kahan (1989, p. 188)

[a]Passports were documents indicating permission from village authorities for a peasant's absence of more than a few weeks

Manifestations of Individual and Collective Dignity: Literacy, Strikes, and Complaints in the 1890–1914 Industrial Spurt

Amid the *rising living standards* that typified the post-emancipation and industrialization era—discovered by Paul Gregory's (1994, 1982) revisionist school, convincingly supported by Mironov and elaborated on by Nafziger and Dennison—Mironov (1999) reports emerging intra-household individualism and an increasingly strong perception of personal dignity. It is crucial to emphasize that the challenge to the hierarchy of coercion that erupted in the closing decades of Tsarism, as evidenced in archive-based contemporary source material, traces not to class solidarity but to trade-union-based complaints and challenges flowing from the individual and labor microcosm of the *obshchina* and its characteristic as a rural artel—*a crafts cooperative and communal village*. Alternatively expressed, the Tsarist Russian trade unions were reconstituted by the institutional heritage of skilled labor on the move in *zemliachestva* (landsman ties) and the mutually insuring village commune and *artel* (skilled workers' cooperative) ethos rather than the Marxist ideology, as Soviet-era historiography would have it.

Let us look at the primary document presented by Ascher (1988, p. 88) on demands presented by workers in St. Petersburg, encapsulated in their petition to the Tsar to be received by His Majesty at the Winter Palace—an event that triggered the "Bloody Sunday" of January 1905. Here are the institutional improvements that these workers demanded in their initial petition points:

> Measures to eliminate ignorance of and arbitrariness toward the Russian people.
>
> 1. The immediate release and return of those who suffered for their political and religious convictions, for striking, and for peasant disorder….
> 2. An immediate proclamation of freedom and inviolability of the person, freedom of speech, press, association and worship.
> 3. Free compulsory and public education, financed by the State.
> 4. Responsibility of the ministers before the people and guarantees that the government will act according to the law.
> 5. Equality of all before the law without any exceptions.
> 6. *Separation of church and state.*

These points are so congruent to each other as if they summarized a primary source compiled by Freeze (1988), comprised of multiple peasant petitions typical of the railroad age: *From Supplication to Revolution—A Documentary Social History of Imperial Russia*. The recurrent demands in these authentic peasant petitions pertain to equal access to free education, equality before the law, the equalization of property rights in land with other estates, and the release of political prisoners. Selected petitions seek democratic rights in terms of universal suffrage. Among the socially and politically heterogeneous petitioners, the weightiest demands in the opening petition concern, impressively, the emphatic rejection of every hierarchy of coercion by peasant-proletarians, followed by industrialists and then students led by a member of the clergy, Georgii Apollonovich Gapon, the leader of the heterogenous procession—believed to be a provocateur from the Okhrana, the *Tsarist secret security police* (Sablinsky, 1976, p. 77)—in a manner that almost could be mistaken for a Bakunian credo à la *God and the State*. By seeking universal equality before the law and the separation of church and state, the peasant workers rejected the crux of ecclesiastical and secular authority. The demand for universal access to education indicates their profound awareness and consciousness of the political, social, and economic utility of literacy education, meaning the utility of human-capital acquisition and accumulation. Importantly, none of the points in the petition seek paternalistic care or resource redistribution. All points, including those dealing with the peasant-proletarians' economic undertakings, demand accountability and transparency of ministerial decision-makers, the right to political participation including legislative processes, and rights of association, with a focus on effective access to rights to assets, including land, on equal terms with other estates.

These demands do not reflect a Marxist-style quest for collective proletarian rights. Rather, they concern the *individual* human rights of peasant-proletarians—an institutional novelty in the context of Imperial Russia.

To get to the root of the issue at hand, I resort to Corrinne Gaudin's (2007) telling account, based on recently opened archives: *Ruling Peasants—Village and State in Late Imperial Russia*. Gaudin's tables and graphs illuminate the peasant perception of self-dignity in litigation rates (criminal cases per 1000 rural inhabitants) in the two closing decades of Tsarism, 1891–1915. Gaudin refers to the increasing frequency of peasants' "dragg[ing] each other to court" in cases of insult and affront to individuals' good reputation and good name (Gaudin, 2007, p. 103). After a kink in the curve in the post-1905 Revolution years of 1906–1907, in 1907–1913 (coinciding with the second industrialization spurt), the litigation rate relating to peasant manifestations of "self-worth" skyrocketed before plummeting in the wake of World War I. Concurrently and in tandem with the longer-run industrialization perspective, litigation rates (civil cases per 1000 rural inhabitants) steadily increased until 1914. In Moscow, and in other regions of industrialized Russia in Tver Province, they peaked in 1908 or so and with the passage of the School Bill 1908 (Brooks, 2003). We can assume that the proximity of industrialized urbanities in those regions pushed up the rural litigation rates (Eklof, 2012).

The documented court cases show a dramatic increase in the proportion of intra-village land disputes in the total civil caseload between 1901 and 1913 in Riazan, Moscow, Tver, and Vladimir. Interestingly in our context, Gaudin refers to the Penza and St. Petersburg regions as manifesting similar patterns of rising frequency of disputes between peasant households over allotment land and the use rights of land renters, and, quite excitingly, of intra-household disagreements over the status of the *bolshak*, the head of household (Gaudin, 2007, p. 108). These suits indicate the near-absence of class solidarity of any type and an upturn in property consciousness and determination to delineate individual property rights in land as a way of obtaining rising returns from the control of investments, as Burbank (2004) observes. Worobec (1995), like Gaudin, stresses that the tendency to pre-mortem household partitions involving patriarchal heads of household intensified as industrialization progressed—an industrialization that, as I have shown, centered on railroad construction as its developmental building block. Frank (1999) shows that in 1890—following the first industrialization spurt—about 20 percent of cases brought before justices of the peace concerned "insults to honor." In the municipal and land-captain courts, those afforded by the imperial bureaucracy, the rate was higher; 40 percent of cases heard before *volost* (cantonal) courts concerned "insult to honor." Frank does emphasize the long-term constitutive importance of honor and reputation in Russian peasant hierarchical society. Nevertheless, a combined analysis of several sources including Mironov (1999) reveals that the perception of personal dignity had been on the rise during the industrial modernization era, pursuant to the upturn in property-rights consciousness.

From Kotsonis' (2011) astute analysis, I infer that the reform legislators had a keen sense of where Tsarist concessions were absolutely indispensable in quelling the 1905 unrest: on the issue of personal dignity and rights. Kotsonis emphasizes that since the reform anticipated "individualization without private property," that is, did not provide sufficient enforcement guarantees for the translation of landed possession into individual rights, while leaving in place the inalienability of property from the peasant estate, the land in question was poor collateral for loans. Even resorting to Peasant Landbank credits—an entitlement to *ukreplienie* land covered by the 1906 reform—could not be fully equated with or understood as the head of household's private property (Kotsonis, 2011, pp. 36, 37).

I counter this by claiming that this in-between stage of individualization without its due corollary—multidimensional property control—irreversibly raised the probability of success in the peasants' demands for the equilibration of their civil status, including the equalization of their rights to landed property with those of the gentry. These demands, demonstrating peasant understanding of the virtues of the individualization of property rights, are evident in Burbank (2004), who refers to the peasants' successful and individualistic use of the systems of rule in the defense of their inheritance rights, and in Macey's (1990) accounts of the Stolypin reform.

All of which leads me to the concluding point in regard to wage labor among literate peasants: Spatial mastery and human-capital accumulation—a cognitive modernizing development—reduced mutual dependency within and among households, allowing demands for personal dignity and material individual rights to be upheld. This paved the way to rising individual investment of skill in other aspects of control of labor and capital returns, creating a virtuous cycle in which factor-productivity increase outpaced population growth. This explains how Russia avoided the Malthusian catastrophe that the scholars of the Soviet school envisaged. The growing individualization of property rights lowered transaction costs and uncertainties in asset exchange, strengthening the incentive function of property rights and abetting the search for novelty and the implementation of agricultural innovation—cumulatively resulting in higher productivity and additional modernization in terms of the individual's emancipation from the yoke of compulsory collectivism (Poznanski, 1992, p. 72).

Figures 10.2 and 10.3 illustrate the transition that occurred.

The advent of the railroads reduced these uncertainties and hazards dramatically, lowering the land-to-labor ratio and allowing an exodus from bondage and a transition to individualism as the means of investment that would assure productivity increase. The model in my dissertation is an adaptation of the initial model for the Penza data, with fifteen land categories that emerged between the emancipation and the second stage of the Stolypin reform (1913) as the dependent variables. The categories reflect long-term decreasing degrees of collectivism in terms of the frequency and mode of repartitions and rotating redistributions of peasant land in

Fig. 10.2 The instrumental transition in self-dignity perception, indicating a shift toward increasing modernization. (Sources: Robbins (1975); Kahan (1989); Mironov (1999, 2012); Brooks (2003); Freeze (1988); Ascher (1988), Pipes (1995))

nadelnoe zemlevladenie (communal usufruct) until *vykup*—redemption in accordance with Section 165 of the 1861 emancipation law—and *ukreplienie*, entitlement under the Stolypin reform statute of November 9, 1906, as well as peasant access to *vnenadelnoe zemlevladenie* (non-allotment land) and the formation of *edinolichnyj otrub*, individualistic holdings of consolidated parcels. The landholding data also include intermediary forms that entailed a high degree of peasant coordination, such as *cherezpolositsa* (strip-farmed land and collectively cultivated non-allotment land).

The model tested was: Land category 1863–1913 = f(distance in km from a *selo* [a group of communes] to the nearest railroad station).

The *uezd* (district) data are divided into an introductory part, documented information on *selos*, groups of village communes, and village-commune tables divided into data on *volosti*, cantons. The last-mentioned tables are of special interest to us in the tests below. Among other statistics, they contain communal-village data on landholding and material for the explanatory part of the model, populations of both sexes, household containing literate members, literate working men, working men, children learning to read divided by gender, and the grand total. There are data on

Individualism in Landholding as the Ultimate Modernization Proxy

(DEPENDENT VARIABLE)

Ratio of literate otkhodniks (wage laborers) to population

(EXPLANATORY VARIABLE)

The Model

Landholding mode—*zemlevladenie*

=*f* (share of literate male wage labor commuting by rail in population)

Fig. 10.3 Literate *Otkhodniks* ride the iron horse: data, variables, and model. (Source of data: I obtained my data from *zemstvo* (rural self-government) statistics edited by V.G. Groman, who is known to be a reliable source, for the Penza region in the northern *chernozem* (black earth) zone, not far from the Volga River system. I was introduced to this material by Professor Mikhail Abramovich Davydov in 2008, when I presented my initial model, *x/50 years repartitions of land in commune = f(distance from the railroads)*. This model simply assumes that the clustering of Russian peasants in village communes, with their mutually insuring physical-asset redistribution collectivism, was the product of the exceptionally high risks to life in the precarious agriculture on the Russian plain—especially from a historical perspective that included the heightened peril of Tatar invasions and more than two centuries of institutionalized serfdom)

the number of women in the population but none on working women, from which I infer that the women in question were members of *tyaglo* (household agricultural labor teams) who did not commute and were not spatially mobile industrial wage workers; the working woman category is absent. In regard to male workers and their placement among working men and literate working men, Column I assigns them to the category of spatially mobile wage labor because they were differently registered than men who continued to work as members of agricultural teams. These statistics also contain data on households that engaged in crafts in an *obshchina*.

Households engaging in crafts in *obshchina* = *f*(distance from *obshchina* to railroad station)
Households engaging in crafts in *obshchina* = *f*(households with literate members in relation to all households in *obshchina*)
Households engaging in crafts = *f*(literate working men/population ratio) including spatial-mobility aspects.

The table below sets forth the variables (Table 10.14).

Table 10.14 Collectivistic and individualistic landholding modalities

Russian	*English*	*Ratio*	*Name*	*Proxy*
Zemlievladenie nadelnoe razverstannoe razpredelonnoe	Collective allotment rotating redistributed land	/all land	**COLLROTALO-FALLAND**	Collectivist dependence, the legacy of serfdom; The yoke of hierarchy of coercion: Backwardness
Ukreplienie po zakonu 9 Noyabria, cherezpolositza	Land entitlement in Stolypin reform, stripfarming redistributed	/all land	**STOLSTRRSH**	Intermediary collectivist individualist form containing risk reduction as to soil quality
Zemlievladenie vnenadelnoe, edinolichnyi otrub	Non-allotment individual consolidated parcel	/all land	**INDCONSO-FALLAND**	The most individualist land holding entailing entrepreneurial mastery and risk-taking: Modernization
Zemlievladenie nadelnoye	Allotment land	/all land	**SERITOGOAL11O-FALLAND**	Total legacy of serfdom—Mutual insurance—Including the elements at individualization in Stolypin reform
Zemlievladenie vnenadelnoe	Non-allotment land	/all land	**ITOGONONA-L11OFAL**	Individualist landholding sum—Albeit containing collective coordination
Rozstayanie od stancji zheleznoy dorogi v obshchinie	Distance from railroad station in *obshchina*	–	**DISTOB**	Technological transport novelty
Gramotnych mushchin robochich	Literate working men	LMR/ITOGOD LMR/MR	**LMR**	Spatial mobility and literacy—Modernization conundrum
Mushchin robochich	Working men	–	**MR**	
Uchiashchihsia detej itogo	Children learning to read	Children learning to read/ITOGOD	**CHILDSH**	Future modernization intensity optimism—Rational expectations of returns to literacy and education
Dush Oboego pola—	Population of both sexes		**ITOGOD**	–

Literate Peasant Landholding and Commuting by Rail for *Otkhod* (Wage Labor): Regressions

Dependent Variable: COLLROTALOFALLAND
Method: ARMA Maximum Likelihood (OPG—BHHH)
Date: 07/25/18 Time: 10:23
Sample: 1 926
Included observations: 868
Convergence achieved after 259 iterations
Coefficient covariance computed using outer product of gradients

Variable	Coefficient	Standard Error	*t*-Statistic	Probability
C	0.691154	0.046245	14.94532	0.0000
LMROFITOGOD	-3.050754	0.655233	-4.655983	0.0000
AR(1)	0.343152	0.009420	36.42870	0.0000
SIGMASQ	0.281651	0.002684	104.9446	0.0000
R-squared	0.113768	Mean dependent variable		0.622638
Adjusted *R*-squared	0.110691	S.D. dependent variable		0.564069
S.E. of regression	0.531935	Akaike information criterion		1.585041
Sum-squared residual	244.4730	Schwarz criterion		1.607005
Log likelihood	-683.9077	Hannan-Quinn criterion		1.593446
F-statistic	36.97128	Durbin-Watson statistic		1.933357
Prob (*F*-statistic)	0.000000			
Inverted AR Roots	0.34			

S.D. standard deviation; S.E. standard error

Dependent Variable: COLLROTALOFALLAND
Method: ARMA Maximum Likelihood (OPG—BHHH)
Date: 07/25/18 Time: 10:30
Sample: 1 926
Included observations: 856
Convergence achieved after 260 iterations
Coefficient covariance computed using outer product of gradients

Variable	Coefficient	Standard Error	*t*-Statistic	Probability
C	0.683253	0.046975	14.54507	0.0000
LMROFMR	-0.596386	0.155528	-3.834594	0.0001
AR(1)	0.339620	0.009430	36.01633	0.0000
SIGMASQ	0.283227	0.002651	106.8533	0.0000
R-squared	0.115118	Mean dependent variable		0.619224
Adjusted *R*-squared	0.112002	S.D. dependent variable		0.566081
S.E. of regression	0.533439	Akaike information criterion		1.592138
Sum-squared residual	242.4423	Schwarz criterion		1.614345

(*continued*)

(continued)

Log likelihood	-677.4349	Hannan-Quinn criterion	1.600641
F-statistic	36.94677	Durbin-Watson statistic	1.943817
Prob(*F*-statistic)	0.000000		
Inverted AR Roots	0.34		

S.D. standard deviation; S.E. standard error

Dependent Variable: COLLROTALOFALLAND
Method: ARMA Maximum Likelihood (OPG—BHHH)
Date: 07/25/18 Time: 10:38
Sample: 1 926
Included observations: 868
Convergence achieved after 257 iterations
Coefficient covariance computed using outer product of gradients

Variable	Coefficient	Standard Error	*t*-Statistic	Probability
C	0.687449	0.046687	14.72464	0.0000
CHILDLSH	-2.172672	0.455117	-4.773871	0.0000
AR(1)	0.341697	0.009261	36.89499	0.0000
SIGMASQ	0.281940	0.002683	105.0646	0.0000
R-squared	0.112858	Mean dependent variable		0.622638
Adjusted *R*-squared	0.109778	S.D. dependent variable		0.564069
S.E. of regression	0.532208	Akaike information criterion		1.586026
Sum-squared residual	244.7240	Schwarz criterion		1.607990
Log likelihood	-684.3353	Hannan-Quinn criterion		1.594431
F-statistic	36.63807	Durbin-Watson statistic		1.935226
Prob(*F*-statistic)	0.000000			
Inverted AR Roots	0.34			

S.D. standard deviation; S.E. standard error

Let us look at the significant elasticity of the most collectivistic type of landholding. The mutually insuring land-rotation system, an institutional remnant of serfdom, entails peasant dependency on land management by the patriarchal authority, the *shkod* (assembly of elders). The larger the share of this land, the less informed are the individual peasant household and, within it, the individual peasant—and, by tautology, the lower is the share of literate commuting wage workers in the population and among working men. The lower also is the future-oriented optimism proxy: children learning to read as the share of the population. The most noteworthy facts are that all three explanatory variables place the equation signs in the theory-congruent direction, signaling a negative correlation, and that all three are significant at a 5 percent level. Considering that neither R-square nor Durbin-Watson (DW) is very impressive, I conclude that factors other than the literate *otkhod*—a relatively recent phenomenon—determined this type of landholding. This inference comports with the historical serfdom legacies of the most collectivist pre-modern insurance system, one that established a rotation among households, based on ***krugovaya poruka***, mutual responsibility for taxes and dues. This system had been utilized by landlords and, after the emancipation, by the state for tax extraction while the peasantry, through land rotation, aimed to ensure that each household would be able to shoulder its tax burden, simultaneously preserving internal harmony (Ma, 2006) and keeping the Tsarist gendarmes at the desired arm's length.

Dependent Variable: INDCONSOFALLAND
Method: ARMA Maximum Likelihood (OPG—BHHH)
Date: 07/25/18 Time: 12:45
Sample: 1 926
Included observations: 866
Convergence achieved after 41 iterations
Coefficient covariance computed using outer product of gradients

Variable	Coefficient	Standard Error	t-Statistic	Probability
C	0.070837	0.028908	2.450395	0.0145
LMROFITOGOD	0.574574	0.150629	3.814499	**0.0001**
AR(1)	0.565044	0.022247	25.39886	0.0000
SIGMASQ	0.030168	0.001158	26.04140	0.0000
R-squared	**0.335366**	Mean dependent variable		0.084832
Adjusted R-squared	0.333053	S.D. dependent variable		0.213173
S.E. of regression	0.174092	Akaike information criterion		−0.640494
Sum-squared residual	26.12544	Schwarz criterion		−0.618490
Log likelihood	281.3338	Hannan-Quinn criterion		−0.632073
F-statistic	144.9849	Durbin-Watson statistic		**2.065982**
Prob(F-statistic)	0.000000			
Inverted AR Roots	0.57			

S.D. standard deviation; S.E. standard error

Dependent Variable: INDCONSOFALLAND
Method: ARMA Maximum Likelihood (OPG—BHHH)
Date: 07/25/18 Time: 12:49
Sample: 1 926
Included observations: 854
Convergence achieved after 43 iterations
Coefficient covariance computed using outer product of gradients

(*continued*)

(continued)

Variable	Coefficient	Standard Error	*t*-Statistic	Probability
C	0.074238	0.029360	2.528566	0.0116
LMROFMR	0.094760	0.033448	2.833025	**0.0047**
AR(1)	0.562553	0.022599	24.89265	0.0000
SIGMASQ	0.030537	0.001194	25.56752	0.0000
R-squared	**0.335068**	Mean dependent variable		0.086024
Adjusted *R*-squared	0.332721	S.D. dependent variable		0.214428
S.E. of regression	0.175160	Akaike information criterion		-0.624484
Sum-squared residual	26.07893	Schwarz criterion		-0.602236
Log likelihood	270.6546	Hannan-Quinn criterion		-0.615964
F-statistic	142.7754	Durbin-Watson statistic		**2.064690**
Prob(*F*-statistic)	0.000000			
Inverted AR Roots	0.56			

S.D. standard deviation; S.E. standard error

Dependent Variable: INDCONSOFALLAND
Method: ARMA Maximum Likelihood (OPG—BHHH)
Date: 07/25/18 Time: 12:54
Sample: 1 926
Included observations: 866
Convergence achieved after 40 iterations
Coefficient covariance computed using outer product of gradients

Variable	Coefficient	Standard. Error	*t*-Statistic	Probability
C	0.069293	0.029147	2.377402	0.0177
CHILDLSH	0.492778	0.131675	3.742372	**0.0002**
AR(1)	0.567279	0.022251	25.49443	0.0000
SIGMASQ	0.030092	0.001147	26.23483	0.0000
R-squared	**0.337036**	Mean dependent variable		0.084832
Adjusted *R*-squared	0.334728	S.D. dependent variable		0.213173
S.E. of regression	0.173873	Akaike information criterion		-0.642914
Sum-squared residual	26.05981	Schwarz criterion		-0.620910
Log likelihood	282.3818	Hannan-Quinn criterion		-0.634493
F-statistic	146.0737	Durbin-Watson statistic		**2.065352**
Prob(*F*-statistic)	0.000000			
Inverted AR Roots	0.57			

S.D. standard deviation; S.E. standard error

The three tables above give the regression results of the most telling land category in my argument—individual consolidated parcel of non-allotment land. The results are significant and *the p-values allow H0 to be refuted*. That is, the ratios of literate wage-earning males to population, of literate wage-earning males to working males, and of children learning to read in the population have an impact on this land-category choice. The Durbin-Watson value is about 2, conveying correct model specification. The R-square in all three equations is 34 percent. Thus, roughly a third of choices of the most individualistic landholding mode is explained by the ratio of *literate wage workers* to population and by the ratio of the same to all working males. The share of children learning to read in the population yields the same result. The signs of the equation are a case in point: The higher the ratio of literate male wage workers to population and to working males, the more likely it is that the peasants of Penza Province will choose the most individualistic landholding mode. Thus, the nexus of spatial mobility and reading skill that this ratio captures allows us to cast off the yoke of collectivist mutual insurance in authoritarian structures, paving the way to an exodus of peasant households from the communal-resource orbit and allowing heads of household to engage in agricultural entrepreneurial innovative risk-taking. Likewise, the share of children learning to read in the population explains 34 percent—one-third—of the choice of this landholding mode. This variable mirrors the future-oriented dynamism that undergirded peasants' assessment of future demand and returns on reading skill, which, according to secondary sources, peasants construed as a craft. Thus, the declining physical distance, an outcome of railroad construction (Sztern, 2017 and Chap. 9) and the phenomenon derived from it—the contraction of cognitive distance to urban agglomerations—increasingly raised the opportunity costs of having children till the land and, in turn, incentivizing parents to enroll their children in school.

Consequently, up to 34 percent of individualism that allows peasants to substitute innovative risk-taking in agriculture for the old ways is explained by their ability to educate their children and gather available information while participating in markets of knowledge, utilizing the knowledge spillover. It also must be noted that the peasant population was growing at this time, depressing this ratio. Thus, the 34 percent explanatory power is lower here than in the equation of land category and physical distance from railroad station, with a 45 percent R-square (Sztern, 2017 and Chap. 9). Even the ratio that I found, however, makes it possible to estimate the strength of a future-oriented dynamism that participates in the interaction between spatial mobility and reading skills. Given that such a dynamism may grow infinitely and more rapidly than the long-term expansion of rail lines, its revolutionary cultural potential portends higher explanatory values in the future.

Dependent Variable: ITOGONONAL11OFAL
Method: ARMA Maximum Likelihood (OPG—BHHH)
Date: 07/26/18 Time: 19:28
Sample: 1 926
Included observations: 868
Convergence achieved after 51 iterations
Coefficient covariance computed using outer product of gradients

Variable	Coefficient	Standard Error	*t*-Statistic	Probability
C	0.194000	0.022913	8.466699	0.0000
LMROFITOGOD	2.145474	0.373028	5.751505	0.0000
AR(1)	0.332324	0.016081	20.66504	0.0000
SIGMASQ	0.098005	0.001609	60.89663	0.0000
R-squared	0.144439	Mean dependent variable		0.240859
Adjusted *R*-squared	0.141468	S.D. dependent variable		0.338649
S.E. of regression	0.313782	Akaike information criterion		0.529096
Sum-squared residual	85.06867	Schwarz criterion		0.551060
Log likelihood	-225.6276	Hannan-Quinn criterion		0.537501
F-statistic	48.62111	Durbin-Watson statistic		2.049781
Prob(*F*-statistic)	0.000000			
Inverted AR Roots	0.33			

S.D. standard deviation; S.E. standard error

Dependent Variable: ITOGONONAL11OFAL
Method: ARMA Maximum Likelihood (OPG—BHHH)
Date: 07/26/18 Time: 19:34
Sample: 1 926
Included observations: 856
Convergence achieved after 52 iterations
Coefficient covariance computed using outer product of gradients

Variable	Coefficient	Standard Error	*t*-Statistic	Probability
C	0.197797	0.022674	8.723678	0.0000
LMROFMR	0.446843	0.076880	5.812250	0.0000
AR(1)	0.330275	0.016210	20.37458	0.0000
SIGMASQ	0.098524	0.001624	60.65177	0.0000
R-squared	0.145741	Mean dependent variable		0.244236
Adjusted *R*-squared	0.142733	S.D. dependent variable		0.339804
S.E. of regression	0.314621	Akaike information criterion		0.535851
Sum-squared residual	84.33619	Schwarz criterion		0.558058
Log likelihood	-225.3444	Hannan-Quinn criterion		0.544355
F-statistic	48.45170	Durbin-Watson statistic		2.054426
Prob(*F*-statistic)	0.000000			
Inverted AR Roots	0.33			

S.D. standard deviation; S.E. standard error

Dependent Variable: ITOGONONAL11OFAL
Method: ARMA Maximum Likelihood (OPG—BHHH)
Date: 07/26/18 Time: 19:39
Sample: 1 926
Included observations: 868
Convergence achieved after 47 iterations
Coefficient covariance computed using outer product of gradients

Variable	Coefficient	Standard Error	*t*-Statistic	Probability
C	0.190307	0.022957	8.289651	0.0000
CHILDLSH	1.761899	0.251102	7.016665	0.0000
AR(1)	0.333788	0.015976	20.89272	0.0000
SIGMASQ	0.097327	0.001577	61.72918	0.0000
R-squared	0.150363	Mean dependent variable		0.240859
Adjusted *R*-squared	0.147412	S.D. dependent variable		0.338649
S.E. of regression	0.312694	Akaike information criterion		0.522188
Sum-squared residual	84.47966	Schwarz criterion		0.544152
Log likelihood	-222.6294	Hannan-Quinn criterion		0.530593
F-statistic	50.96813	Durbin-Watson statistic		2.048539
Prob(*F*-statistic)	0.000000			
Inverted AR Roots	0.33			

S.D. standard deviation; S.E. standard error

The aforesaid is additionally corroborated by the higher elasticity of the share of total non-allotment land to total peasant land. The ratios of literate wage workers to population and to wage-earning men, and of children learning to read to population, are positively related to the total share of non-allotment land in total peasant land, which accounts for most land held in the individualistic household hereditary manner even though some of it is collectively cultivated—a share that lies in between the collectively and individually held portions, as I show below. The regression result is significant at a 5 percent level and the Durbin-Watson value is about 2, indicating correct model specification. The sign of the equations is fully congruent with the theory. Thus, the larger the share of literate commuting wage workers in the population, the greater will be the share of non-allotment landholding in total land. The *R*-square is weaker than in the share of individual consolidated parcels because the grand total includes an in-between landholding mode that is determined by considerations other than access through spatial mobility and reading skill to agglomerations of knowledge in urban industrial economies.

Dependent Variable: INDCONSOFALLAND
Method: ARMA Maximum Likelihood (OPG—BHHH)
Date: 08/11/18 Time: 11:15
Sample: 1 926
Included observations: 866
Convergence achieved after 41 iterations
Coefficient covariance computed using outer product of gradients

Variable	Coefficient	Standard Error	t-Statistic	Probability
C	0.121996	0.030548	3.993524	0.0001
DISTOB	-0.002272	0.000990	-2.295626	0.0219
LMROFITOGOD	0.581589	0.152417	3.815769	0.0001
AR(1)	0.560367	0.022372	25.04727	0.0000
SIGMASQ	0.029920	0.001118	26.75753	0.0000
R-squared	0.340831	Mean dependent variable		0.084832
Adjusted R-squared	0.337768	S.D. dependent variable		0.213173
S.E. of regression	0.173475	Akaike information criterion		-0.646638
Sum-squared residual	25.91065	Schwarz criterion		-0.619133
Log likelihood	284.9942	Hannan-Quinn criterion		-0.636111
F-statistic	111.2973	Durbin-Watson statistic		2.065552
Prob(F-statistic)	0.000000			
Inverted AR Roots	0.56			

S.D. standard deviation; S.E. standard error

Dependent Variable: INDCONSOFALLAND
Method: ARMA Maximum Likelihood (OPG—BHHH)
Date: 08/11/18 Time: 11:26
Sample: 1 926
Included observations: 854
Convergence achieved after 42 iterations
Coefficient covariance computed using outer product of gradients

Variable	Coefficient	Standard Error	t-Statistic	Probability
C	0.125276	0.030866	4.058706	0.0001
DISTOB	-0.002264	0.001004	-2.254204	0.0244
LMROFMR	0.095356	0.034020	2.802919	0.0052
AR(1)	0.557897	0.022745	24.52880	0.0000
SIGMASQ	0.030288	0.001152	26.28116	0.0000
R-squared	0.340497	Mean dependent variable		0.086024
Adjusted R-squared	0.337390	S.D. dependent variable		0.214428
S.E. of regression	0.174546	Akaike information criterion		-0.630593
Sum-squared residual	25.86601	Schwarz criterion		-0.602783
Log likelihood	274.2632	Hannan-Quinn criterion		-0.619943
F-statistic	109.5833	Durbin-Watson statistic		2.064323
Prob(F-statistic)	0.000000			
Inverted AR Roots	0.56			

S.D. standard deviation; S.E. standard error

Dependent Variable: INDCONSOFALLAND
Method: ARMA Maximum Likelihood (OPG—BHHH)
Date: 08/11/18 Time: 11:31
Sample: 1 926
Included observations: 866
Convergence achieved after 42 iterations
Coefficient covariance computed using outer product of gradients

Variable	Coefficient	Standard Error	*t*-Statistic	Probability
C	0.122412	0.030532	4.009308	0.0001
DISTOB	-0.002382	0.000993	-2.399516	0.0166
CHILDLSH	0.518002	0.134671	3.846428	0.0001
AR(1)	0.562242	0.022364	25.14079	0.0000
SIGMASQ	0.029822	0.001106	26.97089	0.0000
R-squared	0.342996	Mean dependent variable		0.084832
Adjusted *R*-squared	0.339944	S.D. dependent variable		0.213173
S.E. of regression	0.173190	Akaike information criterion		-0.649849
Sum-squared residual	25.82552	Schwarz criterion		-0.622344
Log likelihood	286.3848	Hannan-Quinn criterion		-0.639323
F-statistic	112.3737	Durbin-Watson statistic		2.064382
Prob(*F*-statistic)	0.000000			
Inverted AR Roots	0.56			

S.D. standard deviation; S.E. standard error

The three sequence equations above, with two explanatory variables—distance of the village commune from the railroad and reading-skill ratios—simply corroborate my findings. The closer the peasants of Penza Province are to the railroads, the more likely it is that they will choose an individual consolidated parcel of non-allotment land as a share of all land. Thus, collectivism versus individualism in the Russian pre-Revolution *obshchina* (1913) is explained by several determinants: the reduced risk of perishing that traces to proximity to the railroad; the concurrent dwindling of the same risk in the modernization process; the upturn in individuals' demand for mastery over their lives and endeavors; the growing share of the literate peasantry that has satisfied its quest for self-dignity relative to the peasant population at large; and the quest for personally satisfying modern ways of life. The literacy of mobile wage-earning *otkhodniks* as a share in the population explains all by itself 34 percent of the transition to the individualistic landholding mode. This proportion is congruent with the results pertaining to the ratio of literate wage-earning *otkhodniks* to wage-earning males and the ratio of peasant children learning to population. The latter clearly indicates the future orientation of the

Penza region peasantry, who foresee their children's reading skills being transformed into crafts while expecting higher returns on their acquisition of this skill than on the use of their labor in tilling the fields.

Dependent Variable: COLLROTALOFALLAND
Method: ARMA Maximum Likelihood (OPG—BHHH)
Date: 08/11/18 Time: 11:20
Sample: 1 926
Included observations: 868
Convergence achieved after 218 iterations
Coefficient covariance computed using outer product of gradients

Variable	Coefficient	Standard Error	*t*-Statistic	Probability
C	0.498268	0.076225	6.536786	0.0000
DISTOB	0.008536	0.002573	3.317198	0.0009
LMROFITOGOD	-3.073510	0.678409	-4.530471	0.0000
AR(1)	0.302787	0.012372	24.47320	0.0000
SIGMASQ	0.275231	0.004268	64.48388	0.0000
R-squared	0.133969	Mean dependent variable		0.622638
Adjusted *R*-squared	0.129955	S.D. dependent variable		0.564069
S.E. of regression	0.526142	Akaike information criterion		1.563213
Sum-squared residual	238.9003	Schwarz criterion		1.590668
Log likelihood	-673.4345	Hannan-Quinn criterion		1.573719
F-statistic	33.37514	Durbin-Watson statistic		1.891828
Prob(*F*-statistic)	0.000000			
Inverted AR Roots	0.30			

S.D. standard deviation; S.E. standard error

The most collectivistic landholding mode in the two-explanatory-variable model also supports my results and their interpretation. The farther from the railroad a peasant in Penza Province is, the more likely he is to choose the collectivistic and mutually ensuring landholding mode. In this type of landholding, the share of literate wage-earning *otkhodniks* in the population will be lower. Thus, the lower the ratio of literate spatially mobile peasants to population is, the greater will be the dependency on mutual insurance in the traditional rotational landholding practice. The holding itself is explained by the legacies of serfdom rather than by distance from railroads and the share of literate peasants in the population, thus explaining the relatively low *R*-square obtained. Nevertheless, the direction of the change is clear—and the dwindling distance of the commune from the railroad explains, as shown above in the individualistic parcel equations, the crumbling of the *obshchina*, the redistributive commune in Tsarist Russia.

Conclusion: Railroads, Literacy, Individualism, and the Seed-to-Yield Ratio

Above I proposed *spatial mobility and literacy as mutually and dynamically reinforcing interactions, complementary and accommodative of countless rural–urban multipliers*, as the actual and material developmental engine of the pre-Revolution Tsarist Russian peasant's cognitive emancipation from the yoke of servile backwardness. This exodus was facilitated by the "iron horse" (Fogel, 1964), or as I called it the "iron-spider web," of the Tsarist railroads that had been spreading since 1837–1843 and onward to 1914. It was these Tsarist locomotives, I propose, that pulled peasant Russia out of the formal and informal modalities and aspects of bondage that its personalized-patriarchal and paternalizing hierarchies of coercion had sustained until then.

Gerschenkronians emphasize Tsarist Russia's "dual economy," a modernized economy that nevertheless enjoyed the advantages of backwardness, imported novel technology and industry, and kept itself isolated and insulated from the backward agricultural economy that typified the country's 80 percent peasant majority. I argue that the latter constituency, by boarding moving trains and seating its children on school benches, placed itself within the radii of "knowledge spillover" (Fujita, 2001) from increasingly industrializing urban agglomerations while steadily replenishing these agglomerations amid an increasingly modernizing and individualistic agriculture that delivered rising returns. By putting it this way, I find that the real Russian revolution occurred before January 1905 and *a fortiori* before October 1917, meaning that the Gerschenkronian "dual economy" model is static. Instead of that model, I suggest a dynamic correlation among railroads, literacy, and individualism in landholding, manifested in the course of the second stage of Stolypin's reform (1913).

I chose to construct a sequence of three test ratios: (1) literate wage-earning male *otkhodniks* as a share of the population, (2) literate wage-earning male *otkhodniks* as a share of working *otkhodniks*, and (3) children learning to read as a share of the population. All three are explanatory variables for peasants' real-life choice of the individualistic landholding option that became available as the result of the Tsarist concession encapsulated in the Stolypin reform. The ratios of literate *otkhodniks*, I argue, yield evidence of the vehicles of Russia's pre-Revolution modernization. The railroads, transporting spatially mobile and increasingly literate *otkhodniks*, provide and incentivize a forum for information exchange

(Brooks, 2003). In this forum, the economies of the knowledge-contingent asymmetry of power steadily eroded as the ceremonial transmogrified into matters of fact (Veblen, in Hodgson, 2004), allowing and incentivizing the demand for equality before the law, universal access to free education, and political suffrage. Therefore, my chosen proxy for the modernization aspect is spatial mobility: the ratio of literate male wage-earning peasant-proletarian commuters between the rural and urban economies, and that of children learning to read, as percentage shares of the population. The proxy of the ultimate modernization, in turn, is the propensity to choose individualistic consolidated landholding.

Concluding, I refer again to Poznanski (1992, 1985) and the correlation among the individualization of rights, innovative entrepreneurial risk-taking, and factor productivity. Just as I argued that literate wage labor explains 34 percent of landholding individualization, the same phenomenon explains at least in part the rising seed-to-yield ratio and Total Factor Productivity during the post-emancipation and railroad era—mitigating uncertainty, lowering transaction costs, and reinforcing the incentive function of property rights in the long run. Even though the crux of the 1906 reform was bound to the autocratic tradition, as Kotsonis makes clear, the very delegation of aspects of individualization of rights to land to the peasantry had irreversible dimensions that, de facto until de jure, paved the way to intensive resource use amid increases in population and literate population. The pre-Revolution phenomenon discussed here included additional spatial mastery coupled with human-capital accumulation that, in the long run, could pose a sufficiently effective threat from below as to occasion the full transformation of *votchina* (patrimony) land into the inalienable allodial property of the peasant head of household—heralding the dissolution of autocracy in Russia before the 1917 Revolution and the advent of Stalinism eleven years later.

References

Ascher, A. (1988). *The revolution of 1905. Part I: Russia in disarray. Part II: Authority restored.* Stanford University Press.

Atack, J., Bateman, I. A., Haines, F., & Margo, M. (2010). Did railroads induce or follow economic growth? Urbanization and population growth in the American Midwest 1850–1960. *Social Science History, 34*(2), 171–197.

Atkinson, D. (1983). *The end of the Russian land commune 1905–1930.* Stanford University Press.

Bideleux, R. (1990). Agricultural advance under the Russian village commune system. In R. Bartlett (Ed.), *Land commune and peasant community in Russia: Communal forms in Imperial and early Soviet society*. Macmillan in Association with the School of Slavonic and East European Studies, University of London.

Brooks, J. (2003). *When Russia learned to read: Literacy and popular literature 1861–1917*. Northwestern University Press.

Burbank, J. (2004). *Russian peasants go to court: Legal culture in the countryside, 1905–1917*. Indiana University Press.

Burds, J. (1998). *Peasant dreams and market politics: Labor migration and the Russian village 1861–1905*. University of Pittsburgh Press.

Eklof. (2012). Russia and the Soviet Union: Schooling, Citizenship and the Reach of the State, 1870–1945. In Brockliss, L and Sheldon, N (Ed.), *Mass Education and the Limits of State Building c. 1870–1930*.

Engel, A. B. (1996). *Between the fields and the city: Woman work and family in Russia 1861–1914*. Cambridge University Press.

Fogel, R. (1964). *Railroads and American economic growth*. Johns Hopkins University Press.

Frank, S. (1999). *Crime, cultural conflict and justice in rural Russia 1856–1914*. University of California Press.

Freeze, G. (1988). *From supplication to revolution: A documentary social history of Imperial Russia*. Oxford University Press.

Frierson, C. (1993). *Peasant icons: Representations of rural people in late nineteenth century Russia*. Oxford University Press.

Fujita, K. V. (2001). *The spatial economy: Cities regions and international trade*. The MIT Press.

Gaudin, C. (2007). *Ruling peasants: Village and state in late imperial Russia*. Northern Illinois University Press.

Gerschenkron, A. (1962). *Economic backwardness in historical perspective*. The Belknap Press of Harvard University Press.

Gerschenkron, A. (1968). *Continuity in history and other essays*. The Belknap Press of Harvard University Press.

Gintis, H. (2009). *The bounds of reason: Game theory and the unification of the behavioral sciences*. Princeton University Press.

Gregory, P. R. (1982). *Russian national income 1885–1913*. Cambridge University Press.

Gregory, P. R. (1994). *Before command. An economic history of Russia from emancipation to the first five-year plan*. Princeton University Press.

Hesse, G. (1993). Land use systems and property rights. Evolutionary versus institutional economics. In U. Witt (Ed.), *Evolution in markets and institutions*. Physica-Vlg.

Hoch, S. (1986). *Serfdom and social control in Russia. Petrovskoe a village in Tambov*. University of Chicago Press.

Hodgson, G. M. (1999). *Evolution and institutions: On evolutionary economics and the evolution of economics*. Edward Elgar.
Hodgson, G. M. (2004). The Evolution of Institutional Economics- Agency, Structure and Darwinism in American Institutionalism, Routledge.
Johnson, R. (1979). *Peasant and proletarian: The working class of Moscow in the late nineteenth century*. Leicester University Press.
Jones, A. (2013). *Late-imperial Russia and interpretation : Three visions two cultures and one peasantry*. Peter Lang.
Kahan, A. (1989). In R. Weiss (Ed.), *Russian economic history: The nineteenth century*. University of Chicago Press.
Kingston-Mann, E. (1991). Peasant communes and economic innovation: A preliminary inquiry. In E. Kingston-Mann, T. Mixter, & J. Burds (Eds.), *Peasant economy culture and politics of European Russia*. Princeton University Press.
Kotsonis, Y. (2011). *The problem of the individual in the Stolypin reform*. Kritika: Explorations in Russian and Euroasian History Slavic Publishers Volume 12, November 1, Winter 2011 (New Series), pp. 22–55.
Leonard, C. S. (2011). *Agrarian reform in Russia. The road from, serfdom*. Cambridge University Press.
Ma, D. (2006). *Law and commerce in traditional China. An institutional perspective on the 'Great Divergence.'* Seminar Paper, Department of Economic History, Lund University.
Macey, D. (1990). The peasant commune and the Stolypin reforms: Peasant attitudes, 1906–14. In R. Bartlett (Ed.), *Land commune and peasant community in Russia: Communal forms in imperial and early Soviet society*. University of London, Macmillan in Association with the School of Slavonic and East European Studies, University of London.
Metzer, J. (1972). *Some economic aspects of railroad development in Tsarist Russia* [Unpublished doctoral dissertation]. University of Chicago.
Milov, L. (2001). *Velikorusskii pakhar i osobennosti rossijskogo istoricheskogo protsessa*. Biblioteka Gumer-istoria http://www.gumer.info/bibliotek_Buks/History/milov/01.php
Mironov, B. N. (1999). *Socialnaya istoria Rossii perioda Imperii (XVIII-nachalo XX v) genezis lichnosti demokraticheskoj semii grazhdanskogo obshchestva i pravovogo gosudarstva: v dwuch tomach*. Dimitrij Bulanin.
Mironov, B. N. (2012). Nabljudalsia li v Pozdnie Imperskoj Rosii Malthusianskij krizis: Dochody i povinosti Rossijskogo krestianstva, v 1801–1914 gg.
Mokyr, J. (1990). *Lever of riches. Technological creativity and economic progress*. Oxford University Press.
Moon, D. (1999). *The Russian peasantry 1600–1930. The world the peasants made*. Longman.
Nafziger, S. (2007). *Land redistributions and the Russian peasant commune in the 19th century*. EHES, Lund and Department of Economics, Williams College.

Nafziger, S. (2010). Peasant communes and factor markets in late-nineteenth-century Russia. *Explorations in Economic History, 47*(4), 381–402.

Nafziger, S., & Dennisson, T. (2011). *Micro-perspectives on living standards in nineteenth century Russia*. Researchgate.

North, D. C. (1973). *Västerlandets Uppgång*. SNS.

North, D. C. (1990). *Institutions, institutional change and economic performance*. Cambridge University Press.

Penza Province Zemstvo (1913). Itogi otzenochno-statisticheskogo izsledovania Penzeskoj Gubernii pod obshchim rukovodstvom V.G. Gromana. *Podvornaya perepis krestianskogo khozjajstva obrobotana T.B. shubom*. Penza: Rapoport et al.

Pipes, R. (1995). *Russia under the old regime*. Penguin Books.

Poznanski, K. (1985). *The environment for technological change in centrally planned economies*. World Bank Staff Working Papers.

Poznanski, K. (1992). A property rights perspective on the evolution of communist-type economies. In K. Poznanski (Ed.), *Constructing capitalism. The re-emergence of civil society and liberal economy in the post-Communist world*. Westview Press.

Robbins, R. G., Jr. (1975). *Famine in Russia 1891–1892: The Imperial government responds to a crisis*. Columbia University Press.

Sablinsky, W. (1976). *The road to bloody Sunday: Father Gapon and the St. Petersburg massacre of 1905*. Princeton University Press.

Sen, A. (1999). *Development as freedom*. Oxford University Press.

Sheshinski, E. (2010). *Limits in individual choice*. The Hebrew University of Jerusalem.

Shivelbusch, W. (1986). *The railway journey: The industrialization of time and space in the 19th century*. University of California Press.

Smurova, O. V. (2003). *Niezemledelcheski odkhod krestian v stolitsu I ego vlejanie na transformacjiu kulturnoj tradicji*. Izd-vo Kostromskogo gos. technologich. Universiteta.

Sztern, S. (2017). *Russia on the move the railroads and the exodus from compulsory collectivism 1861–1914*. Dissertation. Lund University Press.

Sztern, S. (2018). *Steam engine on the rail and landholding system in-nineteenth century Russia*. Lomonosov State University Economic History Seminar (in Russian).

Veblen, T. (1931). *The theory of the leisure class*. Viking.

Witt, U. (1993). *Evolution in markets and institutions*. Physica- Verlag A Springer Verlag Company.

Worobec, C. D. (1995). *Peasant Russia: Family and community in the post-emancipation period*. Northern Illinois University Press.

Yokoyama, O. (2008). *Russian peasant letters texts and contents*. Harrassowitz Verlag.

CHAPTER 11

Measurable Power: Railroads, Literacy, and the Crafts Artel—Hierarchy in Disarray in Late Imperial Russia

In this chapter, I propose a way to measure the heretofore unexplained techno-cultural "translation" of the traditional rural non-agricultural production organization—the mutually insuring skilled workers' cooperative, the *artel*—into the historically continuous core of industrial trade unions, the institutional harbingers of modernization in pre-1905-revolution Russia. The ratio of spatially mobile literate wage laborers to population, and to working men, introduced in previous chapters, is an explanatory variable for the transition to individualism and rationalism. Peasants' aforementioned choice of individualistic landholding, in turn, correlates positively with the share of children learning to read in the population, my proxy for the human-capital aspects of the kind of development that creates modernization. The *arteli* generated non-agricultural peasant income while incentivizing literacy and lowering the costs of collective action. Thus, they paved the way toward constitutional governance by foreshadowing the protection of intellectual property while contractually consolidating and tacitly carrying knowledge of subversive and artisan skills and stimulating effective bottom-up demand for reform. To anchor these propositions in data, I again use *zemstvo* (rural self-government) statistics for the Penza Province pertaining to the population of literate wage laborers, the distance of village communes from railroad stations, and the ratio of households that engaged in crafts production to households at large. Following Mironov (1999, 2000, 2012)and Gregory (1994, 1982) and countering Gerschenkron,

S. Sztern, *Russia on the Move*, Studies in Economic Transition,
https://doi.org/10.1007/978-3-030-89285-2_11

I argue that the cultural revolutions (Kahan, 1989; Mokyr, 1990; Smurova, 2003) that occurred were non-violent and were catalyzed by the Tsarist railroads—setting the peasant population in motion, incentivizing the exodus from analphabetism, enhancing skill accumulation, and predating 1905.

Introduction: The Evolution of Conventions That Forced the Autocracy into the Concessions of 1905

There was something peculiar about most industrial wage laborers in Late Tsarist Russia: the persistence of their ties to the redistribution of household land-use rights within the frame of the *obshchina*, the pre-revolution village commune. These rights, which inter alia provided social safety insurance in the event of old age and the failure of non-agricultural urban employment, obliged wage-earning peasants to repatriate wage income for the upkeep of their kin in the village. Key among these kin were *bolshaks* (heads of household, in whose hands rested the decision to allow wage-earning peasant sons to obtain internal passports, without which they could not move about, let alone commute to urban centers for paying work (Chap. 7). Moreover, to cope with the possibility of urban industrial conflict with employers, the hierarchy of peasant workers under Tsarist coercion ultimately organized along the traditional patterns of rural skilled workers, establishing cooperative structures that emerged from skilled workers' cooperatives, the *arteli*. These entities were supported by *artel'nye kassy* (Freeze, 1988), pooled resources for intra-trade-union mutual insurance. Therefore, it is a-historical to speak of the proletarian class identity in nineteenth-century Russia as an element that explains the organization of the strike movement and the revolution of 1905 (Ascher, 1988).

It is proposed below that the explanation of the history-specific organization of production and, consequently, of the subversion of autocracy in late Imperial Russia, paradoxically lies in *krugovaya poruka*, the traditional rural mutual-insurance structures. These structures, according to the Slavophile conception, evolved organically. Their implementation varied over time, in response to the topography and the divergent degrees of climate-specific predictability of crop yields, which, interacting with the available technology, determined the demand for mutual household insurance. The Westernizers school, headed by Boris Chicherin, emphasizes, however, that during the serfdom era, predominantly in black-earth regions, the mutual responsibility and aid structures had been enforced by landlords for the purpose of lowering the surveillance costs associated with collecting taxes and dues and for the satisfaction of *barshchina* (corvée labor) obligations. Following the de jure emancipation of the serfs in 1861–1863, *krugovaya poruka* survived natural selection and the adaptation of institutions to become the backbone of a new structure: redemption payments for allodial rights in land (Gerschenkron, 1962, 1968).

The basic constitutive ethos of the *obshchina*, manifested in communal redistribution of assets and the corresponding legal liabilities, including land and chattels, and in the *artel*—the peasant mutual solidarity craft cooperative—underwent a transformation from authority-compliance to rationalism due to peasant exposure to the multiplicity of choices introduced by the railroads. The spontaneous recurrence of the *obshchina* and artel structures among convicts and soldiers (Dostojewski, 1977; Bushnell, 1990) indicates the emerging ethos of *increasingly voluntary rural cooperation under mutual insurance.*

This form of labor organization, emancipated from its constitutive legacy of serfdom, was translated into modern relations of workers vis-à-vis labor foremen as it adapted itself to the needs of urban industrial production (Ascher, 1988), prefiguring the subversive trade-union activity that took the place in Late Imperial Russia. The implementation by the Russian peasantry of the abstract concept of class may have occurred much later, and was also understood by the Russian peasantry as such, through the prism and the historically specific concepts of their rural organization.

Here I suggest that peasants' mutual guarantee of the quality of production and the social-insurance artel organization evolved in classic synergy among spatial mobility (catalyzed by the railroads), acquisition of literacy, and the organization of skilled handicraft manufacturing for export that reduced transaction costs and the uncertainty of subversive challenges to the autocracy by trade unions. This paradox should be viewed against the background of the patronage that the Tsarist regime extended to crafts producers as a way of promoting enlightenment (Salmond, 1996).

The traditional crafts shop with its contractual networks, enforcement of rights and obligations, inventory of tacit knowledge, and ability to orient itself among multiple occupational, income, and spiritual options available to increasingly spatially mobile wandering peasant landsman communities (*zemliachestva*) was contingent on the acquisition of literacy and education. In this manner, the pre-revolution exodus from analphabetism was discontinuously incentivized by spatial mobility and the proliferation of crafts under the patronage of the Tsarist state (Salmond, 1996; Brooks, 2003).

In this process, peasants' ability to give, receive, and exchange information, acquire education, organize, and challenge the traditional hierarchies of patriarchal coercion intensified remarkably. Literate peasants, organized in trade unions and demanding democratizing reforms, eventually posed an effective challenge to the legacies of the personalized patronage and coercion that had survived from the era of Russian serfdom. The railroads, by thrusting the rural structures into flux while adapting them to the urban industrial milieu, forced workers to acquire new factual knowledge with incompatibly greater celerity. Thus, the construction of the Tsarist "iron horse" set a multidimensional modernization avalanche in motion.

Thus far I have identified three aspects of the process of exodus from backwardness that preceded the 1905 revolution: spatial mobility, transition to individualism and rationalism (Chap. 9), and literacy. Now I add a fourth aspect contingent on the third aspect and vice versa: the transformation and implementation of rural-cohesion mechanisms that mitigated the costs of collective action in the translation of pre-modern individual-risk-reducing mutual-responsibility organizations into subversive urban trade unions (Ma, 2006). Foreshadowing future historical findings, the actual vehicles of subversion were encapsulated in the literacy incentivizing artel organization and were additionally enhanced by spatial mobility, creating engines of social progress that challenged the autocracy.[1]

The main empirical findings in this chapter, presented in the Appendix, indicate that crafts production mitigated the risk to individual households' subsistence. This allocation of labor is explained to more than 20 percent R square by the ratio of children learning to read to literate working men. Thus, from a dynamic perspective, individual household risk was reduced by the future-orientated acquisition of literacy among peasant children. Indeed, in Chap. 10 I showed a positive correlation between the share of children learning to read in the population and that of individually cultivated consolidated parcels among all land, indicating that peasants rationally chose individualistic landholding modes and displayed a growing propensity to entrepreneurial risk. Thus, modernization in its interaction

[1] This raises the question of whether Stalinism, including forced collectivization, had been necessary for the modernization of Russia. The answer is no. See Chap. 9.

with the railroads and the cooperative artel was increasingly based on rationalist utility maximization rather than tradition compliance.

I argued in my dissertation and subsequent paper (Sztern, 2017, 2018a) that the railroads catalyzed the 1906 agrarian reform by empirically showing that railroad construction lowered the opportunity cost to peasants who allocated their children's labor to literacy acquisition, a skill that offered a future high return, instead of farm chores. By so doing, it increased the returns to households of their implementation of landholding reforms. This is why I chose the share of children learning to read relative to the population and relative to the proportion of literate working men as my proxy for modernization. My most interesting finding here is that the increase in this share in the black-earth Penza Province in Late Imperial Russia is explained by the share of literate working male adults in the population. This suggests to me that a discontinuous modernization process was under way, in which illiterate parents became economic dependents on literate and educated offspring (Yokoyama, 2008). Below I explain the identity between the variable of literate working men and *otkhod*—wage labor—that the railroads made possible (Spitzer, 2019).

The Impersonalization of Law: The Villagers Association and the Artel

Here I present elements of anecdotal evidence in tentative support of my introductory statements. Freeze (1988, p. 180) asserts that the Russian working class in 1860, growing slowly since the Catherinian era amid its disputes, "bore the stamp of" earlier, that is serfdom-contingent, factory relations. The social control and production relations that were typical of serfdom rested firmly on shared liability for taxes and dues in the Russian village commune, as well as other obligations that rotated use rights in peasant land commensurate with the number of labor teams that each household could deploy. A petition from a deputation of workers in Penza to the provincial governor on March 20, 1861, concerns the pledge of *otkhodniks* (wage-earning peasants) created by the obligation to repatriate their meager wages. These rules established the conditions for working outside the commune and demonstrated the inadequacy of land endowment, giving clear indication of the status of this land-bound labor force. The latter circumstance indicates and emphasizes the importance of local cultural-institutional, meteorological, topographic, and geographic rather than class conditions in the formation of labor associations (Milov, 2001; Burbank, 2004). Moreover, the humble address of the "skilled craftsman [from the ranks of craftsmen] of the Zlatoust Mining Plant petitions [was] *the Most August Monarch! The Most Merciful Sovereign*" (Freeze, 1988, p. 185)—conceptualizing the institution of the Tsar as the protector of the Russian peasant and the peasant-craftsman rather than their despoiler, as Marxian theory would have it (see also Cohen 2000). Similarly, a petition in 1863 to the Finance Ministry-owned Onega Salt Works from *pripisnye* workers (serfs assigned to industrial enterprises) indicates that the relationship with serf-owning gentry estates centered on the workers' locally delineated collective identity rather than adherence to the abstract concept of class (ibid.).

The organic association and organization of labor were set in motion by the *obshchina* with its *zemliachestva* (homesteader) ties, along with the sharing of liability among skilled workers within the structure of the crafts *artel* (Troyat, 1961, p. 99). These were the institutional vehicles of the transformation. They embodied the incentive for mutually guaranteed and quality-controlled labor-supply harbingers of income and human-capital accumulation and risk-reducing redistribution. In this autonomous associational mode, expanding ranks of peasant laborers could present the autocracy with an effective grassroots demand for democratizing concessions. In 1903, Lenin himself proposed that class consciousness be taught (Harding, 1996), tacitly admitting by so saying that such a consciousness did not exist among the peasant masses. The communal-village ethos that evolved in order to mitigate individual households' uncertainty, set in the organized village commune, was a pre-structured form of peasant cooperation that would translate, within the community of itinerant peasant artisans and agricultural workers, into *arteli*—shared-liability wage-labor organizations that traveled spatially in landsman-based networks (*zemlichestva*) (Johnson, 1979). The guarantee of peer-controlled labor quality that the *arteli* offered potential employers (Ransel, 1993, Appendix) allowed capital to accumulate and shifted the authority flowing from the breadwinner's status from sedentary fathers to spatially mobile sons. The latter population posed a credible threat from below to the prevailing hierarchies of coercion that were based on the patriarchal order, creating a nexus of subversion that historically predated the Marxist-Leninist agitation and the formation of the proletariat as a corporate class (Cohen, 2000). To implement the shared-liability labor contract and earn a premium (*bast shoe*) for lowering transaction costs and mitigating the uncertainty of employment for the labor cooperative as a whole (Troyat, 1961, pp. 98–9), at least the labor foremen had to be literate. Consequently, and as stated in Chap. 10, a link took shape among literacy (which allowed knowledge acquisition), seasonal work, and migration—facilitating income-earning opportunities in spatially dispersed crafts and trade employment—and bolstering the leaders' status. The leaders' authority, legitimized by the accumulation of practical matter-of-fact knowledge of and experience in novel industrial technologies, steadily replaced that of the village-bound patriarch, whose traditional experience and social standing historically represented the embodiment of the individual villager's risk insurance.

The strikes of 1870–1880 and their successors in the 1890s, through which child labor below age twelve was banned and women's working hours were limited, eventually also capped men's work day at 11.5 hours (Troyat, 1961, p. 97). By abusing their ability to level fines, employers triggered organized protests that were quashed with excessive force. Interestingly, the workers who were involved in these events organized along *obshchina*–artel lines that entailed mutual aid. The peasantry in conflict addressed itself to its economic pledge and uncertainty by setting up occupationally differentiated mutual-assistance funds—of shoemakers, weavers, paper makers, domestic servants, and so on (Troyat, 1961, 97)—that allowed them to persevere in the face of Tsarist repression.

Workers' demands that were brought before the Tsar on January 9, 1905, created a blueprint for peasant petitions to the Duma in numerous provinces in 1906 (Freeze, 1988, p. 279), repeatedly demanding universal suffrage and free and universally accessible education. The 1905 petition clearly emphasizes individual rights—"*equality of all before the law*" Ascher, 1988, p. 89)—and the de jure and de facto abolition of the collectivist hierarchies of coercion. Again, however, I claim, in a Bakunian (Bakunin, 1970) and not in a Marxian or a classical Liberal spirit, that peasant rural organization during and after the industrialization spurt of the 1890s presented the autocracy with an effective credible threat from below, encapsulated in the emergence of trade-union subversion that made the individualization of land rights in the 1906 Stolypin reform, ratified by the First Duma the same year, the governmental choice that surpassed "inferior optimum" (Ascher, 1988) strategies, such as engaging in territorial conflicts in order to divert subversion and discontent, in its political expectations. The individualization of rights entails, by tautology, the *impersonalization* of rights and transformation of the distribution of entitlement to them (Sztern, 2017). Causally, the skilled workers' *artel* and the peasants' railroad-enabled spatial mobility incentivized literacy acquisition, enforcing the trade-union structures that, by enhancing social-subversion capability, became harbingers of the challenge to the patriarchate—the very institution that, supported by the mainstream Orthodox Church, gave the autocracy its legitimacy. I emphasize, however, the Kahanian nature of the cultural revolution, driven by peasant spatial mobility, literacy, crafts production, and organization. All of these were contingent on the Tsarist-built railroad system and its technology, interacting with the historic organic mutual-insurance entities of the peasantry, the *obshchina* and the artel. Paradoxically, the challenge that these posed to the autocracy followed the diversification and growing strength of individualized control of income and belief systems amid the transition to rational choice among the newly available profusion of options—a composite upheaval that predated a blood-soaked conflict.

Theoretical Proposal: The Pre-Revolution Modernization Loop

Railroad technology first came to Imperial Russia in 1837–1843 (Westwood, 1964). By 1874, it reached the Penza Province, a northern black-earth region that is representative of awakening agricultural Russia in terms of its climatic and topographic conditions and in consideration of its proximity to the Volga River and the canal system. Access to this means of transport, which defied climatic conditions including frozen waterways, set two phenomena in motion. The first was the startling mitigation of the risk of impoverishment, death in famines (Robbins, 1975), and epidemics. Thus, the railroads circumscribed the existential uncertainty that had made rural households dependent on a mode of mutual insurance that was encapsulated in collectivist reciprocal-aid structures. This raises two questions: Do the dwindling cognitive and temporal hazards of travel and the shrinking distance to urban markets explain, at least indirectly, the regional dispersion of the income share of handicrafts production in the peasant budget, which mitigated economic risk over historical time? If the answer is yes, which specific aspects of this process provide the explanation? Below I test, tentatively, the correlation among the share of households involved in the practice of crafts, literacy, and spatial mobility, while acknowledging non-agricultural income in the peasant budget, peasant wage labor in urban industries, and the importation of modern technological expertise in agriculture, healthcare, and artisan skill to the villages.

The railroads did have a countervailing effect—growing social displacement due to increasing migration and seasonal commuting to novel and theretofore unknown institutional and technological environments. Their net impact, however, manifested in population increase, is clear: less risk of death.

The peasant communities strove to mitigate the risks and hazards associated with urban wage labor and migration by organizing along the lines of landsman and craft (artel) networks that emulated the mutual responsibility of the peasant commune. Craft production in spatially mobile *arteli* allowed peasant subversion to take shape while internalizing and reducing the risks associated with the absorption of novelties (Kingston-Mann, 1991). Peasant artisans' mutual insurance and quality assurance were mobile capital-accumulating accelerators of new knowledge, anchored in the ever-present incentive to acquire reading and cognitive skills. The travelling peasants were incentivized to acquire literacy skills, education, and practical knowledge that would give them the social mobility that they needed in order to obtain "clean work" in their novel and uncertainty-intensive exploration of urban employment options (Brooks, 2003; Mironov, 2012). The effective urban-industrial pull and the agglomeration and spillover of knowledge occasioned by the peasants' use of railroads (Fujita et al., 2012), absorbed in the spatially mobile peasant proletarian associations, legitimize the empirical inquiry that follows about the nature of pre-revolution peasant Russia's transition to modernity—an epitomic case of cultural-institutional discontinuity. The discontinuity that I have in mind in this context is the transition to rationalism and individualism, embedded in the dissolution of the authoritarian compulsory collectivist structures that embodied the legacy of serfdom, toward voluntary cooperation within the artel setting and an individualism codified ex post in the 1906 Stolypin reform (Chap. 9).

The Empirical Model and Its Variables

Three explanatory variables embody the railroads' causal effect: the ratio of literate wage-earning, commuting peasants to the total population and to that of working commuting peasants; the share of households that enjoy an income from crafts (hereinafter: craft-producing households) in the population of households; and a prospective developmental variable:

the share of literacy-acquiring boys in the total population and in the population of their role models, literate commuting working men. The share of children learning to read and that among literate working men in the population explains separately, with more than 30 percent R^2 and DW close to 2, peasants' choice of individualistic land categories among the fifteen categories that emerged between the emancipation in 1861 and the second stage of the Stolypin reform (1913) (see also Chap. 9: the stronger explanatory power of distance from *selos*, groups of communal villages). As a new aspect of the "cultural revolution" (Kahan, 1989) that preceded the violent upheaval, I investigate the impact of those among these boys who learned to read vis-à-vis the share of literate working men in households that had crafts income. The frequency of railroad use, I assume, is embedded in the variables of peasant wage-labor, migration-incentivized peasant literacy (Anderson, 1980; Brooks, 2003) and, paradoxically (because it occurred farther away from railroad lines), the acquisition of craft-production skills, enhanced by the share of children learning to read in the peasant population—a crucial development for the dynamic aspects of modernization in terms of the transition to rationalism and individualism.

Introduction to the Empirical Analysis

Materials Used: Models and Data

This chapter is based on statistics suggested for my initial hypothesis (Chap. 9) by Professor MA Davydov 2008 from the Penza Province *zemstvo* (rural self-government) for 1913, published under the supervision of V.G. Groman. The novelty in my resort to this source is its use of data on the proportion of *promysly* (peasant households with an income from crafts) among all households. In my model and in the construction of its ratios, I understand the share of such households as a function of the impact of the railroads on literacy and on the share of children learning to read in the population. Thus, I match the peasant literacy data in the Penza statistics with a sample of distances between peasant villages and railroad stations in the nine *uezds* (districts) of the province as well as the total populations of peasants, literate wage-earning men, and wage-earning men. The Penza authorities did not collect data on working women, least of all literate working women. By implication, women did not engage in wage labor to a sufficient degree and, in turn, did not acquire the spatial mobility that I assume to have motivated the acquisition of literacy. The data also include the variables that I use as proxies for the dynamic aspect of modernization: *uchiashchichsia malchikov* (boys—the more spatially mobile gender) who learned to read. I chose to focus on literacy-acquiring boys because the gendered division of labor assigned the future wage-earning breadwinner role to boys rather than girls. Thus, the ratio of literacy-acquiring boys to literate working men (their role models) is chosen in this study as an indicator of the modernization/cultural evolution variable.

Regression Equation and the Meaning of the Ultimate Dependent Variable: Movement Toward Individualization in Landholding as a Proxy for Modernization

In the pre-modern developmental stage, decisions of peasant households and individuals are assumed to be molded and shaped by temporally prior structures anchored in the authority-contingent, risk-diversifying, and risk-mitigating customs of the *obshchina*, the village commune (Archer, 1995; Hodgson, 2004). Therefore, I select American Evolutionary Institutionalism (AEI) as the appropriate explanatory framework. With the advent of the railroads, which afforded spatial mobility while reducing the mutual dependence of peasant households against natural calamities occasioned by the precarious meteorological conditions of Russian agriculture (Chubarov, 2001; Sztern, 2000), the emerging profusion of individual choice options in their spiritual, intellectual, and economic respects legitimize the application of the bottom-up hedonist utility-maximization assumption of which New Institutional Economics (NIE) is structured (Sheshinski, 2010; Gintis, 2009; Sztern, 2017; North, 1973, 1981, 1990, 1993). I assume the complementarity of the AEI and NIE frameworks (I explain this innovation in Chap. 3) and apply the relative weight theory over time (Hodgson et al., 1997; Boyer & Orlean, 1993; Sztern, 2017). The unfolding of multiple institutions before a spatially mobile peasantry allows risk diversification, rendering the pre-modern mechanisms of mutual insurance, derived from "sharing norms," redundant (Metzer, 1972; Sztern, 2017; Martens, 2004; McCloskey, 2001). This redundancy emancipated the *dvor* (peasant household) from compliance with authority as the path of access to the pool of collective-experience memories that previously mitigated the peasant household's risk of death under the harsh climatic conditions of Russian agriculture.

The main dependent variable in my sequence of models reflects the adaptation of the institutions to the physical structural conditions of life that shape and mold individual preferences (in AEI—the structure to agency perspective): the *land-to-labor ratio, soil quality*, and *climatic conditions* that are not prone to short-term changes. The explanatory exogenous variables are relatively flexible anthropogenic ones, such as the technologies applied (in NIE—the agency-to-structure perspective) (North, 2005),[2] that are assumed to change and bring on marginal and cumulatively discontinuous changes that cause and are caused by institutional mutations. By stating this, I liken the interaction between institutions and technology to drops of water descending on a stone, namely, it subjects relatively constant institutions to irreversible erosion and transformation. Evolutionarily Stable Strategy of survival (ESS) is encapsulated in the rural landholding system. ESS destabilizes and transforms amid peasants' use of railroad technology. The latter incentivizes, with marginal changes in users' cognition, their ability to absorb information, engage in non-ritual learning, accumulate personal knowledge not contingent on authority, and amass the capacity for rational choice. All of these determine the mix of agricultural and non-agricultural production technologies that mitigate risk of death.

Thus, the relative dependent variables in my sequence of models are:

- *The share of non-allotment individually held consolidated parcels of land relative to all peasant land.* I assume that this share changed more slowly than did the share of households that engaged in crafts.
- *The share of households engaging in crafts relative to all households.* I assume that this constituted a historical adaptation and risk-dispersion and -mitigation practice, contingent on regionally relatively constant climatic and soil conditions over time, railroad construction, and the consequent distance to railroad stations of structurally earlier origin.
- The same dependent variable in respect of marginal changes in the *share of literacy-acquiring boys relative to the population of literate working men*; this variable is less adaptable to short-term relative scarcities.
- *The share of literacy-acquiring boys relative to the population of literate working men.* This presupposes a parental household decision,

[2] The distinction between institutions occasioned by the physical environment and those explained by human interaction.

bounded by ritual tradition, relative to the already-established share of the literate *wage-earning* population (*otkhodniks*) in the population, which adapts flexibly on the margin.

I argue with emphasis that the *institutionalized association* encapsulated in *krugovaya poruka* (the labor organization based on mutual liability) was attenuated by peasants' use of railroads and structured the transition from authority to rational cooperation frameworks such as the late nineteenth-century *obshchina*, the artel, and the landsman association, inspired by the cooperative ethos. These settings, absorbed into the emerging urban trade unions, constituted effective vehicles of challenge to autocracy and the ensuing delegation of land rights to individual heads of household manifested in Stolypin's 1906 reform (Chap. 9).

McCloskey (2001), much in line with my reasoning, points to the economic incentives for risk-sharing and diversification that were manifested in the English open-field and strip-farmed landholdings versus enclosed and consolidated parcels. The risks to soil quality attending to farming under precarious conditions of natural disaster were mitigated by strip farming amid low but predictable average income. The standard deviation of income from the low mean allowed planning and insurance to take place. The consolidated land parcels, in contrast, raised the average income but boosted the standard deviation from the mean to a very high level. The resulting acute volatility and unpredictability of income resulted in severe perceived risk of death by starvation.

McCloskey's analysis captures both sides of Smith's insights (Smith, 1998, 2000), explaining clustering and cooperation in terms of rationalistic risk insurance. Like McCloskey, Scott (1976) emphasizes the safety-first principle or the minimization of the perceived risk of death. So does Pallot (1982, 1984) (1999) in her understanding of the Tsarist Russian village commune structure, as well as Eggertsson (1990) in explaining the structure of the pre-modern village.

I posit that the mutual liability that structured the *obshchina*, the artel, and strip farming among the previously tested land categories should be understood as the implementation of evolutionarily stable "safety first" risk-reducing strategies at the individual household level.

In the investigation that follows, I select the confluence of crafts, literacy, and spatial mobility, enhanced by peasant use of the railroads (see Fig. 11.1), and test each of these variables in its relation to the relatively dependent one (which is relatively stable over time). In so doing, I surmise that household crafts production uniquely constituted an empowering and, in terms of the negotiating power of the European Russian peasantry, an emancipating institution for the organization of production. Artisanship, particularly in its characteristic of apprenticeship contracts, incentivized the acquisition of literacy. Along with ***kustar*** (cottage industries) (Brooks, 2003), a cooperative organization of skilled workers in an artel based on written agreements allowed income to accrue, incentivized investment in skills and education, and portended the tacit accumulation of organizational knowledge (Hodgson, 1997). Peasant households' risk of death was thus reduced, paving the way to relative economic and therefore social independence. Under initial conditions of the imperatives of diversifying risk to income and insuring against natural disasters (triggered by crop failures) amid seasonal budget volatility, these characteristics of the artel

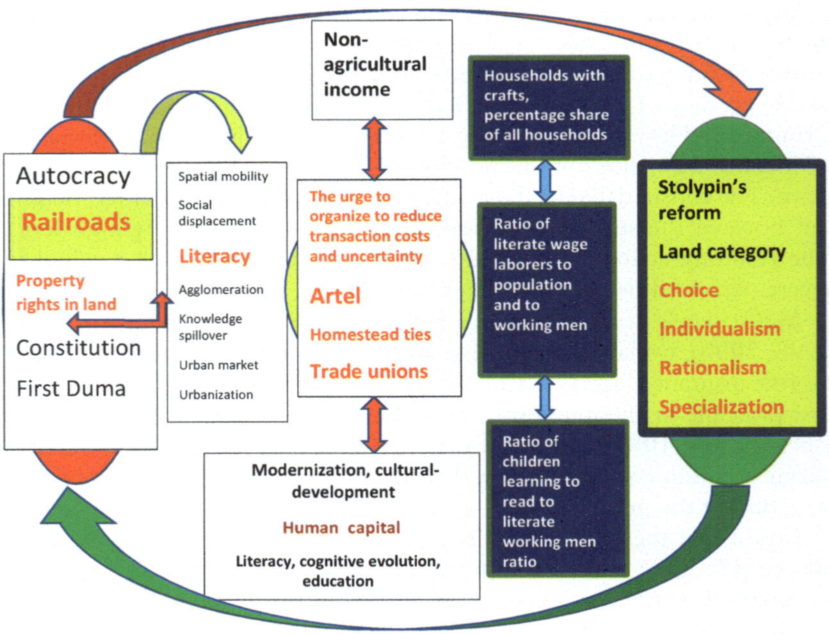

Fig. 11.1 Undermining the autocracy: from railroads to land reform and back. (Sources: Ascher (1988), Gerschenkron (1962), Fujita et al. (2012), Sztern (2017, 2018b), Anderson (1980), Mironov (2012), Johnson (1979), Eklof (1986), Markievich and Castaneda (2017), Martens (2004))

are important. Conversely, the mutual liability and contract production by artisans and skilled workers created "islands of conscious power" (Coase, 1937) that reduced the costs of collective action and mitigated the risks to the individual of absorbing novel technologies along with progressive ideologies (Kingston-Mann, 1991; Witt, 1993).

In the analysis that follows, I elaborate on Tsarist state support of crafts industries as an incentive to the acquisition of literacy, numeracy, and education, the vehicles of enlightenment and cultural modernization.

The Hypothesis

The selected formal models to be tested are:

- Share of craft-producing households among all households = f(distance from village commune to railroad station);
  HwCShare1913 = $\alpha + \beta$ DISTOB1913 + u1913
- Choice of individualistic land category relative to all land = f(share of craft-producing households in all households);
  Indconsofalland1913 = $\alpha - \beta$ HwCShare 1913 − u1913
- Share of craft-producing households among all households = f(children—ratio of literacy-acquiring boys to literate working men);
  HwCShare1913 = $\alpha + \beta$ childshboysoflmr1913 + u1913
- Share of literacy-acquiring children (boys) among literate working men = f(ratio of literate working men to population).
  childshboysoflmr1913 = $\alpha + \beta$ LmrofitogoD1913 + u1913

The residual, u, is the aspects of the marginal change in y that are not explained by the selected marginal impact of x on y variable. The slope of the regression; $\Delta Y/\Delta X$, is interpreted as the marginal effect of X on Y. α is the intercept term, interpreted as the value of Y, the dependent variable when X is zero. Importantly, u as well as α captures the effects of variables omitted from the model. The u term also includes the effect of nonlinearities, errors in measuring the X and Y variables, and unpredictable random effects.

The basic assumptions of the model that yields valid regression results are *homoscedasticity* (the residuals cancel out each other—equal scatter) and *serial independence—no autocorrelation*. That is, the residuals are correlated neither with themselves nor with any of the variables. Another crucial assumption concerns the ***normality of errors; Y given X is distributed as N($\alpha + \beta X$, s^2 − variance)***.

Advised by Professor Michael Keren, I solve the autocorrelation problem by applying the GLS General Least Squares regression equation. If the residuals are autocorrelated and/or their variance is unstable—if heteroscedasticity resulting from the *specification of the model errors* (omitted variables) is detected—the Ordinary Least Squares estimator will be biased and inconsistent. When auto-correlation and/or heteroscedasticity are detected and are the results not of model misspecification but of the data-generating process, the General Least Squares estimation method may be relied on to yield efficient parameter estimates (Vogelvang, 2005, pp. 171, 172). I assume that my autocorrelation is the result of the data-generating process. Therefore, I choose the GLS model to handle the spatial autocorrelation in cross-section and the unstable variances heteroscedasticity to achieve efficient results. Moreover, I generate my models implicitly from the general to the specific and assume that there are theoretical reasons for an AR(1) model when an additional parameter is included in the equation to reduce residual autocorrelation, rendering the estimators efficient.

As for the regression results, I dwell on four crucial indicators: the validity of the p values, the standard deviation of the parameters, the Durbin Watson (DW) value, and the strength (explanatory power) of the R^2 correlation coefficient.

The p values are probabilities that the explanatory variable has no impact on the dependent variable, meaning that the H0 hypothesis is valid. The lower the p-value, the safer it is to reject the null hypothesis. If the probabilities of rejecting a true H0 hypothesis exceed 0.1, 0.05, or 0.01, the H0 hypothesis should be accepted and the conclusion should be that the selected explanatory variable has no impact on the dependent variable. The lower the standard error of the regression and the standard deviation are from the mean of the parameters, the more precise is the parameter (Ramanathan, 1995, pp. 99–104).

The DW test, in turn, applies to ordered time or a spatial in a cross-section series. I provide the latter. My sample consists of two initial *volosti* (cantons or townships) in each *uezd* (district), with the *uezds* numbered 1–9 in descending order. In each volost, there are about fifty observation pairs. In each *uezd* in this sample, there are 100 observation pairs. This gives me about 900 observation pairs in the initial tested ordered sample. Yanguang Chen (2016, pp. 1, 2) writes: "The structural problems of a model can be reflected by residuals, that is, a series of errors between observed values from the real world, and predicted values given by the model. A good model will give random series without the autocorrelation [...]." The DW formula in cross-section is constructed with a one-step space displacement, provided the spatial series are defined in one-dimensional space. A DW value close to 2 means that there is no first-order autocorrelation (Ramanathan, 1995, p. 455), which means no misspecification of the model. As none of the X's in my model constitutes a spatial lag of the dependent variable, the DW test is valid.

Finally, the crucial coefficient of determination—R^2—measures the strength of the correlation or the goodness of fit, the extent to which the regression equation line explains the strength of the actual correlation of the change in the independent variable, x, explaining the change in the dependent variable, y.

Identification of Crucial Variables for the Analysis (Spitzer, 2018)

The crucial aspect of the analysis is the ability to identify the working-male category, the *mushchin robochich*, with the phenomenon of the *otkhodnik*—the-seasonal wage worker and the migrant who travelled by rail. Three factors indicate identity. First, the corresponding category of woman is absent in the zemstvo statistics (those of the rural self-government institution) despite the female contribution to the *tyaglo* (the agricultural team), working alongside men as secondary historical sources advise. The same sources demonstrate that women rather rarely participated in wage labor outside the village and limited themselves largely to geographically restricted intra-village teams (Johnson, 1979). Apparently, so few women did wage labor that they were not recorded in the category "working woman" -"*zhenshchin robochich*" by members of the third group, statisticians employed by the zemstvo. This statistical peculiarity allows us to surmise that men depicted as "working" were participating in *otkhod*: seasonal industrial or agricultural wage labor, hired labor that was used rationally in the expectations of repatriated industrial wage when the village endowment's supply exceeded the demand of working hands (Burds, 1998; Nafziger, 2010), or as skilled workers not organized in *arteli*. The second indicator is specific to the collection of the statistics: the total population of men and women in the village, the column pertaining to men separate from women and another separate column for the category labeled "working men." This category is not identical to the category of "men," which captures all men who worked either in the village, as members of agricultural labor teams, or outside the village, commuting and engaging in wage labor. There can be no explanation for the separate column of "working men" unless this category depicts wage labor, *otkhod*. The very concept of *otkhod* includes the expression "work outside the village." Wage labor was usually performed outside the spatial confines of the village and was very likely, and increasingly likely, to require rail travel. The third indicator, especially valid for this chapter, is literacy. Literacy is directly, although as an untested hypothesis, correlated with the use of railroads and spatial mobility among the peasants (Brooks, 2003; Burds, 1998). Therefore, it is less prevalent among women than among men (Kahan, 1989, p. 171, Table 6.2) in both the rural and the urban environments. The category that I choose as the denominator is the ratio of literacy-acquiring children (boys) to the population. This ratio is sensitive to population densities along the railroads lines (Atack et al., 2010). My proxy for modernization is the ratio of these children to literate working men. This, I believe, gives me solid reason to claim that the category of working men, and especially literate working men, indeed denotes *otkhodniks* who commuted by rail. Moreover, the equation results congruent with this theory indicate, as the fourth aspect, that there is an identity among *otkhodniks* who commuted by rail, wage labor, and this category in the statistics collected by Groman for Penza Province in regard to working men and literate working men (Table 11.1).

The results and their most immediate interpretation flow from the findings of my previous research (Sztern, 2017, 2018b, 2019).

Share of Crafts-Producing Households Among All Households

Kustari (household peasant crafts producers) turned out "sheepskin coats, woolen goods, bast sandals, agricultural implements, furniture, barrels, wheels, musical instruments, clay toys, icons, and much else that people in rural and urban Russia needed (Brooks, 2003, p. 10). Brooks adds that the population of crafts producers included autonomous agents who managed trade with nearby urban markets on their own, along with others who relied on middlemen who traded their produce to longer distances while supplying them with raw materials. It is obvious that those in the latter category were harbingers of urban and regional information exchange. That is, even if they themselves did not travel, they depended on the railroads for their brokers' spatial supremacy. The number of crafts

Table 11.1 The variables

Russian	*English*	*Ratio*	*Name*	*Proxy*
Hozjajstv z promyslami	Households with crafts	To all households	HwCShare	Risk reduction through non-agricultural production
Rozstojanie od stancji zheleznoj dorogi w obshchinie	Distance in village commune Distance from village commune to railroad		Distob	Function of railroads: technological progress—incentives for spatial mobility
Vnenadelnyj jedinolichnyj otrub	Non-allotment individual consolidated parcel	To all land	Indconsofallland	Individualism and rationalism—modernization
Uchiashchichsia malchikov	Literacy-acquiring children (boys)	To literate working men	Childshboysoflmr	Dynamic aspects of transition to modernity
Gramotnych mushchin robochich	Literate working men	To population	LmrofitogoD	The impact of literacy on spatial mobility, and vice versa—transition to modernity

producers during the nineteenth century, calculated for forty provinces of European Russia, is about 1,800,000 (Brooks, 2003, p. 11). In my investigation, it is crucial to note the indispensability of literacy for the relatively entrepreneurial and independent production of crafts because every cottage industry entailed a written contract, giving literate artisans a clear comparative advantage over others. The more artisans were able to bargain, the greater was their return on literacy. Literacy among crafts workers in the late nineteenth century did not exceed 30 percent but was higher among toymakers and icon painters than among others (Brooks, 2003).

In 1897, some 12,000,000 people who legally belonged to the peasant estate lived outside their native villages (Brooks, 2003). Some 75 percent of them continued to live in the countryside while engaging in spatially mobile wage labor in urban industries. For them, the acquisition of literacy was a useful price to pay for the ability to bargain and negotiate wages. This made literacy a vehicle of economic and social ascendance for crafts producers and mobile wage-earning peasants. Above (Chap. 10), I quoted Mironov (2012), who discovered the growing incidence of analphabetism among the landed gentry amid the decline in its economic status and the increasing accumulation of literacy skill among the capital-amassing peasantry. Thus, land possession and ownership followed literacy as indicators of rising (peasantry) and falling (gentry) economic and social and, in turn, political decision-making and negotiating power. This social and economic discontinuity and evolution challenged the previously stable hierarchies of coercion by which the autocracy anchored its legitimacy in patriarchal authority, in tandem with the peasant investment in literacy and additional human-capital acquisition. The transformation in question was not violent and was relatively unattended. Nevertheless, it is crucial for understanding the nature of modernization in pre-revolution late imperial Russia.

To place the potential absorption of the developmental novelty embedded in these institutions in its context, one must understand how production in workers' crafts cooperatives was organized. Paradoxically, this traditional production mode was a forerunner of modernity in that it carries a causal connection between literacy and handicrafts. It is also important to understand the increase in the individual artisan's probability of employment due to shared responsibility for, and guarantee of, the quality of labor supplied within this traditional Russian organization of artisan production, reaching back to the twelfth century, that allowed migrating workers to integrate easily into the organized services, workshops, and factories of the urban landscape. All artels, writes Henri Troyat (1961, p. 98), had registered capital with which they covered the costs of the *vkup* (the gift on admission) and the *novizna* (the gift on being received). These funds insured individual workers against defection or underperformance within the shared-liability network. *Artelshchiki*—members of an artel—opposed any deviation from agreed-upon and mutually guaranteed labor-quality standards. Their reliability, in turn, made them well-to-do. There was no such thing as a "poor or intemperate artelshchik" (Troyat, 99). After agreeing on their own social benefits and on pensions for widows and orphans, they elected a *starosta* (president) and a *pisar* (secretary—an office that had an outspokenly literate contingent). Thus, crafts production was associated with a democratic voting tradition and literacy-dependent structures. Implemented in a modern factory environment, I believe, these institutions acquired transformational modernizing characteristics and introduced members to the option of informed elaboration and insurance against risks of individual failure. If so, *arteli* constituted an important mechanism of collective action that was capable of coping with the persistent challenge of the ruling-authority-sanctioned hierarchy.

I now empirically investigate the correlations among individualized landholding modes in the 1913 phase of the Stolypin reform, the share of households that produced crafts, distance from village commune to railroad station, and the ratio of literacy-acquiring boys to the population of literate wage laborers, whom I assume to be literate ***otkhodniks*** who commuted by rail (see above). I also investigate the explanatory variable of my modernization proxy, the ratio of literacy-acquiring boys to literate working men (see Appendix table).

The sign of the equation between the village commune's distance from the railroad (DISTOB) and the share of craft-producing households (HWCSHARE) among all households is positive. The secondary sources explain that households engaged in crafts production and cottage industry (***kustar***) during the winter, as occurred in non-black-earth provinces as well (Worobec, 1995, p. 31). Those endeavors predated the railroads; of course, such production created a supplement to agricultural income, reducing the risk of pauperization in the event of crop failure due to frost and/or infertile soil conditions. Villages that were farther from railroad stations had less access to urban markets, restricting an influx of agricultural knowledge and income margins that would have allowed innovative investment in land to mitigate the riskiness of subsistence farming. Thus, their risks of maximal loss would be higher. This, in turn, would validate the Gerschenkronian hypothesis of a negative correlation between the risk insurance embedded in land rotation and yield per hectare (Nafziger, 2007) as a self-enforcing vicious cycle that originates in the longitudinal application of the "safety-first" principle at a time of population growth. Such a conception, however, disregards the communal risk-reduction strategies that were resorted to, and the compensation awarded to individual households for the investment in land made, when village-member households implemented agricultural innovations (Kingston-Mann, 1991, p. 43). Against this background, crafts production was a strategy of income-risk reduction and diversification for households. Therefore, the farther from a railroad station a commune was, the greater was the risk of crop failure due to deficient implementation of modern agronomic knowledge. This, in turn, amplified the need for land rotation and mutual insurance and dependency on crafts as a way to smooth the meteorologically seasonal instability of the household's yearly assured agricultural income. At the same time, the combination of agricultural and handicraft income facilitated the peasantry's future transition from compulsory to voluntary cooperative coordination of production, investing the result obtained with historical legitimacy. In my earlier investigations (Sztern, 2017 and Chap. 9), I found that the most collectivistic and mutually insuring form of landholding was positively correlated to the distance from a group of village communes called a *selo* to the nearest railroad station. The R^2 of the foregoing equation has only 15 percent explanatory value because the availability of railroad stations, a relatively recent phenomenon in crafts production, does not explain the centuries-old tradition by which promysly households were dispersed and distributed across the regional and provincial geographical space. I hypothesize that the highest explanatory power should be assigned to the impact of climatic condition and soil quality for the riskiness of agricultural income and for that of literacy—a source of income in itself, defined by the peasantry as crafts (Brooks, 2003)—on the percent distribution of promysly households in the province. It is necessary to point out again that subsistence in Penza, a northern *chernozem* (black earth) province, depended predominantly on agriculture, as was the case in as all fertile black-earth regions. Prone to colder winters than those to the south, however, farmers in Penza relied on crafts production to supplement their income non-redundantly. Given the temporal novelty of railroad availability—thirty-nine years—the positive power of distance from the railroad station in explaining the share of crafts-producing households, discovered above, should not be considered devoid of historical content in respect of the dynamic impact on peasant-household modernization of crafts production in locations relatively far from railroad stations.

Thus, in terms of the results in the Appendix table, one additional kilometer of distance from the *obshchina* to the nearest railroad station (the explanatory variable) instigates a 35 percent increase in the share of craft-producing households in the *obshchina*. The DW value is close to 2, implying no autocorrelation and, therefore, efficient regression results due to the AR (1) term that absorbs the autocorrelation produced by the data-generating process. The probability of refutation of a true H0 hypothesis is 0.00; consequently, the distance from railroad to village has a significant if limited impact on the share of crafts-producing households among all households. The explanatory power of distance from *obshchina* to railroad on the share of crafts-producing households is 16 percent (Appendix table).

The dependent variable is the most individualistic land category (INDCONSOFALLLAND—Table 11.1 and Appendix) among the fifteen categories that emerged in the second (1913) stage of the Stolypin reform (Sztern, 2017 and Chap. 9, testing of full DS *selos* [groups of *obshchinas*]). The share of all land that is non-allotment land—individual consolidated parcels (*wnenadelnoe zemlevladenie, jedinolichnyj otrub*)—is negatively correlated with the share of crafts-producing households among all households (HWCShare). This result is consistent with the preceding one. The reader is reminded again that Penza is a black-soil province, predominantly sustained by agricultural income. The less agricultural subsistence risk households confront, as explained by households' access to the urban market for agricultural produce and the influx of knowledge in agronomy, the more households' dependency on auxiliary income from crafts declines with the declining distance from the nearest railroad station, and the lower is the share of craft-producing households among all households. Drawing on the perceptive and convincing findings of Markievich and Castaneda (2017), I explain below that this mode of landholding, which emerged in Penza in the second stage of the Stolypin reform (the non-allotment consolidated parcel that is cultivated by an individual household), attained the highest per-hectare gain in land productivity in the course of the Stolypin reform. Advised by Markievich's writings, I argue that the expected increase in agricultural returns, in tandem with declining coordination and other transaction costs, made cottage industry among households that opted for individualistic landholding redundant. My results, from 2010 produced in conjunction with Keren (2010), show that this type of holding is located close to a railroad station with 44 percent probability. Adults, including craftsmen who engaged in wage labor, were absorbed either directly into the urban modernizing factory system or into the migrating artel, the landsman artisan cooperative. Landsman community relations created coordination among seasonal workers and migrants (Johnson, 1979; Anderson, 1980; Troyat, 1961) in their urge to utilize the urban labor markets that the readily accessible railroads had made available.

Thus, one household with a share of crafts among all households will correlate with a 6.6 percent negative probability to the peasant choice of an individualistic consolidated parcel of all land. In other words, the lower the risk to the agricultural return, the less dependent on crafts a household will be and the more likely will be its choice of individualistic, high-productivity landholding. Individually cultivated holdings of this type (*otrub*) were the closest to the nearest railroad station. However, the significance level—the p-value—verges on the critical 0.01 if rounded. Thus,

H0 may still be refuted. The strength of the regression indicates that 34 percent of the increase in individualistic landholding among all land is explained by the residual restriction of the share of households that hedge their agricultural risks by producing crafts, correspondingly increasing their dependence on the agricultural income that the railroads made possible while engaging in urban trade along the rail lines. A DW value close to 2 indicates no autocorrelation; thus, the results of the regression are efficient.

Continue to track the results in the Appendix table, it is found, interestingly, that 23 percent of the increase in the share of crafts income households among all households (HWCSHARE) is explained by the ratio of boys among children learning to read to literate working men (CHILDSHBOYSOFLMR). This equation offers the most content of all in the context of this chapter. Boys are conceptualized as future potential wage-earning urban factory workers who commute by rail and repatriate their *otkhodnik* wage income as breadwinners (the numerator of the explanatory variable), while literate working men (the denominator) are already literate wage laborers who commute to the factories (Anderson, 1980). The lower this ratio is and the closer to the railroads a commune is, as one may surmise, the smaller the share of crafts-producing households will be. And the higher this ratio, as the number of boys among children who learn to read grows faster than the population of literate working men, the higher will be the share of crafts-producing households. I define the variable of "ratio of children learning to read to population" as a proxy for modernization because it captures the rising opportunity costs of the employment of children in agricultural field work and the growing incentives to exit analphabetism for the purpose of engaging in crafts. To put this variable to its purpose, the qualification of declining per-capita land endowment (Atkinson, 1983) due to population increase (Jones, 1997) and peasants' rising demand for, and social and economic returns to, literacy skills as a function of their spatial mobility (Brooks, 2003) is needed. Even though—as the secondary sources below demonstrate—the diversion of peasant labor from crafts production to urban factory work in the course of the industrialization and modernization process was additionally incentivized by the use of railroads, literacy is the common denominator that incentivizes the proliferation of crafts, migration to factory labor, and factory labor itself (Anderson, 1980; Brooks, 2003, p. 10). Even as engaging in crafts makes child literacy advantageous, this traditional proto-industrial mode of production acquires the property of an accelerating harbinger of modernization. As the proto-industrial phenomenon of cottage-industry contracts increase in tandem with the upturn in spatial mobility and the availability of middlemen, demand for and returns to child literacy grow. This, in turn, abets an increase in peasants' prospective mobility to urban factory labor, explaining the accelerating pace of industrialization. This aspect of the pre-revolution Tsarist modernization poses an additional challenge to the Gerschenkronian hypothesis of a custom originating in landlords' surveillance of serfs' labor as a mobility barrier to industrialization. According to Gerschenkron's analysis, adult sons of inhabitants of *obshchinas* were bound to the land due to the commune's shared responsibility as the increasingly scarce resource of land was allocated commensurate with the number of labor teams in the household. Crafts production enhanced peasants' acquisition of literacy and allowed non-agricultural income to rise in relative terms while reducing households' risk of pauperization. According to the foregoing findings, this mode of production, when situated in the most collectivistic villages in the *volosti* (cantons) and the province, incentivized *bolshaks* (patriarchal heads of households) to allow literacy-acquiring boys, among the children, to engage in handicrafts. Literate boys constituted future commuters to urban industries, where they would absorb modern practical knowledge and accumulate income. This process, paradoxically, challenged and eroded the authority of the bolshak and, in turn, the determinants of the mobility barrier. Viewed from a dynamic perspective, the intersection of crafts, literacy, and peasant spatial mobility transformed the village-commune structure from compulsory and authoritarian to voluntary, with rationally cooperating or dissolving organizations of production (Sztern, 2017).

Results Table in the Appendix: Each additional boy who learns to read in relation to literate working men will increase the share of crafts-producing households by 75 percent. The significance level of this equation is likewise close to critical. If rounded to 0.05, it would indicate that H0 may still be refuted. The proportion of literacy-acquiring boys to literate working men impacts the share of crafts-producing households among all households. The DW value approaches 2, which means that the results of the equation may still be accepted as efficient. The 23 percent explanatory power of literacy-acquiring boys as a share of literate working men has dynamic diachronic rather than synchronic importance.

The share of literate working men in the population explains more than 70 percent of the share of literacy-acquiring children in the population.

This strong R-square correlation clearly indicates that the role models and the incentive-generating constituency for the future exodus of peasants from analphabetism were wage-earning peasants (*otkhodniks*) who commuted to urban industries, and not the *bolshak* parent generation. Thus, the breadwinner's authority shifted from the tradition-laden hierarchical structures, anchored in the ceremonial knowledge reservoir and experience, toward individualized practical bearers of knowledge[3]—from fathers to sons. Yokoyama's (2008) collection of peasant correspondence between wage-earning (*otkhod*) sons and kin in the villages indicates that the weight of dependence became burdensome to the *bolshaks*. From Anderson's analysis (1980), it is evident that a positive correlation exists between out-migration numbers and peasant literacy percentage shares. Anderson's findings provide additional support for the attribution to the railroads of direct and indirect explanatory power in regard to literacy acquisition and modernization. The convergence of spatiality and literacy is the harbinger of the cultural revolution that came into view before the revolutions of 1905 and 1917.

The foregoing equation results (the Appendix table) ascribe significant explanatory power (53 percent) to the ratio of literate working men to population (LMROFITOGOD)—the explanatory variable—and the ratio of boys among literacy-acquiring children to literate working men (CHILDSHBOYSOFLMR). These results square with the previous findings. Literate working men, whose constituency increases in tandem with the frequency of urban factory labor, incentivize the acquisition of literacy among peasant boys via the repatriation of income, the economic incentives (including risk margins for the parental generation, allowing bolshaks to consider forgoing children's agricultural labor), and the availability of literate commuting adults as cultural role models for boys to acquire craft skills and engage in urban *otkhod* in the future. As out-migration is found to be positively correlated with literacy (Anderson, 1980) and the railroads allowed the frequency of out-migration to increase, the railroad technology—I argue—was the lever of cultural revolution intrinsic to the 1890 industrial spurt that abetted the peasant transition to individualism and rationalism (Sztern, 2017 and Chap. 9) and the *ex post* codification of individual households' property rights in land in Stolypin's 1906–1917

[3] This remark is based on Veblen's (1931) definition of ceremonial and relatively practical knowledge acquisition. The latter characterizes the modernization process, which encapsulates the transition to rationalistic accumulation of knowledge independent of tradition.

reform. This consolidation, coupled with peasants' exodus from the compulsory collectivistic structures of the ***obshchina***, reduced transaction costs and enhanced land productivity (Poznanskii, 1992), allowing specialization of production to accelerate (Markievich & Castaneda, 2017). Extrapolating from these processes, I again find it justified, as I argued at length in Chaps. 8–10, to suggest that the 1917 revolution was not the primary lever of modernization and that Stalinism was not necessary for the liberation of the peasant masses from the yoke of backwardness, diminishing returns, and Malthusian catastrophes.

In this regression (see Appendix table), one percentage share of literate working men in relation to population increase explains roughly a 60 percent increase in the percentage share of literacy-acquiring boys in relation to literate working men. The results are significant at a 5 percent level and the DW value is close to 2, indicating no model misspecification. The R^2 of the regression is 53 percent, quite high in terms of ratios. The share of literate working men in the population explains 53 percent of the share of literacy-acquiring boys in relation to literate working men. In effect, the ratio of working peasants who commute by rail wage to population explains more than 50 percent of the parental generation's decision to allow boys to exit analphabetism by having them learn to read rather than till the soil, in relation to their role models, literate working men (Table 11.2).

Climate and Soil Quality: Peasant Budget Structure, Crafts, and Trade Versus Agriculture Before and During the Industrial Spurt of the 1890s

The post-emancipation peasant economy was burdened with dramatic population increase (Kahan, 1985, 1989). It began in the eighteenth century amid landlord effects—the risk insurance that characterized the serf economy (Hoch, 1986) (Engelgardt in Frierson, 1993), the enforcement of shared liability for taxes and dues, and land redistribution commensurate with the number of labor teams that each household provided. Traditional peasant survival strategies, including ***pomoch*** (rotation of movable assets by means of ***kladka*** [bride price] and ***bratchiny*** [fraternity parties] (Mironov 2000)), provided additional leveling that enhanced mutual protection from famine. In the period of interest in this monograph—the

Table 11.2 Peasant budgets—household income in 13 provinces of European Russia, 1877–1900

Province	*Year*	*Households*	*Individuals*	*Type of households*	*Income (rubles)*					
					Agri-culture	*Live-stock*	*Crafts, trade*	*Other*	*Total*	*Crafts and trade % share*
Novogorod	1879–1880	5	29	Crafts	66	24	165	–	255	65%
Viatka	1880–1883	17	157	Crafts	317	60	301	5	683	44%
Perm	1880	18	110	Crafts	58	24	248	–	330	75%
N. Novo-gorod	1877–1880	14	101	Crafts	99	–	197	7	303	65%
Saratov	1883	1	5	Agricultural	318	40	–	–	358	–
Voronezh	1885–1890	263	2147	Agriculture	263	115	114	107	599	19%
	1880	1	6	Crafts	43	–	270	–	313	86%
Tula	1881	6	52	Agriculture	151	17	202	–	470	43%
	1879–1882	5	44	Crafts	149	22	550	–	721	76%
Vladimir	1880	2	11	Crafts	99	–	118	–	217	54%
Iaroslavl	1879	2	13	Crafts	148	3	245	–	396	62%
Tver	1894	1	5	Agriculture	117	17	29	–	163	18%
	1879–1894	4	33	Crafts	150	16	133	–	299	45%
Kaluga	1896	1313	10,670	Agriculture	240	76	77	5.1	398.1	19%
	1879	2	13	Crafts	102	7	191	–	300	64%
Kherson	1880–1900	126	823	Agriculture	366	15	48	–	429	11%
	1880	1	7	Crafts		–	–	–	–	–
Kuban	1901	7	54	Agriculture	272	130	65	21	588	11%
Avg. per household				Agriculture	253.3	77.5	80.9	20.4	432.2	19%
				Crafts	146.2	25.2	254.6	2.6	428.9	59%
				Total	249.1	75.4	87.7	19.7	431.9	20%
Avg. per capita				Agriculture	31.6	9.7	10.1	2.5	53.9	19%
				Crafts	21.0	3.6	36.5	0.4	61.5	59%
				Total	31.3	9.5	11.0	2.5	54.3	20%

Source: Mironov (2012, p. 180, Table 5.27); calculation in right-hand column: my own

second half of the nineteenth century and, particularly, in the closing decades of Tsarism—another factor in the demographic explosion was the peasants' growing access to railroad technology. As spatial mobility allowed non-agricultural income to accrue, gave access to grain storage, and triggered an inflow of rationalistic knowledge to the peasant villages, thereby addressing the plague of epidemics, in the short run the fecundity and fertility patterns remained un-adapted or vested with novel contents that meshed the traditional survival strategies with institutional innovations (Jones, 1997), resulting in additional population increase. As noted above, the peasants met the economic burden occasioned by the combination of post-emancipation redemption payments and declining per-capita land allotments by increasingly engaging in "domestic industries" (Worobec, 1995, p. 31), namely, crafts production. This agricultural-risk-mitigating endeavor was historically typical of the non-black-earth central industrial provinces: Novogorod, Perm, Viatka Vologda, and Nizhnij Novogorod (Jones, 1997, p. 63; Anderson, 1980, p. 28.). In reference to Nizhnij Novogorod, Worobec (1995, p. 31) explains, "*On average, two workers per household contributed non-agricultural income to the peasant budget.*" According to Mironov's table (above), about half of the peasant budget in the non-black-earth provinces was generated by craft production. Penza Province, located between Nizhnij Novogorod to the north, where crafts generated 65 percent of income, and southern-black-earth Saratov, where 100 percent of income was generated by agriculture, is a northern black-earth area where the peasantry maintained income stability by combining agricultural and crafts production in proportions that varied over time. As inhabitants of a black-earth province, the peasantry in Penza had endured barshchina (corvée labor) obligations during serfdom, a time when tax liabilities could also be met by household crafts production. Relatively speaking, however, this province was one of high soil fertility. Anderson finds a negative correlation between soil fertility and literacy in forty-one provinces of European Russia. Penza Province in 1874–1883 had a low literacy rate among military recruits, at 0–19 percent as against 50–100 percent in Jaroslavl (Anderson, 1980, p. 37, Map 2.4). This northern chernozem province, Penza, was sustained predominantly by agriculture, as the opportunity costs there were prohibitively high. The high literacy rate among Jaroslavl military recruits is positively correlated with the share of income generated by crafts, as may be seen in the table above.

The positive correlation that I found between the share of crafts-producing households and that of literacy-acquiring boys among literate working men in 1913 indicates a modernizing and prospective change in the structure of earnings that occurred between 1883, when the literacy census of military recruits was taken, and 1913, when the Penza zemstvo statistics were compiled. The point of departure for the change, I suggest, is 1874, when the railroad first came to Penza. Some 23 percent of the increase in the share of crafts-producing households is explained by the proportionate increase in literacy-acquiring boys among literate working men (Table 1 Appendix). The latter upturn indicates that reading-skill acquisition among boys for the purpose of crafts production was a relatively new, prospective, dynamic phenomenon rather than a historical constant. Moreover, there is clear evidence of increasing specialization of production in the province: the closer a village was to the nearest railroad station, the more black-earth agriculture benefitted from the dwindling cognitive and temporal distances to the urban market, (Shivelbusch, 1986) allowing the individualization of ownership and rising yields per hectare (Markievich & Castaneda, 2017). Farther away, in contrast, the promise of future "clean work" (Brooks, 2003) in urban crafts, captured by the access-to-railroads function, enhanced the acquisition of reading skills and the engagement in contract cottage-industry activity involving children.

Concluding Discussion

By incentivizing the acquisition of literacy, the spatial mobility that the Tsarist railroads delivered created social-mobility opportunities that the peasantry realized during the state-led industrialization even as it accumulated human and physical capital. The resulting synergies abetted the formation of a developmental nexus of growth that meshed the rural and urban economies and unleashed an intense exchange of production technologies, ideologies, and beliefs about the world (North, 1973). These factors posed a necessary but insufficient challenge to the legacies of the authority-contingent hierarchies of coercion. Nevertheless, the results support the validity of the revisionist analyses of Gregory (1994, 1982), Simms (1977), Mironov (2012), and Nafziger (2010) and counter the Gerschenkronian conception of the Tsarist economy as a "dual" one, in which technology imported from the West diverted the allocation of surpluses from peasant Russia, which remained institutionally relatively backward and culturally static, toward urban industry. This industry, from the Gerschenkronian perspective, was steadily aligning itself with Western standards with the assistance of technology imports that were congruent with the "advantages of backwardness," namely, the absence of vested interests in obsolete modes of production. Tsarist Russia modernized, and its industrial honesty standards became higher and homogeneous, not solely as the Gerschenkronian school proposes—by emulating the role-model Western entrepreneurial ethos during the second industrialization spurt (1907) that followed the technology import. Crafts and trade-related-credit production in shared-responsibility units, the *arteli* of carpenters and merchants (Troyat, 1961), were outgrowths of the traditional rural mutual-insurance practices that had given the *obshchina* culture its structure. These outgrowths, including itinerant *arteli* under landsman organizations, paved the way—by collectively/cooperatively organizing production and migration in a manner that mitigated individual risk—to the awakening of industrial modern Russia through peer pressure and mutual quality control within settings of shared responsibility. These institutional forerunners of trade unions constituted an effective instrument of subversion. Posing a credible threat from below in the course of the industrialization spurt of the 1890s, rural artisans and wage laborers, transmogrifying into an urban labor force, compelled the Late Imperial government to make modernizing concessions. Central among them was the Stolypin reform in 1906, featuring an unprecedented delegation of property rights from the Tsarist votchina (serf-owner) to the peasant *dvor* (household) (Pipes, 1995; Macey, 1990). Although the modern urban factory seemed to divert labor away from crafts production as it absorbed rural labor, making it a substituting endeavor rather than a complementary one, the artel institution, embedded in trade unionism, gave peasant workers ever-strengthening negotiation power and accounts for the success of the pre-revolution urge to industrialize and, in regard to workers' rights, to modernize in late Imperial Russia.

Stolypin's reform, entailing recognition of conquest as the inferior optimum relative to the attainment of popular loyalty and support (Sztern, 2017; Ascher, 1988, 2001; Freeze, 1996, Gaudin, 2007), prescribed the individualization of property rights in land. The implementation of aspects of this reform that resulted in land consolidation and exit from the commune reduced the costs of cooperation and their contingent uncertainty and transaction costs, allowing land productivity in terms of yield per hectare to increase. This reform must not be misconstrued as a process of revolution from above that involved the importation of land-tenure structures of Bismarck's Germany (Pallot, 1999). Just as ex post it codified and encouraged the transition to individualism and rationalism from above, I have shown in this chapter that the Tsarist railroads, by discontinuously boosting demand for and returns to literacy, enhanced by means of the latter the production and organization of artel-led Tsarist Russia toward a transition to individualism and rationalism from below. Thus, Russia was culturally modernizing prior to the 1906 reform and before the revolutions that I have described as retrograde (see also Nafziger and Dennison, 2007; Leonard, 2011). I demonstrated this by calling attention to the modernizing synergy that existed among the peasants' railroad-contingent spatial mobility and the crafts artel, which allowed the geographically local and specific stratification of labor units of peasant origin among the peasant estate, diffusing its ethos among landsmen who migrated in search of urban and interregional industrial employment. In this synergy, literacy was incentivized and subversive modern trade-union activity—combining the seizure of negotiating power and the demand for equality before the law and universal suffrage—progressed. This developmental nexus emphasizes the core characteristic of the technology-driven transition from compulsory collectivism to rational cooperation and individualism, the techno-institutional revolution in Russia's nineteenth-century modernization. As counterfactual as it sounds, physical- and human-capital accumulation amid emerging equality before the law would have allowed peasant Russia to exit from backwardness without experiencing what Orlando Figes calls "the people's tragedy."

Appendix

Table 11.3 Results

Indconshofl.	*Coeff*	*P-Value*	*HWCSHARE*	*Coeff*	*P-Value*	*CHILDSH BOYSofLMR*	*Coeff*	*P-Value*
C	0.110399	0.000100		0.441076	0.000000		-0.008626	0.000000
		3.871635			26.38837			-8.218671
HWCSHARE	-0.065748	0.014500	CHILD SHBOYS ofLMR	0.750064	0.051900	LMRofI TOGOD	0.588942	0.000000
		-2.449534			1.947693			56.71864
AR(1)	0.558377	0.000000		0.499190	0.000000		0.111189	0.024200
		25.30538			12.74584			2.259795
R-squared		0.337379			0.232686			0.534857
Adjusted R-Sq		0.335122			0.228668			0.532426
DW stat		2.071803			1.929965			2.077313
Schwarz crit.		-0.641606			-0.145422			-5,633,726
SD dep var		0.211173			0.243828			0.020738

References

Anderson, B. A. (1980). *Internal migration during modernization in late nineteenth-century Russia*. Princeton University Press.

Archer, M. (1995). *Realist social theory: The morphogenetic approach*. The University of Hertfordshire: Chapter Presented at the 6th International Workshop on Institutional Economics.

Ascher, A. (1988). *The Revolution of 1905: Part I Russia in disarray*. Stanford University Press.

Ascher, A. (2001). *P.A. Stolypin -The Search for Stability in Late Imperial Russia*. Stanford UP.

Atack, J., Bateman, F., Haines, M., & Margo, R. (2010). Did railroads induce or follow economic growth? Urbanization and population growth in the American mid-west 1850–1960. *Social Science History, 34*(2), 171–197.

Atkinson, D. (1983). *The end of the Russia land commune 1905–1930*. Stanford University Press.

Bakunin, M. (1970) *God and the state*. With a new introduction and index of persons by Paul Avrich. Dover Publications.

Boyer, R., & Orlean, A. (1993). How do conventions evolve? In U. Witt (Ed.), *Evolution in markets and institutions*. Physica-Vlg.

Brooks, J. (2003). *When Russia learned to read: Literacy and popular literature, 1861–1917*. Northwestern University Press.

Burbank, J. (2004). *Russian Peasants go to Court - Legal culture in the countryside, 1905–1917*. Indiana University Press.

Burds, J. (1998). *Peasant dreams and market politics: Labor migration and the Russian Village 1861–1905*. University of Pittsburgh Press.

Bushnell (1990). "The Russian Soldiers Artel", 1700–1900- A history and interpretation. In Bartlett, R. (1990) (Ed.), Land commune and peasant community in Russia-communal forms in Imperial and Early Soviet society / Macmillian in Association with the school of Slavonic and East European Studies.

Chen, Y. (2016, January 22). *Spatial autocorrelation approaches to testing residuals from least squares regression*. Department of Geography, College of Urban and Environmental Sciences, Peking University, 100871, Beijing, China.

Chubarov, A. (2001). *The fragile empire: A history of Imperial Russia*. Continuum.

Coase, R. (1937). *The firm, the market, and the law*. University of Chicago Press.

Cohen, G. A. (2000). *Karl Marx's theory of history: A defense*. Clarendon Press.

Davydov, M. A. (2008). Personal communication.

Dostojewski. (1977). *Wspomnienia z Domu Umarlych*. Panstwowy Instytut Wydawniczy.

Eggertsson, T. (1990). *Economic behavior and institutions*. Cambridge University Press.

Engelgardt, P. N. (1993). *Letters from the country, 1872–1887*. Translated and edited by C. Frierson. Oxford UP.

Eklof, B. (1986). *Russian Peasant Schools-Officialdom Village Culture, and Popular Pedagogy, 1861–1914*. University of California Press.

Freeze, G. (1988). *From supplication to revolution: A documentary social history of Imperial Russia*. Oxford University Press.

Freeze, G. (1996). Subversive piety: Religion and political crisis in late Imperial Russia. *The Journal of Modern History, 68*(2), 308–350.

Fujita, M., Krugman, P., & Venables, A. J. (2012). *The spatial economy, cities, regions and international trade*. MIT Press.

Gaudin, C. (2007). *Ruling peasants: Village and state in late Imperial Russia*. Northern Illinois University Press.

Gerschenkron, A. (1962). *Economic backwardness in historical perspective*. The Belknap Press of Harvard University Press.

Gerschenkron, A. (1968). *Continuity in history and other essays*. The Belknap Press of Harvard University Press.

Gintis, H. (2009). *The bounds of reason: Game theory and the unification of the behavioral sciences*. Princeton University Press.

Gregory, P. R. (1982). *Russian national income 1885–1913*. Cambridge University Press.

Gregory, P. R. (1994). *Before command: An economic history of Russia from emancipation to the first five-year plan*. Princeton University Press.

Harding, N. (1996). *Leninism*. Macmillan.

Hoch, S. (1986). *Serfdom and social control in Russia: Petrovskoe, a village in Tambov*. University of Chicago Press.

Hodgson, G. M. (1997). *Notes on habits, institutions and evolution* The Judge Institute of Management Studies, University of Cambridge.

Hodgson, G. M. (2004). *The evolution of institutional economics, agency, structure and Darwinism in American institutionalism*. Routledge.

Hodgson, et al, (1997). *Notes on habits, institutions, and evolution*. The Judge Institute of Management Studies, University of Cambridge.

Johnson, R. (1979). *Peasant and proletarian: The working class of Moscow in the late nineteenth century*. Leicester University Press.

Jones, A. (1997). *Late-Imperial Russia, an interpretation: Three visions, two cultures, one peasantry*. Peter Lang.

Kahan, A. (1985). *The plow, the hammer and the knout—An economic history of eighteenth century Russia*. University of Chicago Press.

Kahan, A. (1989). *Russian economic history: The nineteenth century*. Ed. R. Weiss. University of Chicago Press.

Keren, M. (2010). Personal communication.

Kingston-Mann, E. (1991). Peasant communes and economic innovation: A preliminary inquiry. In E. Kingston-Mann, T. Mixter, & J. Burds (Eds.), *Peasant economy culture and politics of European Russia*. Princeton University Press.

Leonard, C. S. (2011). *Agrarian reform in Russia—The road from serfdom*. Cambridge University Press.

Ma. (2006). *Law and commerce in traditional China. An institutional perspective on the great "Great divergence"*. Seminar paper Economic History Lund university.

Macey, D. (1990). The peasant commune and the Stolypin reforms: Peasant attitudes, 1906–14. In R. Bartlett (Ed.), *Land commune and peasant Community in Russia: Communal forms in Imperial and Early Soviet Society*. University of London, Macmillan, in Association with the School of Slavonic and East European Studies.

Macey, D. (1998). A wager on history: The Stolypin agrarian reforms as a process. In J. Pallot (Ed.), *Christ Church Oxford, Transforming peasants. Society, state and the peasantry, 1861–1930*. Selected Papers from the Fifth World Congress of Central and East European Studies, Warsaw, 1995.

Markievich, A., & Castaneda, D. (2017). *The Stolypin reform and agricultural productivity in late Imperial Russia*. Working Paper No 239 CEFIR/ NES Working Paper Series.

Martens, B. (2004). *The cognitive mechanics of economic development and institutional change*. Routledge.

McCloskey, D. (2001). *English open fields as behavior toward risk, in measurement and meaning in economics*. University of Chicago Press.

Metzer, J. (1972). *Some economic aspects of railroad development in Tsarist Russia*. Ph.D. Diss, Department of Economics, the University of Chicago.

Milov, L. (2001). *Velikorusskii pakhar i osobennosti rossijskogo istoricheskogo protsessa*. Biblioteka Gumer-istoria http://www.gumer.info/bibliotek_Buks/History/milov/01.ph

Mironov, B. N. (1999). *Socialnaya Istoria Rossii Perioda Imperii (XVIII-nachalo XX v) Genezis Lichnosti Demokraticheskoj Semii Grazhdanskogo Obshchestva i Pravovogo Gosudarstva: v Dwuch Tomach*. Dimitrij Bulanin.

Mironov, B. N. (2000). *A social history of Imperial Russia, 1700–1917*. Vol. I. Westview Press.

Mironov, B. N. (2012). *The standard of living and revolutions in Russia, 1700–1917*. Ed. L. G. Freeze. Routledge.

Mokyr, J. (1990). *Lever of riches: Technological creativity and economic progress*. Oxford University Press.

Nafziger, S. (2007). *Land redistributions and the Russian peasant commune in the 19th century*. EHES Lund 2007 and Department of Economics Williams College.

Nafziger, S. (2010). Peasant communes and factor markets in late nineteenth century Russia. *Explorations in Economic History*, *41*(4), 381–402.

Nafziger, S., & Dennisson, T. (2007). *Micro perspectives on 19th-century Russian living standards*. Prepared for a meeting with Social Science History.

North, D. C. (1973). *Västerlandets Uppgång*. SNS.

North, D. C. (1981). *Structure and change in economic history*. W.W. Norton and Company.

North, D. C. (1990). *Institutions, institutional change and economic performance*. Cambridge University Press.

North, D. C. (1993). *Economic performance through time*. Prepared for Presentation as the Prize Lecture in Economic Science in Memory of Alfred Nobel.

North, D. C. (2005). *Understanding the process of economic change*. Princeton University Press.

Pallot, J. (1982). *Social change and peasant landholding in pre-revolutionary Russia*. Oxford: Research Paper 30 School of Geography University of Oxford.

Pallot, J. (Summer 1984). Khutora and otruba in Stolypins program of farm individualization. *Slavic Review, 43* (2), 242–256.

Pallot, J. (1999). *Land reform in Russia 1906–1917: Peasant responses to Stolypin's project of rural transformation*. Clarendon Press.

Penza Province Zemstvo. (1913). Itogi otzenochno-statisticheskogo izsledovania Penzeskoj Gubernii pod obshchim rukovodstvom V.G. Gromana. *Podvornaya perepis krestianskogo khozjajstva obrobotana T.B. shubom*. Penza: Rapoport and Co.

Pipes, R. (1995). *Russia under the old regime*. Penguin Books.

Poznanski, K. (1992). Property rights perspective on evolution of communist-type economies. In K. Poznanski (Ed.), *Constructing capitalism—The re-emergence of civil society and liberal economy in post communist world*. Westview Press, Inc.

Ramanathan, R. (1995). *Introductory econometrics with applications*. The Dryden Press, Harcourt Brace College Publishers.

Robbins, R. G., Jr. (1975). *Famine in Russia 1891–1892: The Imperial government responds to a crisis*. Columbia University Press.

Salmond, W. R. (1996). *Arts and crafts in late Imperial Russia—Reviving the Kustar Art Industries 1817–1917*. Cambridge University Press.

Scott, J. (1976). *The moral economy of the peasant. Rebellion and subsistence in Southeast Asia*. Yale University Press.

Sheshinski, E. (2010) *Limits in individual choice*. Jerusalem: Department of Economics and Center for the Study of Rationality, The Hebrew University of Jerusalem.

Shivelbusch, W. (1986). *The railway journey: The industrialization of time and space in the 19th century*. University of California Press.

Simms, Y. J. (1977). The crisis in the Russian agriculture at the end of the nineteenth century a different view. *Slavic Review, 36*(2), 377–398.

Smith, A. (1998). *An inquiry into the nature and the causes of the wealth of nations.* With the classic Introduction by Ludvig von Mises. Regnery.

Smith, A. (2000). *The theory of moral sentiments.* Prometheus Books.

Smurova, O. V. (2003). *Niezemledelcheski odkhod krestian v stolitsu I ego vlejanie na transformacjiu kulturnoj tradicji.* Izd-vo Kostromskogo gos. technologich. Universiteta.

Spitzer, Y. (2019). Personal communication.

Sztern, S. (2000a). *The Railroad and the Mir. Project description.* Lund University and (1997) The Hebrew University of Jerusalem.

Sztern, S. (2000b). *The Russian commune-village, the obshchina: Its origins, function and character.* Lund University. Lund: Sweden. Paper presented at the Economic History Seminar.

Sztern, S. (2008). *Steam engine on rail and landholding system in nineteenth century Russia.* Lomonosov State University Economic History Seminar (in Russian).

Sztern, S. (2017). *Russia on the move: The railroads and the exodus from compulsory collectivism 1861–1814 and Sztern, S. & Keren, M. was Stalin necessary? The railroads and the crumbling of the Obshchina in Tsarist Russia.* Lund and Jerusalem: PhD dissertation yet unpublished. Economic History, Lund University.

Sztern, S. (2018a). *Railroads to democracy: Individualism, rationalism and literacy: Challenge to democracy in late Imperial Russia.* PEDD Political Economy of Dictatorship and Democracy Conference, Muenster University, Germany, March 2018.

Sztern, S. (2018b, September 5–6). *Individualism and collectivism. Measuring the transition to modernity in Tsarist Russian peasant society.* Penza Province EACES Conference Warsaw Poland.

Sztern, S. (2019). Measurable Power-railroads, literacy, and the crafts Artel: Hierarchy in dissarray in Late Imperial Russia. In *Conference: Israel Economics Society At: The Hebrew University of Jerusalem.*

Troyat, H. (1961). *Daily life in Russia under the last Tsar.* Stanford University Press.

Veblen, T. (1931). *The theory of the leisure class.* Modern.

Vogelvang, B. (2005). *Econometrics—Theory and applications with Eviews.* FT Prentice Hall Financial Times.

Westwood, J. N. (1964). *A history of the Russian railways.* George Allen and Unwin.

Witt, U. (1993). *Evolution in markets and institutions.* Physica-Verlag, A Springer Verlag Company.

Worobec, C. D. (1995). *Peasant Russia family and community in the post-emancipation period.* Northern Illinois University Press.

Yokoyama, O. (2008). *Russian peasant letters texts and contexts.* Harrassowitz Verlag.

CHAPTER 12

Epilogue

Late Imperial Russia's Transition to Modernity seen through the lenses of Penza Province; Railroads, Human Capital, and Subversive Graefian "Commitment Devices" for the Cross-Sectional Study of Fifty Provinces of European Russia, 1913

Stalin Wasn't Necessary

The Kantian intuition that inspired this monograph is twofold. First, it was a tacit cultural and economic transition, spanning over half a century, rather than a time-limited and blood-stained revolution, that cumulatively modernized the steppes economies of the Euroasian continent-nation up to World War I. Second, the transition was catalyzed irreversibly by the development of the railways. The discontinuous manifestation of the post-Crimean War era was followed by the concession of peasant rights in the 1861–1863 emancipation by the Imperial political power structure as reflected in Count Witte's system. This along with the extension of the arms of the Tsarist state across Russia's vast spaces in the form of the Iron Horse—likened to a spider web—is well explained in the opening chapters of this monograph. Thus, my thesis suggests that paradoxically a democratization process emerged during that half-century of interaction between the railroads and the peasant commune village (the *obshchina*) and was codified ex post in the Stolypin reform of 1906. The growing share of the peasant population that carried internal passports attests to an avalanche-like exodus of peasant *otkhodniks*—wage laborers—to the industrial

S. Sztern, *Russia on the Move*, Studies in Economic Transition,
https://doi.org/10.1007/978-3-030-89285-2_12

agglomerations of knowledge in the country's urban centers (Fujita et al., 2001; Burds, 1998). Three voluntarily and rationally knit peasant associations—the landsman-based (*zemliachestvo*) crafts workshop (*artel*) and the village commune—mitigated the risks of seasonal wage work and migration and partly freed the peasants of their dependence on agricultural sources of income (Johnson, 1979; Troyat, 1961). Peasants could now accumulate human capital individually (Brooks, 2003) and form networks on a competence basis (Hodgson, 1999) in contractual labor associations (Coase, 1937), rendering effective the demand for universal suffrage (Ascher, 1988) amid reduced costs of collective action (Barzel, 2002). These third-party enforcement organizations (Barzel, Greif, 2006), I argue, catalyzed the transition from autocracy to constitutional monarchy.

Late Imperial Russia's political rationality (Hayek, 1944) partly determined the routes of the rail lines that were perceived as of the highest priority (Borodkin et al., 2021) in accordance, it seems, with the continuous allocation structures of government expenditure. The structure, established in the eighteenth-century Petrine modernization, lasted into the Soviet and post-Soviet eras, with 80–95 percent of outlays (with some variance over time) devoted to maintaining the military-industrial base of the regime's legitimacy, pursuing the Empire's geopolitical aspirations as reflected in the railways (construction of the Trans-Siberian railroads 1891 [Marks, 1991]) and its wish to improve bureaucratic control, emergent in the Nicolayev railway (1843—Westwood, 1964) that tied Moscow to St Petersburg. The Tsarist state split its available budget resources equally between military uses and administration and allotted the residual, which grew tentatively during the industrial spurt that began in 1890 and the democratizing reforms that ensued in 1905 and lasted until World War I, to prerogatives of the civilian economy such as health and education. In the case of the railways, however, this residual investment was significant in the construction of lines from the southern and southeastern parts of the country because these lines led to grain-export ports. Indeed, the state prioritized these outlays in order to maintain the strategic international creditworthiness of its treasury, which was based on grain exports (Gerschenkron, 1962, 1968). The historically crucial role of success in battle (Hughes, 1998; Anisimov, 1993) was reflected in the primacy given by the state to the military-technology characteristic of rail over its production-technology properties (Martens, 2004). Predominantly, not only the former traits but also the latter ones, however, carried something that the Imperial state, in its role as its own guardian (Freeze, 1996), including its dependence on administration, had not intended: capabilities of democratization. It was this that allowed me to specify a peasant village's distance from the nearest railroad station in the first generation of the railroadization spurt as a variable exogenous to the structures of the peasant economy.

The spirit of the adaptations to the imported spatial technology, which increasingly determined the character of property, political, spiritual intellectual rights, and freedoms in Late Imperial Russia, emerges in the paintings of Isaac Levitan. His "The Vladimirka Road" (1892), the *kandialnaya doroga* (road of the chained convicts) breathes with Biblical Jobian-Dostoevskian empathy for the ostensibly meek. Nevertheless, Dostoevsky's *Wspomnienia z Domu Umarlych* (*Memoires from the House of the Dead*, Dostoevsky, 1977) documents the sophisticated composite strategies of survival that the forced laborers (subversive Old Believers, the Razkol peasantry) adopted. They included precarity-reducing organization, with subversive multi-dimensional redistributive action, and the attitudes toward property that these elicited, all in order to withstand the challenges that forced labor resented. Alms, the gifts of mercy bestowed by surrounding free populations, were subjected to egalitarian sharing norms and mitigated individuals' risk of death, while strict and calculated adherence to wage differentials in the convicts' communities in exile gave these unfortunates a return on their labor. The latter practice reflects the pious Razkol's unshaken belief in the perseverance of the social and economic power of the indomitable human will, dignified in its urge to liberty and the spirit of its mastery over its fate. Adhering to similar forms of resistance, peasant proletarians who found themselves under lockout for having struck in order to better their conditions withstood the hardships of penalization while reserving the resources collected in craftsman cooperative funds (*artelnye kassy*) at the discretion of those in need (Freeze, 1988). Such fundraising was modelled on rural mutual responsibility, individual risk insurance, proof of quality of labor, and contractual association, all parallel to Graef's "commitment devices," third-party-enforced in the sense of its evolutionary economics function (Barzel, 2002).

Countering this seeming triumph over oppression and subservience, Levitan's work "Above Eternal Peace" (1894) harmonizes well with the "People of God" doctrine, the bold participatory parish challenge to the authoritarian pro-autocracy holy synod of the Greek Orthodox mainstream. This painting bears silent witness to the volcanic democratization of ecclesiastical structures that unfolded in the course of the 1890 industrial spurt that was prompted by the centrifugal philosophies documented by Shevzov (2004). This surge of tension coincided with industrialization that had railroad construction at its core, attenuating the patriarchal control of income by senior and *domoleg* village kin, tied to their agricultural commune-village livelihood—countered by the working-peasant sons, known as Pitershchiks, who pioneered integration into urban industries (Smurova, 2003, Burds, 1998, and Chap. 7). This process was manifested in the flight of piously subversive otkhodniks to the Old Belief and the doings of other schismatics (Matosian, 1968) in their escape from the compulsory repatriation of income enforced by the Tsarist gendarmerie (Freeze, 1988; Burds, 1998). The peasants' increasing use of railroads, proxied by the proportion of the village population carrying internal passports, not only incentivized the acquisition of literacy (Brooks, 2003; Sztern, 2017, 2018, 2019) and the accumulation of Veblenian matter-of-fact useful knowledge but also created a social mutation. In this shift, as they caused the share of children learning to read in the population to rise, literate wage-earning sons rendered their illiterate *bolshak* (paterfamilias) fathers socially and economically dependent, challenging the core authority structure that constituted the institutional foundation of the Tsarist empire (Sztern, 2017, 2018).

The revolution encapsulated in the acquisition of human capital, social mobility, the descent into analphabetism of the landed gentry as well as the patriarchal bolshaks (Sztern, 2018), and the ascendance to political power of a peasant offspring generation that commuted by rail and was incentivized to acquire literacy, steadily boosted individual risk-taking. This chain of events traced to the ability to absorb information in the evolving spatial-mobility era, rather than to a class conflict over immediate control of means of production as Marxian conceptions suggest. The findings in this monograph propose that the 1905 upheaval was harmonized with the Bakuninian rejection of the yoke of the superior, a reality embedded in the personalized system of privilege and patronage historically entrenched in Russia, rather than with the aim of eliminating predictable and enforceable economic and political rights enforced by the state structure. The institutions tasked with this act of elimination, grounded in the principle of equality before the law and the elimination of the estate system, were precisely those that the Late Imperial Russian peasantry demanded in its petitions to the Duma (Freeze, 1988). In Levitan's "Ploughed Field at the Evening" (1883), the Black Earth expresses the sunset of the docility of the peasant who is only seemingly and superficially content with his lot as a muzhik farmer; the ominous sulfur-clouded skies express the friction that actually exists (Jackson, 2004, Groninger Museum, and National Gallery). The most tangible feature one senses in the Jewish shoemakers' sons, landscape painting that had been admired by the progressive Russian intelligentsia, is the concealed revolt that erodes the hierarchies of coercion, shaking, reformulating, and shifting the networks of risk-mitigating authority embedded in the use of the spatial-mobility technology of the railroads, which are invisible on this canvas (Russian Landscape in the Age of Tolstoy Exhibition, London, 2004).

These paintings tentatively tear the veil off the Tsarist Russian Janus, a creature that always elicits either a passive or an active discontent that thrives due to its intrinsic organization, specific to its time and place, and its numerous translations over time (Boyer & Orlean, 1993). These autonomous pre-modern mutual-insurance organizations, Bakuninian rather than Chicherenian or Marxian under incentivizing returns to labor, were adapted by convicts and the peasantry as well as soldiers in the spirit of *artel* cooperation, protecting group members from the strong probability of failure in the course of their urban employment and integration in modernizing society while allowing exactly this outcome to occur. *Krugovaya poruka* (mutual-responsibility organizations) traditionally traded the maximal profit manifestations of individualism against "safety first" habits (McCloskey, 2001) in view of the external danger occasioned by the human institutions (North, 2005) and the precarious natural environment. The literary cultural documents are congruent with the observations of Kingston-Mann (1991) and Macey (1998) analyzed in this monograph. Kingston-Mann points to the commune's risk-reducing role in the entrepreneurial cultivation of novel crops such as clover in fallow fields in the course of the transition to modernity, whereas Macey tells the tale of the property conflict embedded in the implementation of the Stolypin reform, emphasizing the profound and ever-present traditional individualism of the Russian peasant. Against the background of the yoke of autocratic oppression portrayed in its gist in the aforementioned works of art, the thirty-verst-radius confinement of the Russian peasant during serfdom (a verst being approximately 1.7 kilometer), as determined by local landlords for their bonded labor (Blum, 1961), and the institutional, cognitive, and ESS (evolutionarily stable survival strategies) post-emancipation legacies, the culturally revolutionizing role of the spatial-mobility technology of the railroads cannot be overstated.

My future research will take a deeper look at the non-Marxian roots of challenge to autocracy in Late Imperial Russia and their impact on the post-Soviet Transition. The historical facts bring the Marxian theory of revolution in Late Imperial Russia into question: One who studies the peasant proletariat phenomenon (Johnson, 1979; Gaudin, 1998) must bear in mind that the landless proletariat accounted for less than 5 percent of the population (Bideleux, 1990). Given the slow adaptation of institutions (North, 1990), Lenin's 1903 theory of Marxian agitation (Harding, 1996) cannot possibly explain the revolution of 1905. The variegations of synergies between material and immaterial assets were stronger among geographical localities than among the peasantry and other estates and classes. Landsman ties (Johnson, 1979), allowing migration and revising the alternative costs of the acquisition of footloose human capital, exerted stronger explanatory power as the effective harbingers of the demand for equality before the law and universal suffrage, structured by mutual symbiotic dependencies between landlord peasant-serfs and newly emancipated peasants, particular to local conditions.

My aim in this monograph and beyond is to advance empirically a two-part thesis. First, the actual "battleships" (Sztern, 2017, 2018, 2019) that challenged the autocracy were, ultimately, the strike-movement organizations that had been powered by the rural organizations, as certified by the peasants' petitions to the Duma in 1906 (Freeze, 1988); second, these were "translations" (Boyer & Orlean, 1993) of the pre-modern risk-reducing, mutual-responsibility rural communal village and the *arteli*, the skilled crafts workers' cooperatives. In my work, I conceptualize them through the contract-based theory of the firm (Coase, 1937), the competence-based theory of the labor organization (Hodgson, 1999), and Greif's (2006) "commitment devices," peer reviewing individual performance in a hostile competitive environment to reduce the individual risk of claims of underperformance and enhance capitalist inclusion. I will investigate the qualitative and quantitatively delineated pace of human-capital accumulation manifested in the regionally specific peasant letters collected by Yokoyama (2008). Was there a correlation between the share of households that accumulated and was able to mobilize the human-capital properties of the crafts *artel* (literacy, years in school), incentivized by reduced distances to the railroad (Brooks, 2003; Sztern, 2017, 2018, 2019), and *the frequency of strike movements in a given locality in 1905*? The regions of Penza and Pskov will bring the matter into focus. Did these informal commitment devices, these pre-modern risk-reduction organizations, outlast Soviet rule to re-emerge and mitigate the uncertainty of the post-Soviet transition? How rigid and institutionally enserfing was the post-emancipation village commune? Does today's Russia have a historical legacy of voluntary individual utility-based labor cooperatives?

Modern research, based on archive sources, documents the microeconomic neoclassical rationality of the peasant commune, its elastic responses to population changes (Nafziger, 2010), and its articulated demand for the enforcement of property rights, increasingly provided by the cantonal court system as manifested in the court-case petitions documented by Burbank (2004). The systematization of Imperial government embedded in these changes increased the predictability and probability of enforcement (Yaney, 1973, 1982; Gaudin, 2007; Sztern, 2017) and the ongoing impersonalization and the objectivization of law. Although Burbank does discuss the railroads and the assumed contingent frequency of peasant reliance on the cantonal courts, a comprehensive and empirically anchored analysis of the railroads access as an explanatory variable related to peasant attitudes to property is still missing. This monograph, I hope, fills the void.

The costs of a personalized arbitrary system of privilege as opposed to an impersonalized legal system are well-documented in Dostoevsky's *Crime and Punishment*. Marmeladova's immiseration-stricken tubercular delusionary memories of the dance with the shawl in the Tsarist court as the source of ultimate guardianship, the in-exchangeable personalized protection of privilege from all encroachments on her and her children's rights, and Rachmaninoff's Concerto no. 3 for Piano and Orchestra in D Minor, opus 30 (1909) tell the saga of the individual at the highest level of peril, separated from the ice and snow by his troika of sledges, postal diligence, and horses steamily galloping on dangerous roads, and the Russian peasant serf, locked in the thirty-verst radius of his allotment in dependence on his specific locality as permitted by the bondage system, the particular commune village, its elders (the *skhod*), and its pre-emancipation landlord (the *pomeshchik*). Who was the Russian peasant who left bloodstains in the snow while exploring the shortest distance of his motherland's vastness, feet wrapped in *onuche* cloth and *valenki* boots? To what extent, if any, did the Imperial state, represented by its ministries of interior and finance as the institutions of the anointed Tsar, cultivate the notion of the *obshchego blaga*, the common good (Anisimov, 1993), as the protector and authoritarian life-insurer of the peasant communities as these communities perceived it? Was the state the guardian of the peasant estate, to which 80 percent of the country's population belonged, as opposed to the Antichrist colonizer (Frank, 1999) and despoiler who cynically used exploitation to maintain the technologically Westernized *votchina* (patrimony) of the war economy, legitimized by conquest and embedded in the continuous diachronic time from Peter I to Stalin and beyond, as proposed by the Gerschenkronian conception? Did it do this under the Petrine slogan (Hughes, 1998) "Money is the artery of war," financed by credit raised on international markets through Prime Minister Vishnegradski's "hunger exports of grains" program, as Atkinson (1983) says? Was the nineteenth-century Russian industrialization, a latecomer relative to Britain that emerged from the country's eighteenth-century predecessor in the buildup of naval power—a grim saga of the iron arms of the imported railroad technology—incentivized by the quest for geopolitical hegemony? By transporting military conscripts and convicts, did the oppressive Tsarist state wrest social and economic control from the peasant village, the *mir*? Whose incentives for industrialization were served by the debacle of the 1855 Crimean War as opposed to the Petrine incentives roughly a century and a half earlier—which had been delivered by the manifest superiority of Charles XII of Sweden in the Battle of Narva, the pinnacle of the Northern War until defeat ensued at Poltava in 1725? Ultimately, did the United States under Ronald Reagan's administration actually challenge the Soviet Union's historically continuous allocation structures in view of the arms race? Was a dual economy led by a progressive military-industrial complex and thriving at the expense of a vast civilian economy's unending sacrifice and its outcome, an economy typified by civilian shortages that lasted into Soviet and post-Soviet times, a distortion (Winicki, 1988)? To sum up the impression that the answers are not fully, and indeed not, in the affirmative, this monograph confronts Gerschenkron's peasant-household rationality, restricted by the reconstitutive role of custom, with Gregory's neoclassical discourse. By so doing, it proposes the perpetually circumventing power of capitalist exchange and asks how backward Late Imperial Russia really was in contrast to the genuine and revolutionizing pre-World War I and October 1917 modernization, as proposed by revisionist scholars (Mironov, 2012; Simms, 1977; Gregory, 1982, 1994; Leonard, 2011; Borodkin, 2008; and Davydov, 2003, personal communication).

Ekaterina Pravilova's (2014) well-researched analysis, based on primary sources, exposes the rising tensions in the late nineteenth century between the centripetal aspiration of the autocracy, represented by its ministries, to retain urgent emergency control of the environment, the land, forests, and water—in a nutshell, everything belonging to nature—and of intellectual property, defined as a public good and domain property, and the centrifugal rise of the claim to allodial private property and professionalism even among dilettante non-government organizations that sought access to and control of the patrimony pool (Pravilova, 2014, p. 132). Abraham Ascher (1988), extensively quoted in this monograph, analyzes with much attention the ostensibly modernizing autocracy's paradoxical assault on the *zemstvo* (rural self-government) congress that anticipated the 1905 revolution. The organizations in question, composed of representatives of the progressive landed nobility, peasant entrepreneurs and third-element professionals, statisticians, agronomists, and medical personnel, were vectors of formal and tacit contractual and capability-oriented collective action (Barzel, 2002). Their purview of activity, set forth in the 1864 Zemstvos Law that followed the emancipation, including the 1861–1863 redemption statutes, was limited to gathering and mapping the peasant estate's living conditions, Doing this during the Industrial spurt served the ambition of Alexey Sergeyevich Yermolov (the conservative right-wing Minister of Agriculture, appointed in 1894) to better the peasantry's lot under the patronage of the Tsarist autocracy as subsequently envisaged by the progressive Prime Minister, Pyotr Arkadyevic Stolypin. The institutional background of the latter's land reform (1906)—the ultimate gravitation point of this monograph—is understood by Macey (1987) as the codification of an ongoing debate during the second half of the nineteenth century and lesser reform sequences aimed at broadening peasant access to the Tsarist stock of inheritable land (the *votchina*).

The main contribution of this monograph relative the sources cited above lies in the nexus it creates between the Tsarist spatial-mobility technology—the importation and development of railroads, expressed in dwindling distance from villages to stations—and the manifestations of peasants' informal and formal attitudes to landed property and, by implication, to other material and immaterial assets. Viewed through the lenses of Pravilova's analysis, the address to the Tsar on January 9, 1905—issued heterogeneously by peasants, clergy, industrialists, and students—followed by peasant petitions to the Duma in 1906 (Freeze, 1988) articulated the grassroots claim to the Tsarist *votchina* (patrimony property). This demand, escalating during the second half of the nineteenth century and embedded in the rising transaction costs, due to specialization, of undelineated landed assets within the peasant estate (Barzel, 1989), was accommodated by Stolypin's 1906 reform. The declining legitimacy of the Tsarist patrimony rights as perceived by the peasantry, expressed in the price of massive protests for non-compliance in 1905 (North 1981), links the peasants' access to the spatial-mobility technology to their growing negotiation power due to the accumulation of physical and human capital for democratization (Pipes 1999). By putting it this way, my thesis establishes a causal relationship between the upturn in 1890–1914 in court cases per thousand of population concerning land data (Gaudin, 2007) and the growing frequency of personal-insult lawsuits per thousand inhabitants as a metric of perceived self-dignity to rising factor productivity, on the one hand (Leonard, 2011), and steadily improving access to railroads, on the other. Borodkin et al. (2021), disclosing the upturn in land prices along railroads lines, demonstrates an increase in demand contingent upon the escalating perceived exchange value of landed assets within the peasant estate, rising income, and improving living standards. This, in turn, is congruent with my findings on the negative correlation between distance from railroad station and the share of individual household-cultivated land of total peasant land. Peasants' choice of the individual consolidated parcel (*wnienadelnyj jedinolichnyj otrub*) in 1913 is explained in large part by the declining distance from railroad stations of a *selo* (a group of peasant villages, 44 percent) and the individual peasant obshchina (communal village, 37 percent). The peasantry's manifest rationalist individualism, the result of broadening possibilities of choice, is explained by its steadily improving ability to handle information (Sheshinski, 2010; Gintis, 2009). This, in turn, allowed living standards to rise, reduced the volatility of yields, and raised the costs of the probability of cooperation relative to those of profit maximization (Markievich & Castaneda, 2017).

In sum, my monograph proposes that the spatial-mobility technology of the railroads instigated the endogenous translation (Boyer & Orlean, 1993) of the traditional risk-mitigating structures into harbingers of human-capital-oriented subversion, challenging the hierarchies of coercion and ultimately liberating the peasant masses from the shackles of their legacy of bondage, analphabetism, and personal subservient dependence. The collective action units that underwent "translation" in their interaction with the aforementioned spatial-mobility technology (Barzel, 2002) pertain especially to the artels, the obshchinas, and the nexus of cooperation among the nobility, the peasantry, and the free-profession, named the zemstvo organizations. These structured the organized and effectively stratified demand for democratizing reform, anchored in the access of 80 percent of the population to *votchina* patrimony, codified in *ukreplienie* land title under Stolypin's 1906 reform, as the only surviving basis of the Tsarist government's legitimacy. Given the growing subversive turn of the country's ecclesiastic structures and the debacle of the Russo-Japanese War (Freeze, 1996), this was the Empire's sole and perestroika-type promise of perpetuation. The two revolutions, of 1905 and of 1917, emerged from neither a Marxian nor a Leninist cultural environment. In my future use of zemstvo statistics to map the modernization of fifty provinces of European Russia in 1913 as a cross-section, I will continue to argue that the murderous Jacobin cruelty embedded in Stalin's modernization, deflated by the price of the return to barbarism, was not only unnecessary but also detrimental to the attainment of the very modernization that dictator intended. Moreover, the source of the innovative democratizing force emerged not only from external invasion of Western ideas and threats of invasions but also, to a significant extent, from cultural institutional matrixes endogenous to Russia.

Rail as an Endogenous or Exogenous Factor: Future Research as an Epilogue

Did Russia's sources of capital formation shift from the state treasury to the banking system? The paper that bears this title, subtitled "The Geographic Expansion of the Railroad Network and the Rise of Entrepreneurial Culture in Late Imperial Russia," analyzes the long-term effects of Late Imperial Russia's preparations for ruble convertibility and transition to the gold standard in 1881–1897, the type of source structure of which the ratio of domestic to foreign investment was composed, and capital originating in Imperial state debt that was allocated to railroad construction. I investigate the effects of these ratios on the geographic expansion of the railroad network and the urgent need to nationalize this means of transport at the end of the century (Owen, 1991). It seems obvious that capital formation explained by the improved international creditworthiness of the Imperial state established a strategic geopolitical interest, contingent on political rationality (Hayek, 1944), that dictated the geographical dispersion of the railroads. The Trans-Siberian railroads of 1891 are a case in point (Marks, 1991). They are rightly conceptualized as having catalyzed the awakening of an entrepreneurial ethos in the economy at large, paradoxically spearheaded by the 80 percent of the population that belonged to the agricultural sector—the liberated *otkhod*, a culture of mobile seasonal wage labor, interacting with and stimulating the growth of the urban industrial economy and vice versa (Sztern, 2017). This paper, based on my assumption of a marginally escalating risk-taking transition to individualism and rationalism in landholding manifested in peasant participation in the Stolypin reform, proposes that a parallel or perhaps even an anticipatory transition occurred in the sources of capital formation, gradually shifting from the state treasury (viz. the Finance Ministry, under the jurisdiction of Count Witte) to private investors whom the banking system courted. Thus, following Gerschenkron's (1962) typology, Russia's second industrial spurt (1907) is assumed to have been facilitated by a shift in the direction of the German industrialization type, in which capital is formed within the banking system. Stolypin's reform was supported by the ascendancy of the Peasant Land Bank, established in 1882 (Klimin, 2002), for which the central banking system ultimately sanctioned risk-taking contingent on the rise of an entrepreneurial culture in urban industry. Did this shift, in turn, affect the goals and geographical dispersion of the railroads as well as the contingent specific character of the growing propensity to entrepreneurship among the peasantry, including households' agricultural output, craft output, and contract workshops for export, creating added value that interacted with the intensifying acquisition of literacy skills and education (Salmond, 1996; Brooks, 2003; Burds, 1998; Eklof, 1986)? If such was the case, did the impact of the railroads gradually shift from exogenous to endogenous (Markievich 2008), affected by the emerging material, and immaterial in terms of human-capital acquisition, property rights? My sources are secondary and primary: the National Accounts of Imperial Russia as used by Gregory (1982) and the structure and capital sources of the investors (Marks, 1991; Barkai, 1973; Owen, 1991; Davydov, 2010).

References

Anisimov, V. E. (1993). *The reforms of Peter the Great: Progress through coercion in Russia*. Sharpe.

Ascher, A. (1988). *The revolution of 1905. Part I: Russia in disarray. Part II: Authority restored*. Stanford University Press.

Atkinson, D. (1983). *The end of the Russian land commune 1905–1930*. Stanford University Press.

Barkai, H. (1973). *Kibbutz efficiency and incentive conundrum*. Research paper The Maurice Falk Institute for Economic Research.
Barzel, Y. (1989). *Economic analysis of property rights*. Cambridge University Press.
Barzel, Y. (2002). *The theory of the state: Economic rights, legal rights and the scope of the state*. Cambridge University Press.
Bideleux, R. (1990). Agricultural advance under the Russian village commune system. In R. Bartlett (Ed.), *Land commune and peasant community in Russia: Communal forms in Imperial and early Soviet society*. Macmillan in Association with the School of Slavonic and East European Studies, University of London.
Blum, J. (1961). *Lord and peasant in Russia from the ninth to the nineteenth century*. Princeton University Press.
Borodkin, L. I.(2008). Discussion.
Borodkin, L. J., Leonard, C. S., Nazarov, Z., Karpenko, M., & Konchakov, R. (2021). Land prices and railroads building, European Russia, 1860 to the Early 1900. *Russian Journal of Economics, 7*(2), 93–104.
Boyer, R., & Orlean, A. (1993). How do conventions evolve? In U. Witt (Ed.), *Evolution in markets and institutions*. Physica-Vlg.
Brooks, J. (2003). *When Russia learned to read: Literacy and popular literature 1861–1917*. Northwestern University Press.
Burbank, J. (2004). *Russian peasants go to court: Legal culture in the countryside, 1905–1917*. Indiana University Press.
Burds, J. (1998). *Peasant dreams and market politics: Labor migration and the Russian village 1861–1905*. University of Pittsburgh Press.
Coase, R. (1937). *The firm, the market and the law*. University of Chicago Press.
Davydov, M. A. (2003). *Ocherki agrarnoj istorii Rossii v konce XIX-nachale XX VV*. Rossijskij Gosudarstvennyj Gumanitarnyj Universitet.
Davydov, M. A. (2010). Vserossijskij rynok v konce XIX- Nachale XX vv: i zheleznodorozhnaya statistika. Rossijskij Gosudarsvennyj Gumanitarnyj Universitet. Aleteia (2010).
Dostoevsky, F. (1977). *Wspomninenia z domu umarlych*. Panstwowy Instytut Wydawniczy.
Eklof, B. (1986). *Russian peasant schools. Village culture and popular pedagogy, 1861–1914*. University of California Press.
Frank, S. (1999). *Crime, cultural conflict and justice in rural Russia 1856–1914*. University of California Press.
Freeze, L. (1988). *From supplication to revolution: a documentary Social history of Imperial Russia*. Oxford University Press.
Freeze, L. (1996, June). Subversive piety: Religion and the political crisis in Late Imperial Russia. *Journal of Modern History, 68*(2), 308–350.
Fujita, M., Krugman, P., & Venables, A. J. (2001). *The spatial economy, Cities regions and international trade*. The MIT Press.

Gaudin, C. (1998). No place to lay my head. Marginalisation and the right to land during the Stolypin reforms. *Slavic Review, 57*(Winter), 747–773.
Gaudin, C. (2007). *Ruling peasants: Village and state in Late Imperial Russia*. Northern Illinois University Press.
Gerschenkron, A. (1962). *Economic backwardness in historical perspective*. The Belknap Press of Harvard University Press.
Gerschenkron, A. (1968). *Continuity in history and other essays*. The Belknap Press of Harvard University Press.
Gintis, H. (2009). *The bounds of reason: Game theory and the unification of the behavioral sciences*. Princeton University Press.
Gregory, P. R. (1982). *Russian national income 1885–1913*. Cambridge University Press.
Gregory, P. R. (1994). *Before command. An economic history of Russia from emancipation to the first five-year plan*. Princeton University Press.
Greif, A. (2006). *Institutions and the path to modern economy: Lessons from medieval trade*. Cambridge University Press.
Harding, N. (1996). *Leninism*. Macmillan.
Hayek, F. A. (1944). *The road to serfdom*. Routledge.
Hodgson, G. M. (1999). *Evolution and institutions: On evolutionary economics and the evolution of economics*. Edward Elgar.
Hughes, L. (1998). *Russia in the age of Peter the Great*. Yale University Press.
Jackson, D. (2004). *The mother land tradition and innovation in Russian landscape painting*. Groninger Museum National Gallery.
Johnson, R. (1979). *Peasant and proletarian: The working class of Moscow in the late nineteenth century*. Leicester University Press.
Kingston-Mann, E. (1991). Peasant communes and economic innovation: A preliminary inquiry. In E. Kingston-Mann, T. Mixter, & J. Burds (Eds.), *Peasant economy culture and politics of European Russia*. Princeton University Press.
Klimin, I. I. (2002). *Stolypinskaya agrarnaya reforma i stanovlenie krestian sobstvennikov v Rossii*. Centr istoricheskich i gumanitarnych issledovani 'Klio'.
Leonard, C. S. (2011). *Agrarian reform in Russia: The road from Serfdom*. Cambridge University Press.
Macey, D. (1987). *Government and peasant in Russia 1861–1906: The prehistory of the Stolypin reforms*. Northern Illinois University Press.
Macey, D. (1998). A wager on history: The Stolypin agrarian reforms as a process. In J. Pallot (1998). Christ Church Oxford, *Transforming peasants. Society, state and the peasantry, 1861–1930*. Selected Papers From the Fifth World Congress of Central and East European Studies, Warsaw, 1995.
Markievich, A. (2008). *Personal Communication*. Lomonosov State University Moscow Economic History Seminar.

Markievich, A., & Castaneda, D. (2017). *The Stolypin Reform and agricultural productivity in Late Imperial Russia.* Working Paper No 239 CEFIR/NES Working Paper Series.

Marks, S. (1991). *Road to power: The Trans-Siberian railroad and the colonization of Asian Russia 1850–1917.* Cornell University Press.

Martens, B. (2004). *The cognitive mechanics of economic development and institutional change.* Routledge.

Matosian, M. (1968). The peasant way of life. In W. S. Vucinich (Ed.), *The peasant in nineteenth century Russia.* Stanford University Press.

McCloskey, D. (2001). *Talk on bourgeois ethics.* Economic History Seminar, Lund University, February 23.

Mironov, B. N. (2012). Nabljudalsia li v Pozdnie Imperskoj Rosii Malthusianskij krizis: Dochody i povinosti Rossijskogo krestianstva, v 1801–1914 gg.

Nafziger, S. (2010). Peasant communes and factor markets in late-nineteenth-century Russia. *Explorations in Economic History, 47*(4), 381–402.

North, D. C. (1981). *Structure and Change in Economic History.* Norton and Company.

North, D. C. (1990). *Institutions, institutional change and economic performance.* Cambridge University Press.

North, D. C. (2005). *Understanding the process of economic change.* Princeton University Press.

Owen, T. (1991). *The corporation under the Russian law 1800–1917.* Cambridge University Press.

Pipes. (1999). *Property and Freedom.* The Harvill Press.

Pravilova, E. (2014). *A public empire: Property and the quest for the common good in Imperial Russia.* Princeton University Press.

Russian Landscape in the Age of Tolstoy Exhibition. London. (2004).

Salmond, W. (1996). *Arts and Crafts in late I Imperial Russia. Reviving the Kustar Art Industries.* Cambridge University Press.

Sheshinski, E. (2010). *Limits in individual choice.* Department of Economics and the Center for the Study of Rationalisty, The Hebrew University of Jerusalem.

Shevzov, V. (2004). *Russian Orthodoxy on the eve of revolution.* Oxford University Press.

Simms, Y. J. (1977). The crisis in the Russian agriculture at the end of the nineteenth century: A different view. *Slavic Review, 36*(3), 377–398.

Smurova, O. V. (2003). *Niezemledelcheski odkhod krestian v stolitsu I ego vlejanie na transformacjiu kulturnoj tradicji.* Izd-vo Kostromskogo gos. technologich. Universiteta.

Sztern, S. (2017). *Russia on the move the railroads and the exodus from compulsory collectivism 1861–1914.* Dissertation. Lund University Press.

Sztern, S. (2018). *Steam engine on the rail and landholding system in-nineteenth century Russia*. Lomonosov State University Economic History Seminar, Moscow (in Russian).

Sztern, S. (2019). Measurable Power-railroads, literacy, and the crafts Artel: Hierarchy in dissarray in Late Imperial Russia. In *Conference: Israel Economics Society At: The Hebrew University of Jerusalem*.

Troyat, H. (1961). *Daily life in Russia under the last Tsar*. Stanford University Press.

Westwood, J. N. (1964). *A history of the Russian railways*. George Allen and Unwin.

Winicki, J. (1988). *The distorted world of Soviet-type economies*. Routledge.

Yaney, G. (1973). *The systematization of Russian government: Social evolution in the domestic administration of Imperial Russia 1711–1905*. University of Illinois Press.

Yaney, G. (1982). *The urge to mobilize: Agrarian reform in Russia, 1861–1913*. University of Illinois Press.

Yokoyama, O. (2008). *Russian peasant letters texts and contents*. Harassowitz Verlag.

Index[1]

[1] Note: Page numbers followed by 'n' refer to notes.

S. Sztern, *Russia on the Move*, Studies in Economic Transition, https://doi.org/10.1007/978-3-030-89285-2

P

T

The manufacturer's authorised representative in the EU is Springer Nature Customer Service Centre GmbH, Europaplatz 3, 69115 Heidelberg, Germany. If you have any concerns regarding our products, please contact ProductSafety@springernature.com

Printed and bound by CPI Group (UK) Ltd, Croydon, CR0 4YY

30/09/2026

02225492-0012